D0672272

THE
ROMANTIC MOVEMENT
BIBLIOGRAPHY
1936–1970

CUMULATED BIBLIOGRAPHY SERIES
Editor, Thomas Schultheiss

Number one: Literature and Language Bibliographies
from **The American Year Book**, 1910-1919

Number two: Articles in American Studies, 1954-1968;
A Cumulation of the Annual Bibliographies from
American Quarterly

Number three: The Romantic Movement Bibliography,
1936-1970; A Master Cumulation from **ELH,
Philological Quarterly**, and **English Language Notes**

Number four: Russian Studies, 1941-1958; A Cumulation
of the Annual Bibliographies from **The Russian Review**

Number five: The Bibliography of Critical Arthurian
Literature, 1922-1962; A master cumulation of the
MLA Arthurian Group bibliographies and **Modern
Language Quarterly** supplements.

Number seven: Articles on the Middle East, 1947-1971;
A Cumulation of the Bibliographies from **Middle East
Journal**

THE
ROMANTIC MOVEMENT
BIBLIOGRAPHY

1936–1970

A Master Cumulation
from
ELH, Philological Quarterly and English Language Notes

VOLUME V
1965 – 1967

Edited and with a Preface
by

A.C. ELKINS, Jr.
Assistant Professor
Department of English Language and Literature
The University of Michigan

and

L.J. FORSTNER
Assistant Professor
Department of English Language and Literature
The University of Michigan

With a Foreword
by

David V. Erdman
Editor
**The Romantic Movement:
A Selective and Critical Bibliography**

THE PIERIAN PRESS
in association with
THE R. R. Bowker Co.
1973

Library of Congress Catalog Card Number 77-172773
ISBN 87650-025-4

The Pierian Press
P.O. Box 1808
Ann Arbor, Mi. 48106

CONTENTS

English Language Notes

Volume IV   Supplement to No. 1   September, 1966

The Romantic Movement:
A Selective and Critical Bibliography
for 1965

Edited by
DAVID V. ERDMAN
with the assistance of KENNETH NEGUS, JAMES S. PATTY,
OLGA RAGUSA, and RAYMOND S. SAYERS

This bibliography, compiled by a joint bibliography committee for groups General Topics II and English IX of the Modern Language Association, is designed to cover a "movement" rather than a period. Thus, though the English section is largely limited to the years 1789-1837, other sections extend over different spans of years.

It is our intent to include, with descriptive and, at times, critical annotation, all books and articles of substantial interest to scholars of English and Continental Romanticism, and critical reviews of such books. We also make note of items of minor but scholarly interest, except those which are adequately listed in the Annual Bibliography of the Association (issued in the May number of *PMLA*). Major and controversial works are given what is intended to be judicious if necessarily very brief review.

The approximate length of a book is indicated by report of the number of pages—or the number of volumes when more than one.

A new feature this year is the inclusion of available 1966 reviews of the 1965 books, to reduce somewhat the unfortunate "review gap." Another innovation is the noting of book prices when available. And this year we have listed some microfilm publications of historical documents.

The editorial committee gratefully acknowledges the help of its collaborators, whose names are given at the heads of the respective sections.

2

To ensure notice in the next issue of the bibliography, authors and publishers are invited to send review copies of relevant books or monographs, and offprints of articles, to: David V. Erdman, Editor, Room 107, The New York Public Library, Fifth Ave. & 42nd St., New York, N.Y. 10018.

CONTENTS

ABBREVIATIONS

AL	American Literature
AR	Antioch Review
ASch	American Scholar
AUMLA	Journal of the Australasian Universities Language and Literature Association
BA	Books Abroad
BB	Bulletin of Bibliography
BC	Book Collector
BJA	British Journal of Aesthetics (London)
BNYPL	Bulletin of the New York Public Library
BuR	Bucknell Review
CAIEF	Cahiers de l'Association internationale des études françaises
C&S	Cultura e scuola
CL	Comparative Literature
CLS	Comparative Literature Studies
Conv	Convivium
CritQ	Critical Quarterly
DJV	Deutsches Jahrbuch für Volkskunde
DR	Dalhousie Review
DRs	Deutsche Rundschau
DUJ	Durham University Journal
DVLG	Deutsche Vierteljahrsschrift für Literaturwissenschaft und Geistesgeschichte
E&S	Essays and Studies by Members of the English Association
ECr	L'Esprit créateur (Minneapolis)
EG	Études germaniques
EIC	(formerly EC) Essays in Criticism (Oxford)
ELH	Journal of English Literary History
ELN	English Language Notes
ES	English Studies
ESA	English Studies in Africa (Johannesburg)
FLe	Fiera letteraria
FM	Le française moderne

FR	French Review
FS	French Studies
GL&L	German Life and Letters
GQ	German Quarterly
GR	Germanic Review
GRM	Germanish-romanische Monatsschrift, Neue Folge
HeineJ	Heine Jahrbuch
HLQ	Huntington Library Quarterly
Höjb	Hölderlin-Jahrbuch
IJES	Indian Journal of English Studies (Calcutta)
IS	Italian Studies
JAAC	Journal of Aesthetics and Art Criticism
JDSG	Jahrbuch der Deutschen Schiller-Gesellschaft
JEGP	Journal of English and Germanic Philology
JFDH	Jahrbuch des Freien Deutschen Hochstifts (Tübingen)
JHI	Journal of the History of Ideas
JMH	Journal of Modern History
JR	Journal of Religion
KR	Kenyon Review
KSJ	Keats-Shelley Journal
L&P	Literature and Psychology (New York)
LC	Library Chronicle (Univ. of Pa.)
LI	Lettere italiane
LJGG	Literaturwissenschaftliches Jahrbuch der Görres-Gesellschaft
MdF	Mercure de France
MHG	Mitteilungen der E. T. A. Hoffmann Gesellschaft
MLN	Modern Language Notes
MLQ	Modern Language Quarterly
MLR	Modern Language Review
MP	Modern Philology
MQ	Midwest Quarterly (Pittsburg, Kansas)
NA	Nuova antologia
N&Q	Notes and Queries
NCF	Nineteenth Century Fiction
NDL	Neue deutsche Literatur
NM	Neuphilologische Mitteilungen
NMQ	New Mexico Quarterly
NRF	Nouvelle revue française
NRs	Neue Rundschau
New Statesman	(formerly NS)
NS	Die neueren Sprachen
NYRB	New York Review of Books
PBSA	Papers of the Bibliographical Society of America
PCTE Bulletin	Pennsylvania Council of Teachers of English
PeI	Le parole e le idee (Napoli)
PELL	Publications in English Language and Literature
Person	The Personalist
PMLA	Publications of the Modern Language Association of America
PQ	Philological Quarterly
PR	Partisan Review
PULC	Princeton University Library Chronicle
QQ	Queen's Quarterly
QR	Quarterly Review
RdP	Revue de Paris
RDM	Revue de deux mondes

4

REI   *Revue des études italiennes*
REL   *Review of English Literature (Leeds)*
RLC   *Revue de littérature comparée*
RLI   *Rassegna della letteratura italiana*
RLMC   *Rivista de letterature moderne e comparate (Firenze)*
RLV   *Revue des langues vivantes (Bruxelles)*
RMS   *Renaissance and Modern Studies (Univ. of Nottingham)*
RomN   *Romance Notes (Univ. of North Carolina)*
RR   *Romanic Review*
RSH   *Revue des sciences humaines*
RUL   *Revue de l'Universitè Laval (Quebec)*
RUO   *Revue de l'Universitè d'Ottawa*
S   *Spectator*
SAQ   *South Atlantic Quarterly*
S&S   *Science & Society*
SB   *Studies in Bibliography: Papers of the Bibliographical Society of the University of Virginia*
SchM   *Schweizer Monatshefte*
SEEJ   *Slavic and East European Journal*
SEL   *Studies in English Literature, 1500-1900 (Rice Univ.)*
SFr   *Studi francesi*
SIR   *Studies in Romanticism (Boston Univ.)*
SN   *Studia neophilologica*
SNL   *Satire Newsletter (State Univ. Coll., Oneonta, N.Y.)*
SoR   *Southern Review (Adelaide, Australia)*
SP   *Studies in Philology*
SR   *Sewanee Review*
SuF   *Sinn und Form*
TLS   *(London) Times Literary Supplement*
TR   *Table Ronde*
UTQ   *University of Toronto Quarterly*
VQR   *Virginia Quarterly Review*
VS   *Victorian Studies (Indiana Univ.)*
WB   *Weimarer Beiträge*
WW   *Wirkendes Wort*
XUS   *Xavier University Studies*
YFS   *Yale French Studies*
YULG   *Yale University Library Gazette*
YR   *Yale Review*
ZDP   *Zeitschrift für deutsche Philologie (Berlin-Bielefeld-München)*

GENERAL

(Compiled by David V. Erdman, with various assistance.)

1. BIBLIOGRAPHY

For previous issues of the present "Bibliography" see the April numbers of *PQ* (1950-1961), then the October (1962-1964), and thereafter the September Supplement to *ELN*. For the most extensive general listing, in all languages, see the "Annual Bibliography" in *PMLA* each May; slight notes listed there will not be repeated in our list.

See also *The Year's Work in Modern Language Studies*, xxv (1964) and xxvi (1965).

See also listings in Bibliography sections below, under English, French, German, Italian, Portuguese.

2. ENVIRONMENT: ART, MUSIC, SOCIETY, POLITICS, RELIGION

Baeumler, Alfred. *Das mythische Weltalter: Bachofens romantische Deutung des Altertums.* Mit einem Nachwort: Bachofen und die Religionsgeschichte. München: Beck, 1965. Pp. 373.

Bearce, George D. "The Festivals of Mewar: The Interaction of India and the West in Early Eighteenth-Century Painting." *SIR*, IV (1965), 121-42.

Cragg, Gerald R. *Reason and Authority in the Eighteenth Century.* Cambridge University Press, 1964. Pp. ix + 349. $7.50.

De Keyser, Eugénie. *The Romantic West 1789-1850.* (Art Ideas History Series.) Geneva: Skira; Cleveland: World, 1965. Pp. 210; ca. 115 plates, half in color. $20.00.
"The tragedy inherent in the works of men like Goya, Delacroix and Turner tells of a Western world overshadowed by revolution. . . ."

Fennessy, R. R., O.F.M. *Burke, Paine and the Rights of Man: A Difference of Political Opinion.* The Hague, Martinus Nijhoff, 1963; New York, W. S. Heinman, 1964. Pp. 274. $12.00.
Rev. by Harvey C. Mansfield, Jr., in *Burke Newsletter,* VI (1965), 443-45.

George, Graham. "Towards a Definition of Romanticism in Music." *QQ,* LXXII (1965), 253-69.

Harris, Tomás. *Goya: Engravings and Lithographs.* Oxford: Cassirer; London: Faber, 1965. 2 vols. 10 and 15 *gns.*

Haskett, Jeanne. "Decembrist N. A. Bestuzhev in Siberian Exile, 1826-55." *SIR,* IV (1965), 185-205.

Hill, Christopher. *Intellectual Origins of the English Revolution.* London: Oxford University Press, 1965. 45s.
Rev. by K. G. Davies in *New Statesman,* April 2, 1965, pp. 535-36.

Langle, Paul Fleuriot de. "Rome in the Early Nineteenth Century: Some Lithographs of Antoine Thomas." *Connoisseur,* CLX (Oct., 1965), 111-14.

Mitchell, Harvey. *The Underground War Against Revolutionary France: The Missions of William Wickham 1794-1800.* Oxford: Clarendon Press; New York: Oxford University Press, 1965. Pp. 286. $5.60.
This important but narrowly focused study begins with a quick survey of the historiography of the counter-revolution, a ferment of ideas from which "emerged a significant influence on the Romantic movement," but concentrates on documenting the British support and organization of counter-revolutionary forces in France in 1793-1800. "It is the object of this book to show that the

counter-revolution in France could never have posed the danger it did had it not been for the objectives of the British government." Mitchell's thesis is that the British (acting through Lord Grenville and his agent William Wickham) only gradually moved from a policy of containment to one of supporting restoration of monarchy. He seems almost not to notice his demonstration that British interference, in producing that "danger," prolonged the war. (D.V.E.)

Pollard, Sidney. "The Genesis of the Managerial Profession: the Experience of the Industrial Revolution in Great Britain." *SIR,* IV (1965), 57-80.

Sánchez Cantón, F. J. *Goya and the Black Paintings.* With an appendix by X. de Salas. London: Faber, 1965. 33 *gns.*
Rev. by David Sylvester, "Here Comes the Bogeyman," in *New Statesman,* April 2, 1965, pp. 542-43.

Reviews of books previously listed:
COBBAN, Alfred, *The Social Interpretation of the French Revolution* (see *ELN,* III, Supp., 4), reviewed severely in *TLS,* Jan. 7, 1965, p. 8; LEFEBVRE, Georges, *The French Revolution from 1793 to 1799* (see *ELN,* III, Supp., 5), rev. by James Joll in *New Statesman,* Feb. 19, 1965, pp. 282-83.

3. CRITICISM

Anderson, George K. *The Legend of the Wandering Jew.* Brown University Press, 1965. Pp. ix + 489. $12.00.
This impressive scholarly work traces the history of one of the most pervasive and enduring legends of western culture from its origins (in the origins of Christianity itself) through its complex evolution down through the ages and into our own generation. So fully and interestingly has Mr. Anderson traced the vicissitudes of the Legend that it is unlikely anyone in the near future can add anything significant to its history. Of particular interest here is the treatment of the Wandering Jew by the Romantics, the literary generations to which Ahasuerus as "sufferer"—like Cain, Manfred, and other inexpiable sinners—appealed most. Shelley, in Mr. Anderson's judgment, was "the first successful creator of a worthy art form" in which Ahasuerus appeared. The figure, as he shows, obsessed the imaginations of major and minor Romantic writers, and especially the Germans who, beginning with Schubart, have worked the Legend well into the twentieth century. If there is a sense of incompleteness about these chapters on the Romantics it is that the oblique but powerful significance of the Legend on such works as *Manfred* and *The Ancient Mariner* is only alluded to. But that is an omission the interested can attempt for themselves, the book having supplied the materials. In addition to the consistently rich history and commentary, Mr. Anderson has provided copious quotations from some rare and little-known sources of the Legend. (A.J.K.)

Baker, Paul R. *The Fortunate Pilgrims: Americans in Italy, 1800-1860.* Harvard University Press, 1964. Pp. x + 264.
Rev. by Anna Laura Lepschy in *IS,* xx (1965), 130-31.

Barineau, Elizabeth. "La *Tribune Romantique* et le Romantisme de 1830." *MP,* LXII, (1965), 302-24.

Beebe, Maurice. *Ivory Towers and Sacred Founts: The Artist as Hero in Fiction from Goethe to Joyce.* New York University Press, 1964. Pp. 323. $6.50.

Rev. by Ruby Cohn in *CL*, xvii (1965), 273-75.
Treats of English, French, and German literature. The polarity of life and art in *Werther* and *Wilhelm Meister* is seen as prototype for the divided artistic ego. Balzac, James, Proust, and Joyce successfully unite the poles. Dickens and Hawthorne are also discussed. Romanticism is treated by Beebe as a stepchild. (I.C.)

Blocker, Harry. "Kant's Theory of the Relation of Imagination and Understanding in Aesthetic Judgements of Taste." *BJA*, v (1965), 37-45.

Burwick, Fred L. "Hölderlin and Arnold: Empedokles on Etna." *CL*, xvii (1965), 24-42.
In structure and emphases Hölderlin influenced Arnold. Both authors see Empedokles as both poet and philosopher; they differed in the portrayal of his approach to death.

Cacchiara, Giuseppe. "Dal preromanticismo al romanticismo. La scoperta della poesia popolare." *C&S*, iii, No. 12 (1964), 13-19.
European forerunners of the study of folklore, Montesquieu, Herder, and Vico, and their legacy to Romanticism.

Connor, Wayne. "*L'Esule* (1832-1834): Literature and 'Home Thoughts from Abroad'," *Italica*, xl (1963), 297-305.
L'Esule, giornale di letteratura antica e moderna, Mâcon, became almost a textbook for students of Italian. Its inspiration was vaguely romantic, and it played a certain role in the formation of a French image of Italy.

Fryer, W. R. "Romantic Literature and the European Age of Revolutions." *RMS*, viii (1964), 53-74.
Considers English, French, and German Romanticism, 1780-1850.

Hertz, Robert N. "English and American Romanticism." *Person*, xlvi, No. 1 (1965), 81-92.
Mostly concerned with American prose writers.

Hoffmann, Michael J. "The House of Usher and Negative Romanticism." *SIR*, v (1965), 158-68.
Inability to establish rational relations between the order of the mind and the order of nature leads to "Negative Romanticism," exemplified by Poe. Emerson the antipode.

Lombard, C. M. "The American Attitude Towards the French Romantics (1800-1861)." *RLC*, xxxix (1965), 358-72.

Mason, Eudo C. "Das englische und das deutsche Shakespeare-Bild." *SchM*, xliv (1964), 73-90.

Massano, Riccardo. "Goethe e Foscolo, 'Werther' e 'Ortis'." Pp. 231-38 in *Atti del IV Congresso dell'Associazione internazionale per gli studi di lingua e letteratura italiana*. Wiesbaden, 1963.

Massey, Irving. "An End to Innocence." *QQ*, lxxii (1965), 178-94.
"Innocence was not some new fad of the romantic revival."

Massey, Irving. "The Romantic Movement: Phrase or Fact?" *DR,* XLIV (1965), 396-412.

Reviews the grounds for objection to the idea of a "Romantic Movement" and adds further arguments. Concludes that "we read the Romantic authors for quite unromantic reasons." "To detect the Romantic elements in a poem is something like detecting its Freudian content—in neither case have we discovered anything that concerns the poem as poem."

Mogan, Joseph J., Jr. "*Pierre* and *Manfred*: Melville's Study of the Byronic Hero." *PELL,* I (1965), 230-40.

Muir, Edwin. *Essays on Literature and Society.* Enlarged and Revised Edition. Harvard University Press, 1965. Pp. 240. $5.25.

Includes chapters on Burns, Scott, Hölderlin, and Jane Austen. Frequent references to Coleridge and Wordsworth.

Maquet, Albert. "Stendhal e Tommaso Grossi." *LI,* XVI (1964), 298-321.

Maquet, A. "Stendhal traducteur de *La Prineide* de Tommaso Grossi." Pp. 477-509 in *Studi in onore di Carlo Pellegrini.* (Biblioteca di Studi Francesi, No. 2.) Torino: Societâ Editrice Internazionale, 1963. Pp. xxxix + 846.

Passage, Charles E. *The Russian Hoffmannists.* The Hague: Mouton & Co., 1963. Pp. 262. 30 Dutch Guilders.

The course of Russian literature is traced from its beginnings in the Petrine era to the 19th century, then more thoroughly through Dostoevskij, with the aim of showing Hoffmann's role as stimulator in the creation of Russia's literary golden age of the past century. In the first third of this century, Russian writers are presented as having the same kind of love affair with German literature, as German authors of the mid-eighteenth century had had with English literature. Attendant on this process was the abandonment of French standards and models for greatly differing ones that were found in a national literature taking new directions. For the Russians of that time, ". . . all German works were Romantic, Klopstock as well as Tieck, Lessing as well as Hoffmann; there were only differences in degree of Romanticism. . . . The unifying principle in all German writers was, for them, a speculative and imaginative quality alien to anything they knew in French, or even in recent English, literature."
Actually, the pervasive and electrifying literary vogue of Hoffmann imitation in Russia was surprisingly short-lived (mainly from 1825 to 1830!), but it was so widespread and profound that several of the major accomplishments of later Russian writers are inconceivable without it. The supreme example is Dostoevskij, a late-comer among Russian Hoffmannists (the works in question range from 1846 to 1880); yet he is the most extensive adapter, selecting and combining, transforming and transcending, so that, one might say, his achievement is comparable with Bach's consummate musical adaptive genius.
The book is admirably thorough, treating first a series of relatively minor figures; then Pushkin and Gogol'; then some "ebb-tide" figures (including Lermontov and Turgenev); then the key chapter on Dostoevskij; and finally a very incisive summary pointing up a great variety of matters concerning Hoffmann's influence in Russia. Three valuable appendices complete the volume: Hoffmann's works; a chronology of Hoffmanniana in Russia; and a list of his works alongside those of Russian Hoffmannists, showing specific parallels.
A high degree of discrimination is applied throughout. The author's zeal does not mislead him to see his own private image of Hoffmann coming through *in toto* wherever one might suspect "influence." On the contrary, Passage shows

a keen awareness of the randomness with which almost any author influences his contemporaries. Thus each chapter paints a markedly different image of Hoffmann. As one would expect, these images are full of distortions, errors, overratings of minor works, and underratings or even total neglect of major ones. The meaning of such things for the authors concerned is skillfully extracted.

The three major Russian authors adapting materials from Hoffmann afford him excellent examples. Pushkin can be described as a "Hoffmannist in spite of himself," for his inclinations were definitely more French than German, and he shared little in the Germanophilia of his contemporaries. Yet in *The Queen of Spades*, and elsewhere, Hoffmann's gambling symbolism and other characteristic figures shine through. Gogol' is a "critical Hoffmannist," parodying the Hoffmannesque in *Dead Souls*. Dostoevskij, the supreme genius, emerges as the disciple who surpasses the master. Thus the section on *The Brothers Karamazov* is the high point of the book by sheer weight of Hoffmann adaptation and greatness of literary art. But the chapter on Dostoevskij is shorter than the importance of its subject matter would demand, since it is largely a summary of Passage's book, *Dostoevski the Adapter* (Chapel Hill, N.C., 1954). The overall tendency of Russian "Hoffmannizing" is a "darkening" of the often bright and colorful world of Hoffmann's fantasies—an expression of the prevailing sombre and pessimistic atmosphere of the times in Russia. There is also a simplification of Hoffmann's complexities. Finally a liberation from him sets in. A multitude of less all-embracing conclusions are listed in the final chapter under "History," "Hoffmannizing Methods and Practices," and "Use of Hoffmann's Motifs." "Dostoevskij's Unique Position" is then presented separately. These findings seem eminently valid, with one major exception: Passage almost completely overlooks the Russians' disregard for the *Märchenmythos* that Hoffmann developed throughout most of his tales. Russian adapters derived a great many isolated motifs and figures from this fantastic "other world" of Hoffmann, such as are found in the third and eighth "vigils" of *Der goldne Topf*; but no comparable *coherent* myth is re-created in Russian literature, not even by Dostoevskij. What *is* adopted and adapted is a combination of psychological and realistic materials and forms. Thus it is *Die Elixiere des Teufels*—Hoffmann's most psychologically and realistically oriented work—that is Dostoevskij's main literary model, and not *Der goldne Topf*, which is actually Hoffmann's most characteristic work in the total picture of his creations, especially in the fundamental nature of its myth.

Passage is partially aware of this (pp. 230 f., 237 f., 241 f.), but such statements tend to be lost amidst less important matters. Thus one could challenge the statement that in Russia, "Hoffmann may be said to have been eaten whole" (p. 238). In spite of the apparent randomness of his widespread influence, there still appears to have been at least one selective principle in operation, leading instinctively away from such coherencies as those of the *Märchenmythos*, and toward those of the psyche and realistic environs. Surely this is a matter of considerable dimensions.

This one reservation, however, detracts relatively little from the overall value of this informative, stimulating, and unusually well-written book. If reprinted, an index should definitely be added to facilitate reference to the wealth of information. (K.N.)

Paulson, Ronald, ed. *The Novelette Before 1900.* Englewood Cliffs: Prentice-Hall, 1965. Pp. 375. $6.95.

Among the ten novelettes presented here, with brief introductions and in highly readable form, are Edgeworth's *Castle Rackrent* (1800), von Kleist's *The Marquise of O—* (1810), and Constant's *Adolphe* (1816).

Peckham, Morse. "Romanticism: The Present State of Theory." *PCTE Bulletin*, No. 12 (Dec., 1965), pp. 31-53.

There has been some progress away from the form of the statement, "Romanticism is ——," towards the statement, "The Romantic situation was ——."

10

Pollin, Burton R. "Poe and Godwin." *NCF,* xx (1965), 237-53.

Rinsler, Norma. "Victor Hugo and the *Poésies allemandes* of Gérard de Nerval." *RLC,* xxxix (1965), 382-95.

Hugo's change from a pictorial to a metaphorical vision, in *Feuilles d'Automne,* reflects translations from German literature which Hugo read and discussed with Nerval.

Rose, Edward J. " 'The Queenly Personality': Walpole, Melville and Mother." *L&P,* xv (1965), 216-29.

Concerned with "how modern as well as Romantic" is *The Mysterious Mother,* referred to by Melville ("the suppressed domestic drama of Horace Walpole") along with *Oedipus Tyrannus* and Shelley's *Cenci.*

Singh, G. "Thomas Hardy and Leopardi: A Study in Affinity and Contrast." *RLMC,* xvii (1964), 120-35.

Insists that Hardy had for the most part arrived independently at his views of life before reading Leopardi or Schopenhauer. Leopardi and Hardy had practically the same philosophy of the universe and of human destiny, but differed in their attitudes. Leopardi was indifferent to the consequences of his writings; Hardy was concerned lest he shock too much.

Smeed, J. W. "Thomas Carlyle and Jean Paul Richter." *CL,* xvi (1964), 226-53.

Close, mainly stylistic analysis demonstrating the strong influence of Jean Paul upon Carlyle starting with *Sartor,* and extending into the later works. The study is valuable not only for Carlyle, but also for Jean Paul, on whose style, word-compounding, and metaphor much interesting light is thrown. (U.G.)

Trousson, Raymond. *Le thème de Prométhée dans la littérature européenne.* Geneva: Droz, 1964. 2 vols. sfr. 60.—

Rev. by H. Dyserink in *Germanistik,* vi (1965), 582-83, and by J. Seznec in *FS,* xix (1965), 51-53.

Presents the historical development of the Prometheus myth on a universal scale from antiquity to Christian times, the decline of the myth in the middle ages, and its revaluation thereafter. It was a truly European theme during the Romantic era. This excellent comparative study offers a valuable synthesis of all previous studies. Confronting the various interpretations of the myth with its original meaning leads to a "démystification" (according to Trousson) and to critical stimulation of the reader. (I.C.)

Wasserman, Earl R., ed. *Aspects of the Eighteenth Century.* The Johns Hopkins Press, 1965. Pp. vi + 346. $7.00.

Seminar lectures by George Boas, J. A. Passmore, Isaiah Berlin, René Wellek, Jean Seznec, R. Wittkower, Edward E. Lowinsky, Maynard Mack, W. J. Bate, Georges May, Heinz Politzer, Alfred Cobban, and Henry Guerlac—of pervasive relevance to the study of Romanticism. Boas ("In Search of the Age of Reason") questions the dividing of history into periods; Passmore examines "The Malleability of Man in Eighteenth-Century Thought" from Locke down through the differing French and English Lockians; Berlin discusses "Herder and the Enlightenment"; Wellek "The Term and Concept of 'Classicism' in Literary History." Seznec, in "Diderot and Historical Painting" (with plates), evaluates hierarchies of painting from Vien through David. Wittkower examines theories of "Imitation, Eclecticism, and Genius," including a brief contrast of the views of Reynolds and Blake. Bate's essay, "The English Poet and the Burden of the Past, 1660-1820," emphasies "the fearful legacy of the great Romantics." Cobban, very briefly, discusses "The Enlightenment and the French Revolution" as related but divergent phenomena. (D.V.E.)

Wellek, René. *Confrontations: Studies in the Intellectual and Literary Relations between Germany, England, and the United States during the Nineteenth Century.* Princeton University Press, 1965. Pp. 221. $5.00.

Rev. by Howard M. Jones in *MLQ,* xxvi (1965), 353-55.
Wellek here collects six previously published papers (the "unpublished" lecture appeared in *SIR* in 1964, after his Preface was written): (1) a contrasting of "German and English Romanticism"; papers on (2) Carlyle's relations with the German Romantics (emphasizing his affinity for Jean Paul Richter) and (3) "Carlyle and the Philosophy of History" (showing how Carlyle studied earlier periods not for their own values but as expressions of his moral views); (4)"De Quincey and the History of Ideas" (destroying Proctor's claims for De Quincey's originality as a thinker); and two papers detailing the impact of German philosophers on (5) "The Minor Transcendentalists" in America and (6) Emerson. He has carefully updated his notes to show the relations of these papers to subsequent scholarship.
Wellek's "positive" articles, in which he explores literary relationships, will save those who use them from numerous errors. The equally detailed third and fourth essays, refutations of the mistaken scholarship of others, are even more interesting for the drama of the pursuit. Did not Professor Wellek's humanity and intellectual integrity forbid such a course, one would be tempted to suggest that his erudition might make an even greater impression were he habitually to lie in wait for the mistakes of his parochial colleagues, rather than setting forth, in logical order and with full documentation, studies in which he has quite successfully tried "to keep the totality of Western thought in mind." (D.H.R.)

Wellek, René. *A History of Modern Criticism: 1750-1950.* Vol. III: *The Age of Transition.* Vol. IV: *The Later Nineteenth Century.* Yale University Press, 1965. $8.50. (63s.); $10 (72s.).

For listing of reviews of Vols. I and II, see *PQ,* xxv, 105.
Among critics belonging more or less to the Romantic Movement, Sainte-Beuve, Carlyle, DeQuincey, Hunt, and Heine are treated extensively in Vol. III; Balzac and, with great emphasis, De Sanctis in Vol. IV; and both volumes are concerned, *passim,* with criticism of Romanticism and the Romantic poets.
The chapter on "French Criticism before 1850," originally printed in *Studi in onore di Carlo Pellegrini* (Turin, 1963), presents a sound and readable survey of the period 1815-1850. Authors who receive more than cursory treatment are: Barante, Guizot, Sismondi, Fauriel, Ampère, Villemain, Chasles, Planche, Saint-Marc Girardin, Nisard, Vinet, Magnin, Pierre Leroux, and Gautier. Inevitably, Wellek covers much the same ground as the relevant passages in Saintsbury, and he lacks the Englishman's bite and drive (just as he lacks his eccentricities and prejudices). But he is judicious and perceptive, and has the advantages of a position in time and cultural background much closer to the expectations of today's student. Bibliographies. (J.S.P.)

Whalley, George. "Literary Romanticism." *QQ,* LXXII (1965), 232-52.

Widmer, Kingsley. *The Literary Rebel.* With a preface by Harry T. Moore. (Crosscurrents: Modern Critiques.) Southern Illinois University Press, 1965. Pp. x + 261. $4.50.

Chapter 3, "The Marriage of Heaven and Hell" (pp. 35-47), is a lucid and defiant essay on Blake's *Marriage* "as an idiosyncratic, nearly unique, work, defying both usual literature and ordinary responses." "Blake, I am arguing, really is a rebel, and rebels should not be reduced to distant metaphysical blandness or ameliorative liberal humanism." The whole book should be valuable reading for students of Romanticism, if only to find why none of the Romantic poets (except Blake) even gets into the index. (D.V.E.)

12

Reviews of books previously listed:

FABRE, Jean, *Lumières et romantisme* (see *ELN*, III, Supp., 8), rev. by A. Gillon in *CL*, XVII (1965), 346-47; FRYE, Northrop, *Romanticism Reconsidered* (see *PQ*, XLIII, 436-37), rev. by Mark Roberts in *EIC*, XV (1965), 118-30; KROEBER, Karl, *The Artifice of Reality* (see *ELN*, III, Supp., 9), rev. by Glauco Cambon in *Criticism*, VII (1965), 382-85; by Morse Peckham in *JEGP*, LXIV (1965), 591-93; LUKACS, Georg, *The Historical Novel* (see *PQ*, XLII, 437), rev. by Edwin Berry Burgum (Lukács "is a pre-Freudian romantic") in *S&S*, XXX (1966), 70-76; RICHARDSON, F. C., *Kleist in France* (see *ELN*, III, Supp., 10), rev. by R. Masson in *EG*, XX (1965), 77-78; WELLEK, René, *Concepts of Criticism* (see *ELN*, III, Supp., 10), rev. by C. S. Brown in *CL*, XVII (1965), 160-63.

ENGLISH

(Compilers and reviewers: E. E. Bostetter, Univ. of Washington; Kenneth Neill Cameron, New York Univ.; Kenneth Curry, Univ. of Tennessee; David V. Erdman, The New York Public Library; Richard Harter Fogle, Tulane Univ.; David Bonnell Green, Boston Univ.; John E. Jordan, Univ. of California, Berkeley; Karl Kroeber, Univ. of Wisconsin; Albert J. Kuhn, Ohio State Univ.; William H. Marshall, Univ. of Pennsylvania; Martin K. Nurmi, Kent State Univ.; David H. Stam, Marlboro College; Donald H. Reiman, Carl Pforzheimer Library; Bennett Weaver, Univ. of Michigan, Emeritus; Stewart C. Wilcox, Univ. of Oklahoma; Carl Woodring, Columbia Univ.)

1. BIBLIOGRAPHY

For eighteenth-century figures see the annotated bibliography, "English Literature, 1660-1800," in *PQ* each July. For the most extensive international coverage of Keats, Shelley, Byron, Hunt, and their circles, see the "Current Bibliography" in annual volumes of *KSJ*. For items of specifically bibliographical interest see the "Selective Checklist of Bibliographical Scholarship" in the annual *SB*. For a wide coverage of journals, with precis of articles, consult the indexed monthly issues of *Abstracts of English Studies*.

See also the "Anglo-German Literary Bibliography" in *JEGP* each July, and the relevant sections of the *Annual Bibliography of English Language and Literature*, XXXVII (1965) [for 1962], XXXVIII (1965) [for 1963]; and *The Year's Work in English Studies*, XLIV (1965) [for 1963]. See also "Recent Studies in English Romanticism," by Richard Harter Fogle, in *SEL*, V (1965), 735-48.

For the most extensive general listing see the "Annual Bibliography" in the May issue of *PMLA*.

In 1965 there was one article on a special subject:

Grieder, Theodore. "Annotated Checklist of the British Drama, 1789-99." *Restoration and 18th Century Theatre Research,* IV (1965), 21-47.

2. ENVIRONMENT: ART, SOCIETY, POLITICS, RELIGION

Abel-Smith, Brian. *The Hospitals, 1800-1948: A Study in Social Administration in England and Wales.* Harvard University Press, 1965. Pp. 528. $9.00.

Aspinall, A., ed. *The Correspondence of George, Prince of Wales, 1770-1812.* Vol. III: 1795-1798. London: Cassell; New York: Oxford University Press, 1965. Pp. 519; plates, genealogical tables. L 6; $19.20.
Rev. in *TLS*, Dec. 2, 1965, p. 1101.
With the Prince's marriage and attempted separation, and his struggle for military promotion, his affairs grow increasingly public, and political.

Beaglehole, T. H. *Thomas Munro and the Development of Administrative Policy in Madras, 1792-1818.* Cambridge University Press, 1965. Pp. 204. $6.50.
Light on contemporary ideas about the nature of British rule in India.

Checkland, S. G. *The Rise of Industrial Society in England 1815-1885.* London: Longmans, 1964; New York: St. Martin's, 1965. Pp. xiv + 471; maps. 35s.; $7.00.
Rev. in *TLS*, May 6, 1965, p. 349; by Mark Blaug in *VS*, ix (1966), 223-24; by R. K. Webb, glowingly, in *YR*, lv (1965), 150-52.
Vigorous and informed economic history, weakened by a complacent and superficial view of the accompanying social ills and protests. (D.V.E.)

Cone, Carl B. *Burke and the Nature of Politics.* [Vol. II:] *The Age of the French Revolution.* University of Kentucky Press, 1964. Pp. 527. $9.00.
Vol. I, *The Age of the American Revolution*, appeared in 1957.
Rev. in *TLS*, Feb. 25, 1965, p. 153; by J. H. Plumb in *NYRB*, iv, No. 1 (Feb. 11, 1965), 14-16.
A detailed, gently analytical narrative of Burke's role as a politician who philosophized. Glides over unpleasant aspects; e.g., from Cone's account (pp. 387-88) of Burke's views on the slave trade—as prudent but humane and as unrelated to his views on the French Revolution—one would never guess that in 1792 Burke *opposed* abolition as "Jacobinical." (D.V.E.)

Cunningham, Gilbert F. *The* Divine Comedy *in English: A Critical Bibliography 1782-1900.* London: Oliver and Boyd, 1965. Pp. 206. 35s.

Deane, Phyllis. *The First Industrial Revolution.* Cambridge University Press, 1965. Pp. viii + 295. $8.00; paper, $2.95.
"An attempt to apply the concepts and techniques of development economics to a vital section of the historical record" (1750-1850). E.g., the chapter on "The Role of Government" overturns the notion that the British government aided the industrial revolution by letting things alone. Miss Deane sees "underlying pressures which ensured that a generation reared in the doctrines of *Laissez-faire* should systematically lay the foundations of modern collectivism." (D.V.E.)

14

Donoughue, Bernard. *British Politics and the American Revolution.*
London: Macmillan, 1965. 42s.
Rev. in *New Statesman*, March 12, 1965, p. 408.

Fetter, Frank W. *Development of British Monetary Orthodoxy, 1797-1875.* Harvard University Press; London: Oxford University Press,
1965. Pp. xiv + 296. $7.25; 58s.
Rev. by H. Scott Gordon in *VS*, ix (1966), 222-23.
The 1797 suspension of gold payment and the Bullion Report of 1810 are
studied in analysis of the gap between events and official theory.

Harlow, Vincent T. *The Founding of the Second British Empire, 1763-1793.* Vol. II: *New Continents and Changing Values.* [Ed. by F. McC.
Madden.] London: Longmans, 1965. Pp. 820. £ 3 10s.
Rev. in *TLS*, April 22, 1965, p. 307.
Loss of the American Colonies did not dismay the builders of an empire of
sea-power based on trade without dominion; the Indian adventure was unforeseen; expanding industry and free trade carried Pitt and his fellow Neo-mercantilists farther and faster than they intended to go.

Hill, Draper. *Mr. Gillray The Caricaturist*: *A Biography.* London:
Phaidon, 1965. Pp. vii + 266; 147 plates. 40s.
Rev. by Osbert Lancaster in *S*, June 4, 1965, p. 725; by Paul Johnson in *New
Statesman*, June 4, 1965, p. 884.

Hobsbawm, E. J. *Labouring Men: Studies in the History of Labor.* New
York: Basic Books, 1965. Pp. 401. $7.50.
Includes reprinted essays on Luddism, Methodism, and the Standard of Living
debate.

Hughes, Edward. *North Country Life in the Eighteenth Century.* Volume II: *Cumberland and Westmorland, 1700-1830.* London: Oxford
University Press for the University of Durham, 1965.

Kaufman, Paul. "The Rise of Community Libraries in Scotland." *PBSA*,
LIX (1965), 233-94.

Luttrell, Barbara. *The Prim Romantic*: *A Biography of Ellis Cornelia
Knight, 1758-1837.* London: Chatto and Windus, 1965. Pp. 240. 30s.
Rev. in *TLS*, Jan. 28, 1965, p. 69.
Miss Knight was in the Hamilton-Nelson entourage for several years.

Macalpine, Ida, and Richard Hunter. "The 'Insanity' of King George
III: a Classic Case of Porphyria." *British Medical Journal*, Jan. 8,
1966, pp. 65-71; editorial comment, pp. 59-60.
When George III went out of his mind it was, in his day's terms, delirium
not insanity; abdominal and muscular pain and mental disturbance ranging to
gross psychosis were symptoms of a hereditary physical illness now identified
as porphyria. The political-psychological interpretation needs revision.

Owen, David. *English Philanthropy, 1660-1960.* Harvard University
Press, 1964; London: Oxford University Press, 1965. Pp. xiii + 610.
$11.95; 70s.
Rev. by D. V. Donnison in *VS*, ix (1966), 243-44.

Peacock, A. J. *Bread or Blood: A Study of the Agrarian Riots in East Anglia in 1816.* With a foreword by E. P. Thompson. London: Gollancz, 1965. Pp. 191. 35s.
Rev. in *TLS*, May 6, 1965, p. 343.
"Those who are interested in the history of the common people will read this book anyway," remarks Thompson. "Those who sentimentalise Regency England need to read it most of all." But it isn't very *readable*. (D.V.E.)

Raymond, John, ed. *The Reminiscences and Recollections of Captain Gronow.* New York: Viking, 1965. Pp. 384. $7.95.

Read, Donald. *The English Provinces, c. 1760-1960: A Study in Influence.* London: Edward Arnold, 1964; New York: St. Martin's, 1965. Pp. xi + 319. 42s; $8.50.

Reid, Loren. "Charles Fox and the People." *Burke Newsletter,* VI (1965), 422-30.

Rolo, P. J. V. *George Canning: Three Biographical Studies.* London: Macmillan; New York: St. Martin's Press, 1965. Pp. 276. 36s; $7.50.
Rev. in *TLS*, March 18, 1965, p. 211, and by Robert Blake in *S*, March 5, 1965, p. 302.
Studies of the man and the politician prepare for the century's first full estimate of Canning's achievements as a statesman. He was a talented man, perhaps ahead of his time in attention to public-relations while not truly interested in liberal Causes; his quality as a Foreign Secretary ranks him "with a Richelieu or a Bismarck."

Roscoe Papers 1792-1831 (Liverpool Central Library). Introduction by John Rowe. Microfilm, 2 reels. Micromethods, No. 95806. £ 10.
The American correspondence (1792-1828) of William Roscoe of Liverpool.

Todd, William B. *A Bibliography of Edmund Burke.* London: Rubert Hart-Davis; New York: Oxford University Press, 1965. Pp. 312. £ 6:6:0; $20.20.

Vassall Letter Books 1769-1800 (Sheffield Central Library). Introduction by W. E. Minchinton. Microfilm 1 reel; Micromethods, No. 3541. £ 5.
The letters, partly from London 1775-1800, of the Jamaica sugar planter William Vassall.

Wellington, Seventh Duke of, ed. *Wellington and His Friends: Letters of the First Duke . . . .* London: Macmillan; New York: St. Martin's Press, 1965. Pp. 317. £ 2 5s; $7.50.
Letters to four of his women friends; candid, of slight historical but much biographical interest. A third of the letters precede the Reform Bill.

Whinney, Margaret Dickens. *Sculpture in Britain, 1530-1830.* London: Penguin, 1965. Pp. xxii + 314. £ 4 4s.
Rev. in *TLS*, March 4, 1965, as definitive for many years. Includes Nollekens, Flaxman, Chantrey.

Whiting, Frederick A. "The Royal Academy Tondo by Michelangelo."
Connoisseur, CLVI (May, 1964), 44-45.
The gift of Sir George Beaumont. The article quotes letters of Beaumont to
Lawrence and Wordsworth.

Review of book previously listed:
HUGHES, Edward, ed., *The Diaries and Correspondence of James Losh* (see
PQ, XLII, 441-42, and XLIII, 441), rev. by R. S. Woof (who is critical of both
text and annotation) in *N&Q,* XII (1965), 433-36.

3. CRITICISM

Abrams, M. H. "Structure and Style in the Greater Romantic Lyric."
Pp. 527-60 in *From Sensibility to Romanticism* (see Hilles, below).
Abrams defines and identifies the sources and analogues of a poetic type that he
calls "the greater Romantic lyric," a classification that includes Coleridge's
"conversation poems," Wordsworth's "Tintern Abbey," Shelley's "Ode to the
West Wind," and Keats's "Ode to a Nightingale," among others. He emphasizes Coleridge as a developer of the form. (D.H.R.)

Harvey, W. J. "Some Notes on the Study of Nineteenth-Century Literature." *MLQ,* XXVI (1965), 93-110.
Looks at scholarship and trends of the last twenty-five years in Victorian
studies with an occasional glance at the early nineteenth century.

Hilles, Frederick W., and Harold Bloom, eds. *From Sensibility to Ro-
manticism: Essays Presented to Frederick A. Pottle.* New York:
Oxford University Press, 1965. Pp. viii + 585; 14 plates. $9.75.
Rev. in *TLS,* Dec. 23, 1965, p. 1198.
Among the essays treating one or more of the Romantic poets in this excel-
lent *Festschrift,* several are more significant than many books in the field.
(D.H.R.)
(See Abrams above; McKillop, Price, below; under Blake see Erdman, Hag-
strum, Hollander; under Byron see Hirsch, Ridenour; under Coleridge see
Coburn; under Keats see Bloom; under Shelley, Wasserman; under Words-
worth see Brooks, Hartman, Ryskamp).

Keats-Shelley Memorial Bulletin, No. XVI, 1965.
Contents: Winifred Gérin, "The Montpensier Miniature of Shelley," pp. 1-11;
A. M. D. Hughes, "The Triumph of Life," pp. 12-20; Neville Rogers, "Shelley's
Spelling: Theory and Practice," pp. 21-25; Desmond King-Hele, "Erasmus
Darwin's Influence on Shelley's Early Poems," pp. 26-28; Herbert Huscher,
"Alexander Mavrocordato," pp. 29-38; Desmond King-Hele, "Shelley and
Nuclear Disarmament and Demonstrations," pp. 39-41; Frederick L. Jones,
"Trelawny and the Sinking of Shelley's Boat," pp. 42-44; Edmund Blunden,
"T. J. Hogg's Library," pp. 45-46.

MacNeice, Louis. *Varieties of Parable.* Cambridge University Press,
1965. Pp. 157. $4.50.
Includes a chapter on the English Romantics, chiefly the "extreme cases,"
Blake and Shelley.

McKillop, Alan D. "Local Attachment and Cosmopolitanism—The
Eighteenth-Century Pattern." Pp. 191-218 in *From Sensibility to
Romanticism* (see Hilles, above).
After tracing two rival traditions—one praising attachment to familiar locali-
ties and the other urging men to be citizens of the world—from classical

literature through the eighteenth century, McKillop comments on their appearances in Wordsworth's poetry.

Price, Martin. "The Picturesque Moment." Pp. 259-92 in *From Sensibility to Romanticism* (see Hilles, above).
Price shows that "the picturesque moment is that phase of speculation . . . where the aesthetic categories are self-sufficient." Gilpin, Uvedale Price, and Richard Payne Knight emphasized variety, happy accident, and playfulness by asserting aesthetic values for the "interesting" as well as the sublime and the beautiful. Wordsworth turned enjoyment of the naturally picturesque toward a new romantic orthodoxy of sublimity later preached by Ruskin and George Eliot. This stimulating essay ranges from Donne to Jane Austen to Saarinen's colleges at Yale. (D.H.R.)

Roston, Murray. *Prophet and Poet: The Bible and the Growth of Romanticism.* Northwestern University Press, 1965. Pp. 204. $4.95.

Wilkie, Brian. *Romantic Poets and Epic Tradition.* University of Wisconsin Press, 1965. Pp. xi + 276. $6.50.
Rev. by Ernest Bernhard-Kabisch in *ELN*, III (1965), 142-47; by S. M. Parrish in *KSJ*, xv (1966), 126-28; by Donald H. Reiman in *JEGP*, LXIV (1965), 747-51.
Starting from the assumption that "we can best understand epic not as a genre governed by fixed rules . . . but as a tradition . . . that operates in an unusual way . . . it typically rejects the past . . . the partial repudiation of earlier epic tradition is itself traditional," Wilkie provides interesting essays on several Romantic works which he feels participate in this paradoxical tradition. Wilkie's best chapter seems to me on Southey and Landor, where Wilkie's approach enables him to do more justice to both the strengths and weaknesses of Southey and Landor than more conventional critiques of these somewhat irritating figures. Treating Wordsworth's *Prelude* as what I have called a "personal epic," Wilkie finds that Wordsworth "tries to render the heroic ideal more spiritual" and "he rhetorically rejects external epic array in favor of what is truly 'heroic argument' and 'genuine prowess,' the inner mind of man." Hence, Wilkie concludes, Wordsworth is a more successful "epic" poet than Southey *because* he takes more liberties with the epic tradition. Following chapters on *The Revolt of Islam* and *Hyperion* (the former providing one of the few sensible studies of a neglected work, the latter perhaps the least original section of the book) are less concerned with the central paradox of Wilkie's thesis, but the final chapter on *Don Juan* can fittingly return to concentration upon negative adherence to tradition as a basis for a better understanding of a major Romantic poem. Wilkie's method of attack seems to me well justified, particularly since he seldom insists on pressing his system beyond moderate limits and his critical readings are regularly sensible and undogmatic. (K.K.)

Reviews of books previously listed:
BENZIGER, James, *Images of Eternity* (see *PQ*, XLII, 443-44), rev. in *TLS*, May 6, 1965, p. 355; BOSTETTER, Edward E., The *Romantic Ventriloquists* (see *PQ*, XLIII, 443), rev. by James V. Baker in *Criticism*, VII (1965), 199-200; by John E. Grant in *KSJ*, XIV (1965), 93-96; by Donald Meeks in *JAAC*, XXIV (1965), 322-23; COHEN, Ralph, *The Art of Discrimination* (see *ELN*, III, Supp., 17), rev. by Josephine Miles in *JAAC*, XXIV (1965), 315-16; JACK, Ian, *English Literature, 1815-1832* (see *PQ*, XLIII, 444), rev. with other vols. as "Keeping Tabs on the Oxford History" by Bruce King in *SR*, LXXIII (1965), 125-29, by Donald H. Reiman in *JEGP*, LXIV (1965), 325-32; RENWICK, W. L., *English Literature, 1789-1815* (see *PQ*, XLIII, 444), rev. by Bruce King as above in *SR*; RODWAY, Allan, *The Romantic Conflict*, rev. by Norton B. Crowell in *NMQ*, XXV (Summer, 1965), 184-85.

18

4. STUDIES OF AUTHORS

AUSTEN

Craik, W. A. *Jane Austen: The Six Novels*. London: Methuen; New York: Barnes & Noble, 1965. Pp. 210. 30s. $6.00.

Jane Austen's novels will apparently stand almost interminable talking about, and Mrs. Craik's book is good talk, on the whole sensible and often quite perceptive. After a very brief introduction, she devotes a chapter to the construction of each of the six completed novels, electing to disregard the juvenilia and unfinished pieces on the plausible grounds that they are unsure guides to artistic intention, and on the more dubious ones that they lack "serious moral *impulse*," and being little concerned with sources or influences, either literary or biographical. Her thesis is that there is a line of development in the six novels corresponding generally to the order in which they were published. Accordingly she regularly points out Austen's trying new techniques in successive works: a new way of handling large groups of characters in *Pride and Prejudice*, a new manner of subordinating the hero and heroine in *Mansfield Park*, a new auctorial unobtrusiveness in *Emma*, a new use of locality in *Persuasion*, and other, often subtly discriminated, differences of style and method. Constant comparisons back and forth tend to make the same points over and over and quote the same passages wearisomely.

Sometimes the reader fears that he has fallen into the hands of a wide-eyed Janian: "no event or character is ever lost sight of or summarily dismissed, no improbable events bring about required conclusions, and no personality is distorted to fit an obviously predetermined fate" (p. 22). But immediately thereafter Mrs. Craik admits that the plot of *Northanger Abbey* is "not a complete success," and later that *Persuasion* has "an imperfect plot"—although she can hardly believe that novel was finished—and she does see other faults. Only with *Emma* is she completely faithful to her Janolatry: "readers find difficulties and imperfections where none exist except what their own preconceptions create" (p. 125). The generally justificatory approach leads to such easy assertions as that important and unimportant scenes are described at the same length in *Northanger Abbey* because emphasis is not determined by length, whereas in *Emma* events "are emphasized by the amount of space given to them" (pp. 24, 156). Or the statement that the "brisk speech rhythms" of Captain Wentworth's opinion early in *Persuasion* that Anne's power over him is gone indicate that this is "what Wentworth thinks rather than what is actually true" (p. 171), without any consideration why brisk speech must infallibly be mistaken. Still, the whole lovingly detailed examination of Jane's workmanship is revealing and welcome. (J.E.J.)

Dooley, D. J. "Pride, Prejudice and Vanity in Elizabeth Bennet." *NCF,* xx (1965), 185-88.

Comments on R. C. Fox's note, *NCF,* xvii (1962), 182-87.

Edwards, Thomas R., Jr. "The Difficult Beauty of *Mansfield Park*." *NCF,* xx (1965), 51-67.

Reads the novel as saying virtue is its own reward—a meaning which is "no failure of the novelist's integrity but its triumph, and a prediction (as *Emma,* for all its radiance, is not) of what fiction was to be for the masters of the next hundred years."

Litz, A. Walton. *Jane Austen, A Study of Her Artistic Development*. New York: Oxford University Press, 1965. Pp. x + 198. $5.75.

Rev. in *TLS,* Dec. 23, p. 1198, and by Frank Kermode in *NYRB,* Oct. 28, 1965, pp. 5-6.
Professor Litz bases his study on the assumption that the history of Austen's writings is a record of the search for aesthetic means to realize a complex vision of life. He sees her successes and her failures as artistic, thus answering

those critics, notably Marvin Mudrick, who believe that her lapses reflect weaknesses of nerve, meek submission of her comic insight to conventional morality. Litz is relatively little interested in biographical events and feels that attempts to identify specific sources are narrowly futile. He stresses rather Austen's general heritage from the eighteenth century of both reason and sensibility, and her gradual absorption of the romantic literary influences of the early nineteenth century. This is a welcome enterprise, performed with critical tact and presented clearly and economically.

Litz's full treatment of the juvenilia relates them admirably to contemporary fiction and traces the development from literary burlesque to realistic creation, finding the latter first in "Lesley Castle," and pointing out many anticipations of later work: *Evelyn* is a forerunner of *Northanger Abbey* and *Sense and Sensibility* in its concern with the "sympathetic imagination," and *Volume the Third* employs some of the atmospheric use of place so obvious in the unfinished *Sanditon*. He insists that the ironic *Lady Susan* is of "literary" origins and an attempt at a subject beyond Austen's control, as she recognized by her abrupt Conclusion. In these early works she learned from the novelists of sensibility what excesses to avoid and also a primary and continued interest in the "effects produced on the human mind by a series of events." And she learned to base the moral defense of the novel not on its matter but on its manner, its art.

The real problem of *Northanger Abbey* and *Sense and Sensibility* Litz sees as inconsistency. The latter is not so satisfactory because Austen had become ensnared in the thematic dualism of later eighteenth-century fiction. *The Watsons* moves in the nineteenth-century world of manners, deals woodenly with yet unassimilated materials, and tries a dramatic single-vision she abandons as she develops an easy merger of scenic presentation and editorial comment. *Pride and Prejudice* returns to dualism but succeeds because of its realization of an ideal form. Elizabeth and Darcy both are compounds of sense and sensibility and they dramatize the conflict between social limitation and the individual will.

Mansfield Park causes most trouble to Litz's developmental thesis. Refusing to see it as a "betrayal" of the ironic vein of *Pride and Prejudice,* he recognizes it as a reversal of the values of that novel and a little inconsistently looks for such reasons as the frustrations of a spinster approaching forty or the parallel with the disturbing career of her cousin Eliza de Feuillide. But he finds more important Austen's consistent tension between romantic and neo-classic attitudes and sees *Mansfield Park* as a probing analysis of the role of art itself, and evidently a "necessary catharsis" before she could go on to *Emma,* in which these conflicts are internalized and with her achieved techniques Austen can demonstrate "the paradox that freedom can only be achieved *through* self-restraint and self-knowledge" (p. 136). *Persuasion* and *Sanditon* are treated with somewhat disappointing brevity, although Litz neatly shows the effects of the revision of *Persuasion,* which he sees as a variation on Austen's persistent theme of search for social identity. He avoids the developmental problem of the curiously regressive parody and burlesque of *Sanditon* by arguing a little facilely that it was intended mainly for family enjoyment.

An appendix on chronology of composition adds to the usefulness of this authoritative work. (J.E.J.)

Moler, Kenneth L. "Fanny Burney's *Cecilia* and Jane Austen's 'Jack and Alice'." *ELN,* III (1965), 40-42.

Ten Harmsel, Henrietta. *Jane Austen: A Study in Fictional Conventions.* The Hague: Mouton, 1964; New York: Humanities Press, 1965. Pp. 206. $7.00.

This study is a deliberately limited approach to Jane Austen. Taking *Northanger Abbey* almost as a showcase of conventions of late eighteenth-century fiction, it proceeds to demonstrate how Austen twists them in her six major novels. The general thesis is that although she began by burlesquing the over-worked devices of sentimental and Gothic novelists, she was after all writing novels herself and in various ways made use of these same conventions. Miss Ten Harmsel includes in her panoply standard portraits of characters: the heroine as perfect, passive, Quixotic, and a creature of finest sensibility; the hero as romantic lover, mentor, and rescuer; and such minor characters as the chaperone, the objecting relative, and the moralizing clergyman. She also treats such plot elements as scandalous love intrigue, the Cinderella-motif, the seduction attempt, and pat endings; and such strains as the didactic impulse and the cult of the picturesque. These she sees Austen revivifying with more or less success by four overlapping means which she calls "transforming agents": bringing new realism to stock devices, causing characters to develop and change, making routine elements fulfill a variety of functions in the context of the novel, and turning on them the play of irony.

Miss Ten Harmsel argues that although in *Northanger Abbey* Austen was chiefly burlesquing the stocks of the trade, as she had in her juvenilia, she was already beginning to transform them. This process went further in *Sense and Sensibility*, in which realism and character development became more prominent, but too slavish following of the conventions of antithetical structure and didacticism limited the achievement. In *Pride and Prejudice* all the transforming agents, especially irony, work effectively: if Jane is the perfect passive heroine, Elizabeth is charmingly fallible, active, and real. Darcy, less successfully, merges the villain and hero roles, and the last part of the book uses convention more melodramatically. Fanny Price, however, is too much the quiescent perfect heroine and the conventions, although modified, still operate too flatly in *Mansfield Park* under the influence of the didactic impulse. *Emma*, on the other hand, succeeds because Austen "internalizes" the conventions. In *Persuasion* a "ripeness is all" theme is carried by a generally subtle and restrained use of the accepted devices presented through the consciousness of Anne Elliot, yet here, as usual, comes the *deus ex machina* of artificial convention in the affair of Mr. Elliot and Mrs. Clay.

The work still smells of the dissertation: it proceeds rather mechanically and is replete with buttressing quotations from authorities, fulsome repetition, and superogatory summations. One might also question the validity of virtually omitting the juvenilia and *Sanditon* from consideration, and the assumption that a character such as Fanny Price could not undergo development because she was presented as perfect. Or wonder whether all these conventions do not owe more than is recognized to eighteenth-century drama. Yet Miss Ten Harmsel's analyses are often perceptive, and her specialized investigation shows a great deal about the mechanics and intricacy of Jane Austen's art. (J.E.J.)

See also Muir ("General 3. Criticism").

Review of book previously listed:

SOUTHAM, B. C., *Jane Austen's Literary Manuscripts* (see *ELN*, III, Supp., 20), rev. in *TLS*, Jan. 21, 1965, p. 48, and by Marilyn Butler in *EIC*, xv (1965), 337-41.

BECKFORD

Rosberry, Eva. "Books From Beckford's Library Now at Barnbougle." *BC*, xiv (1965), 324-34.

BEDDOES

Donner, H. W. "Two German Poems Attributed to T. L. Beddoes." *SN*, xxxvii (1965) 360-66.

BLAKE

Adlard, John. "Mr. Blake's Fairies." *NM*, lxv (1964), 144-60.
Their development is traced through twenty years of Blake's writing.

Bentley, G. E., Jr. "Blake Annotations to Swedenborg's *Heaven and Hell.*" *UTQ,* xxxiv (1965), 290-93.

Blake's signature and three annotations are found in a copy, now in the Houghton Library, of the 1784 edition of *Heaven and Hell.* (A marginal mark alongside sections 333 and 334 is overlooked.) One of the notes refers to another Swedenborg treatise, *Earths in Our Solar System,* 1787. Bentley considers this note "solid evidence suggesting that Blake was reading Swedenborg as early as 1787": without it, he could have taken the title-page date as "solid evidence" suggesting 1784! He treats as merely odd, and of no evidential value, the echoes of Swedenborg's book in Blake's *Marriage of Heaven and Hell* of "about 1793." (D.V.E.)

Blake, William. *The Book of Thel.* Trianon Press for the William Blake Trust, 1965. £ 16.16.

Reviewed in *TLS,* Dec. 2, 1965, p. 1104.

Bronowski, J. *William Blake and the Age of Revolution.* New York: Harper & Row, 1965. Pp. 230, with 16 plates. $5.00.

Rev. by Aileen Ward in *Herald Tribune,* Jan. 23, 1966, pp. 4, 14.
A reissue of *A Man Without a Mask* (1944) with a 15-page introduction, a few corrections of detail, and about fifteen additional notes. An important book to be kept in print, though a larger revision (of mistaken readings of economic history and Blake's allusions to it) would have been welcome. (D.V.E.)

Butlin, Martin. "Blake's 'God Judging Adam' rediscovered." *Burlington Magazine,* cvii (Feb., 1965), 86-89.

An inscription on the color-print usually known as *Elijah* proves it to be the supposedly lost *God Judging Adam.*

Damon, S. Foster. *A Blake Dictionary: The Ideas and Symbols of William Blake.* Brown University Press, 1965. Pp. xii + 460, with 12 plates. $20.00.

Rev. in *TLS,* Sept. 2, 1965, p. 756; by F. W. Bateson in *NYRB,* Oct. 28, 1965, pp. 24-25; by Kathleen Raine in *SR,* lxxiii (1965), 711-19.
Because Blake was true to his own dictum that true sublimity is to be found in "minute particulars," his reader must know as specifically as possible the identity and meaning not only of persons and places in the events in his works but of a great many other things besides. The Sloss and Wallis edition of *The Prophetic Writings* (1926) attempted to provide some of this information in a sort of dictionary but proved to be an unreliable reference work because their understanding of Blake was inadequate. Professor Damon's *Dictionary,* the product of a lifetime of Blake study, is a solider work, and a much fuller one, giving very specific information on virtually all the factual information one needs to have, in addition to short interpretive essays on ideas, symbols, and individual works. His is not a dictionary that records current critical opinion, however, but one that gives the opinions of Professor Damon or of the critics with whom he agrees. His discussion of "The Tyger," for instance, does not suggest that many responsible critics differ quite widely in their readings of this poem. Instead he states quite flatly that Kathleen Raine has "demonstrated" the Tyger to be a creation of Urizen, though few would agree that she has demonstrated any such thing. And in the article on "Mysticism," Professor Damon gives no hint that his opinion of Blake as a mystic is very much a minority view. A personal book such as this one, despite its having the form of an objective reference work with citations from some critics, must be used with caution. But it will be of great value for the enormous amount of information it collects in readily accessible form, together with cross references to the text. It even gives information on matter not mentioned by Blake, as in

the article on "Nudity," which begins "Nudity was a word Blake never used and probably despised as an invention of the blushing Tirzah," and goes on to discuss nakedness instead—though, curiously, no cross reference appears under that word. (M.K.N.)

Erdman, David V., ed. *The Poetry and Prose of William Blake*. Commentary by Harold Bloom. Garden City: Doubleday, 1965. Pp. xxiv + 906. 4 plates. $12.50.

Rev. by F. W. Bateson, extravagantly, in *NYRB*, Oct. 28, 1965, pp. 24-25; by Aileen Ward in the *Herald Tribune*, Jan. 23, 1966, pp. 4, 14.
Textual notes pp. 709-806; Commentary pp. 807-89. "The present text represents a considerable advance in the recovery of erased words and lines and hence a significant advance in the reconstruction of manuscript drafts."
A second printing corrects some errors (an Errata sheet will be supplied by the editor upon request) and improves the index.

Erdman, David V. " 'Terrible Blake in His Pride': An Essay on *The Everlasting Gospel*." Pp. 331-56 in *From Sensibility to Romanticism* (see Hilles ["English 3. Criticism"]).

Elaborates the rationale for Erdman's shortened, integrated version of *The Everlasting Gospel* in his edition of *The Poetry and Prose of William Blake*, pp. 510-16, 791-96 (see above).

Gleckner, Robert F. "Blake and the Senses." *SIR*, v (1965), 1-15.

A clear and cogent analysis of how the "cleansed" and "expanded" senses can make the whole creation appear infinite and holy. (A.J.K.)

Gleckner, Robert F. "Blake's Seasons." *SEL*, v (1965), 533-51.

Blake's seasonal cycle in *Poetical Sketches* "owes almost nothing to the eighteenth-century (least of all to Thomson)"; something to Milton and Spenser; but in it Blake is adapting, reversing, modifying, and even perverting the traditions of poetry and thought which he inherited. A breakthrough (as we say these days) in Blake criticism. (D.V.E.)

Hagstrum, Jean H. "Blake's Blake." Pp. 169-78 (+ 10 plates) in Bluhm, Heinz, ed., *Essays in History and Literature*. Presented by Fellows of The Newberry Library to Stanley Pargellis. Newberry Library: Chicago, 1965. $15.00.

As *dramatis persona* in his own works, Blake appears as artist, as pilgrim and plowman, and as traveller—the change from pilgrim to traveller being a transportation to the sunlit realms of Los.

Hagstrum, Jean H. " 'The Wrath of the Lamb': A Study of William Blake's Conversions." Pp. 311-30 in *From Sensibility to Romanticism* (see Hilles ["English 3. Criticism"]).

Traces Blake through three stages of thought and art: (1) praise of Innocence; (2) attack on the evils of Experience—a revolutionary phase in which Orc's rebellion is not only inevitable but virtuous; (3) return to "Christian love" in which "the 'war of swords' is supplanted by 'intellectual War'."

Harper, George M. "Apocalyptic Vision and Pastoral Dream in Blake's *Four Zoas*." *SAQ*, LXIV (1965), 110-24.

Hollander, John. "Blake and the Metrical Contract." Pp. 293-310 in *From Sensibility to Romanticism* (see Hilles ["English 3. Criticism"]).

Hughes, William R., ed. *Jerusalem: A simplified version . . . with commentary and notes.* London: Allen & Unwin; New York: Barnes & Noble, 1964. Pp. 235. $6.00.

A work of love and care. F. W. Bateson might find *Jerusalem* readable in this abridgement. The explicatory notes are plain and clear. (D.V.E.)

Keynes, Geoffrey. "William Blake and John Gabriel Stedman." *TLS,* May 20, 1965, p. 400.

Stedman, for whose *Narrative* Blake made engravings, left a *Journal*, recently edited by Stanbury Thompson and published by the Mitre Press, London, 1962. Blake occurs prominently in it as a friend, at Johnson's and at Blake's; the influence of Stedman's Joanna upon Blake's Oothoon is now confirmed. (D.V.E.)

Keynes, Geoffrey, ed. *William Blake.* (The Masters: The world's most complete gallery of painting.) London: Knowledge Publications, 1965. Pp. 8 + 15 large color plates. 6s.

Kreiter, Carmen S. "Evolution and William Blake." *SIR,* IV (1965), 110-18.

The details of embryology, anatomy, and evolution in *Urizen* are traced to John Hunter—and William Harvey.

Lewis, Wilmarth S., and Philip Hofer, comps. *'The Beggar's Opera' by Hogarth and Blake.* Harvard and Yale University Presses, 1965. Portfolio of 11 unbound pp.; pp. 30. $100.00.

Not examined.

Nemerov, Howard. "Two Ways of the Imagination." *Carleton Miscellany,* V, No. 4 (1964), pp. 18-41.

A comparison of Wordsworth and Blake.

Ostriker, Alicia. *Vision and Verse in William Blake.* University of Wisconsin Press, 1965. Pp. x + 224. $6.00.

Beginning with a discussion of the metrical traditions Blake inherited, Professor Ostriker places him among the "liberals," as she considers *Poetical Sketches.* She then considers *Innocence and Experience,* pointing out that the forms are simple, with short lines, repetitive diction, and "jingling rhymes," resembling children's verse but employing a good deal of free rhythmic variation, through substitution and inversion. Finally, she takes up the Prophetic Books, first defending them against adverse criticism and then showing that Blake proceeds from septenaries in the earlier works to "a style which almost destroys meter" in the later ones, but a poetic rather than a prose style nevertheless. There seems little hard news here.

The metrical analysis used is based almost entirely on two degrees of accent only, which severely limits what can be done with a lyric like "The Sick Rose," which, to my ear at least, depends on various degrees of accent for its musical effects. As a result, what we are given is a fairly conventional scansion of selected poems or stanzas, together with descriptions of metrical effects that resemble program notes for a symphony concert. In the analysis of "The Tyger," for instance, in the second stanza "there is already something insinuating and ominous in the iambic lines. The fourth stanza, in which the creation of the Tyger culminates, is again all pounding trochees. The fifth, quieter and more fearsome, is again half and half" (p. 76).

It is suggested, at various points, that the metrical analysis can make plain meanings which have escaped other kinds of analysis, but when "The Fly" is said to be "an excellent example of a poem which achieves its ends through surface manipulation" (p. 48), we lose confidence. And when we are told that "As he proceeded in the Prophetic Books, Blake pushed God, his idea of ultimate unity, ever farther back from the fallen world, apparently the better to enjoy the reunion of God and Man, when it came, as it comes on the final plate of *Jerusalem*" (p. 121), there is a disturbing suggestion that the author postulates for Blake a kind of poetical selfhood which, if taken seriously, would vitiate his whole enterprise.

A metrical study of Blake would be most welcome, but it should be made with a more subtle analytical scheme than one which points out iambs and trochees and does little more, and it should be made with a firmer grasp of Blake's meaning. (M.K.N.)

Pinto, Vivian de Sola. "A Neglected Poem of William Blake." Pp. 19-31 in *Critical Essays in English Literature in Honour of Professor Duraiswami*. London: Longmans Green for Annamalai University, 1965.

A sensitive commentary on the "Golden Builders" lyric in *Jerusalem*. (D.V.E.)

Pinto, Vivian de Sola. *William Blake: Selected Writings*. New York: Schocken Books, 1965. Pp. 194. $4.50; paper $1.95.

The selection is very slightly annotated, but the 58-page introduction is sensitive and informative; excellent of its kind. (D.V.E.)

Price, Martin. "Blake: Vision and Satire." Pp. 390-445, in *To the Palace of Wisdom: Studies in Order and Energy from Dryden to Blake*. Garden City: Doubleday, 1964; Anchor Books, 1965. Pp. 468. $5.95; $1.95.

Rev. by Thomas R. Edwards, Jr., in *Criticism*, VII (1965), 106-08.

The Blake chapter caps an impressively Blakean series of essays, throughout which his name and concepts are frequently invoked. The chapter's four sections give thoughtful attention to the songs—and longer poems—of Innocence; to the conception of States and contraries, with a reading of *The Marriage* as a dialectic satire; to the "process of satiric reduction" in Blake's merging of myths, with a valuable comparison of Blake's Urizen and Pope's Dulness; and to Blake's critical remarks on art, especially in the "confrontation of Blake and Reynolds." The whole book explicates the progression of 18th-century concepts as a path leading to Blake's palace. Comparisons involving Wordsworth are also frequent. (D.V.E.)

Roe, Albert S. *William Blake: An Annotated Catalogue*. Andrew Dickson White Museum of Art, Cornell University, Feb. 27-Mar. 29, 1965. Pp. 44, illus.

The Blake Trust traveling exhibition, supplemented by engravings, illustrations to the Bible, illustrations to literary classics, and some book illustrations, mostly from the Rosenwald Collection.

Rose, E. J. "The Symbolism of the Opened Center and Poetic Theory in Blake's *Jerusalem*." *SEL*, v (1965), 587-606.

Fascinating. (D.V.E.)

Tolley, Michael J. "*The Book of Thel* and *Night Thoughts*." *BNYPL*, LXIX (1965), 375-85.

Passages in Young more plausibly account for words, ideas, and moral sentiments in Blake's *Thel* than do previously adduced, but awkwardly dated, sources.

See also five miscellaneous notes on Blake in *N&Q,* xii (1965), 172-84.

See also Widmer ("General 3. Criticism"); MacNeice, Roston ("English 3. Criticism"); Nemerov ("Wordsworth").

Reviews of books previously listed:

ADAMS, Hazard, *William Blake: A Reading of the Shorter Poems*, (see *PQ,* xliii, 447), rev. by Martin K. Nurmi in *Criticism,* vii, (1965), 110-12; BENTLEY, G. E., Jr., and Martin K. Nurmi, *A Blake Bibliography* (see *ELN,* iii, Supp., 21), rev. in *TLS,* Sept. 2, 1965, p. 756, by David V. Erdman in *JEGP,* lxiv (1965), 744-47, and by Geoffrey Keynes in *BC,* xiv (1965), 250-53; HAGSTRUM, Jean H., *William Blake, Poet and Painter* (see *ELN,* iii, Supp., 22), rev. by John E. Grant in *JAAC,* xxiv (1965), 126-28; HIRSCH, E. D., Jr., *Innocence and Experience* (see *ELN,* iii, Supp., 33-34), rev. in *TLS,* Feb. 11, 1965, p. 108, by G. E. Bentley, Jr., devastatingly, in *MP,* lxiii (1965), 77-79, by E. J. Rose, severely, in *DR,* xlv (1965), 103-107, and by Anthony Blunt in *NYRB,* Oct. 28, 1965, pp. 22-23; KEYNES, Geoffrey, *A Study of the Illuminated Books of William Blake* (see *ELN,* iii, Supp., 24), rev. in *TLS,* Dec. 2, 1965, p. 1104, and by John E. Grant in *Nation,* Jan. 25. 1965, p. 91.

BYRON

Bartel, Roland. "Byron's Respect for Language." *PELL,* i (1965), 373-78.

Escarpit, Robert. *Byron: un tableau synoptique de la vie et des oeuvres de Byron et des principaux événements contemporains.* (Ecrivains d'Hier et d'Aujourd'hui, No. 21.) Paris: Editions Pierre Seghers, 1965. Pp. 192.

Gleckner, Robert F. "Ruskin and Byron." *ELN,* iii (1965), 47-51.

Byron's manuscript revisions of a passage in *The Island* (Canto III, ll.63-72) considered in relation to Ruskin's analysis of the lines in manuscript notes for *Fiction, Fair and Foul.*

Hassler, Donald M. "*Marino Faliero,* the Byronic Hero, and *Don Juan.*" *KSJ,* xiv (1965), 55-64.

Hirsch, E. D., Jr. "Byron and the Terrestrial Paradise." Pp. 467-86 in *From Sensibility to Romanticism* (see Hilles ["English 3. Criticism"]).

An important essay that emphasizes "romantic" elements in *Don Juan* "to uncover . . . its inner form." (D.H.R.)

Luke, Hugh J., Jr. "The Publishing of Byron's *Don Juan.*" *PMLA,* lxxx (1965), 199-209.

Considers it "altogether unfortunate" that Byron acquired a radical reputation, from his voluntary and involuntary association (through piratical editions) with radical booksellers,—yet not "altogether unfortunate" either, for although the association ruined his reputation among the respectable, the piracies indicate "a wide sale to the newly emerging English common reader." (D.V.E.)

Marchand, Leslie A. *Byron's Poetry: A Critical Introduction.* Riverside Studies in Literature. Boston: Houghton Mifflin Company, 1965. Pp. vii + 261. $1.95.

Professor Marchand says modestly in his preface that his "only purpose is to furnish to students and general readers some useful observations on Byron's poetry as a whole and on particular poems." In this purpose he succeeds admirably, but he does much more. He provides a meticulous close examination of individual poems considered more or less in chronological order, first whenever relevant in relation to a group of similar poems, as in the case of Popean satires and Oriental tales, and then in relation to the artistic development and changing interests of Byron. The accumulative effect is to provide a more comprehensive and accurate view of Byron's achievements than is provided by any recent special studies such as those by Rutherford and Joseph. Indeed, I know of no other book that performs this particular much-needed service. The book will be of most value for undergraduate and graduate students, for whom it is of course first of all intended, but teachers will profit also from the careful interpretations and sane criticism. For the advanced student the chapters on lesser known and minor poems are especially useful. An annotated selected bibliography is appended. (E.E.B.)

Ridenour, George M. "Byron in 1816: Four Poems from Diodati." Pp. 453-65 in *From Sensibility to Romanticism* (see Hilles ["English 3. Criticism"]).
Treats "Epistle to Augusta," "Darkness," "The Dream," and "A Fragment" ("Could I remount the river of my years").

Thorslev, Peter L., Jr. "Incest as Romantic Symbol." *CLS,* II (1965), 41-58.
Centers on Byron and Shelley.

See also Roston, Wilkie ("English 3. Criticism"); Marshall, Strickland ("French. Stendhal"); Martins ("Portuguese, Brazilian. Alencar").

Reviews of books previously listed:
JOSEPH, M. K., *Byron the Poet* (see *ELN,* III, Supp., 26), rev. by Frederick L. Beaty in *KSJ,* xv (1966), 124-26; by Ian Jack in *Landfall,* xIx (1965), 89-91, and by Andrew Rutherford in *MLR,* LX (1965), 260-61; MARSHALL, William H., *The Structure of Byron's Major Poems* (see *PQ,* xLII, 453), rev. by Andrew Rutherford in *RES,* xvI (1965), 89-90; WEST, Paul, ed., *Byron: A Collection of Critical Essays* (see *PQ,* xLIII, 450), rev. by Ernest J. Lovell, Jr., in *KSJ,* xIv (1965), 89-91.

CLARE
Review of books previously listed:
MARTIN'S *Life* and the ROBINSON-SUMMERFIELD editions of *Later Poems* and *Shepherd's Calendar* (see *ELN,* III, Supp., 27-28), rev. by Radcliffe Squires in *VS,* Ix (1966), 291-92.

COLERIDGE
Appleyard, J. A. *Coleridge's Philosophy of Literature: The Development of a Concept of Poetry 1791-1819.* Harvard University Press, 1965. Pp. xvi + 266. $6.50.
Rev. in *TLS,* June 9, 1966, p. 512.

Boulger, James D. "Christian Skepticism in *The Rime of The Ancient Mariner.*" Pp. 439-52 in *From Sensibility to Romanticism* (see Hilles ["English 3. Criticism"]).
Boulger attempts a reading of the poem mediating between Warren's and Bostetter's, but substantially weakens his argument by ignoring the Gloss. (D.H.R.)

Braekman, W. "The Influence of William Collins on Poems Written by Coleridge in 1793." *RLV,* XXXI (1965), 228-39.
Coleridge was attracted to Collins in 1793, not 1796 as hitherto assumed.

Chandler, Alice. "Structure and Symbol in 'The Rime of the Ancient Mariner'." *MLQ,* XXVI (1965), 401-13.

Chayes, Irene H. "A Coleridgean Reading of 'The Ancient Mariner'." *SIR,* IV (1965), 81-103.
". . . the Mariner's adventures at sea comprise not only psychological and aesthetic experiences which are the subjects of other poems by Coleridge and for the most part have been recognized by his critics, but also experiences which dramatize the epistemological problems dealt with more prominently in his 'philosophical' prose."

Coburn, Kathleen. "Reflections in a Coleridge Mirror: Some Images in His Poems." Pp. 415-37 in *From Sensibility to Romanticism* (see Hilles ["English 3. Criticism"]).
Draws from Coleridge's notebooks clues to the personal meaning of his poetic imagery.

Coburn, Kathleen. *The Interpretation of Man and Nature.* Warton Lecture on English Poetry, British Academy 1963. From the *Proceedings of the British Academy,* XLIX, 95-113. London: Oxford University Press [1965]. 5s.

Coburn, Kathleen. "Who Killed Christabel" [Letter], *TLS,* May 20, 1965, p. 397.

Deschamps, Paul. *La formation de la pensée de Coleridge (1772-1804).* Etudes Anglaises, 15. Paris: Didier, 1964. Pp. 603. 58,00F.
Rev. in *TLS,* Jan. 14, 1965, p. 28.
This fat, valuable study attempts to build Coleridge's personality by bringing together the available strands of biography, temperament, reading, and thought. It synthesizes the best scholarship of the 1950's, notably that of Kathleen Coburn and John Beer. Its full bibliography extends to 1962.
Deschamps shares the current belief that Coleridge's greatest potential value to our time, aside from his major poems, lies in marginalia, notebook entries, cogitations, records of introspection, and *cris du coeur.* His sympathy for Coleridge's eclecticism shows in his own method. He suggests that Coleridge learned from Boyer at Christ's Hospital the rigor of thought in the face of an object or phenomenon that we find applied in the notebooks to the poet's own sensations, passions, and affections. Arguing, like Beer and Woodring, that Kubla Khan is more nearly tyrant than poet, he takes the maiden to be Psyche, whom Kubla had banned from his godless garden of pleasure. Concluding that Coleridge had from childhood a standpoint of Platonic idealism, he frequently paraphrases Platonically: "Le symbole est la représentation dans le monde des apparences d'une réalité appartenant au monde des idées. . . ."
There are small problems. In saying that fancy became assimilated to the primary imagination, he seems to misunderstand the cryptic passage at issue (p. 523). He inserts *sic* at odd places in English quotations, especially when Coleridge is at his most idiomatic, but he has generally understood the positions of those quoted and those quarreled with. Coleridge should be the first to forgive the slightly excessive but purposeful repetitions within the lucid whole. As a bonus, Descramps reprints George Whalley's list of books borrowed at Bristol and Alice Snyder's list of books borrowed at Göttingen. (C.W.)

Eiseley, Loren. "Darwin, Coleridge, and the Theory of Unconscious Creation." *LC,* xxi, No. 1 (Winter, 1965), 7-22.

Empson, William. "The Ancient Mariner." *CritQ,* vi (1964), 298-319.
Concerned with the poem's expression of Coleridge's ambivalent attitude toward the Christian doctrine of guilt and expiation, especially as this seemed to reflect his own personal sense of uncaused guilt.

Forstman, H. Jackson. "Samuel Taylor Coleridge's Notes Toward the Understanding of Doctrine." *JR,* xliv (1964), 310-27.
Using the observations on Christian doctrine found in *Aids to Reflection,* discusses Coleridge's views concerning the proper function and limitation of theological language.

Gardner, Martin, ed. *The Annotated Ancient Mariner: The Rime of the Ancient Mariner,* by Samuel Taylor Coleridge, illustrated by Gustave Doré. New York: Clarkson N. Potter, 1965. Pp. 200. $7.50.
The 1834 text is illustrated by the Doré woodcuts in gem-like reduction, the 1798 text by the same cuts full size; the introduction and notes are clever and informative. (D.V.E.)

Gerber, Richard. "Cybele, Kubla Khan, and Keats." *ES,* xlvi (1965), 369-89.
See Meier below.

Houston, Neal B. "Fletcher Christian and 'The Rime of the Ancient Mariner'." *DR,* xlv (1965), 431-46.
"Had not Coleridge known of the adventures of Christian, the mutineer, there would likely be no moral to the poem"—indeed, by this argument, no poem either.

Knights, L. C. "Idea and Symbol: Some Hints from Coleridge." Pp. 155-68 in *Further Explorations.* Stanford University Press, 1965.
Shows that Coleridge supports (1) most recent attitudes toward symbols and (2) Knight's insistence that symbols involve personal commitment and a change in being for both author and reader. Reprinted from *Metaphor and Symbol,* ed. L. C. Knights and Basil Cottle (Proceedings of the Colston Research Society, Bristol, 1960, Vol. XII). (C.W.)

Meier, Hans Heinrich. "Ancient Light on Kubla's Lines." *ES,* xlvi (1965), 15-29.
Partly in response to Gerber's 1963 article (see *PQ,* xliii, 451). Finds the myth of Adonis, rather than of Cybele, central to the meaning of *Kubla Khan* and considers the parallel to *Paradise Lost* IV. 214 ff. fundamental.
(Another note to Gerber, by Robert F. Fleissner, is given on p. 45 of this issue.) (See Gerber's current article, above.)

Ober, Warren U. "Heart of Darkness: 'The Ancient Mariner' a Hundred Years Later." *DR,* xlv (1965), 333-37.
Conrad reverses Coleridge's theme.

Schulz, Max F. "Coleridge, Wordsworth, and the 1800 Preface to *Lyrical Ballads*." *SEL,* v (1965), 619-39.
Argues for a more complex intellectual-aesthetic genesis of the preface than has usually been admitted.

Sen, Ramendra Kumar. "Imagination in Coleridge and Abhinavagupta: A Critical Analysis of Christian and Saiva Standpoints." *JAAC,* XXIV (1965), 96-107.

Suther, Marshall. *Visions of Xanadu.* Columbia University Press, 1965. Pp. xiv + 297. $7.50.

After explaining his reasons for taking *Kubla Khan* as a complete, coherent, and symbolic poem, Professor Suther traces its symbols, sometimes singly, sometimes in clusters, throughout Coleridge's work, especially in the notebooks and the lesser poems. Although a few of his examples of romantic chasms and women weeping for demon-lovers carry much less conviction than his best examples, he makes the strongest case we have yet had for the unity of the entire poetic canon. The last hundred pages, drawing on the imagistic patterns established in the earlier chapters, offer a close reading of the poem. This book, as dust-jackets say, is one for both specialist and general reader. (C.W.)

See also Muir ("General 3. Criticism"); Roston ("English 3. Critcism').

Reviews of books previously listed:

SCHULZ, Max F., *The Poetic Voices of Coleridge* (see *PQ,* XLIII, 452-53), rev. by George Whalley in *SAQ,* LXIV (1965), 147-49; by R. S. Woof in *N&Q,* XII (1965), 474-76.

CONSTABLE

Reviews of book previously listed:

BECKETT, R. B., ed., *John Constable's Correspondence* (see *ELN,* III, Supp., 30), rev. in *TLS,* Jan. 14, 1965, p. 23, and by Geoffrey Grigson in *New Statesman,* Sept. 3, 1965, pp. 327-28.

CRABBE

Link, Frederick M. "Three Crabbe Letters." *ELN,* II (1965), 200-05.

Sigworth, Oliver F. *Nature's Sternest Painter: Five Essays on the Poetry of George Crabbe.* University of Arizona Press, 1965. Pp. 191. $6.50.

Crabbe's poetry deserves the unromantic readers who will be attracted to it by these unemphatic essays that unfold his virtues and account for the reception his work was given by contemporaries—who liked it for eighteenth-century reasons and disapproved for nineteenth-century ones. The chapter on "Crabbe and the Eighteenth Century" (arguing that his kind of "realism" came to them as no particular shock) is followed by one on "Crabbe in the 'Romantic Movement' " (which desists from placing him in it but offers an examination of the comparison Wordsworth invited, also an excellent survey of Crabbe's gradually widened grasp of social problems). The essay on "Crabbe as Nature Poet" argues that Crabbe could have been such a poet—if he had wished to be. In Chapter 4 he emerges triumphant "as Narrative Poet" (a master in conception and manipulation of character if not in plotting). The final essay surveys the criticism of Crabbe and offers a judicial critique. (D.V.E.)

DARWIN, ERASMUS

See *Keats-Shelley Memorial Bulletin* ("English 3. Criticism").

DeQUINCEY

Goldman, Albert. *The Mine and the Mint: Sources for the Writings of Thomas De Quincey.* Southern Illinois University Press, 1965. Pp. 206. $5.95.

". . . His many works of a scholarly or intellectual nature are almost all derived in the most direct way from printed sources, and in almost every case from a single volume" (p. 9).

Moreux, Françoise. *Thomas DeQuincey, La Vie—L'Homme—L'OEuvre*. (Publications de la Faculté des Lettres et Sciences humaines de Paris, Séries Recherches, XII.) Paris: Presses Universitaires de France, 1964. Pp. 624. 40 Fr.

DeQuincey had a low opinion of the French but a generous enthusiasm for lady authors: he would have been surprised and pleased that a sensitive and cordial study, containing the fullest analysis yet of his work, should have come from a Frenchwoman. Mlle. Moreux divides her book into three parts—the life, the personality, and the work. Her life has little to contribute besides such chapter titles as "Le 'Fardeau de l'incommunicable'" and "La 'Parenthèse Passionée.'" Otherwise it covers the ground fairly routinely, offers no new facts, and does not make use of all those uncovered by Eaton and others. The treatment is sympathetic, sometimes defensive, and perhaps inconsistent. Isn't it a little hard to reconcile a "manie de la persécution" (p. 38) with a "manque total d'égoïsme" (p. 106.)

The section on personality—the shortest of the three—echoes some of the interpretations of the life, especially the perhaps overstressed notion of De-Quincey's inadaptability, which leads to the untenable charge of intellectual stagnation. Short but useful chapters discuss his religious and moral, his philosophical, and his political, economic, and social ideas. Mlle. Moreux acutely sees the ambiguity of his mixed conservatism and liberalism, and argues that sentimental conservatism often balks his intellectual daring and immobilizes him. She also interestingly suggests that his generous sympathy for the suffering of others leads to modern concepts of ennobling men by having confidence in them.

Longest and best of the sections is that on DeQuincey's work, which follows his own classifications of "Divertissantes," "Instructives," and "Passionnées." Most of Mlle. Moreux's comments are not unanticipated, but no other description and analysis on this scale exists. She finds his autobiography sensitive, interpretative, valuable for its insights into the interior life, and interestingly using digressions as Proust did parentheses. DeQuincey's biographical writing she believes reveals a talent for psychological portraiture, but his tales "add nothing to his glory." Her chapter on "L 'Humoriste" is an admirable discussion of a side of DeQuincey which has been most variously received. Under "Instructive" writing she deals with DeQuincey as a critic and historian, devoting a helpful chapter each to his critical theory and his critical methods, noting his logical turn of intuitive criticism, his sympathetic echoing of author's styles, and the relation of his ideas to those of earlier commentators. She is therefore chary of claiming for him great originality, yet does insist that he introduced a new aesthetic idea of "puissance emotionnelle" (p. 349).

Some of Mlle. Moreux's most original contributions come in the last section on DeQuincey's impassioned prose. She perhaps pays too little attention to the writing and rewriting of *Confessions*—dismissing the 1856 version as a monstrosity—but the treatment of the *Suspiria* is understanding and the investigation of the landscape of DeQuincey's dream world perceptively notes the sensitivity of verbal echoes and the general absence of color. A chapter on "L'Artiste" offers a short discussion of his style and a summary conclusion touches on the subject of his influence.

The index is of proper names only and the unusually full bibliography has a number of mistakes. (J.E.J.)

See also Wellek, *Confrontations* and *History* ("General 3. Criticism").

Review of book previously listed:

JORDAN, John E., *DeQuincey to Wordsworth* (see *PQ*, XLII, 458), rev. by Norton B. Crowell in *NMQ*, XXXIV (1964), 212-15.

EDGEWORTH, RICHARD

Clarke, Desmond. *The Ingenious Mr. Edgeworth.* London: Oldbourne, 1965. Pp. 256. 35s.
Rev. in *TLS*, Dec. 30, 1965, p. 1211.
Full length biography of Richard Lovell Edgeworth.

See also Paulson ("General 3. Criticism").

GODWIN

Godwin, William. *Italian Letters: or, The History of the Count de St. Julian.* Ed. by Burton R. Pollin. University of Nebraska Press. $4.50.
First published by George Robinson in 1784, this anonymous Godwin novel, believed lost until recently, is here presented with useful editorial equipment. In an introduction Mr. Pollin concisely discusses the history of the novel, its sources and parallels, some aspects of its structure and technique, and the contemporary reviewers' reaction to it. He carefully indicates the nature of and reason for any departures from the original text. In epistolary form and with expectedly didactic overtones, the somewhat traditional narrative concerns the Marquis de Pescara's betrayal of his friend the Count de St. Julian for the hand of Matilda della Colonna and St. Julian's revenge on the betrayer. (W.H.M.)

Pollin, Burton R. "Verse Satires on William Godwin in the Anti-Jacobin Period." *SNL,* II (1964), 31-40.

See also Pollin ("General 3. Criticism").

Review of book previously listed:
POLLIN, Burton Ralph, *Education and Enlightenment in the Works of William Godwin* (see *PQ*, XLII, 458), rev. by Jack W. Marken in *KSJ*, XIV (1965), 98-100.

HAWKER

Woolf, Cecil. "Some Uncollected Authors XXXIX: Hawker of Morenstow, 1803-1875." *BC,* XIV (1965), 62-65; 202-11.
Robert Stephen Hawker.

HAZLITT

Albrecht, W. P. *Hazlitt and the Creative Imagination.* University of Kansas Press, 1965. Pp. 203. $4.00.
Not received in time to review.

Cain, Roy E. "David Hume and Adam Smith as Sources of the Concept of Sympathy in Hazlitt." *PELL,* I (1965), 133-40.

Kinnaird, John. " 'Philo' and Prudence: A New Hazlitt Criticism of Malthus." *BNYPL,* LXIX (1965), 153-63.

Sikes, Herschel M. " 'The Infernal Hazlitt': *The New Monthly Magazine,* and the *Conversations of James Northcote, R.A.*" Pp. 179-91 in *Essays in History and Literature: Presented by Fellows of The Newberry Library to Stanley Pargellis,* ed. by Heinz Bluhm. Chicago: The Newberry Library, 1965. Pp. 231.

32

Trawick, Leonard M. "Hazlitt, Reynolds, and the Ideal." *SIR,* IV (1965), 240-47.
On abstraction and selectivity of the imagination.

Review of book previously listed:
BAKER, Herschel, *William Hazlitt* (see *PQ,* XLII, 459-60), rev. by Peter Stockham in *BJA,* v (1965), 411-12.

HUNT

Fogle, Stephen F. "Leigh Hunt, Thomas Powell, and the *Florentine Tales.*" *KSJ,* XIV (1965), 79-87.

See also Wellek, *History* ("General 3. Criticism").

Review of book previously listed:
CHENEY, David R., ed., *Musical Evenings* (see *ELN,* III, Supp., 33), rev. by Carolyn W. Houtchens in *KSJ,* XV (1966), 138-39.

KEATS

Birkenhead, Sheila. *Illustrious Friends: The Story of Joseph Severn and his Son Arthur.* London: Hamish Hamilton, 1965. Pp. 393. £ 2 10s.
Rev. in *TLS,* Dec. 30, 1965, p. 1211.

Bloom, Harold. "Keats and the Embarrassments of Poetic Tradition." Pp. 513-26 in *From Sensibility to Romanticism* (see Hilles ["English 3. Criticism"]).
This important essay finds Keats achieving independence from the Miltonic tradition by becoming increasingly naturalistic—the forerunner of Pater and Stevens. Discussion centers on the odes and the second *Hyperion.* (D.H.R.)

Evert, Walter H. *Aesthetic and Myth in the Poetry of Keats.* Princeton University Press, 1965. Pp. x + 325. $6.50.
Rev. in *TLS,* Sept. 23, 1965, p. 828; by Helen E. Haworth in *DR,* XLV (1965), 378-81; by Bernice Slote in *KSJ,* XV (1966), 135-38.
This is a mature and even a major essay in Keats interpretation, despite the fact that only one-third of its 319 pages of text is devoted to Keats's mature poetry. Mr. Evert, it must be said, has good reasons for perpetrating the misproportion. He considers that Keats's thought grew faster than his ability to express it, and was essentially complete a good deal earlier than we generally suppose.
On the question whether Keats *did* think, the author is with C. D. Thorpe and most of us, and against Fairchild and E. C. Pettet. He contributes markedly, however, to the continuing Keatsian dialogue by the skill of his formulation of terms; that is, he successfully evades the false dilemma of philosopher-or-sensualist, neo-Platonist-or-"realist," that has so often plagued our arguments. His interpretation of *Endymion,* consequently, is one of the most satisfying treatments of this inescapable poem in the canon of Keats criticism. Without making a wire-drawn allegory out of it, Evert is able to demonstrate its essential meaning as the quest of the poet.
He sets forth Keats's creed with remarkable precision: "The complete spiritual cycle of individual human life and growth is comparable to the annual cycle of physical life and growth in external nature. These cycles are not only comparable by developmental analogy but are harmonious with each other because identically subject to the influence of a single beneficent power, or law, which manifests itself in and through them. This power is the law of universal harmony, by which all existing things are held in a balanced interrelationship

with each other, and initially discrete elements are fused, through an assimilative growth process, into new, organically integrated entities. The power is best exemplified concretely in the late-Greek conception of the god Apollo" (pp. 30-31). The account fuses myth with Romantic dynamism and the doctrine of symbol, though for the present reviewer Evert, like M. H. Abrams in *The Mirror and the Lamp*, accepts the principle of analogy too simply as a sufficient explanation.

This creed works best with the earlier poems. Accordingly, we hear almost as much about the "Ode to Apollo" as about the "Ode on a Grecian Urn," and certainly more about the "Epistle to John Hamilton Reynolds" in proportion than its poetic value warrants. Yet this, it must be remarked, is an intended consequence of Evert's approach. He deals with the "Epistle" at length because it represents a crisis in Keats's thought. From the "Epistle" on, Keats retreats from his system, from Apollo, and from the imagination to the "self-sufficient beauty of the real world," in "a flight from system in a willing acceptance of whatever response the experience of the moment may bring forth" (p. 224). Only once more, and without knowing it, is Keats able to synthesize—in the final glory of "To Autumn."

The volume is dense in texture, profusely annotated, and fully argued, with previous criticism frankly met. It is one of its virtues that it is both tactful and straightforward. Almost all of its interpretations of individual poems are profitable, although Mr. Evert's anticipations of outrage at his treatment of *The Eve of St. Agnes* are fulfilled in the present reviewer. He raises questions by his division of "thought" and "poetry" throughout, and his method, as with the "Ode to a Nightingale," is not adequate to the structure and dynamics of the individual poem. He is much too kind to Apollonius in *Lamia*, and too certain of the textual solution to "Beauty is Truth, Truth Beauty." But these again, are issues of the approach to Keats's poetry. (R.H.F.)

Gleckner, Robert F. "Keats's Odes: The Problems of the Limited Canon." *SEL*, v (1965), 577-85.

Goldberg, M. A. "John Keats and the Elgin Marbles." *Apollo*, LXXXII (1965), 370-77.

Jones, James Land. "Keats and Yeats: Artificers of the Great Moment." *XUS*, iv (1965), 125-50.
One of the best of Keats-Yeats comparisons. Suggests that Keats might have become Yeatsian in thought had he lived. (R.H.F.)

Magaw, Malcolm. "Yeats and Keats: The Poetics of Romanticism." *BuR*, xii (December, 1965), 87-96.
A succinct, well-balanced, and lucid essay. "As romanticists, Yeats and Keats . . . envision ideal worlds, but these worlds bear diametrically opposite stamps —Yeats's primarily intellectual and artificial, Keats's sensuous and natural." (R.H.F.)

Miller, Bruce E. "On the Meaning of Keats's *Endymion*." *KSJ*, xiv (1965), 33-54.

Rollins, Hyder E., ed. *The Keats Circle: Letters and Papers and More Letters and Poems of the Keats Circle*, 2nd ed. 2 vols. Cambridge: Harvard UP, 1965. Pp. cl + 332; 519, 125. $25.
Since these volumes were fully reviewed at their first publications in 1948 and 1955, the present comment is confined to a welcome to the second edition and a rehearsal of a few salient facts about it. In a new Preface W. J. Bate informs us that it incorporates about 160 corrections by Professor Rollins, in addition to other corrections and additions. The original pagination, however, has been

retained throughout. *The Keats Circle* contains Keatsian materials in the Houghton Library to the year 1878, based primarily on the Lowell collection (1927) and the "Crewe papers," acquired by Harvard in 1941, and comprising the original collection made by R. M. Milnes, Lord Houghton, for his biography of 1848. *More Letters and Poems* is a set of correspondence by and to Fanny Keats de Llanos. It may be remarked that insofar as these letters concern the financial affairs of George and Fanny Keats they should now be read in connection with Bate's *John Keats* (1963) and Robert Gittings' *The Keats Inheritance* (1964). It may also be useful to remind readers that in addition to letters of "the Keats circle" the total collection contains "the Morgan Ms.," a scrapbook of Keatsiana compiled by Richard Woodhouse; and Charles Armitage Brown's *Life of Keats*. (R.H.F.)

Saly, John. "Keats's Answer to Dante: *The Fall of Hyperion.*" *KSJ,* xiv (1965), 65-78.

Sharrock, Roger, ed. *Selected Poems and Letters.* (New Oxford English Series.) London; New York: Oxford University Press, 1965. Pp. iv + 220. $1.55.
A forty-page introduction; twenty-five pages of notes.

Webster, Grant T. "Keats's 'La Belle Dame': A New Source." *ELN,* iii (1965), 42-47.
Sackville's "Induction" to the *Mirror for Magistrates,* via Warton's *History of English Poetry.*

Woodring, Carl. "On Looking into Keats's Voyagers." *KSJ,* xiv (1965), 15-22.
New insights into the reading of a familiar poem. ". . . an attempt to describe explicitly the vertical division between the announced subject of voyaging among books and its primary metaphor of voyaging in the Atlantic." (K.C.)

See also Wilkie ("English 3. Criticism"); Gerber ("Keats").

Reviews of books previously listed:
Bate, Walter Jackson, *John Keats* (see *PQ,* xliii, 456-57), rev. by Barbara Hardy in *BJA,* iv (1964), 379-80, and by Milton Wilson in *SR,* lxxiii (1965), 678-85; Bate, ed., *Keats: A Collection of Critical Essays* (see *ELN,* iii, Supp., 33), rev. by Stuart M. Sperry, Jr., in *KSJ,* xv (1966), 121-23; Gittings, Robert, *The Keats Inheritance* (see *ELN,* iii, Supp., 34), rev. in *KSJ,* xv (1966), 117-21, by John Rutherford, a London solicitor, whose explanation of the "mock hostility" necessitated by a friendly action to obtain a Court ruling collapses the entire structure of Gittings' conjectural reconstruction of quarreling within the Jennings family, based on the supposition that the hostility was genuine (the crucial discovery of Rutherford: that the same person acted "as Solicitor for all parties"); Ward, Aileen, *John Keats* (see *PQ,* xliii, 457-58), rev. by Milton Wilson in *SR,* lxxiii (1965), 678-85.

LAMB

Ades, John I. "Charles Lamb's Judgment of Byron and Shelley." *PELL,* i (1965), 31-38.
"There is a sense of unfairness and blindness in Lamb's categorical rejections of Byron and Shelley, but the passages quoted at least show that he did have his reasons. . . ."

Bishop, Morchard. "Lamb's Mr. M: the First Englishman in Lhasa." *Cornhill,* No. 1046 (Winter, 1965/66), pp. 96-112.

In Thomas Manning's Lhasa journal (1811-1812) lie clues to his enigmatic personality, which seems almost a creation of Elia.

Meserole, Harrison T. "Charles Lamb's Reputation and Influence in America to 1835." *Journal of General Education,* XVI (1965), 281-308.

Reiman, Donald H. "Thematic Unity in Lamb's Familiar Essays." *JEGP,* LXIV, (1965), 470-78.

LAMB, MARY

Blunden, Edmund. "Mary Lamb 1764-1847: A Bicentenary Tribute." *Charles Lamb Society Bulletin,* No. 181 (Jan. 1965), pp. 469-72.

LANDOR

See Wilkie ("English 3. Criticism").

MOORE

Dowden, Wilfred S., ed. *The Letters of Thomas Moore.* Vol. I: 1793-1818. Vol. II: 1818-1847. Oxford: Clarendon Press, 1964 [1965]. £ 9 9s.

Rev. by Hoover H. Jordan in *KSJ,* XV (1966), 132-35, by Peter Quennell in *S,* March 5, 1965, p. 305; by Christopher Ricks in *New Statesman,* March 5, 1965, p. 363.

Contains 1323 letters, the majority published for the first time. Those of most interest to literary historians are the letters to and about Byron, particularly the letters written to Murray, Mary Shelley, Hobhouse, and Kinnaird in connection with the biography of Byron. In general, Moore was a rather pedestrian and perfunctory correspondent, and no startling new light is thrown on him and his times. Nevertheless, we do get interesting glimpses of the social, political, and literary circles in which he moved. The volumes are carefully edited with full annotations, and a valuable glossary of proper names. (E.E.B.)

Quennell, Peter, ed. *The Journal of Thomas Moore, 1818-1831.* New York: Macmillan, 1965. Pp. 256. $4.00; paper $1.95.

Rev. by Walter Laqueur in *NYRB,* Jan. 14, 1965, pp. 16-18.

PEACOCK

Read, Bill. "Thomas Love Peacock: An Enumerative Bibliography." *BB,* XXIV (1963), 32-34; (1964), 70-72; 88-91.

RADCLIFFE

Levy, M. "Une nouvelle source d'Anne Radcliffe: Les Mémoires du Comte de Comminge." *Caliban,* I (1964), 149-56.

ROBINSON

Steinberg, S. H. "The Correspondent of *The Times* in Hamburg-Altona in 1807." Pp. 26-47 in Vol. II. *Festschrift Percy Ernst Schramm.* Wiesbaden: Franz Steiner, 1964.

Henry Crabb Robinson, whose suggestions to John Walter contain "the germ of the modern conception of foreign correspondence."

SCOTT

Chandler, Alice. "Sir Walter Scott and the Medieval Revival." *NCF,* XIX (1965), 315-32.
Scott's place in the intellectual history of medievalism.

Crawford, Thomas. *Scott.* Edinburgh: Oliver and Boyd, 1965. 5s.
Rev. with other books by Martin Dodsworth in *New Statesman,* Aug. 20, 1965, p. 257.

Greene, Militsa. "Pushkin and Sir Walter Scott." *Forum for Modern Language Studies,* I (1965), 207-15.

Parsons, Coleman O. *Witchcraft and Demonology in Scott's Fiction: With Chapters on the Supernatural in Scottish Literature.* Edinburgh and London: Oliver and Boyd; New York: Clarke, Irwin, 1964. Pp. x + 363. $15.00.
Contains an impressive amount of information, the result of many years of study. The topic, central to a study of Scott, is ably and exhaustively treated: the impressive footnotes evidence vast erudition, the judgment is reasonable and well-balanced. The material, arranged by topic, says something about all Scott's fiction. Supplementary chapters concern Hogg, Galt, and Scottish novelists after Scott, *e.g.* Buchan and Stevenson. Chapter V ("Scott's Methods and Achievements") is of interest to readers who are not curious about folklore and the supernatural. The topical arrangement of the work under such headings as Ghosts, Fairies, The Poltergeist, Magic, leads the reader to a comparative study of Scott's handling of these topics wherever found in his works, and the full index provides a guide to individual works. The title of this study does not indicate that other topics are discussed: for instance, Parsons shows that Scott's treatment of sex is more forthright and "modern" than some critics have asserted. Parsons' conclusion to his study is: "The novelist's not always consistent attitude toward phenomena is that of eighteenth-century rationalism, an attitude which has its drawbacks. . . . In long and short Scottish narratives, Sir Walter encompasses the great range of native superstitious belief and sharpens understanding of a tumultuous past through its legendary fears" (p. 285). (K.C.)

Smith, Janet Adam. "Scott and the Idea of Scotland." *University of Edinburgh Journal,* XXI (1964), 198-209, 290-98.

Young, Douglas. *Edinburgh in the Age of Sir Walter Scott.* (The Centers of Civilization Series.) University of Oklahoma, 1965. Pp. xii + 170. $2.75.
Filled with names, dates, and facts about Scottish social and cultural history with emphasis upon the eighteenth and early nineteenth centuries, this study would assist a student beginning his studies in Scottish backgrounds. A somewhat misleading title as the work is concerned with much more than Scott. (K.C.)

See review of Lukács cited at end of "General 3. Criticism."

See also Muir ("General 3. Criticism"); Henry ("Wordsworth").

Reviews of book previously listed:
WELSH, Alexander, *The Hero of the Waverley Novels,* (see *PQ,* XLIII, 460), rev. by R. C. Gordon in *CL,* XVII (1965), 167-71; by Karl Kroeber in *JEGP,* LXIV (1965), 177-85.

SHELLEY, MARY

Bloom, Harold. "Frankenstein, or The New Prometheus." *PR,* XXXII (1965), 611-18.
A critical introduction.

Boas, Louise Schutz. "A Letter About *Shelley and Mary.*" *HLQ,* XXVIII (1965), 283-85.

Luke, Hugh J., Jr. "Sir William Lawrence: Physician to Shelley and Mary." *PELL,* I (1965), 141-52.

Luke, Hugh J., Jr., ed. *The Last Man.* University of Nebraska Press, 1965. Pp. xxi + 342. $5.00.
It is curious in view of the preoccupations of the present with racial anni-hilation that Mary Shelley's *The Last Man* has not been reprinted since 1833. But now at last it has appeared—in paperback and with an illuminating Introduction (which discusses both Mary's career and the reflections of Shelley and Byron and others in the novel's characters). (K.N.C.)

Pollin, Burton R. "Philosophical and Literary Sources of *Frankenstein.*" *CL,* XVII (1965), 97-108.

SHELLEY

Baker, Joseph E. *Shelley's Platonic Answer to a Platonic Attack on Poetry.* University of Iowa Press, 1965. Pp. 72. $1.50.
Rev. by Edwin B. Silverman in *KSJ,* XV (1966), 123-34.
A Defence of Poetry can be considered as primarily Platonic only by per-forming two operations: removing the central theme of the connections of literature with social and psychological factors, and ignoring the philosophical influence from the British empiricists. Baker performs both. He then takes segments that contain language with Platonic overtones and elevates them to a position of dominance. The resulting confusion is compounded by the gener-ally loose and rambling nature of the style. Baker does, however, point out that Plato was—contrary to Shelley's view of him—no egalitarian. His knowl-edge of previous scholarship on the work is limited. (K.N.C.)

Basu, Nitish K., ed. *Shelley's Prometheus Unbound* (with an Introduc-tion and Notes). Calcutta, Patna, Allahabad, 1963.
There is nothing new here; the Introduction and Notes repeat discarded clichés and skip over difficult problems; Zillman's variorum edition is ig-nored; inserted summaries of the action might be useful for high school classes. (K.N.C.)

Boas, Louise S. "Edward Dowden, the Esdailes, and the Shelleys." *N&Q,* XII (1965), 163-66; 227-31.

Cameron, Kenneth Neill, ed. *The Esdaile Notebook: A Volume of Early Poems by Percy Bysshe Shelley.* New York: Alfred A. Knopf, 1964. Pp. xxi + 378. $6.95.
This is the first publication of Shelley's "Esdaile Notebook" in its entirety, although Dowden printed poems from it in 1886 and a proportion of it has been published from other manuscripts. The bulk of the poetry in the Note-book, however, is now made available for the first time. Before the writing of this review Neville Rogers' *The Esdaile Poems* had already appeared (Claren-don Press, 1966). It will be no news to Shelley scholars that the relations

between these two parallel editions have been the subject of considerable attention. The volume by Professor Rogers lies beyond my present scope; one must say, however, that the views of the duties of an editor differ, and that some difference of opinion exists concerning the authorship of certain doubtful poems. Cameron's "minimum clean-up" text represents an interpretation, but it is closer to a literal transcript than is the text of Rogers. On this point see Cameron, pp. 30-31, 331-333; and Rogers, pp. vii-ix.

As editor Mr. Cameron is as always thorough and generous. His introduction provides a helpful discussion of the issues of chronology, an elaborate biographical background, and an analysis of the Notebook's themes. In addition he supplies full commentaries of the individual poems, a "Publication History," and exhaustive textual notes. The poems in question are, as could be anticipated, in the main bad but frequently interesting. Their themes are social and political, less often personal, and sometimes both together. The two are united, as later in Shelley, by an over-arching concept of love. Their chief faults are ideological abstraction; diffuseness or sheer abortiveness in the narrative poems; monotony, manifested in overstrained intensity; and over-facility in rhetoric and experimental metres. The most ambitious efforts, however, notably "Henry and Louisa," "Zeinab and Kathema," and "The Voyage," are also the most successful. The first two of these look forward to the fusion of individual and universal love that occurs later on in *The Revolt of Islam*, and is more skilfully managed in *Epipsychidion and Prometheus Unbound*. (R.H.F.)

Chesser, Eustace. *Shelley and Zastrozzi: Self-Revelations of a Neurotic.* London: Gregg Press and Archive Press, 1965. Pp. 165. 35s.

Rev. in *TLS*, April 29, 1965, p. 333.

Dr. Chesser, an English "medical psychologist," argues, as Edward Carpenter had before him, that Shelley had unconscious homosexual tendencies. He bases this in good part on the fact that some homosexual passages in the *Symposium* are "omitted in Shelley's translation." He argues also that Shelley had suppressed incest tendencies (towards his sisters) and that these are reflected in the use of a hermaphrodite in *The Witch of Atlas* and his advocation of "a sisterly, sexless love." So far as the suppressed-homosexual argument is concerned, it must be noted that the passages in question were not omitted in Shelley's manuscript but later by Mary Shelley and Leigh Hunt when she published the work. (Notopoulos, *The Platonism of Shelley*, pp. 388-89, 540-41). Although Shelley did sometimes depict a "sisterly, sexless love" (as in Panthea and Ione) at others he depicts a decidedly sexual one (as in the conclusion of *Epipsychidion*).

As, according to Freud, whom Dr. Chesser is mostly following (with a dash of Jung), everyone has suppressed homosexual and incest tendencies, all this—if true—would bring Shelley well within the norm and call into question Dr. Chesser's "neurotic" characterization. No one has yet, in fact, demonstrated that Shelley was "neurotic" although many charges have flown. He would seem, in spite of his eccentricities, to have had too strong a sense of identity and direction to be classified as neurotic.

We might note that the only modern biography of Shelley included in Dr. Chesser's book list is Maurois' *Ariel*, that Thomas Jefferson Hogg is called "James Hogg," and that the claim that the edition of *Zastrozzi* which forms the second part of this book is "reprinted for the first time this century" is untrue. It was published by the Golden Cockerel Press in 1955. (K.N.C.)

Duerksen, Roland A. "Shelley in Middlemarch." *KSJ*, XIV (1965), 23-31.

Traces the parallels with Shelley's life and writings in Eliot's portrayal of Ladislaw.

Mortenson, Peter. "Image and Structure in Shelley's Longer Lyrics." *SIR*, IV (1965), 104-10.

Sees structural patterns akin to the seventeenth-century meditative lyric.

Pelletier, Robert R. *"The Revolt of Islam* and *Paradise Lost." KSJ,* xiv (1965), 7-13.

Pollin, Alice and Burton. "In Pursuit of Pearson's Shelley Songs." *Music and Letters,* xLvi (1965), 322-31.
Four of a set of six songs by Henry Hugh Pearson to lyrics by Shelley, rediscovered in the archives of the Novello company.

Pollin, Burton R. "Fanny Godwin's Suicide Re-examined." *Études anglaises,* xviii (1965), 258-68.
Fanny Godwin left London on October 7, 1816, arrived in Bath by the London mail the next day, took a local coach to Bristol (14 miles), and then the stage to Swansea (86 miles). At Swansea she went to an inn, "took tea and retired to rest." In the night she killed herself by drinking a bottle of laudanum. Shelley and Mary were at Bath at this time but Mary's diary records only a "letter from Fanny" and no visit. Pollin argues that Fanny did stop at Bath and either saw Shelley or attempted to see him, that he "somehow failed her," and that it was as a result of this episode—a broken romance is darkly hinted—that she committed suicide. She had, he contends, no thought of suicide when she left London.
There is no reason to suppose any romance between Shelley and Fanny in 1816 (she may have had a crush on him in 1814) and the evidence indicates that she had intended to commit suicide before she left London. Her suicide letter began: "I have long determined that the best thing I could do was to put an end to the existence of a being whose birth was unfortunate, and whose life has only been a series of pain to those persons who have hurt their health in endeavoring to promote her welfare." Godwin, on learning of the tragedy, wrote to Mary: "I did indeed expect it." When her body was found she had only eight shillings and sixpence in her purse. The indication is that Fanny's suicide resulted from a depressed semi-psychotic state of some duration and it was for this reason that she did not stop at Bath. She had determined to end her life and wished to see nobody she knew. (K.N.C.)

Reiman, Donald H., ed. *Shelley's "The Triumph of Life": A Critical Study.* Based on a Text Newly Edited from the Bodleian Manuscript. (Illinois Studies in Language and Literature, No. 55.) University of Illinois Press, 1965. Pp. xviii + 272. $6.00.
Rev. in *TLS,* Jan. 20, 1966, p. 44; by James Rieger in *KSJ,* xv (1966), 128-30.
In 1960 Reiman completed, as a doctoral dissertation, a variorum edition of *The Triumph of Life.* The present book is based on this edition with the explanatory notes and the accumulated comments by past scholars unfortunately removed but with an improved text (helped by G. M. Matthews' text in *Studia Neophilologica* in 1960), fuller textual notes and collation and a longer general commentary (now an Introduction). The textual notes (clearly printed on the page opposite the text) are a model of exactness. The text adheres much more closely to the manuscript than does Matthews' and is generally better (except for a few readings, for example, lines 282 and 435).
Reiman considers his text not as an end in itself but a guide for his interpretation. He makes excellent use of the text in this regard, but the interpretation is more impressive in its details than in its main substance. The "central problem" of the poem he believes to be "the apparent impossibility of reconciling 'good & the means of good'," but this thesis is stated rather than demonstrated, and so too with the basically ethical interpretation which follows. The leaders of humanity are said to be chained to the car of "phenomenal life" because they have been "lustful" sinners whereas the few not captive "resisted evil" (and are even promised a "supermundane salva-

tion"). But no evidence is given to indicate that the chariot is the car of "phenomenal life" or that Shelley even had such a philosophical concept. Furthermore, the implication that Shelley was a religious ascetic is contradicted not only by this poem but by his works in general.

Within this static framework, however, considerable light is shed upon a good many of the poem's problems: for instance, the interpretation of "the object of another's fear" (p. 27); the discussion (pp. 43-44) of the "mutiny within"; the suggestion that Plato is but partially captive (p. 53); some of the parallels with Rousseau's *Julie* (p. 59 ff); the argument (pp. 60-61) that Rousseau's prenatal and early childhood states are neither Platonic nor Wordsworthian; some of the comments on the "phantoms" (p. 82) of the final metamorphosis.

The argument (in Appendix D) that Shelley did not begin the poem until May or June omits reference to the evidence that he began it in February or March. (K.N.C.)

Rieger, James. "Shelley's Pater in Beatrice." *SIR,* IV (1965), 169-84.

St. George, Priscilla P. "The Styles of Good and Evil in "The Sensitive Plant." " *JEGP,* LXIV (1965), 479-88.

Wasserman, Earl R. "Shelley's Last Poetics: A Reconsideration." Pp. 487-511 in *From Sensibility to Romanticism* (see Hilles ["English 3. Criticism"]).

An important analysis of *A Defense of Poetry* and of Shelley's views in the reported dialogue between Shelley and Byron published in the *New Monthly Magazine* . . . , XXIX, pt. 2 (1830), 327-36. (D.H.R.)

Wasserman, Earl R. *Shelley's Prometheus Unbound, A Critical Reading.* The Johns Hopkins Press, 1965. Pp. 222. $5.50.

Wasserman bases his interpretation upon Shelley's statement in "On Life" that individual minds are but "modifications of the one mind." What Shelley meant by this is not clear; he continues to write in later works in terms of individual minds. Wasserman takes it to mean that all reality, subjective and objective, is mind-substance. He then takes the further step of identifying Prometheus with this total substance, "the One Mind" (p. 46), "the totality of being" (p. 166). "Asia is the love divorced from the One Mind when it is enchained by its own dark tyrannical shadow" (p. 70), namely Jupiter. Demogorgon is "infinite potentiality" (p. 133). The theme of the drama is "the history of the One Mind's evolution into perfection" (p. 31); it is "cosmic, not human" (p. 131). These concepts are along the same general lines as Grabo's and Baker's, and they run into the same problem: they make nonsense out of the action. Why should a divorced love (Asia) move "infinite potentiality" (Demogorgon) to overthrow the "shadow" (Jupiter) of "the totality of being" (Prometheus)? Why should the "totality of being" then retire into a cave (which is presumably along with the Caucasus, Earth, Demogorgon, Jupiter and so on only a part of him in the first place)? That there is a philosophical strain in the drama is evident, but it is just as evident that it is peripheral and not central. The drama obviously depicts a social revolution, not the evolution of the universe. As soon as one asserts—and it is simple assertion; the argument cannot be documented—that Prometheus is "the first hypostasis of the "One" (Grabo) or more humbly, "the human mind" (Baker) or "the One Mind," he is hopelessly boxed in. Wasserman's interpretation reminds one of the comment on the naturalist who prepared a detailed report on Vesuvius but failed to note that it was a volcano. The comment comes naturally to mind because Wasserman has a great deal to say about volcanoes. He follows up G. M. Matthews' article on this subject in an illuminating chapter "The Breathing Earth," which explores the geological knowledge of Shelley's day. At times, however, this aspect of the poem seems to be considered primary to the action; thus Demogorgon, formerly "infinite potentiality," now becomes "volcanic Demogorgon" (pp. 161, 170) who will overthrow "the fictitious supreme tyrant" (formerly the "shadow" of the One Mind), or, more specifically "dormant volcanic potentiality" whom only Asia (now "generative love") can "arouse" (p. 176). Why "generative love" should "arouse a volcano" is not made clear, nor how volcanic activity is to bring about "the One Mind's evolution into perfection."

Although Wasserman's study cannot be taken seriously as an interpretation of *Prometheus Unbound*, it makes a series of important and original contributions to the meaning of various passages. These are of two kinds, scientific and classical (for instance, Virgil's "Sixth Eclogue"; on the shell of Proteus; on the horae) as in his previous study of *Adonais*; and he cites passages in Bacon, Gibbon, and others which throw new light on Shelley's meanings. On other matters, however, Wasserman is not quite so original, and one notes frequent—and unacknowledged—echoes from previous critics, particularly from Baker, Pulos, and Clarke. (K.N.C.)

See also Rose ("General 3. Criticism"); *Keats-Shelley Memorial Bulletin*, MacNeice, Wilkie ("English 3. Criticism"); Thorslev ("Byron").

Reviews of books previously listed:
CAMERON, Kenneth Neill, ed., *The Esdaile Notebook* (see *ELN*, III, Supp., 39), rev. by Richard H. Fogle in *KSJ*, XIV (1965), 91-93; by Donald H. Reiman in *MLQ*, XXVI (1965), 341-44; JONES, Frederick L., ed., *The Letters of Percy Bysshe Shelley* (see *ELN*, III, Supp., 39-40), rev. by Stewart C. Wilcox in *KSJ*, XIV (1965), 96-98; O'MALLEY, Glenn, *Shelley and Synesthesia* (see *ELN*, III, Supp., 41-42), rev. by Newell F. Ford in *KSJ*, XV (1966), 130-32; by Donald Weeks in *JAAC*, XXIV (1965), 324; by Lawrence J. Zillman in *ELN*, III (1966), 229-31; WOODMAN, Ross Greig, *The Apocalyptic Vision in the Poetry of Shelley* (see *ELN*, III, Supp., 42), rev. by James Gray in *QQ*, LXXII (1965), 210-11; by Ants Oras in *KSJ*, XIV (1965), 100-102.

SOUTHEY

Curry, Kenneth, ed. *New Letters of Robert Southey*. Vol. I: *1792-1810*. Vol. II: *1811-1838*. Columbia University Press, 1965. 2 vols. $20.00.
Rev. by William Plomer in *S*, Oct. 1, 1965, pp. 414-15.
What we some day must have, a complete edition of Southey's correspondence, would make about 20 volumes the size of each of these. Since about half the letters remain unpublished, one can appreciate Professor Curry's decision to concentrate on a selection of *New Letters*. But his excellent editing of these, plus his occasional rescuing of an old letter from the garbling and emasculating of earlier editors, makes us impatient to have all the rest, old and new, in this form. Even the casual reader will find Southey's letters enjoyable; all will agree with the editor that his style is "straightforward, clear, and unmannered" and that his journal-descriptive letters, often "vignettes of the age," constitute "an unusually vivid record" by "a minute observer with an eye for both significant and odd detail." Many will enjoy the bibliographical talk in these new letters, and students of Coleridge and Wordsworth as well as of Southey and of the periodicals to which he contributed will find them indispensable, while tantalizing; biographical details and glancing dicta will reward anyone interested in Godwin, Lamb, Landor, Scott, and such lesser figures as Dyer and William Taylor. The annotation is precise and itself written with an eye for significant detail; one wishes it went still further.

Curry claims to bring us no large surprises, but the cumulative effect of numerous small ones must considerably revise our knowledge and estimation of Southey's views and attitudes and relationships. Several additions to the canon of his writings, mostly of articles and reviews, are pointed to; many

episodes in his and his friends' lives emerge in greater detail; a group of letters describing the back-stage maneuvering of Wellington in 1815 shed light "upon the duke, the *Quarterly*, and Southey's prestige as a valued contributor"; and, throughout the 1790's, "the full expression of Southey's revolutionary enthusiasm" is restored from the softening attentions of biographers and previous editors. "The correspondence for the entire year 1794 can be particularly recommended for its picture of Southey at Oxford, the view of pantisocracy and Coleridge, and an expression of Southey's zeal for commencing a life of authorship" (I, xiii). And the recovery of Southey's portion of the correspondence with Coleridge following Buonaparte's coup of 1799 corrects our understanding of both writers' politics: Coleridge's "But the French are Children," for example, is in reply to Southey's "The Jacobines [sic] were the men"; it elicits his assertion that "Baboeuf was a great man," whose system of total equalization "would have been wise" "in the orgasm of the Revolution" but came too late—also Southey's appeal to the authority of Mary Wollstonecraft and his declaration that "I am a thorough English republican" (I, 215). We also discover such things as Southey's very slight connection with Godwin, his contempt for Mackintosh ("as sure as the Devil is of Sir James Mackintosh"), and his learning in 1805 that the spy who watched Coleridge and Wordsworth at Stowey in 1797 had been sent by a Southey relative who "was then legacy-hunting after John Southey's fortune, . . . Scott told this to Wordsworth" (I, 392, 401).
Thirty-four appended biographical sketches are extremely helpful. (D.V.E.)

Ober, Kenneth H., and Warren U. Ober. "Zukovskij's Early Translations of the Ballads of Robert Southey." *SEEJ*, ix (1965), 181-90.
Shows, among other things, how the translations improve on the originals.

See also Wilkie ("English 3. Criticism").

WORDSWORTH

Bernhardt-Kabish, Ernest. "Wordsworth: The Monumental Poet." *PQ*, xliv (1965), 503-18.
Relates the "Essay Upon Epitaphs" to Wordsworth's intellectual and artistic development, arguing that Wordsworth's fondness for "epitaphic formula" illuminates much of his work.

Brooks, Cleanth. "Metaphor, Paradox, and Stereotype." *BJA,* v (1965), 315-28.
Includes discussion of Wordsworth.

Brooks, Cleanth. "Wordsworth and Human Suffering: Notes on Two Early Poems." Pp. 373-87 in *From Sensibility to Romanticism* (see Hilles ["English 3. Criticism"]).
"The Old Cumberland Beggar" and "The Ruined Cottage" are the two poems.

Cannon, Walter F. "The Normative Role of Science in Early Victorian Thought." *JHI,* xxv (1964), 487-502.
Interestingly traces (pp. 489-93) Wordsworth's attitude towards science.

Christensen, Francis. "Intellectual Love: The Second Theme of *The Prelude*." *PMLA*, lxxx (1965), 69-75.
Wordsworth's "dedication to intellectual love . . . marks his coming of age."

Davies, Hugh Sykes. "Another New Poem by Wordsworth." *EIC*, xv (1965), 135-61.
The "new poem" is a new interpretation of "A Slumber Did My Spirit Seal":

"the poem is . . . a . . . transformation of the experience [described in the skating scene in *The Prelude*] which had been reawakened in meditating the blank-verse description. . . . [The poet] imagines himself joined with [the earth] and in a trance-like state identified with its diurnal motion" (p. 155). This interpretation is more ingenious than persuasive, and Davies has overlooked a significant piece of documentary evidence (since supplied to *EIC* by Gene Ruoff at the University of Wisconsin), but the article is nonetheless the most sane and thorough study of the "Lucy" poems yet to appear and—fortunately—will consign to oblivion the more erratic speculations of previous commentators. (K.K.)
Davies' interpretation is disputed by R. F. Storch in *EIC*, xv (1965), 473-76.

Grob, Alan. "Wordsworth's "Immortality Ode" and the Search for Identity." *ELH*, xxxii (1965), 32-61.
The first part of the ode is considered in relation to Wordsworth's other poems of 1802 and the later part in relation to later, associated poetic efforts. The conclusion: "the *Ode* alone [of Wordsworth's poems] remains *sui generis* . . . a document of inner revelation and personal conversion." (K.K.)

Hartman, Geoffrey H. "Wordsworth, Inscriptions, and Romantic Nature Poetry." Pp. 389-413 in *From Sensibility to Romanticism* (see Hilles ["English 3. Criticism"]).
Hartman traces the "nature-inscription" through classical epigram, Akenside, and Wordsworth's "Lines left upon a Seat in a Yew-Tree," and shows its apotheosis in "Michael," "Tintern Abbey," and the Lucy and Matthew poems; finally, he relates the tradition to the "free-standing lyric."

Henry, Nathaniel H. "Wordsworth's 'Thorn' an Analogue in Scott's *Heart of Midlothian*." *ELN*, iii (1965), 118-20.

Howe, Evelyn M. "Lady Beaumont, Wordsworth's Friend." *SIR*, iv (1965), 143-57.

James, G. Ingli. "Wordsworth's *Solitary Reaper*." *EIC*, xv (1965), 65-76.
". . . an attempt to examine in greater detail . . . in order to demonstrate not only its complexity of meaning but also its distinctively Wordsworthian character."
Responses by Malcolm Pittock, pp. 243-45; by McD. Emslie, pp. 360-61; and final statement by James, pp. 361-62.

Kenner, Hugh. "The Man of Sense as Buster Keaton." *VQR*, xli (1965), 77-91.
A colorful essay that denominates Wordsworth as the last "Man of Sense," pretending to inhabit a stable world, willing to risk ridiculousness. Alexander Pope, following the perception of Dryden that there are dangers in reasonableness, first showed how the poet can achieve an equilibrium of tension through poetry that is "a transcendent juggling act."

Moorman, Mary. *William Wordsworth*. [Vol. II:] *The Later Years*. Oxford: Clarendon Press; New York: Oxford University Press, 1964 [1965]. Pp. 632. 70s.
Rev. in *TLS*, Jan. 20, 1966, pp. 33-34; by Denis Donoghue in *New Statesman*, Nov. 26, 1965, p. 834.
This book is the second part of a biographical study. The first part, covering the years 1770-1803, was published in 1957. Together they make up a work of some 1247 pages.
It might be helpful to give a summary view of what is contained in the

present volume. The sixteen chapters begin with "The Prelude and the Odes, 1804" and end with "The Close of Day." Between these two chapters we deal first with the death of the brother, John, and with those consequent poems which are called "The Fruits of Sorrow." As though to free themselves, in May, 1808, the Wordsworths move to Allan Bank where, Mary said, William's thoughts for a time are occupied with writing the *Cintra* pamphlet. His concern with the freedom of nations did not, however, keep him from completing *The Excursion* by December of 1811. Meanwhile, early in September of 1808 Coleridge arrived to make "his permanent home" at Allan Bank. The complications which followed grew more and more serious, leading to what is nominated "The Estrangement, 1810-13." Near the close of this period we have the death of little Catherine and, "on the first of December, 1812," that of Thomas.

From this sad place the Wordsworths moved to their final home, Rydal Mount. With great care the author now sets before us the facts of Wordsworth's becoming a civil servant, financial need pressing him to the choice. In the following chapter she deals with the publication of *The Excursion* and "Poems New and Old, 1814-16." Slowly now, yet significantly, Wordsworth's poetry begins to make its way. Following the publication of the *Biographia Literaria* in 1817, and in part because of the excellencies Coleridge noted in Wordsworth's poems, the poet finds himself gaining not only in the admiration of "the undergraduates and young fellows of colleges at Oxford and Cambridge," but more importantly in the judgment of one of the most perceptive minds of all literature, that of John Keats: the praise of this one might o'erweigh a whole university of others.

In Chapter X we have a regretful study of the poet's politics, followed in the next chapter by a patient huddling of *Peter Bell, The River Duddon, Ecclesiastical Sketches*, and other poems. The author gives them their due, as she may, and passes on in Chapter XII to Wordsworth's travels in Wales and in Ireland. By this time Wordsworth's fame is established. We move next into a chapter on "The Poet, the State, and the Church," the impression growing that the materials are somewhat intransigent. And as we pass into "Years of Trouble" and the "Late Harvest" we cannot escape feeling that matters have become so multiplex, so various that they tax all labor and skill to present them in consonant wholeness. Now certain problems in chronology grow seemingly insoluble. Yet what we learn of the latter years is invaluable not only to our knowing Wordsworth but the close-knit family which preserved him still a poet.

Many of those grown old in Wordsworthian scholarship will find materials here either new to them or presented in a new light. Wordsworth's compulsion to write poetry stands out as inexorable. Almost equally inexorable seems the necessity for Dorothy, Mary, and Sara Hutchinson to devote their lives to him. We live with them and with others in an intimacy we have not known before. We are brought understandingly, compassionately into the sad relationship between Wordsworth and Coleridge. The friendship for Scott, Lamb, Robinson, Arnold, Beaumont and others, and the relationship with Keats, Hazlitt, Landor, DeQuincey, Tennyson, Gladstone and many more of the leading men of the time are made clear to us, leaving us well aware that no tuneful rustic was honored by the great universities and no mere recluse was made laureate.

The genius of this book is, as it was in volume one, patience; and the worth of it is immediacy. Working especially with the primary materials at Dove Cottage and in the companionship of Helen Darbishire whose golden gift of knowing has enriched Wordsworthian scholarship, toilsomely seeking, winnowing, sifting, and judging, Moorman has given us a book for which we can be grateful. As one studies the footnotes in this volume he is not only assured of the accuracy of the scholarship but impressed by the devoted care they manifest. And one cannot conclude without confessing that in so brief a review, many instances of significance, many illuminating details, perhaps those very matters which give this book its character remain unnoticed.

The reviewer's last trick of fence is this: read it. (B.W.)

Neft, Walter. "Glory, ein Schüsselwort in der Dichtung William Words-worths." *Neuren Sprachen,* XIV (1965), 31-37.
The "Schüsselwort" is *glory* (and its cognates) in the sense of "splendor" rather than "fame."

Nemerov, Howard. "Two Ways of the Imagination." *Carleton Miscel-lany,* V, no. 4 (1964), pp. 18-41.
An illuminating confrontation by a modern poet (who has himself written some Wordsworthian verse) of Blake's and Wordsworth's treatment of imagi-nation. Nemerov sees both poets as precursors of modern developments in poetry, but concludes that Blake's attitude is the more congenial in the con-temporary world and suggests that the "difficulties" of his language seem less serious as time goes on. (K.K.)

Reed, Mark L. "Wordsworth, Coleridge, and the 'Plan' of the *Lyrical Ballads.*" *UTQ,* XXXIV (1965), 238-53.
Judicious tracing of genesis of *Lyrical Ballads* with sensible judgments on the significance of the authors' recollections and mis-recollections of that genesis. (K.K.)

Rountree, Thomas J. *This Mighty Sum of Things: Wordsworth's Theme of Benevolent Necessity.* University of Alabama Press, 1965. Pp. 142. $4.95.
Although Rountree's thesis, that "Wordsworth's conviction about benevolent necessity is too important as a major frame of reference underpinning many of his greatest poems for it to be taken too easily for granted" is not for this reader convincingly established, in part because the treatment of Hartley's influence seems rather superficial, there are a good many interesting observa-tions made in the course of the argument. Particularly worthy of consideration is Rountree's conviction that there is greater agreement between Wordsworth's ideas *after* 1797 and Godwin's than most critics have believed. (K.K.)

Ryskamp, Charles. "Wordsworth's *Lyrical Ballads* in Their Time." Pp. 357-72 in *From Sensibility to Romanticism* (see Hilles ["English 3. Criticism"]).

Salvesen, Christopher. *The Landscape of Memory.* London: Arnold, (1965). Pp. 208. 30s.
Rev. in *TLS,* Jan. 20, 1966, p. 34; by Denis Donoghue in *New Statesman,* Nov. 26, 1965, p. 834.

San Juan, E. Jr. "Wordsworth's Political Commitment." *DR,* XLV (1965), 299-306.
The author advises: "deviations . . . in . . . Wordsworth's political thought . . . should be liberally interpreted as adaptations of definite ideas and princi-ples to the changing circumstances of his time."

Sellers, W. H. "Wordsworth and Spender: Some Speculation on the Use of Rhyme." *SEL,* V (1965), 641-50.

Taaffe, James G. "The 'Spots of Time' Passage in *The Prelude.*" *ELN,* II (1965), 271-75.

Weaver, Bennett. *Wordsworth: Poet of the Unconquerable Mind.* Edited by Charles L. Proudfit. Ann Arbor: George Wahr, 1965. Pp. 109. $3.65.

This book reprints verbatim seven of Weaver's well-known essays on Wordsworth published between 1934-40 plus an essay from 1960 (which supplies the volume's title). Professional Wordsworthians will be grateful for this handy collection. (K.K.)

Woodring, Carl. *Wordsworth.* Riverside Studies in Literature. Boston: Houghton-Mifflin, (1965). Pp. vii + 227. $1.95.
This is the best general introduction to Wordsworth yet written. In clear, fluent, unpretentious style Woodring presents shrewd and sensible criticisms of all of Wordsworth's significant works. The organization of the book is fundamentally chronological and the relationship of the poet's aims and accomplishments to his biography is never allowed to drop from sight. Two of Woodring's most valuable contributions are his comments upon sound patterns and metrical organizations in many of the poems and his illuminating discussion of Wordsworth's prose. The book's concluding chapter is as fair and penetrating a summation of the poet's limitations and successes as has been achieved in so few pages. The Riverside Series apparently discourages footnoting, but Woodring has smuggled a wealth of scholarly information into the text and provided an excellently annotated bibliography. (K.K.)

Zall, P. M. "Wordsworth on Disinterestedness and on Michelangelo." *BNYPL*, LXIX (1965), 131-34.
Prompted by an encounter with Foscolo in 1824.

See also brief notes by Bernice W. Kliman, Julian I. Lindsay, G. L. Little, and Mark L. Reed in *N&Q*, XII (1965), 409-13, 415-17.

See also Muir, Wilkie ("General 3. Criticism"); Whiting ("English 2. Environment"); Nemerov, Price ("Blake"); Houston ("Coleridge").

Reviews of book previously listed:
HARTMAN, Geoffrey H., *Wordsworth's Poetry* (see *ELN*, III, Supp., 44-45), rev. in *TLS*, Apr. 29, 1965, p. 332; by Daniel Hughes in *Criticism*, VII (1965), 389-91; by Christopher Ricks in *NYRB*, Jan. 28, 1965, pp. 10, 12; by Donald Weeks in *JAAC*, XXIV (1965), 321-22; by A. Fletcher, *YR*, LIV (1965), 595-98.

FRENCH

(Compiled by Carrol Coates, Harpur College; Alfred G. Engstrom, Univ. of North Carolina; and James S. Patty, Vanderbilt Univ.).

1. GENERAL

Astborg, Bertrand d'. *Le mythe de la dame à la licorne.* (Collection "Pierres Vives.") Paris: Editions du Seuil, 1963. Pp. 198.
A fascinating essay on the symbolism of the unicorn and, in particular, on the theme of the pure woman in Romantic literature. (C.C.)

Bailey, Helen Phelps. *Hamlet in France from Voltaire to Laforgue* (*with an Epilogue*). (Histoire des Idées et Critique Littéraire.) Genève: Droz, 1964. Pp. xv + 181.
Rev. by Raymond Trousson in *SFr*, IX (1965), 299-301.

Barineau, Elizabeth. "La *Tribune Romantique* et le Romantisme de 1830." *MP*, LXII (1965), 302-24.
A history of an almost unknown "little magazine," of which three issues (spring, 1830) survive and which reflects the views of Hugo's circle. The principal contributors were Victor Pavie, Nerval, Paul Foucher; the editor was one Cordellier Delanoue. Miss Barineau summarizes every article and identifies the dominant themes and attitudes.

Bassan, Fernande. "Chateaubriand, Lamartine, Nerval and Flaubert in Palestine." *UTQ*, XXXIII (1964), 142-63.
Mostly straight-forward summaries of the four journeys to the Holy Land, stressing the authors' reasons for going there, the accuracy of the accounts they left, and the impact of the journey on them. All four went in search of literary inspiration; Chateaubriand and Lamartine were pilgrims as well as tourists; Nerval and Flaubert were primarily tourists. Esthetically, all were disappointed. The general conclusion: ". . . we owe them, among other things, a new vision of the Holy Land."

Bochner, Jay. "Shakespeare in France: A Survey of Dominant Opinion, 1733-1830." *RLC*, XXXIX (1965), 44-65.
Summarizes the views of Voltaire, Mme de Staël, Chateaubriand, and Stendhal, with emphasis on the first-named and last-named of this group. There is brief treatment of Ducis's adaptations, the visiting English troupes in the 1820's, Hugo, Vigny, and Musset. Stendhal is cast as the leading man: "I would say that only Stendhal consciously attempted to follow in some of Shakespeare's footsteps." This rich and complex subject deserves a richer and more complex treatment. (J.S.P.)

Boman, Erik. *Les grands auteurs. XIXe siècle. 1. Le Romantisme.* Edition à l'usage des écoles. Stockholm: Natur och Kultur, 1964. Pp. 126. Kr. 11.75.
Rev. by Elsa Norström in *Moderna Sprach*, LIX (1965), 376-77.

Bowman, Frank Paul. "Notes Towards the Definition of the Romantic Theater." *ECr*, V (1965), 121-30.
Taking as his starting-point Hassan El Nouty's article "Théâtre et anti-théâtre au dix-neuvième siècle" (*PMLA*, Dec. 1964), Bowman makes an interesting excursion into four curious and neglected plays: Pierre Leroux's *La grève de Samarez*, Charles de Rémusat's *Abélard*, Renan's *Caliban*, and George Sand's *Le diable aux champs*. His purpose is to "look at the relations between dialogue and theater, history and theater, ambiguous polemic and theater." His conclusion tends to refute El Nouty's contentions as to the philosophical implications of the "realism" in Romantic drama, but the use of closet dramas as illustrations weakens his argument. (J.S.P.)

Butor, Michel. *Répertoire II.* Paris: Editions de Minuit, 1964. Pp. 301. 16,50 Fr.
Explorations on nature and techniques of the novel and poetry, including the following essays pertinent to a study of French Romanticism: "Chateaubriand et l'ancienne Amérique" (pp. 152-92), "Les parents pauvres" (pp. 193-98), "Babel en creux" (on Hugo's alexandrines, pp. 199-214), and "Victor Hugo romancier" (pp. 521-42).

Cândido, Antônio. *Tese e antítese.* São Paulo: Cia. Editôra Nacional, 1964.

48

Coiscault-Cavalca, Monique. "Les Romantiques français et les Elisabéthains." *LR,* xix (1965), 121-35 (à suivre).
A survey of references to Elizabethan poets and dramatists (other than Shakespeare) in French periodicals of the period 1820-1848.

Derré, Jean-René. *Le renouvellement de la pensée religieuse en France de 1824 à 1834: Essai sur les origines et la signification du mennaisianisme.* Paris: C. Klincksieck, 1962. Pp. 765.
Rev. by Pierre Moreau in *RLC,* xxxix (1965), 135-44.

Easton, Malcolm. *Artists and Writers in Paris: The Bohemian Idea, 1803-1867.* New York: St. Martin's Press, 1964. Pp. vi + 205. $6.50.
Primarily a study of the artistic rather than the literary side of the Parisian "Bohème," Easton's book is a pleasant and well-researched evocation which blends a factual study of a number of young painters and poets who, in one way or another, earned the epithet "Bohemian" with material taken from fictional treatments of the world of the struggling young artist. The Introduction briefly states the generally inferior situation of the artist in the eighteenth century. In the subsequent chapters, which follow the author's theme from the school of "Meditators" which grew up in the shadow of David to the full-fledged Bohemia of Murger, we can trace the gradual emergence of the full-blown type out of the relatively genteel and aristocratic figures (Géricault and Delacroix in real life, the hero of Nodier's "Le peintre de Salzbourg" in fiction) who dominate the scene at the beginning of the century. Balzac's outstanding fictional artists, the young artists who clustered about Hugo, Vigny's tragic figure of Chatterton, Musset's treatment (in such tales as "Le fils du Titien") of the conflict between art and human passion mark the various stages of the evolution. In his final chapter, Easton shows a certain reaction setting in (Claudel, Baudelaire, the Goncourts). In general, Easton is sound enough on all these matters, though he obviously can only skim the surface of such deep topics as Balzac's image of the artist. Presumably the deliberate brevity of his study is responsible for his failure to delve more deeply into these interesting matters. One may regret, too, that he has Englished his quotations and that his own style rarely matches the dash, color, and charm of many of the figures in his book, who, after all, count among their number the likes of Delacroix, Nerval, and Gautier. This defect is by no means fatal, but it is a distracting blemish. (J.S.P.)

Fenger, Henning. *Georg Brandes et la France: La formation de son esprit et ses goûts littéraires (1842-1872).* (Publications de la Faculté des Lettres et Sciences Humaines de Paris, Série "Recherches," VIII.) Paris: Presses Universitaires de France, 1963. Pp. 207. 20 Fr.
Rev. by Morabito in *SFr,* ix (1965), 184.
Chapter VI ("Le Romantisme français," pp. 89-113) reviews Brandes' criticism of Stendhal, Musset, Sand, Balzac, and Hugo in his formative period. Fenger stresses the affinities, biographical and spiritual, between Brandes and these French authors, e.g.: "Brandes semble tout droit sorti d'un roman de George Sand" (this apropos of Brandes "lutte impitoyable contre la société bourgeoise du temps"). References to all the major French Romantics, as well as to many of the minor ones, are scattered through Fenger's study.

Fortassier, Pierre. "Musique et livret dans les opéras de Berlioz, Gounod, Bizet." *CAIEF,* No. 17 (1965), pp. 37-57.
Interesting analysis of the relationship between words and music, using examples from *La damnation de Faust, La prise de Troie, Les Troyens à Carthage, Faust,* and *Carmen.* After showing how the exigencies of the opera form lead

to distortions (especially abbreviation) of the literary sources and to insipid libretti, Fortassier goes on to show how composers redeem these materials even while wedding music to words.

Gershman, Herbert S., and Kernan B. Whitworth, Jr., eds. *Anthologie des préfaces de romans français.* (Collection "Littérature.") Paris: Julliard, 1965. Pp. 368.

Rev. by G. C. Menichelli in *SFr,* IX (1965), 377.
Originally published with introduction and commentary in English (see *PQ,* XLII, 469-70).

Girard, Alain. *Le journal intime.* (Bibliothèque de Philosophie Contemporaine.) Paris: Presses Universitaires de France, 1964. Pp. xxiii + 638. 30 Fr.

Rev. by Jacques Voisine in *IL,* XVII (1965), 127-28.
A very substantial and interesting study of the *journal intime* as a literary *genre.* Somewhat surprisingly, the author's principal frame of reference is sociological; indeed, this is the chief grievance one might lodge against his book: the psycho-sociological statistics he heaps up in an early section seem rather beside the point, since the sample is so small as to cast doubt on the value of a statistical approach. Yet there is a great deal here to be satisfied with: Girard's delimitation of the subject (he distinguishes the *journal intime* from related and similar *genres,* insisting on taking the words *journal* and *intime* rather literally); his historical sketch of the *genre;* his study of eight representative and significant *journaux intimes* (Maine de Biran, Joubert, Constant, Stendhal, Maurice de Guérin, Vigny, Delacroix, and Amiel); finally, his psychological and sociological conclusions about the *journal intime* and its reflection of the developing concept of the personality.
The center of gravity of the book, occupying a little over half of the space, is the section devoted to the eight *journaux intimes* selected for individual attention. In each of the eight chapters, Girard traces the history of the writing of the journal, and discusses the author's reasons for keeping a journal, his method of keeping it, the relationship of the journal to the author's other writing, the insight the journal gives us into the author's intimate preoccupations, the phases, successes, and failures in his effort to know and define his own nature. The longest and most interesting of these eight chapters are probably those devoted to Maine de Biran and to Amiel. In Girard's view, "Maine de Biran, qui fut dès l'origine le théoricien du journal intime, en est aussi le maître." Amiel is instructive because he represents the substitution of the *journal intime* for life itself; the effort to know himself leads the author nowhere: "Il en arrive à ne plus pouvoir se passer de son journal, qui équivaut à un refus de la vie."
Girard writes with admirable clarity and, despite the primacy of psychology and sociology in his book, spares us the jargons of those disciplines. All in all, if one accepts the rather narrow definition of the *journal intime* adopted here, a very satisfying study. (J.S.P.)

Guise, R. "La fortune de *Lazarille de Tormès* en France au XIXe siècle." *RLC,* XXXIX (1965), 337-57.

Brings out the importance of Louis Viardot's translation of *Lazarillo* (first published as a *feuilleton* in 1836) and his critical comments in his *Etudes sur l'histoire des institutions, de la littérature, du théâtre et des beaux-arts en Espagne* (1835). Viardot was a precursor of the view that *Lazarillo* was intended as satire.

Hytier, Jean. "Coup d'oeil sur le changement des réputations poétiques du XIXe siècle." *RR,* LVI (1965), 107-19.

Amusing survey of oscillations of poetic fame, with particular attention to Delille, Béranger, Musset, Gautier, *et al.*

50

Jensen, C. "The 'Romanticism' of the *Annales de la Littérature et des Arts.*" *FS*, XIX (1965), 341-57.
Published from 1820 to 1829, the *Annales* moved from moderate sympathy toward Romantics of the "throne and altar" stripe to a complete identification with reaction and doctrinaire classicism. The departure of Nodier from the magazine's staff in 1823 marked the turning-point.

Kelly, George A. "Liberalism and Aristocracy in the French Revolution." *JHI*, XXVI (1965), 509-30.
Writing in a style occasionally marred by clichés and loose use of words, Kelly reveals the political views of Mme de Staël, Lanjuinais, and Constant on the rôle of aristocracy in post-Revolutionary society to have been rather conservative: in one way or another, all favored the preservation of an hereditary and privileged nobility. (J.S.P.)

Lombard, C. M. "The American Attitude Towards the French Romantics." *RLC*, XXXIX (1965), 358-71.
Combats earlier findings of Howard Mumford Jones and Frank Luther Mott that there was little interest in French culture and French literature among Americans during the Romantic period. Shows American interest in Rousseau, Mme de Staël, Chateaubriand, Lamartine, Hugo, Vigny, George Sand—but only one detailed mention of Musset.

Marmier, Jean. *La survie d'Horace à l'époque romantique.* Paris: Librairie Marcel Didier, 1965. Pp. 170.
Rev. by J. P. C. in *IL*, XVI (1965), 162-63.
This volume brings together a series of articles originally published in *Les Lettres Romanes* (1963-1964). See *PQ*, XLIII, 465, 476, and *ELN*, III, Supp., 66, 72.

Moreau, Pierre. *Ames et thèmes romantiques.* Paris: J. Corti, 1965. Pp. 316. 40 Fr.

Petitbon, René. *L'influence de la pensée religieuse indienne dans le Romantisme et le Parnasse: Jean Lahor.* Paris: A. G. Nizet, 1962. Pp. 323. 28 Fr.
Chapters II and III (pp. 53-83) of Petitbon's study are, in effect, a refutation of Raymond Schwab's *La renaissance orientale* (1950), which saw the influence of Indian religion and philosophy everywhere. It is only fair to point out that Petitbon is not entirely disinterested: it suits his purpose to enhance Jean Lahor's contributions to this "Oriental Renaissance" and so to downgrade the contributions of his predecessors. Petitbon accepts Schwab's work on the birth and rise of Indian studies (Burnouf *et al.*), and then goes on to diminish the achievements of Cousin, Quinet, and Eckstein, and to deny all Indian influence on Hugo, Vigny, and Lamartine. As for Gautier, "Il ne soupçonne même pas l'existence d'une Inde profonde autre que l'Inde des bayadères." (J.S.P.)

Pézard, André. "Comment Dante conquit la France aux beaux jours du Romantisme (1830-1855)." Pp. 683-706 in *Studi in onore di Carlo Pellegrini.* (Biblioteca di Studi Francesi, 2.) Turin: Società Editrice Internazionale, 1963. Pp. xxxix + 846.
Covers much the same ground as the corresponding chapters of W. P. Friederich's *Dante's Fame Abroad, 1350-1850* (Rome-Chapel Hill, 1950). Pézard, in contrast to Friederich, barely touches Dante's impact on creative writers, concentrating instead on Dante scholarship, criticism, and translation in

France for the period in question (Fiorentino's translation is not mentioned, however). Villemain, Fauriel, and Lamennais are given pride of place (but not of space—no figure is treated at much length). There is some useful material here, but it is hard to say that Pézard adds much to Friederich and those on whom *he* drew (Farinelli, etc.). (J.S.P.)

Pichois, Claude. "L'image de Jean-Paul Richter dans les lettres françaises." *IL,* XVI (1965), 11-16.
A résumé of the author's definitive study of the subject published earlier under the same title (see *ELN,* III, Supp., 49). By their translations and comments, Mme de Staël, the marquis de La Grange, and Nerval introduced Jean-Paul to the French public, which, except for such authors as Vigny and Musset, remained largely indifferent to most of his work.

Reizov, Boris. *Entre le classicisme et le romantisme: La querelle du drame sous le Ier Empire.* University of Leningrad, 1962. Pp. 256.
Rev. by Nina Gourfinkel in *RHT,* VII (1964), 40.

Reizov, B[oris]. *L'historiographie romantique française: 1815-1830.* Moscow: Editions en Langues Etrangères, [1962]. Pp. 808.
Rev. by Pierre Halbwachs in *RHL,* LXV (1965), 532-33.
On Sismondi, Ballanche, le Saint-Simonisme, Rio, Thierry, Barante, Thiers, Mignet, Guizot, Quinet, Michelet, and Cousin.

Seznec, Jean. *John Martin en France.* (All Souls Studies, IV.) London: Faber and Faber, 1964. Pp. 53.
Rev. by J.-B. Barrère in *RLC,* XXXIX (1965), 173.
Seznec weaves a number of allusions to Martin's apocalyptic paintings and engravings into an interesting study of his vogue in France. Quotations from Sainte-Beuve, Balzac, Dumas, Custine, Gautier, Mérimée, Flaubert, Berlioz, *et al.* attest to widespread French acquaintance with Martin's work. Seznec does little with Martin's impact on Hugo; Michelet is treated in somewhat more depth. Seven of Martin's works are reproduced in black-and-white. (J.S.P.)

Siciliano, Italo. *Il Romanticismo francese di Prévost a Sartre.* (Critica e Storia.) Florence: Sansoni, 1964.

Toesca, Maurice, ed. *Le chant romantique.* (Collection Dilecta.) Paris: Editions Albin Michel, 1964. Pp. 285. 15 Fr.
A pretty little anthology of Romantic lyricism, decorated with many delightful illustrations. In addition to the usual chestnuts by major and minor figures (e.g., Félix Arvers's sonnet), there are welcome tidbits by out-of-the-way authors (Ph. Chasles, Hégésippe Moreau, Philothée O'Neddy, Xavier Forneret, Alphonse Esquiros). Unfortunately, many poems are not given in their entirety. (J.S.P.)

Touchard, P. A. *Grandes heures de théâtre à Paris.* Suivi d'un guide des théâtres par Jacques Crepineau. Paris: Perrin, 1965. Pp. 475.
History of three Parisian theaters: La Porte Saint-Martin, the Odéon, and the Théâtre Pigalle.

Wood, John S. *Sondage, 1830-1838. Romanciers français secondaires.* University of Toronto Press, 1965. Pp. 141.
Reports the results of a statistical analysis of 200 minor novels of the period.

52

Reviews of books previously listed:

CHARLTON, D. G., *Secular Religions in France, 1815-1870* (see *ELN*, III, Supp., 47-48), rev. by H. J. Hunt in *FS*, XIX (1965), 72-74, by L. Vergnano in *SFr*, IX (1965), 370-71; FABRE, Jean, *Lumières et romantisme: énergie et nostalgie de Rousseau à Mickiewicz* (see *ELN*, III, Supp., 8), rev. by Adam Gillon in *CL*, XVII (1965), 346-47, by Ch. Guyot in *RHL*, LXV (1965), 129-31, by Werner Kraus in *Archiv für das Studium der neueren Sprachen and Literaturen*, Band 202, Jahrgang 117, 79-80; GEORGE, Albert J., *Short Fiction in France, 1800-1850* (see *ELN*, III, Supp., 48), rev. by C. Cordié in *SFr*, IX (1965), 166-67, by Marguerite Iknayan in *ECr*, V (1965), 182-84; GERSHMAN, Herbert, and Kernan B. Whitworth, Jr., eds., *An Anthology of Critical Prefaces to the Nineteenth-Century Novel* (see *PQ*, XLII, 469-70), rev. by J. Kolbert in *RR*, LV (1965), 135-37; MENICHELLI, Gian Carlo, *Viaggiatori francesi reali o immaginari nell'Italia dell'Ottocento* (see *ELN*, III, Supp., 48), rev. by Jean Bruneau in *RLC*, XXXIX (1965), 479-81; MOREAU, Pierre, *Amours romantiques* (see *ELN*, III, Supp., 49), rev. by Albert J. George in *Symposium*, XIX (1965), 273-74, by Raphaël Molho in *RHL*, LXV (1965), 324-26; REBOUL, Pierre, *Le mythe anglais dans la littérature française sous la restauration* (see *PQ*, XLIII, 465), rev. by Albert-Marie Schmidt in *RSH*, n. s., No. 117, pp. 147-49; RICHARDSON, F .C., *Kleist in France* (see *ELN*, III, Supp., 10), rev. by R. Masson in *EG*, XX (1965), 77-78; SEZNEC, Jean, *Literature and the Visual Arts in Nineteenth-Century France* (see *ELN*, III, Supp., 50), rev. by Alison Fairlie in *FS*, XVIII (1965), 274-76; SHRODER, Maurice Z., *Icarus: The Image of the Artist in French Romanticism* (see *PQ*, XLII, 470), rev. by R. Fargher in *FS*, XVII (1965), 372-73, by Ellen Moers in *RR*, LIV (1965), 302-05; SIMCHES, Seymour O., *Le Romantisme et le goût esthétique du XVIIIe siècle* (see *ELN*, III, Supp., 50), rev. by Petre Ciureanu in *SFr*, IX (1965), 369, by Gita May in *FR*, XXXVIII (1965), 704-05; TEICHMANN, Elizabeth, *La fortune d'Hoffmann en France* (see *ELN*, III, Supp., 50), rev. by André Monchoux in *RLC*, XXXIX (1965), 321-23.

2. STUDIES OF AUTHORS

ALLART

Decreus, Juliette, ed. *Mémoires de H. L. B.: Henry Lytton Bulwer.* University of Houston Press, 1963.

Uffenbeck, Lorin A., ed. *Nouvelles lettres d'Hortense Allart à Sainte-Beuve (1832-1864).* Geneva: Droz, 1965. Pp. 176. 26 Fr.

Rev. by A. G. in *RDM*, Nov. 15, 1965, p. 319, by Maurice Parturier in *NL*, Oct. 7, 1965, p. 5.

BALLANCHE

See Kushner ("Vigny").

See Reizov ("French 1. General").

BALZAC

Adamson, Donald. *"Le Père Goriot*: Notes Towards a Reassessment." *Symposium*, XIX (1965), 101-14.

Survey of recent critical views. Adamson takes Rastignac as "the pivot of the action," but is inconclusive on other points. (C.C.)

Allemand, André. *Honoré de Balzac. Création et passion.* (Collection "La Recherche de l'Absolu.") Paris: Plon, 1965. Pp. 352.

Rev. by Patrick de Rosbo in *NL*, Sept. 9, 1965, p. 5.

Allemand, André. *Unité et structure de l'univers balzacien.* (Collection "Histoire des Mentalités.") Paris: Plon, 1965. Pp. 352. 8.20 Fr.

Amadou, Robert. "En marge d' 'Une Ténébreuse affaire': Saint-Martin et Clément de Ris. (Notes et documents inédits.)" *RSH*, n.s., No. 116 (1964), 477-96.

L'Année Balzacienne 1965. Paris: Garnier, 1965. Pp. 406. 23 Fr.

Sixth volume in series. Table of contents shows the usual heavy concentration on biographical and literary historical studies: M. Fargeaud, "Mme Balzac, son mysticisme et ses enfants," pp. 3-33; R. Amadou, "Balzac et Saint-Martin," pp. 35-60; S. Bérard, "Une enigme balzacienne: la 'spécialité'," pp. 61-82; M. Le Yaouanc, "De Cassin de Kainlis à Louis Lambert," pp. 83-92; R. Chollet, "De 'Dézespérance d'amour' à 'La Duchesse de Langeais,'" pp. 93-120; N. Célestin, "Balzac et la chronique tourangelle," pp. 121-29; R.-L. "L'édition Werdet de 'La Femme de Trente Ans,'" pp. 131-42; A.-M. Meininger, "Balzac et Stendhal en 1837," pp. 143-55; R. Guise, "Balzac lecteur de Gozlan," pp. 157-74; P. Barbéris, R. Guise, P. Citron, R. Fayolle, "Notes sur le 'Curé de Village,'" pp. 175-99; P. Citron, "Aux sources d' 'Une Fille d'Eve,'" pp. 201-15; G. Imbault, "Autour de 'La Rabouilleuse': Le Capitaine Fix et le duel de Frapesle," pp. 217-32; J. Maurice, "La transposition topographique dans 'Une Ténébreuse Affaire,'" pp. 233-38; A. Pugh, "Du 'Cabinet des Antiques' à 'Autre Etude de Femme,'" pp. 239-52; P. Barbéris, "Trois moments de la politique balzacienne," pp. 253-90; R. Pierrot, "Les enseignements du 'Furne corrigé,'" pp. 291-308; B. Paul Métadier, "Balzac précurseur de la caractérologie," pp. 309-16; A. Prioult, B. Tolley, R. Amadou, P. Citron, L. Forestier, "Notes," pp. 317-39; J.-A. Ducourneau et R. Pierrot," Calendrier de la vie de Balzac (Année 1834)," pp. 343-58; P. Barbéris, P. Citron, S. Coulon, R. Guise, A.-M. Meininger, W.-G. Moore, R. Pierrot, J. Sablé, "Revue critique," pp. 359-86; J.-A. Ducourneau, R. Pierrot, R. Rancoeur, "Bibliographie balzacienne (Année 1964)," pp. 387-92 (81 items); W. Conner, Ch. Gould, G. Vipper, A. Zatloukal, "Balzac à l'étranger," pp. 393-97; "Informations et nouvelles," pp. 399-403.

Balzac à Saché. Bulletin de la Société Honoré de Balzac de Touraine. Nos. 8 and 9 [1963, 1964].

No. 8 contains: Mme Archambault, "Propos d'un Néophyte," pp. 3-5; Mlle Coste, "La Maison du Curé de Tours," pp. 6-8; Dr F. Lotte, "Héraldique balzacienne en Touraine," pp. 9-11; J. Maurice, "Dans les Landes de Charlemagne," pp. 12-16; J. Maurice, "Dans la correspondance de Balzac," pp. 17-18; Mme Meininger et M. Havard de la Montagne, "A propos de Surville," pp. 19-25 (contains two unpublished letters from Laure Surville); B. Paul Métadier, "Honoré et Henry," pp. 33-35; M. Tajan, "Une lettre de Mme Hanska. Note graphologique," p. 36 (with photo-reproduction of letter); J.-E. Weelen, "La promesse de mariage de Bernard-François Balzac," pp. 37-40. No. 9 contains: M. Havard de la Montagne, "Bernard-François Balzac et Joseph d'Albert," pp. 3-7; Professeur Hunt, "L'Amour Platonique chez Balzac," pp. 8-15; Boris Lossky, "Le Balzac en robe de chambre de Louis Boulanger au Musée de Tours. Destinée de l'oeuvre," pp. 16-22; J. Maurice, "M. de Savary, hôte de Balzac," pp. 23-39; P. Métadier, "Observation et intuition," pp. 30-39; J.-E. Weelen, "Une espiéglerie de Balzac à Turin: 'Le Cheval de Saint-Martin,'" pp. 40-43; J.-E. Weelen, "Un fonctionnaire scrupuleux: Bernard-François Balzac à Soissons," pp. 44-46; "Documents nouveaux du Musée de Saché. Années 1963-1964," pp. 48-50; "Bibliothèque de Saché: ouvrages et publications." pp. 51-56.

Barbéris, Pierre. "Balzac et la démocratie." *Europe,* XLIII (Jan. 1965), 202-19.

The idea of democracy in the *Comédie humaine.*

Bardèche, Maurice. "Un roman de Balzac: *Béatrix.*" *Ecrits de Paris*, No. 211 (1963), pp. 101-108.

Barricelli, Jean-Pierre. "Demonic Souls. Three Essays on Balzac." *Edda*, LXIV (1964), 209-33, 292-315.
The essays are: "I. Mercadet: the Fascination of Money"; "II. Gambara: the Temptation of Genius"; "III. Vautrin: the Seduction of Crime."
Pierre Descaves and Pierre Barbéris, among others, have already begun to broaden the scope of Balzac criticism beyond *La comédie humaine*. Barricelli is justified in bringing Balzac's theater into the discussion of the demonic type. His entire essay, however, loses focus through irrelevant biographical assertions, pretentious erudition, unnecessary speculation about influence (Balzac on Beckett), and bad style in general. The whole section on *Gambara* is open to question because Barricelli does not take into account the problem of which parts were actually written by Balzac. The author's hope of opening "some fresh avenues of interpretation" is hardly fulfilled. (C.C.)

Béguin, Albert. *Balzac lu et relu.* Préface de Gaëtan Picon. (Collection Pierres Vives.") Paris: Editions du Seuil, 1965. Pp. [252].
Reprints Béguin's earlier study, *Balzac visionnaire* (Skira, 1946), and a number of prefaces to novels in *La comédie humaine*.

Bertault, Philippe. *Balzac and the Human Comedy.* English version by Richard Monges. New York University Press, 1963. Pp. xvi + 212. $6.00 bound; $2.25 paper.
Translation of *Balzac, l'homme et l'oeuvre* (Collection "Connaissance des Lettres"), originally published in 1946.

Bevernis, Christa. "Zu den ästhetischen Anschauungen Balzacs." *Beiträge zur Romanischen Philologie*, III, No. 1 (1964), 5-17.
From a dissertation on "Balzac's esthetic views" (Berlin, 1963), which "attempts to furnish evidence of a realistic esthetic system in Balzac's work." Balzac identifies art and knowledge, taking "art as a document of the times of a peculiar sort." "The 'histoire des moeurs' is the continuation of the old tradition of comedy for Balzac." There is a wealth of reflections on the theory of art in Balzac's articles on contemporary literature, but I think Miss Bevernis exaggerates the unity of Balzac's system of esthetics. I doubt that Balzac "believed *up to his death* [my italics] in the uninterrupted progress of the world. . . ." The article is of value, however, and some of its esthetic insights (e.g., that the typical is, for Balzac, the condensation of natural truths) are incisive. (C.C.)

Bolster, Richard. "Was Balzac a Revolutionary?" *FS,* XIX (1965), 29-33.
Correctly refutes assimilation of Balzac to a revolutionary philosophy by Engels, but the conception and exposition are weak. (C.C.)

Bourdet, Jeanne-Marie. "La petite ville de province dans *la Comédie humaine.*" *Europe*, XLIII (Jan. 1965), 15-26.

Bouvier-Ajam, Maurice. "Les opérations financières de la Maison Nucingen." *Europe*, XLIII (Jan. 1965), 28-53.
Analysis of the depiction of financial tactics in *La maison Nucingen*. Because of the incredulousness of an uninformed public and of personal relations with the Rothschilds, Balzac understated Nucingen's power and wealth.

Bruhat, Jean. "Balzac et la classe ouvrière française." *Europe,* XLIII (Jan. 1965), 74-90.

Supports an observation made by A. Wurmser in *La comédie inhumaine* that "Balzac n'a créé aucun type valable d'ouvrier." Goes on to say that workers are described peripherally, however, and their condition discussed in articles such as "Le catéchisme social." Bruhat notes that Balzac did not know certain elements of the working classes, that he exaggerated their moral degradation, and that he was unaware of contemporary organization among the workers. The discussion (pp. 90-94) between Bernard Guyon and Bruhat is of interest. (C.C.)

Castex, Pierre-Georges. "L'ascension de monsieur Grandet." *Europe,* XLIII (Jan. 1965), 247-63.

Traces Grandet's business affairs, finding a continual close correlation between them and the economic realities of the times. Concludes that Grandet, contrary to Molière's Harpagon, is a man of great will-power who succeeds in dominating his society. While Castex does not take into account the irony with which Grandet is treated in the novel, his view of Grandet as hero is convincing. (C.C.)

Castex, Pierre-Georges, ed. *Eugénie Grandet.* (Classiques Garnier.) Paris: Garnier, 1965. Pp. lxxiv + 371; illus. 8.50 Fr.

Based on the same text as the old Garnier edition by Maurice Allem; critical apparatus considerably expanded.

Cesare, Raffaele de. "Balzac a Roma." Pp. 609-48 in *Studi in onore di Carlo Pellegrini.* (Biblioteca di Studi Francesi, 2.) Turin: Società Editrice Internazionale, 1963. Pp. xxxix + 846.

Cesare, Raffaele de. "Balzac nel maggio 1836." *Contributi dell'Istituto di Filologia Moderna. Serie Francese.* (Pubblicazioni dell'Università Cattolica del Sacro Cuore.) III (1964), 53-185.

Chevalier, Louis. " 'La Comédie humaine': document d'histoire?" *Revue Historique,* LXXXII (1964), 27-48.

Citron, Pierre. *Le médecin de campagne; Le curé de village.* Paris: Publications du Centre National de Téléenseignement, 1964. Pp. 11.

Citron, Pierre. "Les affreux du miroir." *Europe,* XLIII (Jan. 1965), 94-104.

On characters of the *Comédie humaine* who are "des visages de Balzac." Followed by remarks of André Wurmser (pp. 105-09).

Coates, Carrol. "Engagement and Purity in Balzac Criticism." *RR,* LVI (1965), 277-83.

Confrontation of conflicting studies on *La comédie humaine* by Maurice Bardèche (*Une lecture de Balzac*) and André Wurmser (*La comédie inhumaine*). See *ELN,* III, Supp., 52, 58.

Conseil, Gabriel. "L'univers de Balzac." *Bulletin de l'Institut Français de Copenhague,* March, 1963, pp. 167-72.

Dino, Guzine. "L'aspect historique et social des types chez Balzac." *Europe,* XLIII (Jan. 1965), 295-302.

Study originally published in *Dialogues* (1953). Considers the historical realities reflected in Grandet's rise and fortune. Shows that Grandet is more than a nineteenth-century version of Molière's Harpagon (the thesis of Castex's "L'ascension de monsieur Grandet," see above).

Dirkx, Henri. "Notes sur les premières éditions des *Parents pauvres* de Balzac." *Le Livre et l'Estampe*, No. 34 (1963), pp. 137-49.

Drion, H. "De 'Bekerin' van Balzac." *Tirade,* VIII (1964), 31-41.

Druesne, J. "La banque et les affaires dans Balzac." *Siège et Agences. Bulletin Trimestriel de la Société Générale*, No. 46 (1964), pp. 13-28.

Ducourneau, Jean-A. "Balzac et la paternité." *Europe,* XLIII (Jan. 1965), 190-202.
Traces theme through the *Comédie humaine*, but in reference to Balzac's life and his own paternal aspirations.

Dupeyron, Georges. "L'amour, élément d'énergie, dans l'oeuvre de Balzac." *Europe,* XLIII (Jan. 1965), 288-95.

Fam, Lofty. "Les illusions de deux génies littéraires: Balzac et Lamartine." *Bulletin of the Faculty of Arts* (Alexandria), XVII (1963), 279-84.

Fanger, Donald. *Dostoevsky and Romantic Realism. A Study of Dostoevsky in Relation to Balzac, Dickens, and Gogol.* (Harvard Studies in Comparative Literature, 27.) Harvard University Press, 1965. Pp. xii + 307. $7.50.
Chapter 2, "Balzac: The Heightening of Substance" (pp. 28-64), treats Balzac as a sort of visionary observer of physical and social reality. Fanger briefly shows that there was an evolution in Balzac's treatment of Paris, from an inventorial amassing of detail to the fusing of myth with reality in his view of the city. From the analysis of Paris as scene for the drama of *Le père Goriot,* Fanger turns to the character who symbolizes the ultimate reaction of man to urban society: Vautrin, the mysterious rebel, the link between *Le père Goriot* and the two later novels, *Illusions perdues* and *Splendeurs et misères des courtisanes.* Two of Fanger's observations about Balzac will exemplify the quality of his insights. He recognizes, as so many have failed to do, that Balzac "limits the reader's freedom of judgment by guiding it. . . ." This is prevented from becoming "simple didacticism" by the reader's "overriding awareness that the world in which the action takes place is . . . so complete a one that it must have its own laws, its own iron necessities" (p. 40). Secondly, and basic to Fanger's goal of studying certain stages in the evolution from Romanticism to nineteenth-century Realism, his view of Balzac as Romantic Realist seems to me particularly justified. "The details may be, as Balzac claims in his preface, profoundly true, but the manner of the narration is hardly realistic. . . . " (p. 61).
In all four of the writers treated, with occasional reference to others such as Baudelaire, Fanger studies the capital cities which attracted these men as both scene and symbol for their own versions of the myth of modern urban society. Fanger has severely limited the comparative aspect of his study, feeling "simple acknowledgment to be better than facile generalization," but he works well within that limitation. (C.C.)

Fargeaud, Madeleine. "Balzac et 'les Messieurs du Muséum'." *RHL*, LXV (1965), 637-56.

Did Geoffroy Saint-Hilaire inspire Balzac with a "mode d'expression" or simply confirm what the novelist already had in mind? Mme Fargeaud concludes that the influence of Jean-Casimir Lemercier, doctor and naturalist, preceded that of Saint-Hilaire.

Fayolle, Roger. "Notes sur la pensée politique de Balzac dans 'Le médecin de campagne' et 'Le curé de village'." *Europe,* XLIII (Jan. 1965), 302-24.

Fischer, Jan O. "Quelques leçons méthodologiques du réalisme balzacien et stendhalien." *Romanistica Pragensia*, No. 2 (1962), pp. 95-108.

Fischer, Jan O. "Réalisme et procédés." *Europe,* XLIII (Jan. 1965), 221-24.

Novelistic technique is subordinate to "la réalité objective qu'il faut saisir."

Fortassier, Rose. "Balzac et l'opéra." *CAIEF*, No. 17 (1965), pp. 25-36.

Surveys opera in *La comédie humaine*: visits to the "Opéra" and the "Italiens," opera summaries in *Gambara* and *Massimilla Doni* (testimony from Paul Dukas on Balzac's genius in grasping Beethoven's thought), and opera imagery in various novels.

Frijling-Schreuder, E. C. M. "Honoré de Balzac: A Disturbed Boy Who Did Not Get Treatment." Pp. 379-89 in Hendrik M. Ruitenbeek, ed., *The Literary Imagination: Psychoanalysis and the Genius of the Writer*. Chicago: Quadrangle Books, 1965. Pp. 443.

Furber, Donald. "The Fate and Freedom of Balzac's Courtesans." *FR*, XXXIX (1965), 346-53.

An interesting point of interpretation: the courtesans of *La comédie humaine* building "around themselves a life that is frozen into an eternal present" through fear of death. Unfortunately, the article is carelessly executed. Furber does not make clear who are typical representatives of the three classes of courtesans posited, nor what the characteristics of these classes are. He speaks of "Etudes sociales" (i.e., "Etudes de moeurs"?). W. H. van der Gun gives a clearer and more complete analysis of Balzac's courtesans in *La courtisane et son rôle dans la Comédie Humaine de Balzac* (see *ELN*, III, Supp., 55). (C.C.)

Gauthier, Guy. "Balzac au cinéma." *Europe,* XLIII (Jan. 1965), 339-48.

Some 25 films are listed in chronological order. Includes an "Entretien avec Louis Daquin" about reasons that more films are not based on Balzac's works. A more extensive list was given by René Jeanne and Charles Ford, in "Balzac et le cinéma" (*L'Année Balzacienne 1961*), with the contrary observation that a great number of films have been inspired by Balzac. (C.C.)

Gédéon, Léon. "De Bayeux à Cherbourg avec Balzac." Pp. 139-48 in his *Demeures inspirées et sites romanesques*. Paris: Editions de l'Illustration, 1964.

Gédéon, Léon. "Les origines du beau-frère de Balzac." *Les Lettres Françaises*, April 18-24, 1963, pp. 1, 8-9.

A substantial, factual article. (C.C.)

Gendzier, S. J. "Balzac's Changing Attitudes Towards Diderot." *FS,* XIX (1965), 125-43.
Concludes that Balzac "knew Diderot rather thoroughly."

Graaf, Daniel A. de. "Arthur Rimbaud et *Louis Lambert.*" *RLV,* XXX (1964), 350-52.

Guyon, Bernard. "Balzac héraut du capitalisme naissant." *Europe,* XLIII (Jan. 1965), 126-41.

Henriquez, J. (Ki Wist), ed. *Les manuscrits de premier jet d'Honoré de Balzac.* I: *Le manuscrit primaire du "Curé de village" (1837).* II: *Les ajoutés importants, ou manuscrits secondaires.* Brussels: Editions Henriquez, 1964.
Rev. by J. Sablé in *L'Année Balzacienne: 1965,* pp. 382-83.

Hoffmann, Léon-François. *Répertoire géographique de la Comédie humaine.* I. *L'étranger.* Paris: José Corti, 1965. Pp. [171].
Like F. Lotte's dictionaries of characters and literary allusions, and G. B. Raser's *Guide to Balzac's Paris* (see *ELN,* III, Supp., 57), Prof. Hoffmann's work is designed to be a useful tool for the critic, scholar, and general reader, a purpose it will doubtless serve. *La comédie humaine* is surveyed, novel by novel (references to the Pléiade edition), and geographical references are noted, with brief comments for the more significant ones. Only four categories of references are omitted: geographical names characterizing plants and animals, occurring in titles of creative works, forming part of idiomatic expressions, and belonging to titles of nobility. One may regret the omission of names in idiomatic expressions since these might be useful in analyzing prejudices or attitudes towards certain places. There is a bibliography and an index of place names. The index permits an immediate estimate of the frequency with which Balzac referred to certain places: some 360 references to Italy and places in Italy; 184 to Germany; and around 100 references to England, Belgium, Spain, Russia, and Switzerland.
The presentation and arrangement of materials in the *Répertoire* are good; the typography is large and readable (unlike that of Lotte's dictionaries in Vol. XI of the Pléiade edition). We may look forward to the appearance of the second volume, on France, and hope that someone will have the patience to extend these dictionaries to Balzac's writings outside the *Comédie humaine.* (C.C.)

Köpeczi, Béla. "Balzac and the Human Comedy." *New Hungarian Quarterly,* Winter, 1964, pp. 67-86.

Laubriet, Pierre. "A travers les éditions balzaciennes: vagabondage bibliographique." *Europe,* XLIII (Jan. 1965), 276-84.
Reviews four major editions of Balzac's works: "Formes et Reflets," "Club de l'Honnête Homme," "Bibliophiles de l'Originale," and Garnier's series of re-editions of individual novels.

Laubriet, Pierre, ed. *Histoire de la grandeur et de la décadence de César Birotteau.* . . . (Classiques Garnier.) Paris: Garnier, 1964, Pp. clxxv + 417; illus.
Rev. by Raffaele de Cesare in *SFr,* IX (1965), 303-06, by H. J. Hunt in *FS,* XIX (1965), 417-18.
Based on same text as the old Garnier edition by Maurice Allem; critical apparatus expanded in size and diversity of materials (including an outline of César's financial progress).

Lestang, M. de. *Les magistrats vus par Balzac.* Discours prononcé par M. de Lestang à la Cour d'Appel de Limoges. Audience solennelle de rentrée du 16 septembre 1963. Limoges: Imprimerie Charles-Lavauzelle et Cie., 1963.

Lévy, Madeleine. "Balzac et la Suisse." *Europe,* XLIII (Jan. 1965), 322-38.

Maurois, André. "Balzac et l'action." *Europe,* XLIII (Jan. 1965), 3-11.
Reasons for the failure of business projects which were successfully carried out by other people.

Maurois, André. *Prométhée ou la vie de Balzac.* Paris: Hachette, 1965. Pp. 653. 25 Fr.
Rev. by Pierre Abraham in *Europe,* XLIII (Nov. 1965), 353, by Pierre de Boisdeffre in *NL,* April 8, 1965, p. 7, by Charles Dédeyan in *RSH,* N.S. No. 118, pp. 448-52, by Madeleine Marmin in *Etudes Françaises,* I, No. 3, pp. 105-06, by Roger Parelou in *Le Français dans le Monde,* No. 35, p. 51, and by Jean Pommier in *RHL,* LXV (1965), 657-82.
Briefly, this is a good biography, purportedly Maurois' last. Few reviewers will go to the extent of Pommier's 25-page examination, where he practically evokes his own image of Balzac, admitting the quality of Maurois' work, nonetheless. The tone adopted by Maurois is judicious, the scope is adequate, the style clear. Maurois takes the very latest scholarship into account, deftly working selected quotations into his own narrative, with adequate but unobtrusive footnotes. I object, personally, to the use of passages from the novels to evoke Balzac's own life, but Pommier thinks more should have been used. But apart from all reservations on specific emphases or details of technique, Maurois' work is the most up-to-date biography and, probably, the best for some time to come. (C.C.)

Maurois, André. "Prométhée ou la vie de Balzac." *Les Annales, Conferencia,* LXXII (April 1965), 5-17.
A lecture summarizing aims of his biography (see above).

Maurois, André. *Prometheus: The Life of Balzac.* Translated by Norman Denny. London: Bodley Head, 1965. 50 s.
Rev. by John Weightman in *Observer Weekend Review,* Nov. 7, 1965, and by F. W. J. Hemmings in *New Statesman,* Nov. 26, 1965, pp. 848-49.

Mayberry, Fred. "A Dictionary from the Printing-House of Balzac." *Canadian Modern Language Review,* XXII, No. 1 (1965), 58-60.

Meininger, Anne-Marie. "Réalisme et réalités." *Europe,* XLIII (Jan. 1965), 179-88.
"Petits faits vrais" which Balzac assimilated into *La cousine Bette, Une fille d'Eve, La Rabouilleuse, et al.* The facts suggest links between reality and *La comédie humaine,* but a fuller discussion of the creative process or of the esthetic use of the facts is lacking. Noteworthy: remarks by Raymond Jean in the ensuing discussion (pp. 188-90) on Balzac and the "new novelists." (C.C.)

Métadier, B[ernard] Paul. *Balzac à Saché.* Catalogue avec notes et commentaires par B. Paul Métadier. Précédé du "Château de Saché" par J. Maurice. Tours: Imprimerie Centrale, 1961. Pp. 47; illus.

60

Métadier, Bernard Paul. *Balzac au petit matin.* Note liminaire par André
Maurois. . . . Paris: La Palatine, 1965. Pp. [229]; illus. 14.10 Fr.
> Rev. by Philippe Brunetière in *NL*, March 25, 1965, p. 5.
> Balzac's health and state of mind are considered in order to "donner ses
> dimensions humaines. . . . " Métadier chooses to let Balzac be "l'historien de
> [son] propre mal," while the biographer's task of selecting and ordering the
> numerous, lengthy quotations from the correspondence is dissimulated. Balzac
> probably had, among other maladies, a coronary condition and pulmonary
> oedema. Diagnoses of many modern doctors (Dr. Guérin diagnosed syphilitic
> aortitis) seem less probable to Métadier. Evident in the introduction and con-
> clusion is a strong sense of the unity of life and art, a twentieth-century
> reflection of Balzac's monistic world view. (C.C.)

Milner, Max, ed. *Massimilla Doni.* Paris: José Corti, 1964. Pp. 250.
> Rev. by Raffaele de Cesare in *SFr,* VIII, 508-10, by Anne-Marie Meininger in
> *L'Année Balzacienne: 1965,* pp. 361-70.
> A companion edition to that which M. Regard has given of *Gambara* (see
> below). The 76-page introduction ranges over the history of the dual genesis
> of the two musical novels, and the themes (the role of music and opera in
> particular). In addition to reprinting both the first and final versions of the
> text, Milner studies the type of modifications Balzac made in the original.
> Also included in the appendices are the musical examples cited in the novel.
> The footnotes give much information about sources. In every respect, an
> exemplary edition. (C.C.)

Mitterand, Henri. "A propos du style de Balzac." *Europe,* XLIII (Jan.
1965), 145-61.
> Calls for a separation of genetic studies from stylistic studies of the definitive
> text. A much needed voice of reason in the area of Balzac studies. (C.C.)

Mitterand, Henri. "Zola et le 'Rappel'." *Les Cahiers Naturalists,* VI
(1960), 559-608.
> Reproduces Zola's review of *La comédie humaine,* published in *Le Rappel,*
> May 13, 1870.

Nemo, Maxime. "Je hais Balzac." *Europe,* XLIII (Jan. 1965), 324-33.
> Testimony of a Balzacophobe.

Paradissis, A. G. "Balzac's Relationships with the Caricaturists and
Popular Dramatic Satirists of the July Monarchy: an Investigation
Based on an Unpublished Plan for a Satirical Novel." *Australian
Journal of French Studies,* II (1965), 59-81.
> The "plan d'un roman sur Bilboquet, Papa Doliban Ier, etc." is reproduced in
> full. The author compares the plan with Louis Reybaud's *Jérôme Paturot à la
> recherche d'une position sociale* (1842), hypothesizing that "Balzac's manu-
> script represents in the complexity of its plot and satirical situations a con-
> scious or unconscious attempt to surpass Reybaud."

Perrod, Pierre-Antoine. "Au pays des ancêtres d'Honoré de Balzac, dans
le Ségala tarnais." *Les Cahiers de l'Alpe,* No. 6 (1963), pp. 15-20.

Perrod, Pierre-Antoine. "Balzac et l'affaire Peytal." *Europe,* XLIII (Jan.
1965), 171-77.

Regard, Maurice. "Balzac et la politique étrangère." *Europe,* XLIII (Jan.
1965), 110-20.

Regard, Maurice, ed. *Gambara*. Paris: José Corti, 1964. Pp. 190.
Rev. by Raffaele de Cesare in *SFr*, VIII (1965), 508-10, by Anna-Marie Meininger in *L'Année Balzacienne: 1965*, pp. 361-63.
Very nearly every available fact and document has been collected to make this edition essential to the intelligent study of a story whose exact authorial status remains in some doubt (the Marquis de Belloy probably wrote the first draft). The introduction presents facts on the genesis, the origin and validity of the musical theories, and a more complete examination of Balzac's debt to Hoffmann than has been previously given. This edition is complemented by Milner's edition of *Massimilla Doni* (see above). (C.C.)

Regard, Maurice. "La critique des créateurs." *Études Françaises*, I, No. 3 (1965), pp. 67-83.
Ranges from Balzac's views on Stendhal to Claudel's on Verlaine, concentrating on Balzac's and Flaubert's reflections on their own work. These writers have given us a "critique de technicien" which "nous permet de préciser en quoi consiste tel genre littéraire . . . selon les formes personnelles que lui donne chaque artiste, à mesure que l'oeuvre se fait."

Rueff-Duval, Dominique. "Études de certains aspects de la fémininité (*Les secrets de la princesse de Cadignan*)." *Entretiens Psychiatriques*, No. 10 (1964), pp. 239-62.

Seznec, Jean. "Diderot et Sarrasine." Pp. 237-45 in *Diderot Studies IV*. Geneva: Droz, 1963.

Smethurst, Colin, and Bruce Tolley. "The Source of the *Post-Scriptum* of Balzac's *Physiologie du mariage.*" *RLC*, XXXIX (1965), 434-39.

Sullivant, Raymond L. "Antecedents for Balzac's Character, Sir Arthur Ormond, Lord Grenville." *Kentucky Foreign Language Quarterly*, X (1963), 215-19.

Sullivant, Raymond L. "Dating Balzac's *Le rendez-vous.*" *Manuscripta*, VIII (1964), 29-44.

Takayama, Tetsuo. "Réflexions sur *La Recherche de l'absolu.*" *Études de Langue et Littérature Françaises*, No. 4 (1964), pp. 65-77.

Ubersfeld, Annie. "La crise de 1831-1833 dans la vie et l'oeuvre de Balzac." *Europe*, XLIII (Jan. 1965), 55-68.
Followed by remarks of Pierre Barbéris concerning Balzac's social views in 1830 (pp. 68-72).

Weyl, Roland. "Balzac et le fait divers." *Europe*, XLIII (Jan. 1965), 164-70.
The view of legality in *La comédie humaine*.

Wurmser, André. "Variations sur la sincérité de Balzac." *Europe*, XLIII (Jan. 1965), 226-39.
Examines in brief the theme of Wurmser's *La comédie inhumaine* (see *ELN*, III, Supp., 58): Balzac the liar (in fiction and in fact) who unmasked a materialistic society.

Wurmser, André. "Die unmenschliche Komödie." *Sinn und Form,* XVI (1964), 137-59.

Wurmser, André. "Les marxistes, Balzac et Zola." *Les Cahiers Naturalists,* X (1964), 137-48.

Concludes that Zola belongs to the same race as Balzac and that "*Les Rougon-Macquart* requièrent contre le demi-siècle qui suivit *la Comédie humaine.*"

See also Beebe ("General 3. Criticism"); Butor, Easton, Fenger, Seznec ("French 1. General"); Majewski ("Mercier"); Donnelly, Guyon, Weinstein ("Stendhal"); DeCesare ("Italian 3. Belli").

Reviews of works previously listed:

L'Année Balzacienne 1963 (see *PQ,* XLIII, 466), rev. by Geneviève Delattre in *FR,* XXXVIII (1965), 705-06, by M. Reboussin in *MLN,* LXXX (1965), 428-30; BARDÈCHE, Maurice, *Une lecture de Balzac* (see *ELN,* III, Supp., 52), rev. by Carrol Coates in *FR,* XXXIX (1965), 173, by G. Guitard-Auviste in *Le Français dans le Monde,* No. 32, pp. 43-44, and in *NL,* March 11, 1965, p. 10; BEEBE, Maurice, *Ivory Towers and Sacred Founts. The Artist as Hero in Fiction from Goethe to Joyce* (see *ELN,* III, Supp., 53), rev. by Ruby Cohn in *CL,* XVII (1965), 273-75, by John Fletcher in *CLS,* II (1965), 87-89, by Frederick J. Hoffmann in *MP,* LXIII (1965), 179-82; CASTEX, Pierre-Georges, ed., *La maison du chat-qui-pelote; Le bal de Sceaux; La vendetta* (see *ELN,* III, Supp., 53), rev. by M. Reboussin in *MLN,* LXXX (1965), 133-35; DONNARD, J.-H., ed., *Les paysans* (see *ELN,* III, Supp., 54), rev. by Pierre Citron in *L'Année Balzacienne 1965,* pp. 370-74, by H. J. Hunt in *FS,* XIX (1965), 305-306, by Marianne Milhaud in *Europe,* XLIII (Jan. 1965), 286-88, by James Walt in *BA,* XXXIX (1965), 172; DONNARD, J.-H. *Les réalités économiques et sociales dans 'La Comédie humaine'* (see *PQ,* XLIII, 467), rev. by Jean Baumier in *Europe,* XLIII (Jan. 1965), 284-86; LAUBRIET, Pierre, *Un catéchisme esthétique. "Le chef-d'oeuvre inconnu"* (see *PQ,* XLIII, 468), rev. by G. Franceschetti in *SFr,* IX (1965), 375; LAUBRIET, Pierre, *L'intelligence de l'art chez Balzac: d'une esthétique balzacienne* (see *PQ,* XLIII, 468), rev. by A. Kies in *Revue Belge de Philologie et d'Histoire,* XLII (1965), 609-11; PIERROT, Roger, ed., *Correspondance,* t. II (see *PQ,* XLIII, 468), rev. by Raffaele de Cesare in *RLMC,* XVIII (1965), 53-56; PIERROT, Roger, ed., *Correspondance,* t. III (see *ELN,* III, Supp., 56-57), rev. by H. J. Hunt in *FS,* XIX (1965), 304-05; RASER, George B., *Guide to Balzac's Paris* (see *ELN,* III, Supp., 57), rev. by S. Coulon in *L'Année Balzacienne 1965,* p. 386, by Geneviève Delattre in *MLJ,* XLIX (1965), 260-61, by Albert J. Salvan in *FR,* XXXVIII (1965), 705; WURMSER, André, *La comédie inhumaine* (see *ELN,* III, Supp., 58), rev. by Pierre Abraham in *Europe,* XLII (May, 1964), 344-45, by Pierre Barbéris in *L'Année Balzacienne 1965,* pp. 374-82, by Marcel Cornu in *La Pensée,* Aug. 1964, pp. 101-09, by Roland Desné in *Cahiers du Communisme,* Oct. 1964, pp. 118-29, by Jean A. Ducourneau in *L'Express,* July 16, 1964, by Maurice Regard in *Europe,* XLIII (Jan. 1965), 429-30.

BERANGER

See Hytier ("French 1. General"); Wilson ("Stendhal").

BERTRAND

Guiette, R. "Baudelaire et le poème en prose." *Revue Belge de Philologie et d'Histoire,* XLII (1964), 843-52.

Considers influence of Bertrand (among other writers) on the *Petits poèmes en prose.* See brief rev. by S. Robiolio in *SFr,* IX (1965), 578.

Nies, Fr. *Poesie in prosaischer Welt: Untersuchungen zum Prosagedicht bei Aloysius Bertrand und Baudelaire.* (Studia Romanica, 7.) Heidelberg, 1964.

CHASLES

Maixner, Rudolf. "Un aspect de Philarète Chasles." *RLC,* xxxix (1965), 396-405.
Chasles as artisan of literary hoaxes and in particular of the *Scènes des camps et bivouacs hongrois* (1855). As usual, Maixner is interested in the connections between Dalmatia and French literature.

Pichois, Claude. *Philarète Chasles et la vie littéraire au temps du romantisme.* Paris: Librairie José Corti, 1965. 2 vols.
Monsieur Pichois's situation vis-à-vis those who would criticize his study of Chasles is comparable to that of Kittredge vis-à-vis those who would examine him, only more so (ironically, this book was Monsieur Pichois' doctoral dissertation). Years of research into the multifarious activity and the unremitting production of Chasles' "années romantiques" have made him as nearly the master of this huge body of material as it is humanly possible to be. The accuracy and abundance of his information put him out of reach of all but the most niggling criticism: only on a few matters of detail can future researchers correct or amplify it. In short, this is a definitive work if there ever was one. One only regrets a little that all this scrupulous attention—about 500 pages of "life and works" (Vol. I), 350 pages of footnotes, 120 pages of bibliography, an index listing about 2500 names of persons—has gone toward the erection of a monument to a writer who has many respectable claims to our attention but who, after all, was not very exciting or very creative. Moreover, Monsieur Pichois' account only takes Chasles' career up to 1841! He promises to continue his exhaustive (and, one is tempted to believe, exhausting) investigation and to arrive at a conclusion as to Chasles' critical achievement. He modestly regards this massive pyramid, now reaching the half-way mark, as only "une pierre en vue de la synthèse qu'un autre écrira quelque jour: l'histoire de la critique littéraire en France au XIXe siècle." This synthesizer, if he ever appears, will have endless opportunities to be grateful to Monsieur Pichois. (J.S.P.)

CHATEAUBRIAND

Alérion. "Une soeur de Chateaubriand refusée à Remiremont." *L'Intermédiaire des Chercheurs et Curieux,* xv (1965), 783-84.

Bassan, F. "Deux lettres inédites de Chateaubriand: du Ministère des Affaires Étrangères à la publication de la Vie de Rancé." *RHL,* lxv (1965), 273-77.

Cabanis, José. "Chateaubriand, Mme de Beaumont et M. Henri Guillemin." *Table Ronde,* No. 200 (1964), pp. 114-17.

[Carré, Jean-Marie.] *Connaissance de l'étranger.* Mélanges offerts à la mémoire de Jean-Marie Carré. (Coll. "Études de Littérature Étrangère et Comparée," 50.) Paris: M. Didier, 1964. Pp. xx + 528.
Contains material on Chateaubriand and Hugo.

Chalvet, Maurice. "Les exemplaires connus de l'édition princeps de *l'Essai sur les révolutions* de Chateaubriand, Londres, 1797." *Le Livre et l'Estampe,* No. 36 (1963), pp. 309-21.

Chinard, Gilbert. "Libraries and Librairies." *PULC*, XXVII (1965), 127-46.
Concerns collecting, mainly of Chateaubriand. Other relevant matter on pp. 154-56 and the following plates.

Duhamel, Roger. "Chateaubriand et Mme de Staël." *RUO*, XXXIII (April-June, 1963).

Ferrand, Didier. "L'affaire Chateaubriand." *RDM*, Sept. 1, 1965, pp. 118-26.
On the writer's cousin, Armand de Chateaubriand, executed as a spy in 1809.

Guillemin, Henri. *L'homme des "Mémoires d'outre-tombe" avec des fragments inédits des "Mémoires."* Paris: Gallimard, 1965. Pp. 335.
Notice in *BCLF*, No. 230 (Feb. 1965), p. 131, remarks that Guillemin shows Chateaubriand's book "un monument d'imposture." But see Jean Meyer's article below.

Lebègue, Raymond. "Le problème du voyage de Chateaubriand en Amérique." *Journal des Savants*, Troisième Centenaire 1665-1965 (Jan.-March, 1965), pp. 456-65.
Professor Lebègue confirms Bédier's conclusions of 1899: that Chateaubriand could not have seen Louisiana, Florida, the village of the Natchez or the great Mississippi. Sees discrepancies between details in the *Voyage en Amérique* (1827) and the *Mémoires d'outre-tombe* (1834-48) as resulting in part from the long periods of time between his American travels and his matured writings about them.

Levaillant, Maurice, and Georges Moulinier, eds. *Mémoires d'outre-tombe.* Édition nouvelle établie d'après l'édition originelle et des deux dernières copies de texte. (Le Livre de Poche, Nos. 1353-58.) Paris: Librairie Générale Française (exclusiveté Hachette), 1964.

Maixner, Rudolf. "Une diatribe de Bartolomeo Benincasa contre Chateaubriand." *RLC*, XXXVII (1963), 581-86.

Meyer, Jean. "A propos de Chateaubriand: Point de vue d'un historien." *Annales de Bretagne*, LXXII (1965), 311-18.
A partial refutation of some of the implications in Henri Guillemin's *L'homme des "Mémoires d'outre-tombe"* (see above). Superficially read, Chateaubriand's work departs from the facts in its self-interested falsehoods; but "relue et méditée, elle ramène à l'histoire profonde." (A.G.E.)

Moreau, P. *Chateaubriand.* ("Les Écrivains devant Dieu.") Paris: Desclée De Brouwer, 1965. Pp. 138.
Rev. [by Petre Ciureanu] in *SFr*, IX (1965), 371.

Pouilliart, R. "Comment Chateaubriand lut Dante." *LR*, XIX (1965), 335-80.
Continues the more extensive studies of A. Counson and W. P. Friederich on Dante's influence in France. Shows that Chateaubriand's part in spreading Dante's reputation was probably slight ("un vaste mouvement insère *La Divine Comédie* dans le romantisme français. . . ."), though references to Dante helped Chateaubriand mould his own statue for posterity. Yet the evidence of Chateaubriand's interest in Dante, mostly from the *Inferno*, is of value in

revealing Chateaubriand's personal sensitivity—for example, his words on the loneliness of the *selva oscura* ("Rien n'est plus effrayant que cette solitude") and on the bitterness of going up and down others' stairs and eating others' bread, and his response to certain elements in Dante or what he stood for that seemed to Chateaubriand close to his own nature.

Roy, Cl. "Contre et pour Chateaubriand." *RdP*, LXXI (1964), 29-44.
Rev. by G. Franceschetti in *SFr*, VIII (1964), 365-66.

Samitch, M. "Une adaptation poétique de René de Chateaubriand en Bosnie vers 1860 et sa genèse." *Revue de Philologie* (Belgrade), 1963, I-II, 127-39.
On the Franciscan poet Gergo Martitch's *Bijedni Novak* (*Le misérable Novak*), written between 1858-1862 and published in 1886. (Brief summary by P. Jodogne in *SFr*, VIII [1964], 566).

Switzer, Richard, ed. *Voyage en Amérique*. Éd. crit. (Société des Textes Français Modernes.) Paris: Didier, 1964. 2 vols. Pp. lxxiv + 454, pagination suivie.
Rev. by Jean Gaudon in *MLR*, LX (1965), 627-29.

Uffenbeck, L. A. "Charles Didier and Chateaubriand." *RLC*, XXXVII (1963), 587-98.
Synopsis [by Petre Ciureanu] in *SFr*, VIII (1964), 372.

Valette, Rebecca M. "Chateaubriand's Debt to *Les Incas*." *SIR*, II (1963), 177-83.

Welch, M. L. "Visite aux États-Unis d'Amérique." *American Society Legion of Honor Magazine*, XXXVI (1965), 149-64.
Noting that "Chateaubriand's version of America held sway in England for so long," author cites the accounts of Tocqueville and Michel Chevalier after visits in the 1830s, and the accounts of two earlier travelers, Edouard de Montulé (visiting in 1816-17) and Théodore Pavie (1829-30), whose reports afford a startling contrast with those of "the Enchanter."

See also Bassan, Bochner, Butor, Lombard ("French 1. General").

Reviews of books previously listed:
LEHTONEN, Maija, *L'expression imagée dans l'oeuvre de Chateaubriand* (see *ELN*, III, Supp., 59), rev. by Fernande Bassan in *ECr*, V (1965), 180-82, in *FR*, XXXIX (1965), 171-72, and in *RSH*, n.s., No. 118 (April-June, 1965), pp. 292-94; [by Petre Ciureanu] in *SFr*, IX (1965), 564-65; by Stephen Ullman in *FS*, XIX (1965), 297-99. MOUROT, Jean, *Chateaubriand . . . Le génie d'un style* (see *PQ*, XLI, 685), rev. by Michel Otten in *LR*, XIX (1965), 37-40.

CONSTANT

Alexander, Ian W. "La morale 'ouverte' de Benjamin Constant." Pp. 395-410 in *Studi in onore di Carlo Pellegrini*. (Biblioteca di Studi Francesi, 2.) Turin: Società Editrice Internazionale, 1963. Pp. xxxix + 846.

Cordié, Carlo. "Il 'Wallstein' di Benjamin Constant nelle testimonianze dell'autore e di alcuni suoi contemporanei." Pp. 411-54 in *Studi in*

onore di Carlo Pellegrini. (Biblioteca di Studi Francesi, 2.) Turin: Società Editrice Internazionale, 1963. Pp. xxxix + 846.
Includes Jean-Louis Laya's review, which appeared in the *Gazette Nationale ou le Moniteur Universel,* Feb. 16 and March 21, 1809.

Gall, Lothar. *Benjamin Constant, seine politische Ideenwelt und der deutsche Vormärz.* (Veröffentlichungen des Instituts für Europäische Geschichte Mainz, Bd. 30. Abteilung Universalgeschichte.) Wiesbaden: F. Steiner, 1963.
Rev. by Pierre Angel in *Erasmus,* April 25, 1964.

Greshoff, C. J. "*Adolphe* and the Romantic Delusion." *Forum for Modern Language Studies,* I (1965), 30-36.
A good literary analysis of Adolphe as "a very young man who thinks he is a romantic hero but who is not truly committed to a romantic attitude to life." (C.C.)

Luzi, Mario. *Lo stile di Constant.* (Biblioteca delle Silerchie, 90.) Milan: Mondadori, 1963.

Peignot, Jérôme. "*Sola inconstantia constans* ou de Benjamin Constant, professeur de mariage." *NRF,* Jan. 1965, pp. 18-31.
Constant's solitude and troubled relations with women.

Pozzo di Borgo, Olivier, ed. *Ecrits et discours politiques par Benjamin Constant.* Paris: J. J. Pauvert, 1964. 2 vols. Fr. 57.
Rev. by Carlo Cordié in *SFr,* IX (1965), 371, by David Thomson in *FS,* XIX (1965), 299-300, and in *TLS,* May 6, 1965, p. 354.

Thadden, Rudolf v. "Das Mandat Benjamin Constants eine Grundsatzdebatte in der Französischen Kammer 1824." Vol. II, pp. 154-68 in *Festschrift Percy Ernst Schramm.* Wiesbaden: Franz Steiner, 1964.

Thompson, Patrice. "A propos de la récente publication des 'Ecrits politiques de Benjamin Constant' par M. Pozzo di Borgo: La politique, la religion, et la doctrine de la perfectibilité humaine." *RSH,* n.s., No. 117 (1965), pp. 129-45.
Disagrees with Pozzo di Borgo (see above); contends it is a mistake to seek the history of a Protestant soul or a philosophy in "De la religion," where Constant's view is focused on man.

See also Paulson ("General 3. Criticism"); Girard, Kelly ("French 1. General").

Review of book previously listed:
CORDIÉ, Carlo, ed., *Adolphe* (see *ELN,* III, Supp., 61), rev. by Olga Ragusa in *RR,* LVI, 224-25.

COUSIN

Simon, W. M. "The 'Two Cultures' in Nineteenth-Century France: Victor Cousin and Auguste Comte." *JHI,* XXVI (1965), 45-58.
The views of Cousin and Comte were not, in spite of mutual antagonism, completely opposed in the areas of spiritualism and materialism.

See also Petitbon, Reizov ("French 1. General").

DELACROIX
Werner, Alfred. "Artists Who Write." *Art Journal,* xxiv (1965), 342-47.

Delacroix, "more than anyone else in modern times, refutes the thesis that an artist fails when he attempts to express himself in words."

See also Girard ("French 1. General").

DESBORDES-VALMORE
Review of book previously listed:

JASENAS, Elaine, *Marceline Desbordes-Valmore devant la critique* (see *PQ,* XLIII, 472), rev. by Louis Bolle in *RR,* LVI (1965), 305-06.

DUMAS
Bassan, Fernande. "Dumas Père et le drame romantique." *ECr,* v (1965), 174-78.

Surveys Dumas' dramatic work, and concludes that he was the Romantic "dont l'oeuvre dramatique a le mieux réussi de son vivant," and that he is "avant tout un grand créateur."

Bauer, Camille. "Le mythe de d'Artagnan." *FR,* xxxix (1965), 329-36.

Diachronic study of the evolution of a character from 1700 to 1962. Dumas' colorful tableaux gave a place to "le petit peuple dans un passé glorieux."

Eaubonne, Françoise d'. "Un bienfait d'Alexandre Dumas ou les dangers du rewriting." *RdP,* July-Aug. 1965, pp. 77-83.

Abortive effort by Dumas to help an aspiring poet, Clémence Badère.

Montesquiou, Pierre de. *Le vrai d'Artagnan.* Paris: Julliard, 1963.

See also Cândido, Seznec ("French 1. General"); Dale ("Vigny"); DuBruck ("Nerval").

ECKSTEIN
Jensen, C. A. E. "The Romanticism of Ferdinand d'Eckstein." *RLC,* xxxix (1965), 226-42.

Jensen gives a brief biography of this curious figure, in whom a large number of Romantic currents blend, and outlines his religious position and his esthetics, which was basically derived and adapted from the Schlegels.

See also Petitbon ("French 1. General").

GAUTIER
Behrens, Ralph. "Three Poets in Search of Beauty." *Midwest Quarterly,* IV, No. 1 (1962), pp. 11-21.

Influence of the methods of Gautier, Leconte de Lisle, and Baudelaire.

Book, Claude-Marie. "Théophile Gautier et l'Hôtel des Haricots," *RHL,* LXV (1965), 277-86.

An amusing article on Gautier's running battle with the Garde Nationale and his incarcerations in "l'Hôtel des Haricots," its *maison d'arrêt.* (A.G.E.)

68

Cottin, Madeleine. "Marie Mattei inspiratrice de Théophile Gautier," *RHL,* LXV (1965), 421-29.
Offers evidence in support of Jean Pommier's suggestion that Marie Mattei inspired Gautier's poem, "Diamant du coeur," which should thus be restored to her *petit recueil.*

Doyon, René-Louis. "Défis littéraires: Mademoiselle de Maupin." *Les Livrets du Mandarin* rédigés par René-Louis Doyon, 6ᵉ Série, Nos. 9-10 (Oct. 1963—Adieu?), pp. 14-23.

Whyte, Peter. "Deux emprunts de Gautier à Irving," *RLC,* XXXVIII (1964), 572-77.
Shows clearly by a comparison of texts that the "Cauchemar d'un mangeur" (earlier assigned to Nerval, but plausibly restored to Gautier by Jean Richer [*RLC,* XXXV (1961), 251-53]) was in part plagiarized from Lebègue d'Auteuil's translation of "The Adventure of the Mysterious Picture" from Washington Irving's *Tales of a Traveller* (1824)—and urges that Gautier's "La cafetière" was inspired by Irving's "The Bold Dragoon" from the same collection. (A.G.E.)

See also Hytier, Petitbon, Seznec ("French 1. General").

Reviews of books previously listed:
RICHER, Jean, *Une collaboration inconnue: La description du Panthéon de Paul Chenavard par Gautier et Nerval* (see *PQ,* XLIII, 473), rev. by Alfred Du Bruck, *RR,* LVI (1965), 308.

GUERIN, EUGENIE AND MAURICE DE
Moreau, Pierre, ed. *Maurice et Eugénie de Guérin.* Préface de François Mauriac. (Coll. "Les Plus Belles Pages.") Paris: Mercure de France, 1965. Pp. 256.
See Robert Kanters' "Les cercles intérieurs" (*Figaro Littéraire,* Dec. 2, 1965, p. 5) for general comment.

GUERIN, EUGENIE DE
Moreau, Pierre. "Silhouette d'Eugénie de Guérin." *Études Françaises,* I (1965), 3-38.
An attractive and sympathetic account of the life and literary character of this "Sévigné romantique . . . [de qui] Gérard de Nerval eût fait . . . une de ses filles du feu." (A.G.E.)

GUERIN, MAURICE DE
Moreau, Pierre. *Maurice de Guérin, ou les métamorphoses d'un centaure.* (Archives des Lettres Modernes, No. 60.) Paris: Minard, 1965. Pp. 80.

Schärer-Nussberger, Maya. *Maurice de Guérin, l'errance et la demeure.* Paris: Corti, 1965. Pp. 221.

Secretan, Dominique, ed. *Pages choisies.* Manchester University Press, 1965. Pp. xxvi + 101.
Rev. [by Petre Ciureanu] in *SFr,* IX (1965), 572.

See also Girard ("French 1. General").

1968

HUGO

Arnautovitch, M. "Jovan Skerlitch—Victor Hugo," *Annales de la Faculté de Philologie* (Université de Belgrade), II (1962), Belgrade, 1963, pp. 205-41.
Brief summary by P. Jodogne in *SFr*, VIII (1965), 573-74.

Bach, Max. "The Reception of Victor Hugo's First Novels." *Symposium*, XVIII (1964), 142-55.

Bach, Max. "Le Vieux Paris dans *Notre-Dame*: Sources et ressources de Victor Hugo." *PMLA*, LXXX (1965), 321-24 (preceded by two illus. of "Le Plan de Tapisserie").
Shows persuasively and amusingly that numerous errors in archaeological details on old Paris in *Notre-Dame de Paris* stem from Hugo's too hasty examination of old maps—especially that of "Paris vers 1540" executed by Gaignières in 1690 from "le Plan dit de Tapisserie." (A.G.E.)

Barrère, Jean-Bertrand, ed. *Un carnet des "Misérables," octobre-décembre 1860.* Notes et brouillons présentés, déchiffrés et annotés par J.-B. Barrère. (Coll. "Paralogue," No. 2.) Paris: Minard (Lettres Modernes), 1965. Pp. 293.

Barrère, Jean-Bertrand. *Victor Hugo.* (Coll. "Les Grands Écrivains devant Dieu.") Paris: Desclée de Brouwer, 1965. Pp. 144.

Bouvet, Francis, ed. *Oeuvres dramatiques et critiques complètes.* Paris: Jean-Jacques Pauvert, 1963. Pp. xiv + 1747.
The third volume in this handsome publication of Hugo's works includes, in addition to the plays and criticism (*Littérature et philosophie mêlée, William Shakespeare, Le tas de pierres*), an appendix containing *Les tables tournantes de Jersey* and the *Albums spirites.*

Bouvet, Francis, ed. *Oeuvres politiques complètes—Oeuvres diverses.* Paris: Jean-Jacques Pauvert, 1964. Pp. xvi + 1667.
The fourth volume of the Pauvert edition of Hugo's works. Includes, in addition to the political writings, such material as *Le tas de pierres, Le Rhin, Carnets—Albums—Journaux, Mes fils,* and *Victor Hugo raconté par un témoin de sa vie,* along with reproductions of some of Hugo's drawings.

Brombert, Victor. "Victor Hugo, la prison et l'espace," *RSH*, n.s., No. 117 (Jan.-March, 1965), pp. 59-79.
Hugo, who seems at first the singer of freedom and motion, is shown in this remarkable study to have been imaginatively and often grotesquely concerned with imprisonment, to have assembled careful documentation on prison conditions, and to have shown the prison (real or symbolic) as a place of horrible claustration and also as the dwelling-place for the visionary and Promethean spirit—the convict or the poet—who may become transfigured by his ordeal. (A.G.E.)

Burguet, Frantz-André, ed. *Les châtiments,* avec introd. et notes. (Le Livre de Poche, Nos. 1378-79.) Paris: Librarie Générale Française (exclusiveté Hachette), 1964.

Butor, Michel. "Victor Hugo critique," *Critique,* No. 221 (Oct., 1965), pp. 203-26.

70

Apropos of *Promontorium somnii* (see *ELN*, III, Supp., 66), *Oeuvres dramatiques et critiques complètes,* and *Oeuvres politiques complètes, oeuvres diverses.* Shows Hugo's prodigious reading, detailed information, and poetic processes of thought in his comments on literature and men of letters. But even in the demonstration of these few pages one feels crushed by the feverish press of ideas and words. (A.G.E.)

Butor, Michel. "Victor Hugo romancier," *Tel Quel,* No. 16 (1964), pp. 60-77.

Cattaui, Georges. *Orphisme et prophétie chez les poètes français, 1850-1950.* Paris: Plon, 1965.
Material on Hugo and Nerval among the Romantics.

Cellier, Léon. *Autour des "Contemplations": George Sand et Victor Hugo.* (Archives des Lettres Modernes, 44, 110-112. Paris: Minard, 1962. Pp. 35.
Concerns George Sand's correspondence with Hetzel and Hugo on the *Contemplations,* and her two articles on the collection for *La Presse* in 1856 in the series called "Autour de la table." The second article is reproduced *in extenso* and shows George Sand as one of the few early critics (before the youthful Mallarmé, and before Baudelaire and Gautier) to praise a masterpiece that was hardly appreciated in its time.

Danitch-Stanojcitch, J. "Victor Hugo dans la presse serbe du 19e et du commencement du 20e siècle," *Annales de la Faculté de Philologie* (Belgrade, I (1962 [1961]), Pp. 151-89.

Dédéyan, Charles. *Victor Hugo et l'Allemagne.* II: *La maturité (1830-1848).* (Bibliothèque de Littérature et d'Histoire, No. 3.) Paris: Minard, 1965. Pp. 308.

Delalande, Jean. [Victor Hugo à Jersey] *La Revue Francaise,* No. 179 (1965), pp. 19-26.

Émery, Léon. *Trois poètes cosmiques.* Paris: Les Cahiers Libres, 1964.
On Goethe, Hugo, and Claudel.

Fongaro, Antoine. "Mallarmé et Victor Hugo," *RSH,* n.s., No. 120 (1965), pp. 515-27.
Surveys research of numerous scholars (Adile Ayda, Léon Cellier, J.-P. Richard, L. J. Austin, *et al.*) refuting Thibaudet's denial of Hugo's influence on Mallarmé except for a brief period in Mallarmé's youth, and hazards the conclusion that Hugo may well be considered "comme l'inspirateur 'fondamental' de l'essentiel de la poétique mallarméenne."

Franceschetti, G. "Carl Maria von Weber e Victor Hugo." *Aevum,* XXXIX (1965), 137-63.
Rev. by R. Masetti in *SFr,* IX (1965), 569.

Franceschetti, G. *Studi hughiani in Italia nel decennio 1951-1960,* estr. dal vol. *Contributi dell' Instituto di Filologia Moderne,* Serie Francese, III (Milano: Società Editrice Vita e Pensiero, 1964), 454-531.
Rev. in *SFr,* IX (1965), 172.

Gaudon, Jean, ed. *Ce que disent les tables parlantes. Victor Hugo à Jersey.* Paris: Pauvert, 1963. Pp. 112.
Rev. by G. Franceschetti in *SFr,* VIII (1964), 573, by H. J. Hunt in *FS,* XIX (1965), 193-94.

Gaulmier, Jean. "Louis Blanc et Victor Hugo." *Revue de Philosophie* (Belgrade), Nos. 1-2 (1963), pp. 211-29.

Georgel, Pierre. "Vision et imagination plastique dans *Quatrevingt-Treize.*" *LR,* XIX (1965), 3-27.
Demonstrates Hugo's well-known descriptive powers in the use of form, color, and contrasts of light and dark, and his versatile employment of the techniques of painting ("là Delacroix et Goya, ici Fragonard, Boilly, Greuze"), and of sculpture and architecture. But beyond merely visual and plastic evocations are those in which the whole mechanism of poetic creation has been at work in Hugo's terms: "Observation, Imagination, Intuition."

Girard, René. "Monstres et demi-dieux dans l'oeuvre de Hugo." *Symposium,* XIX (1965), 50-57.
A consideration of Hugo's attitudes towards Gwynplaine and Lord David in *L'homme qui rit* and illuminating parallels in "Le crapaud."

Halbwachs, Pierre. "Victor Hugo, la mythologie et les mythes." *La Pensée,* No. 119 (Feb. 1965), pp. 93-102.

"Hugo Turns the Tables." *TLS,* April 22, 1965, p. 308.
Notes at present "something of a Hugo revival in France" and considers ten recent publications related to this phenomenon.

Journet, René, et Guy Robert. *Le mythe du peuple dans "Les Misérables."* Paris: Éditions Sociales, s.d. [1964]. Pp. 215.
Rev. by Jacques Seebacher in *RHL,* LXV (1965), 518-21.

Koch, Herbert. "Victor Hugo and Juliette Drouet: Die Krise des Jahres 1873." *ZFSL,* LXXV (1965), 135-43.

Lambert, Françoise. *Le manuscrit du "Roi s'amuse"* (B.N., n.a.f. 13370). (Annales Littéraires de l'Université de Besançon, LXIII.) Paris: Les Belles Lettres, 1964. Pp. 128.
Rev. by R. Journet in *RHL,* LXV, 709.

Pritchett, V. S. "Hugo's Impersonations." Pp. 103-08 in his *The Working Novelist.* London: Chatto and Windus, 1965.
Hugo is described as a black and white artist whose genius depends upon excess. His myth-making power and superb theatrical sense explain popular admiration for such characters as Quasimodo and Jean Valjean. Pritchett finds it more sensible "to call Hugo 'incurious Dostoevsky' than 'inferior Scott'."

Riffaterre, Michael. "Hugo's *Orientales* Revisited." *American Society of Legion of Honor Magazine,* XXXVI (1965), 103-18.
Shows the need for reappraisal of critical *clichés* on Hugo's use of light and color in *Les Orientales.* The supposedly dominant role of light appears characticaly interrelated here with the idea of darkness; and Hugo's use of color is subtly shown as a product of his inner vision and as part of his effort to free language, rather than as an example of realistic and exact description. (A.G.E.)

Riffaterre, Michael. "Un exemple de comédie symboliste chez Victor Hugo," *ECr*, v (1965), 162-73.
On Hugo's *Mangeront-ils* (1867) of his *Théâtre en liberté* in which the parodies of the brigand Aïrolo function to link fantasy and philosophic intent and provide "le pont entre le symbolisme et le comique."

Riffaterre, Michael. "Victor Hugo and the Universe within the Poet," *American Society of Legion of Honor Magazine*, xxxv (1964), 11-27.

Rinsler, Norma. "Victor Hugo and the *Poésies allemandes* of Gérard de Nerval," *RLC*, xxxix (1965), 382-95.
Suggests that Hugo's understanding of the German poets (especially Goethe and Schiller) may have come through Gérard de Nerval.

Saix, Guillot de. "Une comédie sur l'homosexualité imaginée par Victor Hugo en marge d'Homère." *Arcadie*, ii, No. 123 (1964), 150-51.

Secret, Jean, et Marius Lévy. "Victor Hugo et les caricaturistes," *Jardin des Arts*, No. 123 (1965), pp. 58-65.

Six, André. "Explication française—Victor Hugo: 'A Théophile Gautier'." *IL*, xvii (1965), 40-41.

Sauro, Antonio. *Le Rhin de Victor Hugo: Romantisme et diplomatie.* Bari: Adriatica Editrice, [1964]. Pp. 80.
Rev. by Claude Pichois in *RHL*, lxv (1965), 516-17.

Siccardo, F. "Dante e Victor Hugo." *RLC*, xxxix (1965), 427-33.
Shows Hugo's interest in Dante from the preface of *Les rayons et les ombres* (1840) to his response in 1865 to a request by the Gonfalonier of Florence that he write something for the city's celebration of the 600th anniversary of Dante's birth and his reply in 1866 at receiving the Dante jubilee medal from the Gonfalonier while he himself was at Hauteville-House, like Dante an exile.

Zviguilsky, A. "V. P. Botkine chez Victor Hugo." *RLC*, xxxix (1965), 287-90.
A young Russian's account of his visit to Hugo's home in Paris (in the present Place des Vosges) on July 27, 1835. Affords interesting details as to furniture and sketches in Hugo's *salon*.

See also Rinsler ("General 3. Criticism"); Barineau, Bochner, Butor, Fenger, Lombard, Petitbon, Seznec, ("French 1. General"); Carré ("Chateaubriand"); Dale ("Vigny"); Oliver, Wilson ("Nodier").

Reviews of books previously listed:
ALBOUY, Pierre, *La création mythologique chez Victor Hugo* (see *ELN*, iii, Supp., 63), rev. by Pierre Albouy (the author) in a résumé for *IL*, xvii (1965), 193-95; by J.-B. Barrère in *RSH*, n.s., No. 117 (1965), pp. 149-52; by R. Journet in *RHL*, lxv (1965), 521-23; by Max Milner in *IL*, xvii (1965), 210-11; BARRERE, J. B., *La fantaisie de Victor Hugo, II: 1852-1885* (see *PQ*, xli, 688), rev. by J. Gaudon in *MLR*, lviii (1963), 438-41; CORNAILLE, Roger, et Georges Herscher, eds., *Victor Hugo dessinateur* (see *ELN*, iii, Supp., 67), rev. by Yvan Christ in *La Table Ronde*, No. 195 (April 1964), pp. 142-43; by Pierre Georgel in *RHL*, lxv (1965), 524-25; DÉDÉYAN, Charles, *Victor Hugo et l'Allemagne* (see *ELN*, iii, Supp., 65), rev. by André Monchoux in

RHL, LXV (1965), 709-11; GAUDON, Jean, ed., *Lettres à Juliette Drouet 1833-1883. Le Livre de l'Anniversaire* (see *ELN,* III, Supp., 65), rev. by G. Franceschetti in *SFr,* VIII (1965), 572-73; by Herbert Koch in *ZFSL,* LXXV (1965), 183-84; JOURNET, René, et Guy Robert, *Le manuscrit des Misérables* (see *ELN,* III, Supp., 66), rev. by Jean Onimus, *RSH,* No. 119 (1965), pp. 453-54; by Jacques Seebacher in *RHL,* LXV (1965), 518-21; JOURNET, René, et Guy Robert, eds., *Victor Hugo, Trois Albums* (see *ELN,* III, Supp., 66), rev. by Jean Onimus, *RSH,* n.s., No. 119 (1965), pp. 452-53; by Jacques Seebacher in *RHL,* LXV (1965), 523-24; MALLION, Jean, *Victor Hugo et l'art architectural* (see *ELN,* III, Supp., 66), rev. by M. Milner in *IL,* XVII (1965), 124; PIROUÉ, Georges, *Victor Hugo romancier ou les dessus de l'inconnu: Essai* (see *ELN,* III, Supp., 67), rev. by G. Franceschetti in *SFr,* VIII (1964), 371; PY, Albert, *Les mythes grecs dans la poésie de Victor Hugo* (see *ELN,* III, Supp., 67), rev. by H. J. Hunt in *FS,* XIX (1965), 75-77; by Max Milner in *IL,* XVII (1965), 210; RUSSELL, Olga Wester, *Étude historique et critique des "Burgraves"* . . . (see *PQ,* XLIII, 475), rev. by J. Seebacher in *RHL,* LXV (1965), 517-18; SEEBACHER, Jacques, ed., *Les contemplations* (see *ELN,* III, Supp., 67), rev. by Pierre Albouy in *RHL,* LXV (1965), 711-13; by G. Franceschetti in *SFr,* VIII (1964), 572; by Alfred Glauser in *RR,* LVI (1965), 227-28; by H. J. Hunt in *FS,* XIX (1965), 303-04; THIERRY, J.-J., and Josette Mélèze, eds., *Théâtre complet,* t. II (see *ELN,* III, Supp., 67), rev. by G. Franceschetti in *SFr,* IX (1965), 375-76.

JOUBERT

See Girard ("French 1. General").

LACORDAIRE

Sheppard, Lancelot C. *Lacordaire: A Biographical Essay.* London: Burns and Oates, 1964. Pp. xi + 184.

LAMARTINE

Bénichou, Paul. "Sur les premières élégies de Lamartine." *RHL,* LXV (1965), 27-46.

Bénichou identifies and then scrutinizes the poems which survive from a set of "élégies" which Lamartine put together in June 1816 (nine poems which he later incorporated into the *Méditations* and two which he left in MS.). A close study reveals that these poems, of crucial importance because they are the first in which Lamartine's originality manifested itself, were inspired less by specific love affairs than by poetic tradition. Bénichou's general conclusion is that Lamartine "a beau se donner pour le poète de la sincérité et de la pure effusion: cette poésie qu'il a prétendu être l'écho direct de son âme ne s'en est pas moins formée, comme toute poésie, à distance de la vie vécue."

Chervet, Maurice, ed. *Premières méditations poétiques.* (Les Petits Classiques Bordas.) Paris: Bordas, 1965. Pp. 128.

A school edition, but a solid piece of work, especially welcome in view of the dearth of Lamartine texts in print. Good illustrations. (J.S.P.)

Griffiths, David A. "Au dossier des 'années sombres' d'Alphonse de Lamartine: Lettres inédites de Lamartine à Ernest Legouvé." *SFr,* IX (1965), 75-82.

Sixteen letters from the period 1853-1868, mostly dealing with Lamartine's financial difficulties.

Guitard-Auviste, G[inette]. "Le secret de Jocelyn." *NL,* Sept. 30, 1965, p. 11.

Speculates on the question of how Lamartine came by the abbé Dumont's guilty secret.

74

Letessier, Fernand. "Lamartine en 1867-1868: Lettres inédites sur le crépuscule d'un dieu." *Bulletin de l'Association Guillaume Budé,* 4ᵉ série, No. 2 (June 1965), pp. 242-72.

Nadal, Octave. "Le lac." Pp. 109-17 in his *A mesure haute: aux sources de la poésie.* Paris: Mercure de France, 1964. Pp. 282.
Admitting the abiding hold the poem has on him, Nadal goes on to subject its philosophical content to an analysis à la Poulet and finds "une faille sublime" in the poem: "une contradiction fondamentale s'élève au coeur même de l'amour entre ses deux modes de sentir l'éternel."

Picon, Gaëtan. "Comme une grande image." *NL,* Sept. 30, 1965, p. 11.
A re-appreciation of Lamartine as poet.

Remacle, Madeleine. "*Le Lac* de Lamartine." *Cahiers d'Analyse Textuelles,* No. 6 (1964), pp. 31-43.

See also Bassan, Lombard, Petitbon ("French 1. General"); Fam ("Balzac").

Reviews of books previously listed:
GUYARD, Marius-François, ed., *OEuvres poétiques complètes* (see *ELN,* III, Supp., 68-69), rev. by J.-B. Barrère in *FS,* XIX (1965), 70-72; by Pierre Moreau in *RHL,* LXV (1965), 327, in *TLS,* Oct. 1, 1964, pp. 1-2; VERDIER, Abel, *Les amours italiennes de Lamartine: Graziella et Lena* (see *ELN,* III, Supp., 69), rev. by Marius-François Guyard in *RHL,* LXV (1965), 326-27.

LAMENNAIS

Guillemin, Henri. "La Mennais, notes et documents." *Europe,* XLIII (Sept.-Oct. 1965), 163-86.
Another of Guillemin's iconoclastic onslaughts on Romantic personalities. By the usual ingenious piecing together of biographical evidence, Guillemin convicts Lamennais of prurience, perfidy, perjury, hypocrisy, and avarice. "Au demeurant, le meilleur fils du monde," so to speak (Guillemin rejects the accusation of homosexuality sometimes made against Lamennais.) (J.S.P.)

Le Guillou, Louis. "L'information romaine de Lamennais: lettres inédites de MacCarthy à Lamennais (15 nov. 1832—28 oct. 1834)." *Annales de Bretagne,* LXXI (1964), 373-421.

Simon, A. *Rencontres mennaisiennes en Belgique.* (Académie Royale de Belgique. Classe des lettres et des sciences morales et politiques. Collection in -8°, Vol. LVI, Fasc. 3.) Brussels: Palais des Académies, 1963.
Rev. by G. de Bertier de Sauvigny in *Revue Belge de Philologie et d'Histoire,* XLII (1965), 1061-63.

MAISTRE

Matucci, Mario. "Joseph de Maistre e la teoria della Provvidenza." Pp. 171-211 in *Saggi e Ricerche di Letteratura Francese,* Vol. VI. (Università di Pisa, Istituto di Lingua e Letteratura Francese.) Pisa: Libreria Goliardica Editrice, 1965.
A satisfactory résumé; nothing new in material or approach.

MERCIER

Majewski, Henry F. "L. S. Mercier: A Pre-Romantic View of Paris." *SIR*, v (1965), 16-29.
A study of Mercier's *Tableau de Paris* and related texts reveals a "pre-romantic anguish" foreshadowing the morbid fascination with Parisian corruption felt later by Balzac and Baudelaire. Implicitly, Mercier's picture of Paris is a criticism of the Ancien Régime, a presage of the Revolution, and a challenge to Enlightenment optimism.

MERIMEE

Cermakian, Marianne. "Treize lettres inédites de Prosper Mérimée (1862-1870)." *RHL*, LXV (1965), 430-56.
Supplements her earlier *Lettres à Edward Ellice (1857-1863)* (see *PQ*, XLIII, 477). The letters given here are primarily of biographical interest. They are quite adequately annotated.

Teppe, Julien. "La mystérieuse dictée de Mérimée." *Vie et Langage*, No. 148 (July 1964), pp. 429-33.
Attempts to trace the anecdote of the *dictée de Compiègne* back to its sources. The results indicate we may be dealing with a myth.

See also Seznec ("French 1. General").

Reviews of books previously listed:
BOWMAN, Frank Paul, *Prosper Mérimée: Heroism, Pessimism, and Irony* (see *PQ*, XLII, 476), rev. by Robert Baschet in *RHL*, LXV (1965), 528-30; by Victor Brombert in *RR*, LV (1965), 142-43; by A. Olivero in *SFr*, IX (1965), 376; CERMAKIAN, Marianne, and France Achener, eds., *Lettres à Edward Ellice (1857-1863)* (see *PQ*, XLIII, 477), rev. by Petre Ciureanu in *SFr*, IX (1965), 173-74; KOSKO, Maria, *Le thème de Mateo Falcone* (see *PQ*, XLII, 476), rev. by Frank Paul Bowman in *RR*, LV (1965), 141-42; LÉON, Paul, *Mérimée et son temps* (see *PQ*, XLIII, 477), rev. by Emile Lehouck, *Revue Belge de Philologie et d'Histoire*, XLII (1965), 1127-29; PARTURIER, Maurice, ed., *Correspondance générale*, 2e série, Tome XI (see *ELN*, III, Supp., 71), rev. by Robert Baschet in *RHL*, LXV (1965), 528-30; by Jean Théodoridès in *SC*, VII (1965), 251-52.

MICHELET

Atherton, John. "Michelet: Three Conceptions of Historical Becoming." *SIR*, IV (1965), 220-39.
A stimulating article which has the great merit of linking Michelet the artist and Michelet the historian. Essentially, Atherton organizes the figurative language used by Michelet to describe the process of historical change. He distinguishes "three separate ways of viewing the past: history as process, as natural growth, and as fulfillment. . . . In each case the manner in which history is seen to evolve determines a different role for the historian." The processes converge in the Revolution, and Michelet's *Histoire de la Révolution* represents the culmination and convergence of his three conceptions of becoming. (J.S.P.)

Atherton, John. "The Function of Space in Michelet's Writing." *MLN*, LXXX (1965), 336-46.
Atherton attempts to define the "sense of space" underlying many scenes in the *Histoire de France* and *Histoire de la Révolution*. The technique used here is similar to that used in the longer study listed above, the results a little less compelling but suggestive nevertheless. (J.S.P.)

Pellegrini, Carlo. "Sismondi e Michelet: storia di un'amicizia (con lettere inedite)." *SFr* IX (1965), 25-40.
This friendship began in 1825 and lasted until Sismondi's death. It was deeper than usually realized and based on real affinities in the thought of the two men. The hitherto unpublished letters include seven from Michelet to Sismondi, two from Sismondi to Michelet, and one from Sismondi's widow to Michelet.

Seznec, Jean. "Michelet humaniste et les symboles de l'histoire." Pp. 105-19 in *Saggi e Ricerche di Letteratura Francese,* Vol. III. (Università degli Studi di Pisa, Studi di Filologia Moderna.) Milan: Feltrinelli, 1963.
Studies the influence of the classics on the life and thought of Michelet and especially on his changing conception of his role as a historian. In passing, Seznec offers the interesting idea that Michelet found a Romanticism in antiquity.

Siohan, Mme, ed. *Centenaire du Lycée Michelet à Vanves, 1864-1964. Exposition 20-30 juin 1964. Catalogue.* Préface par A.-M. Praud. Historique du Lycée Michelet par André Michel. Paris: Institut Pédagogique National, 1964.

Talvart, Hector, Joseph Place, and Georges Place. "Michelet." Vol. XV, pp. 37-105 in Talvart, Hector et al. *Bibliographie des auteurs modernes de langue française (1801-1962).* Paris: Editions de la Chronique des Lettres Françaises, 1928-1963. 15 vols.

See also Reizov, Seznec ("French 1. General").

Reviews of books previously listed:
CORNUZ, Jean-Louis, *Jules Michelet: un aspect de la pensée religieuse du XIXe siècle* (see *PQ,* XXXVIII, 184), rev. by André Monchoux in *RLC,* XXXIX (1965), 323-25; MORAZE, Charles, ed., *Introduction à l'histoire universelle: Tableau de la France: Préface à l'Histoire de France* (see *PQ,* XLII, 477), rev. by Claude Digeon in *RHL,* LXV (1965), 134; VIALLANEIX, Paul, ed., *Journal,* Tome II (see *PQ,* XLII, 478), rev. by Oscar A. Haac in *RR,* LV (1965), 139-41.

MUSSET

Bachem, Rose M. "Musset and Browning's *Andrea del Sarto.*" *RLC,* XXXVIII (1964), 248-54.

Denommé, Robert T. "The Motif of the 'Poète maudit' in Musset's *Lorenzaccio.*" *ECr,* V (1965), 138-46.

Dimoff, P. *La genèse de Lorenzaccio.* (Publications de la Société des Textes Français Modernes.) Paris: Didier, 1964.
Reprint of an important study originally published in 1936.

Falconer, Graham. "La genèse de 'Mardoche'." *RHL,* LXV (1965), 47-69.
Presents evidence that this work, from the *Contes d'Espagne et d'Italie,* was composed at two different periods rather than one as commonly supposed.

Grisay-Ebbeler, Aletta. "Un sonnet d'Alfred de Musset: 'Tristesse'." *Cahiers d'Analyse Textuelle,* No. 6 (1964), pp. 44-49.

Guillemin, Henri, ed. *Théâtre complet.* Lausanne: Editions Rencontre, 1964. 4 vols.

Jeune, Simon. "Une étude inconnue de Musset sur Hoffmann." *RLC,* XXXIX (1965), 422-27.
Text of an anonymous review of Hoffmann's *Contes,* published in *Le Temps* (Dec. 1, 1830) and here attributed to Musset.

Shaw, Marjorie, ed. *'Lorenzaccio' and 'Un caprice.'* (Textes Français Classiques et Modernes.) London University Press, 1963.

Sion, Georges. "De Marivaux à Giraudoux ou les sourires de la gravité." *Les Annales. Conferencia,* n.s., No. 172 (1965), pp. 37-50.
Peers behind the dramatic masks of Marivaux, Musset, and Giraudoux, "les princes de la futilité." "Entre les vrais futiles et eux, s'élève un monde de différences: trésors cachés, opulence discrète, gravités estompées, engagements souriants."

See also Bochner, Easton, Hytier, Lombard, Pichois ("French 1. General").

NERVAL

Cargo, Robert T. "Gérard de Nerval's Benoni," *RomN,* VII (Autumn, 1965), 12-15.
Shows that the name Benoni is probably of Biblical origin (Genesis 35.18).

DuBruck, Alfred. *Gérard de Nerval and the German Heritage.* London, The Hague, Paris: Mouton and Co., 1965. Pp. 136.
Proposes "to study and determine the actual extent of the German influence upon Gérard de Nerval." After a rather abbreviated treatment of developments in Nerval scholarship (pp. 11-42) the author considers in three successive chapters Nerval and Hoffmann, Goethe, and Heine, "his most important German sources." Urges that the sort of synthesis needed for a complete understanding of Nerval can be accomplished only by the methods of comparative literature.

DuBruck, Alfred. "More on Nerval's 'Benoni'." *RomN,* VI (Spring 1965), 121.
Supplementing the author's earlier note in *RomN,* IV, 117-18.

DuBruck, Alfred. "Nerval, collaborateur of Dumas père." *Neuphilologische Mitteilungen,* XXV (1964), 481-93.

DuBruck, Alfred. "Nerval's *Léo Burckart*: Message or Confession." *RR,* LVI (1965), 262-71.
Contends that Gérard's changes in the later version of *Léo Burckart* "indicate clearly a preoccupation with personal themes" more significant than any concern with political issues. Urges, moreover, that "*Léo Burckart* deserves a place in anthologies with *Ruy Blas, Fantasio,* and *Chatterton.*"

Duckworth, Colin. "Eugène Scribe and Gérard de Nerval: 'Celui qui tient la corde nous étrangle'." *MLR,* LX (1965), 32-40.
On Philibert Audebrand's long attack on Scribe, culminating in his accusation in the *Gazette de Paris* of Jan. 30, 1859 that one of Gérard's reasons for hanging himself was "le style de M. Scribe et son couronnement quotidien sur tous

nos théâtres." Scribe won his suit against Dollingen (the publisher of the *Gazette de Paris*) and Audebrand, and *Le Figaro* of March 17 announced its purchase of Dollingen's journal.

Françon, Marcel, ed. *L'Académie ou Les membres introuvables*. Reproduction photographique de l'édition originale (1826). Cambridge, Mass.: Schoenhof's, 1961. Pp. iii + 45.
Rev. by Alison Fairlie in *FS*, xix (1965), 74-75.

Freer, Alan J. "Diderot, *Angélique* et *Les confidences de Nicolas*." *SFr*, ix (1965), 283-90.

Geninasca, Jacques. *Une lecture de "El Desdichado"* (Archives Nervaliennes 5), *Archives des Lettres Modernes* (Paris: Lettres Modernes, 1965), 59$^{160-163}$ [1965 (2)], [1]-61.
A detailed attempt, with documented reference to earlier scholarship and criticism, to explain the intricacies of one of Gérard's most exquisitely-wrought sonnets. Following the lead of Léon Cellier, J. W. Kneller and A. S. Gerard, Geninasca questions the text "non seulement de l'extérieur . . . mais de l'intérieur" to find the poem's structure in the logical unity of its images and word meanings. In the "pivotal" line "Suis-je Amour ou Phébus? . . . Lusignan ou Biron," the author finds Amour-Lusignan set off against Phébus-Biron in a dark-light relationship of great variety. The attempt to demonstrate a "system" of relationships between quatrains and tercets in the theme of duality is of interest; but there is evident strain in the author's effort to establish a precise structure for his parallels and contrasts and their interweavings. A teasing logic seems at times to replace any emphatic experience of the poem, which is seen at the last as opening on its own beginning. (A.G.E.)

Glatigny, Michel. *"La main enchantée* de Nerval: Quelques sources du XVIIe siècle." *RSH*, No. 119 (July-Sept., 1965), pp. 329-52.
Cyrano de Bergerac's *Estats et empires du soleil* and *Le pédant joué*; the actor Des Laurier's "Prologue sur un habit" from *Les oeuvres de Bruscambille*; *L'histoire macaronique de Merlin Coccaie* (transl. from Folengo); and Furetière's *Roman comique*.

Jean, Raymond. *Nerval par lui-même*. (Coll. "Écrivains de Toujours," 68.) Paris: Éditions du Seuil, 1964. Pp. 190.
Rev. by John W. Kneller in *FR*, xxxviii, 805-06, by Georges Raillard in *Le Français dans le Monde*, No. 3 (Jan.-Feb., 1965), pp. 47-48; by C. Rosso in *SFr*, viii (1964), 574-75.

Laurent, M. "Explication française. Gérard de Nerval à Ermenonville (*Sylvie*, chap. IX)." *L'École*, March 31, 1962.

Montal, Robert. "A propos de l'*Octavie* de Gérard de Nerval et du voyage d'Italie de 1834." *Thyrse* (Bruxelles), lxvi (1964), 514-17.

Peyrouzet, Edouard. *Gérard de Nerval inconnu*. Paris: José Corti, 1965. Pp. 349.
Rev. by James M. Villas in *FR*, xxxix (1965), 459-60.

Pieltain, Paul. "Encore l'image du Soleil noir." *Cahiers d'Analyse Textuelle*, No. 6 (1964), pp. 102-05.

Prévost, L. "Le Vert Galant [dans l'*Angelique* de Gérard de Nerval]." *Bulletin Folklorique de France,* XXVII (1964), 816.

Richer, Jean, ed. *Aurélia ou Le rêve et la vie, Lettres d'amour.* Avec la collaboration de François Constans, Maria Luisa Belleli, John William Kneller, Jean Senelier. ("Paralogue," No. 1.) Paris: Minard (Lettres Modernes), 1965. Pp. xviii + 359.
A critical edition with contributions by a group of outstanding Nervaliens.

Rinsler, Norma. "Nerval, Méry et deux pièces perdues." *Revue d'Histoire du Théâtre,* XVI (1964), 47-49.
On *La nuit blanche* and *Paris à Pékin,* written in collaboration by Nerval and Joseph Méry. Explains Gérard's omission of the second title from the list of his works that he gave two days before his death to Paul Delacroix by suggesting that the two plays were ultimately one, in that *La nuit blanche* was "la dernière métamorphose" of *Paris à Pékin.* The title has an added significance when one recalls the last words in the last letter of Gérard to his aunt two days before his death: "Ne m'attends pas ce soir, car la nuit sera noire et blanche."

Schuhl, Pierre-Maxime. *Imaginer et réaliser.* Paris: PUF, 1963. Pp. xi + 152.
Rev. by Max Milner in *IL,* XVI (1964), 36.
Has a chapter on Nerval.

Strauss, Walter A. "Gérard de Nerval." *Emory University Quarterly,* XXI (1965), 15-31.
A remarkable demonstration of the idea that, in a sense, the life and writings and death of Nerval mark "the failure of realization of an Orphic synthesis in the first part of the nineteenth century." The essay is focussed especially upon *Aurélia,* "El Desdichado" and "Artémis." Detailed interpretations of the two sonnets are unusually persuasive. Nerval and his work are seen finally as symptomatic of the general situation of man and the arts in the contemporary world. (A.G.E.)

Strauss, Walter. "New Life, Tree of Life: The *Vita Nuova* and Nerval's *Aurélia.*" *Books Abroad (Special Issue): A Homage to Dante* (May 1965), pp. 144-50.
A beautifully written essay that seeks to "bridge the gap" separating Nerval from Dante. Certain similarities between the *Vita Nuova* and *Aurélia* are seen in the light of analogies between Christian and Orphic rebirth; but Nerval's attempt at vision is described as dependent upon hermetic and kabbalistic writings and is seen as poignant evidence of lost belief and eroded values. Further steps apparently lead from Gérard to Mallarmé and thence to Kafka and "the demon of silence." (A.G.E.)

Sullivan, Dennis G. "The Function of the Theater in the Work of Nerval." *MLN,* LXXX (1965), 610-17.
Claims to find the key to *Sylvie* in "the theatrical nature of the 'mariage des enfants' and the underlying idea of the theater of *Aurélia,*" and seeks to show that the idea of "the theater of the world" and the identification of the theater with religion are important in the broader structures of Gérard's work.

Vallery-Radot, Pierre. "Gérard de Nerval, ses années d'enfance racontées par lui-même. Leur influence sur son état mental." *La Presse Médicale,* LXXII (1964), 2735-37.

80

Villas, James M. "Gérard de Nerval and Racine's *La Thébaïde*." *RomN*, VI (Spring, 1965), 116-20.
Shows with careful documentation that Gérard may have taken the first part of the fifth verse of "El Desdichado" ("Dans la nuit du tombeau, Toi qui m'as consolé. . . .") from *La Thébaïde* of Racine (who used the same phrase in *Iphigénie* and in *Athalie*), and suggests the light this may throw on the interpretation of "Toi qui m'as consolé" as referring to Gérard's dead mother, even as the reference in *La Thébaïde* is to Antigone's mother, who had committed suicide. (A.G.E.)

Weber, Jean-Paul. *Domaines thématiques.* (Coll. "Bibliothèque des Idées.") Paris: Gallimard, 1963. Pp. 344.
Includes material on Nerval. (Incorrectly listed in *ELN*, III, Supp., p. 75 as *Problèmes thématiques.*)

See also Rinsler ("General 3. Criticism"); Barineau, Bassan, Easton, Pichois ("French 1. General"); Cattaui, Rinsler ("Hugo"); Whyte ("Gautier")

Reviews of works previously listed:
RICHER, Jean, *Nerval· Expérience et création* (see *ELN*, III, Supp., 74), rev. by Ross Chambers in *AUMLA*, No. 22 (1964), 318-20; by George Raillard in *Le Français dans le Monde*, No. 30 (Jan.-Feb. 1965), pp. 47-48, by Jean Roudaut in *MdF*, April 1965, pp. 740-43; RICHER, Jean, ed., *Oeuvres complémentaires de Gérard de Nerval. VIII. Variétés et fantaisies* (see *ELN*, III, Supp., 74), rev. by Ross Chambers in *AUMLA*, No. 23 (1965), pp. 151-53; by Alfred DuBruck in *RR*, LVI (1965), 307-309; SENELIER, Jean, *Gérard de Nerval: Essai de bibliographie* (see *PQ*, XL, 210), rev. by Raymond Jean in *RHL*, LXV (1965), 531-32; SENELIER, Jean, *Gerard de Nerval: Recherches et découvertes* (see *PQ*, XLIII, 479), rev. by Alfred DuBruck in *RR*, LVI (1965), 308-309; by M. L. in *RHL*, LXV (1965), 331; VIVIER, Marie de, *Gérard de Nerval* (see *ELN*, III, Supp., 75), brief rev. by G. Franceschetti in *SFr*, VIII (1964), 372.

NODIER

Oliver, A. Richard. *Charles Nodier: Pilot of Romanticism.* Syracuse University Press, 1965. Pp. ix + 276; illus. $5.95.
Rev. by R. C. Dale in *ECr*, V (1965), 249-50, by James B. Sanders in *FR*, XXXIX (1965), 172-73.
Sanders writes that Oliver "makes every effort to discern at all times the man behind a romantic legend," and that "Hugo's debt to Nodier is clearly indicated." Dale is annoyed by the style—sprinkled with French expressions, although the poetry is translated. Overall, however, the biography is solid, and Oliver has not fallen into the trap of making a secondary novelist into a man of genius. (C.C.)

Richer, Jean. "Un auto-portrait fantaisiste et douze lettres de Charles Nodier." *RSH*, n.s., No. 120 (1965), pp. 553-72.
Publishes "Définitions," "Composition," and twelve letters (dated between Dec. 5, 1812, and Nov. 28, 1836), assumed to be *inédits.* Calls for new work on Nodier: bibliography, edition of his *écrits critiques*, and at least selected correspondence.

Wilson, N. "Charles Nodier, Victor Hugo, and *Les feuilles d'automne*." *MLR*, LX (1965), 21-31.
Influence of Charles and Marie Nodier on Hugo.

See also Easton, Jensen ("French 1. General"); Guyon ("Stendhal").

RECAMIER
See Peignot ("Constant").

SAINTE-BEUVE
Adam, Antoine, ed. *Port-Royal.* Traduzione di Serena d'Arbela. Florence: G. C. Sansoni, 1964. 2 vols.
Rev. in *SFr,* IX (1965), 173.

Barlow, Norman. *Sainte-Beuve to Baudelaire. A Poetic Legacy.* Duke University Press, 1964. Pp. viii + 226.
Rev. by W. T. Bandy in *MLJ,* XLIX (1965), 340.
"This volume is directed to those students of Baudelaire who, like the author, have been intrigued by the enigma of a poetic affinity between the creator of the *Fleurs du Mal* and the Romantic lyricist in Sainte-Beuve."

Bonnerot, Jean, ed. *Correspondance générale.* Tome XIV (1865). Toulouse: Privat; Paris: Didier, 1964. Pp. 550.

Ciureanu, Petre. "Le prime traduzioni italiane degli scritti del Sainte-Beuve." Pp. 511-34 in *Studi in onore di Carlo Pellegrini.* (Biblioteca di Studi Francesi, 2.) Turin: Società Editrice Internazionale, 1963. Pp. xxxix + 846.

Fongaro, Antoine. "La *Correspondance générale* del Sainte-Beuve." *SFr,* VIII (1964), 86-102.

Galimberti, Cesare. "Sul Leopardi tradotto da Sainte-Beuve." Pp. 85-89 in *Miscellanea di studi offerta a Armando Balduino e Bianca Bianchi per le loro nozze. Vicenza, 30 giugno 1962.* Padova: Seminario di Filologia Moderna dell'Università, 1962.

Guillemin, Henri, ed. *Mes poisons,* précédé de "Sainte-Beuve secret," par Henri Guillemin. (Bibliothèque 10/18, No. 264). Paris: Union Générale d'Edition, 1965. Pp. 192. 4.40 Fr.

Molho, Raphaël. " 'Les Cahiers' de Sainte-Beuve, ou le journal secret d'un critique." *CAIEF,* No. 17 (1965), pp. 111-21.
On the journal kept by Sainte-Beuve from the age of 30 to his death. Molho examines Sainte-Beuve's use of the *Cahiers* and the portrait he draws of himself. The critic's awareness of himself as a constantly changing person is particularly striking in its psychological modernity. (C.C.)

Moreau, Pierre. *La critique selon Sainte-Beuve.* Paris: Société d'Edition d'Enseignement Supérieur, 1964. Pp. [155].
Rev. by Roger Fayolle in *RHL,* LXV (1965), 713-15.
Sainte-Beuve's intellectual background and milieu; his critical thought at various stages. Moreau does not deny Sainte-Beuve's strong dependence on biography in his criticism, but insists that there is an "art critique" whose "allure de causerie" is more complex than it appears. Concise and convincing, for the most part, although Fayolle regrets that "la synthèse finale ne réponde pas tout à fait à la rigueur d'une analyse magistralement conduite." (C.C.)

Muller, Armand. "Montaigne et Sainte-Beuve." *Bulletin de la Société des Amis de Montaigne,* 4ᵉ série, No. 1 (1965), pp. 36-47.

Parturier, Maurice. "Sainte-Beuve et Rémusat." *RHL,* LXV (1965), 689-93.

Peter, Marc. *Autour du 'Port-Royal' de Sainte-Beuve.* Geneva: Jullien, 1963.

Proust, Marcel. *Contre Sainte-Beuve.* Préface de Bernard de Fallois. (Coll. "Idées," 81.) Paris: Gallimard, 1965. Pp. 373. 4.95 Fr.
Rev. by Gonzague Truc in *Ecrits de Paris,* No. 243 (1965), pp. 77-78.
An inexpensive reedition of Proust's work with a new preface.

Steegmuller, Francis, and Norbert Guterman, eds. *Sainte-Beuve: Selected Essays.* (Anchor Books.) Garden City: Doubleday, 1964. Pp. 344. $1.45.
Rev. by Ruth Mulhauser in *MLJ,* XLIX (1965), 265-66.

Watson, Harold, O.S.B. "Sainte-Beuve's Molière: A Romantic Hamlet." *FR,* XXXVIII (1965), 606-18.
Sees Sainte-Beuve's greatest insight "in his reflections on Molière's continual progress in the *poésie* of the comic," but largely rejects his view on Molière in the light of twentieth-century criticism. Helpful analysis of Sainte-Beuve's method. (C.C.)

See also Wellek, *History* ("General 3. Criticism"); Seznec ("French 1. General"); Uffenbeck ("Allart").

Review of book previously listed:
LEHMANN, A. G., *Sainte-Beuve. A Portrait of the Critic, 1804-1842* (see *PQ,* XLII, 480), rev. by R. Pouilliart in *LR,* XIX (1965), 191-92.

SAND

Blount, Paul G. "George Sand and the Victorians." *American Quarterly,* XX (1964), 187-92.

Colin, Georges. "Bibliographie des premières publications des romans de George Sand (suite et fin)." *Le Livre et l'Estampe,* No. 33 (1963), pp. 65-87.
Earlier parts appeared in Nos. 29-30, 31-32.

Colin, Georges. "La première édition de *La Coupe* de George Sand." *Le Livre et l'Estampe,* No. 39-40 (1964), 273-75.

Déon, Michel. "Quand George Sand n'épate plus le bourgeois." *NL,* March 11, 1965, pp. 1, 11.
Observations inspired by the *Correspondance générale,* t. I.

Duchet, Claude, and Michel Launay. "George Sand et l'armée en 1848. Quatre lettres inédites." *RHL,* LXV (1965), 78-91.
Letters to Albert de Joinville.

Guillemin, Henri. *'Elle et lui' de George Sand.* Neuchâtel: Ides et Calendes; Paris: Bibliothèque des Arts, 1964.

Joly, René. "Les livres offerts par George Sand à Gustave Flaubert." *Le Livre et l'Estampe,* No. 38 (1964), pp. 3-20.

Lubin, Georges. "George Sand, est-elle vraiment allée en Bohême?" *Philologica Pragensia,* VII (1964), 336-45.
The conclusion: she did not.

Marix-Spire, Thérèse. "George Sand, *Le Marquis de Villemer.* Centenaire d'une fracassante première, 29 février 1864." *Europe,* XLII (Nov. 1964), 77-81.

Toesca, Maurice. *Le plus grand amour de George Sand.* Paris: Albin Michel, 1965. Pp. 282. 14.25 Fr.
Rev. by J. Cressanges in *NL,* Feb. 25, 1965, p. 4, by Raymond Las Vergnas in *Les Annales, Conferencia,* No. 173 (1965), p. 52.
First published under this title in 1931, then in revised form as *Une autre George Sand* in 1945. This third version takes into account new documents brought to light in the last 15 years. Toesca's principal aim is to portray G. Sand as a woman rather than as a legend: "Elle fut, avant tout, une femme acharnée au travail. Voilà pour l'extérieur. Du point de vue intime, elle fut une mère." Her greatest love was her son, Maurice. Well done. (C.C.)

See also Bowman, Fenger ("French 1. General"); Cellier ("Hugo").

Reviews of books previously listed:
LUBIN, Georges, ed., *Correspondance,* T. I (see *ELN,* III, Supp., 77), rev. by Ginette Guitard-Auviste in *Le Français dans le Monde,* No. 33 (1965), p. 47; SODERGARD, Osten, ed., *Les lettres de George Sand à Sainte-Beuve* (see *ELN,* III, Supp., 77), rev. by A. G. Lehmann in *FS,* XIX (1965), 301-03; VERNOIS, Paul, *Le roman rustique de George Sand à Ramuz. Ses tendances et son évolution (1860-1925)* (see *ELN,* III, Supp., 78), rev. by Alexander P. Hartman in *FR,* XXXVIII (1965), 707-08; by R. Mathé in *RHL,* LXV (1965), 134-36.

SENANCOUR

Raymond, Marcel, ed. *Sur les générations actuelles. Absurdités humaines.* Geneva: Droz; Paris: Minard, 1963. Pp. xxx + 415.
Rev. by Béatrice Le Gall in *RHL,* LXV (1965), 320-31, by Max Milner in *IL,* XVII (1965), 209.
Reproduction of the only edition of this youthful work of Senancour, published anonymously in 1793.

Raymond, Marcel. "Senancour: Deux expériences exemplaires." *Cahiers du Sud,* QII (1965), 239-50.
The first chapter of the author's forthcoming book on Senancour.

STAEL

Balayé, Simone. "Madame de Staël." *Europe,* XLII (Nov. 1964), 65-69.

Berger, Morroe, ed. *Madame de Staël on Politics, Literature, and National Character.* (Anchor Books.) Garden City: Doubleday, 1965. Pp. [xi] + 344. $1.25.

84

Rev. by Wayne Andrews in *Saturday Review*, Jan. 18, 1964, p. 80.
A new translation of selections, mainly from *Considérations sur les principaux événements de la Révolution française, De la littérature*, and *De l'Allemagne*. The introduction is substantial (83 pp.).

Götze, Alfred. "Frau von Staël und Herzog August von Sachsengotha. Mit unveröffentlichten Briefen." *Germanisch-Romanische Monatsschrift*, XV (1965), 26-40.
Includes nine letters from Mme de Staël, dated between Jan. 25, 1804, and April 20, 1805.

Götze, Alfred. "Sechs unveröffentlichte Briefe der Frau von Staël an Frau von Berg und Gräfin Voss." *Archiv für das Studium der neueren Sprachen und Literatur*, CCII (1965), 42-52.
Letters dated between April 19, 1804, and May 5, 1814.

Jasinski, Béatrice W., ed. *Correspondance générale*. Tome II, Deuxième partie: *Lettres diverses (1792-15 mai 1794)*. Paris: J. J. Pauvert, 1965. Pp. [317]. 43.50 Fr.

Launay, Jacques de. "Madame de Staël et la police autrichienne." *La Revue Générale Belge*, No. 10 (1964), pp. 81-88.

Viatte, Auguste. "Ce pauvre M. de Staël." *RUL* XIX (1965), 451-58.
Reevaluation of Mme de Staël's husband, based on her *Correspondence générale*, now being edited by Béatrice W. Jasinski (see *PQ*, XLII, 482; *ELN*, III, Supp., 79; and above).

Zwengel, Otto. *Madame de Staël und Deutschland*. Niederlanken (Taunus): Im Selbstverlag, 1963. Pp. 16.

See also Bochner, Kelly, Lombard, Pichois ("General"); Duhamel ("Chateaubriand"); Peignot ("Constant").

Review of book previously listed:
JASINSKI, Béatrice W., ed., *Correspondance générale*, T. I, Première partie (see *PQ*, XLII, 482), rev. by Albert Delorme in *Revue de Synthèse*, IIIᵉ série, No. 33-34 (1964), pp. 200-201.

STENDHAL

Abravanel, Ernest, ed. *Première journée du Stendhal Club*. (Collection Stendhalienne, No. 7.) Lausanne: Editions du Grand-Chêne, 1965. Pp. 160.
Rev. by C. Cordié in *SFr*, IX (1965), 374; by Gilbert Nigay in *SC*, VIII (1965), 64-66.
Contents: Ernest Abravanel, "Le thème du poison dans l'oeuvre de Stendhal"; Armand Caraccio, "Stendhal et la guerre"; Richard N. Coe, "Quelques réflexions sur Stendhal paysagiste"; Massimo Colesanti, "Sur un livre ayant appartenu à Stendhal: 'Pensées et souvenirs' de Michele Palmieri di Miccichè"; Georges Dethan, "Stendhal et Paris"; Pierre Moreau, "Puissance de volonté et volonté de puissance"; Yves du Parc, "Echos diplomatiques de la mort de Stendhal"; Bruno Pincherle, "Le R. P. Maurice ou la lunette de l'abbé Blanés"; Jean Théodoridès, "Stendhal et les savants de son temps."

Abravanel, E[rnest]. "Stendhal à Marseille." *SC*, VIII (1965), 1-8.
Briefly summarizes Stendhal's various experiences in Marseille (1805-1806,

1829, 1833, 1838): love affairs, readings, impressions of the city and its inhabitants. Abravanel considers the first of Stendhal's stays in Marseille to have influenced him much more than the others.

Barbaranelli, Fernando. "Le théâtre de Civitavecchia au temps de Stendhal." *SC*, VII (1965), 201-07.
Discursive treatment of Stendhal's love for the theater and, more directly, of the Teatro Minozzi, whose productions he often attended. Emphasis is on the building itself (torn down soon after Stendhal's death).

Blackmur, R. P. "The Charterhouse of Parma." *Kenyon Review*, XXVI (1964), 211-31.
A dense and demanding study of the novel in terms of "the poetics of hysteria," "the psychology of caprice."

Caraccio, Armand. *Stendhal*. Translated by Dolores Bagley. New York University Press, 1965. Pp. 221. $6.00.
A translation of Caraccio's *Stendhal: l'homme et l'oeuvre* (Paris: Boivin, 1951).

Carella, Ada. "Un guide de Stendhal en Italie: Charles Duclos." *RDM*, June 15, 1964, pp. 569-79.
Almost entirely about Duclos (1704-1772) and his trip to Italy in 1766-67.

Cordié, Carlo. "Un amico di Stendhal." *Il Mondo*, Aug. 31, 1965, pp. 9-10.
On Michele Palmieri di Miccichè. Cordié reviews and corrects previous scholarship on his relationship with Stendhal.

Del Litto, V[ictor]. "Bibliographie stendhalienne. Année 1963." *SC*, VII (1965), 165-84.
Includes some items for 1961 and 1962, in addition to the basic list of 1963 items.

Del Litto, V[ictor]. "Bibliographie stendhalienne. Année 1964." *SC*, VII (1965), 95-108.
A few items for 1963, 138 items for 1964.

Del Litto, V[ictor]. "Nouveaux inédits sur les 'Mémoires d'un Touriste': une lettre de Stendhal et des notes de Romain Colomb." *SC*, VII (1965), 185-92.
A manuscript recently acquired by the Bibliothèque de Grenoble contains comments and *corrigenda* by Colomb on the *Mémoires* and a letter from Stendhal to Colomb (Aug. 20, 1838).

Del Litto, V[ictor]. "Pourquoi Stendhal n'a pas été 'épicier' à Marseille (D'après des documents inédits)." *SC*, VII (1965), 257-70.
Newly discovered documents throw light on the Marseille episode (1805-1806) and on Stendhal's business dealings with Fortuné Mante and Charles Meunier.

Del Litto, Victor. *La vie de Stendhal*. (Vies et Visages.) Paris: Editions Albin Michel, 1965. Pp. 351. 27 Fr.
This is a biography for the general reader and not for the Stendhal specialists. But the author's eminent position among the latter guarantees that the book is based on irreproachable scholarship. As the title suggests, emphasis is on the

86

life of Stendhal, but the major literary works are discussed and evaluated, normally in rather summary fashion. The book is slightly marred by misprints (e.g., "Stendahl," p. 240) and its form skewed somewhat by "l'insertion entre les chapitres d'anecdotes, citations révélatrices, indications curieuses, etc.," but apparently this slight deformation was imposed on the author by the series editor, who states that this practice "constitue l'une des particularités des livres que nous réalisons." Far outweighing this troublesome feature is the abundant illustration. (J.S.P.)

Dembrowski, M. "Un nouveau 'Rouge et Noir'." *SC,* VII (1965), 133-36.
Echoes of Stendhal's life and work in the writings of two modern Russian authors, Tarsis and Vinogradov.

Dethan, Georges. "Feder ou un Marseillais à Paris." *SC,* VII (1965), 287-94.
A pleasant rehabilitation of this neglected *nouvelle,* left unfinished. Dethan finds in it the "âme stendhalienne."

Donnelly, Jerome. "Stendhal and Thackeray: The Source of *Henry Esmond." RLC,* XXXIX (1965), 372-81.
According to Donnelly, *Le rouge et le noir* is a much more likely source than Balzac's *Le lys dans la vallée,* sometimes suggested. All the evidence offered in support of the author's thesis is internal; Thackeray never mentioned Stendhal.

Doyon, André. "La véritable histoire de 'Madame Tarin'." *SC,* VIII (1965), 193-200.
Reconstructs from legal documents the true story, rather banal and undramatic, of the "modern Brinvilliers" who attracted Stendhal's attention in 1837, as shown by his letter to General Chaudru de Raynal, published by Del Litto in *SC,* VII (1964), 1-13 (see *ELN,* III, Supp., 81).

Félix-Faure, Jacques. "Stendhal, Félix Faure et Louis Crozet ou les tribulations d'Alceste." *SC,* VIII (1965), 44-61.
A history of the three-sided friendship.

Froment-Meurice, Henri. "Stendhal ou une certaine idée des hommes." *Preuves,* No. 176 (Oct. 1965), pp. 42-49.
Develops a view of Stendhal close to Auerbach's (see *Mimesis,* "In the Hôtel de la Mole"): a Stendhal poised uneasily between the Ancien Régime and bourgeois democracy, filled with anxiety by the upheavals of his age, disgusted by the actualities of politics and economics, "un romantique que désole la médiocrité de la société politique, qui ne se console pas de vivre dans des régimes aussi peu aptes à susciter les grand caractères et les belles énergies." But the author suggests that in his last works Stendhal was moving towards anarchistic or anti-social extremism.

Gieling, Théo. "Stendhal lecteur de Saint-Simon, III." *SC,* VII (1965), 100-12.
Conclusion of Gieling's excellent study (see *ELN,* III, Supp., 82). Here the author compares the notes Stendhal made in two different editions of Saint-Simon at two very different periods of his life, and states his general conclusions concerning Stendhal's life-long taste for the memorialist: whereas he disliked Saint-Simon the man, he was greatly drawn to Saint-Simon the writer, admiring his vivid *tableaux de moeurs,* his sense of the comic, his accounts of intrigue and change of fortune in high places, and most especially his style, vigorous, fresh, and bold like his own. (J.S.P.)

Gutwirth, Marcel. "*Le rouge et le noir* as Comedy." *RR*, LVI (1965), 188-94.

An incisive and witty analysis of levels of humor in the novel: comedy of manners, comedy of character, and "what we may call the comedy of happiness." The last-named category involves a comparison with Dante's comedy. This seems a bit forced. Stendhal's comedy may be more than human, but is it divine? (J.S.P.)

Guyon, Bernard. "Balzac et Stendhal romanciers de l'évasion." *SC*, VIII (1965), 25-31.

Rather cautiously suggests the influence of Balzac's story of the escape of the Chevalier de Beauvoir (first published in *Contes bruns*, later incorporated into *La muse du départment*) on a famous episode in *La Chartreuse de Parme*. Guyon thinks Nodier may have been the original source of the anecdote.

Hamon, Paul. "Les Hélie, camarades de Stendhal à l'Ecole centrale de l'Isère." *SC*, VII (1965), 125-32.

Biographical sketches of Ennemond Hélie (1774-1844) and Félix Hélie (1782-1864). Stendhal was on much better terms with the former than with the latter, with whom he had no contact after leaving Grenoble in 1799.

Hastier, Louis. "La dernière amie de Stendhal." *RDM*, Feb. 1, 1965, pp. 406-18.

Essentially a biography of Mme Jules Gaulthier (whose lost novel *Le lieutenant* provided Stendhal with a spring-board to *Lucien Leuwen*), Hastier's article corrects and amplifies information on her given by Mélia, Bouvier, and Martineau; traces the course of Stendhal's friendship with her (using quotations from several letters they exchanged); and conjectures that Stendhal originally gave her the idea for *Le lieutenant*. See comment by V. D. L. in *SC*, VII, 252-53.

Imbert, Henri-François. " 'Armance' et 'Marguerite Aimond'." *SC*, VIII (1965), 9-16.

Imbert does not try to prove the influence of Mme de Cubière's novel (1822) on Stendhal's, but he points out several important parallels: a similar treatment of political background and the same *ton de décence*.

Jansse, Lucien. "Stendhal et l'économie politique." *SC*, VII (1965), 295-308.

Stendhal appears to have been much more interested and much better versed in economics than one would expect.

Kotchetkova, Tatiana. "Nouveaux documents stendhaliens découverts en U.R.S.S." *SC*, VII (1965), 93-99.

Several documents shedding light on Stendhal's activity in the Napoleonic bureaucracy. Two are here reproduced in facsimile.

Léautaud, Paul. "Stendhal Club." Pp. 40-65 in Léautaud, Paul, *Passetemps II*. Paris: Mercure de France, 1964. Pp. 224. 12 Fr.

An article which originally appeared in *L'Ermitage*, March 15, 1903. See rev. by V. D. L. in *SC*, VII (1965), 154-55.

Lunel, Armand. "Stendhal et la Provence." *SC*, VII (1965), 271-82.

To Stendhal, Provence was a sort of substitute Italy, thanks to its landscapes, its architecture, its antiquities, and especially the *naturel* of its people. This feeling for Provence was mostly focused on Avignon, where his Gagnon ancestors had settled after fleeing from Italy.

Maquet, Albert. "Arrigo Beyle Milanese en face de l'Italie dialectale." *CLS,* II (1965), 59-70.
See comment by V. D. L. in *SC,* VIII (1965), 67.

Marshall, J. F. "Stendhal, Byron et les 'Mémoires d'une contemporaine'." *SC,* VII (1965), 247-49.
Ida de Saint-Elme's report of a conversation in which Byron objected to Stendhal's charge that he was an aristocrat.

Métral, Maurice. "Un sous-lieutenant de 18 ans à l'assaut du Saint-Bernard: Stendhal." *30 Jours* (Lausanne), May 5, 1965.
See Ernest Abravanel's scathing review in *SC,* VII (1965), 329-30.

Michel, François. *Fichier stendhalien.* Présenté par Jean Fabre, V. Del Litto et James F. Marshall. Boston: G. K. Hall and Co., 1964. 3 vols.
Rev. by C. Cordié in *SFr,* IX (1965), 374.

Mohrt, Michel. "Stendhal et la série noire." *RdP,* July, 1964, pp. 108-12.
In his *Chroniques italiennes,* Stendhal transformed his police-court material into literature embodying the major themes which run through his novels: *incivisme,* admiration for strong characters who wage war on society. Mohrt suggests a parallel with Faulkner's *Sanctuary,* "né du pastiche du *thriller."*

Ortiz Armengol, Pedro. "A propos d'un centenaire: Stendhal et Unamuno." *SC,* VII (1965), 234-38.
Fundamentally, there was little contact or affinity between these two authors. "Et pourtant Stendhal est présent chez l'écrivain espagnol et il est pour lui une référence importante." A sonnet Unamuno wrote shortly before his death was inspired by a quotation from *Le rouge et le noir.*

Pellegrini, Carlo. "Interpretazione stendhaliana di Firenze in 'Rome, Naples et Florence'." Pp. 363-73 in *Connaissance de l'étranger: mélanges offerts à la mémoire de Jean-Marie Carré.* Paris: Didier, 1965. Pp. xx + 528.
See comment by V. D. L. in *SC,* VII (1965), 253.

Pieyre de Mandiargues, André. "L'amour-passion." *RdP,* Jan. 1965, pp. 41-48.
"The originality of Stendhal's work . . . lies in his exaltation, in a manner similar to that of the Surrealists (and Mandiargues has been a member of the group) of the beauty of passionate love, and also in his sympathetic view of woman" (Henry A. Grubbs, *FR,* XXXIX [1965], 467).

Pirotta, Giuliano, ed. *Vita di Henry Brulard: Ricordi d'egotismo.* Prefazione di Giovanni Macchia. Milan: Adelphi, 1964. Pp. xxv + 643.
Rev. by C. Cordié in *SFr,* IX (1965), 371-73.
In his review, Cordié has high praise for Macchia's preface: "si pone tra i contributi migliori della critica moderna su Stendhal."

Riehn, Christa. "Stendhal en Allemagne: bibliographie (1945-1964)." *SC,* VIII (1965), 79-93.
163 items.

Rothkopf, Carol Z. *The Red and the Black: Chapter Notes and Criticism.* (A Study Master Publication.) New York: American R. D. M. Corporation, 1965. Pp. 80. $1.00.

Clearly, a "cram book," the core of which is a 48-page plot summary. Critical comments are unexceptionable but necessarily brief. (J.S.P.)

Saunders, F. W. "Stendhal et l'enseignement mutuel." *SC,* VII (1965), 113-24.

Passes in review Stendhal's numerous and always favorable allusions to this pedagogical system, and discusses the political and religious implications of the quarrel it aroused and the sources of Stendhal's knowledge of it. No literary parallels are noted.

Simone, Franco. "Stendhal et les Piémontais." *La Stampa,* June 24, 1964.

See brief comment (by V. Del Litto?) in *SC,* VII, 156.

Stein, Meïr. "Promenade stendhalienne au Musée Thorvaldsen à Copenhague." *SC,* VII (1965), 209-33.

Stein first reviews Stendhal's observations on the neo-classic Danish sculptor (his antipathy seems to have been due largely to his admiration for Canova, Thorwaldsen's great rival), then strolls, as it were, through the museum pointing out many of the portrait busts found there and showing their relation to Stendhal's biography. He mentions, too, various documents in the museum's archives of interest to Stendhalians. "Le monde italien de Stendhal est en grande partie identique à celui de Thorvaldsen."

Strickland, Geoffrey. "Stendhal, Byron et John Cam Hobhouse." *SC,* VII (1965), 309-28.

Strickland makes a minute comparison between Hobhouse's and Stendhal's accounts of the latter's encounters with Byron, and comes to the conclusion that Stendhal's version contains many "inexactitudes" and "mensonges probables" (he accepts as genuine, however, the famous letter Stendhal says he received from Byron). Still, Strickland grants Stendhal an extraordinary understanding of Byron's personality and work, notes a Beylist element in Byron, and briefly touches on the influence of Byron on Stendhal.

Théodoridès, Jean. "Victor Jacquemont est-il la clef d'Octave Malivert?" *Lettres Françaises,* Jan. 7-13, 1965.

Cautiously proposes Jacquemont, instead of Custine, as model for the hero of *Armance.* See comment by V. D. L. in *SC,* VII (1965), 253.

Turcaret. "Stendhal e Tocqueville." *Il Mondo,* April 7, 1964, p. 9.

Stendhal was a biased reader of *De la démocratie en Amérique,* seeking confirmation of his anti-democratic prejudices. The anti-American remarks in *Lucien Leuwen* were especially intended to rebut a series of pro-American articles published in Carrel's *Le National* in 1831-1833; furthermore, they indicate Stendhal had read only Part I of Tocqueville's study.

Vaillant, P[ierre]. "Stendhal à la Bibliothèque de Grenoble (1939-1962)." *SC,* VIII (1965), 17-24.

Brief retrospective of the six Stendhal expositions held in this library from 1920 to 1962, followed by a detailed discussion of some of the outstanding items in the 1962 exposition.

Vidal, Gaston. "Une pré-originale demeurée inconnue d'un chapitre de 'La Chartreuse de Parme'." *SC,* VIII (1965), 39-43.

The famous narrative of the battle of Waterloo was originally published in a fashion magazine, *Paris-Élégant*, March 20, 1839, preceded by a brief critical comment which forms the earliest criticism of the novel. There are a few interesting variants from the text as published in volume form.

Weinstein, Leo. "Stendhal's Count Mosca as a Statesman." *PMLA,* LXXX (1965), 210-16.

Carefully examines Mosca's skill in political intrigue in order to settle the difference of critical opinion between Zola and those (including Balzac) who see in Mosca a consummate statesman of the Machiavellian type. Weinstein rather conclusively proves Zola's point, and then attempts to explain why the Count, who is clearly a sympathetic character *and* a bungler in politics, remains a great literary creation. "Mosca is profoundly human: torn between conflicting desires, ambivalent, and credibly complex." (J.S.P.)

Wilson, Bernard E. "An Unpublished Letter of Stendhal." *Newberry Library Bulletin,* VI (1965), 187-95.

A letter of Feb. 9, 1829, to Édouard Mounier (see his reply in Le Divan edition, I, 182-83); deals with Stendhal's effort to obtain a position on the Cour des comptes. There are references to Félix Faure, Béranger, Daru, Pastoret, and Barbé-Marbois.

See also Cândido, Bochner, Fenger, Girard ("French 1. General"); Fischer, Regard ("Balzac"); Maquet ("General 3. Criticism").

Reviews of books previously listed:

BERGES, Consuelo, *Stendhal. Su vida, su mundo, su obra* (see *PQ*, XLIII, 481) —consult reviews listed in *SC,* VII (1965), 176, 179; BROMBERT, Victor, ed., *Stendhal: A Collection of Critical Essays* (see *PQ*, XLII, 482-83), rev. by Henri-François Imbert in *RLC,* XXXIX (1965), 318-20; DECHAMPS, Jules, *Amitiés stendhaliennes en Belgique* (see *ELN,* III, Supp., 81), rev. by A. A. in *Marginales* (Brussels), June, 1964; DÉDEYAN, Charles, *L'Italie dans l'oeuvre romanesque de Stendhal* (see *ELN,* III, Supp., 81), rev. by C. Cordié in *SFr,* IX (1965), 169-70; DURAND, Gilbert, *Le décor mythique de la Chartreuse de Parme: contribution à l'esthétique du romanesque* (see *PQ*, XLII, 484), rev. by René Girard in *Critique* (Paris), XXI (1965), 899-924; LEVIN, Harry, *The Gates of Horn. A Study of Five French Realists* (see *PQ*, XLIII, 484), rev. by R. M. Albérès in *TR,* Nov. 1963, pp. 113-17, by P. Mansell Jones in *FS,* XIX (1965), 67-68, by E. A. E. Naughton in *MP,* LXII (1965), 174-78; MAQUET, Albert, *Deux amis italiens de Stendhal: Giovanni Plana et Carlo Guasco* (see *PQ*, XLIII, 484), rev. by Lionello Sozzi in *SFr,* VIII (1965), 320-22; MARSHALL, James Fred, ed., *Letters to Achille Chaper: Intimate Sketches of Life among Stendhal's Coterie* (see *PQ*, XL, 219), rev. by Albert J. George in *RR,* LIV (1965), 66-67; MARTINEAU, Henri, ed., *Correspondance:* Tome I, 1800-1821 (see *PQ*, XLIII, 484)—consult reviews listed in *SC,* VII, 165-66; TROMPEO, P. P., *Incontri di Stendhal* (see *ELN,* III, Supp., 84), rev. by Raffaele de Cesare in *SC,* VII (1965), 152-53, by C. Cordié in *Il Mondo,* June 30, 1964.

SUE

Nicolas, Jean. "Eugène Sue, robespierriste." *Annales Historiques de la Révolution Française,* XXXVII (Jan.-March, 1965), 79-82.

Extracts from unpublished manuscript of 1857 show Sue as attempting to debunk the conservative-moderate version of the revolution of 9 thermidor. As Sue saw it, Robespierre was trying to end the Terror, but the real Terrorists got to him first.

VIGNY

Angrand, Pierre. "Vigny, indicateur bénévole et malchanceux." *Europe,* XLIII (Sept. 1965), 187-202.
Concludes that Vigny did his best to denounce several alleged conspirators during the Second Empire, because he believed the government was doing its business well enough to deserve his support.

Bowman, Frank Paul. "The Poetic Practices of Vigny's *Poèmes philosophiques.*" *MLR,* LX (1965), 359-68.

Castex, Pierre-Georges. "Camus et Vigny." *IL,* XVII (1965), 145-51.
Rejecting any substantial direct influence of Vigny on Camus, Castex presents parallels of thought and imagery in their writing (life as a prison, for example). Concludes with a brief summary of important points of divergence. A far more solid and convincing confrontation than that proposed by Maurice Weiler in *RdP,* Aug. 1964 (see *ELN,* III, Supp., 87). (C.C.)

Dale, R. C. "*Chatterton* is the Essential Romantic Drama." *ECr,* V (1965), 131-37.
An incisive analysis of *Chatterton* as the first anti-melodrama. Discusses Hugo's *Hernani* and Dumas *père's Antony* as prior victories in the Romantics' campaign against bourgeois values. (C.C.)

Doolittle, James. "Lines 65-66 of Vigny's *Moïse*: Another Suggestion." *MLN,* LXXX (1965), 624-28.

Freiherr von Taube, Otto. "Der elfenbeinerne Turm. Gedanken zu Alfred de Vigny." *NS,* XIV (1965), 110-30.
Vigny's relation to his times.

Friedman, Martin B. "Vigny's Use of Chatterton in *Stello.*" *RLC,* XXXVIII (1964), 262-63.

Haig, Stirling. "Notes on Vigny's Composition." *MLR,* LX (1965), 369-73.
Successive states of two poems: "La colère de Samson" and "La maison du berger."

Kushner, Eva. "Histoire et théâtre chez Vigny." *ECr,* V (1965), 147-61.
Early tragedies and sketches for historical plays show the importance Vigny attached to history. Seeking the reasons for which Vigny turned away from this rich source of drama, the author finds a consciousness of a new task for writers and a complex sense of history as a prelude to the future. Informed and provocative. (C.C.)

Kushner, Eva. "Vigny's Vision of History." *BNYPL,* LXIX (1965), 609-17.
Vigny "voluntarily maintains at all times an attitude of lucid, constructive, stoical despair," rejecting the views of those who would justify the existence of evil in history, e.g. de Maistre, Herder, Ballanche.

Massey, Irving. "Variant Readings from the Manuscript of *Stello,* by Alfred de Vigny." *BNYPL,* LXIX (1965), 164-81, 259-72, 330-40.
An appendix gives Vigny's MS notes in a copy of his *Poëmes.*

Minogue, Valerie. "The Tableau in 'La colère de Samson'." *MLR*, LX (1965), 374-78.

V. Minogue's conclusion that Vigny lacks "control of the deep-seated impulses of his imagination" is based on the misguided observation that "La colère de Samson" fails to offer a realistic *picture* of Samson and Delilah. She sees the images working "outwards and away from the poem," rather than evoking, more likely, an atmosphere through strictly verbal rather than pictorial means. (C.C.)

Saba, Guido. "*Mademoiselle Irnois* di Gobineau e il *Discours de réception* di Vigny: un incontro ideologico letterario." Pp. 533-44 in *Studi di letteratura, storia a filosofia in onore di Bruno Revel*. Florence: Leo S. Olschki, 1965.

Saulnier, Verdun-L. "La renaissance de la Renaissance: autour d'un Mathurin Régnier lu par Alfred de Vigny." *Bibliothèque d'Humanisme et de Renaissance*, XXV (1963), 567-76.

Sungolowsky, Joseph. "Les Juifs et le judaïsme dans l'oeuvre d'Alfred de Vigny." *PMLA*, LXXX (1965), 231-36.

A careful examination of Vigny's varying treatment of Jewish characters in *Poèmes antiques et modernes, La Maréchale d'Ancre, Deuxième consultation du docteur Noir, et al.* In spite of a reputation for anti-Semitism, Vigny's thought shows affinities with Judaic tradition in the rejection of original sin and the acceptance of the Biblical notion of the "Dieu jaloux." Sungolowsky shows, on a basis of literary sensitiveness and familiarity with Jewish tradition, that there is likely an "évolution dans l'attitude de Vigny envers les Israélites." (C.C.)

Teppe, Julien. *Alfred de Vigny et ses amantes*. Paris: Editions de Belleville, 1964.

Viallaneix, Paul. *Vigny par lui-même*. (Ecrivains de Toujours, 69.) Paris: Editions du Seuil, 1964. Pp. [190].

Rev. by Georges Dupeyron in *Europe*, XLIII (July 1965), 331-32, by André Wurmser in *Les Lettres Françaises*, Dec. 3-9, 1964.

See also Bochner, Easton, Girard, Petitbon, Pichois ("French 1. General").

Reviews of books previously listed:

Alfred de Vigny, 1797-1863 (see *ELN*, III, Supp., 84), rev. by F[rançois] Germain in *RHL*, LXV (1965), 328; CASTEX, Pierre-Georges, ed., *Les destinées* (see *ELN*, III, Supp., 85), rev. by F[rançois] Germain in *IL*, XVII (1965), 33-34; GERMAIN, François, *L'imagination d'Alfred de Vigny* (see *PQ*, XLII, 486), rev. by Max Milner in *RHL*, LXV (1965), 131-33, by Joseph Sungolowsky in *RR*, LVI (1965), 147-49; PETRONI, Liano, ed., *Chatterton* (see *ELN*, III, Supp., 87), rev. by Léon Zimmerman in *SFr*, IX (1965), 114-16.

GERMAN

(Compilers and reviewers: Ingeborg Carlson, Arizona State Univ.; Alan Cottrell, Univ. of Washington; Ulrich Gaier, Univ. of California, Davis; Philip Glander, Univ. of California, Berkeley; E. Bernell McIntire, Arizona State Univ.; Kenneth Negus, Rutgers Univ.; Günther Nerjes, Univ. of California, Davis; Laurence Radner, Purdue Univ.).

1. BIBLIOGRAPHY

Frey, John R. "Anglo-German Literary Bibliography for 1964." *JEGP*, LXIV (1965), 523-26.

Germanistik: Internationales Referatenorgan mit bibliographischen Hinweisen. VI. Jg. Tübingen: Niemeyer, 1965.
See especially in each of the four issues: "XVIII. Vergleichende Literaturgeschichte," "XXIX. Goethezeit (1770-1830)," and "XXX. Von der Nachromantik bis zum Realismus (1830-1890)." There are critical reviews of most books; articles and dissertations are listed by their authors. Coverage includes Europe, South Africa, North and South America, and Japan.

Hansel, Johannes. *Bücherkunde für Germanisten: Studienausgabe.* 3. erweiterte Aufl. Berlin: Erich Schmidt, 1965.

Henning, Hans, and Siegfried Seifert, eds. "Internationale Bibliographie zur Deutschen Klassik 1750-1850." *WB*, Folge 9 (1964), pp. 415-80 and 910-76.

Reichert, Walter A., and Otto Springer, eds. "Germanic Languages and Literatures." *PMLA*, LXXX (1965). "18th and early 19th Centuries," 278-85 and "19th and early 20th Centuries," 285-92.

2. GENERAL

Albertsen, Leif Ludwig. "Baggesen zwischen Vorromantik und Biedermeier. Ein Beitrag zum Verständnis der zwischen 1760 und 1765 geborenen deutschen [und dänischen] Dichter." *ZDP*, LXXXIV (1965), 563-80.
The sentimentality of the *Hainbund* "hibernates" in Jean Paul and Kotzebue, breaks out again during Biedermeier. Poets such as Matthisson, Salis-Seewis, Friederike Brun, Usteri, born between Schiller and W. v. Humboldt, remain in a Pre-Romantic stage or find their own way, but do not become actual Romantics. Example: J. I. Baggesen, born in 1764. It is questionable whether this approach by dates of birth yields much. (I.C.)

Baeumer, Max L. "Die romantische Epiphanie des Dionysos." *Monatshefte*, LVII (1965), 25-36.
Deals with varying concepts of Dionysos from Heinse to Nietzsche. The interpretation of the function of this figure for Hölderlin is debatable, and quotations from his works are incorrect. Christ's being "Herakles' Bruder" (p. 231) is in *Der Einzige*, not *Brot und Wein*; "Es scheiden und kehren . . ." (p. 235)

is not from "Diotimas Abschiedsbrief," but from Hyperion's last letter. (I. C. and U. G.)

Barnard, Frederick M. *Zwischen Aufklärung und politischer Romantik. Eine Studie über Herders soziologisch-politisches Denken.* (Philologische Studien und Quellen, 17.) Berlin: Erich Schmidt, 1964. Pp. 230. DM 23.—
Rev. by Felix M. Wassermann in *JEGP*, LXIV (1965), 554-55.
Herder is presented as catalyst of the methods and ideas of the Enlightenment; as founder of political Romanticism and—in distorted re-interpretation —of Prussian and nationalistic fanaticism. (I.C.)

Barvad, F. M. *Herder's Social and Political Thought.* Oxford: Clarendon Press, 1965. 30 s.
Rev. in *TLS*, Oct. 28, 1965, p. 961.

Bausch, Walter. *Theorien des epischen Erzählens in der deutschen Frühromantik.* (Bonner Arbeiten zur deutschen Literatur, 8.) Bonn: Bouvier, 1964. Pp. 179. DM 19.80.
Rev. by K. K. Polheim in *Germanistik*, VI (1965), 452-53.
Emerging from a 1963 dissertation, this work is divided into two parts, "Die Novelle" and "Der Roman." Bausch stresses the novel. The focus of the title on earlier Romanticism is not always maintained. The poets' theoretical statements are played against each other without regard to chronology. The book makes especially interesting reading for F. Schlegel scholars. The discussion of his philosophical and theological works makes use of notebooks of 1797-1801 only recently available but does not draw on unprinted sources. (I.C.)

Börsch-Supan, Eva. "Das Motiv des Gartenraums in Dichtungen des 19. und frühen 20. Jahrhunderts." *DVLG*, XXXIX (1965), 87-124.
This Platonic motif, presented as an "Ur-Sehnsucht" of all mankind, is explored from Goethe's "Am farbigen Abglanz" and the Helena grotto up to Musil and Hesse. The article includes Hölderlin, Novalis, Arnim, Tieck, Eichendorff, Brentano, and E. T. A. Hoffmann. Modern trends are seen in the fairy-tale and the dream. (I.C.)

Burger, Heinz Otto. "Statt eines Vorworts: Glasperlen-Etude über ein schwäbisches Thema." Pp. 9-14 in Burger, Heinz Otto. *'Dasein heisst eine Rolle spielen': Studien zur deutschen Literaturgeschichte.* (Literatur als Kunst) München: Hanser, 1963 [1964].
Inasmuch as Hesse has never described the "real" process of a "Glasperlenspiel," Burger improvises one as an introductory meditation to his fine series of studies. The birthdates of Hölderlin, Uhland, and Mörike (1770-1787-1804), besides being equidistant from each other, mark the pivotal points for German literary development from "Sturm und Drang" through the end of "Klassik." Their death dates (1843-1862-1875) are shown to correspond to the development of poetic realism in Germany. (U.G.)

Eichner, Hans. "The Genesis of German Romanticism." *QQ*, LXXII (1965), 213-31.
Of special interest for F. Schlegel.

Emrich, Wilhelm. *Der Universalismus der deutschen Romantik.* (Abhandlungen der Wissenschaft und der Literatur, Klasse der Literatur 1964, I.) Wiesbaden: Steiner, 1964. Pp. 22.

Fambach, Oscar. "Zur Jenaischen Allgemeinen Literaturzeitung." *DVLG,* xxxviii (1964), 577-91.
Fr. Nicolai's alteration of the signatures of the reviewers in the "Literatur-zeitung" caused a continuous feud. From Gustav Parthey (1842) to Karl Bulling scholars have been trying to detect the identity of the critics. With the same thoroughness as in his comprehensive critical work (see *ELN,* III, Supp., 89-90) Fambach attempts to fill the gaps. (I.C.)

Fassmann, Kurt, ed. *Briefe der Weltliteratur. Deutsche Romantiker.* (Kindler Taschenbuch 3020.) München: Kindler, 1965. Pp. 207. DM 2,50.
Rev. by W. H. Bähr in *Germanistik,* vi (1965), 617-18.
Part of a new series in 24 volumes, from ancient to modern times. There is a short, critical introduction to various aspects of the Romantic period and movement. Contains correspondence of Eichendorff, Brentano and Arnim with Bettina, and the Grimms. Letters are chosen somewhat arbitrarily from No-valis, the Schlegels, Wackenroder, Tieck, and Hoffmann. Treats German Romanticism as part of the European movement. (I.C.)

Hardy, Swana L. *Goethe, Calderon und die romantische Theorie des Dramas.* Heidelberger Forschungen. Heidelberg: Winter, 1964. DM 28.—

Jehle, Mimi. *Das deutsche Kunstmärchen von der Romantik zum Na-turalismus.* (Illinois Studies in Language and Literature.) Illinois University Press, 1964. $2.50.

Jennings, Lee Byron. *The Ludicrous Demon. Aspects of the Grotesque in German Post-Romantic Prose.* (University of California Publica-tions in Modern Philology, Vol. LXXI.) University of California Press, 1963. Pp. 214, $4.50.
Rev. by Jost Hermand in *Monatshefte,* LVII (1965), 403-05, by Roy C. Cowen in *GQ,* xl (1965), 366-67, and by U. Weisstein in *JEGP,* LxIV (1965), 121-23.
The grotesque in German Post-Romantic prose includes the satirical, demonic, strange, bizarre, and droll. Based on a 1955 dissertation (hence preceding Kayser's book of 1957), this study is less vague than Kayser's yet employs some loose definitions. It should be of interest to Heine, Immermann, Ludwig, and Stifter scholars. (I.C.)

Kindermann, H. *Theatergeschichte Europas.* Vol. VI: *Romantik.* Salz-burg: Müller 1964. Pp. 464, DM 40.—
Rev. by W. Paulsen in *BA,* xxxix (1965), 433-34.
Kindermann stresses opera more than in previous volumes, but does not include Wagner.

Kunisch, Hermann, ed. *Literaturwissenschaftliches Jahrbuch.* (Im Auftrage der Görres-Gesellschaft, n.s. IV.) Berlin: Duncker & Hum-blot, 1963. Pp. 330, DM 38.—
G. Fellerer "Der Musiker E.T.A. Hoffmann," R. Mühlher "E.T.A. Hoffmann. Beiträge zu einer Motivinterpretation," W. Zehetmeier "Zu Hölderlins 'Fried-ensfeier', Vers 1-9."

Kurth, Lieselotte E. "Historiographie und historischer Roman: Kritik und Theorie im 18. Jahrhundert." *MLN,* LXXIX (1965), 337-62.

Langen, August. "Zur Lichtsymbolik der deutschen Romantik." Pp.
447-85 in Kuhn, Hugo, and Kurt Schier, eds. *Märchen, Mythos, Dichtung.* München: C. H. Beck, 1963.
Proceeds from Hamann's interpretation of literature as symbolic art, and of
Creation as the symbolic language of God. Symbolism is seen as the essence of
Romantic art. Man and nature, formerly one in the "Golden Age," have
become separated, and man now strives back for the original unity. The poet is
the augur of the sacred hieroglyphics of nature (Novalis, Hoffmann). Light
is the transcendent original symbol from Germanic mythology, and the Old
and New Testament. Romanticism turns toward light as the soul of the universe (Schelling, the Schlegels, Novalis). Treated also is the Christian light
symbolism of Runge's landscapes and its influence on Eichendorff's "Seelen-
aufschwung" in the images of the eagle and lark, which are "birds of the soul."
The view from the mountain top and the religious symbolism of the sunrise
in Jean Paul is likewise placed in this context. Moonlight symbolism expresses
the "urromantisch" thought of the reunification of the separated parts of a
totality, of light and darkness. Finally, the merging of light and sound leads
to the synaesthetic configurations of Brentano, who likewise experienced a
longing for a syncretism. (I.C.)

Langen, August. "Zum Problem der sprachlichen Säkularisation in der
deutschen Dichtung des 18. und 19. Jhdts." *ZDP,* LXXXIII (1964),
Sonderheft, 24-42.

LeSage, Laurent. *Giraudoux, Surrealism and the German Romantic
Ideal.* University of Illinois Press, 1964. $2.00.
First edition 1952.

Lüders, Detlev, ed. *Jahrbuch des Freien Deutschen Hochstifts 1965.*
[*JFDH* 1965] Tübingen: Niemeyer, 1965. Pp. 490. DM 32.—

Mayer, Hans. *Zur deutschen Klassik und Romantik.* Pfullingen: Neske,
1964. Pp. 365. DM 24.50.
Rev. by K. Ziegler in *Germanistik,* VI (1965), 263-64.
A group of essays linked by the theme of the title. "Fragen der Romantik-
forschung" (pp. 263-305) deals with the polarity of Classicism-Romanticism;
"Heinrich von Kleist, der geschichtliche Augenblick" (185-242) with Kleist
as "citoyen radical à la Rousseau." Also in "Jean Pauls Nachruhm" (243-62),
"Wagner: Tristans Schweigen" (346-56), "*Tannhäuser* und die künstlichen
Paradiese" (332-45), and "Nichtmehr und Nochnicht im *Fliegenden Hol-
länder*" (317-31) attempt is made at a sociological and poetological synthesis.
(I.C.)

Menhennet, A. "Wieland's 'Idris und Zenide': The 'Aufklärer' as Romantic." *GL&L,* XVIII (1965), 91-100.

Mittner, Ladislao. *Storia della Letteratura Tedesca. Dal Pietismo al
Romanticismo.* Turin: Einaudi, 1964. Pp. 1042.

Muschg, Walter. "Der Zauber der Abstraktion in der Dichtung."
Euphorion, LVIII (1965), 225-42.
Derives marionettes in modern literature from Kleist and Hoffmann.

Neuere deutsche Literatur. Collective Vol. III of articles from *Wirkendes
Wort,* I-IX. Düsseldorff: Schwann, 1963. Pp. 452, DM 24.—
Rev. by L. Rotsch in *Germanistik,* VI (1965), 69-70.

Contains 44 essays from 1950-59, at present out of print. Photomechanical reprint, with all errors left standing. Romanticism: E. Hock "Eichendorffs Dichterum," W. Hof "Zu Hölderlins *Friedensfeier*," B.v. Wiese "Das Menschenbild Heinrich von Kleists," and "Zwischen Utopie und Wirklichkeit." (I.C.)

Rehm, Walter. *Späte Studien.* Bern: Francke, 1964. Pp. 472, S. Fr. 36.—

Rev. by Oskar Seidlin in *GQ*, xxxviii (1965), 91-93, and by Eugen Thurnher in *Germanistik*, vi (1965), 264-65.
All eight essays appeared separately between 1958 and 1962, were planned as one volume by Rehm, but had to be published posthumously. With vast ramifications, stressed by its extensive bibliography, this book represents a fine necrologue to the great scholar Rehm. A single trend of thought unites those interpretative essays into the one "Problemeinheit": the theme of eternal humanity. Rehm's personality emerges as he was in life: clear, sober, and truly humanistic.
Romanticism: "Jean Pauls vergnügtes Notenleben oder Notenmacher und Notenleser," 7-97; "Prinz Rokoko im alten Garten. Eine Eichendorffstudie," 122-215; "Jacob Burckhard und Eichendorff," 276-344; "Heinrich Wölfflin als Literarhistoriker. Mit einem Anhang ungedruckter Briefe von Michael Bernays, Eduard und Heinrich Wölfflin," 359-459, treating Gessner and Wackenroder. (I.C.)

Rempel, H. *Aufstieg der deutschen Landschaft. Das Heimaterlebnis von Jean Paul bis Adalbert Stifter.* Giessen: Mittelhess. Druck & Verlagsges., 1964. Pp. 199.

Szondi, Peter. *Satz und Gegensatz.* Six Essays. Frankfurt: Insel, 1964. Pp. 104. DM 4.50.

Rev. by K. K. Polheim in *Germanistik*, vi (1965), 429-30, and by B. Allemann in *NRs*, lxxvi (1965), 353-55.
Reprint of "*Amphitryon*, Kleists *Lustspiel nach Molière*" (44-57), and of "Fr. Schlegel und die romantische Ironie: Mit einer Beilage über Tiecks Komödien" (5-24), which is revised. (I.C.)

Thalmann, Marianne. *Romantiker entdecken die Stadt.* (Sammlung Dialog Bd. 6.) München: Nymphenburger Verlagshandlung, 1965. Pp. 160. DM 14.80.

This study of the reorientation of man in an altered structure of city life is based predominantly on Tieck, Brentano, Novalis and Hoffmann. The individual, exposed to a threatening urban life, the lost identity among the masses, the unbourgeois existence in a metropolis, the quick growth of the cities all change man's concept of time and space. Here is a surprising discovery of the asphalt jungle literature in an epoch normally not characterized by such concerns. (I.C.)

Tober, K. "German Romanticism, Part II." *ESA*, viii (1965), 56-63.

For Part I see *ESA*, vii (1964), 157-72.

Voerster, Erika. *Märchen und Novellen im klassisch-romantischen Roman.* (*AKML* 23.) Bonn: Bouvier, 1964. Pp. 412. DM 44.00.

Listed in *ELN*, iii, Supp., 95.
Rev. by K. Kratsch in *Germanistik*, vi (1965), 642.
Investigates novels by Goethe, then Romantic novels, mainly for the structural function of fairy-tale interludes. Included are the romantic story interpolations of: Novalis (*Ofterdingen* and *Lehrlinge von Sais*), F. Schlegel (*Lucinde*), D. Schlegel (*Florentin*), Arnim (*Gräfin Dolores* and *Kronenwächter*), Tieck

(*Sternbald*) and Eichendorff (*Ahnung und Gegenwart* and *Dichter und ihre Gesellen*). Cervantes (*Don Quijote*), Goethe (*Meister*) and Shakespeare (*Hamlet*) serve as models for the theory, origin, and importance of the interludes. (I.C.)

Reviews of books previously listed:

BENNETT, W., *German Verse in Classical Metres* . . . (see *ELN*, III, Supp., 88), rev. by V. A. Oswald in *GQ*, XXXVIII (1965), 67-68; BULLING, K., *Die Rezensenten der Jenaischen Allgemeinen Literaturzeitung* . . . (see *ELN*, III, Supp., 89), rev. by R. Thieberger in *EG*, XIX (1965), 319; FAMBACH, O. *Der romantische Rückfall in der Kritik der Zeit* . . . (see *ELN*, III, Supp., 89-90), rev. by N. Oellers in *ZDP*, LXXXIV (1965), 619-25; HATFIELD, H., *Aesthetic Paganism in German Literature* (see *ELN*, III, Supp., 90), rev. by A. von Gronicka in *MLQ*, XXVI (1965), 482-83; HIMMEL, H., *Geschichte der deutschen Novelle* (see *ELN*, III, Supp., 91), rev. by L. B. Jennings in *GQ*, XXXVIII (1965), 65-67, and by W. Silz in *JEGP*, LXIV (1965), 134-36; *Jahrbuch der Sammlung Kippenberg* (see *ELN*, III, Supp., 91), rev. by A. Fuchs in *EG*, XIX (1965), 49, and by H. A. Maier in *BA*, XXXIX (1965), 50; KUHN, H. and K. SCHIER, eds. *Märchen, Mythos, Dichtung* . . . (see *ELN*, III, Supp., 92), rev. by J. A. Gaertner in *BA*, XXXIX (1965), 50, and by F. Geissler in *ZDP*, LXXXIV (1965), 460-62; LUDERS, D., ed., *Jahrbuch des freien deutschen Hochstifts, 1963* (see *PQ*, XLIII, 434), rev. by R. Ayrault in *EG*, XX (1965), 103-04, and by W. Herwig in *Germanistik*, VI (1965), 461-62; MEYER, H., *Zarte Empirie* (see *ELN*, III, Supp., 93), rev. by A. Anger in *GQ*, XXXVIII (1965), 351-52; SORENSEN, B. A., *Symbol und Symbolismus in den ästhetischen Theorien des 18. Jahrhunderts und der deutschen Romantik* (see *ELN*, III, Supp., 94), rev. by L. Dieckmann in *MP*, LXII (1965), 359-61, and by R. Nak in *Germanistik*, V (1965), 611; THALMANN, M., *The Romantic Fairy Tale* . . . (see *ELN*, III, Supp., 95), rev. by U. Weisstein in *JEGP*, LXIV (1965), 776-79; and by Liselotte Dieckmann in *MLQ*, XXVII (1966), 95-96; WILLSON, A. L., *A Mythical Image: The Ideal of India in German Romanticism* (see *ELN*, III, Supp., 95), rev. by E. Behler in *ZDP*, LXXXIV (1965), 81-86.

3. STUDIES OF AUTHORS

ARNIM, ACHIM VON

Arnim, Achim von. *Isabella von Egypten. Kaiser Karl des Fünften erste Jugendliebe*. Frechen and Cologne: Bartmann, 1964. Pp. 144.
Rev. by G. L. Fink in *Germanistik*, VI (1965), 452.

Liedke, Herbert R. "Vorstudien Achim von Arnims zur 'Gräfin Dolores.' Zweiter Teil. Entwurf und Quellen zur 'Geschichte der verlorenen Erbprinzessin Wenda.' (Zweite Abteilung, siebentes Kapitel)." *JFDH*, 1965, pp. 237-313.
Part I in *JFDH*, 1964, pp. 236-342.

See also Börsch-Supan, Fassmann ("German 2. General").

ARNIM, BETTINA VON

Arnim, Bettina von. *Märchen der Bettina, Armgart und Gisela von Arnim*. Frechen and Cologne: Bartmann, 1965. Pp. 243.

See also Fassmann ("German 2. General").

BONAVENTURA

Kohlschmidt, Werner. "Das Hamlet-Motiv in den *Nachtwachen des Bonaventura*." Pp. 93-102 in *Dichter, Tradition und Zeitgeist*. Bern, München: Francke, 1965. Pp. 390. DM 42.50.

Paulsen, Wolfgang, ed. *Bonaventura: Nachtwachen*. (Universal-Bibliothek 8926/27.) Reclam, 1964. Pp. 180. DM 1.60.

BRENTANO

Fraenger, Wilhelm. *Clemens Brentanos Alhambra. Eine Nachprüfung*. (Castrum Peregrini LXI) Amsterdam: Castrum Peregrini, 1964. Pp. 88. fl. 13.50.

Rev. by Siegfried Sudhof in *Germanistik,* VI (1965), 619-20.

Fraenger perceptively traces the origins of this poem to Brentano's friendship with Caroline Günderode and Emilie Linder, thus to his earliest and latest periods. A clear analysis of the intensely personal nature of the poem and the subtility of the poet's technique. First published in 1935. (P.G.)

Frühwald, Wolfgang. "Zu neueren Brentanoausgaben." *LJGG*, n. s., V (1964), 361-80.

Largely a discussion of recent anthologies of Brentano's lyric poetry. The author evaluates the methods used in selecting and formulating texts. By comparing different versions of the same poem and considering thematic and other internal evidence, he finds numerous examples of willful "restoration" by editors. The anthologies criticized are meant chiefly for popular consumption and do not pretend to great philological exactness; therefore, his criteria do not well apply. He praises the work of Friedhelm Kemp (*Werke*, II [1964], III [1965], Munich: Hanser) and finds here progress towards a definitive edition of Brentano's works. (P.G.)

Kemp, Friedhelm, ed. *Werke*, vol. II. Munich: Hanser, 1964. Pp. 1240.

Rev. by Siegfried Sudhof in *Germanistik,* VI (1965), 102-03.

Kemp, Friedhelm, ed. *Werke*, vol. III, *Sämtliche Märchen*. Munich: Hanser, 1965. Pp. 1134.

See also Börsch-Supan, Fassmann, Thalmann ("German 2. General").

EICHENDORFF

Herrmann, Joachim. "Eichendorff und die Familie Mendelssohn." *Aurora,* XXV (1965), 85-88.

Remarks upon Eichendorff's apparent lack of interest in "die Vertonung seiner Lieder." Perhaps Eichendorff felt that the music did not express the intent of the poem. (L.R.)

Krummacher, Hans-Henrik. "Die volle und vielseitige Erschliessung der 'als ob'-Figuren in Eichendorffs Lyrik." Pp. 55-76 in Krummacher, Hans-Henrik. *Das "als ob" in der Lyrik: Erscheinungsformen und Wandlungen einer Sprachfigur der Metaphorik von der Romantik bis zu Rilke*. Köln-Graz: Böhlau, 1965.

The "als ob" construction is seen as an integral structural feature of the poem which frequently influences rhythm, syntax, imagery and content of the entire poem. Several poems are carefully analysed and the argument convincingly demonstrated. The author states that no poet before or since has used the construction with equal effectiveness. Its use enables the poet to suggest nuances, subtle articulations and relationships of various dimensions such as "des Innen und Aussen, der Natur und des Ich, der Gegenwert und der Erinnerung und Sehnsucht." The author states that Eichendorff has fully exploited this particular possibility of the construction and further attempts of variation might lead to empty formularization. (L.R.)

Kunisch, Hermann. "Joseph von Eichendorff *Das Wiedersehen.* Ein unveröffentlichtes Novellenfragment." *Aurora,* XXV (1965), 7-39.
The author offers the *Novellenfragment,* a facsimile of the handwriting, a discussion of the variants in the original manuscript, an attempt to establish its date of origin and a tentative interpretation, which is derived from the *a priori* assumption that the fragment is based primarily upon Eichendorff's relationship with his brother and the powerful attraction of "Heimat," especially Lubowitz. The author's reasoning is handicapped by a failure to recognize and consider significant Eichendorff symbols and imagery such as light, the instrument, the hour of Pan and death. (L.R.)

Meyer, Hans M. "Eichendorff-Bibliographie 1963-64 und Nachträge aus früheren Jahren." *Aurora,* XXV (1965), 89-92.

Rehm, Walther. "Prinz Rokoko im alten Garten." Pp. 122-214 in Rehm ("German 2. General").
An excellent, well documented discussion of the rococo influence in Eichendorff's garden symbolism. The author argues convincingly that the poet uses the rococo to insinuate a perversion of nature's innocence. The entire analysis implicitly rejects the understanding that nature, in Eichendorff's works, is capable of sin. (L.R.)

Rehm, Walther. "Jacob Burckhardt und Eichendorff." Pp. 276-343 in Rehm ("German 2. General").
As the title suggests, the stress is upon Burckhardt and not Eichendorff. Although Rehm seems to extend himself too much at times in drawing parallels and trying to establish an influence, the work successfully depicts the intrusion of Eichendorff's "Ideenwelt" into the mind and heart of a contemporary. This alone is significant because it has been almost impossible to establish the fact of Eichendorff's influence. (L.R.)

Schwarz, Peter. *Die Bedeutung der Tageszeiten in der Dichtung Eichendorffs: Studien zu Eichendorffs Motivik, Erzählstruktur, Zeitbegriff und Aesthetik auf geistesgeschichtlicher Grundlage. Freiburg* i.B., 1964. Pp. 300.

Seidlin, Oskar. *Versuche über Eichendorff.* Göttingen und Zürich: Vandenhoeck & Ruprecht, 1965. Pp. 303. 19,80 DM.

Worbs, Erich. "Eichendorff in Homburg." *Aurora,* XXV (1965), 74-84.

See also Börsch-Supan, Fassmann, Langen, *Neuere deutsche Literatur* (Hock) ("German 2. General").

FOUQUE, KAROLINE DE LA MOTTE
See Herd ("Hoffmann").

GRIMM, J.
Simons, L. "Ernte des Grimmjahrs." *Leuvense Bijdragen,* LIV (1965), Bijblad 2, pp. 1-6.

Brief reviews of five publications celebrating the centenary of Jacob Grimm's death. Reviewed are: Schoof, W., ed., *Briefwechsel zwischen Jacob und Wilhelm Grimm aus der Jugendzeit* (see *ELN*, III, Supp., 101); Denecke, L. and I-M. Greverus, eds. *Brüder Grimm Gedenken 1963* (Marburg: Elwert, 1963); Fraenger, W. and W. Steinitz, eds., *Jacob Grimm. Zur 100. Wiederkehr seines Todestages. Festschrift des Instituts für deutsche Volkskunde* (Berlin: Akademie, 1963); Kemminghausen, K. S., ed., *Westfälische Märchen und Sagen aus dem Nachlass der Brüder Grimm. Beiträge des Droste-Kreises*, 2nd ed., (Münster: Aschendorff, 1963); and Kemminghausen, K. S. and L. Denecke, eds., *Die Brüder Grimm in Bildern ihrer Zeit* (Kassel: Röth, 1963). (P.G.)

GRIMM, W.

See "Grimm, J."

GRIMM BROTHERS

See Simons ("Grimm, J.") and Fassmann ("German 2. General").

GÜNDERODE, CAROLINE

See Fraenger ("Brentano").

HEINE

Ewen, Frederic, ed. and tr. *Heinrich Heine: It will be a lovely Day. Selections from the Prose Works.* Berlin: Seven Seas, 1965. Pp. 385. DM-Ost 2.85.

Hahn, Karl-Heinz. *Aus der Werkstatt deutscher Dichter: Goethe-Schiller-Heine.* (Beiträge zur Gegenwartsliteratur 25). Halle: Sprache und Literatur, 1963. Pp. 371. DM-Ost 12.—.

Heine-Archiv Düsseldorf, ed. *Heine-Jahrbuch 1965.* Hamburg: Hoffmann und Campe, 1964. Pp. 86. [*HeineJ*, 1965].

Jennings, Lee B. "The Dance of Life and Death in Heine and Immermann." *GL&L*, XVIII (1965), 130-35.

Kaufmann, Hans, ed. *Sämtliche Werke.* (Textrevisionen und, Erläuterungen von Gotthard Erler). 11 vols. München: Kindler, 1964. Ea. vol. DM 3.80.

Rev. by Jost Hermand in *Germanistik*, VI (1965), 126 and 478. Obviously a West-German version of the East-German edition (Berlin: Aufbau 1961 ff.) which, except for the index, is the most complete recent edition. Kindler has incorporated most of the new text and commentary of the 1961 edition—a rather unusual feature for a pocket book series. Only volumes 12-14 are still lacking. (H.G.N.)

Krämer-Badoni, Rudolf. "Briefe aus Paris." Pp. 49-76 in Lehner, Horst, ed. *Auf der Suche nach Frankreich: Der Nachbar im Westen und die deutsche Kultur.* (Schriftenreihe des Inst. f. Auslandsbez. 5). Herrenalb: Erdmann, 1963.

Interprets some significant remarks and statements in the correspondence of Heine. (H.G.N.)

Maché, Ulrich. "Der junge Heine und Goethe." *HeineJ*, 1965, pp. 42-47.

Maché's article with its subtitle "Eine Revision der Auffassung von Heines Verhältnis zu Goethe vor dem Besuch in Weimar (1824)" is as ambivalent and ambiguous as was Heine's attitude towards Goethe. While claiming that scholarship up to now was more inclined to believe in Heine's strong affection for Goethe before his disappointing visit changed this, the material cited can just as easily be used to prove the opposite. It has, moreover, always been quite obvious that Goethe with his indifference to the political and social problems of the restoration period could not hold too much appeal for a Heine, even before their meeting at Weimar.

Maché is certainly correct in pointing out that Heine's knowledge of Goethe's works was then rather limited and that his attitude towards the poet himself was not helped by Varnhagen's refusal to print his essay on Goethe (though he had asked him to write it in the first place). (H.G.N.)

Maliniemi, Irja. "Heinrich Heine in der Literatur Finnlands bis etwa 1920." *Nerthus. Nordisch-deutsche Beiträge*, I (1964), 9-105.

Mann, Michael, ed. *Zeitungsberichte über Musik und Malerei.* (Selections.) Frankfurt: Insel, 1964. Pp. 256. DM 20.00.
Rev. by Jost Hermand in *Germanistik*, VI (1965), 126, by Philipp Veit in *JEGP*, LXIV (1965), 558-59, and in *TLS*, March 25, 1965, p. 227.
This handy little volume makes available some of the original texts of Heine's reports on music and painting for the *Augsburger Allgemeine Zeitung* which up to now were known to most readers only in the revised version of *Lutetia*. Michael Mann thereby makes a remarkable contribution to an understanding of the development and changes in Heine's views; though this reviewer was surprised by Mann's contention that the poet's philosophy of life and art essentially had not undergone any change over the years (p. 7)—a statement that to some extent negates the necessity of Mann's own endeavours. As Veit in his review (see above) already pointed out, Mann may be hard put to prove this—aside from the fact that Heine's limited knowledge of art and particularly music made him a questionable authority in these fields. What makes this volume valuable is not only Mann's careful reproduction of the texts but also his thoroughly documented and detailed notes which should prove helpful in the preparation of a new critical edition which is so badly needed. (H.G.N.)

Mende, Fritz. "Heinrich Heines literarisches Persönlichkeitsideal." *HeineJ*, 1965, pp. 3-16.
Since there is a confusing multitude of contradictory opinions on Heine's literary personality, Mende feels that the poet's own concept can best be found in his works by checking what ideal features worthy of imitation Heine found in people like Lessing, Goethe, Schiller, Jean Paul, Voltaire, Sterne and Mirabeau. Questionable, however, is Mende's claim that the poet's inner discord was not so much part of his character but due to the social and political conditions of his time.
Heine admires the enthusiasm of Schiller and Jean Paul, an enthusiasm with a goal and a willingness to get involved—which he misses in Goethe, "das gross Zeitablehnungsgenie". Yet he castigates any exaggerated pathos and demands common sense in dealing with realities.
Mende sees the most fitting self-characterization in Heine's description of Lessing as the man "mit dem klarsten Kopf und dem schönsten Herzen." While Heine certainly was a poet "engagé", Mende's article sems to overstress the socio-political aspects of Heine's "Persönlichkeitsideal". (H.G.N.)

Schmidt-Künsemüller, Friedrich A. "Georg Herweghs Wandlung zum politischen Radikalismus." *HeineJ* 1965, pp. 68-80.

Seifert, Siegfried. "Der unbewältigte Heine." *NDL*, XIII (1965), 172-79.

Weber, Dietrich. " 'Gesetze des Standpunkts' in Heines Lyrik." *JFDH*, 1965, pp. 369-99.

Zagari, Luciano. "Heine in der italienischen Kritik." *HeineJ*, 1965, pp. 51-63.
This essay is actually a translation of a lecture held in Rome and Milan and published in abbreviated form in *Il Mondo* (June 6, 1964).
Zagari sees the different facets of Heine-criticism as rather typical symptoms of trends in the cultural development of Italian society and intellectual life. According to Zagari the Heine cult of the 19th and early 20th century was marked by what he calls the myth of popular poetry, being anti-rhetorical and anticlassical, the myth of unacademic realistic expression, the myth of Heine's irony and, out of this, the myth of the antithesis. In the 20th century he sees above all a turning away from all this as irrelevant; Heine-criticism concerns itself with those works which are considered as based on pure inspiration— with Benedetto Croce as its best-known exponent. In contemporary criticism Zagari distinguishes two diverging trends, a historical and a stylistical approach; he seems to plead for a synthesis of both. (H.G.N.)

Zagari, Luciano. "La Pomare di Heine e la Crisi del Linguaggio 'lirico'." *Studi Germanici, III* (1965), 5-38.

See also Wellek, *History* ("General 3. Criticism"); DuBruck ("French 1. Nerval").

Review of book previously listed:
HOFRICHTER, L., *Heinrich Heine* (see *ELN*, III, Supp., 105), *QQ*, LXXII, 209-10.

HÖLDERLIN

Alewyn, Richard. "Dominiksgesichter." *HöJb*, XIII (1963/64), 77-78.
Study revealing the origin of this word (twice used by the young Hölderlin) on the 17th century French stage (*Dominique* as the nickname of a well-known comic actor), and its use by Hölderlin to express his scorn for the von Kalb types at the courts.

Baum, Manfred. "Hölderlins Pindar-Fragment 'Das Höchste'." *HöJb*, XIII (1963/64), 65-76.
Fine interpretation of this late piece, leading to the recognition of the principle of "notwendige Gleichheit notwendig verschiedener Prinzipien und reiner Methoden" (74), and involving a close study of Pindar's text as compared with Hölderlin's translation. (U.G.)

Bernd, Clifford A. "The Formal Qualities of Hölderlin's 'Wink für die Darstellung und Sprache'." *MLR*, LX (1965), 400-04.
Study focused upon a pivotal sentence in the essay and revealing a dialectical structure of the whole. Although the fragmentary state of some of the essays may forbid similar investigations, one would welcome further studies in this direction. (U.G.)

Berteaux, Pierre. "Du nouveau sur Hölderlin." *EG*, XX (1965), 172-77.

Puts together some pieces of evidence that Hölderlin was, during his whole life, a "Jacobin attardé," and that his poetry is a cryptic message that can be and has to be deciphered as a document of revolutionary spirit and political engagement. In its one-sidedness highly improbable. (U.G.)

Binder, Wolfgang. "Friedrich Hölderlin: 'Der Winkel von Hardt,' 'Lebensalter,' 'Hälfte des Lebens'." *SchM*, XLV (1965), 583-91.

The three poems which Binder subjects to a fine interpretation have been placed by Hölderlin at the end of the *Nachtgesänge* which Wilmans published. Binder shows that their sequence is meaningful and constitutes a line of thought dealing with the structure of remembrance. Some easier readings of lines could be suggested. (U.G.)

Binder, Wolfgang, and Alfred Kelletat, eds. *Hölderlin-Jahrbuch*. 13. Band (1963/64). Tübingen: Mohr/Siebeck, 1965. Pp. 189. [*HöJb*, XIII].

Contains, aside from the papers which are reviewed here individually (by Staiger, Hölscher, Mojasević, Baum, and Alewyn), poems about and to Hölderlin by Celan and nine Anglo-American poets, the latter introduced by Michael Hamburger. A brief inventory of Hellingrath's "Nachlass" (now part of the Hölderlin archives in Bebenhausen), and some letters taken from this collection follow; three necrologues and two reports conclude the volume.

George, Emery E. "Some New Hölderlin Decipherments from the 'Homburger Folioheft'." *PMLA*, LXXX (1965), 123-40.

Using better photographs of the mss. than Beissner had available in the war years, George is able to detect minor variants to Beissner's text which are certainly valuable. His sequences of possible arrangements of lines, however, lack credibility, mainly from a purely syntactical standpoint. (U.G.)

Hölscher, Uvo. *Empedokles und Hölderlin*. Frankfurt/M.: Insel, 1965. Pp. 65.

A very enlightening study not only as to the relationship between the poet and the ancient philosopher, but also regarding each of them separately. Detailed investigation of Hölderlin's possible sources shows a strong 18th century influence on his image of Empedokles. One of the several points in Hölscher's book which need correction is the following: It is certainly incorrect to see in Empedokles' *death* the loving deed which unites the opposed forces and which ends the "Streit der Welt" (47). *Grund zum Empedokles* as well as version III make it perfectly clear that the aspect of reconciliation is already given by Empedokles' mere *existence*, and that his death is the result of the fictitiousness of divine forces reconciling themselves in a human being. For this reason, Hölscher's reference to Christ's death (at least in the dogmatic meaning) is wrong. On the whole, however, this book fills an important gap in our knowledge about Hölderlin's *Empedokles*, and one would wish equally detailed studies of the poet's use of other sources. (U.G.)

Hölscher, Uvo. "Empedokles von Akragas: Erkenntnis und Reinigung." *HöJb*, XIII (1963/64), 21-43.

See (above) review of Hölscher's book *Empedokles und Hölderlin*, which is an expanded version of this paper read at the Hölderlin-Tagung in 1963.

Lüders, Detlev. "Die unterschiedene Einheit. Eine Grundstruktur im Spätwerk Hölderlins. I. Das Gefüge der Welt in der Hymne 'Der Einzige'." *JFDH*, 1963, pp. 106-38.

The text on which Lüders bases his interpretation is a *potpourri* from all versions of the poem made up in order to constitute an unbroken line of thought. Because of this mixed nature, its credibility is slight. Moreover, Lüders overlooks the "geistige" nature of Christ (cf. *Der Einzige* III, 76 and 64). Obviously, the difference in *nature* of the three semi-gods accounts for the difference in their *performance*, and not, as Lüders points out, an absolute superiority of performance in Christ over the two others. From the "Hesperian" point of judgment, Christ's performance is superior, and therefore, he is "Der Einzige." But since Hölderlin expressly criticizes the subjectivity under which this superiority appears, his opinion seems to be just opposite to Lüders' contention, and his poem turns out to be an essay aiming for purification of "Hesperian" thinking. (U.G.)

Lüders, Detlev. "Die unterschiedene Einheit. Eine Grundstruktur im Spätwerk Hölderlins. II. Welt und Weltlauf. III. Unterschiedene Einheit und Ganzheit." *JFDH*, 1964, pp. 102-19.
Good but unoriginal description of the principle named in the title as appearing in history and in the relationship between "Sein" and "Erkenntnis." (V.G.)

Mojašević, Miljan. "Stille und Mass." *HöJb*, XIII (1963/64), 44-64.
Word study touching upon "Stille," "Mass," "Harmonie," "Freude," "Leid." A main disadvantage is the lack of a clear historical aspect differentiating between the meanings of these terms at different periods in Hölderlin's work— a methodical approach indispensable for a word study but denounced by the author as "unnütze Arbeit" (56). The results are vague and unconvincing. (U.G.)

Ryan, Lawrence J. *Hölderlin's 'Hyperion': Exzentrische Bahn und Dichterberuf.* Stuttgart: Metzler, 1965. Pp. 244.
Rev. by U. Gaier in *GQ*, XXXIX (1966), 244-49.
This study has its definite merit since it shows that Hölderlin's novel cannot be taken too seriously: behind what was long thought to be the expression of a dreamy mind, there appears the constant adherence to strict principles of composition. Ryan's analysis of the novel, however, suffers from one serious impediment: he bases it upon a false definition of "exzentrische Bahn" (see my review listed above for evidence), and therefore the basic categories are inadequate. (U.G.)

Staiger, Emil. "Der Opfertod von Hölderlins Empedokles." *HöJb,* XIII (1963/64), 1-20.
Staiger's tracing back the "Schuld" problem of version I to pietistic sources is of high merit, as is his constant reference to Hegel's early writings for version III. By the fact that the versions never run beyond the second act, however, Staiger seems to have been misled into the assumption that Hölderlin had already spent all of his ideas up to this point and could not fill the remaining three acts. But a comparison of the two great speeches ending version III could reveal the fact that Hölderlin interrupted his work at a point of extreme dramatic tension, where Empedokles' death would be, in Manes' words, actually "schwarze Sünde" (III, 370). Thus, Staiger does not solve the problem as to why Hölderlin's tragedy remained a fragment. (U.G.)

See also Burwick, Muir ("General 3. Criticism"); Börsch-Supan, Kunisch, *Neuere deutsche Literatur* (Hof) ("German 2. General").

HOFFMANN

Erné, Nino, ed. *E. T. A. Hoffmann: Gesammelte Werke.* Hamburg: Standard Verlag, 1964-65. Vol. I: *Romane.* Pp. 769. Vol. II: *Märchen.* Pp. 787. DM 11.50 per vol.

Herd, Rudolf, ed. "Der Kapellmeister Gottmund im 'Delphin' der Karoline de la Motte Fouqué: eine Verkörperung E. T. A. Hoffmanns." *MHG,* x (1963), 27-32.

Kanzog, Klaus. "E. T. A. Hoffmanns Erzählung 'Das Fräulein von Scuderi' als Kriminalgeschichte." *MHG,* xi (1964), 1-11.
A close analysis of the structure and motifs of this early modern "detective story." Kanzog draws the important conclusion: ". . . dass Hoffmann die klassische Strukutr der Kriminalgeschichte, wenn auch nur in Ansätzen, bereits zwanzig Jahre vor Edgar Allan Poe aus einer Gattung entwickelt hat, in der diese Struktur alsbald zu einem Schema umgestaltet und damit in die Trivialliteratur zurückgeholt wird." (K.N.)

Kroll, Erwin. "E. T. A. Hoffmann und Schlesien." *Aurora,* xxiii (1963), 93-100.
Deals mainly with Hoffmann's stay in Glogau, his trip to Silesia in 1819, and his widow's residence in Breslau from 1835 until her death in 1848.

Leitherer, Hans. "Das E. T. A.-Hoffmann-Museum in Bamberg." *MHG,* x (1963), 3-7.

Maekawa, Mitisuke. "Japanische Uebersetzer als Wegbereiter der Dichtung E. T. A. Hoffmanns." *MHG,* x (1963), 16-19.

Müller, Hans von, and Friedrich Schnapp. *Julie Marc: Erinnerungen an E. T. A. Hoffmann (1837).* Bamberg: Fränkischer Tag GmbH & Co., 1965. Pp. 16.
Rev. by W. Segebrecht in *Germanistik,* vi (1965), 632.
These "Erinnerungen" are in a single long letter written by Julie Marc, Hoffmann's former song-pupil, to her cousin, Dr. Friedrich Speyer in Bamberg, on March 15, 1837, and hitherto unpublished. The document is important for Hoffmann both as man and as author because of Julie's role as an unattainable sublimated feminine figure, whose image became the muse of Hoffmann's romantic writings. The occasion for the letter was the appearance of Kunz' *Supplemente zu Ernst Theodor Wilhelm Hoffmann's Leben,* in which Julie and Hoffmann were obviously and shamelessly slandered by this former publisher of Hoffmann's works. In the letter, Julie defends herself and her former teacher in a totally convincing way, and in so doing reveals some new details and perspectives on the teacher-pupil relationship that was so vital to the breakthrough of Hoffmann's literary art. Probably the most important single contribution of the letter is the revelation that from *Julie's* point of view the attraction between them was long and intense, as for Hoffmann, but naturally much more suppressed. The pamphlet should evoke considerable discussion. (K.N.)

Müller, Helmut. *Untersuchungen zum Problem der Formelhaftigkeit bei E. T. A. Hoffmann.* Bern: Haupt, 1964. Pp. 123. 9.80 Swiss Franks.
Rev. by W. Segebrecht in *Germanistik,* vi (1965), 636.

Müller-Seidel, Walter, Wolfgang Kron and Friedrich Schnapp, eds. *E. T. A. Hoffmann. Sämtliche Werke in Fünf Einzelbänden.* Vol. III: *Die Serapionsbrüder.* Vol. IV: *Späte Werke.* Munich: Winkler-Verlag, 1965.
These volumes complete this excellent, well-annotated set. (K.N.)

Negus, Kenneth. *E. T. A. Hoffmann's Other World. The Romantic Author and his "New Mythology."* Philadelphia: Pennsylvania University Press, 1965. Pp. 183. $6.—
Footing on Hoffmann's total production, this important monograph attempts a critical evaluation. The main asset of Hoffmann's narrative art is found to lie in his combining the images and ideas from various sources into the "new mythology" which Fr. Schlegel proposed as substitute for the familiar ancient tradition. This spiritual and artistic conception, born of the union of the poet's inward self with cosmic forces, is symbolized in the three terms "Urzeit, Urquelle, Mittelpunkt" (of the universe). Selecting this leitmotif in the unique and dynamic production of his poet enables Negus to investigate the deeper strata of his imaginary universe. Though all forms of Hoffmann's literature reveal the poetic vision as basis for his mythology, the four major "Märchentypen" *Klein Zaches, Prinzessin Brambilla, Meister Floh,* and above all *Der goldne Topf* represent the "internal security of a primeval world of art in which all his frustrated aspirations in a hostile world seemed fulfilled." The satanic figures of the underworld with their origins in a beet-root appear to the reviewer as a missing link between Faust's Homunculus and Ewers' Alraune. An interesting observation is that the conflict of the two extremes of reality and fantasy softened toward the end of Hoffmann's life. This suggests a classical harmony and the speculation that he might have produced a basically realistic literary art. His foreign adapters, even Dostoewski, ignore his mythical factors. The author furnishes a bibliography of secondary works which deal with Hoffmann's "New Mythology." Consideration of recent publications might have been useful, such as R. Taylor, 1963, A. L. Willson, 1964. (I.C.)

Prawer, S. S. "Hoffmann's Uncanny Guest. A Reading of 'Der Sandmann'." *GL&L,* XVIII (1965), 297-308.
Concentrates on the evil Coppelius-Coppola, and his psychological, moral, and metaphysical significance. Upgrades the tale for its modernity.

Raraty, Maurice Michael. "Hoffmann und die 'ombres chinoises'." *MHG,* XI (1964), 11-23.
This unassumingly entitled article actually offers a genuine contribution to Hoffmann studies: the derivation of certain figures and techniques in his narrative art from puppetry, especially the "shadow-theater" type. Interesting new light is cast on some of Hoffmann's major works, including *Ritter Gluck, Der goldne Topf, Der Sandmann,* conversations of the *Serapionsbrüder, Seltsame Leiden . . ., Prinzessin Brambilla,* and *Kater Murr.* This influence is particularly important in the visual characterization of certain grotesque and surrealistic figures. (K.N.)

Reber, Natalie. *Studien zum Motiv des Doppelgängers bei Dostojewskij und E. T. A. Hoffmann.* Giessen: Wilhelm Schmitz, 1964. Pp. 240.

Salomon, Gerhard. *E. T. A. Hoffmann. Bibliographie.* Hildesheim: Olms, 1963. Pp. 118. DM 16.50.
A photographic reprinting of the second edition (1927) of this standard work.

Schneider, Wolfgang. "E. T. A. Hoffmanns Nachtgesang aus der 'Genovefa' des Malers Müller." *MHG,* XI (1964), 37-48.
Contains a little-known musical text, composed by Hoffmann, to a song connected with the Julia Marc affair, and discussed by the *Serapionsbrüder* in connection with *Der Dichter und der Komponist.*

Stinchcombe, J. "Trakl's 'Elis' poems and E. T. A. Hoffmann's 'Die Bergwerke zu Falun'." *MLR,* LIX (1964), 609-15.

Presents evidence that parts of Trakl's "Elis" poems were derived from Hoffmann's version of the Falun legend, rather than from Hofmannsthal's, as was previously assumed. Trakl apparently knew both; but there is no evidence that he had read the third famous version by Hebel.

Wührl, Paul-Wolfgang. "Hoffmann's Märchentheorie und 'Die Erzählungen aus den tausendundein Nächten'." *MHG*, x (1963), 20-26.

See also Passage ("General 3. Criticism"); DuBruck ("French. Nerval"); Börsch-Supan, Fassmann, Muschg, Thalmann ("German 2. General").

Reviews of books previously listed:
TAYLOR, R., *Hoffmann* (see *ELN*, III, Supp., 111), rev. by W. Segebrecht in *Germanistik*, VI (1965), 117-18; by J. Giraud in *EG*, xx (1965), 75-76; and by G. W. Field in *GQ*, xxxvIII (1965), 76-77; TEICHMANN, E., *La fortune d'Hoffmann en France* (see *PQ*, xLII, 497), rev. by A. Monchoux in *RLC*, xxxIx (1965), 321-23.

JEAN PAUL

Baumann, Gerhart. "Jean Paul: 'Des Luftschiffers Gianozzo Seebuch'." Pp. 399-423 in *Die Wissenschaft von deutscher Sprache und Dichtung: Methoden, Probleme, Aufgaben.* Festschrift Friedrich Maurer. Stuttgart: Ernst Klett, 1963.
Very fine analysis showing the piece as an "Abbreviatur geläufiger Jean-Paul-Themen" (403). Especially laudable is the clear presentation of Jean Paul's humour and its implications as incorporated in Gianozzo, his reflections, and his fate. (U.G.)

Berend, Eduard. *Jean-Paul-Bibliographie.* Neu bearbeitet und ergänzt von Johannes Krogoll. (Veröffentlichungen der deutschen Schillergesellschaft, Bd. 26.) Stuttgart: Ernst Klett, 1963. Pp. xv and 303.
Renewing the 1925 edition and bringing it up to date (end of 1962), this bibliography is an extremely valuable tool for every Jean Paul scholar. In the dichotomy between critical selection and completeness, Krogoll has decided for the latter, thus avoiding all subjectivity, and providing a firm basis for future research. (U.G.)

Endres, Elisabeth. "Die Funktion des Absonderlichen in der Dichtung Jean Pauls." *SchM*, xLIV (1964), 850-60.

Fieguth, Gerhard W., ed. *Jean Paul: Begegnungen mit Zeitgenossen.* Frankfurt/M.: Insel, 1964. Pp. 135. DM 4.50.
Rev. by Joachim Müller in *Germanistik*, VI (1965), 462-63.

Haselberg, Peter von. "Musicisches Vexierstroh: Jean Paul, ein Jakobiner in Deutschland." Pp. 162-82 in *Zeugnisse: Theodor W. Adorno zum 60. Geburtstag.* Im Auftrag des Instituts für Sozialforschung hrsg. von Max Horkheimer. Frankfurt/M.: Europäische Verlagsanstalt, 1963.
By showing Jean Paul's tendency towards disrupting political and intellectual systems in his emphasis upon chance and contingency, v. Haselberg seems to strike a theme which is important for the correct understanding of Jean Paul. But one would wish a more consistent treatment without all of v. Haselberg's jumps from one thought or quotation to another. (U.G.)

Mayer, Gerhart. "Die humorgeprägte Struktur von Jean Pauls 'Flegel-jahren'." *ZDP*, LXXXIII (1964), Heft 4, pp. 409-26.
Somewhat unoriginal but clear discussion of the principles of "Witz" (Vult), "poetische Phantasie" (Walt), "Humor" (narrator) in Jean Paul's novel. (U.G.)

Richter, Helmut. "Wege zu Jean Paul." *SuF*, XV (1963), 462-81.
By showing the historical background to Jean Paul's writings, Richter tries to present him as an important and unduly neglected object of Marxist literary criticism. But if, for instance, the political scene does not furnish events and personalities that could inspire a novelist to compose his book with a consistent plot around one of these personalities, this would not account for an increased emphasis just on the character and its development as Richter would have it (476-78). The reasons must obviously be looked for in the poet's interpretation of his world, and not in the world itself. (U.G.)

See also Smeed, Wellek, *Confrontations* ("General 3. Criticism"); Al-berken, H. Mayer, Rehm, Rempel ("German 2. General").

KLEIST

Cervani, Iole Laurenti. *La narrativa di Heinrich von Kleist*. Udine: Del Bianco Editore, 1962.
Rev. by R. Masson in *EG*, XX (1965), 78.

Crosby, Donald H. "Heinrich von Kleist's 'Oak-Image'." *GQ*, XXXVIII (1965), 14-19.
Examples of the metaphor of the storm-pounded, sometimes defeated oak are pointed out in Kleist's letters and works, with special reference to *Penthesilea*. Then they are traced to La Fontaine, Shakespeare, and Sophocles; contrasted with the examples by these authors; and finally shown to be "a reliable key to Kleist's tragic vision." Kleist's oak-image is distinguished from that of pre-cursors by its tragic irony. "In its finest poetic form it serves as an epitaph for Penthesilea; in its tragic implications, it embraces Kleist's life as well." A revealing contribution to the subject of Kleist's verbal imagery. See "Stern" below. (K.N.)

Haupt, Gunther. *Heinrich von Kleist in Berlin*. Vol. I of Berlinische Reminiszensen (ed. Horst Behrend). Berlin: Haude & Spener, 1963. Pp. 82, DM 9.80.
Rev. by K. Kratzsch in *Germanistik*, VI (1965), 315.
Although it presents no new materials, this little volume is a useful, informa-tive, and well-written summary of Kleist's last two years, with emphasis on Prussia and politics. Eight illustrations. (K.N.)

Horwath, P. "Michael Kohlhaas: Kleists Absicht in der Ueberarbeitung des Phöbus-Fragments." *Monatshefte,* LVII (1964), 49-59.

Hubbs, V. C. "The Concept of Fate in Kleist's 'Schroffenstein'." *Monatshefte,* LVI (1964), 339-45.

Koopmann, Helmut. "Das 'rätselhafte Faktum' und seine Vorgeschichte. Zum analytischen Charakter der Novellen Heinrich von Kleists." *ZDP,* LXXXIV (1965), 508-50.

Parker, John J. "A Motif and Certain Peculiarities of Style in Heinrich von Kleist's 'Prinz Friedrich von Homburg'." *AUMLA,* xxiii (1965), 103-10.
Interprets single crucial words used by Kleist as a unique kind of "motif." They are both a stylistic factor and a pointed expression of Kleist's views on the imperfect order of the world.

Parker, John J. " 'Wenn er den Spruch für ungerecht kann halten, Kasser' ich die Artikel: er ist frei!—, Zum 'Prinzen Friedrich von Homburg' 1185-1186." *GRM,* xiv (1964), 313-14.

Rothe, Eva, and Helmut Sembdner. "Die Kleist-Handschriften und ihr Verbleib." *JDSG,* viii (1964), 324-43.
An up-to-date listing of all known Kleist manuscripts. The brief but highly informative introduction tells the sad tale of the destruction or disappearance of two-thirds of Kleist's literary remains. All known essential information is given, including former locations of lost items, published facsimiles, and the last year in which lost items were known to be extant. (K.N.)

Schunicht, Manfred. "Heinrich von Kleist: 'Der zerbrochene Krug'." *ZDP,* lxxxiv (1965), 550-62.

Stern, Martin. "Die Eiche als Sinnbild bei Heinrich von Kleist." *JDSG,* viii (1964), 199-225.
Sheer accident places two articles on the same Kleist metaphor in this listing. (See "Crosby" above.) Stern's treatment is more extensive, at times going perhaps slightly far afield. Here the background of Kleist's oak-tree imagery is seen in the Hamann and Herder theories of language (especially "Besonnenheit"). The main literary precursors in this case are Homer and Goethe. A great many instances of Kleist's employment of the oak and related images are cited. The conclusion: "Die . . . am Anfang festgestellte Hypertrophie der Metaphorik ist also nicht ein Zeichen intellektueller Schwäche; im Gegenteil, Kleists Bildersprache erschliesst das Innere eines zerrissenen, aber scharfen Geistes, der sich zu Unrecht für ganz 'unaussprechlich' hielt." (K.N.)

Thalmann, Marianne. "Das Jupiterspiel in Kleists Amphitryon." *Maske und Kothurn,* ix (1963), 56-67.

Werlich, Egon. "Kleists 'Bettelweib von Locarno.' Versuch einer Aufwertung des Gehalts." *WW,* xv (1965), 239-57.
A close scrutiny, taking issue with E. Staiger's interpretation.

See also Paulson ("General 3. Criticism"); H. Mayer, Muschg, *Neuere deutsche Literatur* (v. Wiese), Szondi ("German 2. General").

KOTZEBUE, AUGUST VON
Schumacher, Hans, ed. *Die deutschen Kleinstädter. Ein Lustspiel in vier Akten. 1803.* Berlin: de Gruyter, 1964. Pp. 110. DM 6.00.
Rev. by C. Jauslin in *Germanistik,* vi (1965), 112.
Contains a wealth of background information, and important bibliographical and interpretative materials (pp. 84-110). (K.N.)

See also Albertsen ("German 2. General").

LENAU

Minckwitz, Friedrich, ed. *Nikolaus Lenau und Sophie Löwenthal. Die Geschichte einer tragischen Liebe. Briefe und Tagebücher.* Introduction by Minckwitz. Weimar: Kiepenheuer, 1963. DM-Ost 9.50.

Review of book previously listed:

ROOT, W. H., tr., *Nikolaus Lenau: Poems and Letters* (see *ELN*, III, Supp., 115), rev. by H. Schmidt, *JEGP*, LXIV (1965), 126-27.

NOVALIS

Grützmacher, Curt. *Novalis und Philipp Otto Runge. Drei Zentralmotive und ihre Bedeutungssphäre. Die Blume—Das Kind—Das Licht.* München: Eidos Verlag, 1964. Pp. 116.

An informative and enlightening study of the interrelated flower, child and light imagery common to Novalis and Runge. Some readers may miss discussions of Runge's paintings (only his writings are discussed), as well as consideration of the differences between the two men's works arising from the two different art media (painting and poetry). These weaknesses are at least partially offset by the sensitivity and painstaking care in the areas treated. (K.N.)

Kreft, Jürgen. "Die Entstehung der dialektischen Geschichtsmetaphysik aus den Gestalten des utopischen Bewusstseins bei Novalis." *DVLG*, XXXIX (1965), 213-45.

Sees a parallelism and interpenetration of chiliastic and dialectical concepts of history in Novalis' thought. Deals specifically with the new epoch of the future prophesied in *Die Christenheit oder Europa*, supplemented by certain of the "Fragmente."

Worbs, Erich. "Novalis und der schlesische Physiker Johann Wilhelm Ritter." *Aurora,* XXIII (1963), 85-92.

See also Baeumer, Börsch-Supan, Fassmann, Langen, Thalmann ("German 2. General").

Reviews of books previously listed:

VORDTRIEDE, W. *Novalis und die französischen Symbolisten* (see *PQ*, XLIII, 438), rev. by J. J. Anstett in *EG,* XX (1965), 598-99, and by L. Kilchberger in *Monatshefte,* LVII (1965), 77-78.

RÜCKERT

Prang, Helmut. *Friedrich Rückert als Diener und Deuter des Wortes.* (Veröffentlichungen des Fördererkreises der Rückert-Forschung). Schweinfurt: Fördererkreis der Rückert-Forschung, 1963. Pp. 32.

Rev. by Rudolf Majut in *Germanistik,* VI (1965), 133-34, and by the same in *GRM,* XV (1965), 218.

Prang, Helmut. *Friedrich Rückert. Geist und Form der Sprache.* (Schweinfurt: Selbstverlag der Stadt Scwheinfurt.) Wiesbaden: In Kommission bei Otto Harrassowitz, 1963.

Rev. by Rudolf Majut in *GRM,* XV (1965), 216-18.

SCHELLING
Fuhrmann, Horst, and Lisolette Lohrer, eds. *Schelling und Cotta. Brief-wechsel, 1803-1849.* Unter Mitwirkung des Cotta-Archivs im Schiller Nationalmuseum. (Veröffentlichungen der deutschen Schillergesellschaft, Bd. 27.) Stuttgart: Ernst Klett Verlag, 1965. Pp. 360. DM 29.—.

Marquet J. F. "Schelling et le métamorphoses de l'Histoire." *Critique,* XXI, Janvier, No. 212 (1965), pp. 63-72.

Schelling, F. W. J. *Über das Wesen der menschlichen Freiheit.* Stuttgart: Reclam, 1964. Pp. 181. DM 2.40.

See also Baeumer, Langen ("German 2. General").

SCHLEGEL, A. W. and F.
See Fassmann, Langen ("German 2. General").

SCHLEGEL, A. W.
Guthke, Karl S. "Zu August Wilhelm Schlegels Tasso-Kenntnis." *GRM,* XV (1965), 202-05.

Lohner, E., ed. *Geschichte der romantischen Literatur.* Kritische Schriften und Briefe IV. Stuttgart: W. Kohlhammer, 1965.

SCHLEGEL, DOROTHEA
Eichner, Hans. " 'Camilla.' Eine unbekannte Fortsetzung von Dorothea Schlegels Florentin." *JFDH,* 1965, pp. 314-68.

See also Baeumer, Langen ("German 2. General").

SCHLEGEL, F.
Behler, Ernst, Jean-Jacques Anstett, and Hans Eichner, eds. *Kritische Friedrich Schlegel-Ausgabe.* Vol. V, Section 1. *Dichtungen,* ed. Hans Eichner. Pp. 544. DM. 46.—Vol. XVIII, Section 2. *Philosophische Lehrjahre, 1796-1806. Nebst philosophischen Manuskripten aus den Jahren 1796-1806.* Erster Teil, ed. Ernst Behler. Paderborn: Schöningh, 1964. Pp. 580. DM 58.—
Rev. in *TLS,* Jan. 30, 1964, p. 89.

Klin, Eugeniusz. "Friedrich Schlegel an Friedrich Majer. Zwei unbekannte Briefe." *DVLG,*

Klin, Eugeniusz. *Die frühromantische Literaturtheorie Friedrich Schlegels.* (Acta Universitatis Wratislaviensis, No. 26 Germanica Wratislaviensia, VIII.) Wroclaw: Panstwowe Wydawnictwo, 1964. Pp. 132. zl. 10.—
Rev. by Karl Konrad Polheim in *Germanistik,* VI (1965), 464.

Menze, Clemens. *Der Bildungsbegriff des jungen Friedrich Schlegel.* Ratingen: Henn, 1964. Pp. 37. DM 5.80.
Rev. by K. K. Polheim in *Germanistik,* VI (1965), 465.

Oppenberg, Ursala. *Quellenstudien zu Friedrich Schlegels Übersetzungen aus dem Sanskrit.* (Marburger Beiträge zur Germanistik Bd. 7.) Marburg: N. G. Elwert Verlag, 1965. Pp. 135. DM 18.—

Rasch, Wolfdietrich, ed. *Kritische Schriften.* 2nd ed. München: Hanser, 1964. Pp. 710, DM 28.00.
Rev. by L. Uhlig in *Germanistik*, VI (1965), 470.
This edition is valuable since Schlegel's early writings are emphasized. These have not yet appeared in the critical Schlegel edition. Welcome inclusions not found in the first edition are: "Ueber das Studium der griechischen Poesie" in its entirety, and additional "Rezensionen." (B.M.)

Rychner, Max. *Zwischen Mitte und Rand. Aufsätze zur Literatur.* Zürich: Manesse, 1964. Pp. 253. sfr. 14.—
Rev. by Joachim Müller in *Germanistik*, VI (1965), 422.
Has a short impressive essay concerning Friedrich Schlegel's pioneer effort in comparative literature. (B.M.)

Schanze, Helmut. "Shakespeare-Kritik bei Friedrich Schlegel." *GRM*, XV (1965), 40-50.
Schanze traces the development of Schlegel's Shakespeare concept from a subjective identification with Hamlet to objective attempt to plumb artistic laws in dramas such as *Romeo and Juliet, Love's Labor's Lost, Much Ado about Nothing.* Schlegel termed these "Novellen." (B.M.)

Schlegel, Friedrich. *Lucinde.* Friedrich Schleiermacher. *Vertraute Briefe über Friedrich Schlegels 'Lucinde.'* Frankfurt a.M.: Insel, 1964. Pp. 165. DM 4.50.
Rev. by K. K. Polheim in *Germanistik*, VI (1965), 470-71.

Slessarev, Helga. "Die Ironie in Friedrich Schlegels 'Idylle über den Müssigang'." *GQ*, XXXVIII (1965), 286-97.

Starr, Doris. *Über den Begriff des Symbols in der deutschen Klassik und Romantik unter besonderer Berücksichtigung von Friedrich Schlegel.* Reutlingen: Hutzler, 1964. Pp. 103. DM 10.—
Rev. by K. K. Polheim, *Germanistik*, VI (1965), 471.

See also Jensen ("French. Eckstein"); Bausch, Eichner, Fassmann, Jensen, Szondi ("German 2. General"); Negus ("Hoffmann").

TIECK

Grümbaum, Anita. *Von Tiecks Sommernachttraum-Inszenierung zur ersten Aufführung in Stockholm.* Kleine Schriften der Gesellschaft für Theatergeschichte. Berlin: Selbstverlag der Ges. für Theatergeschichte, 1964. Pp. 68.

Sammons, Jeffrey L. "Tieck's 'Franz Sternbald': The Loss of Thematic Control." *SIR*, V (1965), 30-43.
Sammons contends that Tieck's novel is unfinished because he failed to retain a forming principle in the second part of *Sternbald* as new aspects were added. (B.M.)

Scheibe, Friedrich Carl. "Aspekte des Zeitproblems in Tiecks früh-romantischer Dichtung." *GRM*, xv (1965), 50-63.

Goes beyond the concept of "Langeweile" as the cause of lack of fulfillment in *William Lovell*, as proposed by Staiger and Gottrau. Contends that the passage of time is an actual menace to Lovell. In *Der Blonde Eckbert* time loses orientation, is neutralized. 'Waldeinsamkeit' in the first form reflects an eternal present. In the second version transitoriness is emphasized. (B.M.)

See also Börsch-Supan, Fassmann, Thalmann ("German 2. General").

Review of book previously listed:

PESTALOZZI, K., ed., *Ludwig Tieck: Die verkehrte Welt* . . . (see *ELN*, III, Supp., 120), rev. by C. Jauslin, *Germanistik*, VI (1965), 118-19.

UHLAND

Eberle, Josef. *Ludwig Uhland. Festvortag zu seinem hundertsten Todestag bei der Immatrikulationsfeier der Universität Tübingen ar 29.* November 1962. Tübingen: Mohr, 1963. Pp. 25.

Rev. by Joachim Müller in *Germanistik*, VI (1965), 329.

VARNHAGEN

Glander, Philip. *The Letters of Varnhagen von Ense to Richard Monckton Milnes.* (Anglistische Forschungen, Heft 92.) Heidelberg: Carl Winter, 1965. Pp. 34.

WACKENRODER

Kohlschmidt, Werner. "Wackenroder und die Klassik. Versuch einer Präzisierung." Pp. 83-92 in *Dichter, Tradition und Zeitgeist. Gesammelte Studien zur Literaturgeschichte.* Bern und München: Francke, 1965. Pp. 390. DM 42.50.

See also Fassmann, Rehm ("German 2. General").

WERNER

Guinet, Louis. *De lafranc-maçonnerie mystique au sacerdoce ou La vie romantique de Friedrich-Ludwig-Zacharais Werner (1768-1823).* (Publications de la Faculté des Lettres et Sciences Humaines de l'Université de Caen.) Caen: Association des Publications de la Faculté des Lettres et Sciences Humaines de l'Université de Caen, 1964. Pp. 246. Br. F. 20.00.

Reviews of book previously listed:

KOZIELEK, G., *Friedrich Ludwig Zacharias Werner. Sein Weg zur Romantik* (see *ELN*, III, Supp., 122), rev. by J. B. Neveux in *RLC*, XXXIX (1965), 168-71, by R. Ayrault in *EG*, XX (1965), 75, and by H. Moenkemeyer in *JEGP*, LXIV (1965), 555-58.

ITALIAN

(By Olga Ragusa, Columbia University, and William T. Starr, Northwestern University).

1. BIBLIOGRAPHY

Goffis, Cesare Federico. "Rassegna bibliografica. Primo ottocento." *RLI*, LXIX (1965), 466-76.

2. GENERAL

Abbundo, Vinicio. "Una storia della storiografia del Risorgimento." *Conv*, XXXIII (1965), 193-205.
Apropos W. Maturi, *Interpretazione del Risorgimento, Lezioni di storia della storiografia*, Torino, 1962.

Maiolo Molinari, Olga. "I giornali politici romani del periodo napoleonico." *Palatino*, VIII (1964), 221-28.

Piromalli, Antonio. "I Romantici e la polemica contro L'Arcadia." *Ausonia*, XVIII, No. 5-6 (1963), 10-21.

Puppo, Mario. *Poetica e cultura del Romanticismo*. Roma: Canesi editore, 1962. Pp. 314.
Rev. by Alfredo Schiaffini, in *GSLI*, CXXXIX (1962), 624-26.
The essays in the collection were previously unpublished, or have been considerably revised. The first, and longest discusses the poetry of the Romantics from Foscolo to De Sanctis, emphasizes various fundamental themes that appear in Foscolo, Manzoni, Leopardi, and De Sanctis. The central theme is the relation of art to reality. Others are: the Hellenism of the Romantics, aspects of Scalvini's criticism, the formation of the Leopardian concept of lyricism, Manzoni's sense of tragedy, the two redactions of the "Storia della colonna infame," Foscolo in his letters, and the historical novels of Tommaseo.

Stoli Legnani, Emilio. "Il pranzo dell'Ildegonda offerto da T. Grossi agli amici della 'Cameretta'." *Archivo storico Lombardo*, LXXXVIII (1963), 302-09.
While editing a poem of G. B. De Cristoforis in praise of the *Ildegonda*, the author brings to life a curious episode of early milanese Romanticism: the dinner at which were present Manzoni, Porta, Visconti, Berchet and others. The author includes other anecdotes from Manzoni's life.

Review of book previously listed:
RUSSI, Antonio, *Poesia e realtà* (see *PQ*, XLIII, 504), rev. by Olga Ragusa in *RR*, LV (1964), 232-34.

3. STUDIES OF AUTHORS

BELLI

Ansaldi, Giulio R. "La mostra del Belli." *Palatino*, VIII (1964), 87-91.
Principally concerning the importance of the exposition and the errors of the catalogue.

116

Cagli, Bruno, ed. *Tutti i sonetti romaneschi compresi i sonetti rifiutati, gli abbozzi e le note dell'autore.* Vol. 1. Roma: Avanzina e Torracca editori, 1964. Pp. 487.
Rev. by Francesco Biondolillo in *FLe*, XL (March 14, 1965), 5.
First volume of a new edition of Belli's sonnets; the purpose of the edition is to satisfy the most demanding reader. Integral reproduction of all the sonnets, including those rejected, the sketches and notes of the author.

De Cesare, Raffaele. "Il *Balzac* di Belli." *Aevum,* XXXVIII (1964), 194-201.

De Michelis, Eurialo. "Postille al convegno di studi belliani." *Palatino,* VIII (1964), 9-12.
De Michelis situates Belli's sonnets in the realistic-burlesque-plebeian tradition. He reacts against the thesis (pedestrian-Biedermeier) of Praz, which seems to him to limit Belli's poetry.

Felici, Lucio. "Gli appunti in dialetto romanesco di G. G. Belli." *RLI,* LXIX (1965), 354-68.

Orioli, Giovanni. "G. G. Belli e Roma ai suoi giorni (a proposito di una mostra)." *NA,* CDXCIV (1964), 243-54.

Orioli, Giovanni, ed. *Poesie e prose.* Bologna: Cappelli, 1964. Pp. xviii + 179.
Rev. in *FLe*, XL (Jan. 24, 1965), 4.

Orioli, Giovanni. "Belli e i suoi critici." *Studi romani,* X (1962), 549-61.

Pallotino, L., and R. Vighi. *G. G. Belli (1791-1863): Miscellanea per il centenario.* Roma: Ediz. "Palatino," 1963. Pp. 146.

Verdone, Mario. "Sulla 'teatralità' del Belli (a proposito della 'Manfrina')." *Palatino,* VIII (1964), 244-45.

Vighi, Roberto. "Il 'capitolo' romanesco del Belli." *Arcadia.* Accademia Letteraria Italiana. Atti e memorie. Serie 3ª, Vol. IV, fasc. 3ª (1964), 45-71.

Vighi, Roberto. "L'inedito 'Capitolo dei mangioni' di G. G. Belli." *Studi romani,* XII (1964), 425-43.

Vighi, Roberto, ed. *La plebe di Roma: Tutti i sonnetti romaneschi di Giuseppe Gioacchino Belli.* Vol. II. Firenze: G. C. Sansoni, 1964. Pp. 540.

Reviews of books previously listed:
ORIOLI, Giovanni, ed., *Lettre Giornali Zibaldone* (see *PQ,* XLIII, 505), rev. Lucio Felici in *NA,* CDXCIII (1963), 395-99; VIGOLO, Giorgio, *Il genio del Belli* (see *ELN,* III, Supp., 124), rev. by Antonio Piromalli in *NA,* CDXCIV (1964), 250-52.

BERCHET
See Stoli Legnani ("Italian 2. General").

Review of book previously listed:
BERCHET, Giovanni, *Lettere alla marchesa Costanza Arconati* (see *PQ*, XLIII, 505), rev. by Mario Scotti in *GSLI*, CXLII (1965), 137-47.

CATTANEO

Portinari, Folco. "Notizie sullo stile di Carlo Cattaneo." *LI*, XVII (1965), 35-57.

DE SANCTIS

Antonetti, Pierre. "La grammaire et la langue dans la pensée du jeune Francesco de Sanctis." *Annales de la Faculté des Lettres d'Aix* XXXVIII (1964), 173-94.

Consoli, Domenico. "Gli studi sul Romanticismo dopo il De Sanctis." *C&S*, III, N. 11 (1964), 33-43.

De Sanctis, Francesco. *Epistolario (1856-1858) e (1859-1860)* Torino: Einaudi, 1965, 2 vols.

Gifuni, G. B. "Francesco De Sanctis. Letter inedite ad un suo capoelettore: Vincenzo Gervasio." *Rivista di studi crociani*, I (1964), 98-107; 230-47; 364-76.

Landucci, Sergio. "A proposito del De Sanctis politico (Interpretazioni od errori?)." *Belfagor*, XX (1965), 215-26.
An answer to Mirri's criticism of Landucci's *Cultura e ideologia in F. De Sanctis* (Milano, 1964).

Landucci, Sergio. *Cutura e ideologia in Francesco De Sanctis*. Milan: Feltrinelli, 1964. Pp. 512.
Rev. by Claudio Cesa in *Belfagor*, XX (1965), 491-96; by Gian Carlo Giardina in *Conv*, XXXIII (1965), 427-29; by Guido Macera in *Fle*, XIX (Dec. 13, 1964), 5; by Alda Croce in *GSLI*, CXLI (1964), 619-30.

Savarese, Gennaro. "Le 'Considerazioni al Tasso' del Galilei nell'opera di F. De Sanctis." *RLI*, LXIX (1965), 92-111.

See also Puppo ("Italian 2. General").

Review of book previously listed:
CROCE, Elena and Alda, *De Sanctis* (see *ELN*, III, Supp., 125), rev. by Guido Macera in *FLe*, XIX (Dec. 13, 1964), 5.

DI BREME

Review of book previously listed:
DI BREME, *Il romitorio di Sant'Ida* (see *PQ*, XLIII, 506), rev. by Anne Paolucci in *Italica*, XL (1963), 188-92.

FOSCOLO

Antognoni, Oreste, ed. *Liriche scelte, i Sepolcri e le Grazie*. Col commento di Severino Ferrari. 2ª ed. riveduta, corr. e accresciuta. Nuova presentazione di Sergio Romagnoli. Firenze: Sansoni, 1964. Pp. xviii + xvi + 186.

Bianchi, Enrico, ed. *Prose.* Firenze: Salani, 1965. 2 vols. Pp. 645 + 634.

Based on the established text of the National Edition. Contains: *Jacopo Ortis, Viaggio sentimentale,* the Lyons oration, *Della servitù d'Italia, Le donne italiane, Letteratura apologetica,* the Pavia lectures, *Saggi sopra il Petrarca, Discorso storico sul testo del Decamerone,* and the essays on the Italian language and on narrative poems.

Conti, Mario Rosario. "Ugo Foscolo. L'uomo e il poeta." *Iniziativa,* XII, No. 4 (1963), 25-33.

Donadoni, Eugenio. *Ugo Foscolo, pensatore, critico, poeta,* Saggio. 3ª edizione riveduta con un' appesdice critico-bibliografica di Riccardo Scrivano. Firenze: R. Sandron, 1964. Pp. 450.

Fasano, Pino. "L'amicizia Foscolo-Sterne e la traduzione didimea del "Sentimental Journey." *English Miscellany* XIV (1963), 115-69.

This is a thoughtful assessment of the relation of Sterne's work to Foscolo. The author points out the gross critical error of V. Rossi, who invented the "*Proto-Ortis*"; he also reconstructs the various strata of the translation, considered in the light of Foscolo's theory of translation. This is obviously part of a future, more extensive work, in which some of the weaknesses will doubtless be corrected, for example, references to unimportant articles and critics, and the omission of certain important studies. (W.T.S.)

Gambarin, Giovanni. "L'edizione foscoliana del Carrer." *GSLI,* LXXXII (1965), 71-87.

Carrer's edition (*Prose e poesie edite e inedite di Ugo Foscolo,* Venezia, coi tipi del Gondoliere, 1842) occupies a central position in Foscolo criticism. Gambarin has made an important contribution to the history of its composition and publication by examining the Carrer manuscripts at the Museo Civico Correr in Venice. The role played by Giuseppe Guarnieri of Lodi in the preservation and interpretation of Foscolo materials is here brought to light for the first time. Of interest also are the details of Mazzini's abortive collaboration, and the censorship difficulties encountered. (O.R.)

Gambarin, Giovanni, ed. *Prose politische e apologetiche (1817-1827).* (Edizione Nazionale delle *Opere,* XIII.) Firenze: Le Monnier, 1964. Pp. cxxv + 593 + 262.

Rev. by Mario Scotti in *GSLI,* CXLII (1965), 296-310.

The first is a group of three essays, under the collective title supplied by Gambarin "Come far abrogare e modificare la costituzione delle Isole Jonie," which comprise the essays in praise of liberty of the Ionic Islands and the relationship that should be created between the protector nation and the protectorate; the "Mémoire sur l'éducation publique aux Iles Ioniennes," which the Florentine editors attributed to Lord Guilford; and an essay previously published by Viglione among the fragments concerning the History of Parga. A second group of two essays concerns the misfortune of Parga; one had appeared in the *Edinburgh Review,* October, 1819. The article was drastically revised by previous editors, and the confrontation here with the first proofs show what happened to some of Foscolo's writings.

Included in the two volumes is the *Lettera apologetica,* a defense of the political and literary works of Foscolo, written before his exile. (W.T.S.)

Kroeber, Karl. *The Artifice of Reality: Poetic Style in Wordsworth, Foscolo, Keats, and Leopardi.* University of Wisconsin Press, 1964. Pp. 272.

Listed and reviewed last year (see *ELN*, III, Supp., 9) without cross-reference to Foscolo or Leopardi.

Loggia, Giuseppc. *La genesi dello spirito intellettivo e l'anima cosmica, loro processo e fine. La tetrade issia il divenire, dolore, amore e morte. Il dieci novembre, con dedica a F. Lausa e critica ai Sepolcri di Ugo Foscolo.* Roma: Ed. Ricerche, 1963. Pp. 749.

Marotta, Sante. *Nuovo studio sulle "Grazie" di Ugo Foscolo.* Padova: Cedam, 1963. Pp. 80.
Reviewed by Pino Da Prati in *Humanitas,* XX (1965), 125-26.
This is a subtle and constructive analysis of the "Grazie" which appears to be inspired by the critical method and criteria of Armand Caraccio; the author takes into account various other recent studies. (W.T.S.)

May, Frederick. "Mary Wollstonecraft Shelley e il sonetto autoritratto del Foscolo." *GSLI,* CXLI (1964), 390-93.

Moullás, Panachiotis. "Tre lettre inedite di Ugo Foscolo (1826, 1827)." *O* Ερανιστες, Athens, I (1963), 225-34.
Three letters to Andrea Luriotis, from the Luriotis archives, which contain notes about painful parts of Foscolo's life.

Navarria, Aurelio. "La genesi dei *Sepolcri,*" *L'Osservatore politico-letterario,* IX (1963), 78-84.
It is partly true that Foscolo's writings on mythology and Greek culture constitute a sort of Genius of Hellenism, in opposition to Chateaubriand, but the "Sepolcri" is not just an occasional poem.

Provenzal, Dino. "Caratteri dei *Sepolcri.*" *NA,* CDXC (1964), 187-214.
A sound and complete linguistic and stylistic analysis, including a partial vocabulary count with emphasis on some key words found also in the sonnet "Alla sera" and word groups classified around themes.

Radcliff-Umstead, Douglas. "Foscolo and the Early Italian Romantics." *Italica,* XLII (1965), 231-46.

Raya, Gino. "Al Digamma Cottage." *NA,* CDXCIII (1965), 378-81.
Imaginary sketch of an evening at Foscolo's London home.

Scotti, Mario. 'Il 'De Sepulchris Hebraeorum' di Johann Nicolai e i 'Sepolcri' del Foscolo." *GSLI,* CXLI (1964), 492-547.

Zoric, Mate. "Due note su Ugo Foscolo e la Dalmazia." *Studia Romanica et Anglica Zagrebiensia,* 15-16 (1963), 151-183.

See also Massano ("General 3. Criticism"); Zall ("English. Wordsworth"); Puppo ("Italian 2. General").

Review of book previously listed:
FUBINI, Mario, *Ugo Foscolo* (see *PQ,* XLII, 508), rev. by Aldo Vallone in *Italia Che Scrive,* XLVII (1964), 52.

LEOPARDI
Basile, Carlo. *Una giornata con Leopardi* (A che serve un poeta). Milano: Cavallotti, 1965. Pp. 285.

Bataillon, M. "Sicut passer solitarius . . . Sur un thème de Leopardi."
Pp. 535-40 in *Studi in onore di Carlo Pellegrini.* (Biblioteca di Studi
Francesi, No. 2.) Torino: Società Editrice Internazionale, 1963. Pp.
xxxix + 846.
The story of *De passere et ape* from the *Speculum sapientiae* of the pseudo
Saint Cyril is proposed as a source of Leopardi's poem.

Biral, Bruno. "Il sentimento del tempo: Leopardi, Baudelaire, Mon-
tale." *Il Ponte,* xxi (1965), 1156-76.
Biral studies the sentiment of the irrevocable, destructive nature of time, a
basic sentiment in Leopardi, and the absolute nothingness, "come non nate" to
which all material things succumb.

Blasucci, Luigi. "Su una lettera 'insincera' di Giacomo Leopardi. *GSLI,*
cxlii (1965), 88-96.
A reading, in context, of Leopardi's August 3, 1825 letter to Karl De Bunsen,
Prussian Chargé d'Affaires to the Vatican. The accusation of "insincerity" is
shown to be unfounded.

Diamantini, Alessandro. "Giacomo Leopardi e un progetto di lettera
a un giovane del ventesimo secolo." *RLI,* lxviii (1964), 379-81.

Forti, Marco. "L'eredità di Leopardi." *Letteratura,* xxviii, Nos. 69-71
(1964), 91-96.

Frattini Alberto. "Un decennio di studi sul Leopardi (1953-1963)."
C&S, iii, Nos. 11, 12 (1964), 29-32; 20-26.
Some mention also of unusually important publications before 1953.

Frattoni, Oreste. "Descrizioni leopardiane." *Italica,* xlii (1965), 247-
64.

Getto, Giovanni. "Poesia e letteratura nelle *Operette morali.*" *LI,* xvii
(1965), 299-332.

Marletta, Paolo. *Leopardi a Firenze e a Napoli.* Bari: Ediz. del "Centro
librario," 1964. Pp. 47.
Appropriate references to Gelli's writings, whose ideal of "umanità" was not
without influence in the *Operette.* Also interesting, but bitter, the references of
certain misanthropic *Pensieri* to Florentine friends of Leopardi, from whom
he was becoming estranged because of his pessimism. The satire of the *Nuovi
credenti* is directed against the Neapolitan writers. (W.T.S.)

Pichini, Giacomo. "Il pessimismo nella scienza e G. Leopardi." Pp. 7-
47 in Pichini. *Scritti di carattere letterario ed artistico.* Parma: "La
Nazionale," 1964.
This essay (1898-1899) constitutes the reaction of a scientific attitude towards
the excesses of positivism and towards the attitudes of such anthropologists as
Patrizi. Pichini recognizes in Leopardi traces of the ideas of Lavoisier, Helm-
holz, Mayer, Kant, and even some anticipations of Darwin.

Timpanaro, Sebastiano. "Alcune osservazioni sul pensiero di Leopardi."
Critica storica, iii (1964), 397-431.

Examines the latest studies of Leopardi's thought and the perspectives opened by Binni and Luporini. Timpanaro urges a more careful study of Leopardi's pessimism in its cultural ambience, stresses the influence of Giordano upon his philosophy, and insists on his anti-romanticism. He concludes that the poet's pessimism has a permanent and enduring value, which the acquisition of the new theoretical instrument of dialectic logic would not have overcome. (W.T.S.)

See also Singh ("General 3. Criticism"); Puppo ("Italian 2. General"); Kroeber ("Foscolo").

Reviews of books previously listed:
CECCHETTI, Giovanni, *Leopardi e Verga* (see *PQ*, XLII, 509), rev. by Thomas G. Bergin in *Italica*, XL (1963), 376-78; *Leopardi e il Settecento* (see *ELN*, III, Supp., 128), rev. in *TLS*, Feb. 11, 1965, p. 109; SINGH, G., *Leopardi and the Theory of Poetry* (see *ELN*, III, Supp., 129), rev. in *TLS*, Feb. 11, 1965, p. 109, and by Sergio Antonielli in *GSLI*, CXLII (1965), 310-11; TORTORETO, Alessandro, ed., *Bibliografia analitica leopardiana* (see *PQ*, XLIII, 510), rev. by J. G. Fucilla in *Italica*, XL (1963), 374-75.

MANZONI

Alberti, Guglielmo. *Alessandro Manzoni: Introduzione allo studio della sua vita e delle sue opere.* Milano: Garzanti, 1964. Pp. 300.
The interest of this volume, part of a series "Saper tutto," lies principally in the presentation of Manzoni's personality, and in the reading of *I Promessi Sposi*. The penetration of the author's remarks, his point of view as a very democratic Catholic, give this volume a value far above the average work of popularisation. (W.T.S.)

Angelini, Cesare. "Sulla satira." *FLe*, XL (June 27, 1965), 6.

Arbasino, Alberto. "L'Ingegnere e il Manzoni." *Il Verri*, No. 17 (1965), 58-62.
Arbasino points out, among other opinions expressed by Carlo Emilio Gadda, the contention that *I Promessi Sposi* is not a novel of Catholic propaganda, and that it must be interpreted in the light of the author's period. (W.T.S.)

Barbi, Michele. "Note postume sui 'Promessi Sposi.' VII." *Rendiconti dell'Istituto Lombardo.* Classe di Letterature e Scienze morali e storiche XCVIII (1964), 249-60.

Bernardini Marzolla, Ugo. "La cavalleria nel '500 e '600 e gli spunti nei *Promessi sposi* di A. Manzoni." *RLI*, LXIX (1965), 588-617.
An interpretation of the three anti-chivalric episodes in the novel, as a satire on the content and style of the manuals in use in the seventeenth century.

Bezzola, Guido. "Per il testo dell'ode manzoniana 'Qual su le Cinzie cime'." *GSLI*, CXLI (1964), 514-85.
Examines four MSS to constitute the text, discusses Ghisalberti's and Sanesi's conclusions, and gives the authority to the MS Braidense.

Bianchi, Dante. "Il Manzoni alla ricerca dell'assoluto. Svolgimento circolare del suo pensiero da Dio a Dio." *Rendiconti dell'Istituto Lombardo.* Classe di Lettere e Scienze morali e storiche, XCVII (1963), 68-92.
Bianchi finds in Manzoni's activities an ascending circular development towards absolute truth. Starting from the *Carme*, he studies the correctives furnished

by Enrichetta Blondel. From the point of view of religion he examines the letter to Chauvet, and the dialogue *Dell'Invenzione.*

Biral, Bruno. *Pantasecca su don Abbondio.* Venezia: Stamperia di Venezia, 1964. Pp. 35.

This study of don Abbondio's character is one of a series of modern studies in reaction against Pancrazi's position, who limited the character to an expression of simple fear. Biral studies the dynamics of don Abbondio, and insists on the diverse ways in which the author's moral judgments are presented. He seems to react excessively, however, when he sees the priest as shown solely as a product of his society. (W.T.S.)

Bollati, Giulio, ed. *Tragedie.* Torino: Einaudi, 1965. Pp. xxxvi + 382.

Besides the texts of the two tragedies, Bollati publishes in an Appendix the letters of 1845, the complete Preface and the "Notizie storiche" of *Carmagnola* (but not the "Notizie storiche" of *Adelchi*), a group of letters of the period from the announcement of the publication of *Carmagnola* to the abandonment of the presentation of the tragedy at Florence, the notes for *Spartaco,* and the letters to M. Chauvet—all the essentials for understanding Manzoni's plays. According to Bollati, the psychological drama precedes the religious solution; it is the projection of the conscience towards action that is paralyzing; hence the tragedies represent a moment of impossibility of action.

Cambon, Glauco. "Manzoni: il poeta come testimone corale." *Italica,* XLII (1965), 239-47.

Camurri, Antonio. "Motivi musicali nei 'Promessi sposi'." *Idea,* XIX (1963), 626-30.

Caretti, Lanfranco. *Dante, Manzoni e altri studi.* Milano-Napoli: Ricciardi, 1964. Pp. 180.

Casella, Giuseppe. "La gioia di Renzo." *LI,* XVII (1965), 19-34.

Following a suggestion made by Giovanni Getto in his *Letture manzoniane* (Firenze, Sansoni, 1964), Casella analyzes further Manzoni's avoidance of the formula of the love story and the sentimental novel by showing how he consistently plays down the expression of happiness, be it material or spiritual. (O.R.)

De Castris, A. Leone, ed. *Tutte le poesie.* Firenze: Sansoni, 1965. Pp. 663.

An excellent introduction traces Manzoni's development up to *I promessi sposi.* Useful explanatory notes. (O.R.)

De Michelis, Eurialo. "Poesia e morale in Padre Cristoforo." *NA,* CDXCV (1965), 313-34.

A reading of Chapter IV of *I promessi sposi,* which points out parallels between the portrait of Cristoforo and of Federigo (in Chapter XXII) and disputes the current interpretation of the forgiveness scene as a mannerist sketch: it should be understood, instead, as the culmination of the chapter, an important moment in the respresentation of the "ineffabile etico-religioso" in the novel. (O.R.)

De Michelis, Eurialo. *"I Promessi Sposi* come sacra rappresentazione." *NA,* CDXCI (1964), 69-90.

An analysis of Chapter XX, the first of seven chapters that underline the miracle play quality of the novel by opposing good and evil in the meeting first of

Lucia and the Innominato, then of the Innominato and Federigo, and finally of Federigo and Don Abbondio. A forceful reconstruction of the motifs of the Innominato's "conversion." (O.R.)

Di Benedetto, Virgilio. "Nota manzoniana." Pp. 57-65 in Di Benedetto. *Antica prosa italiana ed altri studi.* Napoli: Istituto della stampa, 1963.
Discusses the similarities between the shipwreck and the end of the novel, and refuses to accept the interpretation that there is a distinction between the moments before and after the shipwreck. He refutes those who describe the end of the novel as "languid."

Francia, Ennio. "I personaggi difficili del Manzoni." *NA*, CDXCIII (1965), 187-96.
The characters are Federigo, the Innominato, and Don Abbondio. But aside from this grouping, there is nothing particularly original in the essay. (O.R.)

Getto, Giovani. "I capitoli 'francesi' de *I Promessi Sposi*." Pp. 559-608 in *Studi in onore di Carlo Pellegrini*. (Biblioteca di Studi Francesi, No. 2.) Torino: Società Editrice Internazionale, 1963. Pp. xxxix + 846.
Important contribution to a study of the possible French sources of the episode of the Monaca di Monza. (O.R.)

Ghisalberti, Fausto, ed. *Opere morali e filosofiche*. Milano: Mondadori, 1963. Pp. xvi + 952.
Rev. by Luigi Blasucci in *GSLI*, CXLI (1964), 458-61.

Goudet, Jacques. "La Genèse de l'Adelgise de Manzoni—à propos d'un livre récent." *REI*, X (1964), 240-72.
Goudet argues against two points in Aurelia Accame Bobbio's thesis in her *Storia dell'Adelchi* (Firenze, Le Monnier, 1963): her view of the central importance of a "politics of integration" in *Adelchi*, and her interpretation of Adelchi as a hero of action rather than a melancholy dreamer. Both concepts are the result of a twentieth century reading of *Adelchi*, a misinterpretation of Manzoni's thought. Goudet offers his own explanation of the genesis of the drama and suggests reasons for Manzoni's expression of dissatisfaction with the historical sources on which it is based. Pp. 264-72 contribute to a better understanding of Manzoni's problematic view of the irreconcilability of poetry and history in works of the imagination. See esp. p. 267 for a brief exploration of the theory of knowledge which gave rise to this problem. (O.R.)

Isella, Dante, ed. *Postille al vocabolario della Crusca nell'edizione veronese*. Milano-Napoli, 1964.
Rev. by Fiorenzo Forti in *GSLI*, CXLII (1965), 130-37.

Lonardi, Gilberto. *L'esperienza stilistica del Manzoni tragico*. Firenze: Olschki Editore, 1965. Pp. xv + 156.

Lonardi, Gilberto. "Autodifese manzoniane." *LI*, XVII (1965), 205-208.
Two passages in *Adelchi* (III, 272-3 and 399-402), echoing Racine (*Andromaque*, IV, iv, 1245-8) and Tasso (*Gerus. lib.* XVI, 36), are cited as evidence of Manzoni's difficulty in freeing himself of the attraction of the "couleur romanesque" which in the *Lettre à M. Chauvet* and elsewhere he so strongly decries.

Macchia, G. "L'addio al Lago di Ginevra. Una nota su Manzoni e Rousseau." Pp. 347-50 in *Studi in onore di Carlo Pellegrini*. (Biblioteca di Studi Francesi, No. 2.) Torino: Società Editrice Internazionale, 1963. Pp. xxxix + 846.

Rousseau's letter to Prince Beloselski, 27 May 1775, is proposed as a new source of the "Addio monti."

Mazza, Antonia. "Coincidenze." *VeP*, XLVIII (1965), 6-13.

I Promessi Sposi and *Tom Jones*.

Mazza, Antonia. "Reminiscenze culturali e similitudini manzoniane." *Aevum*, XXXVIII (1964), 202-14.

Quotations and reminiscences, many of them classical, disseminated throughout the first version of *I Promessi sposi*, were frequently transformed into similes in the later version.

Merati, Augusto. "Trovato a Monza un documento relativo alla monacazione di Marianna de Leyva." *Archivo Storico Lombardo*, LXXXVIII (1963), 316-18.

The "cartula di professione" of sister Virginia Maria and of other nuns, among them two accomplices of hers (Sept. 12, 1591).

Monzini, Virginia. "La critica dei 'venticinque'." *Conv*, XXXIII (1965), 360-91.

An original view of the significance of the historical passages in *I promessi sposi* and of the part played by the invisible reader in revealing Manzoni's opinions. Many interesting suggestions that could be developed. The author's conclusion, however, is not stated with clarity. (O.R.)

Mor, Antonio. "A proposito di alcuni giudizi su A. Manzoni." *Studium*, LX (1964), 844-58.

Examines A. Moravia's preface to *I Promessi Sposi*, and the essay "Satira, poesia e rigorismo nei *Promessi sposi*" which appeared in Sommariva's *Incognite religiose della letteratura contemporanea* (1963). He finds both are valid, but that Manzoni really only serves them as an excuse for their own ideas and polemic.

Nava, Giuseppe. "C. E. Gadda lettore di Manzoni." *Belfagor*, XX (1965), 339-52.

Paladino, Vincenzo. *La revisione del romanzo manzoniano e le postille del Visconti*. (Saggi di letteratura italiana diretti da Umberto Bosco, XVI.) Firenze: Le Monnier, 1964. Pp. 157. 1,600 1.

Any study that sheds light on the transition from *Fermo e Lucia* to *I promessi sposi* is in itself important. The present work also reevaluates the contribution of Ermes Visconti to the definition of Romanticism, especially in relation to the role of history in the creation of "reality" (Chap. I). It is well known that at Manzoni's request Visconti read the manuscript of *Fermo e Lucia* and made numerous suggestions for revision. These annotations, which cover Book I, Chaps. 1-7, and Book II, Chap. 2 through Book III, Chap. 7, are divided and discussed by Paladino under three headings: comments regarding the conflict between the general Romantic desire to give complete historical documentation and the exigencies of good story-telling (Chap. II); comments that underline the intrusion of Manzoni's ethical lesson into the representation of characters who should have their own artistic "autonomy" in order to be convincing (Chap. III); and comments that seconded Manzoni in his search for a new narrative language (Chap. IV). It is interesting to note that Manzoni accepted about eighty percent of Visconti's strictures. Mr. Paladino did not escape the pitfall of identifying too closely with Visconti when the latter analyzes the faults of passages later revised or eliminated. This gives the impression of a one-sided discussion. The reader rarely hears Manzoni's voice, while Visconti's often high pitched and emotional, often trenchant and precise exclamations predominate. It seems to me that any reading of *I promessi sposi* that does not take as its point of departure a thorough understanding of Manzoni's Catholicism is bound to be out of focus. In the present case, this shortcoming becomes especially apparent in Paladino's discussion of the character of Gertrude's father (p. 52) and of that of Don Abbondio (p. 95): Paladino almost has Manzoni excuse the former by making him the prototype and the victim of a certain mentality and of the customs of his century; he turns the latter into an appealing kind of anti-hero whose weaknesses must be excused as the weaknesses of Everyman. This is definitely a misreading of Manzoni's intention. (O.R.)

Palanza, Ugo M. "Alessandro Manzoni e il nostro tempo," *Ausonia*, XX, No. 2 (1965), 37-41.

Paratore, Ettore. "Lettura del C. XXI dei 'Promessi Sposi'." *Arcadia*. Accademia Letteraria Italiana. Atti e memorie. Serie 3ª, Vol. IV, fasc. 3ª (1964), 1-28.

Pecci, Giuseppe. "Le illustrazioni dei *Promessi Sposi*." *NA*, CDXCIII (1965), 103-107.
Routine review of some of the illustrators.

Portier, Lucienne. "La Conversion d'Alessandro Manzoni et son refus de la mythologie." *REI*, X (1964), 92-100.
Neither religious scruples nor purely literary considerations (for both of which there is documentary evidence) are primarily responsible for Manzoni's rejection of mythology. As the example of Dante testifies, pagan mythology is not in itself contrary to Christian subject matter. With great sensitivity and perception Mme Portier points out that Manzoni abandoned mythology because it was not meaningful to him. As can be seen in his landscapes, which exist only through and in his characters, Manzoni's world is strictly human and factual. (O.R.)

Prodi, Paolo. "Nel IV Centenario della nascita di Federico Borromeo." *Conv*, XXXIII (1965), 337-59.
Etat présent of historical and biographical studies devoted to the Cardinal, important because the representation of Federigo has been a crucial point in the discussion of the role of history and art in *I promessi sposi*. (O.R.)

Ragusa, Olga. "Imitation and Originality in Manzoni's Romantic Theory." *Pel*, VI (1964), 219-28.

Russo, Luigi. *Personaggi dei "Promessi sposi."* Bari: Laterza, 1965. Pp. 378.
Rev. in *Belfagor*, XX 3 (1965), 379.
This work, originating in university lectures thirty years ago, was first published in 1945. It now incorporates recent critical work on *I Promessi Sposi*. It is perhaps somewhat polemical; it is meant as a refutation, of Crocean origin, of the realistic-psychological embodiment of poetic moments in specific characters; and it is a desire to pay homage to the authentic act of creation. Although the author discusses the oratorical quality of certain chapters, he goes beyond the dichotomy of poet and orator in the humanization of the perfect

image of peace and good in the person of Cardinal Federigo Borromeo. (W.T.S.)

Secchi, Claudio Cesare. "Introduzione alla lettura degli *Inni sacri.*" *Aevum,* XXXVIII (1964), 125-38.

Secchi attempts to relate the *Inni* to Manzoni's experiences as a father, "Il Natale" to the birth of his son Pietro, "Risurrezione" to the death of Luigia Maria Vittorina. Among other discussions, Secchi insists that Manzoni wished to sing of the eternity of the evangelical principles and tried to show that all the values in the Revolution derive from these principles. (W.T.S.)

Travi, Ernesto. "Tre studi manzoniani." *Vita e pensiero,* XLVIII, No. 1 (1965), 55-59.

Asserts the value of certain Italian critical works as expressions of the best Italian prose, especially the *Letture manzoniane* of Getto, *La lirica di A. Manzoni* of C. F. Goffis, and *Manzoni: un discorso che continua,* by M. Gorra. (W.T.S.)

Travi, Ernesto. "O. B. De Saussure: un capitolo delle letture romantiche di A Manzoni." *VI Congresso manzoniano.* Lecco: 1963. Pp. 24.

De Saussure's *Voyages dans les Alpes* as a source of Manzoni's style.

Travi, Ernesto. "La presenza della lirica barocca nel rinnovamento poetico e religioso manzoniano." *VI Congresso manzoniano.* Lecco: 1963. Pp. 12.

Manzoni's interest in baroque poetry revealed by a passage in *Fermo e Lucia.*

Ulivi, Ferruccio. "Le lettre di Manzoni," *Letteratura,* XXIX, Nos. 74-75 (1965), 3-20.

Comments, judgments, some corrections and criticisms concerning Petrocchi's study of Manzoni's *Epistolario* (in *Letteratura*), and on other of Manzoni's works, especially *I Promessi sposi,* with especial consideration of the religion and religious attitudes of the poet.

Ulivi, Ferruccio. " 'Natura caduta' e rappresentazione naturale in Manzoni." *Conv,* XXXII (1964), 584-603.

In the first part Ulivi takes issue with G. Bàrberi Squarotti ("La vigna di Renzo e l'*esempio* della natura caduta," *Cratilo,* I, No. 4, 1963) for postulating an opposition between "mondo umano" and "mondo della natura" in Manzoni. Ulivi cites the probable theological and philosophical sources on which Manzoni drew (especially Pierre Nicole's *Essais de morale*) and which maintain a providential order in both realms. The second part is of the greatest interest because it deals with the whole question of landscape description in 19th-century literature, drawing parallels to painting. Manzoni's procedure is described as differing from the typical Romantic fusion of landscape and feeling. Though in Manzoni there are subtle correlations between the natural and the historico-psychological worlds, his landscapes are never exclusively "landscapes of the mind" but always remain concrete and specific. (O.R.)

Varese, Claudio. *Fermo e Lucia: un'esperienza manzoniana interrotta.* Firenze: La Nuova Italia, 1964. Pp. 157. 1,500 1.

Rev. by Lucio Felici in *NA,* CDXCIV (1965), 547-49.

A seminal work, which for the first time examines the first version of *I promessi sposi* as an independent work and not as a preparatory draft. *Fermo e Lucia* is studied in relation to the *Osservazioni sulla morale cattolica* and the *Discorso su alcuni punti della storia longobardica in Italia* as reflecting Manzoni's intellectual interests between 1817 and 1822, a time when the ideals of the Enlightenment and the historiographical problems raised by Fauriel dominated his thinking. This new perspective leads to a new interpretation of some basic problems in Manzoni criticism: the reasons behind his portrayal of the error-ridden seventeenth century; his presentation of the position of the lower classes as historically conditioned and morally justified; the nature of his democratically oriented Catholicism. The difference between the first and final versions is studied in detail in a careful analysis of the principal characters, whose evolution is no longer attributed to the author's stylistic development but to a shift in his view of man and society. This shift is summarized by Varese as follows: while in *I promessi sposi* there is an opposition between the relative and the absolute (man's errors are contrasted with the truth of reason and faith), in *Fermo e Lucia* the opposition is between two historical periods (man's errors in the seventeenth century are contrasted with the triumph of reason in Manzoni's own times). The Appendix contains Varese's essay "Manzoni e la poetica dell'idillio" (*RLI*, 1961), which analyzes the progressive growth of the idyllic aspect of the novel. (O.R.)

Zanazzo, G. B. "Due matrimoni di sapore manzoniano." *Archivio Veneto*, LXXVI (1965), 25-33.
Documents relating to two "forced" marriages are cited in support of Manzoni's scrupulous adherence to historical reality.

See also Puppo, Stoli Legnani ("Italian 2. General").

Reviews of books previously listed:
ACCAME BOBBIO, Aurelia, *La formazione del linguaggio lirico manzoniano* (see *ELN*, III, Supp., 129), rev. by Cesare Federico Goffis in *RLI*, LXIX (1965), 187-88; DE MICHELIS, Eurialo, *Studi sul Manzoni* (see *PQ*, XLIII, 511), rev. by Jacques Goudet in *REI*, X (1964), 160-61; GETTO, Giovanni, *Letture manzoniane* (see *ELN*, III, Supp., 131), rev. by Olga Ragusa in *RR*, LVI (1965), 225-27; GOUDET, *Catholicisme et poésie dans . . .* I Promessi sposi (see *PQ*, XLIII, 512), rev. by Lionello Sozzi in *GSLI*, CXLI (1964), 141-42; ULIVI, Ferruccio, *Dal Manzoni ai decadenti* (see *ELN*, III, Supp., 132), rev. by Giorgio Bàrberi Squarotti in *LI*, XVII (1965), 364-67.

MONTI
Turri, Anna, ed. "Le carte del *Prometeo* montiano nel Museo della Storia dell'Università di Pavia." *Conv*, XXXIII (1965), 392-96.

PELLICO
Curto, Carlo, ed. *Opere scelte*. Torino: UTET, 1964. Pp. 788.
Thoroughly revised edition making use of newly published materials.

Fucilla, Joseph G. "A Group of Spielberg-Prison Poems by Silvio Pellico." *Annali dell'Istituto Universitario Orientale* (Sezione Romanza), VII (1965), 163-202.
A substantial group of virtually unknown poems, important as source material for *Le mie prigioni*.

PORTA
Guarisco, Carla, ed. *Le poesie*. Milano: Feltrinelli, 1964. 2 vols.
In the introduction to this popular, but well-prepared edition, the editor traces Porta's life and reviews critical opinion of various biographies. Porta's culture and his relationship to Romanticism are particularly well set forth. There is an informative bibliography. The text chosen is that of the Isella edition; it

includes "El lava piatt del Meneghin ch'è mort," and a generous selection of sketches and fragments. Translations have been made following modern philological principles. (W.T.S.)

TOMMASEO

Ciampini, Raffaele, ed. *Salmi e inni sacri tradotti.* Firenze: Sansoni, 1965. Pp. xlvii + 301.

Mattalia, Daniele, ed. *Fede e bellezza.* Milano: Rizzoli, 1963. Pp. 287.
The 1840 text is accompanied by diary pages written for the 1852 edition by the author's defense of his book, by Luigi Piel's letter on Tommaseo's view of France, by Cattaneo's famous review, and various excerpts from Tommaseo's diary and correspondence.

Percoraro, Marco, ed. *Memorie poetiche: Edizione del 1838 con appendice di poesie e redazione del 1858 intitolata "Educazione dell'ingegno."* (Scrittori d'Italia, N. 229). Bari: Laterza, 1964. Pp. 662.
Rev. by Armando Balduino, in *GSLI,* CXLII (1965), 149-58.

Puppo, Mario. "Edizioni del Tommaseo." *Studium,* LX (1965), 234-35.
Discusses editions of Tommaseo's works by Borlenghi, Mattulka, Verzara, and points out some recent significant studies.

See also Puppo ("Italian 2. General").

Review of book previously listed:
CIAMPINI, Raffaele, *L'Ultimo Tommaseo: La versione dei Vangeli* (see *ELN,* III, Supp., 134), rev. by Giovanni Gambarin in *GSLI,* LXXI, (1964), 461-63.

PORTUGUESE

(By Raymond Sayers, Queens College).

1. BIBLIOGRAPHY

Ribeiro Filho, J. S. *Dicionário biobibliográfico de escritores cariocas (1565-1965).* Rio: Livraria Brasiliana, 1965.

2. GENERAL

Cândido, Antônio, e José Aderaldo Castello, eds. *Presença da literatura brasileira: História e antologia.* S. Paulo: Difusão Europeia do Livro, 1963. 3 vols.
Though the selections are well chosen, the most valuable contributions of this book are found in the critical prefaces about the literary movements and the bibliographical and critical notes about the authors. Included among the selections are the preface to *Suspiros poéticos,* a scene from *Mãe,* and the prologue to *Inspirações do claustro.*

Castello, José Aderaldo. *Manifestações literárias da era colonial.* (Roteiro das Grandes Literaturas: A Literatura Brasileira, I.) S. Paulo: Cultrix, 1965. Pp. 256.
The lengthy chapter on "manifestações pre-românticas" begins with a terse analysis of the intellectual background from 1808 to 1836. The author empha-

sizes the anti-Portuguese sentiment of the time, which he believes contributed greatly to the achievement of literary independence by the next generation. His analysis of the periodicals of those years is especially succinct and valuable.

Cavalheiro, Edgard, ed. *O romantismo.* (Panorama da poesia brasileira, II.) Rio: Civilização Brasileira, 1959. Pp. xxxviii + 302.
A much larger volume than Bandeira's anthology of Romanticism. There are 25 poets in the latter and 50 in this book. There are fewer selections in this from the major poets but there are page-long critical prefaces for all. The inclusion of many minor poets makes possible a good picture of the Brazilian Romantic movement. The influence of the Portuguese Romantics and pre-Romantics becomes more evident. Some poets are included whose work is well-nigh inaccessible today; e.g., Otávio Hudson. The introduction is a good history of the development of Brazilian Romanticism.

Coelho, Jacinto do Prado, ed. *Poetas do romantismo.* Com introd. e notas. (Clássicos Portugueses.) Lisboa: Livraria Clássica, 1965. 2 vols. Pp. 94 & 86.
Since this selection omits Garrett, Herculano and Castilho, it is limited chiefly to the ultra-Romantics, plus Maria Browne. The 26 page introduction is characteristically provocative and thorough. A new point of view is found in Prado Coelho's challenge of the idea that Portuguese Romanticism began in 1825; he places the real beginning in 1837 and points out that foreign literary movements usually arrived late in Portugal. The intellectual and social ambiance is well described. A useful companion anthology to *Poetas pre-românticos,* mentioned in *PQ,* XLI (1962), 724.

Dias, Augusto da Costa. *Crise da consciência pequeno-burguesa. I. O nacionalismo literário da geração de 90.* 2.a ed. rev. Lisboa: Portugália, 1964. Pp. liii + 324.
The theme of this interesting book is that two different kinds of nationalism are represented in nineteenth century men of letters: that of Garrett, which is a nationalism *de facto,* and that of Alberto de Oliveira and the *neo-garrettianos,* which was its negation. Garrett's nationalism was founded upon his belief in personal liberty and equality, a position which he had inherited from the philosophers of the enlightenment. The social ideas of *neo-garrettismo,* on the other hand, were anachronistic and based upon the need for a stable society with feudal overtones. Cista Dias sees it as a doctrine fostered by the *petite bourgeoisie,* which by 1890 had lost its function in society. Unlike the liberals of Garrett's time, they had no Revolution to look forward to, and unlike Antero's generation, they could not espouse Proudhon. The result was an anti-intellectualism concealed by a cloak of nostalgia for the past which had important repercussions in Portugal at the time and in the subsequent movement of *saudosismo.*

Nascimento, Cabral do, ed. *Colectânea de versos portugueses do século XII ao século XX.* Com pref. Lisboa: Minerva 1965. Pp. 222.
Includes single poems by such minor Romantics and ultra-Romantics as Freire de Serpa, João de Lemos, Pereira da Canha, Rodrigues Cordeiro, Costa Pereira, Augusto Lima, and Alexandre Braga.

Rocha, Andrée Crabbé, ed. *A epistolografia em Portugal.* Com pref., introd., e notas. Coimbra: Livraria Almedina, 1965. Pp. 444.
An introductory essay on the art of letter writing, selections going from the Infante D. Pedro to Florbela Espanca preceded by critical studies which are usually of more interest than the letters themselves, some well selected bibliographical material, and an interesting *conclusão.* There are previously unpublished letters by the Marquesa de Alorna, Garrett, Herculano, and Camilo.

3. STUDIES OF AUTHORS

a) *Portuguese*

BOCAGE

Correia, Romeu. *Bocage.* (Colecção Vária.) Lisboa: Ulisséia, 1965.

Mourão-Ferreira, David. "O drama de Bocage." *Panorama,* No. 14 (1965), pp. 15-18.

Had Bocage lived fifty years later, he would have found among the Romantics the poetic stimuli and the passionate love—of an Ana Plácido, perhaps—that were denied him in eighteenth century Portugal.

CASTELO BRANCO

Anon. "Um inédito de Camilo." *Boletim da Casa de S. Miguel de Seide.* No. 1 (1964), p. 3.

Bessa, Joaquim C. Moura. "A sepultura de Camilo Castelo Branco." *Tripeiro,* IV (1964), 148-52.

Cerqueira, Eduardo. "Camilo e José Estêvão." *Arquivo do Distrito de Aveiro,* No. 114 (1963), pp. 81-93.

César, Amândio. *A casa assombrada de S. Miguel de Seide.* Vila Nova de Famalicão, Portugal: Câmara Municipal, 1964. Pp. 104.

Includes the diaries of José Augusto Pinto de Magalhães and Fanny Owen. In annotating them, Camilo—who was always fascinated by the story of the two lovers—employed a very suggestive phrase: "Estes documentos provam a que miséria *o romantismo* de há trinta anos podia levar dois desgraçados com o cérebro vazio e cabeça cheia de asneiras." The Emma Bovarys of real life were little different from their fictional sisters and brothers.

Coelho, Jacinto do Prado, ed. *Contos de Camilo Castelo Branco.* Com pref. e notas. (Textos Clássicos.) Lisboa: Verbo, 1963. Pp. 92.

Three short stories: the third part of *Coração, cabeça e estômago* and parts of two *Novelas do Minho.* In a few pages of the preface Prado Coelho, the leading Camilo critic, defines the esthetic values present in Camilo's works, insisting on the "realismo espontâneo, insuperável das suas melhores páginas," and points out that the vast vocabulary is made necessary by this rich, exact realism.

Ferreira, Joaquim. *Memórias de Camilo.* Porto: Domingos Barreira, 1965.

Gomes, Alberto F. *Nótulas camilianas.* Lisboa, 1965. Pp. 84.

Lawton, R. A. "Technique et signification dans *Amor de perdição.*" *Bulletin des Etudes Portguaises et de l'Institut Français au Portugal,* XXV (1964), 77-135.

Luís, Agustina Bessa. "Um pé dentro do mar, outro na aréia." *Tempo Moderno,* No. 15 (1964), pp. 93-105.

Peres, Gustavo D'Avila. As traduções do *Amor de perdicão.* Pref. Vitorino Nemésio. Lisboa: Portugália, 1965. Pp. 146.

Five translations into Spanish and one each into Italian, Swedish, Japanese and possibly Hebrew. The prefaces of these editions are reprinted, along with some critical opinions of Unamuno, Azorín and other critics. The title pages and some illustrations are reproduced. There is also a chapter containing some critical study of the first three editions. The third is the one that has formed the basis of later editions.

CASTILHO

Anon. "António Feliciano de Castilho." *LdP*, No. 70 (1965), pp. 7-10, 14.

Very complete bibliographical information.

GARRETT

Diégues Júnior, Manuel. "Um precursor do folclore: Almeida Garrett." *Revista Brasileira de Folclore*, v (1965), 143-48.

Garrett, the first great Portuguese folklorist, collected ballads and studied folklore in the hope of discovering the true Portuguese spirit. He said, "Nothing is natural that is not of the people." The article is a good appreciation of this aspect of Garrett's work.

Garrett, Almeida. *Frei Luís de Sousa*. Pref. Pedro Calmon. Porto: Tavares Martins.

Garrett, Almeida. *Obra política*. Introd. Augusto da Costa Dias. Lisboa: Portugália, 1965.

Articles from *O Patriota* and other papers of the twenties, including some published in London: *Chaveco Liberal, O Popular*, and *O Precursor*. Also articles that helped to prepare the way for the 1836 revolution, the complete parliamentary speeches, letters, memoirs and biographies.

HERCULANO

Jorge, Maria do Céu Saraiva. "Shakespeare e Alexandre Herculano." *Palestra*, No. 20 (1964), pp. 11-25.

Silva, Maria Beatriz Nizza da, ed. *Alexandre Herculano, o historiador*. Com. introd. (Nossos Clássicos, 76.) Rio: Agir, 1963.

b) *Brazilian*

Coutinho, Afrânio. *A polêmica Alencar-Nabuco*. Rio: Tempo Brasileiro, 1965.

ALENCAR

Doyle, Plínio. "Arquivo literário (No. 8): Centenário de *Iracema*. *Leitura*," Nos. 90-91 (1965), pp. 52-53.

Some contemporary appreciation of Alencar and a contemporary caricature.

Leite, Dante Moreira. *Psicologia e literatura*. (Coleção Textos e Documentos, 8.) S. Paulo: Conselho Estadual de Cultura, Commissão de Literatura, 1964. Pp. 264.

A pioneer book in Brazilian literary criticism. The author uses the psychological approach in studying the problems of creative thought, the literary text, and the reader. In his discussion of *Senhora* and *Luçíola* he states that Alencar's concept of personality as presented in these two books is surprisingly modern.

132

Martins, Heitor. "Byron e *O guarani.*" *Luso-Brazilian Review,* II (1965), 69-74.
Martins documents Alencar's undeniable acquaintance with Byron and points out similarities between *The Corsair* and *O guarani.* However, he does not convince one that Alencar was influenced by *The Corsair* when he wrote his novel. An equally good case for influence in character delineation and plot structure could easily be made for other Romantic works; *Ivanhoe,* for example.

Montenegro, Braga, ed. *Iracema: Lenda do Ceará.* Edição comemorativa do centenário. Com pref. e bibliog. das edições. Fortaleza: Imprensa Universitária do Ceará, 1965.
Postulating that Alencar was the most important Brazilian representative of Romanticism, Braga Montenegro says that he regards *Iracema* as his most romantic work, a *novel-poem* that stands apart in both quality and genre from his other writings.

Santiago, Silviano. "Alegoria e palavra em *Iracema.*" *Luso-Brazilian Review,* II (1965), 55-68.
A brief essay, rich in ideas, which would be an excellent introduction to an edition of *Iracema.* Santiago mentions several aspects of the book that merit further discussion, such as the botanical metaphors used to characterize the heroine and the symbolism of the names. Though Santiago explains that the book is allegorical, he does not defend it from those critics who disapprove of the characters as being unrealistic and vague.

ALMEIDA
Almeida, Manuel Antônio de. *Memórias de um sargento de milícas.* Introd. Antônio Olinto. Rio: Conquista, 1965.

ALVES
Azevedo, Vicente de Paulo. "Castro Alves em São Paulo." *Estado de São Paulo, Suplemento Literário* (1964), 7 Nov., p. 4; 14 Nov., p. 4; 28 Nov., p. 4; 5 Dez., p. 4; 12 Dez., p. 4; 19 Dez., p. 4.
Day by day account of the poet's life in S. Paulo, his affair with Eugênia, his accident and the treatment that he underwent. There are many quotations from letters and other documents.

Castello, José Aderaldo. *Método e interpretação.* (Coleção Ensaio, 39.) S. Paulo: Conselho Estadual de Cultura, Comissão de Literatura, 1965.
Essays on writers, including one on *Revisão de Castro Alves.*

BONIFACIO
Castello, José Aderaldo, ed. *José Bonifácio, o Velho: Poesia.* Com introd. (Nossos Clássicos, 78.) Rio: Agir, 1964.

Rodrigues, José Honório. "O pensamento político e social de José Bonifácio." *Cadernos Brasileiros,* VII (1965), 62-70.
Lamenting that there is no collected edition of José Bonifácio's works (one has apparently just appeared), José Honório says of the Patriarch's contribution to Brazilian political development that "nenhum brasileiro fez tanto em tão pouco tempo." He blames Varnhagen and other nineteenth century historians for the fact that José Bonifácio's reputation is not as high in Brazil as that of Washington in this country.

Toledo, Júlio Sauerbronn de. "José Bonifácio de Andrada e Silva: O maior dos brasileiros." *Kriterion,* XVI (1963) [1965], 223-53.

DIAS

Doyle, Plínio. "Homenagem a Gonçalves Dias." *Leitura,* Nos. 87-88 (1964), pp. 58-59.
Unpublished poem by the poet, sent to José de Alencar in memory of his father, who had just died, and an unpublished letter by the poet written in Lisbon in 1855 in acknowledgment of the receipt of two books.

Meireles, Mário. *Gonçalves Dias e Ana Amélia.* São Luís do Maranhão, 1964. Pp. 84.
A brief chronicle of Gonçalves Dias' emotional life after his meeting with Ana Amélia, based on his poems and letters. Most of the latter are from the Coleção Nogueira da Silva and the Coleção do Instituto Geográfico e Histórico Brasileiro, and many are apparently unpublished.

Merquior, José Guilherme. "O poema do *lá.*" *Cadernos Brasileiros,* VI (1964), vi, 54-60.
Merquior unweaves the rainbow of the "Canção do exílio" in an attempt to demonstrate that the secret of its beauty is the "obstinate unity of feeling that dominates it."

Montello, Josué. "A 'Canção do exílio': Poema indianista." *Comentário,* v (1964), 317-20.

GUIMARAES

Andrews, Norwood H., Jr. "Bernardo Guimarães and the Brazilian Novel of Transition." *Dissertation Abstracts,* XXV (1965), 4140-41.

PORTO-ALEGRE

Lyra, Heitor. "Manoel de Araújo Porto-Alegre: Consul Geral do Brasil em Lisboa de 1866-1879." *Palestra,* No. 23 (1964), pp. 16-22.

QUEIROGA

Eulálio, Alexandre. "João Salomé Queiroga: Folclorista." *Revista Brasileira de Folclore,* III (1963), 225-38.
Essay on Salomé Queiroga followed by a ballad and a short story printed in his *Canhenho* and in the newspaper *O Jequitinhonha.* Queiroga was a Romantic who wanted to produce a national literature based on Brazilian folklore. Though *Maricota e o Padre Chico* seems to most readers to be infra-infra-literature, Eulálio defends its value as an encyclopedia of customs and a repository of the nineteenth century vocabulary of Minas.

VARELA

Barros, Frederico Pessoa de. *Poesia e vida de Fagundes Varela.* S. Paulo: Editôra das Américas, 1965.
Biographical and critical study based on much original research and including much new material, as well as excerpts from hitherto unpublished documents.

SPANISH

(A two-year survey will appear in our next annual.)

English Language Notes

| Volume V | Supplement to No. 1 | September 1967 |

The Romantic Movement
A Selective and Critical Bibliography
for 1966

Edited by

DAVID V. ERDMAN

with the assistance of KENNETH NEGUS and JAMES S. PATTY

This bibliography, compiled by a joint bibliography committee for groups General Topics II and English IX of the Modern Language Association, is designed to cover a "movement" rather than a period. Thus, though the English section is largely limited to the years 1789-1837, other sections extend over different spans of years.

It is our intent to include, with descriptive and, at times, critical annotation, all books and articles of substantial interest to scholars of English and Continental Romanticism, and critical reviews of such books. We also make note of items of minor but scholarly interest, except those which are adequately listed in the Annual Bibliography of the Association (issued in the May number of *PMLA*). Major and controversial works are given what is intended to be judicious if necessarily very brief review.

The approximate length of a book is indicated by report of the number of pages—or the number of volumes when more than one.

A new feature this year is the inclusion of a small selection of studies in American literature which seem relevant to discussions of European Romanticism; supplied by Herbert L. Kleinfield, these are given in the "General" section.

The editorial committee gratefully acknowledges the help of its collaborators, whose names are given at the heads of the respective sections.

2034

To ensure notice in the next issue of the bibliography, authors and publishers are invited to send review copies of relevant books or monographs, and offprints of articles, to: David V. Erdman, Editor, Room 107, The New York Public Library, Fifth Ave. & 42nd St., New York, N.Y. 10018

CONTENTS

ABBREVIATIONS

AL	*American Literature*
AnB	*L'Année Balzacienne*
AnBret	*Annales de Bretagne*
ASch	*American Scholar*
AQ	*American Quarterly*
AUMLA	*Journal of the Australasian Universities Language and Literature Association*
BA	*Books Abroad*
BAGB	*Bulletin de l'Association Guillaume Budé*
BB	*Bulletin of Bibliography*
BC	*Book Collector*
BH	*Bulletin Hispanique*
BHS	*Bulletin of Hispanic Studies*
Biblio	*Bibliofilia*
BJA	*British Journal of Aesthetics (London)*
BLAM	*Bulletin de la Librarie Ancienne et Moderne*
BNYPL	*Bulletin of the New York Public Library*
BNL	*Burke Newsletter*
BRAE	*Boletín de la Real Academia Española*
BRAH	*Boletín de la Real Academia de la Historia*
BuR	*Bucknell Review*
CA	*Cuadarnos Americanos*
CAIEF	*Cahiers de l'Association internationale des études françaises*
C&S	*Cultura e scuola*
CHE	*Cuadarnos de Historia de España*
CL	*Comparative Literature*
CLS	*Comparative Literature Studies*
Conv	*Convivium*
CritQ	*Critical Quarterly*
DJV	*Deutsches Jahrbuch für Volkskunde*
DR	*Dalhousie Review*

DRs   Deutsche Rundschau
DUJ   Durham University Journal
DVLG   Deutsche Vierteljahrsschrift für Literaturwissenschaft und Geistesgeschichte
E&S   Essays and Studies by Members of the English Association
ECr   L'Esprit créateur (Minneapolis)
EG   Études germaniques
EIC   (formerly EC) Essays in Criticism (Oxford)
ELH   Journal of English Literary History
ELN   English Language Notes
ES   English Studies
ESA   English Studies in Africa (Johannesburg)
FL   Le Figaro Littéraire
FLe   Fiera letteraria
FM   Le français moderne
FR   French Review
FS   French Studies
GL&L   German Life and Letters
GQ   German Quarterly
GR   Germanic Review
GRM   Germanish-romanische Monatsschrift, Neue Folge
HeineJ   Heine Jahrbuch
Hisp   Hispania (U.S.A.)
HLQ   Huntington Library Quarterly
Höjb   Hölderlin-Jahrbuch
HR   Hispanic Review
Hum   Humanitas
ICC   Intermédiare des Chercheurs et des Curieux
IJES   Indian Journal of English Studies (Calcutta)
IL   L'Information Littéraire
IS   Italian Studies
JAAC   Journal of Aesthetics and Art Criticism
JDSG   Jahrbuch der Deutschen Schiller-Gesellschaft
JEGP   Journal of English and Germanic Philology
JFDH   Jahrbuch des Freien Deutschen Hochstifts (Tübingen)
JHI   Journal of the History of Ideas
JMH   Journal of Modern History
JR   Journal of Religion
KR   Kenyon Review
KSJ   Keats-Shelley Journal
KSMB   Keats-Shelley Memorial Bulletin
LanM   Les langues modernes
L&P   Literature and Psychology (New York)
LC   Library Chronicle (Univ. of Pa.)
LeE   Le Livre et l'Estampe
LI   Lettere italiane
LR   Les Lettres Romanes
MdF   Mercure de France
MedF   Médecine de France
MHQ   Mitteilungen der E. T. A. Hoffmann, Gesellschaft
MLN   Modern Language Notes
MLQ   Modern Language Quarterly
MLR   Modern Language Review

MP   *Modern Philology*
MQ   *Midwest Quarterly (Pittsburg, Kansas)*
NA   *Nuova antologia*
N&Q   *Notes and Queries*
NCF   *Nineteenth Century Fiction*
NL   *The Newberry Library Bulletin*
NM   *Neuphilologische Mitteilungen*
NMQ   *New Mexico Quarterly*
NRF   *Nouvelle revue française*
NRs   *Neue Rundschau*
New Statesman   *(formerly NS)*
NS   *Die neueren Sprachen*
NYRB   *New York Review of Books*
PBSA   *Papers of the Bibliographical Society of America*
Pel   *Le parole e le idee (Napoli)*
Person *The Personalist*
PLL   *Papers on Language and Literature*
PMLA   *Publications of the Modern Language Association of America*
PQ   *Philological Quarterly*
PR   *Partisan Review*
PULC   *Princeton University Library Chronicle*
QQ   *Queen's Quarterly*
QR   *Quarterly Review*
RBPH   *Revue Belge de philologie et d'histoire*
RdP   *Revue de Paris*
RDM   *Revue des deux mondes*
RdS   *Revue de synthèse*
REI   *Revue des études italiennes*
REL   *Review of English Literature (Leeds)*
RF   *Romanische Forschungen*
RFE   *Revista de Filología Española*
RHT   *Revue d'histoire des théâtre*
RI   *Revista Iberoamericana*
RLC   *Revue de littérature comparée*
RL   *Revista de Literatura*
RLI   *Rassegna della letteratura italiana*
RLMC   *Revista de letterature moderne e comparate (Firenze)*
RLV   *Revue des langues vivantes (Bruxelles)*
RMS   *Renaissance and Modern Studies (Univ. of Nottingham)*
RO   *Revista de Occidente*
RomN   *Romance Notes (Univ. of North Carolina)*
RPP   *Revue politique et parlementaire*
RR   *Romanic Review*
RSH   *Revue des sciences humaines*
RUL   *Revue de l'Université Laval (Quebec)*
RUO   *Revue de l'Université d'Ottawa*
S   *Spectator*
SAQ   *South Atlantic Quarterly*
S&S   *Science & Society*
SB   *Studies in Bibliography: Papers of the Bibliographical Society of the University of Virginia*
SC   *Stendhal Club*
SchM   *Schweizer Monatshefte*

SEEJ *Slavic and East European Journal*
SEL *Studies in English Literature, 1500-1900 (Rice Univ.)*
SFr *Studi francesi*
SIR *Studies in Romanticism (Boston Univ.)*
SN *Studia neophilologica*
SNL *Satire Newsletter (State Univ. Coll., Oneonta, N.Y.)*
SoR *Southern Review (Adelaide, Australia)*
SP *Studies in Philology*
SR *Sewanee Review*
SSL *Studies in Scottish Literature*
SuF *Sinn und Form*
TLS *(London) Times Literary Supplement*
TM *Temps modernes*
TR *Table Ronde*
UTQ *University of Toronto Quarterly*
VeP *Vita e Pensiero*
VQR *Virginia Quarterly Review*
VS *Victorian Studies (Indiana Univ.)*
WB *Weimarer Beiträge*
WW *Wirkendes Wort*
XUS *Xavier University Studies*
YFS *Yale French Studies*
YULG *Yale University Library Gazette*
YR *Yale Review*
ZDP *Zeitschrift für deutsche Philologie (Berlin-Bielefeld-München)*
ZFSL *Zeitschrift für französische Sprache und Literatur*

GENERAL

(Compiled by David V. Erdman, with various assistance.)

1. BIBLIOGRAPHY

For previous issues of the present "Bibliography" see the April numbers of *PQ* (1950-1961), then the October (1962-64), and thereafter the September Supplement to *ELN*. For the most extensive general listing, in all languages, see the "Annual Bibliography" in *PMLA* each May; slight notes listed there will not be repeated in our list.

See also listings in Bibliography sections below, under English, French, German, Italian, Portuguese, Spanish.

2. ENVIRONMENT: ART, MUSIC, SOCIETY, POLITICS, RELIGION

Antal, Frederick. *Classicism and Romanticism: With Other Studies in Art History*. London: Routledge & Kegan Paul, 1966. Pp. 198; 48 plates. £ 3 10s.
Rev. in *TLS*, Dec. 29, 1966, p. 1202.
The title essay explores the strands of Neo-classicism and early Romanticism in French painting, to 1824.

Artz, Frederick B. *From the Renaissance to Romanticism.* University of Chicago Press, 1965. Pp. 311. Paper $2.25.
Rev. by Mario Praz in *MLR*, LXI (1966), 108-09.
Trends in style in art, literature, and music, 1300-1830.

Bingham, Alfred J. "Marie-Joseph Chénier and French Culture during the French Revolution." *MLR*, LXI (1966), 593-600.

Brown, Bruce. "The French Revolution and the Rise of Social Theory." *S&S*, xxx (1966), 385-432.
The first section concerns "The French Revolution and German Thought Up to 1840" and the fourth (pp. 422 ff.), "Marx and the French Revolution."

Carlson, Marvin. *The Theatre of the French Revolution.* Cornell University Press, 1966. Pp. xii + 328. $10.00.
A lively narrative account, with illustrations, chart, and bibliography, of the French theatre from the fall of the Bastille to the rise of Napoleon.

Carozzi, Albert V. "Agassiz's Geological Speculation: The Ice-Age." *SIR*, v (1966), 57-83.

Colbourn, H. Trevor. *The Lamp of Experience: Whig History and the Intellectual Origins of the American Revolution.* University of North Carolina Press, 1965. Pp. 247. $7.50.

Corrigan, Beatrice. "Neapolitan Romanticism and the Social Sciences." *SIR*, v (1966), 113-20.

Crookshank, Anne. "Irish Sculptors from 1750 to 1860." *Apollo*, LXXXIV (1966), 306-13.

Dotson, Esther Gordon. "English Shakespeare Illustration and Eugène Delacroix." Pp. 40-61 in *Essays in Honor of Walter Friedlaender, Marsyas, Studies in the History of Art, Supplement II.* Institute of Fine Arts, New York University, 1965.

Gay, Peter. *The Enlightenment: An Interpretation. Vol. I: The Rise of Modern Paganism.* New York: Alfred A. Knopf, 1966. Pp. xviii + 555. $8.95.
This comprehensive work traces the ascendancy of "paganism" in enlightenment thought, the *philosophes'* fascination with classical antiquity as well as the rise of modern secularism. Although paganism and secularism should be distinguished, they were complementary in the anti-Christianity of the thinkers discussed. Gay takes the warfare between the critical and mythical mentalities as the motivation behind enlightenment thought. After the introductory sections, he offers something like a reconstructed philosophical history, tracing the enlighteners' attitude toward the epochs of the past, from ancient Greece through modern France, and their assessment of the degree to which the critical spirit was embodied in the different ages. There are separate chapters on Voltaire and Hume, but for the most part Gay treats the enlightenment as a loosely unified movement. There are informative discussions of the eighteenth-century evaluations of the Ionians, Socrates, Lucretius, Cicero, Dante, Machiavelli, Montaigne and many others. One of the finest parts of this book is the extensive bibliographical essay with which it concludes. (James H. Stam)

Guehenno, Jean. *Jean-Jacques Rousseau.* Transl. by John and Doreen Weightman. London: Routledge, 1966. 2 vols. 5 gns.
Rev. by George Lichtheim in *New Statesman,* Sept. 16, 1966, pp. 398-99.

Habakkuk, H. J., and M. M. Postan. *The Cambridge Economic History of Europe.* Vol. VI: *The Industrial Revolution and After: Income, Population and Technological Change.* Cambridge University Press, 1965. Pp. xii + 1040 (in two parts). £ 5 5s. and $19.50.
Rev. by A. E. Musson in *VS,* x (1966), 211-13, as valuable chiefly for the 300-page section by D. S. Landes on "Technological Change and Development in Western Europe, 1750-1914."

Knight, David M. "The Atomic Theory and the Elements." *SIR,* v (1966), 185-207.
The views of Davy, Dalton, Boscovich, and others.

Lefebvre, Georges. *The Directory.* Transl. by Robert Baldick. London: Routledge & Kegan Paul, 1966. Pp. 216. 30s.

Lefebvre, Georges. *The Thermidorians.* Transl. by Robert Baldick. London: Routledge & Kegan Paul, 1966. Pp. 216. 30s.

Maier, Hans. *Revolution und Kirche. Studien zur Frühgeschichte der christlichen Demokratie (1789-1901).* 2. erweiterte Aufl. (Freiburger Studien zur Politik und Soziologie.) Freiburg i.Br.: Rombach, 1965. DM 29.00.

McDonald, Joan. *Rousseau and the French Revolution.* University of London, The Athlone Press, 1966. 35s.

Rather, L. J. *Mind and Body in Eighteenth Century Medicine.* A Study based on Jerome Gaub's *De Regimine Mentis.* London: Wellcome Historical Medical Library, 1966. Pp. xii + 275. 30s.
Rev. in *TLS,* Aug. 25, 1966, p. 766, and by G. S. Rousseau in *PQ,* xlv (1966), 512-13.

Rothkrug, Lionel. *Opposition to Louis XIV: The Political and Social Origins of the French Enlightenment.* Princeton University Press, 1965. Pp. xv + 533. $12.50.
An impressive "story of how conditions external to the history of ideas helped to transform the speculative currents of one period into the political doctrines of another." The French monarchy's feebleness in the 18th century and the intense secular theories of the *philosophes* are traced to the "peculiar combination of ecclesiastical defeat and political inadequacy which characterized Louis XIV's reign after 1697." From the attempts of Louis' opponents "to substitute natural laws for mercantilist codes," Voltaire and Condorçet picked up the themes of agrarian and utilitarian optimism.

Rudé, George. *The Crowd in History: A Study of Popular Disturbances in France and England 1730-1848.* New York: John Wiley & Sons, 1964. Pp. 281. $5.95. Paper $2.95.
Rev. by Edward T. Gargan in *Nation,* Feb. 13, 1967, pp. 216-20, with Rudé's *Revolutionary Europe 1783-1815* (Harper & Row, 1966: pp. 350, $6.95).
Includes chapters on Luddism and "Church and King" riots in England; and on the political, food, and collective-bargaining riots of the French Revolution.

Ruitenbeek, Hendrik M., ed. *The Literary Imagination: Psychoanalysis and the Genius of the Writer.* Chicago: Quadrangle Books, 1965. Pp. 443. $7.95.
Reprinted essays include Fritz Wittels on Kleist, F. L. Wells on Hölderlin, Charles Kigerman on Rousseau, and E. C. M. Frijling-Schreuder on Balzac.

Starzinger, Vincent E. *Middlingness: "Juste Milieu" Political Theory in France and England, 1815-48.* University Press of Virginia, 1965. Pp. xiii + 158. $4.00.
A close—and penetrating—analysis of "middle of the road" political thinking, in the two contexts of "the attempts in France and England after the Napoleonic wars to establish middle-class rule as a permanent . . . golden mean. . . ." Brougham and Macaulay in England and Royer-Collard and Guizot in France illustrate "the fatal weakness of the middling mind": caught in its unreal view of the present, it cannot cope with change as creatively as either the radical or the conservative. A fascinating probe. (D.V.E.)

White, James. "Irish Romantic Painting." *Apollo,* LXXXIV (1966), 269-75.

Zapperi, Roberto. *Edmund Burke in Italia.* (Cahiers Vilfredo Pareto: Revue Européenne d'histoire des sciences sociales, 7-8.) Genève: Libraire Droz, 1965. Pp. 62.
Bibliographical study of the history of the *Reflections* in Italy.

3. CRITICISM

Arpiz, Harold. "Educating the Kosmos: 'There Was a Child Went Forth.'" *AQ,* XVIII (1966), 655-66.
Whitman's "There Was a Child Went Forth," generally taken as an illustration of the Romantic tradition because of its lyrical celebration of beauty and innocence in childhood, is reexamined according to the doctrines of phrenology with interesting results.

Bousquet, Jacques. *Les Thèmes du rêve dans la littérature romantique (France, Angleterre, Allemagne). Essai sur la naissance et l'évolution des images.* (Études de Littérature Etrangère et Comparée, 47.) Paris: Didier, 1964. Pp. 656. 50 Fr.
Rev. by Max Milner in *IL,* XVIII (1966), 77-78.
A vast repertory of the themes appearing in the dreams recorded in the Romantic literature of France, Germany, and England. In his review, Milner notes Bousquet's very different perspective from that of Albert Béguin in *L'Ame romantique et le rêve.*

Coiscault-Cavalca, Monique. "Les Romantiques français et les Elisabéthains." *LR,* XX (1966), 38-56, 125-41, 230-46.
Continues study begun in 1965 (see *ELN,* IV, Supp. 48). The first of the three installments listed here is entitled "Sources d'information des critiques français" and lists the books mentioned in French literary reviews of the Romantic period: critical studies (Hazlitt, Tieck, etc.); anthologies and collections of texts, both in English and in French; and histories of the Elizabethan age. The second installment, "Les critiques français devant leurs sources," shows the importance of English dramatic criticism and anthologies (Hazlitt, Lamb, Nathan Drake, J. P. Collier) as intermediaries (to Chasles,

Villemain, *et al.*). French reaction to Elizabethan poets is revealed as similarly second-hand, and translated excerpts weakened and distorted the originals. The third installment, "L'époque élisabéthaine vue par les critiques romantiques français," traces the influence of N. Drake's *Shakespeare and His Time*; Chasles is shown to be more scholarly, complete, and original than the other French critics (Guizot, Ch. Coquerel, Chateaubriand, Villemain).

Early, James. *Romanticism and American Architecture.* New York: A. S. Barnes, 1965. Pp. 171. $8.50, illus.
A consideration of American architecture within the framework of the history of ideas, centering on the ramifications of romantic form in five major considerations; Associationism, the Picturesque, Nature, Functionalism, and Nationalism. (H.L.K.)

Goimard, Jacques, ed. *L'Italie au temps de Stendhal.* (Collection Ages d'Or et Réalités, 6.) Paris: Hachette, 1966. Pp. 295. 38.90 Fr.
Using the format of the handsome series "Génies et Réalités," Hachette has begun a series devoted to the evocation of different periods of culture. The charming and abundant illustrations overshadow the text, which is a miscellany of essays on different facets of Italian life in the Romantic era; politics, religion, literature, opera, art. Of special interest to French readers is the chapter on Stendhal by V. Del Litto, "La patrie du sublime." Del Litto recounts Stendhal's Italian experience and the writings on Italy, assesses the meaning of Italy for Stendhal, and concludes that Stendhal's Italy is both a reflection of reality and a creation of his myth-making power. In a final chapter, Marcel Brion evokes the Italy beloved of literary tourists. (J.S.P.)

Graham, John. "Character Description and Meaning in the Romantic Novel." *SIR,* v (1966), 208-18.
The role of physiognomy in novelistic technique.

Gurian, Jay. "The Romantic Necessity in Literary Naturalism: Jack London." *AL,* xxxviii (1966), 112-20.
An attempt to show that the naturalistic novelist required a romantic hero to embody his vision of causative natural forces working on man and his environment. "Modern romanticism may be defined as the storming [of the world] by private vision and power to comprehend and affect the universe; and London is, very simply, a romantic in his exultation of private visions which he takes to be visions of the modern world." Although typical of the flabby use of "romantic" as a critical term, the effort to analyze the emotional commitments of naturalism is provocative. (H.L.K.)

Hibbard, G. R., ed. *Renaissance and Modern Essays. Presented to Vivian de Sola Pinto in celebration of his seventieth birthday.* With assistance of George A. Panichas and Allan Rodway. London: Routledge and Kegan Paul, 1966. Pp. viii + 235. 40s.
Includes James T. Boulton on Burke's Letter to a Noble Lord (pp. 73-82); G. R. Hibbard on "Crabbe and Shakespeare" (pp. 83-94); and Mario Praz on "Byron and Foscolo" (pp. 101-18).

Karlinsky, Simon. "A Hollow Shape: The Philosophical Tales of Prince Vladimir Odoevsky." *SIR,* v (1966), 169-82.

Kindermann, Heinz. *Theatergeschichte Europas. Romantik.* Vol. VI. Salzburg: Otto Müller, 1964. Pp. 464. DM 40.00.
Rev. by W. Hinck, *Germanistik,* vii (1966), 143-45.
The author reveals the structural "Mehrgesetzlichkeit" of the epoch by viewing

it as a reflector which absorbs and merges innumerable impulses, diffusing them in just as many directions. The Romantic theatre is revealed to be "engaged," and serving as a political factor in the strong nationalistic tendencies of its time, especially for the suppressed peoples. Kindermann recognizes Romanticism as a European movement, its nucleus Germany. Tieck, Hoffmann, and Immermann, as theatre directors, staged productions that included elements of the miraculous and the Gothic, and opened paths to new forms. (Hundreds of informative illustrations, an extensive bibliographical and chronological appendix, and a good index.) (I.C.)

Kraus, Werner. "Französische Aufklärung und deutsche Romantik." *WZUL,* XII (1963), 496-501.

Lentricchia, Frank, Jr. "Harriet Beecher Stowe and the Byron Whirlwind." *BNYPL,* LXX (1966), 218-28.
"Mrs. Stowe's indiscreet excursion into Lord Byron's private life quickly became a topic of national interest."

Levine, Paul. "Reappraisals. The American Novel Begins." *ASch,* XXXV (1965-66), 134-48.
Considers the emergence of the American novel as a particular *genre* sprouting from the "romances" of Charles Brockden Brown.

Lindenberger, Herbert. "On Commentary, Romanticism, and Critical Method: Reflections on Three Recent Books." *MLQ,* XXVII (1966), 212-20.
The three are Karl Kroeber's *Artifice of Reality* (see *ELN,* III, Supp., 9), G. H. Hartman's *Wordsworth's Poetry* (see *ELN,* III, Supp., 44), and G. Roppen's and Richard Sommer's *Strangers and Pilgrims: An Essay on the Metaphor of Journey* (see *ELN,* III, Supp., 18).

Locker, Malka. *Les Romantiques: Allemagne, Angleterre, France.* Paris: Presses du Temps Présent, 1964. Pp. 310. 18 Fr.
Brief, general essays on the principal Romantic figures in the three countries indicated. They were originally published in Yiddish (New York, 1958) as *Romantiker.* The present text is a revision as well as a translation.

Moreau, Pierre. "Le mythe de Don Juan. IV. Don Juan et le donjuanisme dans la poésie et dans le roman: de Byron à Barrès." *Les Annales. Conferencia,* n.s., No. 192 (October 1966), pp. 28-36.
On Byron, Musset, Gautier, G. Sand, Mérimée, Constant, etc.

Peyre, Henri. *Modern Literature. Vol. I: The Literature of France.* New Jersey: Prentice-Hall, 1966. Pp. xiii + 242.
Chapter 4 is devoted to Romanticism.

Poulet, Georges. "Piranèse et les poètes romantiques." *NRF* (Apr. 1, 1966), 660-71; (May 1, 1966), 849-62.
Taking off from Keller's *Piranèse et les romantiques français,* Poulet analyzes passages in Baudelaire, De Quincey, Nodier, Gautier, and Hugo, revealing such motifs as transcendence of space and time, multiplication, repetition, the labyrinth, *approfondissement, creusement,* descent into the inner self, *écroulement, petrifaction.*

Rehder, Helmut, ed. *Literary Symbolism: A Symposium.* University of Texas Press, 1966. Pp. 144. $5.00.

Sambrook, A. J. "A Romantic Theme: The Last Man." *Forum for Modern Language Studies,* II (1965), 25-33.
Mostly on English treatments of the theme (Byron, Campbell, T. L. Beddoes, Mary Shelley, Hood), but the introductory section mentions L.-S. Mercier, *L'An 2440* and *Mon Bonnet de nuit,* and Cousin de Grainville, *Le Dernier Homme* (1805).

Schneider, Marcel. *La Littérature fantastique en France.* (Les Grandes Études Littéraires.) Paris: Fayard, 1964. Pp. 425. 24 Fr.
Covering a great many writers, this study does not deal in depth with any. As might be expected a large part of the book—five of the sixteen chapters—is devoted to the fantastic element in French Romanticism. Giving due recognition to English influences (Walpole, Radcliffe, Lewis, Byron) and to German (Hoffmann), Schneider brings together many useful observations and plot summaries. Sade, Nodier, Hugo, Balzac, Borel, Dumas, Nerval, Gautier, Chasles, and Mérimée are the French authors receiving most attention.

Stern, J. P. *Re-interpretations: Seven Studies in Nineteenth Century German Literature.* London: Thames and Hudson, 1964. Pp. 370.
Rev. by G. E. Bell in *AUMLA,* No. 26, Nov. 1966, pp. 332-35, as "a weighty volume, both quantitatively and qualitatively," ranging through English, French, Spanish, Russian, and Italian literatures as well as German. Chapter 5 is titled "History and Prophecy: Heine."

Thomas, John L. "Romantic Reform in America, 1815-1865." *AQ,* XVII (1965), 656-81.
A study of reform movements in the age of Jackson and Emerson from the viewpoint that sees their object and their spirit in the doctrine of "perfectability." "Alternate routes to the millenium had to be found. One of these [humanitarianism] . . . made reform a branch of prophecy. Another was opened by the idea of a universal reawakening of the great god self [Emersonism] . . . a third . . . an attempt to build the experimental community as a reform model." Bracketing the term "romantic" with "perfectionist" reflects a further ray of the Parringtonean vision, which a generation ago hailed idealism and liberalism as the main arteries of the American corpus. (H.L.K.)

Whalley, George. "Literary Romanticism." *QQ,* LXXII (1966), 232-52.

Woodson, Thomas. "Ahab's Greatness: Prometheus as Narcissus." *ELH,* XXXIII (1966), 350-69.
More than a Byronic or Faustian figure, Ahab embodies man's tormenting quest for mastery of nature and self, and he looms as the titan of American Romanticism.

Woof, R. S. Review of vols. III-IV of *SIR* (1963-65), *N&Q,* XIII (1966), 161-63.

See also Pellegrini ("German. Hölderlin").

Reviews of books previously listed:
BRAND, C. P., *Italy and the English Romantics* (see *PQ,* XXXVII, 135), rev. by John D. Jump in *N&Q,* XIII (1966), 198-99; KROEBER, Karl, *The Artifice of Reality* (see *ELN,* III, Supp., 9), rev. by Henry Gifford in *N&Q,* XIII (1966), 195-96; TROUSSON, Raymond, *Le Thème de Prométhée dans la littérature européenne* (see *ELN,* IV, Supp., 10), rev. by Jean V. Alter in *ECr,* VI (1966), 53-54; by Michel Launay in *RHL,* LXVI (1966), 758-59; by Kurt Wais in *SFr,* X (1966), 113-14.

ENGLISH

(Compilers and reviewers: E. E. Bostetter, Univ. of Washington; Kenneth Neill Cameron, New York Univ.; Kenneth Curry, Univ. of Tennessee; David V. Erdman, New York Public Library; Richard Harter Fogle, Univ. of N. Carolina; David Bonnell Green, Boston Univ.; John E. Jordan, Univ. of California, Berkeley; Karl Kroeber, Univ. of Wisconsin; Albert J. Kuhn, Ohio State Univ.; William H. Marshall, Univ. of Pennsylvania; Martin K. Nurmi, Kent State Univ.; David H. Stam, Newberry Library; Donald H. Reiman, Carl Pforzheimer Library; Carl Woodring, Columbia Univ.)

1. BIBLIOGRAPHY

For eighteenth-century figures see the annotated bibliography, "English Literature, 1660-1800," in *PQ* each July. For the most extensive international coverage of Keats, Shelley, Byron, Hunt, and their circles, see the "Current Bibliography" in annual volumes of *KSJ*. For items of specifically bibliographical interest see the "Selective Checklist of Bibliographical Scholarship" in the annual *SB*. For a wide coverage of journals, with precis of articles, consult the indexed monthly issues of *Abstracts of English Studies*.

See also the "Anglo-German Literary Bibliography" in *JEGP* each July, and the relevant sections of the *Annual Bibliography of English Language and Literature*, and *The Year's Work in English Studies*.

For the most extensive general listing see the "Annual Bibliography" in the May issue of *PMLA*.

Hecht, J. Jean. "The Reign of George III in Recent Historiography: A Bibliographical Essay." *BNYPL,* LXX (1966), 279-304.
A critical guided tour through two decades of historical scholarship.

Stratman, Carl J., ed. *Bibliography of English Printed Tragedy 1565-1900.* Southern Illinois University Press, 1966. Pp. xx + 843. $15.00.
1,483 English printed tragedies (whose first editions appeared before 1900) require 6,852 entries, giving full title-page information, publishing and acting history, and library locations. Byron's tragedies take 143 entries for full listing of printings and editions; Coleridge's 69; Shelley's 44. Lamb's *Woodvil* ("never staged") had 10 printings. Maturin's *Bertram* (performed 22 times in 1816) had 12 printings that year, four the next, eleven more by 1877. One can see the emergence of Elizabethan tragedy in the Romantic period; e.g. Marlowe in 1818, after 18th-century silence.
An appendix gives the location of "extant English tragedy manuscripts."

Todd, William B. "London Printers' Imprints, 1800-1840." *Library,* XXI (1966), 46-59.

2. ENVIRONMENT: ART, SOCIETY, POLITICS, RELIGION

Bartlett, C. J. *Castlereagh.* London: Macmillan, 1966. Pp. 292. 42s.
Rev. in *TLS,* Jan. 5, 1967, p. 5; highly commended, especially on "the actual

power structure of foreign policy," but with the caveat: "Putting Castlereagh into perspective is well enough. Let us not make perspective into whitewash."

Beaglehole, T. H. *Thomas Munro and the Development of Administrative Policy in Madras, 1792-1818.* The Origins of "The Munro System." Cambridge University Press, 1966. Pp. 192 + 1 map. $7.00.

Bolton, G. C. *The Passing of the Irish Act of Union: A Study in Parliamentary Politics.* Oxford University Press, 1966. Pp. viii + 239. $6.10.

Under close scrutiny (focused on "the relations between a colonial ruling minority and the metropolitan power"), the old notion vanishes that Union was achieved, in 1800-01, by "the presence of British troops, reinforced by the relentless corruption of Dublin castle" (p. 216). This lab report excludes notice of the Rebellion and assumes that the "scuffles and manoeuvres" of the "articulate" (i.e. the propertied classes) occurred "without the slightest effect or interest on the part of the submerged peasantry" (222, 84). Valuable within the imposed limits. (D.V.E.)

Brady, Frank. *Boswell's Political Career.* (Yale Studies in English, Vol. 155.) Yale University Press, 1965. Pp. 200. $5.00.

Chambers, J. D., and G. E. Mingay. *The Agricultural Revolution 1750-1880.* London: Batsford, 1966. 45s.

Synthesis of modern studies.

Clark, William Smith. *The Irish Stage in the County Towns 1720 to 1800.* Oxford: Clarendon Press; New York: Oxford University Press, 1966. Pp. 417. $11.20.

Curtin, Philip D. *The Image of Africa: British Ideas and Action, 1780-1850.* University of Wisconsin Press, 1964. Pp. xvii + 526.

Fetter, Frank Whitson. *Development of British Monetary Orthodoxy 1797-1875.* Harvard University Press, 1965. Pp. ix + 296. $7.25.

Rev. by H. Scott Gordon in *VS,* ix (1966), 222-23.

Chapters I ("The Monetary and Banking World of 1797") and II ("The Restriction Period, 1797-1815") are especially pertinent, but the whole book helps us see what the Bullionists and Antibullionists thought they were talking about and thought they were doing. (D.V.E.)

Finer, Ann, and George Savage, eds. *The Selected Letters of Josiah Wedgwood.* London: Cory, Adams and Mackay, 1965. Pp. 375.

Gowing, Lawrence. *Turner: Imagination and Reality.* New York: The Museum of Modern Art, 1966. Pp. 64; 77 illus. $4.95; paper $2.95.

Concentrates on Turner's last twenty years and the "still not altogether comprehensible" change in his pictures, illustrated in exhibited and unexhibited works, intimate sketchbooks, and notes.

Greaves, Margaret. *Regency Patron: Sir George Beaumont.* London: Methuen, 1966. Pp. 163 + 23 plates. 36s.

Rev. in *TLS,* Nov. 17, 1966, p. 1049 and by Geoffrey Grigson in *New Statesman,* Sept. 30, 1966, p. 482.

Grebanier, Bernard. *The Great Shakespeare Forgery.* New York: W. W. Norton, 1965. Pp. 308.
The forgeries perpetrated by William Henry Ireland, 1794-96.

Grigg, David. *The Agricultural Revolution in South Lincolnshire.* Cambridge University Press, 1966. Pp. 234; 22 maps and text-figures. $10.00.

Hair, P. E. H. "The Binding of the Pitmen of the North-East." *DUJ,* xxvii (1965), 1-13.
The developing system of collective bargaining in coal mines.

Hermann, Frank. "Collecting Classics: 3: Mrs. Jameson's *Companion to the most celebrated private galleries of art in London: part 1.*" *Connoisseur,* clxii (May 1966), 31-35.
Includes illustrated account of collections of Robert Peel and Samuel Rogers.

Hermann, Frank. "Dr. Waagen's Works of Art and Artists in England." *Connoisseur,* clxi (1966), 173-77.
Waagen's first tour in 1835 resulted in his three-volume *Works of Art and Artists in England* (1838).

James, Patricia, ed. *The Travel Diaries of Thomas Robert Malthus.* Cambridge University Press, for the Royal Economic Society, 1966. Pp. xvi + 316. $8.50.
Two-thirds of the volume is devoted to Malthus' journal of a trip through Scandinavia in 1799 that provided material for later editions of his *Essay on Population* and was also used by Edward Daniel Clarke in writing his *Travels.* In this journal Malthus emerges as a curious, tolerant man, questioning professors of mineralogy and statistics, merchants and soldiers, farmers and Lapland nomads. He has Cobbett's eye for details of dress, soil, crops, and weather (his saddest moment is when he breaks his thermometer) without Cobbett's axe-grinding belligerence.
Miss James's biographical sketches of Malthus, Clarke, and their companions and her footnotes to the journals are excellent, but the latter are not thoroughly indexed. On the whole, a fine edition, redressing unwarranted prejudices against Malthus, the man, by showing the range of his sympathies. (D.H.R.)

[Kenrick, Samuel] "The Birmingham Riots of 1791: A Contemporary Account." Ed. by John Creasey. *Transactions of the Unitarian Historical Society,* xiii (1965), 111-17.

Kettler, David. *The Social and Political Thought of Adam Ferguson.* Ohio State University Press, 1965. Pp. 325. $6.50.

Letwin, Shirley Robin. *The Pursuit of Certainty: David Hume, Jeremy Bentham, John Stuart Mill, Beatrice Webb.* Cambridge University Press, 1965. Pp. vi + 391. $9.50; 52s 6d.
Rev. by Jeffrey Hart in *BNL,* viii (1966), 620-21; by Anthony Quinton in *New Statesman,* 29 July, 1966, pp. 170-71; and by C. B. Macpherson in "Halevy's Century Revisited," *S&S,* xxxi (1967), 37-47, along with recent books by John B. Stewart (on Hume), Carl Cone (on Burke: see *ELN,* iv, Supp., 13), Alfred Cobban (on Rousseau), and Joseph Hamburger (on James Mill).

The progression from Hume to Webb is interpreted as a progressive degradation of the liberal tradition.

Lindsay, Jack. *J. M. W. Turner*. London: Cory, Adams, and Mackay, 1966.
Rev. by Francis Watson in *S*, July 22, 1967, p. 125.

Liversidge, M. J. H. "James Bourne (1773-1854): an assessment of his life and work." *Connoisseur*, CLXIII (1966), 161-65.
Eleven illustrations of his water colors.

Malins, Edward. *English Landscaping and Literature 1660-1840*. Oxford University Press, 1966. Pp. xiv + 186; 20 plates. 42s.
Rev. in *TLS*, Sept. 22, 1966, p. 875, and by Wylie Sypher in *BNL*, VIII (1966), 629-33.
A small book but with very little waste; we are given close, careful looks at garden after garden—as they were planned, as they were seen and criticized in poetry and novel, and as Mr. Malins reports on what remains of them today. Emphasizes the influence on garden planning of the political ideal of reasoned freedom. (D.V.E.)

Mitchell, Austin. *The Whigs in Opposition 1815-1830*. Oxford University Press, 1966. Pp. 276. $6.10.

Paulson, Ronald, comp. *Hogarth's Graphic Works*. Yale University Press, 1965. 2 vols., 342 plates. $40.00.
Rev. in *TLS*, Feb. 9, 1967, pp. 97-99, where the introduction is called "possibly the best essay on Hogarth that has ever been written."

Price, Cecil, ed. *Letters of Richard Brinsley Sheridan*. Oxford: Clarendon Press, 1966. 3 vols. £ 8 8s.

Price, John Valdimir. "Hume's Concept of Liberty and *The History of England*." *SIR*, V (1966), 139-57.
"Change was the stuff of which history was made, and, as Hume wrote . . . in . . . 1770, 'I believe this is the historical Age and this the historical Nation. . . .'"

Richardson, Joanna. *George IV: A Portrait*. London: Sidgwick & Jackson, 1966. 50s.
Emphasizes the Regent's patronage of the arts.

Rossiter-Smith, H. "Prince Leopold in Westmorland: 25th of 9th Month 1819." *N&Q*, XIII (1966), 164-68.
Quotes diary of Thomas Wilkinson, friend of Wordsworth.

Schumann, Hans-Gerd. *Edmund Burkes Anschauungen vom Gleichgewicht in Staat und Staatensystem: Mit einer Edmund Burke-Bibliographie*. Meisenheim am Glan: Verlag Anton Hain, 1964. Pp. 230.
Rev. by Joseph A. Fihn in *BNL*, VIII (1966), 621-24; said to contain, on new methodological principles, the first study of "the vital significance of the idea of balance of power in Burke's total political thought" including justification of war with France; also a thematically ordered bibliography of 895 items including secondary studies and polemical articles against Burke.

Smith, Robert A. "Burke's Crusade Against the French Revolution: Principles and Prejudices." *BNL*, VII (1966), 552-68.

Spencer, Marion. *R. P. Bonington, 1802-1828.* Nottingham: Castle Museum and Art Gallery, 1965. Pp. 43; 50 plates.
Richard Parkes Bonington, whose short but brilliantly productive life parallels in so many respects the patterns of his most precociously gifted literary contemporaries, has recently been the subject of several monographs and exhibitions. Yet this study is the most valuable thus far: Marion Spencer deals scrupulously with problems of biography, description, and attribution, having flushed out many works from private collections which, if previously not unknown, were certainly unpublished. Moreover, she is cognizant of Bonington's two strains: his strong roots in his native English tradition of landscape painting and water color, best exemplified by Turner and Girtin; and his rapid and original assimilation of the doctrines of the *jeunes romantiques* and Delacroix in France where he lived, except for visits to England and elsewhere on the continent, from 1817 until his untimely death at twenty-six of tuberculosis. The choice of plates is splendid, showing Bonington's forceful yet refined draughtsmanship (Delacroix called it "la touche coquette") and his eclecticism of subject. One laments only the brevity of the monograph and the lack of color plates; one hopes that the long, definitive study by the same author is now in progress, making full use of the unpublished papers of Bonington, Delacroix, Gros, Huet, and their circles. (Marcia Allentuck)

Taylor, E. G. R. *The Mathematical Practitioners of Hanoverian England, 1714-1840.* Cambridge University Press, 1966. Pp. 520; 12 plates. $15.00.

Temperley, Nicholas. "The English Romantic Opera." *VS,* IX (1966), 293-301.
Raymond and Agnes, based on Lewis' *The Monk,* is now revived as "the best of the remarkable series of English Romantic operas" that began in 1834.

Werkmeister, Lucyle. "Theodor Gomperz's Reflections on Burke's Reflections on the Revolution in France." *BNL,* VII (1966), part I, 574-83; explanatory note, 572-3.

Western, J. R. *The English Militia in the Eighteenth Century: The Story of a Political Issue 1660-1802.* London: Routledge & Kegan Paul; Toronto University Press, 1965. Pp. xv + 459. 70s; $11.50.
An account rich with, or burdened with, depending on one's outlook, "personal intrigues and administrative details," as the author concedes (p. 436). "Besides illuminating the changes in the character of the central issues in politics, the story of the militia is helpful in measuring the temperature and atmosphere in which political life was carried on" (p. 440). It is also "perhaps an example of . . . the genius of the English governing class for self preservation" (p. 444).

Wood, J. C. "William Delamotte, 1775-1863." *Apollo,* LXXXIII (1966), 205-07.

Woodhouse, A. S. P. *The Poet and His Faith: Religion and Poetry in England from Spenser to Eliot and Auden.* University of Chicago Press, 1965. Pp. xii + 304. $6.95.

Wrigley, E. A., ed. *Introduction to English Historical Demography from the Sixteenth to the Nineteenth Century.* New York: Basic Books, 1966. Pp. 283. $7.50.

Reviews of books previously listed:
CHEVENIX-TRENCH, Charles, *The Royal Malady* (see *ELN*, III, Supp., 13), rev. as valuable but extremely faulty, by Donald E. Ginter in *BNL*, VII (1966), 593-95; DEANE, Phyllis, *The First Industrial Revolution* (see *ELN*, IV, Supp., 13), rev. by A. E. Musson in *VS*, X (1966), 212; HILL, Draper, *Mr. Gillray, The Charicaturist* (see *ELN*, IV, Supp., 14), rev. by Marcia Allentuck in *BNL*, VIII (1966), 633-35.

3. CRITICISM

Abrams, M. H. "Coleridge, Baudelaire, and Modernist Poetics." Pp. 113-38 in *Poetik und Hermeneutik: Immanente Äesthetik—Ästhetische Reflexion—Lyrik als Paradigma der Moderne*. Munich: Wilhelm Fink, 1966.
Examines the essentially anti-Romantic premises of post-Romantic criticism, under sections headed: "The analogical universe and the poetic image"; "Original sin and fallen nature"; "Nature and art"; and " 'La poésie pure' and the Absolute Poem."

Avery, Gillian, with the assistance of Angela Bull. *Nineteenth Century Children: Heroes and Heroines in English Children's Stories, 1780-1900*. London: Hodder & Stoughton, 1965. Pp. 260; 16 plates. 35s.
Rev. by Mary Elizabeth David in *VS*, IX (1966), 418-21.

Donovan, Robert Alan. *The Shaping Vision: Imagination in the English Novel from Defoe to Dickens*. Cornell University Press, 1966. Pp. 272. $5.75.
Received too late for review this year.

Fussell, Paul. *The Rhetorical World of Augustan Humanism: Ethics and Imagery from Swift to Burke*. Oxford: Clarendon Press, 1965.

Houtchens, Carolyn Washburn, Lawrence Huston, and Houtchens, eds. *The English Romantic Poets and Essayists: A Review of Research and Criticism*. Revised ed. New York University Press, 1966. Pp. xviii + 395. $6.50.
For "The" read "Some"—or "Essayists and Blake and Minor Poets" (Wordsworth, Coleridge, Byron, Shelley, and Keats being in the companion volume revised in 1956 called *The English Romantic Poets*). But the book by any name is welcome, and rightly jacketed as "an indispensable research tool . . . an expert survey"—of bibliographies, editions, biographies, and criticism, up through 1964, of Blake (surveyed by Frye and Nurmi), Lamb (by Barnett and Tave), Hazlitt (by Miss Schneider), Scott (by Hillhouse and Welsh), Southey (by Curry), Campbell (by Hoover Jordan), Moore (by Jordan), Landor (by Super), Hunt (by the Houtchens), DeQuincey (by John Jordan), and—a new and startling addition—Carlyle (by Carlisle Moore).
"Thomas Carlyle was first of all a romantic," Moore argues, akin, however, more to the German than the English romantics; his inclusion here is persuasively justified as serving "not only to bridge but, in many ways, to unite the two periods [Romantic and Victorian] and to illustrate the persistence of romantic ideas and attitudes." Attention to these considerations makes this survey of Carlyle studies particularly valuable for us (the editors of "The Romantic Movement"); we shall continue to exclude him from our list, with Goethe, as more wholly the province of other bibliographers; yet it is our

policy (too little practised) to note occasional studies of the Romantic elements in both. (D.V.E.)

Kostelanetz, Anne. "Romantic Poets and Pontificators." *Minnesota Review,* IV (Summer 1964), 532-43.
An omnibus review.
Books reviewed include Ian Jack, *English Literature 1815-1832;* W. L. Renwick, *English Literature 1798-1815;* E. E. Bostetter, *The Romantic Ventriloquists;* Edward B. Hungerford, *Shores of Darkness;* Hazard Adams, *William Blake;* Harold Bloom, *Blake's Apocalypse;* G. E. Bentley, Jr., *William Blake, Vala or the Four Zoas; Blake's Grave,* ed. S. Foster Damon; Jean H. Hagstrum, *William Blake;* W. J. Bate, *John Keats;* Aileen Ward, *John Keats;* M. R. Ridley, *Keats' Craftsmanship.*

Kroeber, Karl. "Trends in Minor Romantic Narrative Poetry." Pp. 269-92 in *Some British Romantics* (see Logan ["English 3. Criticism"]).
A "Romantic tendency toward *subjective narrative,"* and some other trends, are traced in the poems of Crabbe, Southey, Landor, Hunt, Peacock, Beddoes, Praed, and Hood. With brief comparisons to the major Romantics.

Kumar, Shiv K., ed. *British Romantic Poets: Recent Revaluations.* New York University Press; University of London Press, 1966. Pp. viii + 327. $7.50; paper $2.75.
"Recent" means mainly reprinted from the 1950's; even the "suggestions for further reading" scarcely come into the 1960's—except on Keats. On "Romanticism" there are essays by Peckham and Foakes; on Wordsworth essays by Bush, Raysor, Morgan, and Stallknecht; on Coleridge, by Salinger, Stoll, and House; on Byron, by Wilfred Dowden, Rutherford, and Bowra; on Shelley by Fogle, Baker, and Wilcox. On Keats the four essays include Brooks's famous "Sylvan Historian" piece, Stewart Sperry on *Endymion,* and two articles "written especially for this book": Bernard Blackstone on "The Mind of Keats in His Art" (pp. 257-75) and, by the anthologist himself, "The Meaning of *Hyperion:* A Reassessment" (305-18). The *hubris* of this placement (the Kumar "reassessment" makes a distinction without a difference) derives from approaching Keats via Nietzsche and Bergson and some confusion of negative and positive capability. (If Keats's taking part in the existence of a sparrow is the former, Apollo's flitting into a beauteous star with his lyre to make it "pant with bliss" must be the latter.) (D.V.E.)

Literature in Perspective Series. London: Evans, 1966. 15s. each.
Booklets by Norman Sherry on *Jane Austen;* Margaret Drabble on *Wordsworth;* Fred Inglis on *Keats.* Rev. severely in *TLS,* June 9, 1966, p. 516.

Lodge, David. *Language of Fiction; Essays in Criticism and Verbal Analysis of the English Novel.* London: Routledge & Kegan Paul; New York: Columbia University Press, 1966. Pp. 283. 35s.; $7.50.
Rev. by F. W. Bateson in *New Statesman,* May 20, 1966, p. 734.

Logan, James V., John E. Jordan, and Northrop Frye, eds. *Some British Romantics: A Collection of Essays.* Ohio State University Press, 1966. Pp. 343. $6.00.
Rev. in *TLS,* Sept. 15, 1966, p. 860.
For the individual essays in this volume see: Kroeber above, Ward below; under Blake, Frye; under Clare, Jack; under DeQuincey, Grant; under Hazlitt, Coburn; under Hunt, Fogle; under Lamb, Tillotson; under Landor, Mercier; under Scott, Raleigh.

Reed, Joseph W., Jr. *English Biography in the Early Nineteenth Century 1801-1838.* (Yale Studies in English, Vol. 160.) Yale University Press, 1966. Pp. xi + 180. $5.00; 37s. 6d.
Rev. in *TLS,* Apr. 21, 1966, p. 343.
Reed is concerned with the recognition—and the practise—of biography as a literary art, and his selection of examples is guided by that concern. The most successful conscious imitator of Boswell was Barry O'Meara; most biographers saw no art in Boswell to imitate. We are taken "into the depths" in chapters illustrating the restrictive effect of standards of dignity and suppression and spiritual uplift. A chapter not ironically called "Higher Criticism" deals with the contemporary theory of biography expressed by James Stanfield and Carlyle, both of whom "felt that the solution to contemporary problems lay in the biographer's artistic responsibility." When we get to Southey's *Nelson,* Moore's *Byron,* and Lockhart's *Scott,* in the last three chapters, we are well equipped to appreciate Southey's and Lockhart's successes and Moore's failure and to see how the first two accepted the critical doctrines and dogmas of their times yet "transmuted restrictions into literary power." Considering "what a slippery set of principles biographical criticism rests upon" (p. 165), we must welcome the modest light this essay supplies. (D.V.E.)

Rose, Edgar Smith. "The Anatomy of Imagination." *College English,* XXVII (1966), 346-54.
Reaffirms "the idea of imagination" bequeathed by Coleridge; compares Herrick's and Blake's roses.

Sen, Sailendra Kumar. *English Literary Criticism in the Second Half of the Eighteenth Century: A Reconsideration.* University of Calcutta Press, 1965. Pp. xii + 409. Rs. 15.

Tennyson, G. B. *"Sartor" Called "Resartus": The Genesis, Structure, and Style of Thomas Carlyle's First Major Work.* Princeton University Press, 1965. Pp. viii + 354. $8.50; 68s.
A thorough reconsideration.

Ward, William S. "Periodical Literature." Pp. 292-331 in *Some British Romantics* (see Logan ["English 3. Criticism"]).
A sketch of the shaping of new forms of the review (in 1802), the magazine (1817), and the weekly journal (1808), followed by a survey of the development of critical and scholarly interest in these.

Woodhouse, A. S. P. *The Poet and His Faith: Religion and Poetry in England from Spenser to Eliot and Auden.* University of Chicago Press, 1965. Pp. xii + 304. $6.95.
Two concise, lucid chapters of this posthumously-published study trace religious trends in English thought and poetry from 1660 through 1840—from the impact of the influence of Hobbes and Bacon, through Deism, to the major Romantics. Blake, Coleridge and Wordsworth (as an interacting double-entry), and Shelley receive serious attention. Woodhouse, though writing from the viewpoint of a believer, describes (rather than judges) a variety of genuine religious effects in poetry. The result is illuminating and suggests how much H. N. Fairchild might have achieved, had he studied these poets in the same spirit. (D.H.R.)

Zall, Paul M. "Adam Smith as Literary Critic?" *BNYPL,* LXX (1966), 265-69.
How Wordsworth knew of Smith's literary criticism.

Reviews of books previously listed:
COHEN, Ralph, *The Art of Discrimination* (see *ELN*, III, Supp., 17), rev. by John Chalker in *SN*, XXXVIII (1966), 163-67; DAVIES, Hugh Sykes, and G. E. Watson, eds., *The English Mind* (see *ELN*, III, Supp., 17), rev. by J. G. A. Pocock in *AUMLA*, No. 25, May 1966, pp. 93-100; HILLES, Frederick W. and Harold Bloom, eds., *From Sensibility to Romanticism* (see *ELN*, IV, Supp., 16), rev. in *CQ*, VIII, No. 1 (1966), 95-96; by John D. Jump in *RES*, V (1966), 331-33; by James Kinsley in *MLR*, LXI (1966), 680-83; RODWAY, Allan, *The Romantic Conflict* (see *PQ*, XLIII, 446), rev. by Mario Praz in *ES*, XLVII (1966), 388-89; ROSTON, Murray, *Prophet and Poet* (see *ELN*, IV, Supp., 17), rev. by E. D. Mackerness in *MLR*, XLI (1966), 502-03, and by Donald H. Reiman in *JEGP*, LXV (1966), 605-06; WILKIE, Brian, *Romantic Poets and the Epic Tradition* (see *ELN*, IV, Supp., 17), rev. by John Buxton in *RES*, XVII (1966), 215-17; by William Walling in *Commonweal*, LXXXII (1965), 197-99; by Carl F. Keppler in *Arizona Quarterly*, XXI (1965), 286-88; by James V. Logan in *SAQ*, LXV (1966), 168; by James Scoggins in *College English*, XXVII (1966), 645-46; and by Robert Gleckner in *Criticism*, IX (1967), 93-95.

4. STUDIES OF AUTHORS

AUSTEN

Bradbrook, Frank W. *Jane Austen and Her Predecessors.* Cambridge University Press, 1966. Pp. 179. $5.95.
Rev. by Denis Donaghue in *New Statesman*, May 13, 1966, pp. 698-99.
By "Jane Austen's relationship to her predecessors" Dr. Bradbrook appears to mean her probable knowledge and possible use of anything that was in print by her day. Thus he is not demonstrating her position in the history of the novel, as the title might suggest, or analysing her manipulation of fictional devices, as did Henrietta Ten Harmsel in *Jane Austen: A Study in Fictional Conventions.* He is rather accumulating likely source materials from a variety of genres—periodicals, conduct books, treatises on landscape gardening, plays, poetry, and the novel from Bunyan to Sir Egerton Brydges. The effect is somewhat hit and run—the chapter on "Drama and Poetry" is only eleven pages long—but it is interesting and useful to be able to compare Jane's comments on polite conversation with those of the conduct manuals, and to be reminded that when Elizabeth Bennet refuses to make a garden foursome with Mrs. Hurst, Miss Bingley, and Darcy on the grounds that "the picturesque would be spoilt by admitting a fourth," she is echoing Gilpin. Appendices excerpt some of the least accessible source materials. (J.E.J.)

Gomme, Andor. "On Not Being Persuaded." *EIC*, XVI (1966), 170-84; 480-81 (comment and reply).
Persuasion "is badly flawed" with "the weakness of a sketch in which Jane Austen has not found the opportunity to develop her own most serious interests."

Minter, David L. "Aesthetic Vision and the World of *Emma.*" *NCF*, XXI (1966), 49-59.
Emma tries to force an aesthetic ideal upon her world.

Moler, Kenneth L. " 'Pride and Prejudice' and Edward Cooper's 'Sermons.' " *N&Q*, XIII (1966), 182.

Page, Norman. "Standards of Excellence: Jane Austen's Language." *REL*, VII, No. 3 (July 1966), 91-98.
Discusses Austen's precise use of abstract words like *amiable, elegant, rational, judgement, taste,* and *understanding* to show her approval of intelligence, strength of character, and a manner both pleasing and sincere.

Reviews of books previously listed:

CRAIK, W. A., *Jane Austen: The Six Novels* (see *ELN*, IV, Supp., 18), rev. by H. S. Babb in *NCF*, XXI (1966), 90-92; by Gilbert Ryle in *RES*, XVII (1966), 336-38; and by Ian Watt in *MLQ*, XXVII (1966), 480-84; LITZ, A. Walton, *Jane Austen: A Study of Her Artistic Development* (see *ELN*, IV, Supp., 18-19), rev. by Francis R. Hart in *SAQ*, LXV (1966), 148-50; SOUTHAM, B. C., *Jane Austen's Literary Manuscripts* (see *ELN*, III, Supp., 20), rev. by John Hogan in *MP*, LXIV (1966), 83-84; by J. M. S. Tompkins in *RES*, XVII (1966), 212-13; and by Philip Waldron in *Southern Review* (Adelaide), II (1966), 87-90.

BARRINGTON

Torchiana, Donald T. "The World of Sir Jonah Barrington's *Personal Sketches*." *PQ*, XLV (1966), 321-45.

Overdue appreciation of an anecdotist who has been kept outside the pale of literary history.

BECKFORD

Babb, James T. "William Beckford of Fonthill." *YULG*, XLI (1966), 60-69.

Describes additions to Yale's Beckford collection.

See also Poulet ("French 1. General").

BEDDOES

Scarlett, E. P. "The Doctor of the Dance of Death." *Archives of Internal Medicine* (Chicago), CXVII (1966), 300-04.

See also Sambrook ("General 3. Criticism"); Kroeber ("English 3. Criticism").

BLAKE

Adlard, John. "Blake and the 'Geeta.' " *ES*, XLV (1964), 460-62.

Altizer, Thomas J. J. "William Blake and the Role of Myth in the Radical Christian Vision." *Centennial Review*, IX (1965), 461-82.

Bentley, G. E., Jr. "The Date of Blake's Pickering Manuscript, or, The Way of a Poet with Paper." *SB*, XIX (1966), 232-43.

Bentley, G. E., Jr. "The Printing of Blake's *America*." *SIR*, VI (1966), 46-57.

Blondel, Jacques. "William Blake, 'The Chimney Sweeper': de l'innocence à la violence." *LanM*, LX (March-April 1966), 42-47.

Bogen, Nancy. "An Early Listing of William Blake's *Poetical Sketches*." *ELN*, III (1966), 194-96.

In John Egerton's *Theatrical Remembrancer* (1788).

Burke, Joseph. "The Eidetic and the Borrowed Image: An Interpretation of Blake's Theory and Practice of Art." Pp. 110-127 in Philipp, Franz, and June Stewart, eds. *In Honour of Daryl Lindsay: Essays and Studies*. Melbourne: Oxford University Press, 1964.

Damon, S. Foster. *Blake's* Job: *William Blake's* Illustrations of the Book of Job: *With an Introduction and Commentary.* Brown University Press, 1966. Pp. ix + 66, incl. 22 plates. $6.00.
A valuable and conveniently arranged edition, with fine reproductions of the Harvard proofs, a tabulation and collation of Blake's Biblical inscriptions alongside the original King James texts, and a lucid and instructive if extremely brief Damonian commentary, plate by plate. (D.V.E.)

England, Martha Winburn, and John Sparrow. *Hymns Unbidden: Donne, Herbert, Blake, Emily Dickinson and the Hymnographers.* New York: New York Public Library, 1966. Pp. x + 153. $5.00.
Rev. in *TLS,* May 25, 1967, p. 436.
This little book opens up a whole new area in the literary—and religious—background of Blake and his contemporaries. There have been a few articles, really notes, on Blake and Wesley, but the real significance of the relationship has remained obscure until Mrs. England, who has absorbed all of Wesley and Watts and knows Blake very well, showed us what we have missed. A summary of her study would be difficult and misleading, because a great part of its value arises out of her expository strategy—if that's the proper word—of writing directly, personally, even colloquially in a manner somewhat like the discourse in a very fine classroom lecture to a familiar and thoroughly warmed up audience which not only comes to understand various points but is led to see things as the lecturer sees them. This style is quite appropriate to the matter, because the relationship of Blake and Wesley is not one of direct similarity or "sources" so much as it is one of attitudes and of participation in a common tradition. Her scholarship is impressive, and when called upon she is able to make objective points incisively, with a keen awareness of how far to go and not to go. But her analysis is one that is greatly enlivened and enriched by her personal involvement.
The central section of the book deals with Blake. The first essay, with bibliographical appendices, by John Sparrow succinctly shows the influence of Herbert and Donne on hymnody; and the last essay, by Mrs. England, discusses the hymnody of Watts in the poems of Emily Dickinson.
This is a valuable book and refreshing for its combination of new discoveries, thorough scholarship, and lively style. (M.K.N.)

Fish, Stanley. "Milton's God: Two Defences and a Qualification." *Southern Review* (Adelaide), II (1966), 116-36.
No direct reference to Blake's view, but relevant to a study of it.

Frye, Northrop, ed. *Blake: A Collection of Critical Essays.* Englewood Cliffs, N.J.: Prentice-Hall, 1966. Pp. 182. Paper $1.95.
Thirteen reprinted essays by twelve contemporary critics.

Frye, Northrop. "The Keys to the Gates." Pp. 3-40 in *Some British Romantics* (see Logan ["English 3. Criticism"]).

Frye, Northrop. *The Return of Eden: Five Essays on Milton's Epics.* University of Toronto Press, 1965. Pp. viii + 143. $4.95.
Relevant to Frye's interpretation of Blake's epics.

Gillham, D. G. *Blake's Contrary States: The Songs of Innocence and of Experience as Dramatic Poems.* Cambridge University Press, 1966. Pp. vii + 258. $8.00.
Professor Gillham's reading of the *Songs* is conducted, as he says, "according to the most conservative and orthodox principles," and avoids bringing to

bear on them any perspectives gained from Blake's later work, which "by their obscure and involved construction" are said to "invite a ponderous and mysterious explanation," extended by most critics to the lyrics. Gillham therefore belongs with the let's-avoid-the-elaborate-nonsense writers on Blake, who shy away from the solid body of Blake scholarship and from his later work.

As often seems to happen with those who want to avoid Blake's "system," the *Songs* are not read entirely on their own terms but in some context or other that is supplied by the critic. Though Gillham's subtitle suggests that he will stress the persona in reading the poems as dramatic projections, a good deal of the time he reads them in a rather sketchily described context that includes Paine, Burke, Godwin, Hobbes, and Hume in a way that I do not find especially enlightening because the connections between the poems and these thinkers are so generally drawn. One main point that seems to emerge from this study is a variation of the A. E. Housman idea that "Blake has no message, or 'philosophy,' . . . but offers something better: a serious and responsible consideration of the ways in which human energy may manifest itself" (p. 5). I'm not quite certain what this means, but surely Blake has, if anything, too much message. We are shown again that it is hazardous to try explaining even the early lyrics without knowing what lies beyond them. (M.K.N.)

Grant, John E., and Fred C. Robinson. "Tense and the Sense of Blake's 'The Tyger.' " *PMLA*, LXXXI (1966), 596-603.
A curiously inconclusive critical exchange. Grant seems to accept Robinson's point that "dare" is used as a preterite; Robinson to concede that the spinning implied in "twist" is "metal-working." But Grant insists that the "crucial problem" is the identity of the speaker; his own misreading of that identity (as "benighted *questioner*" or "dramatized frightened speaker") certainly gets in his way again and again. (D.V.E.)

Greenberg, Alvin. "The Real World of Blake's Manuscript Lyrics." *Bucknell Review*, XIII, No. 2 (1965), 26-46.

Halliburton, David G. "Blake's *French Revolution*: The *Figura* and Yesterday's News." *SIR*, V (1966), 158-68.
"The peculiar quality of the poem may be said to consist in the tension arising from an effort to bridge the gap between the tradition of the Christian *figura* and a work such as Joel Barlow's *Columbiad*; to create, if you will, a kind of Old Testament prophecy of yesterday's news."

Hill, Charles G. "Gide and Blake's *Marriage of Heaven and Hell*." *CLS*, III (1966), 21-32.

Hirst, Désirée. "Die Heimlichen Schätze: William Blake's Genius." *Antaios*, VIII (1966), 319-42.

Keynes, Geoffrey, ed. *The Complete Writings of William Blake: with variant readings*. London: Oxford University Press, 1966. Pp. xv + 944. 30s. $7.00.
Rev. in *TLS*, Aug. 18, 1966, p. 752, and by John Holloway in *S*, April 1, 1966, pp. 407-08.
An offset reprinting of the Nonesuch edition of 1957, with numerous substantive corrections and a six-page supplement of new matter. Preservation of the pagination and line-numbering of the Nonesuch is a convenience, but hundreds of significant variants have had to be excluded, and the correction of typographical errors has been minimal.

Lewis, Wilmarth S., and Philip Hofer, comps. *"The Beggar's Opera"* by *Hogarth and Blake.* Yale University Press; Harvard University Press, 1965. Pp. 30; portfolio of 11 plates. $100.00.
Plate 11 is a modern restrike of Blake's original copper plate.

Paley, Morton D. "Method and Meaning in Blake's *Book of Ahania.*" *BNYPL,* LXX (1966), 27-33.

Paley, Morton D. "Tyger of Wrath." *PMLA,* LXXXI (1966), 540-51.
With admirable concision Paley traces the history of interpretations of "The Tyger" and then succeeds in an attempt to deepen and enhance our understanding of the poem by connecting it with the sublime, the Bible, and Boehme. "The Tyger" is "an apostrophe to Wrath as a 'sublime' phenomenon . . . both in the Prophetic sense and as what Boehme calls the First Principle." What the poem asks is "How this can be . . . not whether. . . ." (D.V.E.)

Preston, Kerrison. "A Note on Blake Sources." *Apollo,* LXXXIV (1966), 384-87.
Illustrations from Blake and suggested sources from Rembrandt, Dürer, Bonasone, Bronzino, and Michaelangelo.

Rose, Edward J. "Visionary Forms Dramatic: Grammatical and Iconographical Movement in Blake's Verse and Designs." *Criticism,* VIII (1966), 111-25, with 8 plates.
A most important essay, clarifying "the meaning of visual and verbal direction in Blake's language, symbolism, and designs"—and in the process clearing up a number of cruxes of interpretation. At the end one sees the irrelevance of the recent dispute about verb tense in "The Tyger." (D.V.E.)

Ungaretti, Giuseppe. *Visioni di William Blake.* Milan: Mondadori, 1966. Pp. 560. L. 4.500.
Rev. in *TLS,* May 19, 1966, p. 458.
Translations of Blake's poetry, with introduction and notes.

Wittreich, Joseph Anthony, Jr. "Blake's Philosophy of Contraries: A New Source." *ELN,* IV (1966), 105-10.
Sees Milton's *Reason of Church-Government* as supplying the "struggl of contrarieties" and the intellectual war in Blake's *Marriage of Heaven and Hell.*

See also Woodhouse ("English 3. Criticism").

Reviews of books previously listed:
BENTLEY, G. E., Jr., and Martin K. Nurmi, *A Blake Bibliography* (see *ELN,* III, Supp., 21), rev. by Donald Weeks in *JAAC,* XXIV (1966), 455-56; DAMON, S. Foster, *A Blake Dictionary* (see *ELN,* IV, Supp., 21-22), rev. by David V. Erdman in *JEGP,* LXV (1966), 606-12, and by John E. Grant is *PQ,* XLV (1966), 533-35; HAGSTRUM, Jean H., *William Blake, Poet and Painter* (see *ELN,* III, Supp., 22), rev. by Martin K. Nurmi in *MP,* LXIV (1966), 166-68; HIRSCH, E. D. H., Jr., *Innocence and Experience* (see *ELN,* III, Supp., 33-34), rev. by Margaret Bottrall in *SN,* XXXVIII (1966), 167-69; by Arnold Goldman in *N&Q,* XIII (1966), 234-35; and by Martin K. Nurmi in *JEGP,* LXV (1966), 201-02; HUGHES, William R., ed., *Jerusalem* (see *ELN,* IV, Supp., 23), rev. by G. E. Bentley, Jr., in *MLR,* LXI (1966), 112-13, and by Arnold Goldman in *N&Q,* XIII (1966), 196-98; OSTRIKER, Alicia, *Vision and Verse in William Blake* (see *ELN,* IV, Supp., 23-24), rev. by Hazard Adams in *JAAC,* XXV (1966), 107-09; by G. E. Bentley, Jr., in *MLR,* LXI (1966), 684-85; by James

Benziger in *Criticism*, VIII (1966), 289-93; by John E. Grant in *PQ*, XLV (1966), 536-38; by D. W. Harding in *N&Q*, XIII (1966), 235-36; by George M. Harper in *SAQ*, LXV (1966), 410-11; and by Frederick W. Hilles in *SEL*, VI (1966), 627.

BROUGHAM

See Starzinger ("General 2. Environment").

BYRON

Elledge, W. Paul. "Imagery and Theme in Byron's *Cain*." *KSJ*, XV (1966), 49-57.

A perceptive reading restricted to an examination of the blood-fire, organic-nature, light-darkness, and clay-dust motifs. (K.C.)

Fiess, Edward. "Byron's Dark Blue Ocean and Melville's Rolling Sea." *ELN*, III (1966), 274-78.

Gérin, Winifred. "Byron's Influence on the Brontës." *KSMB*, XVII (1966), 1-19.

Hudson, A. P. "The 'Superstitious' Lord Byron." *SP*, LXIII (1966), 708-21.

Kernan, Alvin B. *The Plot of Satire*. Yale University Press, 1965. Pp. vi + 227. $6.50.

Rev. by Philip Pinkus in *PQ*, XLV (1966), 518-20.

This genre study develops theory, "hopefully, to bring us closer to particular works of art," and the particular work that fills the concluding quarter of the study is *Don Juan*. Kernan uses Byron's poem to help define "the perspective of satire" in relation to the perspectives of the other genres of comedy and tragedy—since *Don Juan* presents a "various, plentiful, turbulent world" and shows it in comic, satiric, and tragic perspectives (epic is mainly there "for purposes of mockery"). The help comes; *Don Juan* puts muscle on the critic's genre definitions. And the hope is fulfilled; the critic's discriminations do bring us closer to Byron's "unusual and distinct" character as "one of the very few romantic satirists." (D.V.E.)

Knight, G. Wilson. *Byron and Shakespeare*. London: Routledge & Kegan Paul, 1966. Pp. xv + 381. 42s.

Rev. in *TLS*, Feb. 23, 1967, p. 148.

A *tour de force* culminating Knight's studies of Byron as "an archetypal and universal figure"—and his studies of the Shakespearean "universe"—this volume is dedicated to the proposition that what Shakespeare conceived, Byron experienced; indeed that Byron was "an incarnation, involving . . . both sex and politics, of Shakespearean drama" (p. 22). There are critical and biographical riches here—even for readers unwilling to suspend disbelief in clairvoyance, astral walking (Byron's astral body, while he lay ill in Greece, met Peel on the streets of London), or "the royal essence" (claimed for Byron as Messiah).

An appendix on the Separation Controversy clarifies Knight's quarrel with his critics, if not the issue itself. (D.V.E.)

Lovell, Ernest J., Jr., ed. *Thomas Medwin: Conversations of Lord Byron*. Princeton University Press, 1966. Pp. 287. $6.50.

Rev. in *TLS*, Oct. 6, 1966, p. 916.

This much-needed edition of one of the most important and enjoyable of the contemporary records of Byron is based "on Medwin's copy (now in the

Houghton Library) of his 'New Edition' of 1824 (the third London edition) heavily annotated by the author and with notes for a new preface." In additions to Medwin's notes, comments have been taken from copies annotated by Lady Byron, Hobhouse, Trelawny, and Sir Charles Napier, who knew Byron in Cephalonia. Other major sources of notes are Hobhouse's review in *Westminister Review*, his suppressed pamphlet: *Exposure of the Misstatements in Captain Medwin's Pretended Conversations*, and unpublished passages from his diary; John Wilson Croker's suppressed review for the *Quarterly Review*; hitherto unpublished comments by Fletcher, Byron's valet, and Teresa Guiccioli; and reviews and letters by John Murray, John Galt, Lady Caroline Lamb, Mary Shelley, Leigh Hunt, and others. Professor Lovell's own notes are thorough and meticulous, providing cross-references to Byron's letters and journals and other sources of information. The result is a fascinating running commentary on Medwin's *Conversations*, in which one witness or interested bystander is played off against another and often against statements by Byron himself in letters or journals. The value of the edition is enhanced by a careful index. Used as intended as a supplement to Professor Lovell's earlier volume, *His Very Self and Voice: Collected Conversations of Lord Byron* (1954), this volume becomes an indispensible reference aid for the Byron scholar. Considered on its own merits, it holds up as excellent entertainment for the general reader. (E.E.B.)

McGann, Jerome. *"Childe Harold's Pilgrimage* I-II: A Collation and Analysis." *KSMB*, XVII (1966), 37-54.
Plots and dates the stages of the poem's composition, correcting the legend of Byron's indifference to publication and to matters of form and aesthetic significance; traces the revision of a relatively disorganized travelogue into "the revolutionary confessional poem which . . . influenced Romantic and post-Romantic art."

Stamm, Rudolf. "Lord Byron's *Cain*: Mysterium der Versuchung." In *Zwischen Vision und Wirklichkeit: Zehn Essays über Shakespeare, Lord Byron, Bernard Shaw, William Butler Yeats, Thomas Stearns Eliot, Eugene O'Neill und Christopher Fry.* Bern und München: Francke Verlag, 1964. Pp. 204.
Cain less a drama of revolt against Christianity than a study of the mysteries of damnation and of love. (Not seen.)

Wright, Austin. "The Byron of *Don Juan.*" In *Six Satirists*, Carnegie Series in English No. 9. Pittsburgh: Carnegie Institution of Technology, 1965. Pp. 100. $2.00.

Young, Ione Dodson, ed. *A Concordance to the Poetry of Byron.* Austin, Texas: Pemberton Press, 1965. 4 vols. $32.50.

See also Hibbard, Sambrook ("General 3. Criticism"); Reed ("English 3. Criticism"); Radcliffe-Umstead ("French. Nerval").

Reviews of book previously listed:
MARCHAND, Leslie A., *Byron's Poetry* (see *ELN*, IV, Supp., 25-26), rev. in *TLS*, Sept. 15, 1966, and by Annette Park in *CLSB*, No. 189 (May 1966), pp. 525-26.

CAMPBELL
Black, Hester M. "The Scene of 'Lord Ullin's Daughter.'" *Bibliotheck*, IV (1965), 245-46.
Loch Goil in Argyllshire.

See also Sambrook ("General 3. Criticism").

CLARE

Grainger, Margaret. *John Clare; Collector of Ballads.* (Peterborough Museum Society, Occasional Papers No. 3.) Peterborough, 1964. Pp. 23.
Rev. by Liliam Haddakin, *MLR*, xli (1966), 295-97.

Green, David Bonnell. "John Clare, John Savage, and 'The Scientific Receptacle.' " *REL,* viii, No. 2 (April 1966), 87-98.
In 1825 Clare contributed eight poems to the *Receptacle,* of which Savage was one of the editors. Prints three lackeyish letters from Savage to Clare, and Clare's previously unreprinted elegy "On the Memory of a Lady," a third sonnet on Robert Bloomfield, and an additional stanza to "Peggy Band." (J.E.J.)

Jack, Ian. "Poems of John Clare's Sanity." Pp. 191-232 in *Some British Romantics* (see Logan ["English 3. Criticism"]).
Urges a recovery of attention to *The Shepherd's Calendar* of 1827, which "contains by far the best of the poems that Clare published." It appeared at a time of waning interest in poetry; it has been dispersed and incompletely represented in most modern editions.

Review of books previously listed:

The ROBINSON-SUMMERFIELD editions of *Later Poems* and *Shepherd's Calendar* (see *ELN,* iii, Supp., 27-28), rev. by Liliam Haddakin in *MLR,* lxi (1966), 295-97—who notes also a *Catalogue of the John Clare Collection in the Northampton Public Library.*

COBBETT

Duff, Gerald A. "An Unpublished William Cobbett Letter." *ELN,* iv (1966), 110-12.

Osborne, John W. *William Cobbett: His Thought and His Times.* Rutgers University Press, 1966. Pp. x + 272. $10.00.
Rev. in *TLS,* Feb. 23, 1967, p. 145.
An important book, built on the mastery of extensive materials, treating Cobbett's ideas schematically if not quite systematically, and calling for a re-interpretation of his career as radical only in technique not in objectives; yet too thin a book, requiring too much summarized narrative and capsulated history, to serve either as a wholly satisfactory political biography or to supply convincing application of the terms of interpretation put forward. It is also a difficult book to quote from fairly, for on any one page Cobbett sounds like a smaller man than he appears in Osborne's final analysis, where his "persistent oversimplification of problems" is only a foil (or a necessary condition?) to his "career as a popular journalist in the teeth of opposition from very powerful quarters." (D.V.E.)

COLERIDGE

Berkoben, L. D. "The Composition of Coleridge's 'Hymn Before Sunrise': Some Mitigating Circumstances." *ELN,* iv (1966), 32-37.
"Evidence from Coleridge's notebooks suggests that Coleridge drew strongly upon his own experiences for the conception and for the execution of much" of the poem.

Blunden, Edmund. "Coleridge's Notebooks." *REL,* VII, No. 1 (January 1966), 25-31.
A general appreciation of the usefulness of the Notebooks, the *Specimens of the Table Talk* (1835), and the *Anima Poetæ* (1895) for earlier generations and the edition by Kathleen Coburn for our own.

Calleo, David P. *Coleridge and the Idea of the Modern State.* (Yale Studies in Political Science, 18.) Yale University Press, 1966. Pp. 157. $5.00.
Rev. in *TLS,* Dec. 15, 1966, p. 1172.
Most of this short work paraphrases late versions of a few essays in *The Friend,* two of Coleridge's last three books, and several passages from the later notebooks. Calleo's analyses sometimes differ from those of John Colmer, whose *Coleridge, Critic of Society* attended to the historical context as well as to theory. Calleo's study applies Coleridge's arguments to political problems of our own day. Students of literature will be drawn out of their shells by his analysis of the secondary imagination as belonging to "an educated aristocracy" (pp. 45, 68-69, 120, 126). He serviceably shows that a more "psychological" theory of the state can be extracted from the notebooks than from *On the Constitution of the Church and State.* (C.W.)

Chayes, Irene H. " 'Kubla Khan' and the Creative Process." *SIR,* VI (1966), 1-21.

Collison, Robert. "Samuel Taylor Coleridge and the *Encyclopaedia Metropolitana.*" *Cahiers d'Histoire Mondiale,* IX (1966), 751-68.

Haven, Richard. "Coleridge and Jacob Boehme: A Further Comment." *N&Q,* XIII (1966), 176-78.
". . . it is difficult to avoid the conclusion that his association of the sound-light-colour theory with an early reading of Boehme is a projection into the past of an idea which in fact belonged to a more recent date."

Hotopf, W. H. N. *Language, Thought and Comprehension: A Case Study of the Writings of I. A. Richards.* Indiana University Press, 1965. Pp. x + 349. $7.95.
Chapter 4 (pp. 63-95) is concerned with Richards' book *Coleridge on Imagination* and with the critics' mistaken readings of it; both topics recur at later points. The probing of sources of confusion in Richards' explication incidentally sharpens the reader's awareness of such sources in Coleridge. Hotopf investigates Richards' logical inconsistencies and his errors in reading Coleridge and concludes that they cannot be explained by Richards' own theories of linguistic causes of error but derive from the latter's psychological make-up. (D.V.E.)

Jackson, J. R. de J. "Coleridge on Shakespeare's Preparation." *REL,* VII, No. 1 (January 1966), 53-62.
When Coleridge was faced by what he regarded as a Shakespearean infelicity, he attempted to justify it as a theatrical device, an instrument for manipulating the audience. The majority of such comments, as those cited here, were not part of Coleridge's lectures, in which he was concerned with the literary excellence of Shakespeare's plays, but occur in marginalia and manuscript remains; "they are the most reliable evidence we have of the personal interests of the author of *Remorse.*" (W.H.M.)

Kaufman, Paul. "New Light on Coleridge as Undergraduate." *REL,* VII, No. 1 (January 1966), 63-70.

The two sources previously unrecognized are Henry Gunning's *Reminiscences of the University, Town, and County of Cambridge, from the Year 1780* (2 vols., 2nd ed., 1855) and *The Life of Robert Owen by Himself* (1857, 1920). The incidents which they recount "do not increase our understanding of his major traits, but they bear fresh witness to both the strong and weak aspects of a personality at ceaseless war with itself."

Little, Geoffrey. *"Lines Written at Shurton Bars* . . .: Coleridge's First Conversation Poem?" *Southern Review* (Adelaide), II (1966), 137-49.

Lyon, Judson S. "Romantic Psychology and the Inner Senses: Coleridge." *PMLA,* LXXXI (1966), 246-60.

Martin, C. G. "Coleridge and Cudworth: A Source for 'The Eolian Harp.' " *N&Q,* XIII (1966), 173-76.
Makes independently the same connection as Schrickx (see below) between Cudworth and "The Eolian Harp"—both inspired, of course, by Vol. I of the *Notebooks.*

Schrickx, W. "Coleridge and the Cambridge Platonists." *REL,* VII, No. 1 (January 1966), 71-91.
The influence exerted upon Coleridge by Ralph Cudworth's *The True Intellectual System of the Universe,* especially his doctrine of "the Plastick Life of Nature," is striking in the theme and treatment of "The Eolian Harp." See Martin (above).

Shelton, John. "The Autograph Manuscript of 'Kubla Khan' and an Interpretation." *REL,* VII, No. 1 (January 1966), 32-42.
Printing the manuscript of the poem in the British Museum, Shelton proposes an interpretation of the poem as it appears here, built largely upon a one-for-one relationship between symbol and referent, by which the poem is concerned with the esthetic experience. (W.H.M.)

Watson, George. *Coleridge the Poet.* London: Routledge & Kegan Paul; New York: Barnes & Noble, 1966. Pp. xi + 147. $4.00.
Rev. in *TLS,* Jan. 12, 1967, p. 28, and by C. B. Cox in *Spectator,* Oct. 14, 1966, p. 487.
Received too late for review this year.

Whalley, George. "Coleridge's Poetical Canon: Selection and Arrangement." *REL,* VIII, No. 1 (January 1966), 9-24.
Tracing the history of editions of Coleridge's poetry, from *Poems on Various Subjects* (1796) through those of Dykes Campbell (1893) and E. H. Coleridge (1912), Whalley proposes some rules for inclusion and exclusion, arrangement, and significantly relating the subcanonical materials to the poems of the canon, by which might be achieved "a collection such as Coleridge himself never saw even in his mind's eye, and never intended." (W.H.M.)

Woodring, Carl. "Christabel of Cumberland." *REL,* VII, No. 1 (January 1966), 43-52.
The influence of the Lakes upon the Conclusion to Part I and Part II, which Coleridge probably wrote at Greta Hall, Keswick, in 1800.

Woof, R. S. "A Coleridge-Wordsworth Manuscript and 'Sarah Hutchinson's Poets.' " *SB,* XIX (1966), 226-31.
Suggests a later dating of the Sarah Hutchinson notebook and collates an earlier Dove Cottage MS.

Yura, Kimiyoshi. "The Involuntary Memory as Discovered by S. T. Coleridge." *Studies in English Literature* (Tokyo), XLII (March 1966), 133-43.

See also Woodhouse ("3. Criticism"); Pottle ("Wordsworth").

Reviews of books previously listed:

APPLEYARD, J.A., *Coleridge's Philosophy of Literature* (see *ELN*, IV, Supp., 26), rev. by John L. Mahoney in *Thought*, XLII (1967), 129-31, and by Carl Woodring in *ELN*, IV (1967), 219-21; GRIGGS, Earl Leslie, *Collected Letters of Coleridge*, Vols. III and IV (see *PQ*, XXXIX, 151), rev. by W. Schrickx in *ES*, XLVII (1966), 70-73; SUTHER, Marshall, *Visions of Xanadu* (see *ELN*, IV, Supp., 29), rev. by James Benziger in *Criticism*, VIII (1966), 289-93, and by John Colmer in *AUMLA*, No. 26, Nov. 1966, pp. 321-22.

CONSTABLE

See Storch ("Wordsworth").

Review of book previously listed:

BECKETT, R. B., ed., *John Constable's Correspondence* (see *ELN*, III, Supp., 30), rev. by D. S. Bland in *N&Q*, XIII (1966), 200.

CRABBE

Chamberlain, Robert L. *George Crabbe*. New York: Twayne, 1965.
With descriptive bibliography.

See also Hibbard ("General 3. Criticism"); Kroeber ("English 3. Criticism").

Reviews of book previously listed:

SIGWORTH, Oliver, *Nature's Sternest Painter* (see *ELN*, IV, Supp., 29), rev. by R. L. Brett in *RES*, VIII (1966), 333-34, and by Arthur Pollard in *MLR*, LXI (1966), 683-84.

DEQUINCEY

Dobree, Bonamy, ed. *Thomas DeQuincey*. New York: Schocken, 1965. Pp. 212. $4.50; paper $1.95.
A fairly representative attempt to present DeQuincey "in his totality" through fifty-three selections, including two letters. The selections are organized under five disparate headings: "Life and Dreams," "Set Pieces," "Portraits of Contemporaries," "Literature," and "General." As the ten-page "Introduction" recognizes, this choice emphasizes the DeQuincey who "teaches by hieroglyphic suggestion" and ignores a range of activity from *Klosterheim* to "Dialogues of Three Templars on Political Economy." Most of the pieces are brief excerpts—some of less than a page in length—printed without indications of their relations to the wholes from which they were taken. The text is from Masson's edition; annotation is minimal. (J.E.J.)

Goldman, Albert. *The Mine and the Mint: Sources for the Writings of Thomas DeQuincey*. Southern Illinois University Press, 1965. Pp. 206. $5.95.
Rev. by David J. Gordon in *Nation*, April 1966, pp. 433-34.
This little book is admirable for its thoroughness, restraint, and general clearheadedness. Goldman finds that DeQuincey is more or less dependent on "literary source materials in something like sixty percent of his writings,"

exclusive of translations, and indeed often used one work while disingenuously giving the impression that he was judiciously weighing several authorities. Resisting the temptation to make wholesale charges of plagiarism, he even defends DeQuincey against some accusations, and argues plausibly that the Opium-Eater had no need to borrow ideas, only stores of facts. Such a state of affairs is certainly not surprising; and perhaps DeQuincey deserves more credit than his critic gives him for providing honestly, if misleadingly, the names of authorities which aided the search. This study's conclusion that DeQuincey should be regarded principally as "a very able literary journalist" is not very startling; its value lies chiefly in the information it gives us about what DeQuincey chose to take and the ways in which he used it. (J.E.J.)

Grant, Douglas. "Thomas DeQuincey." Pp. 143-66 in *Some British Romantics* (see Logan ["English 3. Criticism"]).

Tave, Stuart M. *New Essays by DeQuincey: His Contributions to the* Edinburgh Saturday Post *and the* Edinburgh Evening Post, *1827-28.* Princeton University Press, 1966. Pp. xiii + 412. $10.00.
Starting with Carlyle's reference to DeQuincey's review "in his 'Saturday Post,'" in November 1827 and building on a Bodleian manuscript in which DeQuincey quotes what he said in a political leader for the *Edinburgh Post* on January 26, 1828, Professor Tave recovers thirty-nine articles for the DeQuincey canon. Although he somewhat disconcertingly describes articles as "certainly" DeQuincey's when the evidence will allow only assurance beyond a reasonable doubt, his attributions are generally convincing. The articles themselves are not very notable: they are characteristic DeQuincey rigamarole and play the changes on familiar subjects: Klopstock, the Doctrine of Rent, Junius, and—particularly—Tory politics; the most interesting are his reviews of issues of the *Edinburgh Review* and *Blackwood's Magazine.* More fascinating than the articles is the painstaking process of attribution, which takes up about a fourth of the volume and is a remarkable cross-reference catalogue of DeQuincey's repeated ideas, mannerisms, and stylistic devices. (J.E.J.)

See also Keller, Poulet ("French 1. General").

DRAKE

Snell, W. E. "Nathan Drake, M.D.: A Literary Practitioner and His Illness." *Proceedings of the Royal Society of Medicine,* LVIII (April 1965), 263-66.

GODWIN

Cook, Wayne. "Two Letters of William Godwin." *KSJ,* xv (1966), 9-13. To Aaron Burr and Catherine Wilmot (1809).

Dumas, D. Gilbert. "Things As They Were: The Original Ending of *Caleb Williams.*" *SEL,* vi (1966), 575-97.
A truly "startling" discovery, that Godwin wrote two radically different endings of *Caleb Williams,* replacing a realistic version with a sentimental one shortly before going to press, is established with valuable preciseness— and its implications as to Godwin's doctrinal and artistic ambivalence and as to the critical readings of the novel are shrewdly considered. (D.V.E.)

Godwin. *Four Early Pamphlets (1783-1784): A Defence of the Rockingham Party, Instructions to a Statesman, An Account of the Seminary . . . at Epsom in Surrey, The Herald of Literature.* Facsimile Reproductions, with an Introduction by Burton R. Pollin. Gainesville, Florida: Scholars' Facsimiles and Reprints, 1966. Pp. xx + 319. $7.50.

Three of these pamphlets have slight historical and biographical interest only, but *An Account of the Seminary . . . at Epsom,* Godwin's "Of Education," is perhaps the most concise statement of his basic views on human nature. Pollin's close-packed introduction contains much information (and a few ambiguities). The quality of facsimile reproduction is uneven; pages like 114 and 115 should have been rephotographed before production. (D.H.R.)

Graham, John. "Character Description and Meaning in the Romantic Novel." *SIR,* v (1966), 208-18.

Of particular relevance to Lewis and Godwin.

Marken, Jack W. "William Godwin's History of the United Provinces." *PQ,* xlv (1966), 379-86.

Wardle, Ralph M., ed. *Godwin & Mary, Letters of William Godwin and Mary Wollstonecraft.* University of Kansas Press, 1966. Pp. viii + 125. $4.00.

Professor Wardle prints—all from the Abinger Manuscripts—151 letters in the body of his text and two in an appendix; of the 153 letters, 46 have been previously published in full, 31 in part. The previous publication has been in three separate works, Paul's life of Godwin, Wardle's life of Mary Wollstonecraft, and *Shelley and his Circle* (two items). This is the first time that the letters have been published in one place and in full. (Nine letters, however, are apparently missing from the Abinger Manuscripts.) Thus put together the letters make interesting and often delightful reading. It is refreshing, after all the talk about his cold, philosophical nature, to see Godwin in a frolicksome mood, as in the following comment, after leaving Mary's house: "The rain fell but did not wet me; I wore a charmed skin." Wardle's annotation is generally adequate but sometimes skimpy. More research might have revealed more. (Who is "Mrs. Newton"?) The reference to George Dyson (and other peripheral figures) should have included *Shelley and his Circle,* which contains information not in the earlier biographies. (K.N.C.)

Reviews of book previously listed:

GODWIN, William, *Italian Letters,* ed. Burton R. Pollin (see *ELN,* iv, Supp., 31), rev. by Peter Faulkner in *MLR,* lxii (1967), 117-18, and by Frederick W. Hilles in *SEL,* vi (1966), 611; also in *NCF,* xxi (1966), 297-98.

HAZLITT

Albrecht, W. P. *Hazlitt and the Creative Imagination.* University of Kansas Press, 1965. Pp. 203. $4.00.

Rev. by Daniel Majdiak in *JEGP,* lxv (1966), 613-17, and by Herschel M. Sikes in *MLQ,* xxvii (1966), 228-29. (Listed in *ELN* last year but not reviewed.)

A welcome bringing together and expanding of Professor Albrecht's monograph and essays on Hazlitt published over the past twenty years, this book deals with Hazlitt roughly in the chronological order of his philosophical writings, political works, criticism of art and literature, and familiar essays. The sustaining thesis is that his productions in all areas are informed by a consistent belief in a creative freedom of the human mind and the empirical "reasoning imagination" as the "faculty that determines truth and morality." As he argued for disinterestedness in his early philosophical writings, Hazlitt attacked egotism in his later critical works and even in his familiar essays moved to a "generalized" I. The thematic approach is helpful, if it perhaps slips—despite disclaimers—into supposing more consistency than Hazlitt's journalistic output quite realizes. After all, in 1814 he had moderate praise for Wordsworth's "powers of description and fancy," whereas in 1824 he would allow the poet "no fancy" and "little descriptive power." Albrecht's book is also useful for its careful relation of Hazlitt's thought to predecessors' from Hobbes to Rousseau and its perceptive final chapter on Hazlitt's style. (J.E.J.)

Coburn, Kathleen. "Hazlitt on the Disinterested Imagination." Pp. 167-88 in *Some British Romantics* (see Logan ["English 3. Criticism"]).
". . . is not its very absence sometimes the source of his critical strength?"

Jones, Stanley. "Hazlitt and *John Bull*: A Neglected Letter." *RES,* xvii (1966), 163-70.
Speculates that a letter from Hazlitt to Sarah Walker, printed in *John Bull* for June 22, 1823, and probably chiefly responsible for revealing Hazlitt's authorship of *Liber Amoris,* may have been procured by John Wilson Croker. (J.E.J.)

O'Hara, J. D. "Hazlitt and the Functions of the Imagination." *PMLA,* lxxi (1966), 552-62.
A refinement upon current emphasis on Hazlitt's interest in the sympathetic imagination; it was "supplemented by much use of associational aesthetics and balanced by his responsiveness to the form of the work of art."

HOLCROFT

Baine, Rodney M. *Thomas Holcroft and the Revolutionary Novel.* University of Georgia Monographs, No. 13. University of Georgia Press, 1965. Pp. vi + 126. $3.00.
Emphasizing Holcroft's political courage and intellectual consistency as well as his literary superiority among his contemporaries, this study usefully places him in the various traditions of which he became part. A chapter is devoted to the early works and then to each of three more significant novels: *Anna St. Ives* (1792), *Hugh Trevor* (1794-97), and *Memoirs of Bryan Perdue* (1805). The chapter entitled "The New Jerusalem," exploring in its contemporary context Holcroft's social and political philosophy, is one of the clearest of its kind, of value to both the scholar and the beginning student. (W.H.M.)

HOOD

See Sambrook ("General 3. Criticism"); Kroeber ("English 3. Criticism").

HUNT

Fogle, Stephen F. "Leigh Hunt and the End of Romantic Criticism." Pp. 119-39 in *Some British Romantics* (see Logan ["English 3. Criticism"]).
In Hunt's "most important critical production," his *Imagination and Fancy* of 1844, the great critical terms of Romantic criticism have lost their glow, "and all precision of meaning."

See also Kroeber ("English 3. Criticism").

Review of book previously listed:
CHENEY, David R., ed., *Musical Evenings* (see *ELN,* iii, Supp., 33), rev. by Jean de Palacio in *MLR,* lxi (1966), 294-95.

KEATS

Bush, Douglas. *John Keats: His Life and Writings.* (Masters of World Literature Series.) New York: Macmillan, 1966; London: Weidenfeld and Nicolson, 1967. Pp. 224. $4.95. 21s.
Rev. in *TLS*, Feb. 2, 1967, p. 88.
Received too late for review this year.

"Critical Exchange" by John Bellairs, Philip Waldron, and Manfred Mackenzie. *Southern Review* (Adelaide), I (1965), 58-73,
Bellairs, in "Variations on a Vase," attacks the essays on the "Ode on a Grecian Urn" by Cleanth Brooks, Kenneth Burke, and Earl Wasserman as confusing the poem with "their own teeming and diffuse maunderings." Waldron's "Reply" defends Brooks and briefly Wasserman; Mackenzie's defends Burke.

Green, David B. "An Early Reprinting of Three Poems from Keats's 1820 Volume." *PBSA*, LX (1966), 363.

Halpern, Martin. "Keats and the 'Spirit that Laughest.' " *KSJ*, XV (1966), 69-86.

Hamilton-Edwards, Gerald. "John Keats and the Hammonds." *KSMB*, XVII (1966), 31-36.

Harrold, William E. "Keats's 'Lamia' and Peacock's 'Rododaphne.' " *MLR*, LXI (1966), 579-84.

Hooker, Charlotte Schrader. "The Poet and the Dreamer: A Study of Keats's *The Fall of Hyperion*." *McNeese Review*, XVII (1966), 39-48.

Notopoulos, James A. " 'Truth-Beauty' in the 'Ode on a Grecian Urn' and the Elgin Marbles." *MLR*, LXI (1966), 180-82.
The famous phrase is to be associated with "the new aesthetics of the Elgin Marbles proclaimed by Haydon in his fight against Payne Knight."

Polgar, Mirko. "Keats's Beauty-Truth Identification in the Light of Philosophy." *KSMB*, XVII (1966), 55-62.

Pollin, Burton R. "Keats, Charlotte Smith, and the Nightingale." *N&Q*, XIII (1966), 180-81.
Finds source of ideas and diction in Charlotte Smith's sonnet "On the Departure of the Nightingale."

Sperry, Stuart M. "Keats's First Published Poem." *HLQ*, XXIX (1966), 191-97.
The companion in the sonnet "To Solitude."

Starr, Nathan Comfort. "Negative Capability in Keats's Diction." *KSJ*, XV (1966), 59-68.

Ting, Nai-tung. "The Holy Man and the Snake-Woman. A Study of a Lamia Story in Asian and European Literature." *Fabula*, VIII (1966), 146-91.
"Strangely, in spite of the fact that the Western group [of analogues of the lamia story] has been closely analyzed by experts on Keats and Coleridge, and

the Eastern group has been quite thoroughly investigated in China, no serious attempt has yet been made [before the present study] to set the twain side by side."

Visick, Mary. " 'Tease us out of thought': Keats's *Epistle to Reynolds* and the Odes." *KSJ,* xv (1966), 27-98.

Ware, Malcolm. "Keats's 'Stout Cortez': A Deliberate Error." *ELN,* IV (1966), 113-15.
A familiar point, newly discovered.

See also Kumar ("English 3. Criticism").

Reviews of books previously listed:
EVERT, Walter H., *Aesthetic and Myth in the Poetry of Keats* (see *ELN,* IV, Supp., 32-33), rev. by Mary Lynn Woolley in *JEGP,* LXV (1966), 730-34; ROLLINS, Hyder E., *The Keats Circle* (see *ELN,* IV, Supp., 33-34), rev. by Royal Gettman in *JEGP,* LXV (1966), 341-42; WILSON, Katharine M., *The Nightingale and the Hawk* (see *ELN,* III, Supp., 35), rev. by Miriam Allott in *MLR,* LXI (1966), 114-15.

LAMB

Tillotson, Geoffrey "The Historical Importance of Certain 'Essays of Elia.' " Pp. 89-116 in *Some British Romantics* (see Logan ["English 3. Criticism"]).

Review of book previously listed:
BARNETT, George L., *Charles Lamb: The Evolution of Elia* (see *ELN,* III, Supp., 35), rev. by Derek Roper in *N&Q,* XIII (1966), 194-95.

LANDOR

Mercier, Vivian. "The Future of Landor Criticism." Pp. 43-85 in *Some British Romantics* (see Logan ["English 3. Criticism"]).
". . . is there any English prose writer other than Landor who can be set beside Montaigne without seeming either narrow in range of interest and knowledge or anemic in personality?"

See also Kroeber ("English 3. Criticism").

LEWIS

See Graham ("Godwin").

LOCKHART

Jack, Ian. "Two Biographers: Lockhart and Boswell." In *Johnson, Boswell and Their Circle, Essays Presented to Lawrence Fitzroy Powell in Honour of His Eighty-fourth Birthday,* ed. Mary M. Lascelles *et al.* Oxford: Clarendon Press, 1965.

See also Reed ("English 3. Criticism").

MOORE

McClary, Ben Harris. "The Moore-Irving Letter File." *N&Q,* XIII (1966), 181-82.
The Dowden edition of Moore's letters (see *ELN,* IV, Supp., 35), overlooks

four letters of Moore to Irving, published and "available in Irving scholarship."

See also Reed ("English 3. Criticism").

Reviews of book previously listed:

Dowden, Wilfred S., ed., *The Letters of Thomas Moore* (see *ELN*, IV, Supp., 35), rev. by Robert Brainard Pearsall in *ELN*, III (1966), 310-12, and by Cecil Price in *RES*, XVII (1966), 213-15.

PEACOCK

Kennedy, William F. "Peacock's Economists: Some Mistaken Identities." *NCF*, XXI (1966), 185-91.

Mr. Fax has been mis-identified as Malthus but should be recognized as a Philosophical Radical of 1817. MacQuedy is not simply McCulloch but a typical Utilitarian economist. Peacock was "a more serious student of social problems and ideas" than the accepted identifications stipulate.

See also Kroeber ("English 3. Criticism"); Harrold ("Keats").

PRAED

See Kroeber ("English 3. Criticism").

REYNOLDS

Jones, Leonidas M., ed. *Selected Prose of John Hamilton Reynolds*. Harvard University Press, 1966. Pp. 493. $12.50.

Rev. in *TLS*, Feb. 23, 1967, p. 148.
Received too late for review this year.

ROBINSON

Brown, Eluned, ed. *The London Theatre 1811-1866: Selections from the Diary of Henry Crabb Robinson*. London: Society for Theatre Research, 1966. Pp. 227. 50s.

Rev. in *TLS*, Feb. 23, 1967, p. 146.

SCOTT

Bushnell, Nelson S. "Scott's Mature Achievement as Novelist of Manners." *SSL*, III (1965), 3-29.

Crawford, Thomas. *Scott*. (Writers and Critics Series.) Edinburgh: Oliver and Boyd, 1966. Pp. 119. 5s.

An excellent introduction to Scott's biography, poetry, and fiction. Exploration of Scott's work on ballads as a key to his later work, special chapter on *The Heart of Midlothian*, and suggestions for desirable future studies in Scott (K.C.)

Hart, Francis R. *Scott's Novels: The Plotting of Historic Survival*. Charlottesville: University of Virginia Press, 1966. Pp. xiv + 371. $6.75.

Rev. by Robert C. Gordon in *CL*, XVIII (1966), 368-72.
The serious study of Scott's fiction gains momentum, and Hart's excellent discussion of the Waverley novels will take its place among important critical

investigations of Scott. For his dissection of the novels Hart uses the method of rhetorical and structural analysis introducing into his commentary previous criticism of Scott. Indeed, much of the book is a running dialogue—very often an argument—with Welsh (in particular), Davie, Daiches, Pritchett, Gordon, Lukacs, and others. The novels are grouped under four headings: Tragicomedy of Jacobitism, Opposing Fanaticisms, Historical Picturesque, Falls and Survivals of Ancient Houses. One novel thus illuminates another so that a relative failure such as *Peveril* can clarify *The Heart of Midlothian*. As some novels receive fuller treatment than others, so do some receive higher evaluations— and such evaluations reversing some long-held orthodoxies will cause dissent. The severe downgrading of *Rob Roy,* for instance, is certain to displease its many admirers. Novels conventionally ignored or contemptuously dismissed are rehabilitated—such as *Ivanhoe. The Abbot* too receives high marks, Hart finding the hero Roland "perhaps the most complex and interesting of the heirs of Edward Waverley." Hart attempts to show the necessity for the post-trial chapters in *The Heart of Midlothian* as required for seeing the new world of the Butlers and Deans and the dissipation of the demonic energies released by Staunton and Effie. He would also relate this novel to other novels of "divisive fanaticisms, of cleavages in society caused by conscientious rigidities, the other projections of the difficulties of adjusting the strenuous ideal demands of an ultimate vision of Law to the personal demands of one's natural humanity." In *Old Mortality* Hart finds "a conception of humane law transcending all divisions in the interests of life is defined by significant differentiation on the folk level of the novel" (p. 72).

At the end of his study Hart conveniently states his objectives: "It will be enough if a fairly exhaustive "reading" of over two dozen thick novels helps to dispel or at least to redefine certain orthodoxies. In the matter of form, it is my conclusion that the Author of Waverley could most certainly construct, and that in the better novels thematic richness and coherence are inseparable from formal success. In the best novels the success is augmented by the coordination of an effectively romantic protagonist, a dynamic central experience, a vivid logical pertinence of other character groupings, and even related patterns of symbolic imagery. In the matter of historic vs. nonhistoric subject, I conclude that history is often essential as a limiting cultural condition, often essential as a major threat to the natural stabilities of human character and society, always essential as the occasion for a crisis of cultural continuity and an ordeal of personal identity." (pp. 332-335)

Thus Hart's purpose is made clear; his argumentative stance is sure to invite dissent and rebuttal in future book and article. All to the good: for Scott is now beginning to receive the same serious critical attention accorded Austen and Dickens. (K.C.)

Macintyre, D. G. "Scott and the Waverley Novels." *REL,* VII, No. 3 (July 1966), 9-19.

McClary, Ben Harris. "Washington Irving to Walter Scott: Two Unpublished Letters." *SSL,* III (1965), 114-18.

Ostrowski, Witold. "Walter Scott in Poland, Part II: Adam Mickiewicz and Scott." *SSL,* III (1965), 71-95.

Parsons, Coleman O. "Chapbook Versions of the Waverley Novels." *SSL,* III (1966), 189-220.

Piggott, Stuart. "The Roman Camp and Three Authors." *REL,* VII, No. 3 (July 1966), 21-28.

Pike, B. A. "Scott as Pessimist: A View of St. Ronan's Well." *REL,* VII, No. 3 (July 1966), 29-38.

Raleigh, John Henry. "*Waverley* and *The Fair Maid of Perth.*" Pp. 235-66 in *Some British Romantics* (see Logan ["English 3. Criticism"]).
An analysis of *The Fair Maid* as a sad and defiant opposite of *Waverley*, embodying also, in unique fashion, a national idyl or pastoral. "Taken in this sense, the idyllic part of *The Fair Maid of Perth* is Scott's *The Tempest*, the final act . . . where the wizard brings everything together, resolves all conflicts, and takes his leave."

See also Reed ("English 3. Criticism"); Alciatore ("Stendhal").

Reviews of book previously listed:
PARSONS, Coleman O., *Witchcraft and Demonology in Scott's Fiction* (see *ELN*, IV, Supp., 36), rev. by Nelson S. Bushnell in *SSL*, II (1965), 260-63, and by Andrew Rutherford in *RES*, XVII (1966), 96-97.

SHELLEY, MARY
See Sambrook ("General 3. Criticism").

SHELLEY
Adams, Charles L. "The Structure of *The Cenci.*" *Drama Survey*, IV (Summer 1965), 139-48.

Duerksen, Roland A. *Shelleyan Ideas in Victorian Literature.* London. The Hague, Paris: Mouton, 1966. Pp. i + 208.
Rev. in *TLS*, July 21, 1966, p. 642.
The list of 19th-century writers who were influenced by Shelley includes Browning, Benjamin Disraeli, Charles Kingsley, John Stuart Mill (partly *via* Harriet Taylor), George Eliot (partly *via* George Henry Lewes), William Butler Yeats, Thomas Hardy, and George Bernard Shaw. The influence varied both in degree and in kind. Browning was a devout Shelleyan in his youth and covered up the degree of his devotion. The now visible influence is in the earlier poems (with apparently more influence from *Epipsychidion* on *Sordello* than Professor Duerksen notes). Shelley inspired characters in two novels (Disraeli's *Venetia* and Eliot's *Middlemarch*) and one play, Shaw's *Candida*, as well as in various novels by Mary Shelley (not treated by Duerksen). Yeats regarded *Prometheus Unbound* as a "sacred book" but appears to have little idea of what Shelley was talking about. Shaw and Hardy, on the other hand, were well aware of Shelley's philosophy and acknowledged it as a major influence. (There is perhaps more of Shelley in *The Dynasts* than Duerksen indicates.) Duerksen correctly points out that Shelley had no illusions about an instant Utopia (a charge constantly used against him), but is incorrect in saying that Shelley insisted "on reforming men before society can be re-formed." It was the other way round. Duerksen's study makes it clear that the attacks on Shelley by Arnold, Carlyle, Ruskin and other Victorians came not from a serious examination of his poetry but antipathy to his radical and anti-religious views. To get a more complete picture, Duerksen's study should be supplemented by Sylva Norman's *Flight of the Skylark* which often pursues byways that Duerksen, intent on the main path, neglects. (K.N.C.)

Hunter, Parks C., Jr. "Textual Differences in the Drafts of Shelley's 'Una Favola.' " *SIR*, VI (1966), 58-64.
At first this note seems merely derivative (from Buxton Forman's edition of the Bixby-Shelley notebooks), but a quick check reveals that Shelley's holograph fair copy of "Una Favola" (which, Hunter argues, could not exist because Shelley didn't know enough Italian) resides safely among the Bodleian Shelley MSS, minus the final 27 lines of Garnett's *Relics of Shelley* text (MS Shelley adds. c. 4 [folder 28], ff. 250-53). (D.H.R.)

Hurt, James R. "*Prometheus Unbound* and Aeschylean Dramaturgy."
KSJ, xv (1966), 43-48.
Contrasts certain features of the *Oresteia*—its progression from grief to joy
and the lyrical quality of the *Agamemnon*—with Sophoclean-Aristotelian
tragedy, and shows how these features are paralleled in *Prometheus Unbound.*

Jellicoe, Ann. *Shelley, or The Idealist*. London: Faber & Faber, 1966.
Pp. 111. 16s.
Rev. in *TLS*, May 4, 1967, p. 380.
The text of a play on Shelley's life.

Kendall, Lyle H., Jr. "Leigh Hunt on Shelley's Missing Will: An Unpublished Letter." *KSJ*, xv (1966), 6-7.
To John Gisborne, 23 July 1822.

McGann, Jerome J. "The Secrets of an Elder Day: Shelley after *Hellas*."
KSJ, xv (1966), 25-41.
Argues (partly on the basis of discredited datings and corrupted texts of
Shelley's works) that 1822 saw Shelley reconciling his dualism in a new
poetry of earth like Keats's "To Autumn." (D.H.R.)

Notopoulos, James A. "New Texts of Shelley's Plato." *KSJ*, xv (1966),
99-115.
New passages from the Bodleian MSS supplement Notopoulos' study of
Shelley's translations from Plato and notes on his works in *The Platonism of
Shelley* (1949).

Raben, Joseph. "Coleridge as the Prototype of the Poet in Shelley's
Alastor." *RES*, xvii (August 1966), 278-92.
This article usefully collects numerous references to Shelley's knowledge of
and interest in Coleridge, but it hardly succeeds in convincing us that Coleridge—or any other particular person—has to be *the* "prototype" of the Poet
in *Alastor*. (D.H.R.)

Raben, Joseph. "Shelley's 'Invocation to Misery': An Expanded Text."
JEGP, lxv (1966), 65-74.
Examines the two holograph MSS of Shelley's poem, related lines in the rough
draft in Bodleian MS Shelley adds. e. 12, and Mary Shelley's handling of the
text in her transcript and editions. (D.H.R.)

Rogers, Neville, ed. *Percy Bysshe Shelley, The Esdaile Poems: Early
Minor Poems from the "Esdaile Notebook."* Oxford: Clarendon Press,
1966. 30s.
Rev. in *TLS*, July 14, 1966, p. 616; reply by Rogers and reviewer's response
Aug. 25, 1966, p. 770.
Professor Rogers' long-awaited volume is significant both in itself and as
the first part of his complete edition, still in prospect, of Shelley's poetry.
Obviously some comparison is in order with K. N. Cameron's *The Esdaile
Notebook*, which anticipated Rogers' work in 1964 (see *ELN*, iv, Supp., 37-
38). Since Rogers and Cameron are both expert Shelley editors who have
performed their tasks with full knowledge of the materials and circumstances
involved in them, summary judgment of their respective results would be
presumptuous. Their texts differ chiefly in respect to punctuation; in commentary, Cameron is comprehensive while Rogers is selective. They differ
considerably in their notions of an editor's duties. Cameron furnishes a
"minimum clean-up" text, altered from the manuscripts only when alteration

is absolutely essential for intelligibility, and looks forward to a text addressed not to the general reader but to the textual scholar, which will give a "close approximation of the manuscript, retaining the spelling, punctuation, and so on of the original." Rogers argues persuasively for more extensive alterations, maintaining that "The gulf between mere transcription and editing proper is as wide as the gulf between Shelley's poems as they appear in his manuscripts and the form in which he, or any printer of his day, would have expected them to reach their readers." Shelley's syntax, "wonderful, fluent, classical," is that of a polyglot, and "Its power, and even its sense, can be destroyed if the editor allows himself even a modified system of reliance on the almost always unsystematic punctuation." He remarks that "there will be not a few today to whom it might appear both new and heretical to suggest that the editing of Shelley's manuscripts involves more than their printed reproduction in accordance with a few formulae." On the contrary, "The path, if there is one, can be sought only by a reasoned point-by-point analysis not merely of one or two manuscripts, but of many; nor can this be done without a constant study of Shelley's thought and linguistic equipment." The issue, then, is clearly defined as between two widely divergent notions of what constitutes scholarly objectivity and faithfulness to an author's intentions. Rogers is undoubtedly expressing what is at present a minority opinion in American scholarship, but it is a very important opinion indeed. (R.H.F.)

Rogers, Neville. "The Punctuation of Shelley's Syntax." *KSMB*, xvii (1966), 20-30.
Maintains that Shelley's texts should be edited impressionistically, with minimal dependence on first editions or MSS so far as accidentals are concerned.

Stempel, Daniel. "Shelley and the Ladder of Love." *KSJ*, xv (1966), 15-23.
An important essay demonstrating that Shelley's "is a ladder of love on which the love removes from a higher rung to a lower" and that *Epipsychidion* and "The Extasie" differ more in method than in message. (D.H.R.)

Zillman, Lawrence J., ed. *The Complete Known Drafts of Shelley's Prometheus Unbound*. Ann Arbor: University Microfilms, 1966.
A xerographic reproduction of the literal transcription.

See also Woodhouse ("English 3. Criticism").

Reviews of books previously listed:

BAKER, Joseph E., *Shelley's Platonic Answer to a Platonic Attack on Poetry* (see *ELN*, iv, Supp., 37), rev. by P. H. Butter in *MLR*, LXI (1966), 686, and by E. D. Mackerness in *BJA*, vi (1966), 87-89; CAMERON, Kenneth Neill, ed., *The Esdaile Notebook* (see *ELN*, iv, Supp., 37-38), rev. by Neville Rogers in *RES*, xvii (1966), 97-99; JONES, Frederick L., ed., *Letters of Shelley* (see *ELN*, iii, Supp., 39-40), rev. by Wm. H. Marshall in *JEGP*, LXV (1966), 207-11; O'MALLEY, Glenn, *Shelley and Synesthesia* (see *ELN*, iii, Supp., 41-42), rev. by Lawrence J. Zillman in *ELN*, iii (1966), 229-31; WASSERMAN, Earl R., *Shelley's "Prometheus Unbound"* (see *ELN*, iv, Supp., 40-41), rev. by Seymour Reiter in *NMQ*, xxxv (1966), 375-79; in *TLS*, Aug. 4, 1966, p. 702.

SMITH

Schneider, Duane B. "Sydney Smith in America to 1900: Two Check Lists." *BNYPL*, LXX (1966), 538-43.
Reprintings of his work, 1809-93, and works about him, 1844-1900.

SOUTHEY

See Kroeber, Reed ("English 3. Criticism").

Reviews of book previously listed:

CURRY, Kenneth, ed., *New Letters of Robert Southey* (see *ELN*, IV, Supp., 41-42), rev. by Joanna Richardson in *Listener*, Sept. 23, 1965, p. 466; in *TLS*, Oct. 7, 1965, p. 894, and by C. J. Myers in *DR*, XLVI (1966), 109-11.

TANNAHILL

Crawford, Ronald L. "New Light on Robert Tannahill, the Weaver-Poet of Paisley." *N&Q*, XIII (1966), 184-89.

WORDSWORTH

DeLaura, David J. "The 'Wordsworth' of Pater and Arnold: 'The Supreme Artistic View of Life.' " *SEL*, VI (1966), 651-68.
Laborious delineation of the interrelation of Arnold's preface to the anthology of Wordsworth's poetry of 1879 and Pater's essay on the poet. DeLaura concludes that these "landmarks in Wordsworth criticism" are crucial to the development of the two Victorians' criticism. (K.K.)

Gerlitz, Barbara. "The Immortality Ode: Its Cultural Progeny." *SEL*, VI (1966), 639-49.
Traces influence of Wordsworth's poem on theological writings and attitudes in the nineteenth century. Chief finding: "For the vast majority of nineteenth-century theologians the Ode became another New Testament . . . a powerful challenge to Calvinism." An important essay. (K.K.)

Groom, Bernard. *The Unity of Wordsworth's Poetry*. London: Macmillan; New York: St. Martin's Press, 1966. Pp. xiii + 224. 35s; $7.00.
Rev. in *TLS*, March 2, 1967, p. 168.
A pleasantly persuasive excursion through the whole of Wordsworth's poetry, pointing to admirable qualities in all portions of it, early and late. The pace is brisk, and we must make mental notes as we read, to follow up later; the values to be perceived in various poems are dealt with so swiftly. But this rapid, compendious quality does effect Mr. Groom's purpose, to illustrate "the essential Wordsworth" seen in "an unchanged attitude of soul" despite superficial inconsistencies. (D.V.E.)

Hall, Donald. "Golden Daffodils," *Times Book Review*, Oct. 9, 1966, p. 2.
"I Wandered Lonely as a Cloud" interpreted as an unconscious expression of a capitalistic imagination—"looking at the daffodils was like suddenly coming into a great deal of money . . . problem: 10,000 daffodils at 6 percent is how many daydreams a quarter?" This gay interpretation is the vehicle for expression of shrewd insights into the function of "unconscious intentions" in poetry. (K.K.)

Harvey, W. J. *Poetic Vision in the World of Prose*. (Queen's University, Belfast, Lectures, N.S., No. 29.) Belfast: Queen's University, 1966.
On *The Prelude*.

Heffernan, James A. W. "Wordsworth on Imagination: The Emblemizing Power." *PMLA*, LXXXI (1966), 389-99.
Argues with support of structural analysis that *The White Doe* rather than demonstrating Wordsworth's poetic decline "represents rather a *terminus ad quem* in the gradually heightened exercise of his imaginative power." This

position depends on the belief that "imagination" for Wordsworth should
never be disassociated entirely from "emblemization . . . essentially a process
of meditative discovery, in which the power of an observed natural phenomenon is explained in terms of spiritual significance." (K.K.)

Kaufman, Paul. "To Wordsworth from Archbishop Trench: A Volume
and a Letter." *ELN*, IV (1966), 37-41.
An 1841 presentation of Trench's *Poems* with a letter to Wordsworth me-
morializes "another rivulet flowing from the stream of Wordsworth's influence."

King, Alec. *Wordsworth and the Artist's Vision: An Essay in Interpretation.* London: Athlone Press, University of London, 1966. Pp. vi +
180. $3.40; 21s.
Rev. in *TLS*, Nov. 24, 1966, p. 1101.

Kostelanetz, Anne. "Wordsworth's 'Conversations': A Reading of 'The
Two April Mornings' and 'The Fountain.' " *ELH*, XXXIII (1966), 43-
52.

Lainoff, Seymour. "Wordsworth's 'Answer to Mathetes'; A Re-Ap-
praisal." *ELN*, III (1966), 271-74.

Marsh, Florence G. "Wordsworth's Ode: Obstinate Questionings." *SIR*,
V (1966), 219-30.
An intelligent reading which interprets the *Ode* as "a flawed, if magnificent,
poem," flawed because the poet fails to make the "two structural patterns, two
major images, two themes" which constitute the contrapuntal system of the
poem expressive of a true coherence between "framework and inner vision."
By turning to a divine transcendence, Wordsworth betrays the representation
of a sense of divine immanence which is the finest achievement of the *Ode*.
(K.K.)

Nabholtz, John R. "Wordsworth's Interest in Landscape Design and an
Inscription Poem of 1800." *PELL*, II (1966), 265-69.
The poem is "Inscription for the House (an Outhouse) on the Island of
Grasmere" (Nabholtz mercifully shortens this poem's actual title but retains
its chief attraction, the parenthesis), here interpreted as a significant attack
on the Repton-Brown style of landscape design and an adumbration of the
poet's later ideal of landscape "improvement." (K.K.)

Pottle, Frederick A. "An Important Addition to Yale's Wordsworth-
Coleridge Collection." *YULG*, XLI (1966), 45-59.

Reed, Mark L. *Wordsworth: The Chronology of the Early Years, 1770-
1799.* Harvard University Press, 1966. $9.00.

Ryan, Frank L. "A Wordsworth Sonnet, One Phase of a Structural
Linguistic Analysis." *Studies in English Literature* (Tokyo), XLII
(September 1965), 65-69.

Stang, Richard. "The False Dawn: A Study of the Opening of Wordsworth's *The Prelude*." *ELH*, XXXIII (1966), 53-65.
"Having the whole poem emerge out of what looks like a loss of impetus"
is successful because Wordsworth's skillful handling of imagery enables him

to make the failure of political liberty appear as a false dawn as opposed to the true dawning of consciousness of personal liberty. (K.K.)

Stillinger, Jack, ed. *William Wordsworth: Selected Poems and Prefaces.* (Cambridge Riverside Series.) Boston: Houghton Mifflin, 1965. Pp. xxiv + 582. $3.00; paper $1.95.
Includes 110 poems plus *Prelude* and the more important prefaces; chronological arrangement and excellent annotation. (K.K.)

Storch, R. F. "Wordsworth and Constable." *SIR*, v (1966), 121-38.
The real affinities between poet and painter have eluded critics, because they have been content to observe only superficial resemblances. Careful analysis not of Constable's and Wordsworth's statements *about* art but of the pictures and poems reveals profound likenesses. Storch's interpretations are interesting, and his method should serve as a model for future criticism of relationships between the arts, a kind of criticism which to date has been almost always aesthetically superficial. (K.K.)

Taafe, James G. "Poet and Lover in Wordsworth's 'Lucy' Poems." *MLR*, LXI (1966), 175-79.
By reading the "Lucy" poems in the order in which they appear in the edition of 1815 one finds "a meaningful lyric progression . . . the lover makes a gradual discovery about himself and his temporal world," the discovery being "the vision of unity which can be found with a poet's eye." No worse than previous interpretations based on selective consideration of textual and editorial problems posed by the famous lyrics, but no better either. (K.K.)

Thorslev, Peter L., Jr. "Wordsworth's *Borderers* and the Romantic Villain-Hero." *SIR*, v (1966), 84-103.
The play, Wordsworth's "only attempt to portray villainous heroes or heroic villains of the type so characteristic of European Romanticism," is in fact "a profound critique" of this part of Romanticism: "like Byron's Cain or Manfred, Oswald is an existentialist manqué in an existentialist universe." (K.K.)

Tillotson, Geoffrey. "Wordsworth." *SR*, LXXIV (1966), 421-33.

Townsend, R. C. "John Wordsworth and His Brother's Poetic Development." *PMLA*, LXXXI (1966), 70-78.
Attempts to define developments in Wordsworth's poetry by references to the poet's attitudes toward his brother John. Such definition necessarily tends toward circularity and tenuousness because so little is known of John. "Hazlitt could be describing Wordsworth's conception of his brother" typifies the central vagueness in Townsend's argument. (K.K.)

Welsford, Enid. *Salisbury Plain: A Study in the Development of Wordsworth's Mind and Art.* New York: Barnes and Noble, 1966. Pp. 171. $6.50.
This is an exasperating book. Its organization may be described as picturesque: 15 percent of the total text consists of appendices, and the two central chapters are a "Divagation" and an "Excursus" from "Salisbury Plain." Although there is a confrontation with Hartman in the second appendix, the book contains almost no references to recent criticism, particularly by Americans. In tracing transformations in poems such as *Guilt and Sorrow,* the author properly follows DeSelincourt closely, but often so closely as to add little to his commentaries. Yet this is not a book without value, and some of its faults are probably inseparable from its virtues. Miss Welsford wants to stress that the changes in the "Salisbury" poems so carefully elucidated by

DeSelincourt are indeed keys to major developments in Wordsworth's thinking and artistry. Her central theme—that the poet's experiences while tramping the neighborhood of Stonehenge in the summer of 1793 provided him with a haunting complex of images and conceptions which recur with significant variations at crucial points in many of his poems—would be falsified by too much systematization. And it is difficult to think of many recent critics to whom Miss Welsford might turn for support of her view that the tendency to read Wordsworth as a sort of Blake al fresco is an oversimplification. The rewards of Miss Welsford's approach are best exemplified by her reading of the Excursion. The conventional judgment of this poem depends in part on glossing over the long, complicated history of its composition. Miss Welsford, concentrating on those elements deriving from Wordsworth's experiences, thought, and poetry of the earlier 1790's, is able to emphasize how much in the central argument of the Excursion reflects Wordsworth's most abiding concerns. Simultaneously, because she is aware that the "Salisbury Plain pattern" is so often transformed, she is ready to accept The Prelude, in part, as a preparatory work and to seek an "original" form in the Excursion. "In the passages quoted from The Prelude, Nature is credited with the power to provide 'apt illustrations of the moral world'; but in the Excursion the emblems are not just scattered similies but constituents of a structural pattern, and a structural pattern is an artefact shaped by the poet to serve his own poetic purposes. . ." The consequence of this line of attack is Miss Welsford's opposition to those who stress the apocalyptic aspects of Wordsworth's art, most notably, of course, Hartman. "Professor Hartman . . . is too preoccupied with self-consciousness to give much thought to the creative or social aspects of imagination. But for Wordsworth Mind and Nature not only commune together in mutual love, they also co-operate together in creative activity and with 'blended might' bring to birth new and real events like the vision on Snowdon, the composition of a poem, the building up of higher forms of culture and a better state of society. Of all this Professor Hartman has little to say, and the chief defect of his exegesis is that it leaves out a great deal of what was of the utmost importance to Wordsworth." This argument is today a salutary one, and I only wish Miss Welsford had supported it more effectively by utilizing the results of the rich Wordsworthian scholarship and criticism of the past decade. (K.K.)

Wordsworth, Jonathan. "A New Poem by Wordsworth?" EIC, XVI (1966), 122-23.
Comment upon H. S. Davies' article in EIC, XV (1965), 135-61 (see ELN, IV, Supp., 42-43). Gene W. Ruoff also questions the Davies' article in EIC, XVI (1966), 359-60.

Wordsworth, Jonathan. "A Wordsworth Tragedy." TLS, July 21, 1966, p. 642.
On the destruction of seven pages of Wordsworth's notebooks by Gordon Wordsworth. See also Landon, Carol. "A Wordsworth Tragedy" [Letter] TLS, Sept. 22, 1966, p. 884, on another ms. disposal by Knight, W's editor.

Zall, Paul M., ed. Literary Criticism of William Wordsworth. (Regents Critics Series.) University of Nebraska Press, 1966. Pp. xvii + 212. $4.50; paper $1.60.
A handy collection of the poet's best-known criticism. Includes the original Advertisement, the 1800 and 1802 Prefaces to Lyrical Ballads, and a few of the most quoted letters; those to Fox, Wilson, Lady Beaumont, and Catherine Clarkson. (K.K.)

See also Woodhouse ("English 3. Criticism").

Reviews of books previously listed:
FINK, Zera S., ed., The Early Wordsworthian Milieu (see PQ, XXXVIII, 166),

rev. by Hans Schnyder in *ES*, xlvii (1966), 68-69; Hartman, Geoffrey H., *Wordsworth's Poetry* (see *ELN*, iii, Supp., 44-45), rev. by Morris Dickstein in *PR*, xxxiii (Winter 1966), 139-42; by Robert Langbaum in *ELH*, xxxiii (1966), 271-84; by Herbert Lindenberger in *MLQ*, xxvii (1966), 212-20; by Manfred Mackenzie in *Southern Review* (Adelaide), ii (1966), 174-78; by W. J. B. Owen in *MLR*, lxi (1966), 685-86, and by J. R. Watson in *RES*, xvii (1966), 94-96; Moorman, Mary, *William Wordsworth: The Later Years* (see *ELN*, iv, Supp., 43-44), rev. by Geoffrey Hartman in *NY Herald-Tribune Book Week*, Mar. 6, 1966, p. 4 (an important review); by John E. Jordan in *CQ*, viii (1966), 281-82; by Russell Noyes in *ELN*, iv (1966), 144-48, and by W. J. B. Owen in *RES*, xvii (1966), 334-36; Perkins, David, *Wordsworth and the Poetry of Sincerity* (see *ELN*, iii, Supp., 46), rev. by R. W. King in *MLR*, lxi (1966), 113-14.

FRENCH

(Compiled by Carrol Coates, Harpur College; Alfred G. Engstrom, Univ. of North Carolina; and James S. Patty, Vanderbilt Univ.)

1. GENERAL

Beauchamp, Louis de. *Le Côté de Vinteuil.* Paris: Plon, 1966.
Includes essays on Stendhal, Lamartine, Chateaubriand. The unifying theme is the worldly ambition of the authors studied.

Bornecque, Jacques-Henry. "L'influence des écrivains réalistes et naturalistes sur l'évolution des classes sociales au XIXe siècle." *Philologica Pragensia*, ix (1966), 38-56.
A good many of the examples of visionary social comment are drawn from Romantic writers.

Bowman, Frank Paul. "La 'Confirmatio christianorum per Socratica' dans le romantisme français." *RSH*, n.s., No. 122-123 (1966), pp. 217-26.
Brings together numerous passages (ultimately derived from Rousseau) in which apologists and enemies of Christianity compare and contrast Jesus with Socrates. Bowman believes the Romantic tendency to think in terms of the *figura* explains the frequency of the theme's appearance. Many of the writers mentioned are minor, but Mme de Staël, Ballanche, Bonald, Maistre, Lamennais, Lacordaire, Balzac, and George Sand play roles too.

Christout, Marie-Françoise. *Le Merveilleux et le théâtre du silence en France à partir du XVIIe siècle.* The Hague: Mouton, 1965. Pp. 447.
A study of the role of spectacle in depicting the "marvelous" on the French stage, this book achieves the rare distinction of being stimulating, scholarly, and physically attractive. The contributions of philosophers (e.g., Bachelard) and estheticians (e.g., Souriau) are brought to bear on a great mass of patiently accumulated material. As the book is organized thematically rather than historically, it is difficult to disentangle what is particularly pertinent to French Romanticism. Suffice it to say that there are many references to the theatre of that period (to Gautier's ballets, for example), and that the volume is well indexed. (J.S.P.)

Cronin, Vincent. *The Romantic Way: Four Women in Pursuit of an Ideal.* Boston: Houghton Mifflin, 1966. Pp. 287; illus. $5.95.

Rev. by Marguarita Laski in *Saturday Review*, Feb. 26, 1966, pp. 33-34.
Studies of Caroline de Berry, Marie d'Agoult, Eve de Hanska, and Marie
Bashkirtseff. Laski finds the last "out of place" in the Romantic context.
Cronin hopes that "a definition of love in nineteenth-century France will
emerge from the four portraits." Other well-known women (G. Sand, Madame
Desbordes-Valmore) are rather arbitrarily excluded because they are not
representative or do not "reveal general truths." Readable, but undocumented.
Brief bibliography. (C.C.)

Delmas, A. and Y. *A la recherche des Liaisons dangereuses*. (Collection
Ivoire.) Paris: Mercure de France, 1964. Pp. 486. 30 Fr.
Rev. by L. Versini in *RHL*, LXVI (1966), 726-28.
A very satisfactory study of the critical reaction to Laclos' novel and of its
influence from its publication to the present. The second chapter, "La descente
en enfer (1815-1850)," is most pertinent to this bibliography. Vigny, Musset,
and Gautier receive some attention, but Balzac and especially Stendhal are
the principal exhibits. Stendhal is called "le premier disciple avoué," and
Laclos' influence on him, as well as the general affinities between the two
writers, is well analyzed, although, as in many studies of this kind, the author
tends to find his theme cropping up somewhat more frequently than it would
for an utterly impartial observer. (J.S.P.)

Deniel, Raymond. *Une Image de la famille et de la société sous la
Restauration (1815-1830): étude de la presse catholique*. (Collection
"L'Evolution de la Vie Sociale.") Paris: Les Editions Ouvrières,
1965. Pp. 303. 19.50 Fr.
Deniel weaves together quotations from four leading Catholic newspapers
(*Le Conservateur, La Quotidienne, L'Ami de la Religion, Le Mémorial
Catholique*), organizing them around the basic issues important at the time.
His study reveals the nuances of Catholic opinion in these periodicals as well
as the ideology of the Catholic segments of Restoration society. While Deniel
writes dispassionately, his quotations naturally bolster his view of the situation: in general, these Catholic papers propound a deeply conservative and
traditionalistic image of society, one in which authority is defended and
equated on all levels: ecclesiastical, royal, and paternal. For the authors of
these papers, Chateaubriand, Frayssinous, Maistre, Lamennais, but especially
Bonald, are major oracles. (J.S.P.)

Duhamel, Roger. *Aux sources du romantisme français*. Editions de
l'Université d'Ottawa, 1964. Pp. 223. $3.75.
Not exactly a new synthesis, but more than a manual, Duhamel's book is
hard to classify. Unquestionably, it is a useful compilation, and in certain
places the author juxtaposes materials in a new way or cites an unknown or
little known parallel. On the other hand, many passages repeat the old familiar
ideas. The emphasis here is on the earlier phases of French Romanticism:
Rousseau, Chateaubriand, and Madame de Staël. Courier, Lamennais, Lamartine, and Béranger are squeezed into a rather short chapter as illustrations
of tendencies dominant around 1820. Another chapter brings Nodier, Vigny,
and Hugo into the picture. A final chapter accounts for the appearance and
triumph of Romantic drama in the period 1827-1830. There is no bibliography
(or index), but Duhamel obviously knows the literature, since he cites a good
deal of it in his footnotes. (J.S.P.)

Engler, Winfrid. *Der französischen Roman von 1800 bis zur Gegenwart*.
Berne-Munich: Francke Verlag, 1965. Pp. 299.
Rev. by Wolfgang Drost in *RLMC*, XIX (1966), 246-47.

Fraisse, Simone. "Le Théme d'Antigone dans la pensée française au XIXe et au XXe siècles." *BAGB*, ser. 4 (1966), pp. 250-88.
For the Romantic period, the topics covered are: Ballanche, academic criticism, and Antigone as prefiguration of Joan of Arc.

Gibaudan, René. *La Lyre mystérieuse: Gérard de Nerval, Aloysius Bertrand, Maurice de Guérin, Théophile Gautier, Marceline Desbordes-Valmore.* (Collection "Alternance.") Paris: Les Editions du Scorpion, 1965. Pp. 192. 11 Fr.
Agreeable but superficial essays on the authors listed in the subtitle. Emphasis is on biography. (J.S.P.)

Gougy-François, Marie. *Les Grands Salons féminins.* Paris: Nouvelles Editions Debresse, 1965. Pp. 190.

Gravier, Maurice. "Camilla Collet et la France." *Scandinavica,* IV (1965), 38-53.

Havens, George R. "Pre-Romanticism in France." *ECr,* VI (1966), 63-76.
A neat summary of the movement from about 1700 into the Romantic period proper.

Jean, Raymond. *La Littérature et le réel: de Diderot au "Nouveau Roman."* Paris: Albin Michel, 1965. Pp. 276.
Rev. by André Wurmser in *Europe,* XLIV (January-February 1966), 216-19. Among the essays included are: "Chateaubriand ou rien" (pp. 47-55), "Stendhal dans le miroir" (pp. 56-65).

Kamerbeek, J., Jr. *Tenants et aboutissants de la notion "Couleur locale."* Utrecht: Utrechtse Publikaties voor Algemene Literatuurwetenschap, 1962. Pp. 71.
Rev. by Bodo Richter in *CLS,* III (1966), 299-308.

Keller, Luzius. "Piranèse et les poètes romantiques." *CAIEF,* No. 18 (1966), pp. 179-88.
References to Nodier, Musset, Gautier ("une cinquantaine d'allusions à Piranèse se trouvent dans son oeuvre immense"), Hugo, Baudelaire, and Mallarmé. See also the "Discussion" of this paper, pp. 280-84.

Keller, Luzius. *Piranèse et les romantiques français: le mythe de l'escalier en spirale.* Paris: José Corti, 1966. Pp. 272. 30 Fr.
Primarily a literary-historical approach to this subject (compare the treatment by Georges Poulet, *infra*). In his introduction, Keller follows the development of his theme through Dante, Tasso, and Michelangelo, and thence into English literature, meaning DeQuincey primarily. The chapters directly relevant to a study of French Romanticism: "Musset, Nodier et Balzac," "Théophile Gautier" (the longest chapter), and "Victor Hugo." Ten examples of Piranesi's fantasies, along with half a dozen related works of art by others, are photographically reproduced.

Lobet, Marcel. *La Ceinture de feuillages: essai sur la confession déguisée.* Brussels, 1966. Pp. 213. 13.50 Fr.
Contains an introduction on the general theme announced in the subtitle. Among the writers to whom a chapter is devoted are Stendhal, Constant, Sainte-Beuve, and Musset.

Macchia, Giovanni. *Il Mito di Parigi: saggi e motivi francesi.* Turin: Einaudi, 1965. Pp. 356.
Rev. by Pierre Citron in *RHL,* LXVI (1966), 757-58; by Luigi di Nardis in *Belfagor,* XXI (Jan. 31, 1966), 108-14.
This collection of miscellaneous essays contains chapters on Madame de Staël, J. de Maistre, Balzac, and Stendhal, among others.

Maixner, R. "La retraite parisienne d'Antoine Sorgo-Sorkocević." *RLC,* XL (1966), 467-74.
This native of Ragusa, born in 1775, lived in Paris in 1820-1841 and knew Madame de Staël, Nodier, and Mérimée, among other French Romantics.

Palou, Jean, ed. *Histoires étranges.* Paris: Casterman, 1963. Pp. 370. 13.50 Fr.
Includes tales by Balzac, Nerval, Nodier, Dumas, and Gautier along with a bio-bibliographical study.

Poulet, Georges. "Piranèse et les poètes romantiques français." Pp. 135-87 in his *Trois Essais de mythologie romantique.* Paris: José Corti, 1966. Pp. 189.
Starting from Keller's book, Poulet subjects the material to his characteristic analysis. The theme of self-multiplication is first isolated and defined ("Se multiplier, c'est projeter partout une image de soi qui se cherche sans jamais pouvoir se rejoindre") and then followed through various phases—*gouffre, Babel, creusement, approfondissement, écroulement*—in the works of De-Quincey, Nodier, Beckford, Musset, Gautier, Hugo, and Baudelaire.

Raitt, A. W. *Life and Letters in France: The Nineteenth Century.* London: Nelson, 1965. Pp. xxx + 177. 30s.
Like the other volumes in this series, the present one is primarily a pedagogical device, a handbook designed to give English-speaking students of French literature a compendium of information on the cultural background of the century. This end is accomplished by a series of chapters each organized around a passage from a leading author. Each passage is chosen to represent one of the major historical, social, religious, or artistic movements of the age. Nine of the twenty authors included here are normally classified as Romantics: Madame de Staël, Chateaubriand, Musset, Vigny, Dumas, Stendhal, Lamennais, Balzac, and Hugo. There is nothing really new here, but the book is sound in its choices and affirmations, and should prove useful. (J.S.P.)

Sartre, Jean-Paul. "La conscience de classe chez Flaubert." *TM* (May 1966), pp. 1921-51; (June 1966), pp. 2113-53.
Allusions to the major Romantic writers, and especially to Vigny, apropos of the developing image of the "artist."

Willard, Charity Cannon. "The Remarkable Case of Clotilde de Surville." *ECr,* VI (1966), 108-16.
The story of the hoax perpetrated by Nodier and others; the possible influence of the factual case of Christine de Pisan; Longfellow's interest in Clotilde's poetry.

Reviews of books previously listed:
BAILEY, Helen Phelps, *Hamlet in France from Voltaire to Laforgue* (see *ELN,* IV, Supp., 46), rev. by Robert J. Nelson in *RR,* LVII (1966), 137-40; CHARLTON, D. G., *Secular Religions in France, 1815-1870* (see *ELN,* III,

Supp., 47-48), rev. by Frank Paul Bowman in *MLR*, LXI (1966), 327-28; GEORGE, Albert J., *Short Fiction in France 1800-1850* (see *ELN*, III, Supp., 48), rev. by Jean-Albert Bédé in *Symposium*, XX (1966), 81-83; GUILLEMIN, Henri, *Eclaircissements* (see *PQ*, XLIII, 474), rev. by André Vandegans in *RBPH*, XLIII (1965), 118-20; MARMIER, Jean, *La Survie d'Horace à l'époque romantique* (see *ELN*, IV, Supp., 50), rev. by M. M. in *IL*, XVIII (1966), 78; MILNER, Max, *Le Diable dans la littérature française de Cazotte à Baudelaire* (see *PQ*, XLI, 679), rev. by Robert Jouanny in *SFr*, IX (1965), 506-10; MOLHO, Raphaël, *La Critique littéraire en France au XIXe siècle* (see *ELN*, III, Supp., 49), rev. by Werner Krauss in *Deutsche Literatur Zeitung*, LXXXVII, No. 2 (1966), 119; MOREAU, Pierre, *Ames et thèmes romantiques* (see *ELN*, IV, Supp., 50), rev. anon. in *TLS*, May 26, 1966, pp. 465-67; by Jacques Body in *RLC*, XL (1966), 310-12; SEZNEC, Jean, *John Martin en France* (see *ELN*, IV, Supp., 51), rev. by Jean Bellemin-Noël in *RHL*, LXVI (1966), 729-30; by François Jost in *CL*, XVIII (1966), 372-73; SIMCHES, Seymour O., *Le Romantisme et le goût esthétique du XVIIIe siècle* (see *ELN*, III, Supp., 50), rev. by Gisèle Corbière-Gille in *RR*, LVII (1966), 140-41.

2. STUDIES OF AUTHORS

AGOULT
Reviews of books previously listed:

VIER, Jacques, *La Comtesse d'Agoult et son temps*, tomes III-VI (see *ELN*, III, Supp., 51), rev. by Claude Pichois in *RHL*, LXVI (1966), 343-46; tomes V-VI, rev. by J. Voisine in *IL*, XVII (1965), 125.

ALLART
Reviews of books previously listed:

UFFENBECK, Lorin A., ed., *Nouvelles lettres d'Hortense Allart à Sainte-Beuve (1832-1864)* (see *ELN*, IV, Supp., 52), rev. by Pierre Deguise in *FR*, XXXIX (1966), 942-43; in *SFr*, X (1966), 374-75.

BALLANCHE
See Bowman, Fraisse ("1. General").

BALZAC
Adamson, Donald. *The Genesis of 'Le Cousin Pons.'* (Oxford Modern Languages and Literature Monographs.) Oxford University Press, 1966. Pp. 138; illus. $4.80.
Adamson presents a clear appraisal of facts and questions concerning the genesis of this novel. He rejects the thesis (M. Bardèche, M.-J. Durry) that Balzac rewrote *Le Cousin Pons* as a whole. The argument that Balzac added a longer part to what began as a *nouvelle* is convincing, but seems to me to obscure the structural analysis of the novel. Remarks on dialogue (ch. 8) and on the symbolism of clothes (ch. 9) indicate that the study has critical as well as historical interest. (C.C.)

Affron, Charles. *Patterns of Failure in 'La Comédie humaine.'* (Yale Romantic Studies, Second Series, 15.) Yale University Press, 1966. Pp. ix + 148. $5.00.
Perceptive criticism of a selection of important novels: *César Birotteau, La Cousine Bette, Illusions perdues, Louis Lambert, et al.* Analyzes failures as the blind (C. Birotteau), the depraved (Hector Hulot), the weak (Lucien de Rebempré), and the genius (L. Lambert). (C.C.)

L'Année Balzacienne 1966. Paris: Garnier, 1966. Pp. 475. 28 F. [*AnB*]
Seventh volume in series. Contains: Ph. Havard de la Montagne, "A l'ombre
de quelques clochers parisiens. Oncle et cousins Sallambier," pp. 3-18; Arlette
Michel, "Aspects 'mystiques' des romans de jeunesse," pp. 19-32; K.-E. Sjödén,
"Remarques sur le 'swedenborgisme' balzacien," pp. 33-45; Bruce Tolley,
"Balzac et les saint-simoniens," pp. 49-66; Pierre Barbéris, "Balzac, le baron
Charles Dupin et les statistiques," pp. 67-83; Roland Chollet, "Le second
dixain des 'Contes drolatiques,'" pp. 85-126; Moïse Le Yaouanc, "Introduction à 'Un Drame au bord de la mer,'" pp. 127-56; Max Milner, "Le sens
'psychique' de *Massimilla Doni* et la conception balzacienne de l'âme," pp.
157-69; René Guise, "Un grand homme du roman à la scène ou les illusions
reparaissantes de Balzac," pp. 171-216; Anne-Marie Meininger, "Balzac et
Henry Monnier," pp. 217-44; Jean Pommier, "Eve de Balzac, sa fille, son
amant," pp. 245-85; Albert Prioult, "L'amour sous le masque au bal de
l'Opéra," pp. 287-96; Léon-François Hoffman, "Balzac et les noirs," pp. 297-
308; Gérard David, "L'idée de bonheur dans 'La Comédie humaine,'" pp.
309-56; E. Brua, P. Citron, R. Fortassier, L. Gédéon, H. Godin, J. MacBride,
A.-M. Meininger, J. Pommier, "Notes," pp. 357-96; J.-A. Ducourneau et R.
Pierrot, "Calendrier de la vie de Balzac (Année 1835)," pp. 399-417; P.
Citron, A. Lacaux, P. Laubriet, M. Le Yaouanc, M. Milner, R. Pierrot, M.
Regard, O. Tacca, "Revue critique," pp. 419-49; J.-A. Ducourneau, R. Pierrot,
R. Rancoeur, "Bibliographie balzacienne (Année 1965)," pp. 451-58; C. Gould,
R. Guise, T. Hiraoka et T. Takayama, L.-F. Hoffmann, G. Dierenkovskaia et
G. Vipper, "Balzac à l'étranger," pp. 459-68; "Informations et nouvelles," pp.
469-72.

Anon. *Honoré de Balzac. Bibliographie des oeuvres traduites en roumain
et parues en volumes (1852-1965).* Bucarest: L'Institut Roumain pour
les Relations Culturelles avec l'Etranger, 1965. Pp. 23.

Balzac, Honoré de. *Le Chef-d'oeuvre inconnu.* 13 illustrations de Pablo
Picasso. (Les Peintres du Livre.) Paris: Editions L.C.L., 1966. Pp.
120.

Balzac, Honoré de. *Monographie de la presse parisienne.* Précédée de
"L'histoire véridique du canard" par Gérard de Nerval. Paris: J.-J.
Pauvert, 1965. Pp. 229.

Barbéris, Pierre. *Aux sources de Balzac. Les Romans de jeunesse.*
Préface par Jean-A. Ducourneau. Paris: Bibliophiles de l'Originale,
1965. Pp. xxxii + 451; illus.
Rev. by Arlette Michel in *RSH,* n.s., fasc. 124 (1966), pp. 429-30; by Roger
Pierrot in *AnB* 1966, pp. 437-42.
This is volume 16 of *Romans de jeunesse.*

Barbéris, Pierre. "Mythes balzaciens. II. *Le Curé de village.*" Nouvelle
Critique, Nov. 1965, pp. 106-28.

Bevernis, Christa. "Die Weiterentwicklung der ästhetischen Konzep-
tionen Diderots durch Balzac." *Wissenschaftliche Zeitschrift der
Humboldt-Universität zu Berlin. Gesellschaftsund Sprachwissenschaft-
liche Reihe,* XIII (1964), 179-87.

Brua, Edmond. "Balzac et les deux David de Smyrne." *RHL,* LXVI
(1966), 491-93.

Cabanis, José. "Retour à Balzac." *RdP*, LXXII (June 1965), 19-27.
Cabanis seeks reasons why Balzac's "cruel realism" more often succeeds than his lyricism (examples of atrocious lapses of taste on the same page). His answer is that Balzac's failures are those parts of his writing which are not based on his own experience.

[Chancerel, André]. *Guide de la maison de Balzac.* Paris: Ville de Paris, 1965. Pp. 23; illus.

Citron, Pierre, ed. *La Femme de trente ans.* Chronologie et préface par Pierre Citron. Paris: Garnier-Flammarion, 1965. Pp. 250.
Rev. by Roger Pierrot in *AnB* 1966, pp. 435-36.

Citron, Pierre, ed. *Une Fille d'Eve.* Chronologie et préface par Pierre Citron. Paris: Garnier-Flammarion, 1965. Pp. 192.

Cluzel, Etienne. *"David Séchard* de Balzac, est-il une véritable édition originale?" *BLAM*, March 1965, pp. 58-62; April 1965, pp. 85-89.

Crampton, Hope. "Melmoth in 'La Comédie humaine.' " *MLR*, LXI (1966), 42-50.
Sees *Melmoth réconcilié* as a rejection of "Maturin's teaching about humanity in its relation with the forces of good and evil." Examines other parallels and echoes of Maturin's novel in *La Comédie humaine.*

David, Gérard. "Balzac et le bonheur en bleu et gris." *Bulletin des Lettres,* No. 271 (October 15, 1965), pp. 321-25.

Davin, Emmanuel. "Balzac à Toulon, 1838 et 1845." *Bulletin des Amis du Vieux Toulon,* 1965, pp. 14-20.

Delattre, Geneviève. "Le retour en arrière chez Balzac." *RR,* LVII (1966), 88-98.
A brilliant exploration of novelistic technique, focused primarily on *La Peau de chagrin, Le Curé de Tours,* and *La Cousine Bette.* Mme Delattre finds an essential aspect of Balzac's thought in the "remontée vers le passé d'abord et vers l'origine de toutes choses ensuite. . . ." (C.C.)

Durr, René. "La part de l'Yonne dans le roman de Balzac, *Les Paysans.* La fiction et la réalité, essai d'une voie nouvelle." *Bulletin de la Société des Sciences Historiques et Naturelles de l'Yvonne, 1963-1964* (1965), pp. 187-220.

Frappier-Mazur, Lucienne. "Balzac et les images *reparaissantes*: Lumière et flamme dans *La Comédie humaine.*" *RSH,* n.s., No. 121 (1966), pp. 45-80.

Fischer, Jan O. "Colloque Balzac (Paris, 6-7 novembre 1964)." *Beiträge zur romanischen Philologie,* IV. Jahrgang, Heft 1 (1965), pp. 170-73.

Ganière, Paul. "Dupuytren dans l'oeuvre de Balzac (*La Messe de l'athée,* 1836)." *La Presse Médicale,* December 18, 1965, pp. 3152-54.

Genestet, Marc. "Les archives attestent le réalisme de Balzac." *Cahiers Pédagogiques,* Feb. 1963, pp. 58-61.

Genuzio, Joseph. *Jules Guesde et Emile Zola, ou le socialisme dans l'oeuvre d'Emile Zola.* Bari: Tipografia Levante, 1964.

Germain, François, ed. *L'Enfant maudit.* Edition critique établie avec introduction et relevé des variantes par François Germain. (Publications de l'Université de Dijon, Fasc. XXXIII.) Paris: Les Belles Lettres, 1965. Pp. 364.
Rev. by Arlette Michel in *RSH*, n.s., No. 124 (1966), pp. 431-32.

Godot, Brigitte. "Le Paris du *Père Goriot.*" *Cahiers de Neuilly*, July 1964, pp. 89-95.

Gregg, Richard A. "Balzac and the Women in *The Queen of Spades.*" *SEEJ*, x (1966), 279-82.
Influence of Balzac's *La Peau de chagrin* on Pushkin.

Harcourt, Le Duc d'. "La providence chez Balzac." *RdP*, LXXIII (March 1966), 61-65.
Firm beliefs of Balzac in the beneficent effect of suffering on human character.

Hunt, Joel A. "Balzac and Dostoevsky: Some Elements of Scene." *CLS*, III (1966), 439-43.

Hunt, Joel. "Color Imagery in Dostoevskij and Balzac." *SEEJ*, x (1966), 411-23.
Inconclusive but interesting. (C.C.)

Jean-Nesmy, C. "Les heureuses contradictions de Balzac." *Livres et Lectures*, Dec. 1965, pp. 539-42, 544.

Kolbert, Jack. "André Maurois à la recherche d'un genre: la biographie." *FR*, XXXIX (1966), 671-83.
Analyzes Maurois' search for an ideal biography, up to his recent *Prométhée ou la vie de Balzac.*

La Condamine, Pierre de. "Balzac en Bretagne." *Miroir de l'Histoire*, Aug. 1963, pp. 229-37.

Lafon, Henri-René. "Les anciens du Laveur." *Le Cerf Volant*, No. 49 (1965), pp. 19-22.

Le Yaouanc, Moïse, ed. *Le Lys dans la vallée* Introduction, notes, bibliographie et choix de variantes par Moïse Le Yaouanc. (Classiques Garnier.) Paris: Garnier, 1966. Pp. c + 554; illus. 13.90 F.
Rev. by André Billy in *FL*, July 14, 1966, p. 7.
Text of the Furne edition. Introduction treats the genesis of the novel, characters, themes, language and form, and the critical reception. An "Appendice critique" offers a description of the manuscripts, proofs, and editions, as well as a selection of variant readings.

Lock, Peter W. "Hoarders and Spendthrifts in 'La Comédie humaine.' " *MLR*, LXI (1966), 29-41.
A lucid, informative analysis. (C.C.)

Maquet, Albert. "A proposito del soggiorno di Balzac a Torino nell'agosto 1836. II. Deux témoignages inédits de Charles Boucheron." *SFr,* x (1966), 71-75.
See Simone (below) for part I of this article.

Maurois, André. "La jeunesse de Balzac." *RdP,* LXXII (March 1965), 11-36.
Extract from *Prométhée ou la vie de Balzac* (see *ELN,* IV, Supp., 59).

Méras, Edmond A. "Teaching a Sophomore Honors Seminar in Translation." *FR,* XXXIX (1966), 742-47.
Difficulties of finding suitable Balzac translations in print.

Merrill, Francis E. "Balzac as Sociologist: A Study in the Sociology of Literature." *Sociology and Social Research,* L (1966), 148-59.
For the student of literature, Merrill affirms Balzac's grasp and utilization of valid principles of sociology in *La Comédie humaine.* It is remarkable to find a sociologist of the 1960's confirming claims of nineteenth-century novelists that they were essentially scientists. Merrill considers the *Comédie* as "literary experimentation," and "a mine of information about social interaction." (C.C.)

Moser, Françoise. "Balzac et les médecins." *MedF,* No. 162 (May 1965), pp. 14-16.

Mount, A. J. *The Physical Setting in Balzac's Comédie Humaine.* University of Hull Publications, 1966.
Rev. by Claude Elsen in *TR,* No. 226 (November 1966), 154-55.

Nykrog, Per. *La Pensée de Balzac dans 'La Comédie humaine.' Esquisse de quelques concepts-clé.* Munksgaard and Copenhagen: Scandinavian University Books, 1965. Pp. 414. 60 Dan. Kr.
Rev. by H. J. Hunt in *FS,* XX (1966), 416-18; by Arlette Michel in *RSH,* n. s., No. 124 (1966), 430-31; by Norman Suckling in *Erasmus,* XVIII (1966), 358-62.

Picard, Leo. "Balzac en de sociale achtergrond van onze Vlaamse literatur." *Nieuw Vlaams Tijdschrift,* XVIII (1965), 389-400.

Pierrot, Roger, ed. *Contes drolatiques, précédés de La Comédie humaine (Oeuvres ébauchées,* II: *Préfaces).* Etablissement du texte, notices et notes par Roger Pierrot. Index de la *Comédie humaine* par Fernand Lotte. Tome XI. (Bibliothèque de la Pléiade.) Paris: Gallimard, 1965. [2e éd.] Pp. 1742.
In this revised and corrected edition, Fernand Lotte's Indexes have been expanded by fourteen pages to take into account recent scholarship. Names of reappearing characters are now indicated by an asterisk. A cursory check reveals that certain errors remain. An allusion to Diderot's *Le Neveu de Rameau* missed in the first printings of the Index is now given incorrectly as v, 507—it should be v, 594. Marianna Gambara is still incorrectly listed as "Marianina." Béatrix de Rochefide is listed as *comtesse* instead of *marquise.* Errors notwithstanding, these indexes (literary allusions and characters of the *Comédie*) are tremendously useful. This volume also assembles prefaces written or commissioned by Balzac in an accessible location. (C.C.)

Pierrot, Roger, ed. *Correspondance.* Tome IV (*1840-Avril 1845*). Paris: Garnier, 1966. Pp. iv + 931; illus. 30.85 Fr.

Pierrot, Roger. "La pensée politique, sociale et économique de Balzac." *Revue des Travaux de l'Académie des Sciences Morales et Politiques*, 118e année, 4e série (1er semestre 1965), pp. 156-71.
Reprinted, slightly modified, in *RPP*, No. 757 (June 1965), pp. 51-61.
Main elements of theories based on, but surpassing, Balzac's metaphysics: sympathy for republicanism, hostility to the United States and England; monarchy and religion as necessary restraints for individual thought and passion; awareness of dangerous social and economic disequilibrium. Perceptive analysis. (C.C.)

Pugh, Anthony R. "Balzac's Beethoven: A Note on Gambara." *RomN*, VIII (1966), 43-46.
A comment on Beethoven which Balzac actually transposed from the Renduel translation of Hoffmann's *Kreisleriana*. A valuable note. (C.C.)

Pugh, Anthony R. "Ten Years of Balzac Studies." *Modern Languages*, XLVI (September 1965), 91-97.
Rev. by H. G. Hall in *SFr*, x (1966), 372-73.

Reizov, B. "Rastignac et son problème." *Europe*, XLIV (July-August 1966), 223-30.
Concludes that Rastignac is not a rascal, but rather the average man of his time whose soul echoes "la lutte entre deux systèmes philosophiques, l'utilitarisme et la doctrine de l'impératif catégorique."

Savage, Catharine H. "The Romantic *Père Goriot*." *SIR*, v (1966), 104-12.
Suggests that *Le Père Goriot* is badly structured, not because of conflict between the stories of Rastignac and Goriot, but "because of their conflicting ethic." The author accepts Balzac's presentation of Rastignac as a young noble, however, when it seems that his values are more those of an ambitious young bourgeois. An article of considerable interest. (C.C.)

Simone, Franco. "A proposito del soggiorno di Balzac a Torino nell'agosto 1836. I. Sugli amici Torinesi di Balzac e, in particolare, su Constanzo Gazzera." *SFr*, x (1966), 69-70.
See Maquet (above) for part II.

Simone, Franco. "Un romanzo esemplare di Balzac: *Les Paysans*." Vol. II, pp. 1095-1118 in *Studi in onore di Italo Siciliano*. (Biblioteca dell' Archivum Romanicum, Ser. I, Vol. 86.) Florence: Leo S. Olschki, 1965. 2 vols. Pp. 1238.

Steinmann, Jean. *Littérature d'hier et d'aujourd'hui*. [Bruges:] Desclée du Brouwer [1963].
Contains material on Balzac and Nerval.

Välikangas, Olli. *Les termes d'appellation et d'interpellation dans La Comédie humaine de Balzac*. (Memoires de la Société Néophilologique de Helsinki, XXVIII.) Helsinki: Société Néophilologique, 1965. Pp. 506. $6.00.

Vaulx, Bernard de. "Balzac a-t-il aimé la vertu?" *Les Amis de Saint François*, n.s., VI (1965), 142-63.
An inventory of the *justes* in *La Comédie humaine*. Positive conclusion: Balzac loved virtue and wanted to make it interesting. (C.C.)

See also Ruitenbeek, Starzinger ("General 2. Environment"); Bowman, Delmas, Macchia, Palou ("French 1. General"); Viatte ("Chateaubriand"); Florenne, Le Yaouanc, Meininger ("Stendhal").

Reviews of works previously listed:

ALLEMAND, André, *Honoré de Balzac: création et passion* (see *ELN*, IV, Supp., 52), rev. by Spire Pitou in *BA*, XL (1966), 292; ALLEMAND, André, *Unité et structure de l'univers balzacien* (see *ELN*, IV, Supp., 53), rev. by Albert Delorme in *RdS*, LXXXVII (1966), 187-88, and by G. Joffre in *RUL*, XXI (1966), 213-14; *AnB 1964* (see *ELN*, III, Supp., 51-52), rev. by Albert Delorme in *RdS*, LXXXVII (1966), 181-84, and by André Lacaux in *RHL*, LXVI (1966), 341-42; *AnB 1965* (see *ELN*, IV, Supp., 53), rev. by Albert Delorme in *RdS*, LXXXVII (1966), 184-86; by Carrol F. Coates in *BA*, XL (1966), 421; by Yves Florenne in *Le Monde*, July 28, 1965, p. 9, and by Albert J. Salvan in *FR*, XL (1966), 295-97, in *SFr*, X (1966), 373-74; BARDÈCHE, Maurice, *Une Lecture de Balzac* (see *ELN*, III, Supp., 52), rev. by Edmond Beaujon in *Journal de Genève*, Nov. 20-21, 1965, pp. 1, 3; by V.-H. Debidour in *Le Bulletin des Lettres*, No. 264 (Jan. 15, 1965), pp. 1-5; by Marcel Reboussin in *MLN*, LXXXI (1966), 354-57, and by Maurice Regard in *AnB 1966*, pp. 446-49; BEEBE, Maurice, *Ivory Towers and Sacred Founts* (see *ELN*, III, Supp., 53), rev. by Roy Pascal in *MLR*, LXI (1966), 118-19, and by Olga M. Vickery in *Criticism*, VIII (1966), 298-300; BÉGUIN, Albert, *Balzac lu et relu* (see *ELN*, IV, Supp., 54), rev. by André Bourgeois in *BA*, XL (1966), 292; BÉRARD, Suzanne Jean, *La Genèse d'un roman de Balzac. Illusions perdues, 1837* (see *PQ*, LXIII, 466), rev. by Aimé Depuy in *Revue d'Histoire Moderne et Contemporaine*, XI (1964), 145-47; CASTEX, Pierre-Georges, ed., *Eugénie Grandet* (see *ELN*, IV, Supp., 55), rev. by Carrol F. Coates in *FR*, XXXIX (1966), 942; by Albert Delorme in *RdS*, LXXXVII (1966), 179-80; by H. J. Hunt in *FS*, XX (1966), 81-82; by Pierre Laubriet in *AnB 1966*, pp. 482-32, and by Jacques Robichez in *IL*, XVIII (1966), 28-29; CESARE, Raffaele de, "Balzac nel maggio 1836" (see *ELN*, IV, Supp., 55), rev. by P[ierre] Laubriet in *RHL*, LXVI (1966), 328-30; DONNARD, J.-H., ed., *Les Paysans* (see *ELN*, III, Supp., 54), rev. by Pierre Barbéris in *RHL*, LXV (1965), 494-502; FANGER, Donald, *Dostoevsky and Romantic Realism* (see *ELN*, IV, Supp., 56), rev. by Robert L. Strong, Jr., in *SEEJ*, IX (1966), 469-71; HOFFMANN, Léon-François, *Répertoire géographique de La Comédie humaine. I. L'Etranger* (see *ELN*, IV, Supp., 58), rev. by Pierre Laubriet in *AnB 1966*, pp. 424-26, and by R[aymond] P[ouilliart] in *LR*, XX (1966), 197, in *SFr*, X (1966), 374; LAUBRIET, Pierre, ed., *Histoire de la grandeur et de la décadence de César Birotteau* (see *ELN*, IV, Supp., 58), rev. by Pierre Citron in *AnB 1966*, pp. 426-28; by Carrol F. Coates in *FR*, XXXIX (1966), 942; by Albert Delorme in *RdS*, LXXXVII (1966), 178-79, and by W. G. Moore in *MLR*, LXI (1966), 136-37; MAUROIS, André, *Prométhée ou la vie de Balzac* (see *ELN*, IV, Supp., 59), rev. by Sidney D. Braun in *RR*, LVII (1966), 141-44; by Carrol F. Coates in *FR*, XXXIX (1966), 941-42; by Roger Parelon in *Le Français dans le Monde*, No. 35 (1965), p. 51; by Spire Pitou in *BA*, XL (1966), 300, and by Maurice Regard in *AnB 1966*, pp. 419-20; MÉTADIER, Bernard Paul, *Balzac au petit matin* (see *ELN*, IV, Supp., 60), rev. by Moïse Le Yaouanc in *AnB 1966*, pp. 442-44; MILNER, Max, ed., *Massimilla Doni* (see *ELN*, IV, Supp., 60), rev. by P[ierre] Laubriet in *RHL*, LXVI (1966), 332-36; OLIVER, E. J., *Honoré de Balzac* (see *ELN*, IV, Supp., 56), rev. by Albert J. Salvan in *FR*, XL (1966), 297-98; PIERROT, Roger, ed., *Correspondance*, t. II (see *PQ*, XLIII, 468), rev. by Anthony R. Pugh in *MLR*, LXI (1966), 132-36, t. III (see *ELN*, III, Supp., 56), rev. by Pierre Citron in *RHL*, LXVI (1966), 336-37; by V. D[el] L[itto] in *SC*, VIII (1966), 190-92; by Albert Delorme in *RdS*, LXXXVII (1966); by Jean Pommier in *Revue des Travaux de l'Académie des Sciences Morales et Politiques*, 117e Année, 4e Série (1er semestre 1964), pp. 414-16; by R. Pouilliart in *LR*, XX (1966), 83-84, and by Anthony R. Pugh in *MLR*, LXI (1966), 132-36; REGARD, Maurice, ed., *Gambara* (see *ELN*, IV, Supp., 61), rev. by Pierre Laubriet in *RHL*, xlvi (1966), 330-32; Wurmser, André, *La Comédie inhumaine* (see *ELN*, iii, Supp., 58), rev. by Jean-Hervé Donnard in *RHL*, lxvi (1966), 338-41, and by Marcel Reboussin in *MLN*, lxxxi (1966), 107-10.

BERTRAND

Hubert, Renée Riese. "La technique de la peinture dans le poème en prose." *CAIEF*, No. 18 (1966), pp. 169-78.

Distinguishes Bertrand from his most notable successors (Baudelaire and Rimbaud).

Review of book previously listed:

Nies, Fritz, *Poesie in prosaischer Welt* (see *ELN*, iv, Supp., 63), rev. by D. J. Mossop in *FS*, xx (1966), 204-05.

BONALD

Jallut, Maurice. "Bonald contre le libéralisme." *L'Ordre Français*, May 1965.

Saudoul, Guy. "Le vicomte de Bonald." *L'Ordre Français*, Feb. 1965.

See also Deniel ("1. General").

BOREL

Belleli, Maria Luisa. "Il licantrope immorale." *Il Mondo*, Oct. 19, 1965.

BOYER

Cluzel, Etienne. "Un romantique hugolâtre et idolâtre: Philoxène Boyer." *BLAM*, No. 87 (August-September 1966), pp. 143-47.

Mostly on Boyer's relations with Hugo.

CHASLES

Review of book previously listed:

Pichois, Claude, *Philarète Chasles et la vie littéraire au temps du romantisme* (see *ELN*, iv, Supp., 63), rev. by Raymond Pouilliart in *LR*, xx (1966), 81-83.

CHATEAUBRIAND

See also Krömer ("Spanish 2. General") and Dendle ("Soler").

Barthes, Roland, ed. *La Vie de Rancé*, précédé de *La Voyageuse de nuit* [by Barthes]. (Le Monde en 10/18, No. 234.) Paris: Union Générale d'Edition, 1965.

Bouloiseau, Marc, ed. *Mémoires d'outre-tombe*. (Classiques pour Notre Temps.) Paris: Alpina, 1966. 25.95 Fr.

Bulletin de la Société Chateaubriand, n.s., 8 (1964), Pp. 109.

For survey of contents, see *SFr*, x, 164-65.

Cabanis, José. "Anniversaire d'un pamphlet" [*De Buonaparte et des Bourbons*]. *RdP*, lxxii (1965), 93-98.

Sees Chateaubriand's political ambition as explaining not only his life but his style and a fundamental aspect of his genius. Thus the artifice of much of his early work tends to disappear with *De Buonaparte et des Bourbons*. Later, in the *Mémoires d'outre-tombe* his sense of the loss of youth and of approaching death affords a comparable note of reality.

Cabanis, José. "Non, H. Guillemin, le vicomte n'était pas un vilain Monsieur!" *NL*, Feb. 11, 1965.

Chalvet, Maurice. "Les Exemplaires connus de l'édition princeps de l'*Essai sur les révolutions*, de Chateaubriand." *LeE*, No. 36 (1963), pp. 309-21.

Christophorov, Pierre. "Le Voyage de Chateaubriand en Espagne (à propos d'une discussion littéraire)." Pp. 193-223 in *Connaissance de l'étranger: Mélanges offerts à la mémoire de Jean-Marie Carré*. Paris: Marcel Didier, 1964. Pp. xx + 529; illus.

Duhamel, Roger. "Chateaubriand et Mme de Staël." *RUO*, XXXIII (1963), 117-38.

Gautier, J.-M. *Le Style des "Mémoires d'outre-tombe" de Chateaubriand*. Nouvelle édition. Genève: Droz, 1964. Pp. 209.
Rev. by Arveiller in *FM*, XXXIV (1966), 226-29.
Arveiller notes that Gautier examines the vocabulary (in comparison with that of contemporary dictionaries)—then the sentence construction—then the images. Cites Mourot's examination of the sonorities in his fine thesis.

Jouhandeau, Marcel. *Divertissements*. Paris: Gallimard, 1965. Pp. 150. 9 Fr.
Includes a study of *La Vie de Rancé*.

Lebègue, Raymond. "Structure et but du *Voyage en Amérique* de Chateaubriand." Pp. 273-85 in *Connaissance de l'étranger: Mélanges offerts à la mémoire de Jean-Marie Carré*. Paris: Marcel Didier, 1964. Pp. xx + 529.

L'Osservatore Romano. Comments by Francesco Casnati (Jan. 1, 1965), and by "S.L." (May 14 and 21, 1965).

Remacle, Louis. "Situer le texte: A propos d'une description de Chateaubriand." *Cahiers d'Analyse Textuelle*, No. 7 (1965), 110-15.
Demonstrates how J. Vianey's interpretation of a descriptive passage in *Le Génie du Christianisme* is invalidated by failure to consider its details in context.

Richard, Jean-Pierre. "Chateaubriand et la rêverie du négatif." *Critique*, No. 226 (March 1966), pp. 195-214.

Richard, Jean-Pierre. "Chateaubriand, la civilisation, l'histoire." *NRF*, XIV (1966), 298-306, 478-87.
Sees Chateaubriand as a strange *hybrid*, caught in his human conscience between the political and historical past of royalty and the world of future change—in Chateaubriand's own words, "démocrate par nature, aristocrate par moeurs."

Tapié, Victor-L. *Chateaubriand par lui-même*. (Coll. "Ecrivains de Toujours," 71.) Paris: Éditions du Seuil, 1965. Illus. Pp. 190. 4.90 Fr.

Vaulx, Bernard de. "Chateaubriand sur la sellette." *Écrits de Paris*, No. 241 (1965), 101-06.

Viatte, Auguste. "Chateaubriand, Balzac: l'argent et l'ambition." *RUL,* xx (1965), 24-31.

See also Beauchamps, Deniel, Duhamel, Jean ("1. General"); Arnold ("Senancour").

Reviews of books previously listed:

LEHTONEN, Maija, *L'Expression imagée dans l'oeuvre de Chateaubriand* (see *ELN*, III, Supp., 59), rev. by Fernande Bassan in *Symposium,* xx (1966), 87-89; by J.-Cl. Chevalier in *FM,* xxxIV (1966), 233-35, and by Jean Mourot in *RHL,* LXVI (1966), 519-23; LEVAILLANT, Maurice, *Chateaubriand, prince des songes* (see *PQ,* XLI, 684), rev. by P. Huard in *RdS,* LXXXVII (1966), 175-76; MOREAU, Pierre, *Chateaubriand* (see *ELN,* IV, Supp., 64), rev. by Francesco Casnati in *L'Osservatore Romano,* May 14, 1965; MOUROT, Jean, *Etudes sur les premières oeuvres de Chateaubriand* (see *PQ,* XLIII, 471), rev. by Pierre Christophorov in *RHL,* LXVI (1966), 517-19; VIAL, André, *Chateaubriand et le temps perdu* (see *PQ,* XLIII, 471), rev. by Raymond Pouilliart in *LR,* xx (1966), 80-81.

CONSTANT

Baelen, Jean. *Benjamin Constant et Napoléon.* Paris: J. Peyronnet, 1965. Pp. 248.

Rev. by A. d'Ad. in *Archivio Storico Italiano,* Disp. III (1965), 415-16.

Bastid, Paul. *Benjamin Constant et sa doctrine.* Paris: Armand Colin, 1966. 2 vols. Pp. 1112. 85 Fr.

Rev. by Pierre Clarac in *IL,* xVIII (1966), 162, by Charles Melchior de Molènes in *RPP,* No. 771 (October 1966), pp. 79-89.
Pt. I, "L'homme et le citoyen"; Pt. II, "L'oeuvre et les idées." A monumental view of Constant as lover, writer, citizen. Ideas—on freedom, religion, constitutionalism, economy, etc.—are analyzed in detail. Bastid denies A. France's accusation that Constant "professa la liberté sans y croire." Claims for Constant an originality apart from superficial resemblances to the thought of Montesquieu. (C.C.)

Courtney, C. P. "Benjamin Constant et Nathaniel May. Documents inédits." *RHL,* LXVI (1966), 162-78.

Deguise, Pierre. *Benjamin Constant méconnu: Le livre de la religion, avec des documents inédits.* Geneva: Droz, 1966. Pp. x + 309; illus. 50.40 Fr.

An inquiry into the "rapports de l'homme et de son oeuvre." An important work, designed to show Constant as more than the author of *Adolphe.* In the introductory chapter, Deguise examines in detail the complex history of Sainte-Beuve's judgments of Constant.

Delbouille, Paul. "Propos sur Benjamin Constant." *RLV,* xxxII (1966), 420-33.

Reviews recent works on Constant by Derré, Hogue, Pozzo di Borgo, Cordié, Roulin et Roth, Deguise.

Derré, Jean-René, ed. *Wallstein, tragédie en cinq actes et en vers de Benjamin Constant;* édition critique, publiée avec de nombreuses variantes et des documents inédits, par Jean-René Derré. (Bibliothèque de la Faculté des Lettres de Lyon, Fasc. X, grande série.) Paris: Les Belles Lettres, 1965. Pp. 262. 20 Fr.

Rev. by A. Monchoux in *RLC,* XL (1966), 481-84.

Fairlie, Alison. "The Art of Constant's *Adolphe*: Creation of Character."
Forum for Modern Language Studies, II **(1966), 253-63.**
Excellent treatment of Ellénore as a complex character in her own right, with
similar considerations on the Baron de T. and the Comte de P. (C.C.)

Fairlie, Alison. "The Art of Constant's *Adolphe*: Structure and Style."
FS, XX (1966), 226-42.
Fairlie sketches a description of the style of *Adolphe* (with brief reference to
Constant's conception of style): presence of the physical world, precision,
epigrammatic turns, concentrated sentences. The article is not completely
satisfactory in the establishment of a theoretical basis, but is provocative.
(C.C.)

Frautschi, R. L. "Various Points of View in Benjamin Constant's
Adolphe." *Kentucky Foreign Language Quarterly*, XII (1965), 225-
30.

Girard, Alain. "Benjamin Constant et le livre 'De la réligion' devant la
critique." *RHL*, LXVI (1966), 115-26.

Letessier, Fernand. "La romancière Louise d'Estournelles de Constant
(1792-1860) et ses amis." *BAGB*, Ser. 4, No. 4 (December 1964),
pp. 464-78.

Lobet, Marcel. "Du mal de Sade à Benjamin Constant." *La Revue
Générale Belge*, Cᵉ Année (September 1964), pp. 21-33.

Nicolas, Claire. "Pourquoi Ellénore est-elle Polonaise?" *RHL*, LXVI
(1966), 85-93.
Suggests Louvet de Couvray's *Amours du chevalier de Faublas* as a source
for the Polish elements of *Adolphe*.

Oliver, Andrew. "Existe-t-il un 'Journal intime' inédit de Benjamin
Constant?" *RSH*, n.s., No. 122-23 (1966), pp. 211-15.

Pichois, Claude. "Pour un double centenaire." *RHL*, LXVI (1966), 1-2.

Pozzo di Borgo, Olivier. "Un libéral devant une dictature." *RHL*, LXVI
(1966), 94-114.
Examines Constant's apparent opportunism in politics. Concludes that he was
faithful not to a man but to ideas, to belief in freedom.

Roth, Charles. "Nouveaux fragments du brouillon autographe de Benjamin Constant pour la 'Préface' à la deuxième édition d' 'Adolphe.' "
RHL, LXVI (1966), 158-60.

See also Lobet ("1. General"); Cordey ("Staël").

Reviews of works previously listed:
CORDIÉ, Carlo, ed., *Adolphe* (see *ELN*, III, Supp., 61), rev. by Béatrice Le
Gall in *RHL*, LXVI (1966), 183-84, and by Alison Fairlie in *MLR*, LXI (1966),
519-20; HOGUE, H[elen] H. S., *Of Changes in Benjamin Constant's Books on
Religions* (see *ELN*, III, Supp., 61); rev. by F. T. H. Fletcher in *FS*, XX
(1966), 80-81; by Béatrice Le Gall in *RHL*, LXVI (1966), 182-83, and by
Renée Waldinger in *RR*, LVII (1966), 303-04.

COUSIN

Chauchard, Paul. "Quand Victor Cousin réhabilite Saint Thomas d'Aquin." *TR*, No. 213 (October 1965), pp. 125-30.

Will, Frederic. *Flumen Historicum: Victor Cousin's Aesthetic and Its Sources.* (University of North Carolina Studies in Comparative Literature, 36.) University of North Carolina Press, 1965. Pp. 97.
Sees Plato as a primary source, both as direct influence and indirect (via Plotinus, Shaftesbury, Burke, Reid, Winckelmann, Quatremère de Quincy, Kant, and Hegel).

DELÉCLUZE

Baschet, Robert. "Delécluze à Florence." *SC*, IX (1966), 27-54.
Reprints, with introduction, an unpublished notebook Delécluze kept on his Italian journey (1823).

DESBORDES-VALMORE

Barret, Andrée. "Une poésie de circonstance." *Europe*, XLII (November-December 1964), 82-85.

DUMAS

Arnaboldi, Jean, ed. *Le Grand Dictionnaire de cuisine.* Paris: Cercle du Livre Précieux, 1965. Pp. lxvi + 569.

Cluzel, Etienne. "Le véritable abbé Faria et celui du roman de *Monte-Cristo* (suite et fin)." *BLAM*, 45e Année, n.s., No. 78, (October 1965), pp. 173-75.

Juin, Hubert, ed. *Les Mille et un fantômes.* Préface d'H. J. Verviers: Gérard & Cie.; Paris: L'Inter, 1965. Pp. 758.

Sigaux, Gilbert, ed. *Ange Pitou.* Tomes I-II. Précédé de "La véritable Ange Pitou" par Gilbert Sigaux. Lausanne: Editions Rencontre, 1965. Pp. 1030.

Sigaux, Gilbert, ed. *Le Comte de Monte-Cristo.* Préface de Gilbert Sigaux. Levallois-Perret: Cercle du Bibliophile, 1965. 3 vols. Pp. 1431.

Sigaux, Gilbert, ed. *La Comtesse de Charmy.* Précédée de "Vérité et roman dans *Mémoires d'un médecin*" par Gilbert Sigaux. Lausanne: Editions Rencontre, 1965. 3 vols. Pp. 1676.

Sigaux, Gilbert, ed. *Joseph Balsamo.* Préface de Gilbert Sigaux. Levallois-Perret: Cercle du Bibliophile, 1965. Pp. 469.

Sigaux, Gilbert, ed. *Le Vicomte de Bragelonne.* Préface de Gilbert Sigaux. Levallois-Perret: Cercle du Bibliophile, 1965. 4 vols. Pp. 1887.

See also Palou ("1. General"); Bach ("Sainte-Beuve").

FAURIEL

Ibrovac, Miodrag. *Claude Fauriel et la fortune européenne des poésies populaires grecque et serbe: étude d'histoire romantique, suivie du cours de Fauriel professé en Sorbonne (1831-1832).* (Études de Littérature Etrangère et Comparée, 52.) Paris: Marcel Didier, 1966. Pp. 719. 95 Fr.

Rev. by André Billy in *FL*, Aug. 11, 1966, p. 4. A monument of sound, old-fashioned literary history. An idea of the huge mass of erudition heaped up here can be gained from noting that the index contains references to about 2,500 persons. Ibrovac's study is unusually comparative in that, in addition to the French (Madame de Staël, Nodier, Mérimée, Hugo, N. Lemercier, J.-J. Ampère, *et al.*) and Balkan personalities necessarily involved, more or less prominent roles are held by Manzoni, Pushkin, Goethe, Grimm, Byron, and Scott, to mention only the most prominent. More than a third of the text is given over to an edition of Fauriel's course on "La Poésie populaire des Serbes et des Grecs." Early sections of the book are devoted to the rise of interest in folk poetry, the modern phase of Philhellenism, and to Fauriel's life and work in general. The study is centered in Fauriel's two great works, *Les Chants populaires de la Grèce moderne* (1824), and the above-mentioned Sorbonne course. All this is accompanied by abundant illustration and by various appendices. (J.S.P.)

FOURIER

Lehouck, Emile. *Fourier aujourd'hui.* (Dossiers des Lettres Nouvelles.) Paris: Denoël, 1966. 15.40 Fr.

GAUTIER

Binney, Edwin. *Les Ballets de Théophile Gautier.* Paris: Nizet, 1965. Pp. 443 + 30 pl.

Rev. by H. van der Tuin in *RLC*, XL (1966), 314-16.

Cottin, Madeleine. "Bons Baisers d'Espagne. Une correspondance inédite de Théophile Gautier [1840]." *Nouvelles Littéraires*, Sept. 2, 1965.

Cottin, Madeleine. *"Emaux et camées*, musée de poche." *CAIEF*, No. 18 (1966), pp. 215-26.

Spencer, M. C. "Théophile Gautier and the *Figaro*." *FS*, XX (1966), 134-38.

Suggests possible emendations in Spoelberch de Lovenjoul's attributions to Gautier of articles in the *Figaro* between October 1836 and May 1838.

Tomić, Josip. "Théophile Gautier a-t-il habité l'Hôtel de Lauzun?" *Studia Romanica et Anglica Zagrabiensa*, Nos. 13-14 (July-December 1962), pp. 141-52.

Apparently not. The problem could have been more simply treated by reading Gautier's article "Le club des haschischins," in the *RDM*, Feb. 1, 1846.

Van der Tuin, H. "La Fortune de Théophile Gautier en Hollande (1830-1900)." *RLC*, XL (1966), 212-25.

Shows interest, especially of *la critique hollandaise*, in Gautier's work, but sees the extent of his direct influence on the poets and prose writers of Holland as still unclear.

See also Christout, Keller, Palou ("1. General"); Poulet, Whyte ("Nerval"); Bach ("Sainte-Beuve"); and numerous entries under Nodier.

GUÉRIN

L'Amitié Guérinienne. 34ᵉ Année, No. 2 (1966), pp. 29-56.
Contains: "Deux lettres de Maurice de Guérin," pp. 29-53; Maria Teresa Maiorana, "Maurice de Guérin et le thème de la nature," pp. 34-42; Maria Teresa Maiorana, "Une traduction espagnole de cinq lettres de Maurice de Guérin" [introduction to an Argentine translation of Guérin], pp. 42-43; "Les Chroniques," pp. 44-56.

[Barthe, Chanoine Fernand. (F.B.)] "Trois Lettres inédites de Maurice de Guérin" [à son père, 18 juin 1826; 24 mai 1827; 12 avril 1828], *L'Amitié Guérinienne*, Nos. 1-2, 1965.

Moreau, Pierre, ed. *Les Plus Belles Pages de Maurice et Eugénie de Guérin.* Présentées par François Mauriac. Paris: Mercure de France, 1965. Pp. 256. 16 Fr.

Schärer-Nussberger, Maya. *Maurice de Guérin: l'errance et la demeure.* Paris: José Corti, 1965. Pp. 219.
A psycho-philosophical study after the manner of Poulet. Quotations from Guérin's work are arranged so as to form a coherent view of the author's poetic or imaginary universe and to give his soul a poetic biography in which attitudes and feelings function as events (the death of Marie de la Morvonnais is the only biographical episode of the usual type which plays a role in the "new life" created for the poet by the critic). The book culminates in a long chapter devoted to the two great prose poems "Le centaure" and "La bacchante." Here *l'errance* becomes *la demeure*, as the poet's pantheism merges the mobility of his being with the rhythms of the universe.
Rev. by M. M. in *IL*, xviii (1966), 116, and by Marjorie Shaw in *FS*, xx (1966), 414-15.

Reviews of books previously listed:
MOREAU, Pierre, ed., *Maurice et Eugénie de Guérin* (see *ELN*, iv, Supp., 68), rev. by M. Jeanneret in *SFr*, x (1966), 376-77; SECRETAN, Dominique, ed., *Pages choisies* (see *ELN*, iv, Supp., 68), rev. by Marjorie Shaw in *FS*, xx (1966), 415-16.

HUGO

Albouy, Pierre, ed. *L'Ane.* Éd. critique. ("Cahiers Victor Hugo," 3.) Paris: Flammarion, 1966. Pp. 345. 38 Fr.

Barrère, Jean-Bertrand. *Victor Hugo à l'oeuvre. Le poète en exil et en voyage.* (Bibliothèque Française et Romane. Série C: Études Littéraires, XI.) Paris: Klincksieck, 1965. Pp. 326. 30 Fr.
Rev. in *TLS*, May 26, 1966, pp. 465-67.

Bedner, J. *"Le Rhin" de Victor Hugo. Commentaires sur un récit de voyage.* Groningen: J. B. Wolters, 1965. Pp. vii + 171. 12.90 Fr.

Bozzoli, Adriano. "Per l'interpretazione dell' Ode salvadoriana 'Per la morte di Victor Hugo' [end of May, 1885]." *LI*, January-March 1965.

Bronne, Carlo. "Victor Hugo et la fin du Second Empire." *Synthèses* [Brussels], Nos. 242-243 (July-August 1966), 76-82.

Burguet, F.-A., ed. *Les Travailleurs de la mer*. Préface de Gaétan Picon. (Coll. "Le Livre de Poche," Nos. 1560-61-62.) Paris: Librairie Générale Française (exclusivité Hachette), 1965. 5 Fr.

Comeau, Paul T. " 'Le Satyre' dans *La Légende des siècles* de Victor Hugo." *FR*, XXXIX (1966), 849-61.
After examining various philosophical interpretations of "Le Satyre," concludes that the question of the poem's meaning is still far from being resolved.

Delalande, Jean. "Documents inédits sur 'Le Revenant' des *Contemplations*." *RHL*, LXVI (1966), 314-16.
Cites evidence for dating composition of "Le Revenant" at Aug. 18, 1854 rather than in August 1843 (the date given by Hugo).

Dumas, André, ed. *La Légende des siècles*. ("Classiques Garnier.") Paris: Garnier, 1964. Pp. xxx + 903. Illus.
Valuable notes, pp. 809-82.

Fabre, Jean. "L'idée polonaise dans les *Misérables*." Pp. 256-66 in *Connaissance de l'étranger: Mélanges offerts à la mémoire de Jean-Marie Carré*. Paris: Marcel Didier, 1964. Pp. xx + 529.

Garçon, Maurice. "Les Héros de roman écrivent l'histoire." *Les Annales*, October 1965.
On Parisian society of the period 1830-1848 as seen by H. Monnier, Eugène Süe, Victor Hugo, and Balzac.

Gaudon, Jean. *Victor Hugo (1802-1885)*. An exhibition of autograph letters, manuscripts, prints and books. University of Manchester. Feb. 4-March 13, 1965. Introduction par Jean Gaudon. Manchester, 1965.

Gaudon, Jean. "Victor Hugo et le dragon poète." *Europe*, XLIV (1966), 52-69.
On Charles Dubois de Gennes, who was rescued from over five years of military humiliation and torture through the intervention of the Hugos.

Gaulmier, Jean. "Connaissance de Victor Hugo" [avec une lettre du 21 9bre (1871)?]. *Bulletin de la Faculté des Lettres de Strasbourg*, February 1965.

Henrard, Annie. " 'Pauca Meae' ou la descente aux Enfers, de Victor Hugo." *Marche Romane*, XIV (1964), 129-34.

"Jehovah's Clarion." *TLS*, May 26, 1966, pp. 465-67.
Ostensibly writing a front-page review article on four recent books concerned with Hugo (Maurois' *Victor Hugo and His World*, Barrère's *Victor Hugo à l'oeuvre* and *Victor Hugo*, and Moreau's *Ames et thèmes romantiques*), the anonymous writer attempts to survey Hugo's accomplishments and limitations as a poet, cites "the hollow reverberation" of Hugo's language, his reliance "on noise and on the external associations of words," his "melodramatic language and imagery," and concludes that "the verdict on Hugo must surely be, not the greatest French poet, but a magnificent craftsman, a brilliant technical innovator . . . a flawed genius. . . ."

Journet, René, and Guy Robert, eds. *Boîte aux lettres.* Ed. critique. ("Cahiers Victor Hugo," 2.) Paris: Flammarion, 1965. Pp. 190.
Rev. by Gilbert B. in *RUL*, XXI (1966), 434, and by G. Franceschetti in *SFr*, X (1966), 375.

Journet, René, and Guy Robert, eds. *Journal de ce que j'apprends chaque jour (juillet 1846-février 1848).* Éd. critique. ("Cahiers Victor Hugo," publiés avec le concours du Centre National de la Recherche Scientifique, No. 1.) Paris: Flammarion, 1965. Pp. 283. 19.50 Fr.
Rev. by B. F. Bart in *FR*, XL (1966), 150.

Lambert, François, ed. *Epîtres.* ("Cahiers Victor Hugo," 4.) Paris: Flammarion, 1966. Pp. 144. 16 Fr.

Letessier, Fernand. "Victor Hugo et Ymbert Galloix." *RHL*, LXVI (1966), 487-90.
On an unfortunate young man of letters whom Hugo called "un penseur qui meurt de misère!"

Maurois, André. *Victor Hugo.* ("Les Écrivains par l'image.") Paris: Hachette, 1966. Pp. 144. 20 Fr.

Maurois, André. *Victor Hugo and His World.* Transl. from the French by Oliver Bernard. London: Thames and Hudson, 1966. Pp. 143. Illus. 25s.
Maurois' commentary on Hugo, his family, associates, and contemporaries, accompanied by 115 illustrations, gives an unusually vivid sense of "Victor Hugo and his world." But see adverse review by anon. writer in *TLS*, May 26, 1966, pp. 465-67.

Mercié, Jean-Luc. *Victor Hugo et une inconnue: Clara Duchastel, documents inédits.* (Archives des Lettres Modernes, No. 67.) Paris: Minard, 1966. Pp. 41. Illus. 6 Fr.
On a friend of Léopoldine and Mme Hugo. In the author's words, "un aspect minuscule mais absolument inconnu de la biographie de Victor Hugo."

Prasteau, Jean. "Harvard et Princeton traquent à prix d'or les manuscrits de Victor Hugo." *FL*, July 28, 1966.
Cites the remarkable resurrection of interest in Hugo since the Liberation and describes the program of discussions at the College de France on Hugo (July 27-July 30, 1966) by the Association Internationale des Études Françaises.

Showalter, English, Jr. "De *Madame de la Pommeraye à Ruy Blas.*" *RHL*, LXVI (1966), 238-52.
Sees Don Salluste as more capable of interesting us than Ruy Blas.

Süpek, Ottó. "L'Influence de Victor Hugo en Hongrie à l'époque des réformes (1831-1848)." *Acta Litteraria Academiae Scientiarum Hungaricae*, VIII, No. 1-2, 1965.

See also Keller, Poulet ("1. General"); Cluzel ("Boyer"); Bach ("Sainte-Beuve").

Reviews of books previously listed:
ALBOUY, Pierre, *La Création mythologique chez Victor Hugo* (see *ELN*, III,

Supp., 63), long rev. article by Giancarlo Franceschetti in *SFr*, x (1966), 106-10; ALBOUY, Pierre, ed., *Oeuvres poétiques. I: Avant l'exil, 1802-1851* (see *ELN*, III, Supp., 63), rev. by Jean Gaudon in *MLR*, LXI (1966), 520-21; BARRERE, J.-B., ed., *Un Carnet des "Misérables"* (see *ELN*, IV, Supp., 69), rev. by G. Franceschetti in *SFr*, x (1966), 375-76; by H. J. Hunt in *FS*, xx (1966), 306, and by R. P[ouilliart] in *LR*, xx (1966), 286-87; BARRERE, J.-B., *Victor Hugo* (see *ELN*, IV, Supp., 69), rev. by H. J. Hunt in *FS*, xx (1966), 307; DÉDÉYAN, Charles, *Victor Hugo et l'Allemagne. I: La Formation (1802-1830)* (see *ELN*, III, Supp., 65), rev. by Pierre Georgel in *LR*, xx (1966), 183-88; PY, Albert, *Les mythes grecs dans la poésie de Victor Hugo* (see *ELN*, III, Supp., 67), rev. by R. Trousson in *RBPH*, XLIII (1965), 734-37; THIERRY, J.-J., and Josette Mélèze, eds., *Théâtre complet* (see *ELN*, III, Supp., 67), rev. very unfavorably by Jean Gaudon in *MLR*, LXI (1966), 520-21.

JOUBERT

Gaudemar, Paul de. "La signification du thème de la pudeur dans la pensée morale et sociale de Joubert." *Annales Publiées par la Faculté des Lettres de Toulouse. Homo,* IV (May 1965).

LACORDAIRE

See Bowman ("1. General").

LAMARTINE

Berthelot, Marcel. "L'origine de la pensée politique de Lamartine et les dernières années de la Restauration, 1826-1830." *Annales de l'Académie de Mâcon, 1962-1963* (1965).

Chervet, Maurice, ed. *Secondes Journées européennes d'études lamartiniennes, Mâcon, 18 au 20 septembre 1965: Actes du Congrès, II.* Mâcon: Comité Permanent d'Etudes Lamartiniennes, 1966. Pp. 141. 18 Fr.

Reprints the following papers presented at the congress mentioned in the title: VI. Topentcharov, "Lamartine et la Bulgarie" (pp. 11-16); le baron Pierre Nothomb, "Traces de Lamartine dans le Nord-Est" (pp. 17-22); Charles Fournet, "Lamartine et le poète romantique genevois Jacques Imbert Galloix" (pp. 23-24); Luigi de Nardis, "L'influence de Lamartine sur les poèmes de jeunesse de Mallarmé" (pp. 35-43); A. J. Steele, "Lamartine et la poésie vitale" (pp. 45-59); Louis Charvet, "Découverte de *Saül* ou pérennité de Lamartine" (pp. 61-66); Christian Croisille, "*La vigne et la maison*: constantes et évolution de la poésie lamartinienne" (pp. 67-84); Jean Gaulmier, "Gobineau lecteur de Lamartine" (pp. 85-93); A. Mabille de Poncheville, "Quelques amis de Lamartine restés dans l'ombre" (pp. 95-103); Marius-François Guyard, "Un héritier rebelle de Lamartine: Lautréamont" (pp. 105-14); Georges Poulet, "Lamartine et les exigences du souvenir total" (pp. 115-26); Maurice Chervet, "Lamartine et le terroir" (pp. 127-33); and "Discours prononcé par M. Gaëtan Picon à la séance de clôture du congrès" (pp. 135-40).

Dopp, P. H. "Les contrefaçons belges de Lamartine (suite). XXIX. Un choix de poésies nouvelles de Lamartine à Bruxelles en 1850." *LeE*, No. 45-46 (1966), pp. 109-18.

Apropos of a volume issued by Kiessling containing 26 poems first published in the *OEuvres complètes* (Edition des souscripteurs).

Fargeton, Alphonse. "Lamartine à Cormartin." *Annales de l'Académie de Mâcon, 1962-1963* (1965).

Faure, Dr Robert. "Souvenirs sur une amie de Lamartine: Nica de Pierreclau." *Annales de l'Académie de Mâcon, 1962-1963* (1965).

Lacombrade, Christian. "A propos du platonisme de Lamartine." *Bulletin de l'Université de Toulouse*, February 1965.

Letessier, Fernand. "Glanes lamartiniennes. I. Deux billets inédits. II. Deux projets de poèmes avortés." *BAGB*, ser. 3 (March 1965), pp. 118-25.

Mabille de Poncheville, A. "Amis de Lamartine oubliés." *BLAM*, n.s., No. 84 (April 1966), pp. 85-87.
Brief notes on three of Lamartine's constituents in the Départment du Nord.

Nothomb, Pierre. "Lamartine, son cousin Bonaparte et les Ardennes." *Bulletin de l'Académie Royale de Langue et de Littérature Française,* XLIII, No. 3 (1965), 217-23.
Traces the rather complicated and tenuous family connection between Lamartine and the Bonapartes.

Redman, Harry, Jr., and B. C. Weber. "Lamartine's Impressions of Malta." *Journal of the Faculty of Arts of the Royal University of Malta,* xxx (1965), 38-43.

See also Beauchamps ("1. General").

Reviews of book previously listed:
VERDIER, Abel, *Les Amours italiennes de Lamartine: Graziella et Lena* (see *ELN*, III, Supp., 69), rev. by Maurice Hougardy in *RBPH*, XLIV (1966), 254-55, and by Fernand Letessier in *BAGB*, ser. 4 (1966), pp. 156-57.

LAMENNAIS

Bréhat, René. *Lamennais ou le prophète Féli.* Paris: Nouvelles Editions Latines, 1966. Pp. 187. 10 Fr.
A revised version of the author's *Lamennais le trop chrétien* (1941). Now, as then, the book is a passionate, partisan account of the fiery Breton priest. Unfortunately, Bréhat has retained the arbitrary geographical organization, which tends to obscure the development of Lamennais' career, especially in the earlier sections. The passage of a quarter century has had, however, some interesting effects. In 1941, a passage on pp. 27-28 reads as follows: "Babeuf, premier des précurseurs, le Picard . . . Saint-Simon, de Paris, et Fourier, de Besançon . . . Proudhon, le Franc-Comtois . . . Cabet, voyageur en Icarie, né en Bourgogne . . . Marx, d'outre-Rhin . . . Guesde, descendu froidement du Nord, et Jaurès, monté tout chaud du Midi . . . Lénine, au sang slave et peut-être mongol, génie à cheval sur l'Europe et sur l'Asie . . . *Hitler, jailli du centre géographique même de la vieille Europe . . .*: il faut de tout pour faire un monde, pour faire un monde nouveau." In 1966, the italicized passage has disappeared (p. 15). In the later version (p. 21), we learn that the birthplace of Lamennais was destroyed during the Liberation (but since rebuilt). On another level, Bréhat has eliminated the modest bibliography at the end and replaced it with several pages of quotations designed to attest to Lamennais' relevance and influence today: Pope John XXIII, for instance, is quoted as saying "Pacem in terris." All in all, Bréhat's little book is vivid, agreeable reading but decidedly lightweight (not that he is unaware of modern Lamennais scholarship). (J.S.P.)

Gambaro, A. "Un nuovo Lamennais nella monumentale opera di J.-R. Derré." *Bollettino Storico-Bibliografico,* LXII (1964), 199-228.
See résumé by Petre Ciureanu in *SFr,* IX (1965), 565. Derré's book is, of course, his *Lamennais, ses amis et le mouvement des idées à l'époque romantique, 1824-1834* (see *PQ,* XLII (1963), 475).

Guillemin, Henri. "Dix lettres inédites de la Mennais." *Europe,* No. 449 (September 1966), pp. 107-20.
Letters written in 1822-1824 to the Comte de Senfft, Austrian diplomat in Paris. Guillemin's commentary relates the letters to Lamennais' life and to future developments and briefly turns a baleful light on Lamennais' financial interests.

Guillemin, Henri. "Dossiers secrets. Cassure d'un destin. 1834. La Mennais publie ses *Paroles d'un Croyant.*" *Journal de Genève,* July 17-18, 1965.

Le Guillou, Louis. *L'Evolution de la pensée religieuse de Lamennais.* Paris: Armand Colin, 1966. Pp. 507. 39 Fr.
Rev. anon. in *Les Annales. Conferencia,* n.s., No. 191 (September 1966), p. 60.
This is a conscientious, methodical study, rather sympathetic to Lamennais although the author evidently writes from within the Roman Church. A certain stress is given to those points where the present ecumenical movement within Catholicism seems to justify Lamennais' protests, but Le Guillou cautiously refrains from judging him on certain issues. One has the impression that the author is eager to display, and at length, the unpublished letters and other documents which he has turned up in his investigation. Indeed, he tends to quote almost too fully from the published sources as well. Of course, there is justification for such extensive quotations. Especially important is the Ventura-Lamennais correspondence published in an appendix (but most are from Ventura to Lamennais rather than the other way around). (J.S.P.)

Le Guillou, Louis. "Les idées religieuses en Angleterre en 1833: lettres inédites de MacCarthy à Lamennais (9 mars-29 novembre 1833)." *AnBret,* LXXII (1965), 385-406.
Seven letters from Charles Justin MacCarthy to Lamennais. MacCarthy was much taken with Lamennais, but the English hierarchy opposed the Frenchman's views or was unaware of them. There are references to Montalembert, Rio, and other members of Lamennais' circle.

Le Guillou, Louis. "Une amitié exemplaire: Lamennais et Benoît d'Azy; lettres inédites 1833-1850." *RSH,* n.s., No. 121 (January-March 1966), pp. 13-44.
Twenty letters from Denis Benoît d'Azy to Lamennais. Le Guillou gives a brief sketch of Lamennais' friend and of their friendship.

Letessier, Fernand. "Autour d'une conversation de Lamennais (Décembre 1833)" *BAGB,* ser. 4 (1966), pp. 340-61.
Concerns an article published by Amédée Gabourd, anticlerical journalist and historian, in *L'Ami des Lois* (Le Mans), July 4, 1835. Gabourd's article, reprinted in its entirety, reports on his conversation with Lamennais.

See also Bowman, Deniel ("1. General").

Review of book previously listed:
VERUCCI, Guido, *Félicité Lamennais: Dal cattolicesimo autoritario al radi-*

calismo democratico (see *ELN*, III, Supp., 70), rev. by Sandro Fontana in *VeP*, June 1965.

LASSAILLY

Kaye, Eldon. *Charles Lassailly (1806-1843)*. Geneva: Droz, 1962. Pp. 145.

Rev. by Fernande Bassan in *RSH*, n.s., No. 121 (1966), pp. 133-35.

LATOUCHE

Hoffmann, Léon-François, ed. *Dernières lettres de deux amans de Barcelone*. ("A la Découverte." Publications du Département des Langues Romanes de l'Université de Princeton.) Paris: Presses Universitaires de France, 1966. Pp. xxvii + 182: 8 Fr.

Reprints this 1821 novel by Latouche and L.-F. L'Héritier. The introduction traces the history of the epidemic in Barcelona and its literary and political ramifications in France (the novel is, in effect, a piece of republican propaganda). A few footnotes at the end complete the annotation.

MAISTRE

Lebrun, R. A. *Throne and Altar: The Political and Religious Thought of Joseph de Maistre*. University of Ottowa Press, 1965. Pp. vi + 170.

Lovie, Jacques, and Joannès Chetail, eds. *Du Pape*. (Les Classiques de la Pensée Politique, 2.) Geneva: Droz, 1966. Pp. xxxviii + 368. 42 Fr.

Aside from generalities about J. de Maistre and *Du Pape,* the introduction is valuable for its detailed examination of the complicated negotiations between the author and various Papal authorities. The text reprinted is that of the second edition (1821), but the variants from other editions are also given. All in all, a sound piece of editing. (J.S.P.)

See also Deniel, Macchia ("1. General").

MARMIER

Monchoux, André. "Un romantique français ami de l'Allemagne: Xavier Marmier." Pp. 85-97 in *Connaissance de l'étranger. Mélanges offerts à la mémoire de Jean-Marie Carré*. Paris: Marcel Didier, 1964. Pp. xx + 529.

Moreau, Pierre. "Xavier de Marmier et *The Night Side of Society*." Pp. 98-107 in *Connaissance de l'étranger. Mélanges offerts à la mémoire de Jean-Marie Carré*. Paris: Marcel Didier, 1964. Pp. xx + 529.

MÉRIMÉE

Bouissou, Dr. Roger. "Mérimée et l'épidémie de choléra de 1865." *MedF*, No. 163 (1965).

Gaulmier, Jean. "Mérimée, Gobineau et les Bohémiens." *RHL*, LXVI (1966), 675-91.

By way of introduction to two unpublished letters from Gobineau to Mérimée, providing him with information about the Gypsies and their language, Gaulmier summarizes the relations between the two writers.

Parturier, Maurice. "Une lettre inédite de Prosper Mérimée." *RSH*, n.s., No. 120 (1965), pp. 573-75.
A letter to Stefano Conti of Jan. 18, 1841.
See also Maixner ("1. General"); Maixner ("Nodier").

MICHELET
Alff, Wilhelm. *Michelets Ideen.* (Kölner Romanistische Arbeiten, Neue Folge. Heft 30.) Geneva: Droz; Paris: Minard, 1966. Pp. 105. 26 Fr.
Rev. by André Abbou in *RSH*, n.s., No. 124 (1966), pp. 434-36.

Cadot, Michel. "Autour du *Michelet et son temps* de J.-M. Carré. Nouvelles orientations en face de problèmes anciens." Pp. 73-84 in *Connaissance de l'étranger. Mélanges offerts à la mémoire de Jean-Marie Carré.* Paris: Marcel Didier, 1964. Pp. xx + 529.

Faure, Elie. "Michelet." Pp. 63-108 in his *Les Constructeurs.* (Bibliothèque Médiations.) Paris: Gonthier, 1966. Pp. 235. 5.85 Fr.

Lardenoy, Etienne. "Historiens falsificateurs de l'histoire." *Ecrits de Paris*, June 1965.

Mettra, Claude, ed. *Histoire de France*, Tomes I and II. Lausanne: Editions Rencontre, 1965. 2 vols. 13.20 Fr. each.
These two volumes go from the origins through the thirteenth century.

Saint-Denis, E. de. "Michelet et la genèse de 'La Mer.' " *BAGB*, No. 4 (1965), pp. 561-79.

Viallaneix, Paul, ed. *Des Jésuites.* (Libertés, 35.) Paris: Pauvert, 1966. Pp. 261. 3 Fr.
Reproduces the text of the fifth edition of Michelet and Quinet's polemic. Viallaneix's introduction (pp. 9-31) recreates the controversy between Church and State over education, and links the two writers to the embryonic stirrings of liberal-minded theology.

MUSSET
Bourgeois, André. "Le goût du naturel chez Musset dramaturge." *Rice University Studies*, LI, No. 3 (1965), 3-22.

Chollet, Roland, ed. *Théâtre complet.* Préface, chronologie, notices et relevé des variantes par Roland Chollet. (Coll. "Les Tréteaux du Monde.") Lausanne: La Guilde du Livre, 1964. Pp. 1420.
Rev. by Claude Duchet in *RHL*, LXVI (1966), 730-32.

Jeune, Simon. "Musset caché." *RHL*, LXVI (1966), 419-38.
Musset's collaboration on *Le Temps*, from October 1830 to June 1831; attribution of a number of unsigned articles on literature and theatre to Musset.

Jeune, Simon. " 'On ne badine pas avec l'amour' et sa source impure." *RHT*, XVIII (1966), 199-209.
Sources in Victor Ducange, *Agathe*, and Paul de Kock, *L'Homme de la nature et l'homme policé.*

Jeune, Simon. "Souffles étrangers et inspiration personnelle dans 'Les Caprices de Marianne.' " *RSH*, n.s., No. 121 (1966), pp. 81-96.

Lebois, André. *Vues sur le théâtre de Musset.* Avignon: Aubanel, 1966. 9 Fr.

Mauzi, Robert. "Les fantoches d'Alfred de Musset." *RHL,* LXVI (1966), 257-82.
Penetrating analysis of a character type found in the comedies of 1833-1834: *A quoi rêvent les jeunes filles, Les Caprices de Marianne, Fantasio,* and *On ne badine pas avec l'amour.* Seen as a character without inner resources, reacting automatically according to his position or title. Influenced by Hoffmann's characters, especially Duke Irénéus of *Kater Murr.* (C.C.)

Rothschild, Suzanne Arvedon. *A Critical and Historical Study of Alfred de Musset's Barberine.* Paris: Impr. I.A.C., 1965. Pp. vi + 202.

Simon, John Kenneth. "The Presence of Musset in Modern French Drama." *FR,* XL (1966), 27-38.
Parallels of theme and style between Musset and Giraudoux, Anouilh, Sartre, and Camus.

Starobinski, Jean. "Note sur le bouffon romantique." *Cahiers du Sud,* LXI (1966), 270-75.
Analysis of the character, Fantasio. Starobinski says that the Romantic buffoon has become a hero, the mouthpiece of the tragic consciousness. (C.C.)

See also Delmas, Keller, Lobet, Poulet ("1. General"); Bach ("Sainte-Beuve"); Moreau ("Sand"); Jeune ("Stendhal").

NERVAL

[Artaud, Antoine.] "Sur les Chimères" [lettre à G. Lebreton, Rodez, 7 mars 1946, à la suite d'un article de la revue *Fontaine,* No. 44, 1945]. *Tel Quel,* No. 22, 1965.

Body, Jacques. "Gérard de Nerval et les chansons populaires." *Société Française de Littérature Comparée. Actes du 6e Congrès National.* Paris: Marcel Didier, 1965.

Chambers, R. "*Promenades et Souvenirs* de Nerval." *Essays in French Literature,* No. 2, November 1965, pp. 43-65.
Brief rev. by A. Fongaro in *SFr,* X (1966), 376.

Dhaenens, Jacques. "A propos de l'établissement du texte de 'El Desdichado.'" *SFr,* X (1966), 286-89.
Suggests the following chronological order for the four texts of the sonnet "El Desdichado": 1) l'édition originale: parue dans *Le Mousquetaire* du 10 décembre 1853; 2) le manuscrit Lombard; 3) le manuscrit Éluard; 4) l'édition des *Filles du Feu* (1854). Says only J. Geninasca's edition (see *ELN,* IV [1966], 78) "rendait *exactement* le texte."

Françon, Marcel. "Note on F. Schlegel and Gérard de Nerval." *RomN,* VIII (1966), 38-42.
Supplementary details on Nerval's borrowings from Friedrich Schlegel.

Guédenet, P. "De la réflexion critique à l'action romanesque: Les *Nuits d'Octobre* de Gérard de Nerval." *ECr,* IV (Winter 1964), 228-33.

Guillaume, Jean, s.j., ed. *"Les Chimères" de Nerval.* Éd. critique. (Académie Royale de Langue et de Littérature Française.) Bruxelles: Palais des Académies, 1966. Pp. 171 + 12 planches (portefeuille).
The plates include materials indicated and reproductions of the following MSS: I ("El Desdichado"); II ("Artemis"): MS Alfred Lombard; III ("Le Destin" [i.e., "El Desdichado"]); IV ("Artemis"); V ("Erythrea"): MS Paul Eluard; VI. Classement des documents; VII (First quatrain of first sonnet of "Le Christ aux Oliviers"): Page de *l'Autographe* reproduisant le MS Nadar; VIII (MS Nadar, incl. "Vers dorés"); IX (6 sonnets. MS Michel Dumesnil de Gramont *a*); X-XII (MS Alfred Lombard [letter]).

Moreau, Pierre. *Sylvie et ses soeurs nervaliennes.* Paris: Société d'Édition d'Enseignement Supérieur, 1966. Pp. 101. 7 Fr.
Rev. by Raphaël Molho in *RSH*, n.s., No. 124 (1966), pp. 432-34.

Moulin, Jeanine. "Langage de la poésie." *Les Annales,* LXXIII, n.s., No. 192 (October 1966), 37-41.
Discussion of Nerval on p. 41: "Gérard de Nerval fut le premier écrivain français à bouleverser les normes du langage poétique." Author finds the essential work of Nerval in *Les Chimères* and *Aurélia*: "C'est là qu'avant Rimbaud, les symbolistes et les surréalistes, il misa sur la magie du verbe plutôt que sur la logique et délivra le poème de la narration suivie."

Nelson, Roy Jay. "L'Analyse visuelle de l'harmonie vocalique dans le vers français." *FR*, XL (1966), 377-86.
Pp. 381-83 concern "El Desdichado."

Pellegrin, Jean. "Commentaire sur 'El Desdichado.' " *Cahiers du Sud,* LIII (1966), 276-95.
Urges common sense and emphasis on Gérard's own texts in interpreting his works.

Pia, Pascal. "Gérard de Nerval et son oeuvre." *Carrefour,* May 19, 1965.

Poulet, Georges. "Nerval, Gautier et le type biondo e grassotto." *CAIEF,* No. 18 (1966), pp. 189-204.

Poulet, Georges. *Trois Essais de mythologie romantique: Nerval, Gautier, Piranèse.* Paris: Librairie Jose Corti, 1966. Pp. 192. 9 Fr.
"Sylvie ou la pensée de Nerval"; "Nerval, Gautier et la blonde aux yeux noirs" (pp. 13-134).

Radcliff-Umstead, Douglas. "Cainism and Gérard de Nerval." *PQ*, XLV (1966), 395-408.
Represents Nerval as contributing "Cainism" to French literature—i.e., "the exalting of Cain as a wronged hero and not as an envious villain." Sees Adoniram in the *Voyage en Orient* as mirroring the Dandy's aesthetic revolt, and Nerval as apparently furnishing a sort of link between Byron and the French Dandies, and Nietzsche.

Redman, Harry, Jr., and B. C. Weber. "Gérard de Nerval and His Stop-Over in Malta: Fact and Fancy." *Scientia,* XXX (1965), 10-13.

Whyte, Peter. "Gérard de Nerval, inspirateur d'un conte de Gautier, *Deux acteurs pour un rôle.*" *RLC*, XL (1966), 474-78.
On Gautier's borrowings for his tale, which appeared in *Le Musée des*

Familles for July 1841, from Nerval's *Les Amours de Vienne* (*Revue de Paris*, March 1, 1841).

See also Palou ("1. General"); Steinmann ("Balzac"); Hytier ("Vigny").

Reviews of books previously listed:

DUBRUCK, Alfred, *Gérard de Nerval and the German Heritage* (see *ELN*, IV, Supp., 77), rev. by Ross Chambers in *AUMLA*, No. 24 (November 1965), pp. 326-28; GENINASCA, Jacques, *Une Lecture de "El Desdichado"* (see *ELN*, IV, Supp., 78), rev. by Ross Chambers in *AUMLA*, No. 25 (May 1966), pp. 149-51; JEAN, Raymond, *Nerval par lui-même* (see *ELN*, IV, Supp., 78), rev. by Ross Chambers in *AUMLA*, No. 24 (November 1965), pp. 328-30; RICHER, Jean, et al., *Aurélia ou le rêve et la vie. Lettres d'amour* (see *ELN*, IV, Supp., 79), rev. by James M. Villas in *FR*, XL (1966), 299-301; RICHER, Jean, *Nerval, expérience et création* (see *ELN*, III, Supp., 74), rev. by H. van der Tuin in *Neophilologus*, L (1966), 285-86; RICHER, Jean, ed., *OEuvres complémentaires de Gérard de Nerval*. Tome II: *La Vie du théâtre*; Tome VIII: *Variétés et fantaisies* (see *PQ*, XLIII, 478; *ELN*, III, Supp., 74), rev. by H. van der Tuin in *Neophilologus*, L (1966), 384-85.

NODIER

Maixner, Rudolf. "Sur certains pseudo-bardes du XVIIIᵉ et XIXᵉ siècle." Pp. 106-11 in *Société Française de Littérature Comparée. Actes du VIᵉ Congrès National* (Rennes, 23-25 mai 1963). Paris: Marcel Didier, 1965.

Ryner, Han. "Charles Nodier." *Cahiers des Amis de Han Ryner*, n.s., No. 74 (September 1964), pp. 20-22.

See also Keller, Palou, Willard ("1. General"); Letessier ("Constant").

Reviews of work previously listed:

OLIVER, A. Richard, *Charles Nodier: Pilot of Romanticism* (see *ELN*, IV, Supp., 80), rev. by Victor Brombert in *RR*, LVII (1966), 305-07; by Jean Decottignies in *RHL*, LXVI (1966), 728-29; by Sylvia Raphael in *FS*, XX (1966), 82-83, and by D. P. Scales in *AUMLA*, No. 25 (1966), pp. 148-49.

OZANAM

Morawski, Kalist. "Les études dantesques de Frédéric Ozanam." *L'Alighieri: Rassegna Bibliografica Dantesca*, IV, No. 2 (1963), 74-83.

Summarizes contents of Ozanam's various studies on Dante, stressing his original contributions to Dante scholarship and his general agreement with modern interpretations of Dante.

PONSARD

Ambrière, François. "François Ponsard et 'Le Lion amoureux.' " *Les Annales. Conferencia*, n.s., No. 188 (June 1966), 38-48.

A rehabilitation of Ponsard's play, accompanied by a sketch of Ponsard's career.

QUINET

See Viallaneix ("Michelet").

REYNAUD

Griffiths, David Albert. *Jean Reynaud encyclopédiste de l'époque*

romantique, d'après sa correspondance inédite. Paris: Marcel Rivière, 1965. Pp. 483.
Rev. by Pierre Moreau in *RLC,* XL (1966), 145-51.

SAINTE-BEUVE

Bach, Max. "Sainte-Beuve critique du théâtre de son temps." *PMLA,* LXXXI (1966), 563-74.

Bruno, Francesco. "Sainte-Beuve." *Ausonia,* XX, No. 3 (1965), 53-56.

Chadbourne, Richard M. "Symbolic Landscapes in Sainte-Beuve's Early Criticism." *PMLA,* LXXX (1965), 217-30.
A fine analysis of imagery and its role in Sainte-Beuve's criticism. Runs "from the *Premiers lundis* through the *Portraits de femmes* and *Portraits contemporains,*" suggesting that Sainte-Beuve is too often read for his views on specific writers, missing the cumulative effect of his topographical images. (C.C.)

Gautier, Léopold. "Töpffer et Sainte-Beuve." *RDM,* March 15, 1966, pp. 262-68.
Sainte-Beuve's relations with the Genevan writer, Rodolphe Töpffer.

Kanes, Martin. "Autour de *Thérèse Raquin*: un dialogue entre Zola et Sainte-Beuve." *Les Cahiers Naturalistes,* XII (1966), 23-31.
Prints letters exchanged between June 19, 1865 and July 13, 1868.

Laffitte, Sophie. "Gogol et Sainte-Beuve." *Oxford Slavonic Papers,* XI (1964), 56-59.

See also Lobet ("1. General"); Deguise ("Constant"); Viallaneix ("Vigny").

Reviews of works previously listed:
BONNEROT, Jean, ed., *Correspondance générale,* t. XIII (see *PQ,* XLIII, 480), rev. by Albert Delorme in *RdS,* LXXXVII (1966), 190-91; t. XIV (see *ELN,* IV, Supp., 81), rev. by A. Lytton Sells in *RR,* LVII (1966), 144-45, and by Raphaël Molho in *RHL,* LXVI (1966), 733-37; MOREAU, Pierre, *La Critique selon Sainte-Beuve* (see *ELN,* IV, Supp., 81), rev. by M[ax] M[ilner] in *IL,* XVIII (1966), 79.

SAND

Amezaga, Elias. *Jorje Sand: Aurora Dupin íntima.* Bilbao: Sendo Ed., 1965. Pp. 795. 200 Pesetos.
Rev. by Georges Lubin in *RHL,* LXVI (1966), 526-28.

Cassou, Jean. "George Sand et le secret du XIXe siècle." Pp. 53-73 in his *Parti pris. Essais et colloques.* Paris: Albin Michel, 1964. Pp. 215.
First published in *MdF,* December 1961.

Colin, Georges. *Bibliographie des premières publications des romans de George Sand.* Bruxelles: Société des Bibliophiles et Iconophiles de Belgique, 1965. Pp. 175. 200 F. belges.
Rev. by Henri Godin in *FS,* XX (1966), 83-84, and by Georges Lubin in *SFr,* IX (1965), 570.
Godin notes that this is a corrected *tirage à part* of a bibliography published serially in *LeE* between 1961 and 1963 (see *ELN,* IV, Supp., 82).

Courville, Luce de. "Une lettre inédite de George Sand à la Bibliothèque de Nantes (à Charles Dugast-Matifeux, 19 avril 1857)." *AnBret*, LXXV (1965), 437-40.

Gaulmier, Jean. "Un exemple d'utilisation immédiate du folklore: genèse et structure des *Maîtres sonneurs*." Pp. 143-50 in *Société Française de Littérature Comparée. Actes du VIe Congrès National* (Rennes, 23-25 mai 1963). Paris: Marcel Didier, 1965.

Gaulmier, J[ean]. "Gobineau et George Sand (d'après des documents inédits)." *ZFSL*, LXXVI (1966), 99-107.
Includes four letters from Gobineau, dated 1871-1872.

Lombard, C. M. "George Sand's Image in America." *RLC*, XL (1966), 177-86.
Shows a change from the early "cold reception" to a more tolerant and even enthusiastic view of George Sand.

Lubin, Georges, ed. *Correspondance* (1832-juin 1835). Tome II. Paris: Garnier, 1966. Pp. xxi + 1013. Illus. 39.40 F.
Rev. in *SFr*, X (1966), 376.

Moreau, Pierre. "Musset, Sténio, Don Juan." *RHL*, LXVI (1966), 253-56.
Musset as model for Sténio in *Lélia*.

Pommier, Jean. *George Sand et le rêve monastique. Spiridion*. Paris: Nizet, 1966. Pp. 124. 7.50 Fr.

Salomon, Pierre et J. Mallion, eds. *La Mare au diable. François le Champi*. Edition augmentée d'une chronologie de George Sand. (Classiques Garnier.) Paris: Garnier, 1965. Pp. xlvi + 443.

Sand, George. *Les Beaux Messieurs de Bois-Doré*. (Grand Ecran Littéraire.) Paris: Gründ, 1966. Pp. 512. 17.52 Fr.

Sand, George. "Une lettre inédite (30 décembre 1825)." *Biblio*, XXXIII (January 1965), 19.

Toesca, Maurice. "Une vraie femme: George Sand." *A la Page*, No. 17 (November 1965), 1692-95.

Vernois, Paul. "Le destin du roman rustique de George Sand à Ramuz (1860-1925)." *IL*, XVII (1965), 196-203.

See also Bowman, Gougy-François, Gravier ("1. General"); Bach ("Sainte-Beuve").

Reviews of works previously listed:
LUBIN, Georges, ed., *Correspondance*. Tome I (1812-1831) (see *ELN*, III, Supp., 77), rev. by T. G. S. Combe in *FS*, XX (1966), 84-86; by Maxine G. Cutler in *BA*, XL (1966), 54; by Albert Delorme in *RdS*, LXXXVII (1966), 176-77, and by Annarosa Poli in *SFr*, X (1966), 103-06; SODERGARD, Osten, ed., *Les Lettres de George Sand à Sainte-Beuve* (see *ELN*, III, Supp., 77), rev. by Emilie Noulet in *Critique. Revue Générale des Publications Françaises et Etrangères*, XXII (1966), 92-94.

SÉNANCOUR

Arnold, Werner. "Ennui—Spleen—Nausée—Tristesse: Vier Formen literarischen Ungenügens an der Welt." *NS,* xv (1966), 159-73.

Giorgi, Giorgetto. "Sénancour e Proust." *SFr,* ix (1965), 290-96.

Finds in Sénancour, as in Proust, a great stress not only upon recollection based on involuntary memory but also upon the impressionistic, metaphorical vision of reality.

Le Gall, Béatrice. *L'Imaginaire chez Sénancour.* Paris: Corti, 1966. 2 vols.

Discussed in some detail by the author in *IL,* xviii (1966), 193-98. Considers in turn Sénancour's youth; his early works (*Aldomen, Les Rêveries,* and *Oberman*); and the writings of his maturity and old age (*De l'amour, Les Libres Méditations, Les Traditions morales,* and *Isabelle*).

Raymond, Marcel. "Adieu à Sénancour." *NRF,* xiv (1966), 283-90.

Raymond, Marcel. *Sénancour. Sensations et révélations.* Paris: Librairie José Corti, 1965. Pp. 256. 22 Fr.

[Sénancour, E.-J.-B. Pivert de.] *Oberman.* Précéde de *L'Espace désenchanté de Sénancour* par Georges Borgeaud. ("Le Monde en 10/18," Nos. 272-74.) Union Générale d'Éditions, 1965.

Review of book previously listed:

RAYMOND, Marcel, ed., *Sénancour: Sur les générations actuelles. Absurdités humaines* (see *ELN,* iv, Supp., 83), rev. by Renée Waldinger in *RR,* lvii (1966), 304-05.

STAEL

Anon. "Madame de Staël à la Nationale." *BLAM,* xLvie Année, n.s., No. 85 (May 1966), p. 111.

Balayé, Simone. "Corinne et les amis de Madame de Staël." *RHL,* lxvi (1966), 139-49.

Balayé, Simone, ed. *Dix années d'exil.* Précédé d'une "Esquisse pour un portrait de Madame de Staël" par Emmanuel d'Astier. Introduction et notes par Simone Balayé. [Texte établi par Paul Gautier.] (Coll. "Le Monde en 10/18.) Paris: Union Générale d'Editions, 1966. Pp. xxxix + 281. 6.60 Fr.

Rev. by Francis B. Conem in *RSH,* N. S., Fasc. 124 (1966), pp. 426-29.

Baude, Michel. "Un protégé de Madame de Staël: Pierre-Hyacinthe Azaës d'après des documents inédits." *RHL,* lxvi (1966), 149-52.

Bédé, Jean-Albert. "Madame de Staël, Rousseau et le suicide." *RHL,* lxvi (1966), 52-70.

Bibliothèque Nationale. *Madame de Staël et l'Europe.* Paris: Bibliothèque Nationale, 1966. Pp. xxiii + 138; 7 plates.

Catalogue from the commemorative exhibition: chronology, references to numerous unpublished documents.

Cahiers Staëliens. No. 3 (1965).
Contains: Comtesse Jean de Pange, "Chronique et nouvelles brèves," pp. 1-3; Simone Balayé, "Christopher Herold," p. 4; Léopold Gautier, "Lettres inédites de Mme de Staël à François Gautier de Tournay," pp. 5-14; Simone Balayé, "Mme de Staël et le Dr Koreff," pp. 15-32; André Doyon, "Les bagages de Mme de Staël," pp. 33-42.

Cahiers Staëliens. No. 4 (1966).
Rev. in *SFr,* x (1966), 368-69.
Contains: Comtesse Jean de Pange, "Chronique et nouvelles brèves," pp. 1-3; Norman King, "Un récit inédit du grand voyage de Madame de Staël (1812-1813)," pp. 4-23; Georges Solovieff, "Madame de Staël et le poète russe Tioutchev," pp. 24-26; Georges Solovieff, "Une lettre inédite de Madame de Staël au Consul Lebrun," pp. 27-31; bibliographie, pp. 32-33.

Cordey, Pierre. *Madame de Staël.* (Egéries et Femmes de Lettres.) Lausanne: Editions Rencontre, 1966. Pp. 320. 13.55 Fr.

Cordey, Pierre. *Madame de Staël et Benjamin Constant sur les bords du Léman.* (Les Paysages de l'Amour.) Lausanne: Payot, 1966. Pp. 240. 28 Fr.

Eaubonne, Françoise d'. *Une Femme témoin de son siècle: Germaine de Staël.* Paris: Flammarion, 1966. Pp. 288. 25 Fr.

Eaubonne, Françoise d'. *Germaine de Staël.* Paris: Albin Michel, 1966.
Rev. by André Thérive in *RDM,* Dec. 1, 1966, pp. 441-43.

Gorsse, Pierre de. "Germaine de Staël dans les orages de son temps." *Les Annales. Conferencia,* n.s., No. 187 (May 1966), pp. 5-20.

Grosclaude, Pierre. "La pensée politique de Madame de Staël." *RPP,* No. 772 (November 1966), pp. 58-69.
The role of feeling in the evolution of Germaine's political ideas; freedom and equality as principal themes.

Guillemin, Henri. *Madame de Staël et Napoléon ou Germaine et le Caïd ingrat.* Bienne: Editions du Panorama, 1966. Pp. 271. 12.60 Sw. Fr.

Guisan, Gilbert. "Madame de Staël et la critique en Suisse romande." *RHL,* LXVI (1966), 153-57.

Jasinski, Béatrice W. "Madame de Staël, l'Angleterre de 1813-1814 et les 'Considérations sur la Révolution française.'" *RHL,* LXVI (1966), 12-24.
Maintains convincingly that Mme. de Staël's limited portrait of England in the *Considérations* does not prove her a poor observer. (C.C.)

Le Gall, Béatrice. "Le paysage chez Madame de Staël." *RHL,* LXVI (1966), 38-51.

Luppé, Robert de. "Extrait inédit par Madame de Staël des 'Deux Phèdres' de A. W. Schlegel (1807)." *RHL,* LXVI (1966), 127-30.

Man, Paul de. "Madame de Staël et Jean-Jacques Rousseau." *Preuves,* XVIe Année (December 1966), pp. 35-40.

M[asson], A[ndré]. "Le bi-centenaire de Mme de Staël." *RLC,* XL (1966), 492-95.

Mönch, Walter. "Madame de Staël und ihr Buch 'Über die Literatur.'" *ZFSL,* LXXVI (1966), 133-53.

Monchoux, André. "Madame de Staël interprète de Kant." *RHL,* LXVI (1966), 71-84.

Pange, Comtesse Jean de. "Extraits d'un journal d'enfance d'Albertine de Staël." *RHL,* LXVI (1966), 3-11.

Pange, Comtesse Jean de. "Le 'Grand voyage' de Mme de Staël, d'après un carnet de route inédit." Pp. 347-62 in *Connaissance de l'étranger. Mélanges offerts à la mémoire de Jean-Marie Carré.* Paris: Marcel Didier, 1964. Pp. xx + 529; illus.
First publication of notes which served as a basis for Mme. de Staël's *Dix années d'exil.*

Pange, Victor de, ed. *The Unpublished Correspondence of Madame de Staël and the Duke of Wellington.* Transl. Harold Kurtz. Foreword Jean de Pange. London: Cassell, 1965.
Rev. by Joanna Richardson in *The Listener,* LXXIV, No. 1900 (Aug. 26, 1965), 315.

Poulet, Georges. "La pensée critique de Mme de Staël." *Preuves,* XVIe Année (December 1966), pp. 27-35.

Riberette, Pierre. "L'Exposition 'Madame de Staël et l'Europe.'" *Revue de l'Institut Napoléon,* No. 100 (1966), pp. 159-60.

Solovieff, Georges. "Madame de Staël vue par ses contemporains." *RHL,* LXVI (1966), 130-39.

Starobinski, Jean. "Suicide et mélancolie chez Mme de Staël." *Preuves,* XVIe Année (December 1966), pp. 41-48.

See also Bowman, Duhamel, Gougy-François, Gravier, Macchia, Maixner ("1. General"); Deguise, Pichois ("Constant"); Pellegrini ("Stendhal").

Reviews of works previously listed:
JASINSKI, Béatrice W., ed., *Correspondance générale,* t. I, 1ere et 2e parties (see *PQ,* XLII, 482; *ELN* III, Supp., 79), rev. by Claudette Delhez-Sarlet in *RBPH,* XLIII (1965), 626-29; t. II, 1ere partie (see *PQ,* XL, 215), rev. by J. Dechamps in *FS,* XIX (1965), 65-67, and by Claudette Delhez-Sarlet in *RBPH,* XLIII (1965), 626-29; t. II, 2e partie (see *ELN,* IV, Supp., 84), rev. by Albert Delorme in *RdS,* LXXXVII (1966), 173-74, in *SFr,* X (1966), 163-64.

STENDHAL

Alciatore, Jules C. "Quelques remarques sur Stendhal et les héroïnes de Walter Scott." *SC,* VIII (1966), 339-45.
Although he pronounced Scott's depiction of love feeble and inaccurate, Stendhal was actually drawn to several of his heroines. Their simplicity and courage may have influenced his conception of the character of Mathilde.

Ampola, Filippo. *Fra uomini e poeti.* Pisa: Nistri-Lischi, 1963.
Includes an essay on Stendhal.

Atherton, John. *Stendhal.* (Studies in Modern European Literature and Thought.) New York: Hillary House, 1965. Pp. 126. $2.50.
Rev. anon. in *TLS*, March 4, 1965, p. 165; by R. F. Jackson in *AUMLA* No. 25 (May 1966), pp. 151-53, and by Grahame Jones in *SC*, VIII (1966), 274-75. The author uses the novels and autobiographical writings as sources for the elements of a portrait of Stendhal. The first chapter presents the novelist's *ondoyant et divers* temperament. The rest of the book is primarily given over to the novels; their heroes, themes, and emotional effects are treated under such headings as "Opposition" (the conflict of Stendhal's heroes with society), "The Image of Self," "Strategy and Passion" (head vs heart), "La marche ordinaire du 19e siècle" (Stendhal's social satire, especially in *Lucien Leuwen*), "Boredom" (mostly based on *Lamiel*), "A Style Too Abrupt, Too Harsh," and "The Beylist Hero." There are many stimulating ideas along the way, e.g., that Stendhal's novels are anti-*Bildungsromane*: "The novels do not describe a learning process but pose a problem which is debated with an ever increasing degree of subtlety and penetration" (p. 56). All in all, a good brief introduction to Stendhal the man and the novelist or, rather, the man-who-wrote-novels. (J.S.P.)

Barbaranelli, Fernando. "Un incontro ideale nella Civitavecchia dell' Ottocento." *L'Urbe*, July-August 1964.
Apropos of Gregory XVI's visit to Civitavecchia in May 1835. See comment by C. Cordié in *RLMC*, XVIII (1965), 157.

Baudoin, Henri. "A propos d'un 'Voyage à Rome' (Stendhal et Cie, II)." *SC*, VIII (1966), 255-66.
Using a diary kept by the Vicomtesse d'Haussonville while visiting Rome in the summer of 1840, Baudoin proposes the Vicomtesse as the citadel besieged by Stendhal in "la guerre Earline."

Baumont, Michel. "La dernière année de Julien Sorel (printemps de 1830-printemps de 1831): réflexions historiques." *SC*, VIII (1966), 346-52.
Slightly modifies the chronology proposed by Martineau, and raises the question why Stendhal created "le récit impossible que nous connaissons."

Blanchard, Camille. "Un plateau satyrique relatif à Stendhal." *Bulletin de l'Académie Delphinale*, 1964 [1965].

Bonfantini, Mario. "Ancora su Baudelaire e Stendhal: risultanze della 'Correspondance.'" Pp. 113-15 in *Studi di letteratura, storia e filosofia in onore di Bruno Revel*. (Biblioteca dell'Archivum Romanicum, serie 2, vol. 74.) Florence: Leo S. Olschki, 1965. Pp. xx + 662.

Bossu, Jean, *et al.* "Stendhal maçon." *ICC*, May 1966, columns 515-19.

Boyer, Ferdinand. "Le chevalier Micheroux, Stendhal et la Pasta." *SFr*, X (1966), 290-95.
Details of Micheroux's activities as reflected in police reports on him. His relations with La Pasta, the singer, and Stendhal (the three all lodged under the same roof ca. 1821-1822).

Canosa Donate, J. "Stendhal vu par les Espagnols." *SC*, IX (1966), 22-26.
Disputes Eugenio d'Ors's view of Stendhal as primarily a materialist and sensualist (see the author's earlier article with this title, *SC*, VI [1964], 141-48).

Caraccio, Armand. "Nouvelles 'Variétés stendhaliennes.' " Pp. 9-96 in his *Mélanges franco-italiens de littérature*. (Publications de la Faculté des Lettres et Sciences Humaines de Grenoble.) Paris: Presses Universitaires de France, 1966. Pp. 388. 20 Fr.
Rev. by J. M. in *BAGB*, ser. 4 (1966), p. 394.
Brings together a valuable set of articles published in various places since about 1950: "Stendhal touriste," "Stendhal: du tourisme au roman," "Stendhal et le 'Jugement dernier' de Michel-Ange," "Le 'Dolce stil nuovo' de Stendhal," "Stendhal alchimiste du sentiment," "Stendhal devant la musique," "Stendhal et la guerre," and "La leçon de Stendhal."

Casamassima, Franco. "Sur une note énigmatique de 'Lucien Leuwen.' " *SC*, IX (1966), 1-10.
Clarification of one of Stendhal's mysterious marginal notes in the MS.

Chantreau, Alain. "A propos d'une lettre de Stendhal à Dubois, directeur du Globe.' " *SC*, VIII (1966), 237-54.
Suggests Stendhal himself wrote two anti-Saint-Simonian letters published in *Le Producteur*, March 5 and May 1, 1826.

Del Litto, V. "Bibliographie stendhalienne: année 1965." *SC*, IX (1966), 95-110.
Includes supplement for 1964. In all, 161 items.

Del Litto, V. "Corrections et additions inédites pour la deuxième édition de 'la Chartreuse de Parme.' " *SC*, VIII (1966), 197-222.
Complete transcription of Stendhal's corrections and additions made in an interfoliated copy which he intended to serve as basis for a second edition. This material was known only in fragments hitherto. Del Litto regards these annotations as numerically less important than those of the Chaper copy, but there are entries of biographical interest, and some of the variant readings are valuable.

Del Litto, V., ed. *La Chartreuse de Parme*. Facsimile de l'exemplaire personnel de l'auteur. Paris: Cercle du Livre Précieux, 1966. 3 vols. 170 Fr.

D'Huart, Suzanne. "Pierre Daru et Henri Beyle: Correspondance inédite." *SC*, VIII (1966), 113-53.
Forty-five letters from Daru to Stendhal in the period 1806-1808, six letters exchanged between them in 1812. All deal with Stendhal's administrative work in Germany and Russia. Copious annotation. An unpublished portrait of Daru.

D'Huart, Suzanne. "Une lettre inédite de Stendhal à Alphonse Périer." *SC*, VIII (1966), 223-27.
The only known letter from Stendhal to his boyhood friend, this one was written from Brunswick, July 22, 1807. The history of their friendship is briefly recounted.

Doyon, André. "Impression d'Italie. Lettre inédite de Stendhal à la comtesse Daru." *SC*, VIII (1966), 155-58.
A letter written from Tremezzina, on Lake Como, Sept. 22, 1813.

Doyon, André. "Le dossier de la mort de Stendhal." *SC*, IX (1966), 13-17.
Reprints all the official documents bearing on Stendhal's death. They substantiate the traditional version.

Dufour, L. "Stendhal et la météorologie." *SC*, VIII (1966), 281-324.
A chronological list of all references to actual weather conditions in Stendhal's writings (naturally, the autobiographical writings and the letters are the principal sources), with comments drawn from various documents serving to check on his accuracy. Aside from their value to meteorologists, Stendhal's remarks reveal in him, not surprisingly, "un réel esprit d'observation," especially in regard to nuances of atmospheric phenomena. But his descriptions are few in number and usually brief, in line with his dislike of descriptions à la Walter Scott. Dufour's other important conclusions likewise tend to confirm what we know and suspect of Stendhal.

Dunan, Marcel. "Le système continental, Pierre Daru . . . et Stendhal." *Revue de l'Institut Napoléon*, No. 99 (1966), pp. 89-93.

Engelson, S. "Stendhal annonciateur." *Synthèses* (Brussels), XIX (1964), Nos. 217-218, pp. 295-301.

Florenne, Yves. "Revue des livres." *Le Monde*, July 28, 1965, p. 9.
In reviewing *AnB 1965*, Florenne suggests that Balzac and Stendhal might have met in 1837 at Custine's

Gaulmier, Jean. "En marge de 'La Chartreuse de Parme': Gobineau et Stendhal." *SC*, IX (1966), 19-21.
Gobineau's admiration for Stendhal; the affinities between the two men; Gobineau's projected statue for Duke Melzi (see chapter 2 of the novel).

Girard, René. *Deceit, Desire, and the Novel: Self and Other in Literary Structure*. Translated by Yvonne Freccero. The Johns Hopkins Press, 1965. Pp. 318. $6.95.
Rev. in *Choice*, III (1966), 766, and by B. Kreissman in *Library Journal*, XCI (1966), 1226.
An application of the concept of "triangular desire" (desiring subject-desired object-the Other) to a number of major novels from Cervantes to the present. Stendhal, Dostoevsky, and Proust are the principal sources of illustrative material for the author's thesis: "The great novelists reveal the imitative nature of desire" (p. 14), whereas "In the nineteenth century spontaneity becomes a universal dogma, succeeding imitation" (p. 15). ". . . These new individualisms . . . merely hide a new form of imitation" (*ibid.*). Romantic and neo-Romantic works "reflect the presence of a mediator without revealing it" (p. 17), while truly novelistic ("romanesque") works reveal this presence. Girard's references to Stendhal are numerous, and several of his insights will, if nothing else, arouse controversy. For example, he sees Stendhal as a novelist who has outgrown the *idéologues*. Similarly, the early *De l'amour* is a "romantic" work, whereas in the novels there is no crystallization: "true love does not transfigure." Girard's approach is often too systematic, and he reveals some strange prejudices; but he has opened a discussion which should be fruitful. (J.S.P.)

Goodheart, Eugene. "Style and Energy in *The Charterhouse of Parma*." *Symposium*, XX (1966), 117-34.
The great characters in the novel are not merely expressions of natural energy but artists of the personality, supreme stylists in the moral sphere, where

(according to Stendhal) absolutes no longer exist and the self must constantly be recreated.

Gyergyai, Albert. "Stendhal en Hongrie. Bibliographie." *SC,* IX (1966), 89-93.

It appears that Stendhal had no impact in Hungary until the late 19th century. The bibliography lists Hungarian translations of Stendhal's works (mostly novels) and book-length critical studies.

Hemmings, F. W. J. *Stendhal: A Study of His Novels.* Oxford: Clarendon Press, 1964. Pp. xvii + 232. 42s.

Rev. anon. in *Economist,* Aug. 1, 1964, p. 481; in *TLS,* July 30, 1964, p. 666; by Jules C. Alciatore in *MP,* LXIII (1965), 168-71, and in *SC,* VII (1965), 147-51; by Richard N. Coe in *Southern Review* (Adelaide), I (1965), 74-79; by Joanna Richardson in *Listener,* Dec. 24, 1964, p. 1021, and by Robert Taubman in *New Statesman,* Sept. 11, 1964, p. 360.

Hemmings' book, as one might expect of the author of very fine studies on Zola, is a very intelligent and well-informed work. The opening chapter tells the story of Stendhal's delayed vocation as a novelist. Then Hemmings synthesizes, furnishing some general observations on recurring motifs and devices. But the heart of the book is the series of chapters devoted to the four major novels. Hemmings' approach, in very general terms, is to concentrate on the hero; for the purposes of this book, he treats each novel as a novelized biography. Beyond this, it is difficult to say in just what genre the author is working. At times, he is dealing with problems of sources and other such literary-historical matters; at other times, he is tracking down symbols; at still other times, and most often, he is talking about the character of the hero (to mention just a few of the approaches used). All this is ingeniously woven together, and Hemmings easily bears the reader along with his clear and fluent presentation. From a scholarly point of view, this is an excellent introduction to Stendhal (with a fine selected bibliography at the end). Critically, one could wish for a more forthright stand, more passionate identification with either the novelist or the latter's heroes. (J.S.P.)

Jeune, Simon. "Une recension inconnue de 'Le Rouge et le Noir.' " *SC,* VIII (1966), 167-77.

Reprints a review published in *Le Temps,* Jan. 26, 1831. Jeune thinks Musset is the probable author, in view of the "curieux mélange de désinvolture et de perspicacité."

Kronenberger, Louis. "Stendhal's *Charterhouse*: Supreme Study of Worldliness." *Michigan Quarterly Review,* V (1966), 163-71.

Praise for Stendhal's treatment of "immensely superior people" whose "satisfaction lies in living for and with one another." (The same article was published in *Encounter,* July 1966, pp. 32-38.)

Laurent, Jacques. *La Fin de Lamiel.* Paris: Julliard, 1966. Pp. 185.

In his brief review, V. D. L. dismisses this attempt to finish Stendhal's novel as "une aimable fantaisie" (see *SC,* IX [1966], 68).

Le Yaouanc, Moïse. "De Kératry à Stendhal et Balzac." *AnB,* LXXII (1965), 369-84.

Explores the relationships, literary and personal, between Kératry and his two great contemporaries; explains Kératry's use of the name "Frédéric Styndall" for the hero of his novel, and Stendhal's adoption of "Frédérick" as part of his pseudonym in 1839.

Lorain, Alexandre. *L'Expression de l'hypothèse en français moderne—*

antéposition et postposition. (Les Lettres Modernes.) Paris: M. J. Minard, 194. Pp. 128.
Rev. by L. C. Harmer in *FS,* xx (1966), 110-11.
Contains section on Stendhal.

Martineau, Henri. "Un texte inédit d'Henri Martineau sur 'Féder.'" *SC,* viii (1966), 159-65.
Martineau's recently discovered article sees in *Féder* "un petit roman" foreshadowing comic studies of manners which unfortunately Stendhal did not live to write.

May, Gita. "Préromantisme rousseauiste et égotisme stendhalien: convergence et divergences." *ECr,* vi (1966), 97-107.
A valuable summary of Rousseau's influence on Stendhal's esthetics and on Beylisme.

Meininger, Anne-Marie. "Balzac et Stendhal encore." Pp. 385-88 in *AnB* 1966. Paris: Garnier, 1966. Pp. 474.
Shows the probable influence of scenes in *La Chartreuse de Parme* on *Le Curé de village* and *Splendeurs et misères des courtisanes.*

Moreau, Pierre. "L'égotisme de Montaigne et de Stendhal." *Bulletin de la Société des Amis de Montaigne,* ser. 4, No. 5 (January-March 1966), pp. 8-25.
Moreau finds common ground in three areas: lucidity in analysis, the sense of inner complexity, and intellectual dilettantism. The emphasis is on Stendhal. No attempt is made to show the influence of Montaigne on Stendhal.

Pellegrini, Carlo. "L'interpretazione stendhaliana di Firenze in *Rome, Naples et Florence.*" Pp. 363-73 in *Connaissance de l'étranger. Mélanges offerts à la mémoire de Jean-Marie Carré.* Paris: Marcel Didier, 1964. Pp. xx + 529.

Pellegrini, Carlo. "Stendhal contre Madame de Staël à propos de Napoléon." *RHL,* lxvi (1966), 25-37.
Stendhal's reaction to Madame de Staël's criticism of the dictator should not be explained as literary jealousy (Del Litto's thesis): it stemmed from his admiration for Napoleon and from his own artistic nature, these two elements of his character being intertwined.

Raimondi, Giuseppe. "Stendhal e i 'Bolognesi.'" *Palatina,* No. 33 (January-March 1966), pp. 74-78.
On Stendhal's reaction to the Bolognese School of painters and its influence on him. See résumé in *SC,* ix (1966), 70.

Reizov, Boris. "Stendhal et Benvenuto Cellini (Sur le problème des sources de *La Chartreuse de Parme*)." *SC,* viii (1966), 325-38.
Studies the general influence of Cellini's *Autobiography* on Stendhal's novel. This influence is not confined to the episode of Fabrice's escape from the Farnese Tower. In particular, the theme of predictions owes something to Cellini. But this theme becomes entangled with others, and Reizov shows how Stendhal's conception of his novel shifted as he allowed them to interact. "De là ce désaccord entre les prédictions et la réalité, qui recouvre d'un voile de mystère tout le destin de Fabrice del Dongo."

Riehn, Christa. "Stendhal en Allemagne. Bibliographie (1824-1944)."
SC, IX (1966), 73-88. (à suivre)
113 items added to those listed earlier (*SC,* Oct. 15, 1965).

Sequanus. "Stendhal, maçon." *ICC,* August 1966, columns 808-09.

Strauss, André. *La Fortune de Stendhal en Angleterre.* (Bibliothèque des
Langues Modernes, 5.) Paris: Marcel Didier, 1966. Pp. 243. 50 Fr.
A strange book, perhaps because of the dearth of material. Yet the author
promises a sequel to the present volume, which only goes to about 1900.
There are many dubious generalizations about the state of English culture and
political life in Stendhal's time, a long discussion of Stendhal as English
"gentleman," and a number of passages that discuss the novels without reference to England or the English. To show how the ground was prepared for
the reception of Stendhal's novels, the author mostly confines himself to
quoting from the articles Stendhal wrote for British magazines. Thus, in a
short chapter on the preparation for *La Chartreuse de Parme,* we are informed
that Stendhal had written a criticism of Grossi's poem on the assassination of
Prina and that Silvio Pellico's description of Fabrice's very prison-tower was
known in England. The corresponding chapter on *Le Rouge et le noir* uses
a similar approach, but manages to avoid any direct reference to anything
English for much longer, and closes with a few textual comparisons between
the original French of Stendhal's novel and an *American* translation published
in 1898. In dealing with the influence of Stendhal in England, Strauss's most
important chapter is devoted to a comparison of *Washington Square* and *Le
Rouge et le noir.* There are places where the author accomplishes more or less
what one is led to expect by the title, but the author's general aim and critical
approach remain obscure, to say the least. (J.S.P.)

Théodoridès, Jean. "A propos de 'Philibert Lescall.'" *SC,* VIII (1966),
182-85.
Proposes Victor Jacquemont as model for Stendhal's hero.

Vellay, Edouard. "Stendhal maçon." *ICC,* June 1966, columns 571-72.

Wilson, Bernard E. "Une lettre inédite de Stendhal à Edouard Mounier."
SC, VIII (1966), 228-36.
Translation of an article published in *NL* (1965). See *ELN,* IV, Supp., 90.

See also Goimard ("General 3. Criticism"); Delmas, Jean, Lobet, Macchia ("French 1. General"); Maquet ("Italian 3. Grossi").

Reviews of books previously listed:
DEL LITTO, Victor, *La Vie de Stendhal* (see *ELN,* IV, Supp., 85-86), rev. by
C. Cordié in *SFr,* IX (1965), 373-74; MARTINEAU, Henri, ed., *Correspondance*:
Tome I, 1800-1821 (see *PQ,* XLIII, 484), rev. by Massimo Colesanti in *SFr,* IX
(1965), 501-05.

VIGNY

Abirached, Robert, ed. *Poèmes.* Précédés de "Vigny ou le feu de la
raison" par Robert Abirached. (Coll. "Le Monde en 10/18.") Paris:
Union Générale d'Editions, 1965. Pp. 314.

Barnett, Marguerite, transl. and ed. *The Military Condition.* Introduced
by John Cruikshank. (The Oxford Library of French Classics.) London: Oxford University Press, 1964. Pp. xv + 206.

Castex, Pierre-Georges. "La réflexion politique d'Alfred de Vigny." *Revue des Travaux de l'Académie des Sciences Morales et Politiques*, cxvii^e Année, 4e Série (1er semestre 1964), pp. 119-32.
Rejecting recent attacks on Vigny's character, Castex demonstrates a consistency in the poet's political thought, that of an "aristocrate de bonne volonté," upholding his class but supporting a stable Republican government.

Castex, Pierre-Georges. *Vigny: Stello; Servitude et grandeur militaires.* (Les Cours de Sorbonne: Littérature Française.) Paris: Centre de Documentation Universitaire, 1963.

Catala, J.-A. *Alfred de Vigny. Poète et vigneron.* Angoulême: Société Anonyme des Journaux et Imprimeries de la Charente, 1964. Pp. 24.

Catala, J.-A. and René Pomeau, eds. *Lettres à Philippe Soulet, régisseur au Maine-Giraud et à Eugène Paignon*; avec une introduction et des notes de J.-A. Catala, suivies de "Vigny au Maine-Giraud en 1827 d'après un carnet inédit," par J.-A. Catala et René Pomeau. Angouléme: Société Anonyme des Journaux et Imprimeries de la Charente, 1965. Pp. 203.
Rev. by Christiane Lefranc in *RHL*, LXVI (1966), 523-26.

Catala, J.-A. *Sept lettres à Philippe Soulet, régisseur au Maine-Giraud.* Présentation de J.-A. Catala. Angoulême: Editions Coquemard, 1964.
From the *Bulletins et Mémoires de la Sociéte Archéologique et Historique de la Charente*, 1962-1963.

Eigeldinger, Marc. *Alfred de Vigny.* Un tableau synoptique de la vie et des oeuvres d'Alfred de Vigny et des événements artistiques, littéraires et historiques de son époque. Une suite iconographique accompagnée d'un commentaire sur Alfred de Vigny et son temps. Une étude sur l'écrivain par Marc Eigeldinger. Un choix de textes d'Alfred de Vigny. Un choix de jugements. Une bibliographie. (Ecrivains d'hier et d'aujourd'hui, 19.) Paris: Pierre Séghers, 1965. Pp. 190.

Gelineau, Pierre. *Alfred de Vigny ou Celui qui a passionément cru en l'homme.* Angoulême: Société Anonyme des Journaux et Imprimeries de la Charente, 1965. Pp. 16.
Talk given at Blanzac, Sept. 26, 1964.

Germain, François, ed. *Servitude et grandeur militaires.* Introduction, sommaire biographique, notes et relevé des variantes par François Germain. (Classiques Garnier.) Paris: Garnier, 1965. Pp. lxxxii + 365; illus.
Careful and extensive documentation on genesis of the work, sources of inspiration, Vigny's intentions for the work, reality and invention underlying its composition, etc. Of particular interest is the first appendix, a collection of Vigny's writings relative to the *Servitude* from his *Journal,* correspondence, and other works. (C.C.)

Hytier, Jean. "L'illusion de modernité à travers la poésie française." *RR*, LVII (1966), 241-51.

A survey of the sense of modernity in five poets: Villon, Du Bellay, Chénier, Vigny, Nerval.

Kurz, Harry. "Alfred de Vigny's Ideas on Government and the United States." *The American Society Legion of Honor Magazine,* XXXVII (1966), 43-54.

Massey, Irving. "Alfred de Vigny: Notes for *Stello* in the Musée de Condé." *MP,* LXIII (1966), 246-51.

Massey, Irving. "Verlaine and Vigny: The Use and Abuse of Sources." *RomN,* VII (1966), 123-26.

Oldham, Ronald. "Le symbole chez Alfred de Vigny." *Humanities Association Bulletin,* XVI, No. 1 (1965), 41-44.

Poulet, Louis. "Alfred de Vigny et Giacomo Leopardi." *Nuovo Casanostra,* XCVII (1964), lxxxi, 35-46.

Roy, G. Ross. "Burns in France." *RLC,* XXXIX (1965), 450-52.
Letter from Vigny, Oct. 26, 1862.

Viallaneix, Paul, ed. *Oeuvres complètes.* Préface, présentation et notes de Paul Viallaneix. (L'Intégrale.) Paris: Editions du Seuil, 1965. Pp. 663.
Rev. by Joseph Bertrand in *La Revue Générale Belge.* No. 8 (August 1965), 97-99.
Includes "Portrait de Vigny" by Sainte-Beuve.

Weber, Jean-Paul. "L'analyse thématique, hier, aujourd'hui, demain." *Études Françaises,* II (February 1966), 29-71.
A rejoinder to Raymond Picard's *Nouvelle Critique ou nouvelle imposture.* A long section (pp. 43-61) treats the theme of *l'horloge* in Vigny's work. (C.C.)

See also Delmas, Sartre ("1. General"); Bach ("Sainte-Beuve").

Reviews of work previously listed:
CASTEX, Pierre-Georges, ed., *Les Destinées* (see *ELN,* III, Supp., 85), rev. by R. Fargher in *FS,* XX (1966), 200-01, and by Roger Pierrot in *RHL,* LXVI (1966), 342-43.

GERMAN

(Compilers and reviewers: Ingeborg Carlson, Arizona State Univ.; Ulrich Gaier, Univ. of Calif., Davis; Philip Glander, Univ. of Calif., Berkeley; E. Bernell McIntire, Arizona State Univ.; Kenneth Negus, Rutgers Univ.; Günther Nerjes, Univ. of Calif., Davis; Laurence R. Radner, Purdue Univ.; Josef S. Thanner, Rutgers Univ.)

1. BIBLIOGRAPHY

Eppelsheimer, Hans W., ed. *Bibliographie der deutschen Literaturwissenschaft.* Bd.6, 1963-1964. Bearbeitet von Clemens Köttelwelsch.

Ständige Mitarbeiterin Hildegard Hüttermann. Frankfurt/M: Klostermann, 1965. Pp. xxxix + 431. Br. DM 77.50, Lw. DM 86.50.
Rev. by L.Uhlig in *Germanistik*, VII (1966), 550.

Frey, John R. "Anglo-German Literary Bibliography for 1965." *JEGP*, LXV (1966), 516-20.

Germanistik: Internationales Referatenorgan mit bibliographischen Hinweisen. VII. Jg. Tübingen: Niemeyer, 1966.
See especially in each of the four issues: "XVIII. Vergleichende Literaturgeschichte," "XXIX. Goethezeit (1770-1830)," and "XXX. Von der Nachromantik bis zum Realismus (1830-1890)." Most books are reviewed. All items are listed by their authors. Coverage includes publications in Europe, South Africa, North and South America, Australia, and Japan.

Körner, Josef. *Bibliographisches Handbuch des deutschen Schrifttums*. Unveränderter Nachdruck der 3., völlig umgearbeiteten und wesentlich vermehrten Aufl. Bern and München: Francke, 1966. Pp. 644. DM 68.00.
Rev. by L. Uhlig in *Germanistik*, VII (1966), 554-55.
A reprinting of the 1949 edition.

Morgan, Bayard Quincey. *A Critical Bibliography of German Literature in English Translations 1481-1927*. 2nd revised edition. Supplement Embracing the Years 1928-1955. New York and London: Scarecrow Press, 1965. 2 vols. $10.00 and $14.00.
Rev. by L. Newman in *MLR*, LXI (1966), 722-24.

Müller, Joachim. "Romantikforschung II." (Beilage Forschungsberichte Literaturwissenschaft 10.) *DU*, XVII (1966), 1-16.
For Part I see *PQ*, XLIII (1964), 486. Critical and penetrating résumés of general works on Romanticism in 1963 and 1964 with illuminating quotations. Major works not mentioned: Fambach, Gérard, Sorensen, Plard, Voerster, Wilson. New editions and secondary works on individual poets extensively reviewed. (I.C.)

Schmitt, Franz Anselm. *Stoff- und Motivgeschichte der deutschen Literatur. Eine Bibliographie*. Begründet von Kurt Bauerhorst; 2., neubearbeitete und stark erweiterte Aufl. Berlin: de Gruyter, 1965. Pp. 332. DM 58.00.
Rev. by G.-L. Fink in *Germanistik*, VII (1966), 557-58, and by G. Favier in *EG*, XXI (1966), 636-37.

2. GENERAL

Barnard, Frederick M. *Herder's Social and Political Thought. From Enlightenment to Nationalism*. Oxford: Clarendon Press, 1965. Pp. xxii + 189. 30s.
Rev. by H. D. Irmscher in *Germanistik*, VII (1966), 592, and by M. Rouché in *EG*, XXI (1966), 610-11.
More detailed than its 1964 version in German under the title *Zwischen Aufklärung und politischer Romantik* (see *ELN*, IV, Supp., 94). A study on Herder's sociological-political thinking. (I.C.)

Brinkmann, Hennig. *Studien zur Geschichte der deutschen Sprache und Literatur.* Bd. I: *Sprache*; Bd. II: *Literatur.* Düsseldorf: Schwann, 1965-66. DM 44.00 and 44.00.
Rev. by R. Schützeichel in *Germanistik,* vII (1966), 486-87.
Vol. II contains "Die Idee des Lebens in der deutschen Romantik" (376-435).

Bulling, Karl. *Die Rezensenten der Jenaischen Allgemeinen Literaturzeitung im dritten Jahrzehnt ihres Bestehens 1824-1833.* Weimar: Böhlau, 1965. Pp. 304. DM 23.00.
A continuation of a previously published study (see *ELN,* III, Supp., 89).

Dornheim, Alfredo. "Schöpferisches Gestalten in Lyrik und Prosa der Spätromantik und Gegenwart." *Boletin de Estudios Germanicos,* v (1964), 55-68.
In line with Kohlschmidt and Höllerer, Dornheim recognizes Romantic idealism in its speculative nihilism (which he ascribes to characters of Jean Paul, Brentano, Hoffmann, and Kleist), as the nucleus of the disintegration that leads to the decadence of modern German literature. The modern "passive hero" is considered a descendent of *Taugenichts.* And yet the creative impulses that emanate from the inwardness of the same period, especially Novalis and again Eichendorff, serve Rilke, Hesse, Krolow, and Kaschnitz to regain their lost balance. (I.C.)

Droz, Jacques. *Le romantisme allemand et l'état. Résistance et collaboration dans l'Allemagne napoléonienne.* Paris: Payot, 1966. Pp. 310. 21 Fr.
Rev. in *TLS,* May 4, 1967, p. [369].
Rev. by G. Fink in *Germanistik,* vII (1966), 598.
Continues a previous work on the impact of the French Revolution on Germany. Conservative rather than revolutionary forces are considered the major motivating forces. Thus *not* Prussia's neutralism but Austria's catholic Romanticism instigated the Wars of Liberation, which are seen as restorative attempts of conservative circles, and not products of revolutionary liberalism. (I.C.)

Fuerst, Norbert. *The Victorian Age of German Literature.* Eight Essays. Pennsylvania State University Press, 1966. Pp. 206.
Rev. by I. Carlson in *Germanistik,* vIII (1967), 138-39.
In Romanticism the most important references are to Eichendorff and Heine.

Jahrbuch der Deutschen Schillergesellschaft, IX, 1965. [*JDSG*]
Rev. by Uhlig in *Germanistik,* vII (1966), 552-54.
Benno v. Wiese's "Das Problem der ästhetischen Versöhnung bei Schiller und Hegel" is a confrontation of Schiller's sentimental and Hegel's Romantic aestheticism (167-88). In Fritz Martini's "Kleists 'Der zerbrochene Krug': Bauformen des Lustspiels" the comical element of the play is seen in the contrast between the mask and the reality of the judge (373-419). See articles by Mommsen (under "Hölderlin"), Sembdner (under "Grimm Brothers") and Paulsen (under "Bonaventura").

Jolles-Mazzucchetti, Lavinia. "Mignon von Goethe bis Hauptmann." *SchM,* xxxxv (1965), 359-72.
Translated and abridged version of previously published article. See *ELN,* III, Supp., 93, under "Mazzucchetti." Makes reference to Arnim, Brentano, Eichendorff, and Hoffmann.

Kabel, Rolf, ed. *Eduard Devrient. Aus seinen Tagebüchern.* Weimar: Böhlau, 1964. 2 vols. MDN 28.10 and 26.40.
Vol. I: Berlin-Dresden, 1836-52; Vol. II: Karlsruhe, 1852-70. These diaries were obviously intended for later publication. They contain interesting items of "Zeitgeschichte," criticism of theatrical performances, and splendid characterizations of Rahel, Tieck, O. Ludwig, Gutzkow, Holtei, and Richard Wagner. An invaluable source-book. (I.C.)

Kahn, Robert. "Some Recent Definitions of German Romanticism, or the Case Against Dialectics." *RUS,* L (1964), 3-26.
Wellek's dialectic concept of a unified European Romantic movement impresses Kahn as a sweeping generalization. He proposes restricting the term to the German concept—basically what this section of our bibliography represents. Kahn allows little room for biographical or socio-political background research, and concentrates on the poetic works themselves in an undogmatic "multiplicitarian" spirit. This seems to differ little from "werkimmanente" interpretation. (I.C.)

Klin, Eugeniusz. "August Ferdinand Bernhardi und das frühromantische Milieu." *GW,* X (1966), 75-122.

Kluckhohn, Paul. *Die Auffassung der Liebe in der Literatur des 18. Jahrhunderts und in der deutschen Romantik.* Tübingen: Niemeyer, 1966. Pp. 651. DM 46.00.
This third printing of the 1922 edition is unaltered, with the exception of an added name-index.

Kunisch, Hermann, ed. *Literaturwissenschaftliches Jahrbuch.* Im Auftrage der Görres-Gesellschaft, N.S. V. Berlin: Duncker & Humblot, 1964. Pp. 507. DM 38.00.
Eudo C. Mason in "Wir sehen uns wieder" (79-109) discusses the motif of reunification with a beloved soul in the hereafter. Besides Goethe and Schiller, he treats Hölderlin (*Hyperion* and *Menons Klagen um Diotima*) and Novalis, for whom this transcendental idea was the pivot. Eugeniusz Klin sets off the critical attempts of the Berlin group, including the Schlegels and Tieck, as counterbalance to the *Xenien*; then concentrates on "August Ferdinand Bernhardis Kritik der zeitgenössischen Literatur" (111-42). Winfried Weier points out Kleist's immanent and transilient conception of death in "Entwicklungsphasen des Todesproblems in der deutschen Tragödie zwischen Idealismus und Realismus" (143-75). Marianne Thalmann's "Romantik und Manierismus" is a by-product of her book (*ELN,* III, Supp., 95), centered on Tieck. (I.C.)

Kunszery, Gyula. "Das Bild des Ungartums in der deutschen Romantik." *ALitASH,* VI (1964), 267-85.

Lebe, Reinhard. *Ein deutsches Hoftheater in Romantik und Biedermeier. Die Kasseler Bühne zur Zeit Feiges und Spohrs.* Kassel: Röth, 1964.

Lüders, Detlev, ed. *Jahrbuch des Freien Deutschen Hochstifts 1965.* Tübingen: Niemeyer, 1965. Pp. 517. DM 32.00. [*JFDH* 1965]

Müller-Seidel, Walter and Wolfgang Preisendanz, eds. *Formenwandel. Festschrift zum 65. Geburtstag von Paul Böckmann.* Hoffmann und Campe: Hamburg, 1964. Pp. 520. DM 48.00.
Rev. by L. Uhlig, *Germanistik,* VII (1966), 344-45.

The articles radiate outward from the center of Goethe to all epochs of German literature. Roy Pascal, in "Ein Traum, was sonst?," attempts to interpret the final verses of *Prinz Friedrich von Homburg* (351-622). Benno von Wiese, in "Immermanns *Münchhausen* und der Roman der Romantik," traces the influence of the Romantic novel (363-82). Louis L. Hammerich, in "Trochäen bei Heinrich Heine. Zugleich ein Beitrag zum Werdegang eines alten Germanisten," (393-409), offers wistful personal conclusions. (I.C.)

Puccini, Mario. "Testimonianze di una nuova poetica negli epistolari dei primi romantici tedeschi." *Letteratura*, XXVIII (1964), 209-17.

Purdie, Edna. *Studies in German Literature of the 18th Century. Some Aspects of Literary Affiliation.* London: Athlone Press, 1965. Pp. 224. 40s.
Rev. by Roy Pascal, *MLR*, LXI (1966), 537-38.

Rapp, Eleonore. *Die Marionette im romantischen Weltgefühl. Ein Beitrag zur deutschen Geistesgeschichte.* (Forschung und Lehre, I) Bochum: Deutsches Institut für Puppenspiel, 1964.

Rehder, Helmut, ed. *Literary Symbolism, A Symposium.* University of Texas Press, 1965. Pp. 144.
Five participants of the 5th annual symposium of the Texas Dept. of Germanic Languages and Literatures tackle symbolism from Herder to Expressionism. In his introduction Rehder stakes out the term between "referential and emotive utterance" and "secret code for the initiated." Only one paper deals specifically with German Romanticism: contrasting two passages from *Heinrich von Ofterdingen*, J. Christopher Middleton discusses "Two Mountain Scenes in Novalis and the Question of Symbolic Style" (85-109). He makes special reference to Klingsohr's symbolic *Märchen* and provides evidence for his views from Novalis' sources, which even include reproductions of cabalistic drawings. (I.C.)

Rychner, Max. *Aufsätze zur Literatur*, Zürich: Manesse Verlag, 1966. Pp. 561. sfr. 16.60.
Rev. by Joachim Müller in *Germanistik*, VII (1966), 556-57.
Deals in part with Jean Paul, Novalis, and Fr. Schlegel.

Stern, J. P. *Re-interpretations. Seven Studies in Nineteenth-Century German Literature.* New York: Basic Books, 1964. Pp. 370. $7.50.
Consists of seven essays on seven writers from Grillparzer to Fontane, with Rilke's spirit in the background, all generalized as realists of "historical consciousness" who follow the Goethe heritage and represent their century. "They are distinguished above all by their special combination of the prophetic and the archaic, of the existential and the parochial, of the elements of the worldly innocence and the reflective profundity." "History and Prophecy" (208-39) is the only chapter devoted to Romanticism. The subtitle supplies the cue: Heine is the grandfather of modern German journalists with a philosophical background of pantheistic and Spinozistic beliefs. Stern recognizes him as a Romantic who re-interprets the real world on the basis of his own individual experience. Bibliography and notes on the same page as the text are a boon to the reader. Quotations in translation without bibliographical source are frustrating. (I.C.)

Thalmann, Marianne. "Formen und Verformen durch die Vergeistigung der Farben." *JWGV*, LXVIII (1964), 124-48.
The varying shapes and shades of environment play a major part here in the

creative process of the Romantic poet. Thalmann concentrates on the anti-naturalistic effects that Tieck, Novalis, Brentano, and Hoffmann attain through their spiritualization of color and alienation of form. (I.C.)

Thorslev, Peter L. "Incest as a Romantic Symbol." *CLS*, II (1965), 41-58.

Discussed are Schiller's *Braut*, Tieck's *Eckbert*. Typical for "romantic" love are the "Schicksalstragödien" of Schiller Epigones and their narrative equivalent of German "Schauerroman" and English Gothic novels (Walpole and Lewis). Romantics condemn parent-child incest (the Cenci theme), stepson-stepmother incest (*Don Carlos* and *Parisina*), idealize consciously committed sibling incest (Goethe's Mignon; Byron, Shelley, Chateaubriand, and Hawthorne) as symbol for the narcissistic sensibility and intellectual solipsism of the hero. Thorslev is apparently not aware of Shelley's indebtedness to Goethe's "Warum gabst du uns die tiefen Blicke . . ." in his metaphors of the loved one's soul as a mirror-image of the lover's own. (I.C.)

Tober, K. "German Romanticism." Part I: *ESA* VII (1964), 152-72; Part II: *ESA* VIII (1965), 56-63.

Tober offers a philological explanation of the German word "romantisch," treats the revaluation of Romanticism between 1870 and 1963, and analyzes German thought in philosophy and literature around 1800 and the theory of Romantic writing. He outlines the development of Romantic literature in Germany and traces the three historical phases. For Older Romanticism, Jena 1797-1804, he sees Novalis as the poetic climax. Younger Romanticism with centers from Heidelberg to Vienna, 1805-15, is dedicated to music and a German Renaissance as shown in collections like *Des Knaben Wunderhorn*. Late Romanticism, 1815-30, which was geographically scattered, has a lingering influence up to the present. Catholicism is countered by a Pietistic awakening, mysticism by the scientific trend toward objectivism and realism. Tober points to oscillations between the last two phases. This should also have included the *unio mystica* in Novalis. An amusing misprint is "Hymen an die Nacht." (I.C.)

Urbanowicz, Mieczysław. *Zdziejów literatury niemieckiej na Slasku w pierwszej polowie XIX wieku* (Aus der Geschichte der deutschen Literatur in Schlesien in der ersten Hälfte des XIX. Jahrhunderts.) Wroclaw: Warszawa Kraków: Zakład Narodowy im. Ossolinskich, 1964. Pp. 196. Br. zl 31.

Rev. by M. Szyrocki, *Germanistik*, VII (1966), 297.
This work on Silesian literature understandably deals with poets of mainly local importance. Interesting, however, for Eichendorff scholars who can manage Polish. (I.C.)

Wachsmuth, Andreas B. "Goethe und die Romantik." *WZUL*, XII (1963), 503-13.

Zagari, Luciano. *Studi di letteratura tedesca dell'Ottocento.* (Collana di Cultura, 7.) Roma: Edizioni dell'Ateneo, 1965. Pp. 239. L. 3.200.

Rev. by G. Luciani in *EG*, XXI (1966), and by J. Brummack in *Germanistik*, VII (1966), 615-16.
Deals with Heine in "La Pomare di Heine e la crisi del linguaggio 'lirico' " (121-54) and "Heine nella critica italiana" (221-32); and with Hölderlin's *Friedensfeier*. (I.C.)

Reviews of books previously listed:

BARNARD, F. M., *Zwischen Aufklärung und politischer Romantik* (see *ELN*,

III, Supp., 88), rev. by E. J. Engel in *MLR*, LXI (1966), 539-40; BAUSCH, W., *Theorien des epischen Erzählens* . . . (see *ELN*, III, Supp., 88), rev. by G.-L. Fink in *EG*, XXI (1966), 302-03; BRUGGEMANN, W., *Spanisches Theater und deutsche Romantik* (see *ELN*, III, Supp., 89), rev. by R. Ayrault in *EG*, XXI (1966), 301-02, and by E. Schwarz in *CL*, XVIII (1966), 79-80; FAMBACH, O., *Der romantische Rückfall* . . . (see *ELN*, III, Supp., 89), rev. by G.-L. Fink in *EG*, XXI (1966), 121-22; GÉRARD, R., *L'orient et la pensée romantique allemande* (see *ELN*, III, Supp., 90), rev. by L. Dieckmann in *GQ*, XXXIX (1966), 240-42; HARDY, S. L., *Goethe, Calderon und die romantische Theorie des Romans* (see *ELN*, IV, Supp., 95), rev. by M. Franzbach in *GRM*, XVI (1966), 437-38; HATFIELD, H., *Aesthetic Paganism* . . . (see *ELN*, III, Supp., 90), rev. by L. Uhlig in *Germanistik*, VII (1966), 89-90; LUDERS, D., *JFDH 1964* (see *ELN*, III, Supp., 92), rev. by W. Herwig in *Germanistik*, VII (1966), 92-93, and by R. Ayrault in *EG*, XXI (1966), 126-27; MEYER, H., *Zarte Empirie* (see *ELN*, III, Supp., 93), rev. by W. M. Calder in *GL&L*, XIX (1966), 134-35, and by T. C. van Stockum in *Neophilologus*, L (1966), 185-87; SORENSEN, B. A., *Symbol und Symbolismus* . . . (see *ELN*, III, Supp., 94), rev. by G.-L. Fink in *EG*, XXI (1966), 125-26; THALMANN, M., *The Romantic Fairy Tale* (see *ELN*, III, Supp., 93), rev. by L. Dieckmann in *MLQ*, XXVII (1966), 95-96; THALMANN, M., *Romantik und Manierismus* (see *ELN*, III, Supp., 95), rev. by M. Dyck in *Monatshefte*, LVII (1966), 179-80; THALMANN, M., *Romantiker entdecken die Stadt* (see *ELN*, IV, Supp., 97), rev. by K. Riha in *GRM*, XVI (1966), 321-22, and by G.-L. Fink in *Germanistik*, VII (1966), 613-14; VOERSTER, E., *Märchen und Novellen* . . . (see *ELN*, IV, Supp., 97), rev. by G.-L. Fink in *EG*, XXI (1966), 468; WILLSON, A. L., *A Mythical Image: The Ideal of India in German Romanticism* (see *ELN*, III, Supp., 95), rev. by R. Immerwahr in *JEGP*, LXV (1966), 400-03; by G. Renée in *GQ*, XXXIX (1966); by L. Uhlig in *Germanistik*, VII (1966), 101-02; by R. Ayrault in *EG*, XXI (1966), 301-02; by J. Schröder in *Archiv*, CXVII (1965), 202, and by R. L. Kahn in *MLQ*, XXVII (1966), 358-59.

3. STUDIES OF AUTHORS

ARNIM, ACHIM VON

Migge, Walther, ed. *Sämtliche Romane und Erzählungen.* Vol. III. Munich: Hanser, 1965. Pp. 867. DM 31.

Rev. by Siegfried Scheibe in *Germanistik*, VII (1966), 591.

Peyraube, Jacques. "La sensibilité d'Arnim dans sa correspondance avec Bettina." *EG*, XXI (1966), 188-204.

See also Jolles-Mazzucchetti ("German 2. General").

ARNIM, BETTINA VON

See "Peyraube" ("Arnim, Achim von").

BONAVENTURA

Paulsen, Wolfgang, ed. *Bonaventura. Nachtwachen.* (Universal-Bibliothek 8926/27). Stuttgart: Reclam, 1964. Pp. 180. DM 1.60.

This welcome addition to its series contains not only a well-edited text (a re-working of E. Frank's edition of 1912, with reference to the first edition of 1805), but also a brief discussion of the work's textual problems, thorough notes, a selective bibliography, and an up-to-date postscript. In the last-mentioned, Paulsen completely rejects all previous speculations as to the work's authorship, and boldly professes the agnostic position. In his critical discussion, he stresses novel-like aspects and the modernity of this classic of Romantic nihilism. (K.N.)

Paulsen, Wolfgang. "Bonaventuras 'Nachtwachen' im literarischen Raum: Sprache und Struktur." *JDSG,* IX (1965), 447-510.
This valuable treatise revolves mainly around stylistic and structural matters, but it also delves into broad areas of German literary history, and finds illuminating parallels as well as influences on and from Bonaventura. The *Nachtwachen* is regarded as primarily a product of Romanticism, yet also as showing significant influences from the Reformation period (Hans Sachs), Baroque (the *Vanitas* theme and Shakespeare), and Enlightenment (freethinking). Parallels with Friedrich Schlegel, Jean Paul, Kleist, Brentano, Hoffmann, and popular literature (the Gothic novel) are profitably drawn. It is concluded that, of all of Bonaventura's contemporaries, Jean Paul bears closest resemblances to him—though no identification of the latter with him is implied. The most intriguing section is the structural and thematic analysis of the work on the basis of the *Fastnachtspiel* and the development of devil motifs. In summing up, Paulsen finds the work to be "anti-Faustian," even "anti-Goethean" in character: "Bonaventuras Weltbild wäre . . . nicht nur die Religion eines gefallenen Engels, sondern auch invertierter klassischer Humanismus." Though at times slightly speculative, this lengthy article is a gold mine of insights into Bonaventura and related areas. (K.N.)

Sammons, Jeffrey L. *The Nachtwachen von Bonaventura: A Structural Interpretation.* (Studies in German Literature, Vol. 5.) London, The Hague, Paris: Mouton, 1965. Pp. 128. Hfl. 18.00.
Rev. by W. Paulsen in *Germanistik,* VII (1966), 431-32.

See also Hermand ("Jean Paul").

BRENTANO
Hoffmann, Werner. *Clemens Brentano. Leben und Werk.* Bern and Munich: Francke, 1966. Pp. 452. DM 34.00.
An ambitious undertaking and in many ways successful. The account of the poet's life is best. His love affairs, tortured self-examination, religious crises are vividly presented, but the repeated interpretation of his life as the search for a lost mother is an oversimplification. Discussions of the poetry alternate with biographical chapters, thereby showing the intimate relations between life and works, but these literary discussions are much too superficial. The book is carefully written and documented, in style, however, often redundant, with a disturbing tendency towards psychological analysis. Despite shortcomings, the book is indispensible for knowledge of Brentano. (P. G.)

Mennemeier, Franz Norbert. "Rückblick auf Brentanos 'Godwi.' Ein Roman 'ohne Tendenz.' " *WW,* XVI (1966), 24-33.
Brentano's novel often is falsely judged by standards of classical art. The stylistic principles noted in this study—purposeful lack of intention, spontaneity, destruction of illusion—prove Brentano's disregard for conventional narration. *Godwi,* however imperfect, puts into practice theories of Romantic literature. A good discussion of the Romantic poet's attitude towards his creation is included. (P. G.)

See also Dornheim, Jolles-Mazzucchetti, Thalmann, Tober ("German 2. General"); Paulsen ("Bonaventura").

CHAMISSO
Loeb, Ernst. "Symbol und Wirklichkeit des Schattens in Chamissos *Peter Schlemihl.*" *GRM,* XV (1965), 398-408.
When Chamisso was asked "Was *ist* der Schatten?" he evaded the issue to the delight of innumerable scholars. Loeb quotes their views, omitting Fitzell who

interprets the shadow as "Scheinwert" of society's false standards. Loeb develops the essence of the shadow as an error of Schlemihl, who thinks he can buy light without shadow, an easy way of life. Less of the shadow *and* fortune leads to his finding his true self. Truth is revealed to him in nature, according to the world view of Chamisso both as poet and as scientist. The beard of the unknown vagabond not only points to the Hebrew origin of the word "Schlemihl," as indicated by Loeb, but also to the legend of the eternal wanderer, in his almost Kafkaesque and so very modern search for an answer to the enigma of life. (I.C.)

EICHENDORFF

Gsteiger, Manfred. "Schiller und Eichendorff." *SchM,* xxxv (1965), 592-96.

Lüthi, Hans Jürg. *Dichtung und Dichter bei Joseph von Eichendorff.* Bern: Francke Verlag, 1966. Pp. 311. S. Fr. 37.50.

Schodrok, Christine. "Wilhelm von Eichendorff, des Dichters Bruder." *Aurora,* xxvi (1966), 7-21.

If only Wilhelm von Eichendorff, our poet's "Herzensbruder," were less of an enigma, we could, more easily, achieve a greater understanding of the poet. If nothing else, Christine Schodrok's carefully documented vignette gives us some insight concerning the pain and, paradoxically, the positive value of *separation* which is an integral structural feature of the poet's works. (L.R.)

Seidlin, Oskar. *Versuche über Eichendorff.* Göttingen und Zurich: Vandenheeck & Ruprecht, 1965. Pp. 303. DM 19.80.

Oskar Seidlin is one of the first to sound the depths of Eichendorff's poetry by treating such questions as: Who am I? What is the meaning of "das Dichterische," the creative energy, within me? What is the movement of my mind, my fantasy? What are my selves? What have I forgotten and what do I remember? What is my fear and my desire ("Sehnsucht")? The author points to the fascinating four-dimensional aspect of Eichendorff's world best described by the words "raum- und zeitartig." The last two chapters are especially valuable.

If our author did not love the poet, he would not have spent so many years with him. This gives the reviewer courage to voice a startling criticism which is not meant to be negative but constructive. Many of Seidlin's important conclusions are a distortion of Eichendorff's *poetic* structure. He states: "Der Frühling, der die Hüllen sprengt und das Tor ins neue Leben öffnet bis hin zu dem letzten Tor, das zu Gott führt, er ist es auch, der den Menschen in den streng geschlossenen Kreis festbindet, aus dem die Urformen und -gewalten kreatürlicher Existenz stets erneut aufsteigen" (222-23). We *know* that it is spring that awakens Venus. But Fortunato says to Florio, "Jeder lobt Gott auf seine Weise . . . und alle *Stimmen* zusammen machen den *Frühling* (II, 307). Put this into a simple equation, solve it for spring, and it suggests that praising God results in the awakening of Venus. This is an impossible solution. Seidlin's own reasoning suggests the fallacy. He sees just *one* spring when there are *two.* Two springs, so *very much alike* that man is deceived. This duality is the absolute *foundation* of Eichendorff's universe. Because Seidlin did not see this, much of his work is a collection of evidence drawn from two *different* realities which, until page 257, he assumes are one. One example: he states: "Wo die Welt jeden festen Umriss verliert, wo die Wirklichkeit vor dem Zauber der unendlichen Möglichkeiten versinkt, wo alles sich auflöst in Klang und Licht und Farbe, da ist die Annihilierung vollzogen, in der die Fülle des Alls mit der Leere des Nichts zusammenfällt. Der Boden versinkt, jeder Halt fällt für den, der sich nicht bewahren will, und, ausgesetzt den Uferlosigkeiten, die kein Horizont begrenzt, bleibt nichts andres als ein Gleiten in einem Raume, der kein Oben und kein Unten mehr kennt: 'Hoch

Himmel über mir und Himmel drunter,/Inmitten wie so klein mein schwacher Kahn!' (I, 44)" (p. 200). These two lines of poetry are not negative, as the author insists, but positive. The poem "Auf offener See" is thus utterly distorted. Seidlin "saw" one reality while the poem speaks of the other. After all, the speaker in the poem says, "Walt' Gott, ihm hab' ich alles übergeben." This is "sich bewahren wollen" and not "sich nicht bewahren wollen"! Thus Seidlin sees a negative reality "wo alles sich auflöst in Klang und Licht und Farbe." At the end of *Das Marmorbild* we read: "Der Morgen schien ihnen, in langen, goldenen Strahlen über die Fläche schiessend, gerade entgegen. Die Bäume standen hell angeglüht, unzählige Lerchen sangen schwirrend in der klaren Luft. Und so zogen die Glücklichen fröhlich durch die überglänzten Auen in das blühende Mailand hinunter" (II, 346). Does not all become light, color, song? This is man's movement toward the Ineffable Light of the Perfect Day. In "Jugendandacht," the third poem (I, 275), light, color, song merge to *form a woman.* Assuming a form, the author's "fester Umriss," is also a spiritual error as this poem instructs us. Each process may be either positive or negative depending upon the nature of man's involvement. This lack of distinction colors the reasoned analysis in every chapter, and results in a distortion of the poet's intent. If I were to describe the poet's technique, I would borrow from another field and call it the *principle of equivalence.* (L.R.)

Sörenson, Bengt Algott. "Zum Problem des Symbolischen und Allegorischen in Eichendorff's epischem Bilderstil." *Aurora,* XXVI (1966), 50-56.

The author takes issue with Werner Kohlschmidt's suggestion that Eichendorff's "Formelhaftigkeit" tends to vitiate the symbolic nature of his imagery and "reduces" it to the allegorical. The essential characteristic of the symbol is defined as "die emotionale und irrationale Ausstrahlungskraft, durch die die Idee im Leser evoziert wird" (50). The "Idee" of *Das Marmorbild,* which is used to document the issue, is defined as a struggle between heathen, demonic forces and Christian forces *for* the soul of Florio. The attempt is abortive, and for the following reasons. The novella does not depict the *struggle for* Florio's soul but the *deception which lames* it. The landscape scenes do not depict "die Nachtseite der Natur" (55) but portray *the spiritual dimension of Florio's own song.* In the entire novella, whatever relates to the world of Venus is first within the youth before it becomes "Landschaft." (L.R.)

Worbs, Erich. "Eichendorff und das Meer." *Aurora,* XXVI (1966), 57-66.

In his *Tagebücher* Eichendorff describes the impact which the sea made upon him on his first visit in 1805. The author cites numerous passages and poems that substantiate his assertion that the ocean is part of Eichendorff's "Seelenlandschaft." (38) The point is incontestable, and yet, no interpretation is provided which might show *how* the sea is woven into the poet's "Hieroglyphenschrift." (L.R.)

See also Dornheim, Fuerst, Jolles-Mazzucchetti, Urbanowicz ("German 2. General").

GRIMM, J.

Santoli, Vittorio. "Alle origini della storia letteraria nazionale (a proposito di G. G. Gervinius e J. Grimm)." *RLMC,* XVIII (1966), 5-19.

GRIMM BROTHERS

Grimm, Jacob and Wilhelm, eds. *Deutsche Sagen. Nachwort von Lutz Röhrich.* Munich: Winkler, 1965. Pp. 649. DM 22.80.

Rev. by G.-L. Fink in *Germanistik,* VII (1966), 671.

Schmidt-Barrien, Heinrich. "Fragen zu den plattdeutschen Märchen der Brüder Grimm." *Muttersprache,* LXXVI (1966), 277-79.

Schoof, Wilhelm. *Die Brüder Grimm in Berlin.* (Berliner Reminiszensen, Vol. V.) Berlin: Hauder and Spener, 1964. Pp. 112. DM 9.80.
Rev. by I.-M. Barth in *Germanistik,* VII (1966), 267.

Schoof, Wilhelm. "Die englischen und französischen Beziehungen der Brüder Grimm." *WW,* XVI (1966), 394-407.
Useful references to the Grimm *Nachlass.*

Schoof, Wilhelm. "Die verlorene Handschrift. Aus den Erinnerungen eines alten Grimmforschers." *SchR,* LXV (1966), 353-54.
The story of the acquisition of the Grimm-Savigny correspondence for publication.

Schoof, Wilhelm. "Savigny und die Brüder Grimm." *SZ,* LXXXIX (1966), 67-70.

Schulte-Kemminghausen, Karl. "Die wissenschaftlichen Beziehungen der Brüder Grimm zu Westfalen. Ein Beitrag zum Grimm-Jubiläum." *Westfälische Zeitschrift,* CXIII (1966), 179-242.

Sembdner, Helmut. "Heinrich von Kleist im Urteil der Brüder Grimm. Unbekannte Rezensionen." *JDSG,* IX (1965), 420-46.
Reprint of an anonymous review of Kleist's *Erzählungen* in an attempt to identify Wilhelm Grimm as the author. Comparison with similar passages in Grimm's letters is not convincing, but comparison with other earlier anonymous reviews of Kleist's works points conclusively to one author. This is an important topic in view of the Grimms' early recognition of Kleist's genius. Kleist as reference in the *Wörterbuch* is also discussed. (P.G.)

Wegehaupt, Heinz, and Renate Reipert, eds. *150 Jahre "Kinder- und Hausmärchen" der Brüder Grimm. Bibliographie und Materialien zu einer Ausstellung der Deutschen Staatsbibliothek.* Berlin: Deutsche Staatsbibliothek, 1964. Pp. 111. MDN 6.50.

Zaunert, Paul, ed. *Deutsche Märchen seit Grimm (Neue Ausgabe bearbeitet und mit Nachweisen versehen von Elfriede Moser-Rath).* Düsseldorf and Cologne: Diederichs, 1964. Pp. 353. DM 14.80.
Rev. by G. Gröber-Glück in *Germanistik,* VII (1966), 333.

HEINE

Becker, Eva D. "Heinrich Heine. Ein Forschungsbericht 1945-1965." *DU,* XVIII, Heft 4 (September, 1965), Beilage.

Eisner, Fritz H. "Verschollene Briefe an Heine. Ein neuer Fund." *HeineJ 1966,* pp. 68-89.

Galley, Eberhard. "Heine im literarischen Streit mit Gutzkow. Mit unbekannten Manuskripten aus Heines Nachlass." *HeineJ 1966,* pp. 3-40.

Harich, Wolfgang, ed. *Zur Geschichte der Religion und Philosophie in*

Deutschland. (Sammlung Insel, 17.) Frankfurt a. M.: Insel-Verlag, 1966. Pp. 244. Lw. DM 7.00.
Rev. by J. Hermand in *Germanistik*, VII (1966), 623.

Heine, Heinrich. *Deutschland: Ein Wintermärchen.* Mit Vorwort des Dichters und Anmerkungen. (Reclams Universalbibliothek.) Stuttgart: Reclam, 1966. Pp. 80.

Heine, Heinrich. *Gedichte.* 2. Auflage. (Bibliothek der Weltliteratur.) Berlin und Weimar: Aufbau Verlag, 1966. Pp. 751. DM-Ost 9.00.

Heine, Heinrich. *Reisebilder.* (Bibliothek der Weltliteratur.) Berlin und Weimar: Aufbau Verlag, 1966. Pp. 575. DM-Ost 8.70.

Heine, Heinrich. *Zur Geschichte der Religion und Philosophie in Deutschland.* Anhang: "Briefe über Deutschland" und "Aus den Geständnissen." Mit einem Essay 'Heinrich Heine und das Schulgeheimnis der deutschen Philosophie' von Wolfgang Harich. (Universal Bibliothek, Bd. 296.) Leipzig: Reclam, 1966. Pp. 269. DM-Ost 2.00.
Rev. by J. Hermand in *Germanistik*, VII (1966), 624.

Heine Archiv Düsseldorf, ed. *Heine Jahrbuch 1966.* Hamburg: Hoffmann und Campe, 1965. [*HeineJ 1966*]. Pp. 132.

"Heine Literatur 1964/1965 mit Nachträgen." *HeineJ 1966*, pp. 121-23.

Hofrichter, Laura. *Heinrich Heine. Biographie seiner Dichtung.* (Kleine Vandenhoeck-Reihe.) Göttingen: Vandenhoeck & Ruprecht, 1966. Pp. 190. DM 7.80.
Rev. by J. Hermand in *Germanistik*, VII (1966), 625.

Kubacki, W. "Heinrich Heine und Polen." *HeineJ 1966*, pp. 90-106.
The tone of this article quite understandably is influenced somewhat by Heine's *Zwei Ritter* and—less understandably—by Kubacki's listing Goethe, Byron, Pushkin, Mickiewicz, Slowacki, and Krasiński as the greatest poets of the era. In line with this we learn that Heine paid only one short visit to Poland. Actually, Heine saw little more than Posen (now Poznań) which was then part of Prussia. His report on both Germans and Poles of that region displeased the former even more than the latter. While Kubacki admits that there were no contacts of any kind between Heine and the above-mentioned Polish romanticists, he goes to great length to point out accidental similarities and apparent affinities. Most valuable in his article is the listing of an astonishingly large number of Polish translations of Heine which attest to the general interest in him. Starting about 1836 there was a definite upsurge in the second half of the century culminating in the eighties. Kubacki refers to a list of some sixty Polish writers. It does not surprise us that translations of Heine's prose were much more successful than those of his poems. This, to some extent, also applies to the Heine-scholarship of our century, which has undergone a definite revival within the last fifteen years. (H.G.N.)

Moenkemeyer, Heinz. "Die deutschen Erstdrucke von Heines 'Doktor Faust.'" *HeineJ 1966*, pp. 58-67.

Moenkemeyer, Heinz. "Two Printings of the First Edition of Heinrich Heine's Dance Poem 'Der Doktor Faust.'" *The Library Chronicle of the University of Pennsylvania*, XXXII, No. 1 (1966), 61-73.

Noethlich, Werner. "Was geschah mit Heines Nachlass?" *HeineJ 1966*, pp. 107-120.

Söhn, Gerhart. *Heinrich Heine in seiner Vaterstadt Düsseldorf.* Düsseldorf: Triltsch, 1966. Pp. 69. DM 8.80.

Spann, Meno. *Heine.* (Studies in Modern European Literature and Thought.) New York: Hillary House, 1966. Pp. 111. $3.00.

Vontin, Walther, ed. *Reisebilder.* Teilausgabe; 1.-5. Tsd. Hamburg: Hoffmann und Campe, 1966. Pp. 431. Lw. DM 19.80.
Rev. by J. Hermand in *Germanistik,* VII (1966), 623.

Weiss, Gerhard. "Die Entstehung von Heines 'Doktor Faust.' Ein Beispiel deutsch-englisch-französischer Freundschaft." *HeineJ 1966*, pp. 41-57.
The pretentious subtitle is rather misleading since friendship had precious little to do with the fate of Heine's "Tanzpoem." Weiss himself makes it quite clear that business interests were chiefly responsible for the creation and the changes in *Doktor Faust.*
It was mainly on the suggestion of Benjamin Lumley, director of "Her Majesty's Theatre" in London, that Heine wrote his ballet in order to outdo "The Drury Lane Theatre," a new rival company. The signing of Jenny Lind, the Swedish Nightingale, so Weiss speculates, gave Lumley and his theatre the necessary attraction, and Heine's ballet became superfluous. Yet Heine was paid the tidy sum of 6000 francs. It seems much more likely that the considerable artistic and technical difficulties of the "poem," which by then was encumbered by more "Erläuterungen" than actual text, had made a performance impracticable, if not impossible.
The French part of the friendship is obviously derived from Weiss's assertion that it was Gautier who brought about the personal connection between Heine and Lumley—a claim for which he does not provide any documentation. Even the French translations of *Doktor Faust,* intended for the *Revue des deux Mondes,* were never published. (H.G.N.)

See also Fuerst, Müller-Seidel, Stern, Zagari ("German 2. General").

Reviews of books previously listed:
GALLEY, E., *Heinrich Heine* (see *ELN,* III, Supp., 103), rev. by J. L. Simmons in *GQ,* XXXIX (1966), 249-50; HEINE-ARCHIV, *Heine-Jahrbuch 1964* (see *ELN,* III, Supp., 104), rev. by G. Bianquis, *EG,* XXI (1966), 119-20; MANN, M., ed., *Zeitungsberichte über Musik und Malerei* (see *ELN,* III, Supp., 105), rev. by H. S. Reiss, *GQ,* XXXIX (1966), 250-51.

HOFFMANN
Cramer, Thomas. *Das Groteske bei E. T. A. Hoffmann.* München: Fink, 1966. Pp. 215. DM 28.00.
Rev. by W. Segebrecht in *Germanistik,* VII (1966), 596-97.
This book follows in the trail of Elli Desalm's *E. T. A. Hoffmann und das Groteske* (Bonn, 1930), and W. Kayser's (1957) and Lee B. Jennings' (1963) basic works on the grotesque in German literature. Hoffmann studies needed updating in this area, and for this reason alone the book is welcome. Yet it leaves much to be desired. Its definition of the grotesque is too broad and too remote from commonly accepted concepts (". . . der Umschlag der Komik ins Irrationale durch das Zerreissen des Nexus zwischen Ursache und Wirkung"). The all-important visual and emotional aspects of the grotesque are almost wholly neglected. Thus Hoffmann's basic role as a "Malerdichter"

of the grotesque fails to emerge; and the intriguing simultaneity of fear and amusement conveyed by the grotesque is scarcely an issue. Far too few passages are thus really relevant to what is generally known as "grotesque." In the area of literary history, Cramer may be starting a fad aimed at "deromanticizing" Hoffmann—a risky undertaking, to say the least. Some passages serve as highly intelligent commentaries to works (e.g. the analysis of the style of *Der goldne Topf*, 37-55). Toward the end are some valuable findings on the sources of the grotesque from the Viennese theatre. But as a whole the book rests on uncomfortably shaky foundations of aesthetics and literary history. (K. N.)

Erné, Nino, ed. *Gesammelte Werke*. Bd. 3, 4, 5. Hamburg: Standard Verlag, 1965. DM 11.50 ea.
Rev. (unfavorably) by W. Segebrecht in *Germanistik*, VII (1966), 90-91 (Vol. 3 & 4) and 422-23 (Vol. 5).

Jeune, Simon. "Une étude inconnue de Musset sur Hoffmann." *RLC*, XXXIX (1965), 422-27.

Kanzog, Klaus. "E. T. A. Hoffmann-Literatur 1962-1965. Eine Bibliographie." *MHG*, XII (1966), 33-40.

Köpp, Claus F. "Realismus in E. T. A. Hoffmanns Erzählung 'Prinzessin Brambilla.' " *WB*, XII (1966), 57-80.
In line with recent attempts to "deromanticize" Hoffmann (see "Cramer"), the author attempts to make an allegory out of this tale that has been heretofore regarded (even by Hoffmann himself) as a fanciful capriccio. According to Köpp, the story "really" deals with social criticism—class struggle, political activism, and visionary utopianism. Hoffmann's growing realism toward the end of his life is undeniable, but surely it is of a deeper nature, and above all totally devoid of the heavy-handed kind of purposiveness indicated here. (K.N.)

Maucher, Gisela. "Das Problem der dichterischen Wirklichkeit im Prosawerk von E. T. A. Hoffmann und E. A. Poe." *MHG*, XII (1966), 31-32.
Summary of the authoress' dissertation, Washington University, St. Louis, Mo., 1964.

McGlathery, James M. "The Suicide Motif in E. T. A. Hoffmann's 'Der goldne Topf.' " *Monatshefte*, LVIII (1966), 115-23.
Proposes the notion that Anselmus commits suicide at the end of the story. Parallel cases in Hoffmann's works (especially *Der Sandmann*) lend some plausibility to this new idea, and Biblical background is interesting in itself. Yet the sum total of evidence for this bizarre interpretation seems meagre. (K.N.)

Mitteilungen der E. T. A. Hoffmann-Gesellschaft. Sitz in Bamberg. 12. Heft 1966 [*MHG*, XII (1966)].
Contains, in addition to articles listed separately by author in this section: a listing of Hoffmann programs (both musical and literary) given on radio and television in 1965; and "Notizen," including a portion of Julia Marc's funeral sermon (hitherto unpublished), and a few other short but important biographical items. (K.N.)

Müller, Dieter. "Zeit der Automate. Zum Automatenproblem bei Hoffmann." *MHG*, XII (1966), 1-10.
Finds an important and sharp distinction between Kleist's marionette and Hoffmann's automatons in the latter's strongly demonic features. (K. N.)

Reber, Natalie. *Studien zum Motiv des Doppelgängers bei Dostojevskij und E. T. A. Hoffmann.* (Marburger Abhandlungen zur Geschichte und Kultur Osteuropas, Band 6.) Giessen: Wilhelm Schmitz, 1964. Pp. 240. DM 27.00.

Rev. by A. von Gronicka in *JEGP,* LXV (1966), 554-57, and by G. Bianquis in *EG,* XXI (1966), 458-59.

This comparative analysis is a substantial contribution to two major areas of Hoffmann studies: his influence in Russia, treated by Charles Passage in *Dostoevski the Adapter* and *The Russian Hoffmannists*; and his ubiquitous *Doppelgänger,* examined by Kraus, Roehl, and Chapius. Dr. Reber does not investigate influences primarily, as Passage does, but instead makes a parallel phenomenological comparison of the two authors' *Doppelgänger.* This book differs from others on Hoffmann's double figures in its wealth of detail, which is kept in strict order, and is consistently aimed from the dual standpoint of psychology and metaphysics. The origin of the *Doppelgängertum* in both cases is a fundamentally dualistic world-view. In Hoffmann's works, however, there are more varied and mature forms of the double than in Dostoevski's, who abandoned the more pronounced types of this figure after his early works. The analysis of Hoffmann's works yields various aspects of the *Doppelgänger:* the psychological (*Die Elixiere des Teufels*), the mythical (*Der goldne Topf, Klein Zaches, Prinzessin Brambilla*), the satirical (*Kater Murr* and others), and the pathological. In an additional chapter are assembled the tangible forms and symbols of *Doppelgängertum* (the mirror, magic spectacles, automatons, portraits, and others). Seldom has a subject been so neatly laid out in Hoffmann scholarship.

The conclusions at the end of the Hoffmann section, however, are not quite so invulnerable. Although it is undeniable that there are definitely antithetical features in many a Hoffmann double, there does not have to ensue a Hegelian synthesis to resolve conflict. In fact, let it be submitted here that most of Hoffmann's resolutions of *Doppelgänger* antagonisms are anything but neat— ranging from *Ritter Gluck* to *Meister Floh.* Nor does the spiral ascent to paradise, as applied to *Doppelgängertum,* seem to follow logically from the body of the Hoffmann section.

The conclusion to the whole book, however, is altogether successful. Clearly established are some close similarities of Hoffmann's and Dostoevski's dualisms and *Doppelgänger* figures; but far more impressive are the differences, which are found principally in their respective solutions of the *Doppelgänger* problem. Dostoevski ultimately finds his in Christian love; Hoffmann, when he does, in a non-Christian vision of a Golden Age. A lengthy, valuable bibliography is appended. (K.N.)

Segebrecht, Wulf. "Hoffmanns Todesdarstellungen." *MHG,* XII (1966), 11-19.

Actually deals more with Hoffmann's personal confrontations with death than with literary representations thereof. *Kater Murr, Die Elixiere des Teufels,* and *Des Vetters Eckfenster* ("Todesnähe") provide the main literary examples. The author takes issue with previous Hoffmann scholarship in the matter of "Todessehnsucht," which, as he convincingly shows, is generally superseded by a love for life. (K. N.)

Terras, Victor. "E. T. A. Hoffmanns Polyphonische Erzählkunst." *GQ,* XXXIX (1966), 549-69.

Deals with "musical" structures in Hoffmann's narrative technique.

Wittkopp-Ménardeau, Gabrielle. *E. T. A. Hoffmann in Selbstzeugnissen und Bilddokumenten.* Reinbeck bei Hamburg: Rowohlt, 1966. Pp. 113. DM 2.80.

Rev. by W. Segebrecht in *Germanistik,* VII (1966), 614-15.

Wöllner, Günter. "Romantische Züge in der Partitur der 'Lustigen Musikanten.' " *MHG*, XII (1966), 20-30.

See also Kindermann ("General 3. Criticism"); Dornheim, Jolles-Mazzucchetti, Thalmann ("German 2. General"); Paulsen ("Bonaventura").

Reviews of books previously listed:

NEGUS, K., *E. T. A. Hoffmann's Other World* (see *ELN*, IV, Supp., 107), rev. by J. D. Zipes in *GR*, XLI (1966), 145-46, and by W. Segebrecht in *Germanistik*, VII (1966), 429; SCHNAPP, F., ed., *Schriften zur Musik* . . . (see *ELN*, III, Supp., 110), rev. by J. F. A. Ricci in *EG*, XXI (1966), 615-16; TAYLOR, R., *Hoffmann* (see *ELN*, III, Supp., 111), rev. by E. Stopp in *GL&L*, XIX (1966), 135-36; WERNER, H.-G., *E. T. A. Hoffmann* (see *PQ*, XLIII, 494-95), rev. (unfavorably) by J. Ricci in *EG*, XXI (1966), 117.

HÖLDERLIN

Bach, Emmon. "*Einst* and *Jetzt* in Hölderlin's Works." *DBGU*, V (1965), 143-56.

Bach tries to show in Hölderlin's work the development of a *Denkfigur* "einst-jetzt-einst," which he considers to be cyclic and unfortunately links with Hölderlin's concept of "excentrische Bahn" (which implies development from point to point). A cyclic concept of history would exist if the same thing and area could, after completion of a cycle, re-enter the same development. This, however, is not the case here, since the "einst" of the future is not a simple repetition of the past "einst." (U.G.)

Beissner, Friedrich. *Individualität in Hölderlins Dichtung. Ein Vortrag.* (Herausgegeben von der literarischen Vereinigung Winterthur.) Winterthur: W. Vogel, 1965. Pp. 46.

Discussing Hölderlin's difficulties in incorporating actuality into his poems, Beissner reveals an important difference between Schiller's reduction of poetic matter to infinity and the treatment of individual names in Hölderlin's poetry. Individuality, as with Klopstock and Rilke, is used as a counterweight to balance the abstractness of enthusiasm; the relationship between the two principles is shown in several instructive examples to be different for the sacred forms of tragedy, epic, hymn, and for the lower genres of comedy, idyl, and elegy. This paper seems to be an important step forward in the recognition of Hölderlin's treatment of poetic matter which is so intimately linked with his poetics. (U.G.)

Benn, M. B. "The Dramatic Structure of Hölderlin's 'Empedokles.' " *MLR*, LXII (1967), 92-97.

A dramatic plot involving Empedokles' return to Agrigent after once having decided to throw himself into Aetna would be "a radically defective plan" (93) in Benn's opinion; he therefore tries to prove that the first version was planned to have only three acts, thus acknowledging only one unaltered decision by the hero. The arguments brought forward are circumstantial: the length of acts 1 and 2, the improbability of a change in Empedokles upon the persuasion by two girls, distance between Agrigent and Aetna. Changing reasons and motives for the suicide are not considered. Benn's acknowledgment of the fact that the dramatic structure of version II "would probably have been very much the same as in I" (i.e., three acts, no return to Agrigent) is a self-defeating contradiction to his whole point, since Hölderlin's title page for version II reads: "Ein Trauerspiel in fünf Acten." (U.G.)

George, Emery E. "A Family of Disputed Readings in Hölderlin's Hymn 'Der Rhein.' " *MLR*, LXI (1966), 619-34.

The author shows, in a comparison between Hölderlin's ms. H[3] and Seckendorf's publication of the poem in *Musenalmanach für das Jahr 1808*, that of 8 "disputed readings," two might be read otherwise than Beissner proposes in the StA (v.89 "gründet" for "gegründet," v.180 "Da" for "Dann"). The slightness of his results and the dubitability of his criteria do not warrant the doubts raised by George about Beissner's editing techniques. (U.G.)

Hölderlin, Friedrich. *Hyperion or The Hermit in Greece*. Translated by Willard R. Trask. With a Foreword by Alexander Gode-von Aesch. New York and Toronto: The New American Library; London: The New English Library, 1965. Pp. 170.
The first translation into English is a good one, as far as I can judge, although the carefully balanced harmony of Hölderlin's periods in many instances is not reproduced. The foreword completely misses the idea of the "resolution of dissonances in a particular character" which, according to Hölderlin, is the intent of his novel, and sees in *Hyperion* "a fundamentally tragic view of life, of existence," "somehow synonymous with the symptomatic significance of the existentialist curse" (14). (U.G.)

Jaccottet, Philippe. "Hölderlin." *NRF*, xv (Février, 1967), 221-32.
This study tries to reduce Hölderlin's life and poetry to a few basic concepts— experience of sacred infinity, of instability, of an interior contrast in ideas and values. Simple and existential as these basic concepts may be, their relationship as established by Hölderlin is extremely complex: Jaccottet, therefore, does not seem justified in disparaging Hölderlin's controlled complexity as compared with the simplicity that dominates during the time of mental disorder. (U.G.)

Lachmann, Eduard. *Der Versöhnende. Hölderlins Christushymnen*. Salzburg: Otto Müller, 1966. Pp. 145. S. 105.
Nothing better could be said about the book, its content and importance than what Lachmann himself professes: Es "sollte einmal *sine ira et studio* über Hölderlins Christushymnen berichtet werden, und der Verfasser bedauert, dass das ihm selbst infolge unausweichlicher Polemik nicht beschieden war" (91). But even without the all-pervading polemics, Lachmann's views would not have done much to clarify Hölderlin's poetry: to him, for instance, the poet's interpretation of Dionysos is only "subjektive Verschleierung" (24) with which it is unnecessary to deal since it is the real forces behind all those words and opinions that have chosen the poet's soul as a battle-field; hence, Hölderlin is passive (24), and everything that stems from his own mental activity is a negligible distortion of the "real" Christ and the "real" Dionysos. (U.G.)

Leonhard, Rudolf. "Hölderlin." *SuF*, Sonderheft 2 (1966): *Probleme des Romans*, 1317-42.
A rather superficial essay touching most Hölderlin questions; there is no central idea, and a tendency to link Hölderlin with Marxist concepts. (U.G.)

de Man, Paul. "L'image de Rousseau dans la poésie de Hölderlin." *DBGU*, v (1965), 157-83.
This study is sketchy for the first stages of Hölderlin's development (the intensive preoccupation with Rousseau in Waltershausen is not even mentioned), but it culminates in an interesting interpretation of "Der Rhein." According to de Man, Hölderlin views Rousseau here as the first to "reaffirm the ontologic priority of consciousness over the object of the senses" (178; cf.174), and thus to direct the fate of the Occident into its proper course. One should, however, take the fact into consideration that Hölderlin (1) contrasts Rousseau, "den Fremden," with the demi-gods and thus differentiates him from a "Göttersohn," and that (2) he uses Rousseau not as a pivotal figure in history,

but as an example for a certain attitude possible for many. The crucial line distorted by de Man is v.139: "Wem *aber, wie* Rousseau, dir. . ." (U.G.)

Mieth, Günter. "Zu Hölderlins ästhetischen Anschauungen." *WZUL*, XII (1963), 516-19.
Too simplistic, this essay tries to sum up Hölderlin's theoretical development between 1793 and 1798, and to find a foreshadowing of Lukács' theory of aesthetic reflection (517). The term "Ästhetik der Vermittlung" used by Mieth (519) might prove helpful. (U.G.)

Mommsen, Momme. "Hölderlins Lösung von Schiller. Zu Hölderlins Gedichten 'An Herkules' und 'Die Eichbäume' und den Ubersetzungen aus Ovid, Vergil und Euripides." *JDSG*, IX (1965), 203-44.
A very enlightening study of Hölderlin's struggle to overcome Schiller's influence upon him and his work as evidenced by some letters, poems, and translations which can be dated early 1796. Interesting hints are given to Schiller references in Hölderlin, and to Hölderlin references in Schiller. I would suggest an even earlier stage in this process of separation, visible for instance in the metrical version of *Hyperion*. (U.G.)

Pellegrini, Alessandro. *Friedrich Hölderlin. Sein Bild in der Forschung.* Berlin: de Gruyter, 1965. Pp. 594. DM 84.00.
Although some of the judgments and views in this book may seem already historic in fast-developing Hölderlin research (the Italian version appeared in 1956) this overall picture of Hölderlin interpretation is invaluable, if only for the sheer amount of material covered, and its palatable form. Two chapters are new in the German version: " 'Friedensfeier'—die Krise in der Hölderlin-Forschung," and "Die neueste Hölderlin-Forschung" (through 1960). An important aspect of this book is that it could very well serve as an introductory text to any seminar on the history and methods of literary criticism; it thus presents an interesting counterweight to Wellek and Warren though naturally remaining more limited in scope. (U.G.)

Pezold, Klaus. "Zur Interpretation von Hölderlins 'Empedokles'-Fragmenten." *WZUL*, XII (1963), 519-24.
Shows in Hölderlin's concept of Empedokles' death a development from example to sacrifice. This development is linked to Hölderlin's changing view of the historical situation of his time. More of Hölderlin's specifically historical thought could have been included in this interesting study. (U.G.)

Stammerjohann, Harro. "Ein Exempel aus der Wirkungsgeschichte Hölderlins: *Hälfte des Lebens.*" *EG*, XXII (1966), 388-93.
Enumerates instances of omission and of publication of this poem plus some of the well-known criticisms of Hölderlin. Uninteresting. (U.G.)

See also Ruitenbeek ("General 2. Environment"); Kunisch, Zagari ("German 2. General").

JEAN PAUL

Birznieks, Paul. "Jean Paul's Early Theory of Communication." *GR*, XLI (May 1966), 186-201.
This study deals somewhat inadequately with an interesting subject: Jean Paul's early epistolary novel *Abelard und Heloise* serves as an example for the contention that, with young Richter, "the value of a work of literature is only functional and instrumental" (201). But there is neither an interpretation of the work under this aspect nor are Jean Paul's theoretical statements taken from this early period; one would also wish a fuller discussion of the

various influences from English philosophy upon Jean Paul as mentioned by Birznieks, as well as a discussion of Jean Paul's later development. (U.G.)

Haberstroh, Hans. "Zum Erscheinen des 18. Bandes der Historisch-Kritischen Ausgabe." *Hesperus,* XXVIII (1966), 12-18.
Summary of the volume with some remarks about and quotations from the included essays.

Hartmann, Karl. "Jean Paul und sein unglücklicher Sohn Maximilian Ernst Emanuel." *Hesperus,* XXVIII (1966), 36-43.
Provides some biographical insight into Jean Paul's dealing with his son who died of "Nervenfieber" in 1821.

Hartwig, Wolfgang, ed. *Jean Paul. Ein Lesebuch für unsere Zeit.* Berlin and Weimar: Aufbau Verlag, 1966. Pp. 487.

Hermand, Jost. "Jean Pauls *Seebuch.*" *Euphorion,* LX (1966), 91-109.
Gianozzo is shown to be an *Anti-Titan,* criticized by Jean Paul for his extreme subjectivism. The story thus marks for Hermand a turning-point in Jean Paul's life and thought: an expression of disillusionment with previous ideals and with the concepts of "Kraft" and "Genialität." One could have stressed that the satiric attacks levelled against society by Gianozzo are not invalidated by the fact that Jean Paul, in turn, satirizes Gianozzo, and that therefore a total satire comparable to Bonaventura's *Nachtwachen* is created. (U.G.)

Muschg, Walter. *Gedenkrede auf Jean Paul.* (Francke-Druck, 2.) Bern: Francke, 1964.
Muschg gives a good and unbiased picture of modern understanding of Jean Paul as opposed to the one-sided enthusiasm of his contemporaries and the equally one-sided indifference of 19th-century realists. (U.G.)

Neumann, Peter Horst. *Jean Pauls "Flegeljahre."* (Palaestra, vol. 245) Göttingen, 1966. Pp. 119. DM 16.80.
The primary target of this important book is the solution of the problem of whether *Flegeljahre* is a fragment or not. The methods used follow the "linguistic" tradition set by Herman Meyer's essay on the novel in *Zarte Empirie*: chains of motifs and images are shown to be placed with utmost precision, distinguishing the characters, and combining widely separated parts of the novel. One will object to inconclusive points here and there, but the overall picture confirms the musical structure that Meyer had pointed out; in addition, however, Neumann succeeds in demonstrating a condensation and "Engführung" of motifs in the final chapters that have not been noticed before and that, to him, indicate a kind of completion of the novel. One might, however, argue that this "Engführung" is due to the catastrophe and inner crisis described in these chapters and does not necessitate an ending to the epic flow of events, which admittedly is broken off abruptly. Thus, Jean Paul was probably "correct" in thinking about the possibility of continuing the novel even though he had reached an ending which satisfied him from the point of view of motifs and images (*Vorschule der Aesthetik,* §72 of the 1813 edition). (U.G.)

Smeed, J. W. *Jean Paul's Dreams.* Oxford University Press, for the University of Durham, 1966. 30s.
Rev. in *TLS,* April 21, 1966, p. 349.

Smeed, J. W. "Surrealist Features in Jean Paul's Art." *GL&L,* XIX (October 1965), 26-33.
Smeed shows that the term "surrealist" should not be used for some phe-

nomena of the grotesque in Jean Paul's writings since they can always be shown to have a functional meaning in the context (which distinguishes them from *l'écriture automatique*). One wonders, however, why Smeed has used the term in the first place. (U.G.)

See also Dornheim, Rychner ("German 2. General"); Paulsen ("Bona-ventura").

Review of book previously listed:
BEREND, E., *Jean Paul-Bibliographie* (see *ELN*, III, Supp., 111), rev. by H. Plard in *EG*, XXI (1966), 111-12.

KERNER

Cottrell, Alan P. "Justinus Kerner: 'Der Grundton der Natur.'" *GQ*, XXXIX (1966), 173-86.
A close interpretation of the sonnet, "Wenn der Wald im Winde rauscht. . . ."

Notter, Friedrich. "Justinus Kerner." In Notter, *Eduard Mörike und andere Essays*, ed. Walter Hagen. Marbach am Neckar: Schiller-Nationalmuseum, 1966. Pp. 134.
An early (1842) and still valid evaluation of Justinus Kerner, his works and his poetic talent, now easily available. With instructive concluding remarks by the editor. (J.Th.)

KLEIST

Adler, H. G. "Heinrich von Kleists Prosastil." *Muttersprache*, LXXVI (1966), 161-64.

Baumgärtel, Gerhard. "Zur Frage der Wandlung in Kleists 'Prinz Fried-rich von Homburg.'" *GRM*, XVI (1966), 264-77.
Baumgärtel does not see a possibility of change in Homburg's life or men-tality. The prince, actually shocked by his being pardoned, finds himself—despite all glory—thrown back into the dichotomy of "heart" and "idea," "soul" and "law," and thus is deprived of the often-cited new possibilities in life, for the two absolutes do not permeate each other. This reviewer, however, feels that Baumgärtel, despite his methodical logic, depends too exclusively on existential interpretation to be completely convincing; Kleist himself cannot be so unequivocally identified with the fictitious prince. (J.Th.)

Catholy, Eckehard. "Der preussische Hoftheater-Stil und seine Auswir-kungen auf die Bühnen-Rezeption von Kleists Schauspiel 'Prinz Fried-rich von Homburg.'" In Müller-Seidel, *Kleist und die Gesellschaft* (see below), 75-94.
Catholy traces the staging and reception of Kleist's *Prinz Friedrich von Homburg* to our times.

Conrady, Karl Otto. "Notizen über den Dichter ohne Gesellschaft." In Müller-Seidel, *Kleist und die Gesellschaft* (see below), 67-74.
Conrady, as the only speaker in this "discussion," makes an attempt at clari-fying the various possibilities of analyzing the relationship between author and society. The rest is notes. (J.Th.)

Demisch, Heinz. *Heinrich von Kleist. Schicksal im Zeichen der Bewusstseinsseele*. Stuttgart: Freies Geistesleben, 1964. Pp. 149.
As a mental exercise, an interesting anthroposophic exploration of Kleist

before the background of Rudolf Steiner's "Hall of Fame"; having little interest, however, for the literary historian or critic. (J.Th.)

Dürst, Rolf. *Heinrich von Kleist. Dichter zwischen Ursprung und Endzeit. Kleists Werk im Licht idealistischer Eschatologie.* Bern: Francke, 1965. Pp. x + 220.
Rev. (favorably) by Lawrence Ryan in *Germanistik,* VII (1966), 418-19.
Kleist's image of the marionette is, as is natural, the starting point for interpretations of Kleist's works. These interpretations depend, however, as the subtitle suggests, solely on philosophical explications set in accord with Hegelian philosophy—a rare and, as this reviewer feels, somewhat weird undertaking. (J.Th.)

Dyer, D. G. "Junker Wenzel von Tronka." *GL&L,* XVIII (1965), 252-57.

Herd, E. W. "Form and Intention in Kleist's 'Prinz Friedrich von Homburg.'" *Seminar,* II (1966), 1-14.

Hoffmeister, Werner. "Heinrich von Kleists 'Findling.'" *Monatshefte,* LVIII (1966), 49-63.
Hoffmeister uses the various motifs of the story to probe into transcendental values of existence. He achieves a favorable analysis and interpretation of *Der Findling,* and finds that what is often considered improbable here is artistically logical and thematically relevant; for the improbable permeates the entire structure of the story. We can perceive that empirical probability is abandoned in favor of the creation of the symbol of an inner experience, a transcending poetic concept. (J.Th.)

Ide, Heinz. "Kleist im Niemandsland?" In Müller-Seidel, *Kleist und die Gesellschaft* (see below), 33-66.
Kleist's "societal experiences" are here rehabilitated, i.e., he cannot be understood as the "absolute ego" nor as an isolated human being fighting lonesomely with his fate and capabilities. Ide analyzes especially Kleist's periods of depression and withdrawal; he concludes most satisfyingly that Kleist's isolated situation stems from the turmoil of the times. Kleist's strong societal engagement is seen in his belief that his destination was to regenerate the human being through his artistic endeavors for which he prepared himself during his periods of withdrawal. This provides for the conclusion that Kleist, fundamentally, never was in a no-man's-land. (J.Th.)

Kleist, Heinrich von. *Prinz Friedrich von Homburg. Ein Schauspiel.* Nach der Heidelberger Handschrift hrsg. von Richard Samuel, unter Mitwirkung von Dorothea Coverlid. Berlin: E. Schmidt, 1964. Pp. 248.
Rev. by E. Haufe in *Germanistik,* VII (1966), 259.

Lefèvre, Manfred. "Bericht über die Vortragsveranstaltung der Heinrich-von-Kleist-Gesellschaft am 5. Dezember 1964." In Müller-Seidel, *Kleist und die Gesellschaft* (see below), 95-98.

Michaelis, Rolf. *Heinrich von Kleist.* (Friedrichs Dramatiker des Welttheaters, V.) Velber b. Hannover: Friedrich, 1965. Pp. 119.
Selected bibliography (pp. 118-19).

Müller-Seidel, W., ed. *Heinrich von Kleist und die Gesellschaft. Eine Diskussion.* Mit Beiträgen von E. Catholy, K. O. Conrady, H. Ide und

Walter Müller-Seidel. (Jahresgabe der Heinrich-von-Kleist-Gesell-schaft 1964.) Berlin: E. Schmidt, 1965. Pp. 98.

Müller-Seidel, Walter. "Kleist und die Gesellschaft. Eine Einführung." In Müller-Seidel, *Kleist und die Gesellschaft* (see above), 19-31.

Instead of pointing out the various ways the relationship between author and society can manifest itself, Müller-Seidel somewhat artificially sets up—especially against G. Blöcker's *Heinrich von Kleist oder Das absolute Ich* (Berlin, 1960) the truistic notion that Kleist was not an author "without a society." (J.Th.)

Nakamura, S. "Bemerkungen über Heinrich von Kleist an dem Wende-punkt von 1799—im Hinblick auf seine Dichtungen." *DB*, xxxv (1965), 65-79.

Parker, John J. "Kleists Schauspiel 'Prinz Friedrich von Homburg.' Ein in jeder Hinsicht politisches Werk?" *GRM*, N.F. xvi (1966), 43-52.

The article denies political intentions in Kleist's drama and soundly rejects all interpretations that attempt to make Kleist's political views central to the play. (J.Th.)

Schrimpf, Hans Joachim. "Tragedy and Comedy in the Works of Hein-rich von Kleist." *Monatshefte*, LVIII (1966), 193-208.

A lecture in which Kleist's central symbol, the marionette, is seen as having its own center of gravity as well as being endangered by the relativity of the environment. These elements then are examined—unfortunately in lecture form—as the source for both the tragic and comic forms of Kleist's works. (J.Th.)

Sembdner, Helmut. *Heinrich von Kleists Lebensspuren. Dokumente und Berichte der Zeitgenossen.* 2nd ed. (Sammlung Dieterich, Bd. 172.) Bremen: Schünemann, 1964. Pp. 557.

Simon, Ernst. "Auf dem Wege zur zweiten Naivität—Schiller und Kleist." *NSammlung*, IV (1964), 525-35.

Streller, Siegfried. "Heinrich von Kleist und die Romantik. Thesen zum Referat." *WZUL*, XII (1965), 514-15.

Thalheim, Hans-Günther. "Kleists 'Prinz Friedrich von Homburg.' " *WB*, XI (1965), 483-550.

Turk, Horst. *Dramensprache als geordnete Sprache. Untersuchungen zu Kleists "Penthesilea."* (Abhandlungen zur Kunst-, Musik- und Liter-aturwissenschaft, XXXI.) Bonn: Bouvier, 1965. Pp. viii + 195.

Rev. by L. Ryan in *Germanistik*, VII (1966), 435.

Turk, Horst. "Penthesilea. Sprache des Gefühls oder des Affekts?" *Jahrbuch der Wittheit zu Bremen*, VIII (1964), 221-40.

See also Ruitenbeek ("General 2. Environment"); Dornheim, Kunisch, Martini, Müller-Seidel ("German 2. General"); Paulsen ("Bonaven-tura"); Sembner ("Grimm Brothers"); Müller, D. ("Hoffmann").

LENAU

Cowen, Roy Chadwell. "The Significance of Gottfried Keller's Poem *An Lenau.*" *Symposium,* XIX (1965), 352-58.
In his self-styled isolation, Keller felt imprisoned in himself, his creative powers drying. In a poem of Lenauan tenor and form as homage to the poet, Keller signifies how reading the work of a related lonesome spirit had necromantic effects on his death-like dormancy. (I.C.)

Minckwitz, Friedrich, ed. *Nikolaus Lenau und Sophie Löwenthal. Die Geschichte einer tragischen Liebe.* Briefe und Tagebücher. Weimar: Liepenheuer, 1963. Pp. 471. MDN 9.50.
Rev. by E. Thurnher in *Germanistik,* VI (1965), 132-33.
In spite of the melodramatic title this is an edition—though abridged—of Lenau's diary and letters to Sophie, and of Max's and Sophie's letters to Lenau after his collapse. There is no new material, the introduction makes no use of recent secondary literature, and there is no critical apparatus. (I.C.)

Rieder, Heinz, ed. *Nikolaus Lenau. Gedichte.* (Reclam 1449.) Stuttgart: Reclam, 1965. Pp. 80. DM .90.
All phases of mood and artistic form are represented in this selection of Lenau's poems, even lengthy ones like *Die Heideschenke.* Perhaps the clattering *Auf meinen ausgebälgten Geier* should have been omitted for Lenau's sake. An appendix provides dates, a brief biography, and a list of his works. Reider quotes primarily sources that lend Lenau the air of an early beatnik, not the traditional Byronesque Weltschmerz-aureole that fascinated the ladies. Immense subjectivism is seen as the reason for his failure to create an *Ideendichtung* in his epic poems. Lenau's only theme is his ego, with nature as a mirror of the landscape of his soul. In the melancholic cult of feeling, Lenau's mental collapse is foreshadowed. Rieder's interpretation seems exaggerated, e.g.: "Unbewusst spürte er in sich die zwangshafte Gesetzmässigkeit, in der sein Leben der Umnachtung zutrieb." (I.C.)

MÜLLER, WILHELM

Augustin, Hermann. "Ein treues Lied." *SchM,* XLVI (1966), 85-97.
On Wilhelm Müller's poem "Der Lindenbaum."

Just, Klaus Günther. "Wilhelm Müller und seine Liederzyklen." In Just, K. G. *Übergänge. Probleme und Gestalten der Literatur.* Bern: Francke, 1966. Pp. 231.
Rev. as article (*ZDP,* LXXXIII [1964], 452-471) by A. Cottrell in *ELN,* III (1965), 116.

NOVALIS

Kuczynski, Jürgen. "Diltheys Novalisbild und die Wirklichkeit. Einige Überlegungen—leider noch nicht mehr." *WB,* XII (1966), 27-56.
By citing quotations which overemphasize the practical aspect of Novalis' life and writings, Kuczynski seeks to show that the writings of Novalis are characterized by "magischer Materialismus"—which borders on dialectical materialism. (B.M.)

Löffler, Dieter. "Über das Wunderbare in Novalis' Roman 'Heinrich von Ofterdingen': Thesen zum Referat." *WZUL,* XII (1962-4), 524-25.

Mähl, Hans-Joachim. "Novalis-Zitate in Goethes Gesprächen? Corrigenda zu Friedrich Wilhelm Riemers 'Mitteilungen über Goethe.' " *Euphorion,* LIX (1965), 150-59.

In a short, carefully written article Mähl shows that a number of excerpts which have been accepted as originating from Goethe were actually written by Novalis. Since these deal with the aesthetics of art, some reevaluation of Goethe's ideas based in part on these spurious lines will be necessary. (B.M.)

Schipperges, Heinrich. "Grundzüge einer 'polarischen' Medizin bei Novalis." *Antaios,* VII (1965), 196-208.

See also Kunisch, Rehder, Rychner, Thalmann, Tober ("German 2. General").

Reviews of book previously listed:
GRUTZMACHER, C., *Novalis und Philipp Otto Runge* (see *ELN,* IV, Supp., 111), rev. by K. Negus in *GQ,* XXXIX (1966), 242-44, and by G. Schulz in *Germanistik,* VII (1966), 250-51.

SCHELLING

Bradish, Joseph A. von. "Deutsche Romantik und Schellings Religions-philosophie." Pp. 196-202 in Bradish, Joseph A. von. *Von Walther von der Vogelweide bis Anton Wildgans.* Wien: Bergland Verlag, 1965. Pp. 225.
In a collection of journal articles and lectures produced over a period of more than fifty years appear two articles which deal with Schelling. This first one points out Schelling's belief in the need for a synthesis of the finite with the infinite, the real and the ideal. The second article, "Steinkopf on Schelling," has only general historical interest. No attempt has been made to consider recent scholarship in any of the older articles. (B. M.)

Fuhrmann, Horst, ed. *Schelling und Cotta. Briefwechsel 1803-1849.* Stuttgart: Ernst Klett, 1965. Pp. 360. DM 29.00.
Rev. by G. Favier in *EG,* XXI (1966), 113-15.

See also Deguise ("French 2. Constant").

SCHLEGEL, A. W. AND F.

Patsch, Hermann. "Zwei ungedruckte Brieffragmente August Wilhelm Schlegel an Friedrich Schlegel." *Euphorion,* LIX (1965), 401-11.
Since only six letters and one fragment written by A. W. Schlegel to Friedrich Schlegel have come down to us, any additional material is valuable. These deal mainly with matters concerning publication of material in *Athenaeum.* (B. M.)

Schmitt, Albert R. "Wielands Urteil über die Brüder Schlegel mit ungedruckten Briefen des Dichters an Carl August Böttiger." *JEGP,* LXV (1966), 637-61.
This is a well-written and liberally documented article, which contributes positive information as to Wieland's attitude toward F. and A. W. Schlegel after 1799. Wieland, mercilessly attacked by the Schlegels, is still tolerant and just. (B. M.)

See also Kunisch ("German 2. General").

SCHLEGEL, A. W.

Patsch, Hermann. "Ungedrucktes von August Wilhelm Schlegel aus dem

Nachlass Friedrich Schleiermachers." *Euphorion,* LX (1966), 294-302.

These fragments include: a parody of the Lord's Prayer, which ridicules Kotzebue; a satire of Lafontaine; and a comparison of Kant and Fichte.

See also Deguise ("French 2. Constant"); Luppé ("French 4. Staël").

Review of book previously listed:

SCHLEGEL, A. W., *Die Kuntslehre: Kritische Schriften und Briefe II* . . . (see *PQ,* XLIII, 501), rev. by R. Ayrault in *EG,* XXI (1966), 597.

See also Krömer ("Spanish 2. General") and Dendle ("Spanish 3. Lopez Soler").

SCHLEGEL, DOROTHEA

Thornton, Karin Stuebben. "Enlightenment and Romanticism in the Work of Dorothea Schlegel." *GQ,* XXXIX (1966), 162-72.

This well-organized article describes Dorothea's literary "hack work" prior to and after the writing of *Florentin,* and points out the concepts of enlightened idealism which appear in Dorothea's novel and run counter to the philosophy of the Schlegels. These, it is contended, are borrowed from Moses Mendelsohn's "Humanitätsreligion" and attest to the remaining influence of the Enlightenment on Dorothea's life. (B. M.)

SCHLEGEL, FRIEDRICH

Eichner, Hans "Unbekannte Briefe von und an Friedrich Schlegel." *JEGP,* LXV (1966), 511-15.

All of these five letters are business letters. One substantiates the date of the first correspondence between F. Schlegel and F. L. Stolberg. The rest have no more than historical interest. (B. M.)

Ishii, Yasuo. "Das wesentlich Romantische in Fr. Schlegels Aufsätzen in der Zeitschrift 'Athenäum.' " *DB,* No. 36, (1966), pp. 119-30.

Klin, Eugenius. *Die frühromantische Literaturtheorie Friedrich Schlegels.* (Acta Universitatis Wratislaviensis, 26, Germanica Wratislaviensia VIII.) Wroclaw, 1964. Pp. 134. zl. 10.00.

Rev. by R. Ayrault in *EG,* XXI (1966), 456-58.

Pohlheim, Karl Konrad. *Die Arabeske. Ansichten und Ideen aus Friedrich Schlegels Poetik.* München-Paderborn-Wien: Schöninghs, 1966. Pp. 406. DM 34.00.

Stelzmann, Rainulf. "Goethe, Friedrich Schlegel und Schleiermacher: Eine verhüllte Kritik im 'Walpurgisnachtstraum.' " *Archiv,* CCIII (October 1966), 195-203.

This is a well written, thoroughly documented piece of work. If the reader is willing to make one or two concessions toward statements that are not substantiated, the article may be accepted as a possible explanation of "Weltkind" in "Walpurgisnachtstraum." (B. M.)

See also Françon ("French 4. Nerval"); Rychner ("German 2. General"); Paulsen ("Bonaventura").

Reviews of books previously listed:
BEHLER, Ernst, ed., *Kritische Fr.-Schlegel-Ausgabe*, I, 5 I, 6 II, 12 II, 13 (see *ELN*, III, Supp., 119), rev. by Richard Samuels in *Germanistik*, VII (1966), 264-67; RASCH, W., ed., *Kritische Schriften* (see *ELN*, IV, Supp., 113), rev. by R. Ayrault in *EG*, XX (1965), 598.

SCHLEIERMACHER

See Stelzmann ("F. Schlegel").

TIECK

Koskenniemi, Inna. *John Webster's 'The White Devil' and Ludwig Tieck's 'Vittoria Accorombona'. A Study of two related works.* (Annales Universitatis Turkuensis, B, Vol. 97.) University of Turku, 1966.

Nobuoka, Yorio. "Ludwig Tiecks Novelle 'Die Reisenden.' Ein Beitrag zu seiner späteren Dichtung." *Forschungberichte zur Germanistik*, VII (1965), 13-32.

Stern, Martin. "Die wunderlichen Fata der 'Insel Felsenburg'. Tiecks Anteil an der Neuausgabe von J.G. Schnabels Roman (1828)." *DVLG*, XL (1966), 109-15.
Stern uses Tieck's letters to explain his relationship to the 1828 edition of Schnabel's novel, *Die Insel Felsenburg*. Contrary to the rather widespread belief, Stern shows that Tieck was *not* the editor of this edition, but rather that he only wrote a foreword without having seen the new abbreviated edition. (B. M.)

Tecchi, Bonaventura. "La fiaba nell' opera di Wieland e in quella di Tieck." *Studi Germanici*, III (1965), 301-20.

Tieck, Ludwig. *Die verkehrte Welt.* (Komedia, Deutsche Lustspiele vom Barock bis zur Gegenwart.) Berlin: de Gruyter, 1964. Pp. 147. DM 6.00.
Rev. by R. Ayrault in *EG*, XXI, (1966), 112-13.

Tieck, Ludwig. *Franz Sternbalds Wanderungen*, Stuttgart: Reclam, 1966. Pp. 586. DM 14.80.

See also Kindermann, Thorslev ("General 3. Criticism"); Kabel, Kunisch, Thalmann ("German 2. General"); Kohlschmidt ("Wackenroder").

Review of book previously listed:
TRAINER, J., *Ludwig Tieck. From Gothic to Romantik* (see *ELN*, III, Supp., 121), rev. by Lawrence Ryan in *Germanistik*, VII, 268, and by Egon Schwarz in *JEGP*, LXV, 403-04.

VARNHAGEN VON ENSE, K.

Review of book previously listed:
GLANDER, Philip, *Letters of Varnhagen von Ense to Richard Monckton Milnes* (see *ELN*, III, Supp., 114), rev. by Horst Oppel in *NS*, XV (1966), 149.

VARNHAGEN VON ENSE, RAHEL

Kemp, Friedhelm, ed. *Rahel Varnhagen, Briefwechsel mit Alexander von der Marwitz, Karl von Finckenstein, Wilhelm Bokelmann,*

Raphael d'Urquijo. (Lebensläufe, Biographien, Erinnerungen, Briefe,
Vol. VIII). Munich: Kösel, 1966. Pp. 466. DM 19.80.
Valuable new edition of Rahel's letters. The excellent *Nachwort* does much
to correct false notions concerning Rahel, traceable to earlier editors; and by
wise editing Kemp guides the reader through the labyrinth of Rahel's correspondence. Much more annotation is still needed for a complete understanding,
but the references in this edition are helpful and for the most part exact.
(P. G.)

See also Kabel ("German 2. General").

WACKENRODER

Kohlschmidt, Werner. "Bemerkungen zu Wackenroders und Tiecks
Anteil an den 'Phantasien über die Kunst.' " Pp. 88-99 in *Philologia
deutsch: Festschrift zum 70. Geburtstag von Walter Henzen.* Bern:
Francke, 1965.
Rev. by R. Hinderling in *Germanistik* vii (1966), 490-91, and by G. Zink
in *EG*, xxi (1966), 599.
Kohlschmidt maintains, on the basis of stylistic comparisons, that Tieck, not
Wackenroder, was the author of "Märchen von einem nackten Heligen" and
"Fragment aus einem Briefe Joseph Berglingers," which appeared in *Phantasien
über die Kunst.* (B. M.)

WERNER

Guinet, Louis. *De la franc-maçonnerie mystique au sacerdoce ou la vie
romantique de Friedrich-Ludwig-Zacharias Werner (1768-1823).*
Caen: Association des Publications de la Faculté des Lettres et
Sciences Humaines de l'Université de Caen, 1964. Pp. 247.
In his biography of Zacharias Werner, Guinet utilizes the publications of the
past four decades by Oswald Floeck and Erich Jenisch. He incorporates *in
nuce* his own findings (expressed in the exhaustive study *Zacharias Werner
et l'ésotérisme maçonnique.* Paris: La Haye, Mouton & Co., 1962) on the
significant influence of the esoteric elements of the Masonic Order on Werner's
thought, conversion, and ordination. Guinet avoids the bias of Vierling
(*Zacharias Werner.* Paris: Didier, 1908) and Hankamer (*Zacharias Werner.*
Bonn: F. Cohen, 1920) and produces, before the background of the times of
Werner's contemporary admirers and of critics, a psychologically oriented,
concise biography without giving in to the flamboyance of the subject matter.
(J.Th.)

Jennings, Lee B. "The Freezing Flame: Zacharias Werner and the
Twenty-Fourth of February." *Symposium,* xx (1966), 24-42.
A sympathetic re-examination, if not of the aesthetic value of the work, then
of the genuine involvement of Z. Werner: the accoutrements of the play are
lauded as forming a parable on Werner's concept of the world, the freezing
flame or the trap of existence—which the author describes as having tragic
quality inasmuch as there is to be found "the lament that there is a bondage
at the heart of life which can scarcely be surmounted." (J.Th.)

Kozielek, Gerard. "Unbekannte Gedichte vom Verfasser des 'Vierund-
zwanzigsten Februar.' " *GW,* ix (1964), 85-103.

Moenkemeyer, Heinz. "The Son's Fatal Homecoming in Werner and
Camus." *MLQ,* xxvii (1966), 51-67.
A valuable study that compares Werner's *Der vierundzwanzigste Februar* and
Camus' *Le Malentendu* with exemplary discrimination and depth. Although

both dramas possess "an analogous archetypal pattern of plot," and other secondary similarities, the article is ultimately a study in contrasts, culminating in the final words of the two works: "the hope-denying 'Non!' of the old servant in *Le Malentendu,* and the assertion of God's mercy in Werner's play: "Gottes Gnad' ist ewig! Amen!' " (K.N.)

Review of book previously listed:

KOZIELEK, G., *Friedrich Ludwig Zacharias Werner* (see *ELN,* III, Supp., 122), rev. by S. B. Neveu in *RLC,* XXXIX (1966), 168-70, and by L. B. Jennings in *GQ,* XXXIX (1966), 372-74.

ITALIAN

(By Olga Ragusa, Columbia University, and William T. Starr, Northwestern University).

1. BIBLIOGRAPHY

Goffis, Cesare Federico. "Rassegna bibliografica. Primo ottocento." *RLI,* LXIX (1965), 720-26; LXX (1966), 181-88.

2. GENERAL

Battaglia, Salvatore. *Il problema della lingua dal Baretti al Manzoni.* Napoli: Liguori, 1965. Pp. 238. L 3300.

Bertacchini, Renato. *Il romanzo italiano dell'Ottocento dagli scottiani a Verga.* (Universale Studium, 76). Roma: Editrice Studium, 1964. 2a ediz. Pp. 196.
Rev. by Giorgio De Blasi in *GSLI,* CXLIII (1966), 471-72.
Clear and highly informative. Indispensable reference for work in the nineteenth century Italian novel, based on a number of recent partial studies. The theoretical positions of the Milanese Romanticists and their reception of Scott; the historical novels of the Risorgimento; Tommaseo's *Fede e bellezza;* an excellent, comprehensive chapter on *I promessi sposi.* (O. R.)

Corrigan, Beatrice. "Neapolitan Romanticism and the Social Conscience." *SIR,* v (1966), 113-20.
Shows the originality of Antonio Ranieri's *Ginevra* and of Francesco Mastriani's *I vermi,* both of which helped to establish an important theme in Neapolitan literature. (W.T.S.)

Fubini, Mario. *Romanticismo italiano, saggi di storia della critica e della letteratura.* Bari: Laterza, 1965. 3rd ed. Pp. 362.

Mangini, Nicola. "G. Modena e il teatro italiano del primo ottocento." *Atti della Deputazione di Storia patria per le Venezie,* 1965, pp. 11-47.
On the basis of the *Epistolario* (1955) and the *Scritti e discorsi* (1957) published by the Istituto par la Storia del Risorgimento and some additional research, Mangini traces the effects of the great actor on the renewal of the Italian stage. The relations of stage and literature are illuminated by an examination of the historical situation and the restrictions of the censor, which

excluded tragedies of Foscolo and Manzoni. The analysis and discussion of romantic taste and its evolution is well done. (W.T.S.)

Piromalli, Antonio, "Momenti della cultura livornese nell'ottocento." *Ausonia,* XXI (1966), 25-31.

Rinaldi, Mario. *Felice Romani. Dal melodrama classico al melodrama romantico.* Roma: Ed. De Sanctis, 1965. Pp. 533.

Rinaldi has written an interesting account of the life of the librettist, but the promise of the subtitle is not fulfilled, principally because of the lack of critical analysis on which a study of the transition must be based. The terms of the problem are not clarified and no thoroughly valid conclusions are reached. Rinaldi draws information from dramas and comedies that offer completely different concepts of life, unequal in literary and historical value. (W.T.S.)

Sansone, Mario. "Romagnosi e la poesia ilichiastica." Pp. 528-545 in *Studi di varia umanità in onore di Francesco Flora.* Milano: Mondadori, 1963.

On Romagnosi's "Della poesia considerata rispetto alle diverse età delle nazioni" and the "conciliatory" spirit characteristic of Italian Romanticism.

Titta Rosa, Giovanni. *I lumi a Milano, pagine di civiltà lombarda.* Milano: Martelli, 1964. Pp. 344.

The first part is a highly readable account of cultural life in Milan between 1750 and 1900. A good chapter, "Dal *Caffè* alla Scapigliatura," and chapters on Foscolo, Manzoni, *Il Conciliatore,* and Cattaneo. (O.R.)

Treves, Piero, ed. *Lo studio dell'antichità classica nell'Ottocento.* (La letteratura italiana—Storia e testi, 72.) Milano-Napoli: Ricciardi, 1962. Pp. xlvi + 1293.

3. STUDIES OF AUTHORS

BELLI

Orioli, Giovanni. "Quattro lettere inedite di Giuseppe Gioacchino Belli." *Capitolium,* XL (1965), 438-41.

Four of the nine letters acquired by the Comune di Roma in 1936 are of considerable biographical interest: three addressed to Belli's friend Raffaelli Bertinelli, and one to Count Francesco Maria Torricelli.

Vigolo, Giorgio, ed. *Er giorno der guidizzio e altri 200 sonetti.* Milano: Mondadori, 1965. Pp. 366.

Includes useful notes by the editor as well as Belli's own notes.

CATTANEO

Brancato, Francesco. "Carlo Cattaneo e l'opposizione democratica in Sicilia e a Napoli nel 1860." *NQM,* I (1963), 1-26.

Boneschi, M., ed. *Scritti politici.* Firenze: Le Monnier, 1964. 4 vols.

Brancato, Francesco. "Il pensiero storico di Carlo Cattaneo." *NQM,* III (1965), 326-35.

Ramelli, Adriane. "Un ritratto sconosciuto di Carlo Cattaneo alla Biblioteca cantonale di Lugano." *La Martinella,* XVII (1963), 273-75.

DE SANCTIS

Borsellino, Nino, ed. Francesco De Sanctis. *Verso il realismo—Prolusioni e lezioni zurighesi sulla poesia cavalleresca, frammenti di estetica, saggi di metodo critico.* (Opere, Vol. VII.) Torino: Einaudi, 1965. Pp. li + 345.
Rev. by Giuseppe Izzi in *GSLI,* CXLIII (1966), 288-95.
A disparate collection of works belonging to different periods of De Sanctis' activity and here brought together in somewhat artificial unity. The Introduction is good, especially with respect to the *Lezioni sulla poesia cavalleresca.*

Gifuni, G. B. "Francesco De Sanctis. Lettere inedite ad un suo capo elettore: Vincenzo Gervasio." *Rivista di studi crociani,* No. 3 (1965), 79-98; 199-209.
This completes the publication of unpublished material, begun in 1964. (See *ELN,* IV, Supp., 117.)

Macera, Guido. "Pensieri su De Sanctis: Il politico militante." *Realtà del Mezzogiorno,* V (1965), 133-58.

Talamo, Giuseppe, ed. *Opere di Francesco De Sanctis.* A cura di Carlo Muscetta. XX. *Epistolario (1859-1860).* Torino: Einaudi, 1965. Pp. lix + 353.
Rev. by Giorgio Petrocchi, *FLe,* XL (October 3, 1965), 3.

Tondo, Michele. "Orientamenti dei moderni studi desanctisiani." *Annali della Facoltà di Lettere e filosofia* (Bari: Cressata), IX (1964), 5-23.
A review of significant books and articles after 1949, from Contini to S. Romagnoli and R. Wellek, not forgetting the Marxist critics, Alderisi, C. Salinari, and V. Gerretana.

Reviews of books previously listed:
ANTONETTI, Pierre, *Francesco De Sanctis et la culture française* and *Francesco De Sanctis (1817-1883)* (see *ELN,* III, Supp., 124), rev. by Arshi Pipa in *RR,* LVII (1966), 234-36; CROCE, Elena and Alda, *De Sanctis* (see *PQ,* XLIII, 506), rev. by Gennaro Savarese, in *Rivista di studi crociani,* No. 1 (1965), pp. 65-71; DE SANCTIS, Francesco, *Epistolario 1856-1858 e 1859-1860* (see *ELN,* IV, Supp., 117), rev. by Renato Bertacchini in *NA,* CDXCVII (1966), 542-46.

FOSCOLO

Casnati, Francesco. "Un amore comasco del Foscolo." *La Martinella,* XVIII (1964), 409-15.

Chiappelli, Fredi. "Cultura classica e 'mente poetica' nel Foscolo." *LI,* XVIII (1966), 262-66.
Corrects a wide-spread opinion derived from Giorgio Pasquali's 1920 *Filologia e storia* regarding Foscolo's lack of vocation for philological studies. Shows how the poet by intuition alone had correctly reconstructed a fragment of Callimachus.

Dionisotti, Carlo. "Venezia e il noviziato poetico del Foscolo." *LI,* XVIII (1966), 11-27.

Fasano, Pino. "*Laura e Lauretta.* Il primo romanzo di Ugo Foscolo." *RLI,* LXX (1966), 65-86.
Admitting the value of V. Rossi's study of the *Ortis* (*GSLI,* LXVII [1917]),

especially as a starting point of critical interpretation and evaluation of the *Ultime lettere,* Fasano shows the inacceptability of Rossi's results. (W.T.S.)

Fittoni, Mario. "Due note foscoliane." *Ausonia,* xx, No. 6 (1965), 47-48.

Interpretation of *Sepolcri,* vv. 42-43, and vv. 124-126.

Fischetti, Giuseppe. "L'episodio di Elettra nei *Sepolcri* del Foscolo." *GSLI,* cxliii (1966), 321-77.

A close, exhaustive analysis of sources for vv. 241-253, especially in the light of Foscolo's translations from the *Iliad.* Two separate sections study analogous passages in Pindar and Monti.

Gambarin, Giovanni. "Foscolo e la lingua inglese." *PeI,* vii (1965), 47-8.

May, Frederick. "A Foscolo Fragment in English." *MLR,* lix (1964), 41-42.

The English rendering of the first paragraph of the "Notizia intorno a Didimo Chierico" in Alice Werner's *The Humour of Italy* (1892).

Reggio, Ercole. "Foscolo, scrittore europeo." *NA,* cdxcvii (1966), 62-81.

A review of Foscolo's works, with emphasis on *Ortis,* the *Viaggio Sentimentale,* and the literary essays of his English period, against the background of neo-classical-romantic Europe.

Tenerani, Luciano. "Sul neoclassicismo di Ugo Foscolo." *Ausonia,* xxi, No. 2 (1966), 45-50.

Some of the neoclassic elements in Foscolo's poetry are shown to be the expression of the poet's innermost self, and not merely an echo of preceding poets. (W.T.S.)

Toffanin, Giuseppe. "Giovanni Gambarin, ed. *Ugo Foscolo. Prose politiche e apologetiche. . . .*" *PeI,* vi (1964), 259-60.

Toffanin criticizes severely the *Lettera apologetica,* because of its bad form, the product of an exuberant imagination, unrevised.

T., S. "Gli scritti politici del Foscolo relativi alla età napoleonica." *Bolletino italiano di studi napoleonici,* iii (1964), ix, 19-24.

See also Hibbard ("General 3. Criticism") and Titta Rosa ("Italian 2. General").

GIUSTI

Giusti, Giuseppe. *Poesie.* Firenze: Salani, 1965. Pp. 422.

Viviani, Alberto. "Giuseppe Giusti: Su un'autobiografia che non fu mai scritta." *La Martinella,* xvii (1963), 333-37.

GROSSI

Maquet, Albert. "Stendhal e Tommaso Grossi." *LI,* xvi (1964), 298-321.

A passage from Stendhal's *Rome Naples et Florence* is used to throw light on Grossi's difficulties with the Austrian authorities.

LEOPARDI

Binni, Walter. *Corso sul Leopardi.* Anno accademico 1964-1965. Roma: Edizioni dell'Ateneo, 1965. Pp. 214. L 2000.

Boneschi, Franceso. "Il romanticismo e Leopardi." *Idea,* XX (1964), 750-53.

Bosco, Umberto. *Titanismo e pietà in Giacomo Leopardi.* Roma: Ed. De Sanctis, 1965. Pp. 91. L 1200.

Carini, Nello. *Giacomo Leopardi critico e traduttore di Omero.* Assisi: Porziuncola, 1964.

Carini, Nello. *Virgilio nell'opera filologica di Giacomo Leopardi.* Assisi: Porziuncola, 1964.

Chioccioni, Pietro. *Napoli e i Campi Flegrei. Virgilio e Leopardi.* Roma: A. Staderini, 1965. Pp. 61. L 1200.

Corti, Maria. "Passero solitario in Arcadia." *Paragone,* XVII, No. 194 (1966), 14-25.

One source of "Il Passero solitario" may be found in an Eclogue of the *Arcadia* of Sannazaro. The author insists on the insight this reminiscence gives into Leopardi's poetry.

Frattini, Alberto. *Critica e fortuna dei Canti di Giacomo Leopardi.* Con altri studi e postille sulla critica leopardiana contemporanea. Brescia: La Scuola, 1965. Pp. 198. L 1500.

Fubini, Mario. "Un canto e una stagione poetica del Leopardi." *Nuovo casanostra,* XCVII (1964), lxxxi, 5-26.

Giuliano, Antonio. "Appunti. Giacomo Leopardi, Carlotta Lenzoni, Pietro Tenerani." *Paragone,* XVII, No. 193 (1966), 87-94.

Greco, Mario. *Giacomo Leopardi.* Taranto: Athena editrice, 1964.

Hartley, K. H. "Florian and the 'vecchiarel bianco' in Leopardi's 'Canto Notturno di un Pastore Errante dell'Asia.' " *AUMLA,* No. 23 (1966), 117-21.

Examines relationships between Petrarch's sonnet, Florian's *Le Voyage,* and Leopardi's poem.

Monteverdi, Angelo. "Scomposizione e analisi del canto di G. Leopardi 'A se stesso.' " II, 745-55, in *Studi in onore de G. Schiaffini.* Roma: Ed. dell'Ateneo, 1965.

This is a metrical, syntactical, and morphological study of the poem intended to show the rhythms, hidden and apparent, that circulate throughout. The author adheres more closely to the critical theory of Flora than to that of Croce, but is especially close to Binni, to whom he grants the final word. His conclusions and observations must be kept in mind henceforth. (W.T.S.)

Nurigiani, Giorgio. *Giacomo Leopardi e la sua poesia.* Roma: Editrice Scena illustrata, 1965.

Origo, Iris, and John Heath-Stubbs, eds. *Giacomo Leopardi.* Oxford University Press, 1966. Pp. 312. 35s.
Rev. in *TLS,* July 7, 1966, p. 597.

Pacella, Giuseppe. "Elenchi di letture leopardiane," *GSLI,* cxliii (1966), 557-77.
Brings together a number of lists of readings kept by Leopardi himself, some already published. The period covered is 1819-1828. An index of names is appended.

Peruzzi, Emilio. "L'ultimo canto leopardiano." *LI,* xviii (1966), 28-68.
An excellent, detailed study and analysis of "Il tramonto della luna." (W.T.S.)

Poulet, Louis. "Alfred de Vigny e Giacomo Leopardi." *Nuovo casanostra,* xcvii, lxxxi (1964), 35-46.

Rantifer *(pseud.). Giacomo Leopardi.* Appunti. Roma: Stabilimento tip. V. Ferri, 1965. Pp. 87.

Santoro, Mario. "Leopardi e il Settecento." *NTemp,* xiv, 3 (1965), 22-24.

Savarese, Gennaro. "Un tentativo giovanile del Leopardi: la *Maria Antonietta,*" *RLI,* lxx (1966), 3-22.
Concerning the first draft of *Maria Antonietta,* which Leopardi began, July 30, 1816. This is an excellent study of the origins of the work that was to have been a five-act verse tragedy, its influences and indications of the future poetic activity of Leopardi.

Singh, Ghan Shyam. "John Addington Symonds e Giacomo Leopardi." *GSLI,* cxliii (1966), 407-19.
Symonds' interest in Leopardi as reflected in his early poetic production and in his *Essays Speculative and Suggestive.*

Timpanaro, Sebastiano. "Di alcune falsificazioni di scritti leopardiani." *GSLI,* cxliii (1966), 88-119.
Of fundamental importance for establishing the correct *corpus* of Leopardi's works. Deals with three commonly cited drafts of "L'infinito," a draft of "Idillio alla natura," as well as other works.

Tortoreto, Alessandro. "Giacomo Leopardi nel suo epistolario." *Atti dell'Accademia roveretana degli agiati,* ccxiii (1964), 67-80.

V(ian), N(ello). "Autografi di lettere del Leopardi." *GSLI,* cxliii (1966), 470-71.
Places nine autographed letters, reported as unfound in the 1949 edition of the *Lettere,* in the Vatican.

Whitfield, J. H. *Giacomo Leopardi.* Con una premessa dell'autore alla I ed. in lingua italiana. Napoli: Scalabrini, 1964.

See also Battaglia ("Italian 2. General").

Reviews of books previously listed:
Leopardi e il Settecento (see *ELN,* iii, Supp., 128), rev. by Giovanni Cecchetti in *Italica,* xliii (1966), 197-99, and by J. H. Whitfield in *TLS,* Feb. 11, 1965;

SINGH, G., *Leopardi and the Theory of Poetry* (see *ELN*, III, Supp., 129), rev. by Nicholas J. Perella in *Italica*, XLII (1965), 433-36.

MANZONI

Altieri Biagi, Maria Luisa. "Vile meccanico." *Lingua nostra*, XXVI (1965), 1-12.

The expression is used by Manzoni in Chapter IV of *I promessi sposi*, as indicative of a typical "Seicento" attitude. Altieri Biagi shows that the expression was linked to an aristocratic conception of science as opposed to technology, and traces the principal phases of the history of ethical judgments on practical activities.

Angelini, Cesare. *Capitoli sul Manzoni vecchi e nuovi*. Milano: Mondadori, 1966. Pp. 323. L 2800.

Collection of previously published articles and notes by a sensitive and appreciative critic of Manzoni.

Aprile, Arturo. *Lo spirito religioso nell'opera di Alessandro Manzoni*. Palermo: Tip. Fiamma serafica, [1965?]. Pp. 16.

Arruga, Franco Lorenzo. "Alessandro Manzoni e la 'lezione'del teatro musicale italiano.' " *VeP*, XLVIII (1965), 369-75.

Bàrberi Squarotti, Giorgio. *Teoria e prove dello stile del Manzoni*. Milano: Silva, 1965.

A fine analysis of the stylistic devices used by Manzoni (extended similitudes, rhetorical questions, repetitions, adversative formulas, exhortatives), placed within the framework of an ideological position defined as a view of the redemption of "fallen nature."

Battaglia, Salvatore. "Il conte del Sagrato." *FeL*, X (1964), 422-25.

Bodini, Vittorio. "Manzoni e Cervantes: 'Scendeva dalla soglia. . . .' " *Letteratura*, XXIX, Nos. 76-77 (1965), 99-101.

An accurate stylistic analysis of the passage from *I promessi sposi* and a comparison of it with the beginning of Cervantes' *El Casamiento engañoso*. Adds little to the broad question of the relationships involved. (W.T.S.)

Bosco, Umberto. "Il capitolo XVIII dei 'Promessi sposi.' " Pp. 105-116 in *Studi in onore di Italo Siciliano*. (Biblioteca dell'"Archivum Romanicum," I, 86.) Firenze: Leo S. Olschki, 1966. Pp. 1238.

Reading of the chapter that marks the passage from the second to the third part of the book. Manzoni as miniature painter of minor characters; deepening of the figures of Lucia and Renzo; the Innominato as the Romantic hero who strains against constraint; the theme of solitude; the nature of Don Rodrigo's "passion." Manzoni's subject is history, not love.

Bruno, Giorgetti, and Pino Ferrini. *Sulle orme di tre grandi*. Rimini: Tip. Garattoni, 1964. Pp. 142. L 850.

Manzoni, Dante, and Francis of Assisi.

Cernecca, Domenico. "L'inversione del soggetto nella frase dei *Promessi sposi*." *Studia Romanica et Anglica Zagrabiensia*, 15-16 (1963), 49-98.

Chandler, S. B. "Point of View in the Descriptions of *I Promessi sposi*." *Italica*, XLIII (1966), 386-403.
Skillful analysis which underscores Manzoni's extraordinary craftsmanship in portraying his man-centered and God-directed universe. (O.R.)

Chandler, S. B. "The Portrait of Federigo Borromeo in *I promessi sposi*." *PQ*, XLIV (1965), 519-26.
Chandler feels that while Manzoni presented the Innominato convincingly as a total example of evil, his presentation of the Cardinal is equivocal. In his need to proclaim the Cardinal's superiority and to reply to supposed objections of Borromeo's contemporaries, Manzoni reveals his own uncertainty and pessimism. (W.T.S.)

Contini, Gianfranco. "Onomastico manzoniano." *Corriere della Sera*, Aug. 20, 1965.
A brief discussion of the origin and derivation of names in Manzoni's works, with a witty recall of Baldini's work on this subject (1956).

De Castris, Arcangelo Leone. *L'impegno del Manzoni*. Firenze: Sansoni, 1965. Pp. 340.
In this dense study De Castris aims at a coherent interpretation of Manzoni's inner development. De Castris' reconstruction of Manzoni's poetics and of his formation is an attempt to understand the two fundamental points of his experience: the composition of *I promessi sposi* and the repudiation of the novel. The author is interested in the theoretical, ethical, and imaginative tensions that in balance or in imbalance determined Manzoni's creativity. His account is presented as a critical proposition.
Manzoni's commitment is clarified as antilyrical, since it tends towards a moralization of history, although it is based on a religious ideal which is in essence lyrical. The dichotomy real-ideal is imputed not to establish Christian values, but to poetic interpretation. In its structure *I promessi sposi* attempts to overcome this dichotomy. The center of the expressive system of the novel is in the dialectical relationship between the two operations, the integration of the real in the ideal, and the descent of the ideal towards the real.
In the first twenty-five chapters the characters are particularized animations of reality, faithful representations of the times. Later, they no longer serve history, but are simply inserted into the great actions, which they neither aid nor clarify. Manzoni comes to recognize that he has not revealed the suffering and the thoughts of men through their acts, but that he has invented facts to adapt to men's feelings. The happy ending dispels the notion of complete historical truth, and reveals a Manzoni embittered by his disillusionment in revolution. (W.T.S.)

De Michelis, Eurialo. "Manzoni o il potere di Dio." *FLe*, XLI (Sept. 22, 1966), 10-11.

De Michelis, Eurialo. "Onomastica manzoniana." *NA*, CDXCVIII (1966), 9-27.
Comments on G. Contini's "Onomastica manzoniana" (see above). Minute study of the sources used by Manzoni for naming his characters and of the changes in names from *Fermo e Lucia* to *I promessi sposi*.

Getto, Giovanni. "Manzoni e Rousseau." Pp. 467-494 in *Studi in onore di Italo Siciliano*. (Biblioteca dell'"Archivum Romanicum," I, 86.) Firenze: Leo S. Olschki, 1966. Pp. 1238.
Specific references to Rousseau in *Sulla morale cattolica*; echoes of *Lettre à*

M. d'Alembert in the digression on love in *Fermo e Lucia*; Rousseau reminiscences in *Promessi sposi*, especially in Manzoni's attitude to nature; Lucia and Julie; Julie and Gertrude. Fundamental difference between the two writers.

Maggi, Raffaello. *Volto e anima della Monaca di Monza.* Milano: Giuffré, 1964. 2nd ed. Pp. vii + 433.
Rev. by Quirino Frandella, *Conv,* xxii (1964), 652-55.
This is not a study of the character in Manzoni's novel, but of Maria Virginia de Leyva, the historical figure on which Manzoni based his nun. Maggi associates the two, however, pointing out that Manzoni was acquainted with the documents used in this psychoanalytic and neuropsychological study of abnormal behavior.

Messina, Michele, ed. *I promessi sposi.* Storia milanese del secolo XVII. Pagine scelte dal *Fermo e Lucia* e da *I promessi sposi* del 1827. Appendice e pagine critiche. Messina-Firenze: G. D'Anna, 1964. Pp. xvi + 989. L 1850.

Nava, Giuseppe. "Recenti studi manzoniani." *Paragone,* xvi, No. 190 (1965), 171-76.
Discusses the presentation of the tragedies by G. Bollati (Einaudi), and the work of A. Leone De Castris, *A. Manzoni tra ideologia e storicismo.* Many positive aspects are emphasized, especially in the first of the two works, but it is an error to demand a theoretical adhesion by Manzoni, foreign to his cultural world. In other words, if the poetic value of Manzoni's work is recognized, the culture which subtends it should not be judged negatively. (W.T.S.)

Negri, Renzo. "Un giudizio verriano sul Manzoni." *Conv,* xxxiv (1966), 510-12.
Reports Alessandro Verri's comment on *Imbonati* and suggests possible relationships between Verri's *Notti romane* and *I promessi sposi.*

Negri, Renzo. "Lettura manzoniana: Martino." *VeP,* xlviii (1965), 555-61.

Orioli, G., E. Allegretti, G. Manacorda, L. Felici, eds. *Alessandro Manzoni. Tutte le Opere e Saggio di F. De Sanctis.* Roma: Avanzini e Torraca, 1965. Pp. 1401.
This volume fulfills the demand for completeness. The Casa del Manzoni text is used, completed by autograph MSS. L. Felici introduces the four De Sanctis essays, G. Orioli the poems and tragedies, E. Allegretti *I promessi sposi,* G. Manacorda the historical and philosophical writings, and L. Felici the literary and linguistic writings. The introduction to the novel is thoughtful but not always convincing. Allegretti denies the autonomy of the characters, who are limited by the ethico-religious inspiration of the author. Lucia lives behind a barrier of proverbs and precepts which she has too rigorously assimilated. Yet the ethico-religious inspiration and the barrier of proverbs seem to be the very structure of Manzoni's ideology. (W.T.S.)

Palanza, Ugo Maria. *Il Manzoni e noi. Avviamento alla lettura dei'Promessi sposi.*' Napoli: Loffredo, 1965. Pp. 227. L 1000.

Petrocchi, Giorgio. "Diario manzoniano." *LI,* xviii (1966), 267-78.
Comments on the topos of the "strange" behavior of members of the upper classes, on the connotations of "galantuomo, galantuomini," on Manzoni's

remarks regarding the 17th century writer Virginio Cesarini, on the portrait of Gertrude's father in *Fermo e Lucia,* and on the reports of Manzoni's last illness and death, which appeared in the daily press.

Pompilj, Luigi. "Schede manzoniane." *NA,* CDXCVI (1966), 379-86.
On the "tracking shot" effect of the initial landscape description in *I promessi sposi,* the photographic "blow up" of Don Abbondio in Chapter VIII, and the figure of Lucia as closer to Ermengarda than to Agnese.

Russo, Luigi, ed. *Alessandro Manzoni. Adelchi.* Firenze: G.C. Sansoni, 1964. Pp. lv + 135. L 800.

Travi, Ernesto. "Il Cardinale Federigo Borromeo e la poetica manzoniana della 'placida commozione.' " *LI,* XVIII (1966), 92-97.

Ulivi, Ferruccio. *Il romanticismo e Alessandro Manzoni.* Bologna: Cappelli Editore, 1965. Pp. 219. L 600.
In spite of its title, this is only incidentally a study of Manzoni in relation to Romanticism. It is rather an excellent introduction to the writer's work and personality, with good pages on *I promessi sposi.* (O.R.)

See also Battaglia, Titta Rosa ("Italian 2. General").

Reviews of books previously listed:
DE CASTRIS, ed., *Tutte le poesie* (see *ELN,* IV, Supp., 122), rev. by Giovanni Orioli in *NA,* CDXCVI (1966), 107-09, and by P. De Tommaseo in *Belfagor,* XXI (1966), 119-20; GETTO, Giovanni, *Letture manzoniane* (see *ELN,* III, Supp., 131), rev. by Jacques Goudet in *REI,* XI (1965), 522-25, and by Joseph F. De Simone in *Italica,* XLIII (1966), 85-86; LONARDI, Gilberto, *L'esperienza stilistica del Manzoni tragico* (see *ELN,* IV, Supp., 123), rev. by Aurelia Accame Bobbio in *LI,* XVIII (1966), 325-27, and by Angelo R. Pupino in *Conv,* XXXIV (1966), 543-47; PALADINO, Vicenzo, *La revisione del romanzo manzoniano e le postille del Visconti* (see *ELN,* IV, Supp., 124), rev. by Beatrice Corrigan in *Italica,* XLIII (1966), 320-22, and by Cesare Federico Goffis in *RLI,* LXX (1966), 183.

PELLICO

Gordon, Lewis Hall. "An Unpublished Letter of Silvio Pellico." *Italica,* XLIII (1966), 375-85.
Addressed to Marchese Felice di San Tommaso, from Turin, 27 August 1835.

Vallone, Aldo. "Il *Pellico* di C. Curto." *L'Italia che scrive,* XLVIII, Nos. 7-8 (1965), 317.

Review of book previously listed:
KAUCHTCHISCHWILLI, Nina. *Silvio Pellico e la Russia* (see *ELN,* III, Supp., 134), rev. by Mario Scotti in *GSLI,* CXLIII (1966), 451-56.

PORTA

Gallardo, Piero, ed. *Carlo Porta. Poesie scelte.* Torino: UTET, 1964. Pp. 324.
An enlarged edition of P. Gallardo's *Porta e Belli* (1954), with an introduction which places Porta in his time. A good glossary.

TOMMASEO

Astaldi, Maria Luisa. *Tommaseo come era.* Firenze: Sansoni, 1966. Pp. 758.
Rev. by Nunzio Cossu, in *NA,* CDXCVIII (1966), 402-06.

An interesting, well-written biographical novel of the life of Tommaseo, which insists more on Tommaseo the man, the patriot, and the Catholic, rather than on the poet and savant, as in the biographies of Flora and Borlenghi. Tommaseo's work gains from a reading of this biography. The author's feminine intuition is perhaps what Tommaseo needed. (W.T.S.)

Di Biase, Carmine. "Il 'credo' di Niccolò Tommaseo." *Studium*, CXII (1966), 16-28.

Making generous use of his *Dell'Italia*, Di Biase illustrates Tommaseo's profession of Christian faith, and comments amply (with evident competency in regard to the text and to the Catholic and romantic problems involved) on the declaration of orthodoxy. (W.T.S.)

Di Biase, Carmine. "La 'Comunicazione degli affetti' in Niccolò Tommaseo." *Ausonia*, XXI (May-Aug., 1966), 56-70.

A study of mysticism, the quest for unity and love, in the poetic works and personality of Tommaseo.

See also Bertacchini ("Italian 2. General").

PORTUGUESE

(By Raymond Sayers, Queens College)

1. BIBLIOGRAPHY

Pinheiro, Maciel. *O Rio de Janeiro através das revistas. I. Revista do Instituto Histórico e Geográfico Brasileiro.* (Coleção Vieira Fazenda, 6.) Rio: Livraria Brasiliana, 1965. Pp. 309.

Sousa, José Galante de, e Regina Lúcia de Lemos Gill. *Indice de biobibliografia brasileira.* Rio: Instituto Nacional do Livro, 1963. Pp. 440.

See also Macedo.

2. GENERAL

Amora, Antônio Soares. *Classicismo e romantismo do Brasil.* (Coleção Ensaio, 43.) São Paulo: Conselho Estadual de Cultura, Commissão de Literatura, 1966. Pp. 152.

In one essay, Soares Amora analyzes the reason for the failure of *Niterói: Revista Brasiliense* and the success of *O Panorama: Jornal Literário e Instrutivo.* If the first, with all its solidity and brilliance, had a most ephemeral existence, whereas the second lasted for 21 years, it was because the former rose far above the bounds of the Brazilian intelligence and specifically Brazilian problems while the latter was directed at a public whose taste the editors understood well. In addition to this excellent article, there is one on Gonçalves de Magalhães', "Ensaio sôbre a história da literatura do Brasil," in which the author relates it to other histories of the time and to the Romantic aesthetic, and there is a new version of the study of *Iracema* and *Atala*, reviewed in *ELN*, III, Supp., 120-36.

Faria, Maria Alice. "Os acadêmicos paulistas e Victor Hugo." *Estado de São Paulo, Suplemento Literário* (1966), 30 July, p. 4; 6 Aug., p. 4.

Meyer, Augusto. "Do alexandrino." *A forma secreta,* Rio: Lidador, 1965, pp. 160-64.
Some notes on the nineteenth century alexandrine.

Rossi, Giuseppe Carlo. *Geschichte der portugiesischen Literatur.* Aus dem Italianischen übersetzt von Erika Rossi. Tübingen: Niemeyer, 1964. Pp. 426. DM 46.00.
A comprehensive survey of Portuguese literature from the 12th century to the present, with the 16th century (Camoes) and the second half of the 19th as culminating points.

3. STUDIES OF AUTHORS

a) *Portuguese*

BOCAGE
See Garrett.

CASTELO BRANCO
Abreu, José de. "Mais um problema camiliano." *Revista de Portugal,* XXXI (1966), 239-41.
A study of a *feuilleton* inspired by Camilo's adultery trial.

Alves, Natércia, e A. Coimbra Martins, eds. *Aventuras de Basílio Fernandes enxertado.* Lisboa: Parceria António Maria Fereira, 1966.

Alves, Natércia, e R. Andersen Leitão, ed. *Memórias do cárcere.* Vol. I. Lisboa: Parceria António Maria Fereira, 1966.

Bastos, Carlos. "Rapsódia camiliana incluindo uma carta importante inédita do grande romancista sobre poetas e prosadores do Porto." *Tripeiro,* v (1965), i, 1-5.
A rambling essay on Camilo and two fellow poets, Artagett and Vivó, who worked together in the Customs House, and who experienced parallel economic difficulties.

Cabral, Alexandre, ed. *Onde está a felicidade?* Lisboa: Parceria António Maria Pereira, 1966.

Castelo Branco, Camilo. *Amor de perdição e outras novelas.* Introd. Fernando Mendonça. São Paulo: Boa Leitura, 1965. Pp. 319.

Ferreira, Joaquim, ed. *Memórias de Camilo extraídas das suas obras.* Porto: Domingos Barreira, 1966. Pp. 637.

Girodon, Jean. "L'Armoire aux amants: Camilo et l'*Heptameron*." *Bulletin des Etudes Portugaises,* XXVI (1965), 223-34.
Well written article detailing the relation between the 32nd novella of the *Heptameron* and Camilo's defense of Vieira de Castro, who had been exiled for the murder of his adulterous wife.

Gracias, Bernardino. *Camilo suicida.* Lisboa: Tipografia da E.N.P., 1966. Pp. 190.

Lemos, Ester de, ed. *Vinte horas de liteira*. Lisboa: Parceria António Maria Pereira, 1966.

Review of book previously listed:
CABRAL, Alexandre, ed. *As polêmicas de Camilo* (see *PQ*, XLIII, 517), rev. by Antônio Cândido in *Bulletin des Etudes Portugaises*, XXVI (1965), 242-45.

CASTILHO

Santos, Guilherme de Oliveira, ed. *Há 100 anos: Algumas cartas inéditas de José Feliciano de Castilho*. Com Introd. e notas. Lisboa: Livraria Portugal. Pp. 49.

Andrade, Miranda de. "Bocage visto por Almeida Garrett." *Ocidente,* LXX (1966), 75-81.
Garrett considered Bocage's versification monotonous and his language stilted, and he was distressed by Bocage's admiration of Filinto Elício.

GARRETT

Andrade, Miranda de. "Um ensaio de Garrett sobre a poesia portuguesa." *Ocidente*, LXX (1966), 4-14.

Mendes, João. "Três cartas de Almeida Garrett." *Brotéria*, LXXXIII (1966), 392-95.
The most interesting of the three letters deals with a play that Garrett was writing, *A volta do proscrito*. The other two tell of his nostalgia for the province of Minho.

Reali, Erilde. "Il 'Meio Albuquerque' di Almeida Garrett." *Annali Istituto Universitario Orientale*, Napoli, Sezione Romanza, VIII (1966), 71-82.

HERCULANO

Santos, Mariana A. Machado. *Alexandre Herculano e a Biblioteca da Ajuda*. Coimbra, 1965. Pp. 84.
Informative study of Garrett's contribution as a librarian: his thoroughness and seriousness in collecting and preserving books and manuscripts and in organizing the library. The author, who is the present librarian, describes the library and the people who worked with Herculano.

b) *Brazilian*

ALENCAR

Alencar, José de. *Iracema*. Nota M. Cavalcanti Proença. Introd. biográfica Brito Broca. Vocab. Cândido Juca Filho. Bibliog. Plínio Doyle. Rio: José Olympio, 1965. Pp. 424.

Martins, Fran, ed. "José de Alencar." *Clã*, No. 21 (1965), pp. 1-92.
This number devoted to the Alencar centenary contains three full length, hitherto unpublished articles: "A comédia humana de José de Alencar," by Josué Montello; "Ecologia de um poema," by Raimundo Girão; and "José de Alencar e a lenda indígena," by Alencar Fernandes. Montello points out that there is little similarity between Balzac and Alencar. Girão studies rather well the background of *Iracema* and publishes a useful glossary for the book.

In general, however, the tone of this special number of *Clã* is panegyric rather than scholarly.

Mendes, Oscar, ed. *José de Alencar: Romances urbanos*. Com pref. (Nossos Clássicos, 83.) Rio: Agir, 1965.

Menezes, Raimundo, de. *José de Alencar: Literato e político*. São Paulo: Livraria Martins, 1965. Pp. 424.

The virtues of this biography are obvious: completeness, thorough documentation, and good organization. All phases of Alencar's career are well treated. The background of novels, plays, *crônicas*, and critical essays is all here, and the works themselves are analyzed. The approach is not critical but biographical and historical, and the book is useful as a contribution to intellectual history. There is no index, unfortunately, and bibliographical data at times are insufficient. The bibliography of unpublished writings is very helpful.

Meyer, Augusto, ed. *Iracema*. Introds. Machado de Assis, Rachel de Queiroz e Alceu Amoroso Lima. Rio: Instituto Nacional do Livro, 1965. Pp. 271.

See also Almeida.

ALMEIDA

Rebêlo, Marques. "O Rio das *Milícias* e de Alencar." *Comentário*, VI (1965), 332-40.

Rio as seen through the eyes of Manuel Antônio de Almeida and José de Alencar and in relation to their biographies.

ALVES

Azevedo, Vicente de. "Os amores de Castro Alves." *Estado de São Paulo, Suplemento Literário* (1966), 19; 26 Mar. 23; 30 Apr., p. 4.

Merquior, José Guilherme. "O navio negreiro." *Cadernos Brasileiros,* VIII (1966), iii, 40-45.

Passos, Alexandre. *O humanismo de Castro Alves*. Rio: Ministério da Educação e Cultura, 1965.

BONIFACIO

Anon. *Bi-centenário do patriarca da independência do Brasil José Bonifácio de Andrada e Silva (1763-1963)*. Ed. promovida pela Mesa da Câmara dos Deputados. Brasília: Biblioteca da Câmara dos Deputados, 1964.

DIAS

Anon. *Exposição comemorativa do centenário da morte de Gonçalves Dias*. Rio: Biblioteca Nacional, 1964. Pp. 45.

Machado, José Pedro. "Uma carta de Gonçalves Dias sobre a língua portuguesa." *Revista de Portugal*, XXXI (1966), 47-51.

Raymundo, Maria Antonieta Villela, ed. *Antologia. Com introd.* São Paulo: Melhoramentos, 1966.

GUIMARAES

Andrews, Norwood, Jr. "A Modern Classification of Bernardo Guimarães' Prose Narratives." *Luso-Brazilian Review*, III (1966), ii, 58-82.
So little has been written about Guimarães that it is most appropriate to have this excellent new analysis of his fiction. Mr. Andrews rightly points out that "there is little to distinguish his novels and short stories aesthetically from other Romantic productions besides a pronounced element of local color. . . ." In fact, it might be added that it is the local color that gives whatever life there is to these cliché-ridden books. In the course of the essay, Professor Andrews classifies the two most famous novels, *Isaura* and *Rosaura*, as polemics and sociological and excludes them from the list of "creative prose narratives" with which he concludes. Whatever their merits may be, they are novels as much as the *História de uma moça rica* is a play or "O navio negreiro" is a poem, and they must be grouped with his other fiction.

MACEDO

Macedo, Joaquim Manuel de. *Um passeio pela cidade do Rio de Janeiro*. Introd. Astrojildo Pereira. Rio: Edições do Ouro.

Moreira, José Marcelo. *Indice alfabético e remissivo do* Ano biográfico *de Joaquim Manuel de Macedo*. Pref. Hélio Vianna. Rio: Arquivo Nacional, 1965.

SOUSANDRADE

Avila, Afonso. "Sousândrade: El poeta y la conciencia crítica." *Revista de Cultura Brasileña*, No. 12 (1965), pp. 105-15.
A discussion of the problem of judging the writer who is more advanced than his contemporaries. Even the three most competent critics of his time, Sílvio Romero, Araripe Júnior, and Veríssimo, were equally at a loss in the face of Sousândrade's anticolonialism and stylistic innovations. The article is a good contribution to the cause of reestablishing Sousândrade's literary reputation.

Campos, Augusto de, e Haroldo de, eds. *Sousândrade: Poesia*. (Nossos Clássicos, 85.) Rio: Agir, 1966. Pp. 92.
A briefer anthology than *Revisão de Sousândrade* (See *ELN*, III, Supp., 144-45). The 16-page introductory essay presents more briefly the main points made in the brothers Campos' introduction to the *Revisão*: the *barroquismo*, the conversational—ironic tendencies that recall Tristan Corbière and Laforgue, and the stylistic devices that made it difficult for other Romantics to appreciate Sousândrade.

Crespo, Angel, y Pilar Gómez Bedate. "Noticia de Sousândrade." *Revista de Cultura Brasileña*, No. (1965), pp. 68-104.
In this thorough article, there are interesting sections on Sousândrade criticism—almost inexistent before the Campos brothers' *Revisão de Sousândrade* —on his position in literature, presymbolism rather than Romanticism; on his literary affiliations, Baudelaire, Pound and Joyce. In discussing *O Guesa*, the authors emphasize its Pan-Americanism. After all, two editions of it were published in New York.

VARELA

Azevedo, Vicente de. *A vida atormentada de Fagundes Varela*. São Paulo: Livraria Martins.

SPANISH

(By Brian J. Dendle, University of Michigan)

1. BIBLIOGRAPHY

Simón Díaz, José. "Los clásicos españoles en la prensa diaria de Madrid (1830-1900)." *RL* xxiii (1963), 209-240, and xxiv (1963), 201-37.

Lists references to Spanish classical and neoclassical authors in the Madrid press, 1830-1900.

2. GENERAL

Alberich, José. "Ambigüedad y humorismo en las *Sonatas* de Valle Inclán." *HR*, xxxiii (1965), 360-82.

Valle Inclán's satire of Romantic themes in the *Sonatas*.

Anes Alvarez, Gonzalo. "Ecos de la revolución francesa en España. Algunos datos y documentos." *CHE*, xxxv-xxxvi (1962), 274-314.

Measures adopted to isolate Spain from the contagion of revolution, the difficulties of French refugees in Spain (even the priests were treated with the greatest of suspicion), sympathy for revolutionary ideas among Spanish artisans and peasants. The Appendix includes relevant official documents and an anonymous letter to Godoy denouncing popular enthusiasm for the French Revolution.

Ciplijauskaite, Birute. *El poeta y la poesía (del Romanticismo a la poesía social)*. Madrid: Insula, 1966. Pp. 504.

Chapter I treats neoclassical and Romantic concepts of poetry, the Romantic poet's sense of mission, and the importance of imagination and inspiration to the Romantic. Espronceda, Zorrilla, and Bécquer, among others, illustrate the study.

Defourneaux, Marcellin. "La historia religiosa de la Revolución Francesa vista por Pablo de Olavide." *BRAH,* clvi (April 1965), 113-89.

Text of previously unpublished chapter of Olavide's *El Evangelio en triunfo*. Olavide warns against the Jacobin excesses of the French Legislative Assembly, atheism, *danzas lúbricas*, and the infamous followers of Voltaire. He considers religion a moral restraining force useful to the State.

Díaz-Plaja, Guillermo. "Una càtedra de retòrica 1822-1935." *Boletín de la Real Academia de Buenas Letras de Barcelona,* xxix (1961-1962), 47-79.

History of the Chair of Rhetoric in the University of Barcelona, dealing mainly with the early years. Details of the careers and literary theories of Milà i Fontanals and Pablo Piferrer. Piferrer's influence on Bécquer is established by textual comparison (footnote 26, pp. 58-59).

Dufourcq, Charles-Emmanuel. "Un officier de Murat en Catalogne." *Boletín de la Real Academia de Buenas Letras de Barcelona,* xxix (1961-1962), 319-44.

Baron Nicolas Desvernois was stationed in Catalonia 1810-1811. Interesting details of the difficulties of discipline which the French had with their troops (mainly German and Neapolitan) and of the reprisals against the *guerrilleros*.

Gómez de la Serna, Gaspar. "Viaje a Sargadelos." *RO*, II (1964), 304-26.

Fascinating portrayal of an entrepreneur of the Enlightenment. Antonio Raimundo Ibáñez, the first Marqués de Sargadelos, attempted to create an industrial complex in Galicia in the closing years of the 18th century. Accused of treason by patriots at the time of the French invasion, he was brutally murdered. His death exemplifies popular hostility to the *ilustrados*.

González, López, Emilio. *Historia de la literatura española: la edad moderna (siglos XVIII y XIX)*. New York: Las Américas, 1965. Pp. 861.

Lucid exposition of the works of the major figures of the pre-Romantic and Romantic periods. Contains a wealth of detail on even minor writers. Professor González' main concern is with Romanticism as a literary phenomenon; unlike Peers, he is more interested in the works of the Romantics than in their literary theories. Detailed bibliography. A useful work of reference.

Juretschke, Hans. *Los afrancesados en la guerra de la independencia*. Madrid: Ediciones Rialp, 1962. Pp. 283.

Examines the attempts at social and political reforms in those regions of Spain under the control of Napoleon, the difficult situation of Spanish officials in occupied territory, and the divers motives, ranging from idealistic to opportunist, of those who collaborated with the French. The term *afrancesado* must be used with caution: it was not employed in a political sense before 1811 and later served also to designate the *constitucionalistas*. The Constitution of Cádiz must in part be viewed as a reply to the Constitution of Bayonne. Interestingly, the term *liberal* first appears in Spanish official language in the decrees of Napoleon; we must also thank the *afrancesados* for the new sense of the word *constitución*. However, *afrancesado* collaboration with the French must in part be held responsible for the violent reaction against liberalism under Fernando VII.

Krömer, Wolfram. "*Europeo* und *Conciliatore*, Abhängigkeit und Bedeutung der ersten romantischen Zeitschrift in Spanien." *RF*, LXXV (1963), 377-92.

López Soler and Monteggia do not slavishly imitate *Il Conciliatore* in their articles in *El Europeo*; they differ from the Italian review in their melancholy and in their interest in the Middle Ages. Professor Krömer recognizes the influence of Chateaubriand and A. W. Schlegel. (Cf. Dendle, "López Soler," under "Studies of Authors.")

Mandel, Oscar. "La leyenda de Don Juan." *Asomante*, XXII, No. 1 (January 1966), 7-20, and No. 2 (April 1966), 7-23.

Traces the legend and myth of Don Juan. The essential element of Don Juan is not rebellion but the triumph of sensuality. With the Romantics, Don Juan becomes a feminine, rather than masculine, ideal.

Martínez Cachero, L. A. "Modernidad del pensamiento socioeconómico de Alvaro Flórez Estrada." *Arch*, XII (1962), 267-82.

Flórez Estrada's approval of the *desamortización* but opposition to the sale of Church lands.

Morodo, Raúl, and Elías Díaz. "Tendencias y grupos políticos en las

Cortes de Cádiz y en las de 1820." *Cuadernos Hispanoamericanos,* No. 201 (1966), 637-75.
Statistical analysis by profession of the votes on the abolition of the Inquisition, the freedom of the press, and the abolition of feudal jurisdictions, in the *Cortes* of Cádiz. Three main tendencies can be seen: the reactionaries (landowners, clergy), the moderates (government officials), and the liberals or progressives (army officers and merchants). The subsequent development of these tendencies during the *trienio*; the reasons for the failure of liberalism in 1823. A lucid analysis which should prove invaluable to any student of this period.

Mourelle Lema, Manuel. "Datos inéditos para una biografía de Vicente Salvá." *BRAE,* xlv (1965), 497-505.
Documents concerning Salvá's academic and political career.

Romero Mendoza, Pedro. *Siete ensayos sobre el romanticismo español.* Vol. I. Cáceres: Servicios Culturales de la Excma. Diputación Provincial de Cáceres, 1960. Pp. 526.
This first volume contains five lengthy essays dealing with the *ambiente romántico* (Madrid in the Romantic period, the theatres, the political clubs), the origins and characteristics of Spanish Romanticism (foreign influences, the liquidation of old ideas, Romantic subjectivism), Larra and *costumbrismo,* Romantic poetry (Rivas, Espronceda, Zorrilla, Arolas, la Avellaneda, Coronado, Pastor Díaz, Bermúdez de Castro, Miguel de los Santos Alvarez, Enrique Gil, Ros de Olano, Bécquer, and lesser figures), and the Romantic theatre (the actors, dramatists such as Martínez de la Rosa, Larra, Rivas, García Gutiérrez, Hartzenbusch, Gil y Zárate, Zorrilla, la Avellaneda). Although based on obvious scholarship, the criticism is nevertheless somewhat impressionistic. 46 plates (mostly portraits of Romantic authors).

Ruiz de Galarreta, Juan. *Ensayo sobre el humorismo en las Sonatas del Valle Inclán.* La Plata: Edición Municipalidad de La Plata, 1962. Pp. 296.
Rev. by Gerard Cox Flynn in *HR,* xxxiii (1965), 71-73.
Valle Inclán's *desvalorización* of Romantic topics not only in the *Sonatas* but also in his later works. Romantic attitudes become objects of ridicule when viewed with the corrosive detachment of the Marqués de Bradomín.

Santillán, Ramón de. *Memorias (1815-1856).* Edición y notas de Ana María Berazaluce. Introducción de Federico Suárez. Pamplona: Colección Histórico del Estudio General de Navarra, Serie Siglo XIX, No. 3, 1960. 2 vols.
Santillán served in the Spanish Army until 1825 and later had a distinguished career in the financial departments of the Spanish civil service. Santillán describes Riego's uprising in 1820 and the campaigns of *liberales* and *absolutistas* 1822-1823, exposes the many defects of the Spanish taxation system, and offers his comments on Mendizábal as a person (too temperamental) and as an administrator (intelligent). Although prosaic to the extreme, the mémoires throw light on the attitudes of a *liberal moderado* opposed to all extremes.

Seco, Serrano, Carlos. "Godoy y Jovellanos." *Arch,* xii (1962), 238-66.
The internal contradictions of Godoy's foreign policy. The impact of the French Revolution on Spain. Godoy was not hostile to Jovellanos. Responsibility for Jovellanos' imprisonment rests with Caballero.

Zavala, Iris M. "Forner y Blanco: Dos vertientes del siglo XVIII." *CA,* xxv (1966), 128-38.
The thought of two generations revealed in the contrasting attitudes of Blanco and Forner towards religion.

3. STUDIES OF AUTHORS

ALCALA GALIANO

La Válgoma, Dalmiro de. "Alcalá-Galiano y el Duque de Rivas, en la Real Academia de la Historia." *BRAH,* CLVII (1965), 190-212.
Their presence in the *Academia.*

Marías, Julián. "Antonio Alcalá Galiano 1789-1865." *BRAE,* XLV (1965), 407-20.
An attempt at understanding "quién quiso ser Antonio Alcalá Galiano." His life-long Romanticism.

ARRIAZA

Marcos, Fernando. "Algo más sobre Arriaza." *RL,* xxIV (1963), 145-47.
Historical background to Arriaza's stay in London 1810-1812. His duties included the defense of Spanish interests against Blanco White's attacks in *El Español.*

AVELLANEDA

Carlos, Alberto J. "*René, Werther* y *La Nouvelle Héloïse* en la primera novela de la Avellaneda." *RI,* xxxI (1965), 223-38.
Compares Sab to René, Werther, and Saint-Preux.

Percas Ponsetti, Helena. "Sobre la Avellaneda y su novela *Sab.*" *RI,* xxvIII (1962), 347-57.
Sab is strongly abolitionist. Romantic characters and sentiments in the novel.

BÉCQUER

Ayllón, Cándido. "Bécquer: su realidad poética." *Hum,* vI (1965), 201-16.
Lucid exposition of Bécquer's poetic aims, themes, and style. Analysis of many *rimas.* Professor Ayllón concludes that the keynote of Bécquer's work is *fervor.* A useful article.

Balbín, Rafael de. "Sobre un poema becqueriano desconocido." *RL,* xxv (1964), 91-96.
Overdetailed analysis of a quatrain which hardly deserves the effort.

Díez Taboada, Juan Marín. "Sobre la rima XV de G.A. Bécquer." *RL,* xxII (1962), 91-96.
Explication of *Rima XV.* Suggested textual emendation. Bécquer's lyrical approach contrasted with Espronceda's epic vision in *El estudiante de Salamanca.*

Esquer Torres, Ramón. "Reminiscencias de nuestros clásicos en Bécquer." *BRAE,* XLV (1965), 185-201.
Fleeting traces of Garcilaso, the *vida-sueño* theme, Manrique, Argensola, Luis de León, and the *Song of Songs.* Mainly concerned with the juvenile poems.

Esquer Torres, Ramón. "Presencia de Espronceda en Bécquer." *RFE,*
XLVI (1963), 329-41.
Influence of Espronceda on juvenile poems and on *Rima IX.*

Hartsook, John H. "Bécquer and Enrique Gil." *Hisp,* XLVIII (1965),
800-05.
Gil's *La violeta* and Bécquer's *Rima LIII* similar in rhythm. Also thematic
similarities between the two poets.

Matas, Julio. "Bécquer en el teatro." *Universidad de La Habana,* CLIX
(1963), 71-86.
Similarities in style and attitude toward nature in the *zarzuelas* and *rimas.*
Bécquer's comic vein can be seen in his prose works.

Pageard, R. "Les premiers articles littéraires de Bécquer." *BH,* LXIV
(1962), 260.

Torres-Morales, José A. "Bécquer y Martí." *La Torre,* XXXIX (July
1962), 127-42.
Modernismo begins with Bécquer. Similarities of form, imagery and vocabulary in Bécquer and Martí.

Young, Caroline. "The *Cantables* of Bécquer's Theatre." *RomN,* VI
(1965), 126-30.
Certain verses of Bécquer's *zarzuelas* similar in theme and form to the *rimas.*

See also Díaz-Plaja, Guillermo ("2. General"), and Guerrero, Fuensanta ("Campillo").

BLANCO
See Zavala, Iris ("2. General").

BOHL VON FABER
See Herrero, Javier ("Fernán Caballero").

BRETON DE LOS HERREROS
Allen, Rupert. "The Romantic element in Bretón's *Muérete—!Y verás!*"
HR, XXXIV (1966), 218-27.
The libido as an essential element of the Romantic's worldview. Bretón's play
approves of Romantic idealism.

CAMPILLO
Guerrero, Fuensanta. "Vida y obras de Narciso Campillo." *RL,* XXV
(1964), 69-106.
Life and works of Bécquer's friend. His anticlericalism. A summary of his
Retórica y poética. Bibliography.

CIENFUEGOS
Cano, José Luis. "Un centenario olvidado: Cienfuegos." *RO,* 2d ser.,
II (1964), 365-69.
Cienfuegos' friendship with Quintana; his humanitarianism.

ESPRONCEDA
Allen, Rupert C. "El elemento coherente de *El estudiante de Salamanca:*
la ironía." *Hispanófila,* No. 17 (1963), 105-15.
Analysis of the conceptual basis of the poem. The similarity in the deaths of
Elvira and Don Félix is ironic.

Foster, David William. "A Note on Espronceda's Use of the Romance Meter in *El estudiante de Salamanca.*" *RomN,* VII (Autumn 1965), 16-20.
Romance used as a structuring device.

Martinengo, Alessandro. *Polimorfismo nel "Diablo mundo" d'Espronceda.* Turin: Bottega d'Erasmo, 1962. Pp. 141.
Rev. by Joaquín Casalduero, *HR,* XXXIV (1966), 84-85.
Sources of *El diablo mundo* in *Faust,* Byron, Voltaire's *L'Ingénu,* Béranger, and French Social Romanticism. The form of the poem reflects its theme, the great theatre of the world.

Paolini, Gilberto. "Reflexiones sobre *El diablo mundo* de Espronceda." *DHR,* V (Spring 1966), 1-7.
Adán as aspiration of Espronceda; the Romantic revolt.

See also Díez Taboada, J. M. ("Bécquer"), Esquer Torres R. ("Bécquer"), and Marrast, R. ("Lista").

ESTÉBANEZ CALDERON

Buendía, Felicidad, ed. *Cristianos y moriscos.* Madrid: Aguilar, 1964. Pp. 145.
Text of *Cristianos y moriscos,* with preface, notes and bibliography.

Manzanares de Cirre, M. "El arabismo romántico en Estébanez Calderón, 'El Solitario.' " *PMLA,* LXXVII (1962), 414-18.
Estébanez Calderón's activities as student and teacher of Arabic. His poems and tales on oriental themes. The novel *Cristianos y moriscos.* His passion for *literatura aljamiada.*

FERNAN CABALLERO

Benítez, Rubén. "Una posible fuente española del *Fausto* de Estanislao del Campo." *RI,* XXXI (1965), 151-71.
A rustic's description of an opera in *La Gaviota* is imitated by Del Campo.

Herrero, Javier. *Fernán Caballero: un nuevo planteamiento.* Madrid: Editorial Gredos, 1963. Pp. 346.
A detailed treatment of the life and ideas not only of Fernán Caballero but also of her parents, Juan Nicolás Böhl von Faber and Frasquita de Larrea. Our concept of the development of the Spanish novel in the nineteenth century must be modified, for Herrero establishes that much of Fernán Caballero's work precedes the *costumbristas* and Balzac. She was collecting popular material before 1825; *La familia de Alvareda* and *Elia* were written prior to 1833. Pages 130-141 offer samples of the work of Doña Frasquita. Bibliography.

Herrero, Javier. "Un poema desconocido de Gabriel García Tassara a Fernán Caballero." *BHS,* XLII (1965), 117-19.
The poem throws some light on Romantic influences on Fernán Caballero.

Horrent, J. "Sur *La Gaviota* de Fernán Caballero." *RLV,* XXXII (1966), 227-37.
Analysis of *La Gaviota,* above all of the personality of Marisalada.

GIL
See Hartsook, J. H. ("Bécquer").

HARTZENBUSCH
Sparks, Amy. "Honor in Hartzenbusch's *Refundición* of Calderón's *El médico de su honra.*" *Hisp,* XLIX (1966), 410-13.
Hartzenbusch attaches less importance to honor as a motivating force than does Calderón.

JOVELLANOS
Artola, Miguel. "El pensamiento político de Jovellanos según la instrucción inédita a la 'Junta de Real Hacienda y Legislación.' " *Arch,* XII (1962), 210-16.
The text of Jovellanos' *Instrucción* of 1809; he is a rationalist in his defense of the natural rights of man, and not a traditionalist *avant la lettre,* as certain critics have claimed.

Caso González, José. "Cartas inéditas de Jovellanos." *Arch,* XIII (1963), 292-310.
Thirteen letters of Jovellanos, one of Campomanes. Letter 7 gives Jovellanos' views on harmony and meter in poetry, and on the inadvisability of publishing verse under one's own name.

Caso González, José. "Notas sobre la prisión de Jovellanos en 1801." *Arch,* XII (1962), 217-37.
The difficulties created in Spain by the illness and death of Pius VI in 1799. Religious and political motives for Jovellanos' imprisonment.

Ricard, Robert. "Jovellanos y la nobleza." *Atlántida,* III (1965), 456-72.
Discusses treatment of this problem by Sánchez Agesta and Jean Sarrailh. Ricard cannot accept Sarrailh's interpretation. Jovellanos is not hostile to the nobility *per se.*

See also Seco Serrano, Carlos ("2. General").

LARRA
Caravaca, Francisco. "Notas sobre las fuentes literarias del costumbrismo de Larra." *RHM,* XXIX (1963), 1-22.
The superficial nature of Larra's culture. His sources: Horace, Addison, Mercier, Boileau, and above all, Jouy.

Rumeau, A. "Le premier séjour de Mariano José de Larra en France 1813-1818)." *BH,* LXIV bis (1962), 600-12.
Larra's father resided in Bordeaux and Paris before accepting a position as physician to Fernando VII's brother in 1817. The influence of French schooling on Larra.

Umbral, Francisco. *Larra, anatomía de un dandy.* Madrid: Ediciones Alfaguara, 1965. Pp. 281.
An attempt at understanding Larra's personality obviously inspired by Sartre's study of Baudelaire. Larra's rootlessness, satanism, narcissism. The Appendix consists of extracts from nine of Larra's articles which Umbral considers to be autobiographical.

See also Herrero, Javier ("Fernán Caballero").

LISTA

Marrast, R. "Lista et Espronceda, fragments inédits du *Pelayo*." *BH*, LXIV bis (1962), 526-37.

Text of fourteen *octavas* by Lista which were in part used by Espronceda in his *Pelayo*.

LOPEZ SOLER

Dendle, Brian J. "Two sources of López Soler's Articles in *El Europeo*." *SIR*, V (Autumn 1965), 44-50.

Establishes by textual comparisons López Soler's debt to Chateaubriand and, by way of Böhl von Faber, to A.W. Schlegel.

See also Krömer, Wolfram ("2. General").

MARTINEZ DE LA ROSA

Romero Tobar, Leonardo. "Notas sobre Martínez de la Rosa (En el centenario de su muerte)." *RL*, XXII (1962), 83-90.

Biographical notes.

Romero Tobar, Leonardo. "Una oda desconocida de Martínez de la Rosa." *RL*, XXI (1962), 72-82.

Ode in Italian to celebrate the return of Pius IX to Rome in 1850; also, a contemporary Spanish translation.

MELÉNDEZ VALDÉS

Demerson, G. "Sur une oeuvre perdue de Meléndez Valdés: la traduction de l'Enéide." *BH*, LXIV bis (1962), 424-36.

Text of surviving fragment (294 lines) of Meléndez Valdés' translation of the *Aeneid*.

Demerson, G. "Tres cartas—dos de ellas inéditas—de Meléndez Valdés a D. Ramón Cáseda." *BRAE*, XLV (1965), 117-39.

Throws some light on the artistic and literary tastes of Meléndez Valdés.

MORATIN

Andioc, René. "Leandro Fernández de Moratín hôte de la France." *RLC*, XXXVII (1963), 268-78.

Documents concerning Moratín in the *Archives Nationales*. Moratín, *étranger dangereux*, was under police surveillance as a suspected revolutionary.

Effross, Susi Hillburn. "Leandro Fernández de Moratín in England." *Hisp*, XLVIII (1965), 43-50.

The virtues and defects of the English, according to the notes made by the somewhat jaundiced Moratín during his visit of 1792-1793.

Montero Padilla, José. "Leandro Fernández de Moratín." *BBMP*, XXXIX (1963), 180-94.

Moratín's childhood, loves, and final solitude. Moratín is a Romantic in his melancholy and in his feeling for nature. Because *El sí de las niñas* is auto-biographical and portrays the triumph of sentiment, it is Spain's first Romantic play.

Montero Padilla, José. "Moratín y su magisterio." *BBMP*, XXXVIII (1962), 173-77.

Importance of Moratín to Ventura de la Vega, Enrique Gaspar, Pérez Galdós.

OCHOA

Randolph, Donald Allen. *Eugenio de Ochoa y el romanticismo español*. (University of California Publications in Modern Philology, Vol. LXXV.) Berkeley and Los Angeles: University of California Press, 1966. Pp. 189.

A well-organized presentation of a wealth of detail on every aspect of Ochoa's literary career. Professor Randolph's study not only covers Ochoa's labors as editor, dramatist, novelist, poet, and critic, but also offers a full treatment of Ochoa's considerable achievements as translator. The Appendix to Chapter VI gives the text of the previously unpublished didactic poem "La sopa del convento." Bibliography of Ochoa's works.

PIFERRER

Carnicer, Ramón. *Vida y obra de Pablo Piferrer*. Madrid: Instituto Miguel de Cervantes, 1963. Pp. 398.

Piferrer's life as revealed in his letters and presented in the context of a year-by-year account of events in Barcelona (which includes the interesting revelation of the existence of Republican sentiment in Catalonia in the late 1830's). Piferrer's struggles with ill health, the vicissitudes of his career as librarian and teacher, his evolution from revolutionary to conservative. Piferrer praised German and Scottish Romanticism as expressions of the national soul; he considered French Romantic drama, however, to be degenerate and immoral. He disliked baroque architecture but commended Gothic art as a manifestation of the *espíritu popular*. It is worth noting that Piferrer considered Balmes to be egoistic and indifferent to the sufferings of others. The Appendix includes a list of Piferrer's sources for *Recuerdos y bellezas de España*, extracts from *Recuerdos* and from his articles, and the text of 17 poems. Bibliography.

See also Díaz-Plaja, Guillermo ("2. General").

QUEROL

Guarner, Luis. "Poesías desconocidas de Vicente W. Querol." *RL*, xxv (1964), 135-94, and xxvi (1964), 117-98.

Text of poems written by Querol during his student years (1852-1858) plus a few poems from the later years. Includes *romances históricos* and poems with oriental themes. The influence of Zorrilla and Espronceda is obvious.

QUINTANA

Dérozier, Albert. "Les étapes de la vie officielle de Manuel Josef Quintana." *BH*, LXVI (1964), 363-90.

Details of Quintana's official career as revealed in his dossier in the *Ministerio de Hacienda*. Quintana accepted a pension from Fernando VII in 1829. Also reproduces his speech to the throne in the *Cortes* of 1834, in which he comments on the killing of the friars and the Carlist rebellion.

Pageaux, D. H. "La genèse de l'oeuvre poétique de M. J. Quintana." *RLC*, xxxvii (1963), 227-67.

Unity of ideology and style in the poems written 1788-1808.

See also Cano, J. L. ("Cienfuegos").

RIVAS

Fernández Larraín, Sergio. "Algo del Duque de Rivas a través de un epistolario en el primer centenario de su muerte: 1865-1965." *Atenea*

(Santiago de Chile), CLXI (1966), 124-249.

Historical background and text of 86 letters written by Rivas to Narváez in the period 1844-1865, mainly covering Rivas' years in Naples and Paris.

Rosales, Luis. "Vida y andanzas del Duque de Rivas." *BRAE*, XLV (1965), 396-406.

Summary of Rivas' life. Rosales praises the *impulso narrativo* and *realismo* of *El moro expósito.*

Saro, Pilar de. "Algunos textos raros de y sobre el Duque de Rivas." *RL*, XXI (1962), 82-85.

Two poems and one letter of Rivas, and two references to Rivas in contemporary newspapers.

See also La Válgoma ("Alcalá Galiano").

RODRIGUEZ RUBI

Burgos, Ana María. "Vida y obra de Tomás Rodríguez Rubí." *RL*, XXIII (1963), 65-102.

The life of this prolific dramatist. Mentions his early poems, his *artículos de costumbres,* and his melodramatic novel, *El hermano del mar.* His numerous dramatic works are listed with date of *estreno* and some indication of contemporary reception.

SEGOVIA

González Molleda, María Luisa. "Antonio María Segovia." *RL*, XXIV (1963), 101-24.

Concise presentation of life, works, and ideas of the *costumbrista* Segovia. Bibliography.

ZORRILLA

Abellán, José Luis. "Don Juan: interpretación y mito." *Horizontes*, V (April 1962), 8-19.

A summary of various theories concerning Don Juan. In Zorrilla, Don Juan becomes a myth, a myth in which the inherent contradictions of Don Juan's nature are resolved. Professor Abellán also suggests, not without humor, reasons for Don Juan's continued popularity in Spain.

Davidson, Ned. "Zorrilla, Darío, and 'Yo soy aquel.'" *RomN*, VI (1965), 131-34.

Comparison of poetic autobiographies of Zorrilla and Darío.

Rubio Fernández, Luz. "Variaciones estilísticas del *Tenorio.*" *RL*, XIX (1961), 55-92.

Zorrilla's corrections of the manuscript of *Don Juan Tenorio.*

English Language Notes

| Volume VI | Supplement to No. 1 | September 1968 |

The Romantic Movement
A Selective and Critical Bibliography
for 1967

Edited by

DAVID V. ERDMAN

with the assistance of KENNETH NEGUS and JAMES S. PATTY

This bibliography, compiled by a joint bibliography committee for groups General Topics II and English IX of the Modern Language Association, is designed to cover a "movement" rather than a period. Thus, though the English section is largely limited to the years 1789-1837, other sections extend over different spans of years.

It is our intent to include, with descriptive and, at times, critical annotation, all books and articles of substantial interest to scholars of English and Continental Romanticism, and critical reviews of such books. We also make note of items of minor but scholarly interest, except those which are adequately listed in the Annual Bibliography of the Association (issued in the May number of *PMLA*). Major and controversial works are given what is intended to be judicious if necessarily very brief review.

The approximate length of a book is indicated by report of the number of pages—or the number of volumes when more than one. Book prices are noted when available. Delays in printing and binding produced a great number of books dated 1966 or 1967 but actually published in 1967 or 1968; when our listed date differs from that of the title or imprint page, we have been guided by publishers' notices. But some "1967" books in our list may technically belong to 1968. We continue the practice of including available 1968 reviews of listed books.

The editorial committee gratefully acknowledges the help of its collaborators, whose names are given at the heads of the respective sections.

To ensure notice in the next issue of the bibliography, authors and publishers are invited to send review copies of relevant books or monographs, and offprints of articles, to: David V. Erdman, English Department, State University of New York, Stony Brook, N.Y. 11790.

CONTENTS

ABBREVIATIONS

AL	*American Literature*
AnB	*L'Année Balzacienne*
AnBret	*Annales de Bretagne*
AN&Q	*American Notes & Queries*
Arch	*Archivum*
Archiv	*Archiv für das Studium der Neuren Sprachen und Literaturen*
Arh	*Archivo Hispalesne*
AQ	*American Quarterly*
ASch	*American Scholar*
AUMLA	*Journal of the Australasian Universities Language and Literature Association*
Aurora	*Aurora: Eichendorff-Almanach*
BA	*Books Abroad*
BAGB	*Bulletin de l'Association Guillaume Budé*
BB	*Bulletin of Bibliography*
BBMP	*Boletín de la Biblioteca de Menéndez Pelayo*
BC	*Book Collector*
BH	*Bulletin Hispanique*
BHS	*Bulletin of Hispanic Studies*
BNYPL	*Bulletin of the New York Public Library*
BNL	*Burke Newsletter*
BRAE	*Boletín de la Real Academia Española*
BRAH	*Boletín de la Real Academia de la Historia*
BSUF	*Ball State University Forum*
BuR	*Bucknell Review*
CA	*Cuadarnos Americanos*
CAIEF	*Cahiers de l'Association international des études françaises*
C&S	*Cultura e scuola*
CHA	*Cuadernos Hispanoamericanos* (*Madrid*)
CL	*Comparative Literature*
CLJ	*Cornell Library Journal*
CLS	*Comparative Literature Studies*
Conv	*Convivium*
CritQ	*Critical Quarterly*
CQ	*Cambridge Quarterly*
DR	*Dalhousie Review*
DU	*Deutschunterricht*

ELN 6 Supp. (1968) 1 – 158

DUJ Durham University Journal
DVLG Deutsche Vierteljahrsschrift für Literaturwissenschaft und Geistesgeschichte

EA Études Anglaises
E&S Essays and Studies by Members of the English Association
ECr L'Esprit créateur (Minneapolis)
EG Études germaniques
EHR English Historical Review
EIC Essays in Criticism (Oxford)
ELH Journal of English Literary History
ELN English Language Notes
ES English Studies
ESA English Studies in Africa (Johannesburg)
ESPSL O Estado de São Paulo, Supplemento Literária

FL Le Figaro Littéraire
FLe Fiera letteraria
FM Le français moderne
FMLS Forum for Modern Language Studies (U. of St. Andrews)
FMod Filología Moderna
FR French Review
FS French Studies

GL&L German Life and Letters
GQ German Quarterly
GR Germanic Review
GRM Germanish-romanische Monatsschrift, Neue Folge
GSLI Giornale Storica della Letteratura Italiana

HeineJ Heine Jahrbuch
Hispano Hisponófila (Madrid)
HLB Harvard Library Bulletin
HLQ Huntington Library Quarterly
Höjb Hölderlin-Jahrbuch
HR Hispanic Review
Hum Humanitas

IL L'Information Littéraire

JAAC Journal of Aesthetics and Art Criticism
JBS Journal of British Studies
JEGP Journal of English and Germanic Philology
JFDH Jahrbuch des Freien Deutschen Hochstifts (Tübingen)
JHI Journal of the History of Ideas
JJPG Jahrbuch der Jean-Paul-Gesellschaft
JMH Journal of Modern History
JR Journal of Religion

KFLQ Kentucky Foreign Language Quarterly
KR Kenyon Review
KSJ Keats-Shelley Journal
KSMB Keats-Shelley Memorial Bulletin

L&P Literature and Psychology (New York)
LC Library Chronicle (Univ. of Pennsylvania)
LI Lettere italiane

2172

LJGG	*Literaturwissenschaftliches Jahrbuch der Görres-Gesellschaft*
LR	*Les Lettres Romanes*
MedF	*Médecine de France*
MHG	*Mitteilungen der E.T.A. Hofmann-Gesellschaft*
MLJ	*Modern Language Journal*
MLN	*Modern Language Notes*
MLQ	*Modern Language Quarterly*
MLR	*Modern Language Review*
MP	*Modern Philology*
MQ	*Midwest Quarterly (Pittsburg, Kansas)*
MSE	*Massachusetts Studies in English*
NA	*Nuova antologia*
N&Q	*Notes and Queries*
NCF	*Nineteenth Century Fiction*
Neophil	*Neophilogus (Groningen)*
NL	*The Newberry Library Bulletin*
NMQ	*New Mexico Quarterly*
NR	*New Republic*
NRF	*Nouvelle revue française*
	New Statesman (formerly NS)
NS	*Die neueren Sprachen*
NYRB	*New York Review of Books*
OGS	*Oxford German Studies*
PBSA	*Papers of the Bibliographical Society of America*
PEGS	*Publications of the English Goethe Society*
Pel	*Le parole e le idee (Napoli)*
Person	*The Personalist*
PLL	*Papers on Language and Literature*
PMLA	*Publications of the Modern Language Association of America*
PQ	*Philological Quarterly*
PR	*Partisan Review*
PSA	*Papeles de Son Armadans*
PULC	*Princeton University Library Chronicle*
QR	*Quarterly Review*
RBPH	*Revue Belge de philologie et d'histoire*
RdP	*Revue de Paris*
RDM	*Revue des deux mondes*
RdS	*Revue de synthèse*
REI	*Revue des études italiennes*
REL	*Review of English Literature (Leeds)*
RES	*Review of English Studies*
RF	*Romanische Forschungen*
RFE	*Revista de Filología Española*
RHL	*Revue d'Histoire Littéraire de la France*
RHM	*Revista Hispánica Moderna*
RHT	*Revue d'histoire du théâtre*
RLC	*Revue de littérature comparée*
RL	*Revista de Literatura*
RLI	*Rassegna della letteratura italiana*
RLMC	*Revista de letterature moderne e comparate (Firenze)*

RO   *Revista de Occidente*
RomN   *Romance Notes (Univ. of North Carolina)*
RR   *Romanic Review*
RSH   *Revue des sciences humaines*

Serif   *The Serif (Kent, Ohio)*
S   *Spectator*
SAQ   *South Atlantic Quarterly*
S&S   *Science & Society*
SB   *Studies in Bibliography: Papers of the Bibliographical Society of the University of Virginia*
SC   *Stendhal Club*
SEL   *Studies in English Literature, 1500-1900 (Rice Univ.)*
SFr   *Studi francesi*
SIB   *Studies in Burke and His Time*
SIR   *Studies in Romanticism (Boston Univ.)*
SN   *Studia neophilologica*
SoR   *Southern Review (Adelaide, Australia)*
SoR(La) *Southern Review (Louisiana)*
SP   *Studies in Philology*
SR   *Sewanee Review*
SSL   *Studies in Scottish Literature (Texas Tech. College, Lubbock)*
SuF   *Sinn und Form*

TLS   *(London) Times Literary Supplement*
TR   *Table Ronde*

UR   *University Review (Kansas City, Missouri)*
UTQ   *University of Toronto Quarterly*

VQR   *Virginia Quarterly Review*
VS   *Victorian Studies (Indiana Univ.)*

WHR   *Western Humanities Review*
WW   *Wirkendes Wort*

YFS   *Yale French Studies*
YR   *Yale Review*

ZDA   *Zeitschrift für deutsches Altertum und deutsche Literatur*
ZFSL   *Zeitschrift für französische Sprache und Literatur*
ZRP   *Zeitschrift für Romanische Philologie (Halle)*

GENERAL

(Compiled by David V. Erdman with the assistance of Irene H. Chayes; Herbert L. Kleinfield, C. W. Post College; and others.)

(See also "General" sections under each language heading.)

1. BIBLIOGRAPHY

For previous issues of the present "Bibliography" see the April numbers of *PQ* (1950-1961), then the October (1962-1964), and thereafter the

September Supplement to *ELN*. For the most extensive general list-ing, in all languages, see the "Annual Bibliography" in *PMLA* each May; slight notes listed there will not be repeated in our list.

Bailey, Richard W., et al. "1966 Annual Bibliography on Style." *Style*, I (1967), 257-81.

See also listings in Bibliography sections below, under English, French, German, Italian, Portuguese, Spanish.

2. ENVIRONMENT: ART, MUSIC, SOCIETY, POLITICS, RELIGION

Behrens, C. B. A. *The Ancien Régime*. London: Thames and Hudson, 1967. Pp. 215. 35s.; paper 18s.
Rev. in *TLS*, Sept. 28, 1967, p. 901.

Coute, David. *The Left in Europe since 1789*. New York: McGraw-Hill, 1966. Pp. 256. $2.45.
Rev. by Heniz Lubasz in *JMH*, xxxix (1967), 317-18.

Davis, David Brion. *The Problem of Slavery in Western Culture*. Vol. I. Cornell University Press, 1967. Pp. 505. $10.00.
Rev. by M.I. Finley in *NYRB*, Jan. 26, 1967, pp. 6-10.

Flinn, M. W. *The Origins of the Industrial Revolution*. (Problems and Perspectives in History.) New York: Barnes & Noble, 1966. Pp. x + 114. Paper $1.75.

Glacken, Clarence J. *Traces on the Rhodian Shore: Nature and Culture in Western Thought from Ancient Times to the End of the Eighteenth Century*. University of California Press, 1967. Pp. 763. $15.00.
Rev. by D.P. Walker in *NYRB*, Dec. 21, 1967, pp. 36-37

Glover, Richard. "The French Fleet, 1807-1814; Britain's Problem; and Madison's Opportunity." *JMH*, xxxix (1967), 233-52.

Haskell, Francis, and Francis Watson. *The Age of the Grand Tour*. Lon-don: Elek, 1967. £8 8s.
Rev. by Peter Vansittart in S. Dec. 29, 1967, p. 815.

Hitchcock, James. "The Romantic Rebel on the Campus." *YR*, LVII (1967), 31-37.
"The student-radical style of politics, with its charismatic leadership, its extrav-agant rhetoric and emotional songs, its distinctive clothes, its mystique of youth, and its preference for a semi-private language, is part of the romantic's ageless search for a transcendence of society and the self and the discovery of a nameless higher reality."
Radicals among today's youth rebel in a romantic manner against both bour-geois social values and traditional liberal thought. The sense of romantic used here is "idealized," "intuitive," "antirational." An alert dissection of our public attitude. (H.L.K.)

Kranzberg, Melvin, and Carroll W. Pursell, Jr., eds. *The Emergence of Modern Industrial Society: Earliest Times to 1900.* (Technology in Western Civilization, Vol. I.) Oxford University Press, 1967. Pp. xii + 802, illus. $8.50.

Reaches "1600-1750" by page 105; a broadly conceived, richly detailed, survey textbook by a panel of specialists treating the history of technology in many roots and branches, from "Instrumentation" and "The Beginning of Electricity" to "Social Impact" and "The Invention of Invention."

Lively, Jack, ed. *The Enlightenment.* (Problems and Perspectives in History.) New York: Barnes & Noble, 1967. Pp. xvi + 200. Paper $2.50.

Twenty-one "Select Documents" exhibiting the Enlightenment in eight categories; nine illustrating "The Reaction to the Enlightenment"; followed by 21 excerpts from modern historians' discussions of "Problems of Historiography."

Resnick, Daniel P. *The White Terror and the Political Reaction after Waterloo.* (Harvard Historical Studies, 77.) Harvard University Press, 1966. Pp. ix + 152. $4.25.

A carefully documented study. Though the magnitude of the White Terror and repressive measures of 1815-16 was subsequently exaggerated by both Right and Left, "this early association of royalism with reaction was to do irreparable harm to the political future of the legitimist monarchical movement in France."

Rosenblum, Robert. *Transformations in Late Eighteenth Century Art.* Princeton University Press, 1967. Pp. xxvi + 203; 215 plates. $10.00.

How minor and relatively obscure developments in Neoclassical art (painting, drawing, graphics, sculpture, and architecture) prepared the way for the revolutionary changes of the later nineteenth and twentieth centuries. Among the artists discussed are David, Gros, Ingres, Carstens, Flaxman, Cumberland, Fuseli, and Blake. The star exhibits, with which this admirable study is brought to a close, are drawings by Blake and Ingres which both foreshadow early Analytical Cubism. (I.H.C.)

Simpson, Robert, ed. *The Symphony.* Vol. I. Baltimore: Penguin Books, 1966. Pp. 381. $3.65.

Haydn to Dvořák.

Talmon, J. L. *Romanticism and Revolt: Europe 1815-1848.* London; Thames and Hudson, 1967.

Rev. by George Lichtheim in *New Statesman,* July 7, 1967, p. 19.

A sort of "instant history" of "forces and trends which were at work everywhere" between 1789 and 1848, with more "Romanticism" in the title and the picture captions than in the sound track. The brief chapter directly devoted to literature (pp. 136-65) is the least well digested (it ends misquoting Coleridge and then misquoting him again as "Wordsworth"). Pretentious.

Vereker, Charles. *Eighteenth-Century Optimism: A Study of the Inter-relations of Moral and Social Theory in English and French Thought between 1689 and 1789.* Liverpool University Press, 1967. Pp. viii + 317. 45s.

An absorbing analysis of the (sequentially) "metaphysical," "empiricist," and "redemptive" optimism of a century whose trust in reason has survived but whose trust in a benevolent (reasonable) Nature has not. Particularly interesting is the critique of the "redemptive optimism" preceeding the French Revolution, dealt with in chapters headed "Paradise Lost," "Natural Goodness," and "The Redeemed Society." Vereker is concerned to escape the optimists' assumption "that a dynamic and revolutionary doctrine was really static and simple."

Waters, Edward N. "Franz Liszt to Richard Pohl." *SIR*, VI (1967), 193-202.

Reviews of books previously listed:
GAY, Peter, *The Enlightenment* (see *ELN*, V, Supp., 6), rev. by W.R. Fryer in *SIB*, IX, 784-88; by R.R. Palmer in *JMH*, XXXIX (1967), 164-66; and by John Weightman in *NYRB*, Jan. 12, 1967, pp. 4-8; RUDÉ, George, *Revolutionary Europe*, 1783-1815 (see *ELN*, V, Supp., 7), rev. by C.B.A. Behrens in *NYRB*, Oct. 26, 1967, pp. 30-32, and by Crane Brinton in *JMH*, XXXIX (1967), p. 184.

3. CRITICISM

Adams, Robert Martin. *Nil: Episodes in the Literary Conquest of Void During the Nineteenth Century.* Oxford University Press, 1967. Pp. 249. $6.00.
Rev. by Denis Donoghue in *NYRB*, Mar. 9, 1967, pp. 16-19, and by Julian Moynahan in *NR*, June 3, 1967, pp. 34-36.

Barfield, Owen. *Romanticism Comes of Age.* New and augmented edition. Wesleyan University Press, 1967. Pp. 254. $6.50.
Chiefly Goethe and Coleridge, in light of the "anthroposophy" of Rudolf Steiner. Most of the essays were written between 1929 and 1944.

Brion, Marcel. "La musique, l'amour et la littérature." *RdP*, LXXIV (Dec. 1967), 3-10.
The role of music in the loves and writings of Balzac, Tolstoy, Stendhal, and Goethe.

Buchen, Irving H. "The Modern Visionary Tradition and Romanticism." *WHR*, XXI (1967), 21-29.

Fletcher, Ian, ed. *Romantic Mythologies.* London: Routledge & Kegan Paul; New York: Barnes & Noble, 1967. Pp. xiii + 297; 16 plates. 50s; $9.50.
Rev. in *TLS*, Oct. 26, 1967, p. 1011; and by Gabriel Pearson in *New Statesman*, June 9, 1967, pp. 800-01.
Focus is on the latter part of the nineteenth century, but the eight essays run from Hawthorne and Barnes to Beardsley, Wagner, and Forster, after a lucid and richly documented (and illustrated) survey by A.J.L. Busst of "The Image of the Androgyne in the Nineteenth Century" (pp. 1-96). Busst begins after, and does not refer to, Blake—whose use of this image is nevertheless clarified by this study. Treated closely are Ballanche, Novalis, Mallarmé, and Balzac.

Garber, Frederick. "Self, Society, Value and the Romantic Hero." *CL*, XIX (1967), 321-33.
Self-awareness is assumed to be the basic problem of the Romantic hero from Werther to Julien Sorel. Stress is placed on the paradoxical and ambivalent

attitude of the hero toward society. Garber does not indicate that this sickness unto death is not found exclusively in Romantic heroes. What about Kierkegaard and Kafka? And is Hölderlin's disintegration under pressure into madness really "comparatively rare"? Examples from Nietzsche to van Hoddie point to the contrary. (I.H.C.)

Lyon, Melvin E. "Walden Pond as a Symbol." *PMLA*, LXXXII (1967), 289-300.
A searching critique of *Walden* in its romantic qualities, particularly as a symbol of rebirth. (H.L.K.)

Majewski, Henry F. "Mercier and the Preromantic Myth of the End of the World." *SIR*, VII (1967), 1-14.

Miller, Perry. "The Romantic Dilemma in American Nationalism and the Concept of Nature." Pp. 197-207 in *Nature's Nation*. Harvard University Press, 1967. Pp. 298. $7.50.
Rev. by Max Byrd in *NR*, June 17, 1967, pp. 22-24.

Proffer, Carl R. "Gogol's Definition of Romanticism." *SIR*, VI (1967), 120-27.

Rea, J. "Classicism and Romanticism in Poe's 'Ligeia.' " *BSUF*, VIII (Winter 1967), 25-29.

Reizov, B. G. "U istokov romanticheckoj Estetiki" ("At the sources of Romantic esthetics"). *Izvestija Akademii Nauk S. S. S. R. Serija Literatury i Jazyka*, XXVI (1967), 308-20.

Rogers, Neville. "The Poetic Process: Notes on Some Observations by Keats, Rilke and Others." *KSMB*, XVIII (1967), 26-35.

Schenck, H. G. *The Mind of the European Romantics: An Essay in Cultural History*. Preface by Isaiah Berlin. London: Constable, 1966; New York: Frederick Ungar, 1967. Pp. xxiv + 303; 17 illus. 50s.; $9.00.
Rev. by Robert M. Adams in *NYRB*, Feb. 15, 1968, pp. 25-27, and by A.G. Lehmann in *FMLS*, III (1967), 406-10.
This misnamed "essay" suffers from fundamental confusions of category. Chapter headings—"Forebodings and Nostalgia for the Past," "The Lure of Nothingness," "The Cult of the Ego"—echo literary themes, although they apply to many non-literary figures and non-artists, including such oddities as King Ludwig II of Bavaria and Paul Morphy, an "intuitive" chessmaster. At the same time, the author curiously downgrades literature itself, regarding it as a matter of "style" and "poetic diction." In selecting his evidence, he prefers to go to historians or biographers rather than to critics, and biography, or supposed biography, is the common meeting-ground for the heterogeneous *dramatis personae*. In the chapter entitled "Nature Mysticism," for example, *The Prelude* is bracketed with Beethoven's *Pastoral Symphony*, Thoreau's essay on walking, and Turner's painting *Snowstorm with a Steamship* because all "originated" in inspiring contact with the out-of-doors. The "sturdy Wordsworth, who enjoyed any kind of weather," is mentioned again later in contrast with the hypersensitive Nietzsche, who fled the damps of Venice.

Nietzsche is more congenial to Schenck than the poets, especially the English, and the book might have been better if its subject had been frankly the evolution of the Nietzschean "mind," which in the terms of Lovejoy's classic essay would probably qualify as one of the various Romanticisms. Yet sometimes even Nietzsche is strangely served by this author. On the last page, a quotation from *Human—All Too Human* which calls for a movement *beyond* metaphysics is said to epitomize the "deep-rooted metaphysical urge so characteristic of the Romantics." (I.H.C.)

Strauch, Carl F. "Emerson and the Doctrine of Sympathy." *SIR*, vi (1967), 152-74.

Sussel, Philippe, ed. *Le Romantisme.* (Les Métamorphoses de l'Humanité.) Paris: Editions Planète, 1967. Pp. 253. 63 Fr.
Intended primarily for the coffee tables of the Occident, this book proposes to synthesize literary, esthetic, religious, political, and economic developments throughout the world in the period 1800-1850, albeit with a certain emphasis on Europe and the Americas. Lavish illustration and a cluttered arrangement of the accompanying texts tend to frustrate this grandiose scheme. Still, it is valuable to see events in, say, Japan and Russia correlated with the familiar story of English, French, and German Romanticism. (J.S.P.)

Thorlby, Anthony, ed. *The Romantic Movement.* London: Longmans, 1967; New York: Barnes & Noble, 1968. Pp. xv + 176. Paper 12s. 6d.; $2.50.
Rev. in *TLS*, Oct. 26, 1967, p. 1011.
A lively editorial monologue weaves connections among 26 excerpts from Lovejoy, Babbitt, Peckham, Fogle, Lukács, Barth, Cobban, *et tous ceux*. Followed by a meagre but stimulatingly juxtaposed selection of "Documents" from Rousseau, Burke, Blake . . . Manzoni, Sand, Kierkegaard.

Weimann, Robert. *"New Criticism" und die Entwicklung bürgerlicher Literaturwissenshaft.* Halle: Niemeyer Verlag, 1962. Pp. 364. DM. 25.50.
Rev. by Lee Baxandall in *S&S*, xxix (1965), 346-49.

Witemeyer, Hugh E. " 'Line' and 'Round' in Emerson's 'Uriel.' " *PMLA*, LXXXII (1967), 98-103.

Reviews of books previously listed:
BEEBE, Maurice, *Ivory Towers and Sacred Founts: The Artist as Hero in Fiction from Goethe to Joyce* (see *ELN*, iv, Supp., 6-7), rev. by John P. Anton in *JAAC*, xxvi (1967), 271-73; BOUSQUET, Jacques, *Les Thémes du rêve dans la littérature romantique (France, Angleterre, Allemagne)* (see *ELN*, v, Supp., 8) rev. by J.-B. Barrère in *RBPH*, XLV (1967), 155-57; PEYRE, Henri, *Modern Literature. Vol. I: The Literature of France* (see *ELN*, v, Supp., 10), rev. anon. in *TLS*, June 9, 1966, p. 516; by Sidney D. Braun in *Criticism*, ix (1967), 204-06; and by R.T. Sussex in *AUMLA*, No. 26 (Nov. 1966); WELLEK, René, *A History of Modern Criticism: 1750-1950,* Vols. III and IV (see *ELN*, iv, Supp., 11), rev. anon. in *AL*, xxxviii (1966), 269-70; in *TLS*, Aug. 31, 1967, p. 782; in *VQR*, xlii (1966), lx-lxi; by Wayne C. Booth in *Book Week*, Feb. 27, 1967; by D. Donoghue in *Encounter*, xxviii (June 1967), 80; by R.H. Fogle in *Criticism*, ix (1967), 197; by Ronald Hafter in *DR*, Winter, 1965-1966, p. 352 (Vol. iii only); by Lee T. Lemon in *JAAC*, xxv (1966), 231-32; by Robie Macauley in *New York Times Book Review*, Jan. 6, 1966, pp. 6-7, 27; by Walter J. Ong in *YR*, LV (1966), 585-89; by Peter Pfaff in *Germanistik*, viii (1967), 751-52; and by Earl Rovit in *ASch*, xxxv (1966), 550.

ENGLISH

(Compilers and reviewers: Kenneth T. Abrams, State Univ. of New York, Stony Brook; E. E. Bostetter, Univ. of Washington; Kenneth Neill Cameron, New York Univ.; Irene H. Chayes, Silver Spring, Md.; Kenneth Curry, Univ. of Tennessee; David V. Erdman, State Univ. of New York, Stony Brook; Richard Harter Fogle, Univ. of N. Carolina; John E. Jordan, Univ. of California, Berkeley; Karl Kroeber, Univ. of Wisconsin; Albert J. Kuhn, Ohio State Univ.; †William H. Marshall, Univ. of N. Carolina; Donald H. Reiman, Carl Pforzheimer Library; David H. Stam, Newberry Library)

1. BIBLIOGRAPHY

For eighteenth-century figures see the annotated bibliography, "English Literature, 1660-1800," in *PQ* each July, also the *Johnsonian Newsletter* and the *Burke Newsletter* (since Fall 1967, *Studies in Burke and His Times*). For the most extensive international coverage of Keats, Shelley, Byron, Hunt, and their circles, see the "Current Bibliography" in annual volumes of *KSJ*. See also the *Blake Newsletter* and the "Selective Checklist of Bibliographical Scholarship" in *SB*. For a wide coverage of journals, with precis of articles, consult the indexed monthly issues of *Abstracts of English Studies*.

See also the "Anglo-German Literary Bibliography" in *JEGP* each July, and the relevant sections of the *Annual Bibliography of English Language and Literature*, and *The Year's Work in English Studies*.

For the most extensive general listing see the "Annual Bibliography" in the May issue of *PMLA*.

Egerer, J. W. *A Bibliography of Robert Burns*. Edinburgh: Oliver and Boyd, 1964. Pp. 396.
Rev. in *PBSA*, LXII (1968), 156.

Fogle, Richard Harter. *Romantic Poets and Prose Writers*. (Goldentree Bibliographies.) New York: Appleton-Century-Crofts, 1967. Pp. viii + 87. $1.35.
A selective guide to scholarship in the twentieth century, covering the authors in this "English" section, with categorical subdivisions, as well as an introductory listing of historical, critical, and bibliographical items. Works of "special importance" are starred, with, of course, some controversial choices. (D.V.E.)

Havighurst, Alfred F. "Paperbacks on British History." *JBS*, VI (1967), 124-65.

Hemlow, Joyce. "Preparing a Catalogue of the Burney Family Correspondence 1749-1878." *BNYPL*, LXX (1967), 486-95.
Catalogue being published by The New York Public Library in 1968, of 10,000 letters by over a thousand persons.

Review of book previously listed:
MAYO, Robert D., *The English Novel in the Magazines* (see *PQ*, XLII, 440), rev. by Ian Watt in *Library*, XIX (1964 [1968]), 314-16.

2. ENVIRONMENT: ART, SOCIETY, POLITICS, RELIGION

The Anti-Jacobin; or Weekly Examiner. London, 1797. 2 vols. (pp. 1297). Complete reprint. Hildesheim, W. Germany: Georg Olms, 1967. DM. 94,—.

Aspinall, A., ed. *The Later Correspondence of George III.* Vol. III: 1798-1901. Cambridge University Press, 1967. Pp. xxxii + 671. $27.50.
Volumes I (1783-93) and II (1793-97) appeared in 1962 and 1963 and were listed (*PQ*, XLII, 441; XLIII, 440), but the present note will refer to all three. Three more are to come.
The introductory essays are pithy and thorough. The apparatuses of notes, tables, sources, and indexes make this and the other Aspinall collection (of *The Correspondence of George Prince of Wales*) handy guides to the official and unofficial persons of the British court. The documents—a selection of all known letters and memoranda "of any real importance" in private and public archives—are copious (1) from and to members of the royal family—with increasing significance as the princes grow older and enter diplomatic and military life—and (2) from Pitt, Dundas, Grenville, Portland, and other ministers, with ocasional royal replies or instructions. There is only a fair sprinkling of (3) miscellaneous confidential reports—on everything from the state of the navy or the political circumstances of Sweden to the latest audit of the debts of the Prince of Wales. There is much detail in the correspondence about places and pensions; very little in the rare cabinet minute or memorandum of political espionage or arrest, the accompanying reports having, presumably, vanished, unless, perhaps, still withheld from public use.
Each volume has its surprises, such as the details of a strong but frustrated revolt of cabinet doves in 1797, otherwise almost lost to history. More often the surviving record is bare just where the original correspondence must have been fraught with importance (and promptly destroyed). Few and thin are the reliques of 1792 when the nation moved to war; more frequent but terse are reports during the naval mutinies and the Irish rebellion. The swift, brief notes of the king (he never employed a secretary) disclose his strong interest in patronage and his determined opposition to peace-making and other measures of "expediency." (D.V.E.)

Bamford, Samuel. *Passages in the Life of a Radical.* Introduction by Tim Hilton. London: McGibbon & Kee, 1967. 45s.
Reprint of a classic.

Beazley, Elisabeth. *Madocks and the Wonder of Wales.* London: Faber and Faber, 1967. Pp. 276. 36s.
William Madocks' land-reclamation schemes in North Wales fascinated Shelley, Peacock, Hogg—and Faust. A mass of unpublished correspondence is drawn upon for this full-length biography.

Boulton, James T. "Edmund Burke's *Letter to a Noble Lord*: Apologia and Manifesto." *BNL*, VIII (1967), 695-701.

Burrow, John W. *Evolution and Society: A Study in Victorian Social Theory.* Cambridge University Press, 1967. Pp. 295. $8.50.
Rev. by Noel Annan in *NYRB,* May 18, 1967, pp. 13-17.

Chapman, Gerald W. *Edmund Burke: The Practical Imagination.* Harvard University Press, 1967. Pp. x + 350. $5.95.
Rev. in *TLS,* March 7, 1968, p. 232.
"He might sympathize like a saint, but he calculated like a politician" (p. 115). Chapman supplies a reading of Burke that is sensitive, critical, judicious, and highly to be recommended. He is, however, in such accord with Burke's "heroic despair" that, even while noting that Burke saw some matters "in the twisted lights and dark glass of his passion," Chapman takes the facts and realities to be pretty much what Burke declared them to be. There is little sense of Burke's alarms as self-fulfilling. (D.V.E.)

Cone, Carl B. "Dr. Richard Price—A Character." *BNL,* VIII (1966-67), 638-45.

The Correspondence of Edmund Burke. Vol. V: July 1782-June 1789. Edited by Holden Furber with the assistance of P.J. Marshall. Vol. VI: July 1789-December 1791. Edited by Alfred Cobban and Robert A. Smith. Cambridge University Press; University of Chicago Press, 1967. £6; $13.50 each.
It is fascinating to see the French Revolution enter Burke's correspondence ("every step taken . . . a New prodigy"), to read his private distrust and criticism of Marie Antoinette, to follow his great involvement with the *émigrés,* and to see what the editors call his "seeing . . . into the real nature of political changes" exemplified in such details as the stipulation that the great army that must be sent in to suppress that "strange, nameless, wild, enthusiastic thing" in France ought, if possible, to be ignorant of the French language. (D.V.E.)

Derry, John W. *The Radical Tradition: Tom Paine to Lloyd George.* New York: St. Martins; London: Macmillan, 1967. Pp. 435. $10.00; 50s.

Fulford, Roger. *Samuel Whitbread, A Study in Opposition.* London: Macmillan, 1967. 50s.
Rev. by Gareth Stedman Jones in *New Statesman,* Dec. 1, 1967, p. 768.

George, M. Dorothy. *Hogarth to Cruikshank: Social Change in Graphic Satire.* London: Allen Lane, The Penguin Press, 1967. Pp. 224. £5 5s.
Rev. in *TLS,* Dec. 21, 1967, p. 1232.

Ginter, Donald E., ed. *Whig Organization in the General Election of 1790: Selections from the Blair Adam Papers.* University of California Press, 1967. Pp. 1x + 276. $8.00.
Correspondence of Whig party organizers directed by William Adam and the Duke of Portland (from 1784 through 1790) shows a more "political" and unified party structure than historians since Namier have supposed for this period. A valuable supplement to John Brooke's introduction to the *History of Parliament* (see *ELN,* III, Supp., 15). (D.V.E.)

Gipson, Lawrence Henry. *The Triumphant Empire*. Part I: The Empire Beyond the Storm, 1770-1776. Part II: A Summary of the Series. Part III: Historiography. New York: Alfred A. Knopf, 1967. Pp. 454. $10.00.
Rev. in *TLS*, Sept. 28, 1967.
Thirteenth and concluding volume of *The British Empire Before the American Revolution*.

Hardie, Martin. *Water-Colour Painting in Britain*. II: The Romantic Period. Ed. by Dudley Snelgrove with Jonathan Mayne and Basil Taylor. London: Batsford, 1967. 242 plates. £6 6s.
Rev. in *TLS*, Nov. 16, 1967, p. 1079.
Contains chapters on "Early Eighteenth Century Painters," "Eighteenth Century Romantics," and "William Blake and Henry Fuseli."

Hayter, Alethea. *A Sultry Month*. London: Faber and Faber, 1965. Pp. 224. 30s.
Rev. by Willard B. Pope in *KSJ*, xvi (1967), 104-05.
The month extended from June 18 to July 13, 1846, and included the time of Haydon's suicide.

Herdan, Innes and Gustav, trans. *The World of Hogarth: Lichtenberg's Commentaries on Hogarth's Engravings*. New York: Houghton Mifflin, 1967. Pp. 297. $12.50.
Rev. by Francis Haskell in *NYRB*, Apr. 6, 1967, pp. 5-6.

Highfill, Philip H., Jr. "Charles Surface in Regency Retirement." *SP*, Extra Series, No. 4 (January 1967), 135-66.
The seventy-seven letters to Thomas Coutts by the actor William "Gentleman" Smith (1730-1819) from 1806 to 1819 "in many subtle ways widens our understanding of the changing status of the acting profession." Smith created the role of Charles Surface.

Hill, Christopher. *Reformation to Industrial Revolution: a social and economic history of Britain, 1530-1780*. London: Weidenfeld & Nicolson, 1967. Pp. 254. 42s.

Horn, D. B., ed. *English Historical Documents 1714-1815*. London: Methuen, 1967. Pp. 126. 22s. 6d.
A slight selection "from Volumes X and XI of *English Historical Documents*," illustrated in haste (the print captioned "Caricature of Pitt and Dundas at the beginning of the French War" is visibly dated "1 May 1798").

Huxley, Gervas. *Lady Elizabeth and the Grosvenors: Life in a Whig Family*. London: Oxford University Press, 1965. Pp. 187. 35s.
Rev. in *History*, lii (1967), 354.

Knight, David M. "The Scientists As Sage." *SIR*, vi (1967), 65-88.
An examination of the philosophical context and implications in which Davy wrote *Consolations in Travel* and Oersted *The Soul of Nature*.

Krumbhaar, E. B. *Isaac Cruikshank, A Catalogue Raisonné with a Sketch of his Life and Work.* University of Pennsylvania Press, 1966. Pp. 177; plates. $20.00.
Rev. by Ronald Paulson in *BNL,* VIII (1967), 746-47.

Macmillan, David S. *Scotland and Australia, 1788-1850.* Oxford: Clarendon Press, 1967. Pp. 434. £3 15s.

Marples, Morris. *Romantics at School.* London: Faber & Faber; New York: Barnes & Noble, 1967. Pp. 206. 30s; $5.00.
Rev. in *TLS,* Dec. 28, 1967, p. 1262, and by Robert M. Adams in *NYRB,* Feb. 15, 1968, pp. 25-27.

Millar, Oliver. *Zoffany and his "Tribuna."* London: Routledge, 1967. Pp. 60; 39 plates. 35s.
Zoffany's conversation piece of English connoisseurs in the Uffizi Palace, considered historically as a document of the Grand Tour.

Millard, Charles W. "A Diplomatic Portrait: Lawrence's 'The Persian Ambassador.' " *Apollo,* LXXXV (1967), 115-21.
Full-color portrait of Mirza Abu'l Hassan Khan, object of much attention in 1810.

Mitchell, Austin. *The Whigs in Opposition 1815-1830.* London: Oxford University Press, 1967. Pp. 276. 38s; $6.10.
Rev. by Gareth Stedman Jones in *New Statesman,* Dec. 1, 1967, p. 768.

Newsome, David. *The Wilberforces and Henry Manning: The Parting of Friends.* Harvard University Press, 1966. Pp. 486. $12.00.

O'Gorman, F. *The Whig Party and the French Revolution.* London: Macmillan; New York: St. Martin's Press, 1967. Pp. xv + 270. $9.00.
This is a thoughtful and compendious study (much documentation is cited, though sparingly quoted; a good deal of it new) of politicians adapting their opinions and behavior to the unprecedented circumstances, up through 1794, set in train by the French Revolution. As the Whig Party was split into two, then into three, it was the Foxites, remaining in opposition to the war and the repression of constitutional liberties, who emerged as the vehicle for the development of a "more modern concept of the ideological unity and institutional coherence of a political party." O'Gorman takes time to differentiate the particulars of character and interaction and resists "facile attempts to explain the Portland schism [for example] within the bounds of any one theory of politics or human nature." (D.V.E.)

Parsons, Coleman O. " 'Pilgrims of Research' in the British Museum: 1820-1862." *QR,* CCCV (1967), 54-66.
Readers located in an old admissions ledger include Isaac Disraeli, Allan Cunningham, Thomas Campbell, George Dyer, William Hone, John Gibson Lockhart, Thomas DeQuincey, John Galt, William Gifford, Benjamin Robert Haydon, Thomas Love Peacock, William Godwin, Thomas Lovell Beddoes, and Charles Lamb.

Richardson, Joanna. *George the Magnificent*: *A Portrait of King George IV*. New York: Harcourt, Brace & World, 1967. Pp. 410. $6.95.
Rev. by J.P. Kenyon in *NYRB*, June 15, 1967, pp. 26-28.

Rollinson, William. *A History of Man in the Lake District*. London: Dent, 1967. Pp. 162. £2 2s.
Rev. in *TLS*, Oct. 19, 1967, p. 990.

St. Clair, William. *Lord Elgin and the Marbles*. Oxford University Press, 1967.
Rev. by Peter Quennell in *S*, July 7, 1967, p. 18.

Stewart, W. A. C., and W. P. McCann. *The Educational Innovators 1750-1880*. London: Macmillan, 1967. 70s.
Rev. by Harry Ree in *New Statesman*, Jan. 26, 1968, p. 115.

Whinney, Margaret, and Rupert Gunnis. *The Collection of Models by John Flaxman* R.A. *at University College London*: *A Catalogue and Introduction*. University of London: The Athlone Press; New York: Oxford University Press. Pp. viii + 72; 24 plates. 55s; $8.80.
A documented catalogue of 120 of Flaxman's plaster models for family monuments—all that survived the bombing of 1941. An earlier catalogue by Talfourd Ely, in 1900, listed 219 models. Oddly the present publication attempts no listing of the objects lost.

Wilkins, Burleigh Taylor. *The Problem of Burke's Political Philosophy*. Oxford University Press, 1967. Pp. 257. $7.70.
Rev. by Francis Canavan in *SIB*, IX (1967), 820-23.

See also Rosenblum ("General 2. Environment"), Jack ("Keats").

Reviews of books previously listed:
CONE, Carl B., *Burke and the Nature of Politics* (see *ELN*, IV, Supp., 13), rev. by Louis I. Bredvold in *BLN*, VIII (1966-67), 646-52; MALINS, E., *English Landscaping and Literature 1660-1840* (see *ELN*, V, Supp., 15), rev. by R.W. Ketton-Cremer in *ES*, XLVIII (1967), 349-50; PAULSON, Ronald, comp., *Hogarth's Graphic Works* (see *ELN*, V, Supp., 15), rev. by Francis Haskell in *NYRB*, Apr. 6, 1967, pp. 5-6.

3. CRITICISM

Auden, W. H., ed., with notes by George R. Creeger. *Nineteenth-Century Minor Poets*. London: Faber, 1967.
Rev. by Timothy Hilton in *New Statesman*, July 28, 1967, p. 120, and as "Auden's Minor Birds" by Anthony Burgess in *S*, Aug. 11, 1967, pp. 161-62.

Barnes, T. R. "The Romantics." Pp. 165-227 in *English Verse*: *Voice and Movement from Wyatt to Yeats*. Cambridge University Press, 1967. Pp. ix + 324. $6.50; paper $2.25.
A sensitive, elementary guided tour. Blake is dealt with in pp. 151-65.

Bernhardt-Kabisch, Ernest. "The Epitaph and the Romantic Poets: A Survey." *HLQ*, XXX (1967), 113-46.

Bostetter, Edward. "Recent Studies in the Nineteenth Century." *SEL,* VII (1967), 741-66.

An omnibus review that includes the work of Mark Reed, Bernard Groom, James Scoggins, and Roger Murray on Wordsworth; George Watson on Coleridge; G. Wilson Knight on Byron; James Rieger on Shelley; Mario D'Avanzo on Keats. See respective listings of these books, below.

Boulton, James T. *Arbitrary Power: An Eighteenth-Century Obsession.* (Inaugural Lecture.) University of Nottingham [1967]. Pp. 24. 2s. 6d.

Examines the fear of, and fascination by, tyrannous power in imaginative literature from Defoe to Coleridge as a neglected but vital literary tradition, manifestations of which have usually been dismissed as partisan politics or else ignored in the political aspect. The concluding suggestion that the Romantics came more directly or immediately to grips with the question should provoke fuller consideration of their "agony." (D.V.E.)

Bronson, B. H. "When Was Neoclassicism?" Pp. 13-35 in Anderson, Howard, and John S. Shea, eds., *Studies in Criticism and Aesthetics, 1660-1800.* Essays in Honor of Samuel Holt Monk. University of Minnesota Press, 1967. Pp. 419. $10.00.

Chatman, Seymour, and Samuel R. Levin, eds. *Essays on the Language of Literature.* Boston: Houghton Mifflin, 1967. Pp. 450. $7.50.

Eigner, Edwin Moss. *Robert Louis Stevenson and Romantic Tradition.* Princeton University Press, 1966. Pp. 258. $6.00.

Fletcher, Richard M. *English Romantic Drama, 1795-1843; a critical history.* New York: Exposition Press, 1967. Pp. 226. $6.50.

Gordon, Ian A. *The Movement of English Prose.* Indiana University Press, 1967. Pp. vii + 182. $5.75.

Chapters 14 and 15 define the "new classical prose" of Johnson, Gibbon, and Burke—and the development of "romantic prose" in Burke, the terror and sentimental novelists, and the essayists (especially in the nineteenth-century magazines).

Gregory, Hoosag K. "Cowper's Love of Subhuman Nature: A Psychoanalytic Approach." *PQ,* XLVI (1967), 42-57.

Irwin, David. *English Neoclassical Art, Studies in Inspiration and Taste.* Greenwich, Connecticut: New York Graphic Society, 1966. Pp. 230; 157 plates. $13.50.

Criticized and refined upon by Ronald Paulson in *SIB,* IX, 815-20.

An uninspired assemblage of the fairly available information about Barry, Fuseli, West, Kauffmann, Banks, Flaxman, Reynolds, Blake, and a few other artists of the Antique, the Gothic, the Sublime and Wicked, and the Romantic. Useful plates, increasing the available reproductions of the work, e.g., of Mortimer, Hamilton, Barry. (D.V.E.)

Kemper, Claudette. "Irony Anew, with Occasional Reference to Byron and Browning." *SEL,* VII (1967), 704-19.

Linnér, Sven. "The Structure and Functions of Literary Comparisons." *JAAC,* xxvi (1967), 169-79.
"With a few exceptions, my examples are chosen from criticism dealing with English Romanticism."

Merton, Stephen. *Mark Rutherford (William Hale White).* New York: Twayne, 1967. Pp. 189. $3.95.
A sensitive, balanced study of this "representative Victorian" whose intellectual stimulators were Wordsworth *and* Byron, Shelley, and Carlyle. (D.V.E.)

Paulson, Ronald. *Satire and the Novel in Eighteenth-Century England.* Yale University Press, 1967. Pp. 318. $8.50.
Includes an analysis of the novel of manners up to Jane Austen.

Sherbo, Arthur. *Christopher Smart, Scholar of the University.* Michigan State University Press, 1967. Pp. 303. $8.50.

Stevenson, John. "Arcadia Re-Settled: Pastoral Poetry and Romantic Theory." *SEL,* vii (1967), 629-38.

Reviews of books previously listed:
BOSTETTER, Edward E., *The Romantic Ventriloquists* (see *PQ,* xliii, 443), rev. by Richard H. Fogle in *JEGP,* lxvi, (1967), 155-56; KROEBER, Karl, *The Artifice of Reality* (see *ELN,* iii, Supp., 9), rev. by Alan Grob in *MP,* lxiv (1967), 264-68; LODGE, David, *Language of Fiction* (see *ELN,* v, Supp., 18), rev. by W.J. Harvey in *EIC,* xvii (1967), 231-37; LOGAN, James V. et al, *Some British Romantics* (see *ELN,* v, Supp., 18), rev. by Lawrence W. Houtchens in *ELN,* v (1967), 65-67; MARSHALL, W.H., *Byron, Shelley, Hunt and "The Liberal"* (see *PQ,* xl, 176), rev. by C.A. Bodelsen in *ES* xlvii (1967), 175-76; ROPPEN, Georg, and Richard SOMNER, *Strangers and Pilgrims* (see *ELN,* iii, Supp., 18) rev. by B.M. Wolvekamp-Baxter in *ES,* xlviii (1967), 355-57; WILKIE, Brian, *Romantic Poets and Epic Tradition* (see *ELN,* iv, Supp., 17), rev. by M.N. Nagler in *CL,* xix (1967), 380-81; and by Stuart Sperry in *MP,* lxiv (1967), 263-64.

4. STUDIES OF AUTHORS

AUSTEN
Burroway, Janet. "The Irony of the Insufferable Prig: *Mansfield Park.*" *CritQ,* ix, No. 2 (1967), 127-38.

Donovan, Robert Alan. *The Shaping Vision. Imagination in the English Novel from Defoe to Dickens.* Cornell University Press, 1966. Pp. ix + 272. $5.75.
Distinguishing between the "outer form" or genre of a literary work and the "inner form" (the objective expression of the author's imaginative vision, of his way of looking at experience as the stuff of his work), Mr. Donovan proposes that by the first half of the eighteenth century the outer form of the

English novel had moved so far toward establishment that the history of the novel from Defoe to Dickens is largely that of "the growing complexity and sophistication" of the inner form, which developed "to contain and display the imaginative vision." Discussing *Mansfield Park* as one novel among nine which illustrate the evolution, Donovan regards this work, though less attractive than other Austen novels, as a product of the same imaginative vision that shaped them. Essentially, this comprehends "a universe ruled by moral necessity," in which character determines action but the aggregate of action does not really define character. "Jane Austen's world . . . is ruled, not by a mechanistic conception of causality, but by a more or less deterministic one." The men and women populating this world, though "trapped in their characters somewhat like crabs trapped in shells which . . . they can neither change nor outgrow," nevertheless have a freedom of choice within the scope of possibility that is theirs: "the impulse to action arises out of character, but it is directed by circumstance, and even more importantly, by circumstance as it is appraised by a fallible intelligence." Quite clearly, this world, seen in its moral and (ultimately) literary reflections, contains both order and variation. In his delineation of it, Donovan has made a significant and persuasive contribution, to stand beside those of Trilling, Mudrick, Wright, and others. (W.H.M.)

Fleishman, Avrom. *"Mansfield Park* in Its Time." *NCF,* xxii (1967), 1-18.
In censuring the "libertine morality" of the Romantic movement, it is argued, this novel reverts to the taste and style of the Augustan age.

Harvey, W. J. "The Plot of *Emma." EIC,* xvii (1967), 48-63.

Knoepflmacher, U. C. "The Importance of Being Frank: Character and Letter-Writing in *Emma." SEL,* vii (1967), 639-58.

Lochhead, Marion. "Jane Austen and the Seven Deadly Sins." *QR,* cccv (1967), 429-36.

Lynch, P. R. "Speculation at Mansfield Parsonage." *N&Q,* xiv (1967), 21-22.
Explains the card game of speculation in *Mansfield Park.*

Nash, Ralph. "The Time Scheme for *Pride and Prejudice." ELN,* iv (1967), 194-97.
Internal evidence, Nash argues, is stronger for dating the composition 1799 and 1802 than 1811-12.

Poirer, Richard. *A World Elsewhere: The Place of Style in American Literature.* New York: Oxford University Press, 1966. Pp. xi + 257. $5.75
Rev. by Walker Gibson in *ELN,* v (1967), 70-73, who discusses Poirer's "exciting comparison of *Huckleberry Finn* and *Emma."*

Waldron, Philip. "Style in *Emma."* Pp. 59-70 in Colmer, John, ed. *Approaches to the Novel.* Adelaide: Rigby, 1966. Pp. x + 136.

White, Edward M. "A Critical Theory of *Mansfield Park." SEL,* vii (1967), 659-77.

See also Paulson ("3. Criticism").

Reviews of books previously listed:
BRADBROOK, Frank W., *Jane Austen and Her Predecessors* (see *ELN*, V, Supp., 20), rev. by John Wiltshire in *CQ*, II (1967), 184-193; CRAIK, W.A., *Jane Austen: The Six Novels* (see *ELN*, IV, Supp., 18), rev. by John Wiltshire in *CQ*, *II* (1967), 184-193; LITZ, A. Walton, *Jane Austen: A Study of Her Artistic Development* (see *ELN*, IV, Supp., 18-19), rev. by Howard S. Babb in *MP*, LXV (1967), 81-83, and by John Wiltshire in *CQ*, II (1967), 184-93.

BARRINGTON
Staples, Hugh B., ed. *The Ireland of Sir Jonah Barrington: Selections from His Personal Sketches.* University of Washington Press, 1967. Pp. xxvii + 328. $7.50.
Mr. Staples has "done what a modern editor would do had Sir Jonah submitted the manuscript to him—excise the prolix and the platitudinous," reducing the original heterogeneous memoirs to about one third and rearranging them in "some kind of logical order"—with a few helpful notes.

BLAKE
Adlard, John. "The Annandale Druids: A Blake Crux." *N&Q*, XIV (1967), 19-20.

Altizer, Thomas J. J. *The New Apocalypse: The Radical Christian Vision of William Blake.* Michigan State University Press, 1967. Pp. xxi + 226.
Blake returned to Christianity's original apocalyptic faith by passing through "an interior reversal and transformation of the Western Christian tradition." Before Blake this had been possible only in the non-verbal arts. Unlike their mystical counterparts, Blake's epics "are genuine works of literature. . . directed to the imaginative faculties of every man." Altizer, hammering with deftly wielded blocks of quotation from Blake and Hegel, forges "a new and radical form of faith . . . both mystical and contemporary at once." For the metaphysically or theologically minded, this celebration of the death of God in the awaking of Albion is absorbing and self-annihilating. (D.V.E.)

Ansari, Asloob Ahmad. *Arrows of Intellect: A Study in William Blake's Gospel of the Imagination.* Aligarh, India: Naya Kitabghar, 1965. Pp. 248. Rs. 20.00.
A "fresh inroad upon the dark and misty regions of Blake's symbolic mythology," with "religious creativity" at the end of the trail.

Baine, Rodney M. "Blake's 'Tyger': The Nature of the Beast." *PQ*, XLVI (1967), 488-98.
Links with Lavater, Swedenborg, Fuseli.

Bentley, G. E., Jr. "Blake's Hesiod." *Library*, XX (1965), 315-20.

Bentley, G. E., Jr., ed. *Tiriel: Facsimile and Transcript of the Manuscript, Reproduction of the Drawings, and a Commentary on the Poem.* Oxford: Clarendon Press; New York: Oxford University Press, 1967. Pp. 94; 25 plates. 60s; $9.60.
Most notable in this first separate edition of *Tiriel* are the drawings—all that have been traced (nine of the twelve recorded)—assembled and published with the text for the first time. In contrast to the rough state of the manuscript, they

are carefully composed and executed, in a style which Blake never exactly repeated but which is strikingly close to that of his "transforming" Neoclassical contemporaries - see Rosenblum ("General 2. Environment").
Bentley's newly transcribed text differs from Gleckner's and Erdman's only in deletions and a few uncertain readings. (For comment, see D.V. Erdman, *Blake Newsletter*, Dec. 15, 1967, p. 11.) The critical commentary depends largely on earlier interpretations. (I.H.C.)

Butlin, Martin. *William Blake.* (Tate Gallery Little Book Series.) London: Tate Gallery Publications Department, 1966. Pp. 16; 33 plates, 9 in color.
A handy sample-book of the variety of designs in the Tate collection, with a judicious and informative introductory essay. Butlin, despite the "bafflingly wide" range of the subjects of the twelve large color prints of ca. 1795, which he calls "arguably Blake's greatest works," is convinced that the group was conceived as a whole. He points helpfully to clues suggesting that each print illustrates a stage in man's Fall. (D.V.E.)

Connolly, Thomas E., and George R. Levine. "Pictorial and Poetic Design in Two Songs of Innocence." *PMLA,* LXXXII (1967), 257-64.
See Paley, below.

Doherty, F. M. J. "Blake's 'The Tyger' and Henry Needler." *PQ,* XLVI (1967), 566-67.
Needler's "Copy of Verses" as the covert target of Blake's poem.

Dorfman, Deborah. "Blake in 1863 and 1880: The Gilchrist *Life.*" *BNYPL,* LXXI (1967), 216-38.
Examines the changes made in the 1880 edition as reflecting "the real and lasting accomplishments of the Blake revival" as well as a growing tendency to read the poems "as personal history in disguise."

Douglas, Dennis. "Blake and the Grotesque." *Balcony/The Sydney Review,* No. 6 (Summer 1967), pp. 9-16.
Blake's "willingness to disturb the reader's sense of equilibrium" (aptly illustrated and briefly sorted into four varieties: "the 'metaphysical' grotesque," "the satiric grotesque," "the fanciful grotesque," and "the macabre-grotesque") is suggestively related to his willingness to preach "the revolution and the apocalypse at one and the same time." I should like to see Mr. Douglas carry out the program he sketches here. (D.V.E.)

Douglas, Dennis. "Blake's 'Europe': A Note on The Preludium." *AUMLA,* No. 23 (May 1965), pp. 111-16.

Erdman, David V. "The Binding (et cetera) of *Vala.*" *Library,* XIX (1964 [1968]), 112-29.
Article reviewing the facsimile *Vala or The Four Zoas,* ed. G. E. Bentley, Jr., 1963 (see *PQ,* XLIII, 1964, 448); revisions bring the textual corrections and additions abreast of the 2nd printing, 1966, of the Doubleday *Blake.* Strictly nondefinitive about the chronology of the growth of the MS.

Friedman, John Block. "The Cosmology of Praise: Smart's *Jubilate Agno.*" *PMLA,* LXXXII (1967), 250-56.
Did Smart intend his poem as "the expression of a world view with moral imperatives, which we might compare with Blake's prophetic books? Or was the

poem undertaken . . . as a kind of therapy or daily exercise in faith . . . ?" The truth "lies somewhere in between."

Harrold, William. "Blake's 'Tyger' and Vaughan's 'Cock-Crowing.' " *N&Q*, XIV (1967), 20-21.
Close similarities claimed.

Hardy, Ann. "Blake and Fuseli—The View from Eden." *Alphabet*, No. 12 (August 1966), pp. 39-51.

Hilles, Frederick W. "A 'New' Blake Letter." *YR*, LVII, No. 1 (1967), 85-89.
Transcript and discussion of a letter from Blake to Hayley, 16 July 1804, now in the author's collection.
But "Mr. Hoare: from" should read "Mr. Hoare, fears"; and "I will again read Clarissa & they [?the letters in that book] must be admirable" should have been transcribed and queried thus: "I will again read Clarissa &c [;] they [? Richardson's novels] must be admirable." (D.V.E.)

Kaplan, Fred. " 'The Tyger' and Its Maker: Blake's Vision of Art and the Artist." *SEL*, VII (1967), 617-27.

Keynes, Geoffrey, ed. *Milton: A Poem*. Paris: The Trianon Press for the William Blake Trust, London, 1967. Pp. 16; 51 plates. 48 gns.
Reviewed, from an esoteric bias, in *TLS*, Sept. 14, 1967, p. 280; this bias criticized by John E. Grant and defended by the reviewer Nov. 2, p. 1045, eliciting a letter from Keynes Nov. 9, p. 1069; further exchange by Grant and the reviewer Dec. 7, p. 1197.

Keynes, Geoffrey, ed. *Songs of Innocence and of Experience*. New York: Orion Press; Paris: Trianon Press, 1967. Pp. xvii + 204; 55 plates. Boxed, $20.00.
The color plates are a simplified by-product of the hand-colored Blake Trust facsimile of 1955, generally inferior in color and line. (It is a pity that one of the more simply colored originals was not chosen for this edition.) Sir Geoffrey's brief notes of "tentative explanation," though "deliberately . . . superficial," are useful in calling attention to curious graphic details. (D.V.E.)

Lemaitre, Henri. "A propos de William Blake." *EA*, XX (1967), 290-96. 3 plates.

Paley, Morton D., ed. *Blake Newsletter*. Nos. 1-3 (1967).
Contains various lists, queries, notes informal (No. 3 begins with "Damoniana") and formal (e.g. notes of explication and of textual emendation), and a sprinkling of controversy: the reading of "The Little Boy Found" by T.E. Connolly and G.R. Levine in *PMLA* (see above) is attacked by John E. Grant in No. 2 (pp. 7-9) and defended by Connolly and Levine in No. 3 (pp. 17-18); Paley's 1966 "Tyger" article is debated by M.J. Tolley and Paley in No. 2 (pp. 10-14); a discussion of textual problems in *The Four Zoas* is begun by W.H. Stevenson in No. 3 (pp. 13-16) and continued this year in No. 4 (March 1968), pp. 6-8.

Spicer, Harold. "Biblical Sources of William Blake's *America*." *BSUF*, VIII, No. 3 (1967), 23-29.

Williams, Raymond. "Prelude to Alienation." *Dissent*, XI (1964), 303-15.
Blake, Wordsworth, and subsequently Carlyle afford early but deep insight into the complex of "alienation."

See also Fletcher ("General 3. Criticism"); Hardie ("English 2. Environment"); Barnes ("3. Criticism").

Reviews of books previously listed:
BENTLEY, G.E., Jr., and Martin K. NURMI, *A Blake Bibliography* (see *ELN*, III, Supp., 21), rev. by Peter Ure in *RES*, XVIII (1967), 83-86; DAMON, S. Foster, *A Blake Dictionary* (see *ELN*, IV, Supp., 21-22), rev. by John E. Grant in *PQ*, XLVI (1967), 328-29; and by Michael J. Tolley in *SoR*, II (1967), 269-77; ENGLAND, Martha Winburn, and John SPARROW, *Hymns Unbidden* (see *ELN* V, Supp., 22), rev. by R.L. Colie in *MLQ*, XXVIII (1967), 496-97; by Edna Parks in *Notes* (Music Library Assn.) March, 1968, pp. 487-88; and by Erik Routley in *Bulletin* (Hymn Soc. of Great Britain and Ireland), VI (1967), 111-13; ERDMAN, David V. and Harold BLOOM, eds., *The Poetry and Prose* (see *ELN*, IV, Supp., 22), rev. by Michael J. Tolley in *SoR*, II (1967), 269-77; GILHAM, D.G., *Blake's Contrary States* (see *ELN*, V, Supp., 22-23), rev. by Margaret Bottral in *CritQ*, IX (1967), 189-90; by John E. Grant in *PQ*, XLVI (1967), 329-30; and by U. Laredo in *ESA*, X (1967), 200; HIRSCH, E.D., Jr., *Innocence and Experience* (see *ELN*, III, Supp., 22-23), rev. by Peter Ure in *RES*, XVIII (1967), 83-86; KEYNES, Geoffrey, ed., *The Complete Writings* (see *ELN*, V, Supp., 23), rev. by John E. Grant in *PQ*, XLVI (1967), 327-28; and by Michael J. Tolley in *SoR*, II (1967), 269-77; OSTRIKER, Alicia, *Vision and Verse in William Blake* (see *ELN*, IV, Supp., 23-24), rev. by Martin K. Nurmi in *JEGP*, LXVI (1967), 461-63; by Margaret Shook in *MP*, LXV (1967), 79-81; and by Michael J. Tolley in *SoR*, II (1967), 269-77.

BYRON

Brownstein, Rachel Mayer. "Byron's *Don Juan*: Some Reasons for the Rhymes." *MLQ*, XXVIII (1967), 177-91.

Eliot, C.W.J. "Lord Byron, Early Travellers and the Monastery at Delphi." *American Journal of Archaeology*, LXXI (1967), 283-91; Plates 85-86.

Gleckner, Robert F. *Byron and the Ruins of Paradise*. The Johns Hopkins Press, 1967. Pp xxiv + 365. $8.95.
Rev. by G. M. Matthews in *NYRB*, May 23, 1968, pp. 23-28.
This book is the most serious and sustained attempt yet made to examine Byron's poems as a canon presenting a fundamentally consistent and coherent vision of man and life. The vision is the "frighteningly dark" prophetic one of "man's eternal fall and damnation in the hell of human existence," the ruins of paradise. It is not a theological vision, though Byron frequently adopts the biblical metaphor: God is not a meaningful presence in his universe, and Paradise is simply a mocking dream of man, the lonely mental outlaw wandering through the wasteland of this world to a futile end, doomed as much by his virtues, his desire for good, as by his vices. Since Gleckner sees this vision as bleakly informing all the poetry, he finds the distinctions usually drawn between the romantic-melancholy Byron of *Childe Harold* and the satiric-comic Byron of *Don Juan* relatively unimportant, even irrelevant. The "private-public" Byron of the letters (and the narrator of *Don Juan*) is essentially a pose behind which hides the real Byron who is truly revealed only in the serious poetry. Consequently most of the book is concerned with this poetry, only twenty to thirty pages being alloted to *Beppo* and *Don Juan*. Indeed, two-thirds of the book is

devoted to the poetry Byron wrote before *Childe Harold* III. No previous modern critic has devoted such systematic discussion to and claimed such importance for the early poems—the *Hours of Idleness,* the satires, the "Oriental" tales, the first two cantos of *Childe Harold, Hebrew Melodies*—as stages in the development of a self-conscious and serious artist searching for the most effective form and voice in which to express his vision. This leads Gleckner from time to time into over-subtle analyses, as in carefully distinguishing three voices in the first two cantos of *Childe Harold*—the protagonist, the narrator, and the poet. But certainly he has demonstrated most impressively that later patterns of thought and imagery are perceptible in the earliest poems, and consistently and deliberately developed in successive poems; and this becomes his justification for the cursory treatment of the later poems in themselves. The major difference between earlier and later poems is that Byron's existential vision grew ever more intense and unrelieved; and therefore the function of poetry increasingly became for him a means "To maintain one's sanity in an insane world," a way of confronting and controlling the meaninglessness of existence, of creating "out of despair a coherent vision of the causes of that despair in history and himself" sufficient to sustain him against apathy or surrender. Thus Gleckner is led by his own remorseless thesis to find *Don Juan a* "grim" poem, an "ultimately despairing fable for our time," having fundamentally to do "not with morality or immorality but with nothingness, with a world devoid of value and humanity."

As this brief survey suggests, Gleckner's study with all its virtues cannot avoid the dangers of repetitiveness and reductiveness inherent in the pursuit of so single-minded a theme. The qualities that distinguish one poem from another, that give them power and vitality and excitement, tend to be blurred or buried. All poems are anatomized down to the same bony structure. Though in an admirable effort to escape the biographical trap Gleckner concentrates upon poems detached from the life, he goes to the opposite extreme and eliminates the humor and gusto that more than anything else finally gave sanity to the vision of nothingness; the zestful delight in the absurd that counteracts the despair. And he tends to discount or ignore—as in his discussion of *Childe Harold* and the later plays—the pull toward existential action (sexual, psychological, revolutionary) that is certainly as strong and essential a characteristic as the existential despair of the "ruin amid ruins." But the important thing is that Gleckner has written for the first time the kind of critical study of Byron that has been taken for granted in the approach to the other romantics. He has treated Byron seriously as a serious poet, and has proved how profitable it is to view the poetry as a coherent unit. He has opened up all kinds of dramatic possibilities for future critics of Byron. (E.E.B.)

Hagelman, Charles W., Jr., and Robert J. Barnes, eds. *A Concordance to Byron's Don Juan.* Cornell University Press, 1967. Pp. xiii + 981. $12.00

Rev. by Leslie A. Marchand in *KSJ,* xvii (1968), 132-33.

The publication of a concordance to *Don Juan* by itself is justified by the poem's bulk—this volume is a bit longer than the whole Arnold concordance or the whole Yeats one (which excludes the plays)—and by the fact that only this quarter of Byron's work has appeared in a complete and accurate text. The *Don Juan* list is programed to be merged, ultimately, into a concordance of a complete modern edition. Yet in that case certain "common" but uncommon words, harmlessly omitted from this index, will need to be re-inserted. In a complete concordance we will want to be able to compare, for example, the distributions of archaisms.

Archaic "dost," "hadst," and "shalt," omitted from the four-volume *Concordance to the Poetry of Byron* by Ione Dodson Young (1965; listed in *ELN,* v Supp., 26), are also omitted here—though their frequencies in *Don Juan* are given. On the other hand, "betwixt" and "howe'er," omitted here but given in Young, have frequency figures (1 and 12 respectively) which show that Young caught all the occurrences in *Don Juan;* what we lack for comparison is a frequency for "however" outside *Don Juan* (where it is 28). Evidently one needn't wait to make fairly solid comparisons of the vocabularies of *Childe Harold, Don Juan,* the tales, the plays—except that the number of "partially listed" words in Young is very large. (D.V.E.)

Lombardi, Thomas W. "Hogg to Byron to Davenport: An Unpublished Byron Letter." *BNYPL,* LXXI (1967), 39-46.

Marshall, William H. "The Byron Collection in Memory of Meyer Davis, Jr." *LC,* XXXIII (1967), 8-29.
This sampling of the "richness and variety" of a recent gift collection includes a will of 1809, some of Byron's own books, first editions, and manuscript poems and letters, some seen to supply missing biographical links.

Marshall, William H. "The Byron Will of 1809." *LC,* XXXIII (1967), 97-114.
This will, not hitherto seen by biographers, affords perspective on Byron's later wills—showing, for example, a concern for Augusta's welfare long before the intensification of their relationship. Text transcribed in full, with annotation.

McGann, Jerome J. "Byron, Teresa, and *Sardanapalus.*" *KSMB,* XVIII (1967), 7-22.
"To a large extent Myrrha probably did grow out of Byron's experience of Teresa, but it is neither likely nor true that Byron's idea of Teresa was quite the same as Teresa's."

McGann, Jerome. "The Composition, Revision, and Meaning of *Childe Harold's Pilgrimage III.*" *BNYPL,* LXXI (1967), 415-30.

Steffan, Truman Guy. "Some 1813 Byron Letters." *KSJ,* XVI (1967), 9-21.
Four unpublished letters and two memoranda from the University of Texas Library.

Thompson, James R. "Byron's Plays and *Don Juan*: Genre and Myth." *BuR,* XV, No. 3 (1967), 22-38.

See also brief notes by Elmer L. Brooks, John D. Jump, Hugh T. Keenan, J.C. Maxwell, and T.G. Steffan in *N&Q,* XIV (1967), 295-303.

See also Bostetter, Kemper ("3. Criticism"); Reizov ("French. Staël").

Reviews of books previously listed:
KNIGHT, G. Wilson, *Byron and Shakespeare* (see *ELN,* V, Supp., 25), rev. by John D. Jump in *CritQ,* IX (1967), 93-94; LOVELL, Ernest J., ed., *Medwin's Conversations of Lord Byron* (see *ELN,* V, Supp., 25-26), rev. by Peter L. Thorslev, Jr., in *KSJ,* XVI (1967), 97-99; YOUNG, Ione Dodson, ed., *A Concordance to the Poetry of Byron* (see *ELN,* V, Supp., 26), rev. by Leslie A. Marchand in *KSJ,* XVI (1967), 96-97.

CLARE

Doherty, Francis. "An Unpublished Letter of Lady Caroline Lamb to Clare." *N&Q,* xiv (1967), 297-99.

Green, David Bonnell. "New Letters of John Clare to Taylor and Hessey." *SP,* lxiv (1967), 720-34.
"The seven new letters . . . add to our knowledge . . . of Clare's relations with Lamb, H.F. Cary, John Hamilton Reynolds, Allan Cunningham, and other literary contemporaries and supplement our awareness of his social and political views."

COBBETT

Review of book previously listed:
Osborne, John W., *William Cobbett* (see *ELN,* v, Supp., 27), rev. by Gertrude Himmelfarb in *VS,* xi (1967), 240-41.

COLERIDGE

Hassler, Donald M. "Coleridge, Darwin, and The Dome." *Serif,* iv, No. 3 (1967), 28-31.
"It is a tribute to Coleridge's greater rhetorical skill that Xanadu has become part of our heritage whereas the Temple of Nature has not."

Healey, George H. "A Sleeper in New Bond Street." *CLJ,* No. 2 (Spring 1967), pp. 49-62.

Kelly, Michael J. "Coleridge and Dream Phenomenology." *MSE,* i, No. 1 (1967), 1-7.

San Juan, E., Jr. "Coleridge's 'The Eolian Harp' as Lyric Paradigm." *Person,* xlviii, No. 1 (1967), 77-88.

Schulz, Max F. "Comforts and Consolations: An Unwritten Work by S. T. Coleridge." *Coranto,* iv, No. 2 (1967), 3-11.
Between 1804 and 1806 "Comforts and Consolations" loomed large for Coleridge as a literary project.

Simmons, J. L. "Coleridge's 'Dejection: an Ode': a Poet's Regeneration." *UR,* xxxiii (1967), 212-18.

Stempel, David. "Coleridge and Organic Form: The English Tradition." *SIR,* vi (1967), 89-97.
Hume's contribution to the idea.

Sundell, Michael G. "The Theme of Self-Realization in 'Frost at Midnight.'" *SIR,* vii (1967), 34-39.

Walsh, William. *Coleridge: The Work and the Relevance.* London: Chatto and Windus, 1967.
Rev. with Yarlott's *Coleridge* and Rader's *Wordsworth* as "Conflicts" by John Barrell in *New Statesman,* Aug. 25 1967, p. 232
William Walsh begins his book on Coleridge by announcing that it is "addressed both to the general reader and the student of literature. . . ." If that is to say that it is superficial, then such a warning should be taken seriously. There is

nothing new in Walsh's discussions of Coleridge's biography, his criticism, his poetry, his theory, and his critics. Walsh beats a consistent drum: he favors the concrete and dismisses all, in the poetry and in the prose, that is "apt to float away into a thin, and to modern nostrils distasteful, philosophic air." Such a view transforms Coleridge into someone who must be nearly indistinguishable from Walsh, and, indeed, it is one of the stylistic faults of the book that it is often difficult to distinguish the subject from its author. Walsh's antipathy to Wordsworth and to English romanticism makes it difficult for him to deal with his subject. He strains to turn Coleridge into a "realist." Couple these with the nature of his simplistic case for Coleridge's relevance, and one has an undistinguished study. (K.T.A.)

Warfel, Harry R. "Image vs. Abstraction: Coleridge vs. Pope and the Tests of Poetry." In Schulz, Max F. et al, eds., *Essays in American and English Literature presented to Bruce Robert McElderry, Jr.* Ohio University Press, 1967. Pp. xiv + 334. $6.50.

Watson, George. *Coleridge the Poet.* New York: Barnes & Noble, 1966. Pp. xi + 147. $4.00.

Rev. by R.L. Brett in *CritQ*, ix (1967), 188-89.

Mr. Watson firmly states his purpose: "to show how little substance there has ever been in the myth of his [Coleridge's] defeat or abdication as a poet—to reveal, in fact, how successful a poet he was and how critical a poet." Watson demonstrates that Coleridge was a *successful* poet really because he was a *critical* poet, because he could write in a continuing tradition, significantly adapting to his particular needs the conscious imitation of established literary forms in which he excelled (and imitation in this sense is carefully distinguished from Aristotelian *mimesis*). The translations of *Wallenstein* are most successful when most Shakespearean, "Frost at Midnight" is in imitation of Cowper, *The Ancient Mariner* of Medieval ballad, "Christabel" of Gothic horror, and "Kubla Khan" of two contrasting styles of poetry, the descriptive and "fanciful" in the first thirty-six lines, "a programme for imaginative creation" in the last eighteen. To Watson symbolism seems to be the mark of the successful adaptation of established forms, especially in the "magic triad," though there is no demonstrable inevitability moving a poem from the imitative to the symbolic. Coleridge's achievement is in individuality: "his own poetry never seems so much itself as when it is pretending to be something else."

The first of Watson's three propositions, that Coleridge did not abdicate as a poet, does not really follow from the other two. That in his early years Coleridge "was a great poet, and great not merely in aspiration but by virtue of what he actually did," is a suggestion rarely disputed. But it does not follow that he sustained his performance through other years. Emphasizing the critical nature of good poetry, Watson tends to relate the roles of *poet* and of *sage;* yet the worlds of poetry and philosophy, though contiguous and occasionally merging at the edges, are essentially distinct, and in middle years Coleridge moved the center of his activities from one to the other; or, as Watson admits toward the end of his book, somewhat to the confusion of at least one reader, "What rather happened was that, at the age of thirty, he ceased to be a prolific poet and became an occasional one." The reason which Watson assigns to the change is as applicable to Wordsworth as to Coleridge, so that, implicitly, we no longer need seek a center of imperfection in the poetic being of the one and not in the other: the concern of the poems of the productive years was "the loss-and-gain of growing up," a theme that could hardly be sustained as the immediate consciousness of the transition faded.

Although this book, like others, refutes the myth that Coleridge "failed to achieve his promise as a poet and a sage," it makes little headway against the myth of Coleridge's poetic abdication. The two provinces, one measured by qualitative and the other by temporal standards, are simply not related. The attempt to impose such a relation upon the raw materials contributes significantly to the weakness of the book. But there are other factors. Asserting in the Preface that he has "not usually referred to the views of others unless for some special purpose," Watson really ignores much recent scholarship which has already met some of the points that he makes. Nor does he give sufficient attention to the intellectual background of so *critical* a poet. Though yoking Coleridge and Wordsworth in their withdrawal from the major role of poet, Watson suggests no reason that the older Romantics should be particularly concerned with "the loss-and-gain of growing up." And perhaps finally, though he proposes arguing his case on the formal examination of Coleridge's poems, Watson occasionally overlooks such aspects of individual works as the dramatic structure of "The Eolian Harp"; here, disregarding the essential juxtaposition of two views of life and two levels of response to the microcosm and the larger world, Mr. Watson asserts that "Sara is merely a nuisance."
At the center of the book, nevertheless, remains the proposition that Coleridge was a good poet because in the highest sense he was a critical poet, demonstrating his originality by "annexing the past to his art as no English poet had done before him." (W.H.M.)

Yarlott, Geoffrey. *Coleridge and the Abyssinian Maid.* London: Methuen, 1967.
Rev. rather severely by C.B. Cox in *S*, June 30, pp. 770-71; by John Barrell in *New Statesman*, Aug. 25, p. 232; and in *TLS*, July 27, 1967, p. 686; letter of reply from author in *TLS*, Aug. 10, 1967, p. 732.

Zall, Paul M. "Coleridge and Sonnets from Various Authors." *CLJ*, No. 2 (Spring 1967), pp. 49-62.
Reprinted in 1968 in a separate booklet, with facsimile of the Huntington copy of Coleridge's sheet of sonnets and the text of Bowles's 21 sonnets of 1789: *Coleridge's "Sonnets from Various Authors" bound with Rev. W.L. Bowles' "Sonnets" annotated by Paul M. Zall.* Glendale, California: La Siesta Press. Pp. 68. (Waking from siesta, Zall inserts two sheets of errata.)
Coleridge's keen interest in Bowles is seen as a reflection of his shift from political to social revolution. Bowles "provided a model for poetry of revolution aimed at social happiness and moral order, just as Milton had provided the model for political revolution." In 1797 he found a new model in Wordsworth. (D.V.E.)

Zall, P. M. "Coleridge's Unpublished Revisions to 'Osorio.' " *BNYPL*, LXXI (1967), 516-23.

Zall, P. M. "Sam Spitfire; or, Coleridge in *The Satirist.*" *BNYPL*, LXXI (1967), 239-44.

See also Barfield ("General 3. Criticism"); Bostetter ("English 3. Criticism").

Reviews of books previously listed:
APPLEYARD, J.A., *Coleridge's Philosophy of Literature* (See *ELN*, IV, Supp., 26), rev. by R.L. Brett in *CritQ*, IX (1967), 188-89; by John Colmer (enthusiastically) in *MLR*, LXII (1967), 514-15; and by R.H. Fogle in *MLQ*, XXVIII (1967),

113-14; CALLEO, David P., *Coleridge and the Idea of the Modern State* (see *ELN*, V, Supp., 28), rev. by David V. Erdman in *Political Science Quarterly*, LXXXIII (1968), 94-96; and by R.J. White in *N&Q*, XIV (1967), 315-16; DESCHAMPS, Paul, *La formation de la pensee de Coleridge* (See *ELN*, IV, Supp., 27), rev. by John Colmer, in *MLR*, LXII (1967), 514-15; SUTHER, Marshall, *Visions of Xanadu* (See *ELN*, IV, Supp., 29), rev. by J.B. Beer in *RES*, XVIII (1967), 87-90; and by John Colmer in *MLR*, LXII (1967), 514-15.

COLERIDGE, SARA
Martin, C. G. "Sara Coleridge: An Unpublished Letter." *N&Q*, XIV (1967), 51-52.

CONSTABLE
Reynolds, Graham. *Constable: The Natural Painter.* London: Adams & Mackay Cory; New York: McGraw-Hill, 1965. Pp. 238. £5 5s; $17.50.
Rev. by E.D.H. Johnson in *VS*, X (1967), 303-05.

CRABBE
Mills, Howard, ed. *George Crabbe: Tales, 1812 and other selected poems.* Cambridge University Press, 1967. Pp. xxxviii + 445. $9.50; paper $2.75.
Rev. in *TLS*, Sept. 21, 1967, p. 841.
A vigorous introduction, with a broad selection of complete poems or sections. Sees in the dynamic part of Crabbe's "mixture of inertia and originality" a struggle of escape from the 18th-century way of presenting character; an over-whelming of didactic elements by "a poem's sheer fictional life." (D.V.E.)

Thomas, W. K. "Crabbe's Borough: The Process of Montage." *UTQ*, XXXVI (1967), 181-91.
On the composite nature of the town.

Review of book previously listed:
CHAMBERLAIN, Robert L., George *Crabbe* (see *ELN*, V, Supp., 30), rev. by Arthur Pollard in *MLR*, XLII (1967), 319.

CROKER
Poole, Bernard, ed. *The Croker Papers.* London: Batsford, 1967. 50s.
An abridgement of Louis Jennings' three-volume work of 1884.
Rev. by Robert Blake in *S*, March 31, 1967, p. 370; and by Paul Johnson (with other books) under title "A Very Bad Man?" *New Statesman*, Apr. 14, 1967, p. 512.

DEQUINCEY
Burwick, Fredrick, ed. *Selected Essays on Rhetoric by Thomas De Quincey.* Southern Illinois University Press, 1967. Pp. xlviii + 272 (numbered 81-352). $7.
A convenient collection of DeQuincey's principal writings on rhetoric. The 38 page introduction is the fullest available discussion of DeQuincey's contribution to the field and the first to demonstrate his merging of Scottish association and German aesthetics, including the relation of his concept of "mind play" to Schiller's *Spieltrieb*. The text is by slightly enlarged photo-offset from Masson's

Collected Writings, Vol. x (1889-90)—accounting for the curious page numbering. One wishes it had been possible to provide a corrected text, or at least to improve on Masson's less-than-adequate notes. "Language," of which Masson says "place of original not ascertained," was first published in a slightly different version in *Hogg's Instructor,* vi (1851) under the title "On the Present Stage of the English Language." (J.E.J.)

Hopkins, Robert. "De Quincey on War and the Pastoral Design of *The English Mail-Coach.*" *SIR,* vi (1967), 129-51.

Review of book previously listed:

GOLDMAN, Albert, *The Mine and Mint* (see *ELN,* iv, Supp., 29-30), rev. by Derek Roper in *RES,* xviii (1967), 215-16.

GALT

Kinsley, J., ed. *Annals of the Parish or The Chronicle of Dalmailing during the Ministry of The Rev. Micah Balwhidder.* London: Oxford University Press, 1967. Pp. 242. 25s.

Rev. in *TLS,* Dec. 28, 1967, p. 1257.

GODWIN

Duerksen, Roland A. "Caleb Williams, Political Justice, and Billy Budd." *AL,* xxxviii (1966), 372-76.

Finds parallels in the treatment by Godwin and Melville of innocence, justice, duty, and virtue.

Palacio, Jean de. "État présent des études Godwiniennes: A propos de deux livres récents." *EA,* xx (1967), 149-59.

A review of recent Godwin studies with special attention given to Burton Pollin's *Education and Enlightenment in the Works of William Godwin* (see *PQ,* xlii, 548).

Pollin, Burton R. *Godwin Criticism: A Synoptic Bibliography.* University of Toronto Press, 1967. Pp. xlvi + 659. $18.50.

3,500 entries in more than ten languages, up through 1966, have been annotated, and coded as A, R, P, C, M, B, etc. (article, review, passage, short comment, mention, book, etc. on Godwin), with a few journalistic writings *by* Godwin slipped in (coded G) simply because "not . . . listed in bibliographies as yet"—and because there was not room in this volume to include a full bibliography of Godwin's works. (But we are promised a revision and extension of the already quite substantial Godwin bibliography in Mr. Pollin's *Education and Enlightenment* volume of 1962.)

The chatty, candid Introduction must be read—for obiter dicta on the tribulations of compilation and of coping with the logic of a computer. The fascinated will also read the preface by George W. Logemann on the philosophy and techniques of programming whereby "in the future" a work of this kind shall be both wholly under the compiler's control and "automatically . . . completely free from errors" (as the present work is plainly not)—and to help one get the hang of this initially puzzling format. The explanation of symbols is not where the Introduction says it belongs, nor is it noted in the Contents; the adjective "major" is not where it belongs in the heading of Index VI (a selective duplication of the main list). But all eleven Indices do have their uses, and the whole volume is both valuable and efficient. (D.V.E.)

Pollin, Burton. "Nicholson's Lost Portrait of William Godwin: A Study in Phrenology." *KSJ*, xvi (1967), 51-60.

Rothstein, Eric. "Allusion and Analogy in *The Romance of Caleb Williams.*" *UTQ*, xxxvii (1967), 18-30.

Storch, Rudolph F. "Metaphors of Private Guilt and Social Rebellion in Godwin's *Caleb Williams.*" *ELH*, xxxiv (1967), 188-207.

See also Grob ("Wordsworth").

Review of book previously listed:
POLLIN, Burton R., ed. *Italian Letters, or the History of Count de St. Julian* (see *ELN*, iv, Supp., 31), rev. by Peter Faulkner in *MLR*, lxii (1967), 117-18.

HAZLITT
Albrecht, W. P., and J. D. O'Hara. "More on Hazlitt and the Functions of the Imagination." *PMLA*, lxxxiii (1968), 151-54.
A critical exchange.

Cockburn, Alexander. "Fun at a Funeral Feast." *New Statesman*, July 21, 1967, p. 94.
Discusses the question of whether Hazlitt's published remarks about Gifford would be considered libelous today.

Reviews of book previously listed:
ALBRECHT, W.P., *Hazlitt and the Creative Imagination* (see *ELN*, v, Supp., 32-33), rev. by Sylvan Barnet in *KSJ*, xvi (1967), 106-07; and by Stanley Jones in *RES*, xviii (1967), 346-47.

HOGG
See Lombardi ("Byron").

HOLCROFT
Review of book previously listed:
BLAINE, Rodney M., *Thomas Holcroft and the Revolutionary Novel* (see *ELN*, v, Supp., 32), rev. by Peter Faulkner in *MLR*, lxii (1967), 117-18.

HUNT
Cheney, David R. "Leigh Hunt's 'Evening the First' of *Musical Evenings.*" *KSMB*, xviii (1967), 39-42, with plate.
Newly discovered documents suggest that "Evening the First" may have been completed.

Leigh Hunt on Eight Sonnets of Dante. Introd. by Rhodes Dunlap. Typographic Laboratory. University of Iowa School of Journalism, 1965. Pp. x + 22. $2.00.
Rev. by Carl Woodring in *KSJ*, xvi (1967), 107-08.

Gittings, Robert. "Leigh Hunt's *Examiner.*" *TLS*, Nov. 23, 1967, p. 1111.
A report on four years' reading of "almost every word of this extraordinary production."

JEFFREY

Morgan, Peter F. "Principles and Perspectives in Jeffrey's Criticism." *SSL,* IV (1967), 179-93.

KEATS

Bush, Douglas. *John Keats: His Life and Writings.* (Masters of World Literature Series.) New York: Macmillan, 1966. Pp. 224. $4.95.

The author himself calls this book a "skiff," sailing in the wake of the "richly laden ship" of Walter Jackson Bate, to whom he addresses his dedication. The critical emphasis is the familiar evolutionary-ethical, and the probable limitations of a series audience are scrupulously recognized. For more incisive evaluations, new readers should still go to Bush's earlier and shorter studies of Keats. (I.H.C.)

Chayes, Irene H. "Dreamer, Poet, and Poem in *The Fall of Hyperion.*" *PQ,* XLVI (1967), 499-515.

The Fall of Hyperion is not an abortive attempt to revise *Hyperion,* but a new work in its own right whose subject is the creative process, the experience of composing an epic, and the relation of the narrator to both.

D'Avanzo, Mario L. "Keats's and Vergil's Underworlds: Source and Meaning in Book II of *Endymion.*" *KSJ,* XVI (1967), 61-72.

Parallels with *Aeneid,* Bk. VI; Endymion as "the Aeneas of Romanticism."

Gordon, Ian A. "Keats and the English Pindaric." *REL,* VIII, No. 2 (April 1967), 9-23.

Haworth, Helen E. "The Redemption of Cynthia." *Humanities Association Bulletin,* XVIII (Fall 1967), 80-91.

A study of *Endymion.*

Jack, Ian. *Keats and the Mirror of Art.* Oxford: Clarendon Press, 1967. Pp. xxiii + 309; 42 plates. $10.10.

Rev. by Jack Stillinger in *KSJ,* XVIII (1968), 121-23.

An interesting new attempt, if not the first, to relate descriptive passages in Keats's poetry to particular paintings and works of sculpture, by artists ranging from Raphael to John Martin. The evidence is usually persuasive, and the critical implications are obviously important. Unfortunately, Jack's interest in identifying specific sources, sometimes several for a relatively short passage, tends to leave the poems themselves fragmented and unresolved. (I.H.C.)

Mayhead, Robin. *John Keats.* Cambridge University Press, 1967. Pp. 127. 17s 6d; Paper 8s 6d.

Rev. in *TLS,* Sept. 7, 1967, p. 801.

A useful brief survey of Keats's most significant poetry. The arrangement is in general chronological, though Mr. Mayhead quite reasonably departs from chronology in order to take the "great odes" as a group and a climax. The book is aimed at "readers in other English speaking countries, countries where English is a second language, or even for whom English is a foreign language." It should indeed be helpful to Keats students everywhere, since Mr. Mayhead's analyses and interpretations are both sensitive and sensible. Mild exception might be taken to the author's statement that Keats's scholarship is chiefly biographical. This passes over the elaborate explications of the past twenty-five years. (R.H.F.)

Olney, Clarke. "Keats as John Foster's 'Man of Decision.' " *KSJ*, XVI (1967), 6-8.

Ormerod, David. "Nature's Eremite: Keats and the Liturgy of Passion." *KSJ*, XVI (1967), 73-77.

Osler, Alan. "Keats and Baldwin's 'Pantheon.' " *MLR*, LXII (1967), 221-25.
Suggested source for passages in *Endymion* and *Hyperion*.

Robinson, Dwight E. "A Question of the Imprint of Wedgwood in the Longer Poems of Keats." *KSJ*, XVI (1967), 23-28.
Illustrated article continuing Robinson's earlier one on Wedgwood and Keats in *KSJ*, XII (1963), 11-35.

Rogers, Robert. "Keats's Strenuous Tongue: A Study of 'Ode on Melancholy.' " *L&P*, XVII (1967), 2-12.
Discussed by Aileen Ward, "The Psychoanalytic Theory of Poetic Form: A Comment," pp. 33-35.

Russell, Stanley C. " 'Self-Destroying' Love in Keats." *KSJ*, XVI (1967), 79-91.

Stillinger, Jack, ed. *The Letters of Charles Armitage Brown*. Harvard University Press; Oxford University Press, 1966. Pp. 438. $12.00; £4 16s.
Rev. in *TLS*, Dec. 22, 1966, p. 1190; by Miriam Allott in *N&Q*, XIV (1967), 316-18; by R.W. King in *RES*, XVIII (1967), 347-48; by William H. Marshall in *JEGP*, LXVI (1967), 159-62; and by Joanna Richardson in *KSJ*, XVI (1967), 94-96.

Wills, Garry. "Classicism in Keats's Chapman Sonnet." *EIC*, XVII (1967), 456-60.

See also notes on Keats by Bhabatosh Chatterjee, J. C. Maxwell, H. D. Purcell, and J.-C. Salle in *N&Q*, XIV (1967), 23-24.

See also Bostetter ("English 3. Criticism").

Reviews of books previously listed:
BUSH, Douglas, *John Keats* (see *ELN*, V, Supp., 34), rev. by C.B. Cox in *S*, Feb. 3, 1967, p. 140; and by David Perkins in *KSJ*, XVI (1967), 93-94; EVERT, Walter, *Aesthetic and Myth in the Poetry of Keats* (see *ELN*, IV, Supp., 32-33), rev. by David Perkins in *KSJ*, XVI (1967), 93-94.

LAMB
Standley, Fed L. "Charles Lamb: An Unpublished Album Verse." *ELN*, V (1967), 33-34.
"The Boy, the Mother, and the Butterfly," three quatrains, 1827. (Possibly instructive analogue to Blake's "The Fly.")

See also Green ("Clare").

LANDOR

Prasher, A. La Vonne. "The Censorship of Landor's *Imaginary Conversations." Bulletin of the John Rylands Library*, XLIX (1967), 427-63.

Review of book previously listed:

VITAUX, Pierre, *L'oeuvre de Walter Savage Landor* (see *ELN, III*, Supp., 36), rev. by Geoffrey Carnall in *MLR*, LXII (1967), 710-11.

LEWIS

Bishop, Morchard. "A Terrible Tangle." *TLS*, Oct. 19, 1967, p. 989.

A look at "the actual contents" of *Tales of Terror*, once attributed to Lewis but since rejected as a parody of his *Tales of Wonder*, finds them uncommonly good and suggests that some of them may be Lewis parodying himself.

MOORE

McClary, Ben Harris. "Another Moore Letter." *N&Q*, XIV (1967), 24-25.

Review of book previously listed:

DOWDEN, Wilfred S., ed., *The Letters of Thomas Moore* (see *ELN*, IV, Supp., 35), rev. by Ernest J. Lovell, Jr., in *SR*, LXXV (1967), 358-64.

PEACOCK

Sage, Judith Ann. "George Meredith and Thomas Love Peacock: A Note on Literary Influence." *ELN*, IV (1967), 279-83.

REYNOLDS

Reviews of book previously listed:

JONES, Leonidas M., ed., *Selected Prose of John Hamilton Reynolds* (see *ELN*, v, Supp., 36), rev. by E.E. Bostetter (see above, "English 3. Criticism"); by James T. Boulton in *ES*, XLVIII (1967), 462-63; by William H. Marshall in *KSJ*, XVII (1968), 123-26; and by Jack Stillinger in *JEGP*, LXVI (1967), 465-67.

SCOTT

Anderson, James. "Sir Walter Scott as Historical Novelist." *SSL*, IV (1966-67), 29-41, 63-78, 155-78; v (July 1967), 14-27, 83-97, and to be continued.

Contents: Part I. Scott's opinions on historical fiction. Part II. Scott's practice in historical fiction. Part III. *Old Mortality*. Part IV. *A Legend of Montrose*.

Falle, George. "Sir Walter Scott as Editor of Dryden and Swift." *UTQ*, XXXVI (1967), 161-80.

Hook, Andrew D. *"The Bride of Lammermoor*: A Reexamination." *NCF*, XXII (1967), 111-26.

The novel exhibits a "creative balancing of the romance and realism of old world and new."

Kilroy, James F. "Narrative Techniques in *The Master of Ballantrae." SSL*, v (1967), 98-106.

Lauber, John. *Sir Walter Scott*. New York: Twayne Publishers, 1966. (Twayne's English Authors Series, No. 39.) Pp. 166. $3.95.

A brief account of Scott's life, poetry, criticism of fiction, and novels, together with a special examination of select novels and a concluding consideration of the Waverley Novels and "Their Place in Literature." The book does not contain any new discoveries for the scholar; it seems to be intended to fill a niche in the Twayne's English Authors Series and designed for the beginner who must work up Scott for an examination since the discussions so carefully balance praise and censure. The beginning student, however, will find Thomas Crawford's *Scott* (1965) not only more satisfactory but also briefer (118 pp.); and the advanced student will find the fresh and stimulating studies of Welsh and Hart much more to his purpose. (K.C.)

Parker, W. M. "Scott and Russian Literature." *QR*, cccv (1967), 172-78.

Ruff, William, and Ward Hellstrom. "Some Uncollected Poems of Sir Walter Scott: A Census." *N&Q*, xiv (1968), 292-94.

See also Nuñez de Arenas and Romero Mendoza ("Spanish 2. General").

Reviews of books previously listed:
CRAWFORD, Thomas, *Sir Walter Scott* (see *ELN*, v, Supp., 36), rev. by Coleman O. Parsons in *SSL*, iv (1966), 113-18; DONOVAN, Robert Alan, *The Shaping Vision: Imagination in the English Novel from Defoe to Dickens* (see *ELN*, v, Supp., 17) (contains study of *Redgauntlet*), rev. by Lionel Stevenson in *SAQ*, lxvi (1967), 272-73; HART, Francis R., *Scott's Novels* (see *ELN*, v, Supp., 36-37), rev. by David Daiches in *MLQ*, xxix (1967), 117-20; by Coleman O. Parsons in *SSL*, iv (1966), 113-18; and by W.L. Renwick in *MLR*, lxii (1967), 709-10; PARSONS, Coleman O., *Witchcraft and Demonology in Scott's Fiction* (see *ELN*, iv, Supp., 36), rev. by D.M. Mennie in *N&Q*, xiv (1967), 33-34.

SHELLEY, MARY
Fleck, P. D. "Mary Shelley's Notes to Shelley's Poems and *Frankenstein*." *SIR*, vi (1967), 226-54.
The article examines the two works mentioned in its title "to ascertain whether they . . . reveal a certain hostility towards Shelley's Romanticism" (p. 226). In a well-argued study of this probably moot question, Fleck points out some interesting parallels (and contrasts) between *Frankenstein* and *Alastor*. (D.H.R.)

Luke, Hugh J., Jr., ed. *The Last Man* (see *ELN*, iv, Supp., 37), rev. by J.M.S. Tompkins in *KSJ*, xvi (1967), 108-09.

Pollin, Burton R. "Mary Shelley as the Parvenue." *REL*, viii, No. 3 (1967), 9-21.

SHELLEY
Bass, Eben. "The Fourth Element in 'Ode to the West Wind.'" *PLL*, iii (1967), 327-38.

Bateson, F. W. "Shelley on Wordsworth: Two Unpublished Stanzas from 'Peter Bell the Third.'" *EIC*, xvii (1967), 125-29.
The omitted stanzas "provide an unexpected sidelight on the gossip . . . about Wordsworth's private life."

Echeron, J. C. "Shelley on Wordsworth." *ESA*, IX, No. 2 (1966), 119-45.

Fogle, Richard Harter. "Dante and Shelley's *Adonais*." *BuR*, XV, No. 3 (1967), 11-21.

Halliburton, David G. "Shelley's 'Gothic' Novels." *KSJ*, XVI (1967), 39-49.
This casual essay attempts "to examine the merits" of *Zastrozzi* and *St. Irvyne* "as novels" and to study their relevance for Shelley's later work and for the tradition of the Gothic novel. It is only mildly successful. (One index to the scholarly care of the piece is that the publication date for *St. Irvyne* is given incorrectly.) There is still room for a detailed study of Shelley's novels and the questions that Halliburton raises. (D.H.R.)

King-Hele, Desmond. "Shelley and Dr. Lind." *KSMB*, XVIII (1967), 1-6.
A sage and rebel, Lind introduced Shelley to Plato, Godwin, Darwin, and the habit of printing pamphlets.

Luke, Hugh J., Jr. "An Overlooked Obituary Notice of Shelley." *PLL*, II (1966), 38-46.
From *Rambler's Magazine* for 1822-23.

Massey, Irving. "The First Edition of Shelley's *Poetical Works* (1839): Some Manuscript Sources." *KSJ*, XVI (1967), 29-38.
Finding that the texts of certain poems first published in 1839 came from one of Mary Shelley's copybooks (Bodleian MS Shelley adds. d. 9), Massey compares the texts in that notebook with other transcripts by Mary, with Shelley's holographs in the Bodleian notebooks, with *Poetical Works* (1839), and (occasionally) with Thomas Hutchinson's Oxford edition.

Norman, Sylva. "Twentieth-Century Theories on Shelley." *Texas Studies in Literature and Language*, IX (1967), 223-37.

Pollin, Burton R. " 'Ozymandias' and the Dormouse." *DR*, XLVII (1967), 361-67.
On the meaning of the pseudonym "Glirastes," with which Shelley signed his "Ozymandias."

Raben, Joseph. "Shelley's 'The Boat on the Serchio': The Evidence of the Manuscript." *PQ*, XLVI (1967), 58-68.
Raben argues that "an examination of the available manuscripts and a close analysis of the published version reveal" that "the 'poem' now called 'The Boat on the Serchio' is an unassimilated composite of manuscript fragments intended for a variety of poems" and "that some of them were probably composed in 1817 and 1818." He is, however, unsuccessful in attempting (pp. 62-63) to date Bodleian MS Shelley adds. e. 17 earlier than 1821: "Lines written on Hearing the News of the Death of Napoleon" (May-November 1821) is exactly adjacent to the draft of "The Boat on the Serchio" (pp. 208-202 *reverso* and pp. 218-208 *reverso*), and the notebook also contains "Charles the First" (1821-22). Nor is there any apparent connection between the MSS of "The Boat" fragments and either *Rosalind and Helen* or the translations from Virgil in what Raben calls "adds. e. 4" (really "e. 4"; "adds. e. 4" has been renumbered "adds. d. 3" and there is no longer a Shelley MS in the Bodleian numbered "adds. e. 4"). (D.H.R.)

ELN   6 Supp. (1968)   1 – 158

37

Raine, Kathleen. "A Defense of Shelley's Poetry." *SoR(La)*, III (1967), 856-73.

Reiman, Donald H. "Roman Scenes in *Prometheus Unbound* III.iv." *PQ*, XLVI (1967), 69-78.
This essay explicates two passages of the drama (III.iv.111-121 and III.iv.164-179) in the light of the scenes in Rome on which these descriptions are based—the Sala della Biga in the Vatican Museum and various baroque groupings that feature Egyptian obelisks.

Reiter, Seymour. *A Study of Shelley's Poetry*. University of New Mexico Press, 1967. Pp. 335. $8.95.
Rev. in *TLS*, 22 Feb., 1968.
This is not really a "study" of Shelley's poetry but a series of summaries (with liberal quotations). Reiter is enthusiastic about Shelley (which is a fine thing these days), recognizes something of his social philosophy, but is usually content to skim along on the surface and ignore difficulties. There are, for instance, many knotty problems in *The Triumph of Life*, but one would never guess it from Reiter's breezy ten-page outline. Sometimes he just gives up. *Alastor* gets a five-page summary (70 lines taken up by quotations). *Adonais* is dismissed in six pages, *The Witch of Atlas* in one. Although *Prometheus Unbound* gets a full dress treatment in 13 pages, these contain little beyond a summary of the action. Prometheus is Prometheus, Jupiter is Jupiter, and so on. This is puzzling because we are informed in the Preface that "My explication interprets every difficulty in the poem." Actually it interprets nothing. On the other hand such often neglected poems as *The Revolt of Islam, The Masque of Anarchy, Peter Bell the Third*, and *Swellfoot the Tyrant* are discussed in some detail, usually quite intelligently, and with useful background material. (How, though, one might ask, did Mammon become "Church" and Purganax "Government"?) The book ends on a note of almost utter confusion in its treatment of the poems to Jane Williams, as Reiter is misled by Ivan Roe's unsupported and unsupportable theory that Hogg was the father of William Shelley, and then argues that "We meet not as then we parted" was addressed to Mary and not to Jane and deals with Shelley's reaction to Mary's "confession" of William's paternity! (K.N.C.)

Ridenour, George M., ed. *Shelley: A Collection of Critical Essays*. Englewood Cliffs, N. J.: Prentice-Hall, 1965. Pp. 182. $3.95.
Rev. by Glenn O'Malley in *KSJ*, XVI (1967), 110-12.

Rieger, James. *The Mutiny Within: The Heresies of Percy Bysshe Shelley*. New York: Braziller, 1967. Pp. 283. $6.50; Paper $2.95.
Rev. by Stuart Curran in *KSJ*, XVII (1968), 130-32; and by G.M. Matthews in *NYRB*, Apr. 20, 1967, pp. 21-23.
The new material uncovered in this study is slight: a few sentences in a Godwin manuscript that might bear on *Caleb Williams;* a reference in *Queen Mab* to the religious war against the Albigenses; some background for Polidori's *The Vampyre*. Mostly it is theory, and theory of a rather high-flown character. Some of the theories are simply assertions, some seem to be based on invention rather than discovery, some are so confused that it is hard to tell what they are. Generally they are ushered in with a trumpet blast and then collapse into very little. For instance we are told — indeed, Mary Shelley herself tells us— that Beatrice in *Valperga* is a "Paterin" heretic and we are led to believe that

this is somehow to produce revelations about *The Cenci*, but nothing is forthcoming. Similarly we are led to believe that the Rosicrucianism and the *Rose Croix* will throw new light on *The Wandering Jew* and *Queen Mab*, but no such light is shed. A study of Gnosticism is to explain Shelley's serpent lore and other matters, but everything of relevance on this will be found in Grabo's *The Magic Plant* (1936). This then leads us to Demogorgon and his "snakelike Doom," which produces the following: "Imagination becomes a Doom for one revolutionary Hour by taking the twisted body of the Ophite Nun." We are warned that the "temptation to equate Asia with Sophia Prunicos should be resisted." (It is, indeed, not difficult to resist.)

The author is even less persuasive when he enters the realm of biography. He theorizes that Shelley deliberately capsized the *Don Juan*, which means that he not only committed suicide but murdered Williams and Vivian. In order to support this theory—which runs counter to the mass of evidence—Rieger argues that the *Don Juan* was not "as is generally supposed" an "open" (undecked) boat. This he bases on a drawing now in the British Museum. This must be the drawing noted in Sotheby's Catalogue for December 16-17, 1963 (item No. 530) and reproduced in Glynn Grylls's *Trelawny* (p. 80). But this drawing shows that although there was a small cabin, five feet long, in the stern, the rest of the boat, about 20 feet, was undecked. Hence, the boat could have been swamped by waves, which is the only point of any consequence. On the basis of one journal entry by Polidori, Rieger suggests that Mary took the idea for *Frankenstein* from Polidori and hints that she destroyed her journal from May 1815 to July 1816 in order to hide the theft. The Polidori journal entry records a talk between Shelley and Polidori "about principles—Whether man was to be thought merely an instrument." Who initiated the conversation is not recorded, and, in any case, the word "instrument" is clearly being used in a social not a physical sense. (K.N.C.)

Schulze, Earl J. *Shelley's Theory of Poetry: A Reappraisal.* The Hague, Paris: Mouton, 1966. Pp. 237. 29 Dutch Guilders.
Rev. by Joseph DeRocco in *KSJ*, xvii (1968), 128-30.
Received too late for review.

Swaminathan, S. R. "Shelley's 'Triumph of Life.'" *N&Q*, xiv (1967), 305-06.

Reviews of books previously listed:
O'MALLEY, Glenn, *Shelley and Synesthesia* (see *ELN*, iii, Supp., 41-42), rev. by Richard H. Fogle in *JEGP*, lxvi (1967), 158-59; REIMAN, Donald H., *Shelley's "The Triumph of Life": A Critical Study* (see *ELN*, iv, Supp., 39-40), rev. by P.H. Butter in *MLR*, lxii (1967), 319-20; and by R.A. Foakes in *RES*, xviii (1967), 216-17; ROGERS, Neville, ed., *The Esdaile Poems* (see *ELN*, v, Supp., 39), rev. by P.H. Butter in *MLR*, xlii (1967), 711-12; by Anthea Morrison in *DUJ*, xxviii (1967), 171-72; and by Lawrence J. Zillman in *KSJ*, xvi (1967), 102-03; WASSERMAN, Earl R., *Shelley's "Prometheus Unbound"* (see *ELN*, iii, Supp., 40-41), rev. by Harold Bloom in *ELN*, iv; (1967), 303-04; by Donald H. Reiman in *KSJ*, xvi, (1967), 99-102; and by Melvin T. Solve in *Arizona Quarterly*, xxii (1966), 184-86.

SMITH

Schneider, Duane B. "Unpublished Letters of Sydney Smith." *N&Q*, xiv (1967), 307-08.

SOUTHEY

Curry, Kenneth. "The Published Letters of Robert Southey: a Checklist." *BNYPL,* LXXI (1967), 158-64.

Martin, C. G. "Robert Southey: Two Unpublished Letters." *N&Q,* XIV (1967), 295.

WORDSWORTH

Curtis, Jared R. "William Wordsworth and English Poetry of the Sixteenth and Seventeenth Centuries." *CLJ,* No. 1 (Winter 1966), pp. 28-39.

Echeruo, J. C. "Shelley on Wordsworth," *ESA,* IX (1966), 117-45.

Ellis, Amanda M. *Rebels and Conservatives: Dorothy and William Wordsworth and Their Circle.* Indiana University Press, 1967. Pp. xiv + 367. $10.00.
This is a panoramic study that circles the lives of the Wordsworths, leaving them for vignettes of those whose careers abutted theirs, and returning for further narrative. Such a method defies chronology and forces upon Professor Ellis much repetition and an occasional contradiction and factual error. The book was seventeen years in the making, and perhaps the long passage of time accounts for some of these flaws. Since the author had already achieved success in historical fiction with *Elizabeth, the Woman,* and in legends with *Legends and Tales of the Rockies,* perhaps she wished to bridge the gap between fiction and scholarship. Her attempt, despite 600 bibliographical items appended to a narrative unencumbered by footnotes, will serve as an introduction to the "legends and tales" of the Wordsworth circle. Dorothy Wordsworth finds yet another champion, this time for both her muse-like qualities and for her womanliness. (K.T.A.)

Finch, John A. " 'The Ruined Cottage' Restored: Three Stages of Composition, 1795-1798." *JEGP,* LXVI (1967), 179-99.
Valuable study of evidence for defining the chronology of composition of what was to become the first book of *The Excursion.* The "first stage" of composition, when the poem was called "Incipient Madness" can be dated only roughly, between the limits of September 1795 and early 1797. The "second stage," a developmental one, begins in the spring of 1797 and ends in June, 1797. The "third stage," which brought the poem to "the essential shape and content it was to retain," occupies the first two and a half months of 1798. (K.K.)

Gill, Stephen C. "Wordsworth's 'Never Failing Principle of Joy.' " *ELN,* XXXIV (1967), 208-24.
Laborious and none-too-original effort to show Wordsworth's changing conception of the nature and function of "joy." (K.K.)

Grob, Alan. "Wordsworth and Godwin: A Reassessment." *SIR,* VI (1967), 98-119.
"Wordsworth's disagreement with Godwin and 'the whole tribe of authors of that class' involved not particular points of doctrine but the far more sweeping rejection of a false methodology which sought to reason man into those great moral truths which could only influence and alter him when implanted in his heart by the workings of experience . . . or the writings of mighty poets." A valid argument which would have been even more salutary thirty years ago, when prevailing conceptions of Wordsworth's "philosophy" were much simpler than they are today. (K.K.)

Heffernan, James A. W. "Wordsworth and Dennis: The Discrimination of Feelings." *PMLA,* LXXXII (1967), 430-36.
Dennis provided Wordsworth with the "means for defining the special feelings produced by the qualitative effect of thought upon emotion." These special feelings became increasingly important to Wordsworth as he matured, and we must understand how he regarded them if we are to comprehend his development (both as poet and critic) *after* 1800. Whether or not the direct influence of Dennis is as important as Heffernan implies, his insistence that Wordsworth's conception of the nature of "emotion" evolved significantly is a valuable contribution to more balanced evaluations of Wordsworth's total accomplishment. (K.K.)

Heffernan, James A. W. "Wordsworth on the Sublime: The Quest for Interfusion." *SEL,* VII (1967), 605-15.
Wordsworth's developing value for "interfusion" derives from the concept of the sublime enunciated by Burke, but Wordsworth "achieves a sublimity that is peculiarly his own: the sense of a unity which transcends multiplicity without destroying it." (K.K.)

Hertz, Neil H. "Wordsworth and the Tears of Adam." *SIR,* VII (1967), 15-33.
Analogies of method and point of view between the final two books of *Paradise Lost* and "The Ruined Cottage."

James, G. Ingli, and Howard Mills. "Wordsworth's Unknown. Two Points of View." *Anglo-Welsh Review,* XV, No. 36, (Summer 1966), 67-76.

Jordan, John E. "The Hewing of *Peter Bell*." *SEL,* VII (1967), 559-603.
Useful if unexciting study of the development of the poem in manuscript and revisions in various editions between 1819 and 1845. (K.K.)

King, Alec. *Wordsworth and the Artist's Vision: An Essay in Interpretation.* Athlone Press, University of London, 1966. Pp. vi + 180. 21s.
This book is aptly titled, for it is a long essay that maintains that Wordsworth's best poetry, "written after his apprenticeship to poetry was over and before he moved towards more orthodox attitudes, is best understood as an artist's vision, not as the work of a poetic philosopher or an observer of country ways." Professor King, of Monash University in Melbourne, makes an impressive case for such a view. Using modern painters' theories of seeing, he does for Wordsworth what Harold Bloom did for Shelley through the use of Buber's I-thou relationship. King's book, then, is not merely a critical book on Wordsworth's poetry, but it is a book about seeing, an instructional eye opener. From the vantage point of artistic vision, King is able to deal persuasively with an integration of Wordsworth's vision with his morality: "The senses, for Wordsworth, were not merely agents of the classifying brain, they were moral agents." King's argument is against Wordsworth as a subjective poet and for a view of him as a poet of " 'out there', in the firm contours and processes of living things." Along the way, King is able to skillfully relate Wordsworth's theory of poetic diction to that of the seventeenth century and to face squarely the question of Wordsworth's understanding of the world of spirit. "[Wordsworth] looked at things with no less sense of their palpable material presence than a scientist does; but looking with the whole of his personal spirit he saw their life, not merely their measurable matter-of-factness; and further he saw the one life that rolled through them and through all things. They became, not mere things, but presences filling the earth with something that spoke to and answered his own body and spirit, and in communion with which he saw what he belonged to and with a sober certainty of waking joy." If that sounds pas-

sionate, it grows out of the passion of conviction that King has won earlier by his perceptive modification of our customary understanding of what Wordsworth meant by "joy."

This book is well written, quite a delightful and insightful essay, but it has a messianic tone which can become abrasive, as it does in the final chapter when King addresses himself to the major spiritual problems of the twentieth century and attempts to demonstrate how Wordsworth's poetry will help us to solve them. Whether Wordsworth and/or the artist will save us is moot, but that King depicts Wordsworth as one of those artistic visionaries "seeking the visible world in themselves" is very much to the point. (K.T.A.)

Langbaum, Robert. "The Evolution of Soul in Wordsworth's Poetry." *PMLA,* LXXXII (1967), 265-72.

An extremely well written and lucid argument that "it is the main purport of Wordsworth's poetry to show the spiritual significance of this world, to show that we evolve a soul or identity through experience and that the very process of evolution is what we mean by the soul." Langbaum skillfully defines the fashion in which Wordsworth uses ideas of Plato, Locke, and Hartley to develop his unique "naturalistic revelation." A major critical contribution. (K.K.)

Liversidge, J. H. "John Ruskin and William Boxall: Unpublished Correspondence." *Apollo,* LXXXV (1967), 39-44.
Letter of Wordsworth to Boxall, May 21, 1846.

Montgomery, Marion. "Stranger in a Strange Land: Wordsworth in England, 1802." *MQ,* VIII (1965), 307-17.
On five sonnets which Wordsworth wrote in London in 1802.

Moorman, Mary. "The True Portraiture of William Wordsworth." *CLJ,* No. 3 (Autumn 1967), pp. 26-50.

Murray, Roger N. *Wordsworth's Style: Figures and Themes in the Lyrical Ballads of 1800.* University of Nebraska Press, 1967. Pp. ix + 166. $4.75.
Rev. by Karl Kroeber in *Style,* I (1967), 165-68.
This is the best detailed study of Wordsworth's style that I have encountered. Although Professor Murray's scope is limited (as is indicated by his title) and his claims for the significance of his findings are invariably modest, he presents a penetrating analysis of Wordsworth's language and special handling of poetic figures which should form the basis for all future investigations into this topic. Murray's basic technique consists in analyzing with extreme care Wordsworth's diction, the analyses leading to demonstrations of how particular word-choices are determined by the theme and substance of each poem. Perhaps the central feature of his findings is illustrated by his comment on Wordsworth's "equivocation"—his particular mode of paradox: "Wordsworth characteristically imposes rather strict limitations on his language through his contexts; his themes are profound, but few, and when we cast about for 'chance' networks of meaning, we meet, coming and going, the same themes. The magic alternatives of the Wordsworthian term appear to be to explore, on the one hand, its ties with the realm of literal and scrupulous fact, and, on the other hand, its ties with a realm in which the soul of man and the soul of nature commune. The key words, like his key natural objects, are media that communicate between these realms. . . ." Murray discusses, besides equivocation, Wordsworth's repetition, his use of transitive and intransitive verbs, his preferred forms of synecdoche

and personification, and his "concrete metaphors." To these last especially, Murray attributes Wordsworth's power to "convince us of his sincerity and profundity," demonstrating how, by avoiding "strong" metaphors, "The poet . . . does not make metaphors; he discovers the veritable homologies among things." Equally impressive is the discussion of the nature and importance of Wordsworth's special forms of personification. Here, as throughout the book, Murray stresses that "the purpose of drawing the human realm and the realm of nature into closer proximity in our thinking is the purpose that apparently governs all of Wordsworth's figures . . . certain of our traditional rhetorical divisions are in his case not applicable and . . . the underlying reason . . . is that the rhetorical divisions themselves in some instances rest on an assumed discontinuity between the animate and inanimate realms of being, an assumption that is not in accord with Wordsworth's view. . . ." Virtually every page of this gracefully written little book is rewarding. Murray's meticulously supported evaluations not only illuminate Wordsworth's particular attainment in the 1800 *Lyrical Ballads* but also, by implication, force the reader to reconsider the standard presuppositions about Romantic poetic style in general. One looks forward with keen pleasure to Professor Murray's proposed study of Wordsworth's later style. (K.K.)

Owen, W. J. B., ed. *Wordsworth and Coleridge: Lyrical Ballads, 1798.* London: Oxford University Press, 1967. Pp. xxxi + 179. 10s 6d.
Rev. in *TLS,* Sept. 21, 1967, p. 841.

Potts, Abbie Findlay. *The Elegiac Mode: Poetic Form in Wordsworth and Other Elegists.* Cornell University Press, 1967. Pp. x + 460. $9.00.

This is an impressive book. Its range, its erudition, its forthrightness are all, as Professor Carl Woodring, who saw it through the press, has put it in his afterword, "the mellow fruit of a lifetime of reading, teaching, and meditating." If the fruit is not as "mellow" as one might like at times, there is a tanginess to its judgments, to its wide-ranging suggestiveness that should both stimulate the taste and whet the appetite for new challenges and serious reconsiderations of both poets and poems in fresh contexts.
The late Professor Potts, who died in 1964, displays an understanding of classical elegy that is significant in itself. That she applies it to the poetry of the nineteenth and twentieth centuries, centering on Wordsworth's elegiac verse, is both the most valuable and the most controversial contribution of her long study. The best sense of the elegist is that of a "meditative and revelatory vision for its own sake, satisfying the hunger of man to see, to know, to understand." Elegy is, too, "a procedural form" and not merely a personal voice. Its music is flute sound, best adapted in English to the fourteener of the ballad stanza. Professor Potts is a skilled reader of metrical patterns, and her skill allows us new ways to hear a different music in the early poems of Wordsworth and Coleridge. When she turns her full attention to Wordsworth's poetry (in more than a third of her book) it is to demonstrate that his elegiac verse links the elegiac past and future. Her discussions of "Peter Bell" and *The Excursion* are impressive attempts to resurrect poems that do not stand high on our critical scale. In such analyses, and in her discussion of the *Poems of National Independence and Liberty,* she displays the strengths of looking at these poems under a new generic light and the weaknesses of mistaking illumination for poetic accomplishment. In this regard, her study of Wordsworth's sources and reading displays his debts to literary tradition, both ancient and contemporary, but perhaps, like Robert Mayo's article on "The Contemporanety of the *Lyrical Ballads,*" distorts his originality. Her theory of Wordsworth's poetic development depends upon a highly controversial premise, and, if granted, an enlightening one: poetry is a movement toward "ethical

clarity"; hence elegaic poetry is a superior mode. The poems of "powerful obscurity" thus get devalued, and *The Excursion* and the *Poems of National Independence and Liberty* rise dramatically on her normative scale.

Wordsworth's career is the "paradigm of an elegaic poet in an elegaic age." If this leads Professor Potts to turn every Wordsworth fault into a virtue of the elegist, it allows her at the same time to place Wordsworth in a poetic context that stretches back to the Greek and Latin elegists and extends forward through the nineteenth century to link him with such modern poets as Yeats and Lawrence. (K.T.A.)

Rader, Melvin. *Wordsworth; A Philosophical Approach.* Oxford: Clarendon Press, 1967. Pp. x + 217. $6.10.

In 1931 Professor Rader published in *Presiding Ideas in Wordsworth's Poetry* the first significant philosophic analysis of Wordsworth's poetry based on contrasts between earlier and later versions of *The Prelude,* made available, of course, by De Selincourt's edition. *Presiding Ideas* deserves an important place in the history of Wordsworthian studies. Unfortunately, Professor Rader's new book will not assist in the proper assessment of his earlier work. The new book reproduces the substance of the earlier monograph. What additions are made contribute little of major value to Wordsworthian scholarship of 1967, in large measure because Professor Rader has not made good use of the wealth of scholarship-criticism of the past decade. This is a pity, because he has lost none of his ability to explain lucidly the ideas contained within poetic figures, and he retains his skill at recognizing acute insights when he does notice more recent criticism, e.g., his comment on C.C. Clarke's *Romantic Paradox,* p. 186. (K.K.)

Rayan, Krishna. "Statement by Omission; the Case of *The Prelude.*" *EIC,* XVII (1967), 448-55.

Reed, Mark L. *Wordsworth: The Chronology of the Early Years, 1770-1799.* Harvard University Press, 1967. Pp. xi + 369. $9.00.

What Professor Reed has given us, in skeletal and often cryptic barebones entries, is an indispensible outline of Wordsworth's first thirty years. He tells us where the poet was, what he was doing, with whom he was visiting, and what he was writing. Some of the entries, culled from a massive number of manuscript and published sources, provide genuine correctives of the dating for events in Wordsworth's career.

This book provides the raw material for future biographical and textual studies. But the user must care a good deal about the details of Wordsworth's career, and he must display a good deal of patience, to get from Reed's book the information that can be found in it. That Wordsworth eats cheese in May 1798 or that Dorothy finds bird's eggs on a particular day may not be significant for even the dedicated scholar, but such information is, often by mere juxtaposition, tied up with Wordsworth's first meeting with Hazlitt or Dorothy's relationship with Coleridge. While this is primarily a work of factual data, it provides endless possibilities for imaginative conjecture.

The appendices offer Reed's judgments on some crucial issues for which the chronology itself only provides a welter of confusing and sometimes contradictory evidence. These judgments weigh the evidence and discriminate among the data, and Professor Reed's judgments are informed and discreet. They provide correctives to the biographies and, perhaps more important, to the textual notes of the De Selincourt and Darbishire edition. On occasion Reed overwhelms one with evidence, and one must be familiar with much of the manuscript description to follow his argument.

For this painstakingly amassed data we must all be grateful, sift and refine it as we may. Patience is also in order, since the next projected volume will, at this pace, extend the chronicle only as far as 1807. Wordsworth lived to 1850.

It is to be noted, in caution, that Reed is reluctant to assert; he deals in degrees of probability—"probably," "perhaps," and "possibly" in descending order. His reluctance, however, is not coyness but grows out of a humility earned by those who have handled the manuscript material. (K.T.A.)

Ross, Donald, Jr. "The Prelude, VIII." *AN&Q,* v (1967), 147-48.
Explores lines 70-115 as alluding to "Kubla Khan."

Scoggins, James. *Imagination and Fancy: Complementary Modes in the Poetry of Wordsworth.* University of Nebraska Press, 1967. Pp. ix + 264. $5.50.
The admirable presupposition upon which the organization of this study is founded is that "if Wordsworth's poetry requires no commentary . . . it most certainly requires a context. An important part of that context, embodied in Wordsworth's classification and arrangement of his poems, has not been accorded a sufficiently sympathetic hearing." The hearing Professor Scoggins accords, however, is not deeply sympathetic. Although the two central chapters are rightly devoted to the classifications and arrangements of the 1815 edition, the analysis of Wordsworth's categories and orderings of poems within categories is mechanically desultory. One reason for the fatigued treatment of what one would expect to be the heart of a study concerned with Wordsworth's concepts of imagination and fancy appears in subsequent chapters, where Scoggins asserts a close connection—indeed sometimes a virtual identity—between, first, Wordsworth's conception of imagination and the sublime, and then between fancy and the beautiful. There may be value in the associations, though Scoggins' argument would be more persuasive did he not avoid the sticky yet relevant problem of the "picturesque." For example, one of Wordsworth's interesting comments on the sublime (overlooked by Scoggins) is contained in his note explaining why "picturesque" was dropped from the title of the poem we know as *Descriptive Sketches.* In fact, Scoggins believes he can improve on Wordsworth. " . . . I have made it a point to distinguish carefully between poems that I have characterized as poems of imagination and those so designated by Wordsworth. I have done this simply because many of the poems in this group do not conform to his own comments on the nature and aims of the poetic imagination. . . . indeed, almost the last third of the 'Poems of Imagination' in the De Selincourt edition." (pp. 187-88) The reason Wordsworth so grossly misclassified his own works is "a decline in both his poetic and critical powers" between 1809 and 1815. However steep the poet's decline, Scoggins is plainly less interested in what a sympathetic study of Wordsworth's arrangements and classifications might reveal than in showing how these can be used to support his interpretation of their key terms. Like a good many promising dissertations (of which this book reminds one in several ways, most notably in its overload of unhelpful references), *Imagination and Fancy* is marred by conflicting aims and methods. Its subject, however, is a good one, and Scoggins deserves credit for his endeavor to grapple with a major issue in Wordsworth's poetics. (K.K.)

Scoggins, James. "The Preface to *Lyrical Ballads*: A Revolution in Dispute." Pp. 380-98 in Anderson, Howard, and John S. Shea, eds., *Studies in Criticism and Aesthetics, 1660-1800*: Essays in Honor of Samuel Holt Monk. University of Minnesota Press, 1967. Pp. 419. $10.00.

Shaver, Chester L., ed. *The Letters of William and Dorothy Wordsworth.* Arranged and edited by Ernest De Selincourt. Second edition, revised.

Volume I. *The Early Years 1787-1805.* Oxford: Clarendon Press, 1967. Pp. xxxiii + 729. $14.40.

Rev. by Patrick Anderson in *S,* July 28, 1967, pp. 104-05.

Professor Shaver's new volume supersedes the great work of De Selincourt in *The Early Letters* of 1935 and in the supplement to *The Later Years* of 1939, which contained 17 letters from the early period. Shaver's revision combines the supplementary material with that of the original volume and adds twenty-six letters published since 1939. Furthermore, Shaver includes 14 letters hitherto unpublished, of which at least numbers 109, 130, 200A, and 264 are notably important. Numbers 173, 174, and 175 are of considerable value in helping up to understand Wordsworth's legal-financial maneuvers in 1802. Throughout Shaver's editing appears to me impeccable, but what makes his edition a genuine godsend to the ordinary Wordsworthian is his copious but succinctly worded annotations. These seem to me beyond praise. At—literally—hundreds of places Shaver provides information about correspondents, subjects and places and people referred to, and relevant social-historical events which endow the letters with an interest and significance which otherwise they could have only for the most knowledgeable specialists. This edition is a truly magnificent achievement: thousands of students of Romantic literature will be deeply in Shaver's debt in the years to come. (K.K.)

Shaver, Chester L. "Three Unpublished Wordsworth Letters." *N&Q,* XIV (1967), 14-18.

St. George, Priscilla P. "Wordsworth's Personal Experiment in *The Borderers.*" *EA,* xx (1967), 254-64.

Wordsworth, Jonathan. "A Wordsworth Letter." *TLS,* July 27, 1967, p. 673.

Gives the text of a letter to Southey written in 1805.

See also Williams ("Blake"); Bateson, Echeron ("Shelley").

Reviews of books previously listed:

GROOM, Bernard, *The Unity of Wordsworth's Poetry* (see *ELN,* v, Supp., 41), rev. severely in *TLS;* HARTMAN, Geoffrey H., *Wordsworth's Poetry* (see *ELN,* III, Supp., 44-45), rev. by R.S. Woof in *N&Q,* XIV (1967), 313-15; KING, Alec, *Wordsworth and the Artist's Vision* (see *ELN,* v, Supp., 42), rev. by R.S. Woof in *DUJ,* XXVIII (1967), 170-71; MOORMAN, Mary, *William Wordsworth: The Later Years* (See *ELN,* IV, Supp., 43-44), rev. by Donald J. Gray in *VS,* x (1967), 297-99; and by Mark L. Reed in *N&Q,* XIV (1967), 28-30; REED, Mark L., *Wordsworth: The Chronology of the Early Years, 1770-99* (see *ELN,* v, Supp., 42), rev. in *TLS,* Sept. 7, 1967, p. 801; and by Jack Stillinger in *JEGP,* LXVI (1967), 463-65; SALVESEN, Christopher, *The Landscape of Memory* (see *ELN,* IV, Supp., 45), rev. by James Applethwaite in *SAQ,* LXVI (1967), 273-74; by J.T. Ogden in *JEGP,* LXVI (1967), 156-58; and by J.R. Watson in RES, XVIII (1967), 86-87; WELSFORD, Enid, *Salisbury Plain* (see *ELN,* v, Supp., 43-44), rev. by Stephen Gill in *EIC,* XVII (1967), 362-67.

See also Bostetter ("English 3. Criticism").

FRENCH

(Compiled by Carrol Coates, State University of New York, Binghamton: Alfred G. Engstrom, Univ. of North Carolina; and James S. Patty, Vanderbilt Univ.)

1. GENERAL

Cadot, Michel. *La Russie dans la vie intellectuelle française (1839-1856)*. (L'Histoire sans Frontières, 7.) Paris: Fayard, 1967. Pp. 641. 29.50 Fr.

An exhaustive study of this topic, Cadot's book breaks over the chronological limits of its title, especially for the period leading up to 1839. Indeed, it amounts to an inquest into Russian influence on French culture during the whole Romantic period, and nearly every major French Romantic writer figures in it, notably Chateaubriand, Balzac, Michelet, and Mérimée. Only Custine is treated at length; in fact, the chapters devoted to *La Russie en 1839* form the crux of the book. Cadot's basic divisions are: "Les Russes à Paris," "Les voyageurs en Russie," " 'La Russie en 1839' de Custine," "La Russie temporelle," "La Russie spirituelle," and "La Russie et l'Occident." All in all, this is a monument of literary historical erudition in the old-fashioned comparative literature tradition; the sixty-page bibliography is indicative. (J.S.P.)

Charvet, P. E. *A Literary History of France*. Vol. IV: *The Nineteenth Century, 1789-1870*. London: Benn; New York: Barnes and Noble, 1967. Pp. xvi + 395. $12.50.

Coiscault-Cavalca, M. "Les Romantiques français et les Elisabéthains (Suite)." *LR,* XXI (1967), 141-57, 250-70.

Author by author survey of French criticism and comment on Elizabethan writers; a continuation and conclusion (?) of the study begun in 1965 (see *ELN,* IV, Supp., 48, and V, Supp., 8-9).

Décote, Georges. "Irrationalisme et illuminisme au XVIIIe siècle." *Le Français dans le Monde,* No. 49 (1967), pp. 7-11.

A superficial survey of scholarly studies (Viatte, etc.) of the subject since about 1925.

Derche, Roland. *Etudes de textes français. Nouvelle série. V. XIXe siècle. (Des Memoires d'Outre-Tombe aux Contemplations.)*. Paris: Société d'Edition d'Enseignement Supérieur, 1966. Pp. 251.

Rev. by Petre Ciureanu in *SFr,* XI (1967), 368.

Explications de texte of passages from Chateaubriand, Sainte-Beuve ("Ma Muse," *Vie, Poésies et pensées de Joseph Delorme*), Stendhal, Balzac, Nerval, and Hugo.

Descotes, Maurice. *La Légende de Napoléon et les écrivains français du XIXe siècle*. (Bibliothèque de Littérature et d'Histoire, 9.) Paris: Lettres Modernes (Minard), 1967. Pp. 279. 44 Fr.

Descotes has deftly packed a wealth of information into a series of very solid essays on Napoleon as seen by Madame de Staël (this chapter includes a large number of parallel passages from B. Constant), Chateaubriand, Lamartine, Vigny, Stendhal, Hugo, and Balzac. He compares their statements and insinuations with the facts and with modern interpretations of controversial issues (e.g., the murder of the Duc d'Enghien), examines the biographical and textual sources of their attitudes, and follows in considerable detail the general evolution of the images of Napoleon erected by these particular writers. Descotes wears his erudition gracefully, and he writes clearly and coolly; but he manages to be pungent and incisive as well. (J.S.P.)

Dimakis, Jean. "La 'Société de la morale chrétienne' de Paris et son action en faveur des Grecs lors de l'Insurrection de 1821." *Balkan Studies,* VII (1966), 27-48.

Fischer, Jan O. "En marge d'une histoire de la littérature française du XIXᵉ siècle (Questions de méthode, intensions [sic], résultats, problèmes ouverts)." *Philologica Pragensia,* X (1967), 222-32.
A sort of review of a history of French literature of the 19th and 20th centuries, Vol. I (covering the period 1789-1870), published in Czech in 1966 under the direction of Fischer himself. As suggested by the subtitle in parentheses, some general questions are here discussed, e.g., Romanticism and its relation to Realism.

FitzLyon, April. *The Price of Genius: A Life of Pauline Viardot.* London: Calder, 1964. Pp. 520. £22s.

Garber, Frederick. "Self, Society, Value and the Romantic Hero." *CL,* XIX (1967), 321-33.
Sketches elements of his theme from Werther to Julien Sorel and sees the latter's "ironic compromise" (when he chooses to make a moral stance of hypocrisy) as looking to our time.

Garçon, Maurice. "Les Procès littéraires." *Les Annales,* n.s. No. 205 (November 1967), pp. 3-20.
Traces the judicial trials of publications of fourteen men of letters in France from Béranger (1821) through Lucien Descaves (1890), the latter of whom marks a sort of *terminus ad quem* for the practice.

Giacomelli Deslex, Marcella. *Caratteri del romanticismo francese.* (Università degli Studi di Torino, Facoltà di Magistero.) Turin: Tirrenia, 1966. Pp. 49. L. 800.

Graña, César. *Bohemian versus Bourgeois: French Society and the French Man of Letters in the Nineteenth Century.* New York: Basic Books, 1964.
A "sociological analysis of a literary period," primarily that of the July Monarchy. There are passing references to many of the French Romantics.

Grojnowski, Daniel. "Poésie et chanson: de Béranger à Verlaine." *Critique* (Paris), XXIV (1967), 768-81.
On the contribution of Béranger and Nerval to the development of the *chanson* as conceived by Verlaine.

Guest, Ivor. *The Romantic Ballet in Paris.* With an Introduction by Lillian Moore. Wesleyan University Press, 1966. Pp. 314. $15.00.
Rev. by Clive Barnes in *New York Times Book Review,* Feb. 12, 1967, p. 6;

by Selma Jeanne Cohen in *JAAC*, XXVI (1967), 137-38; and by Carl Wildman in *New Statesman*, Nov. 18, 1966, p. 753.

This handsome volume, attractively illustrated and amply documented, presents the external history of the French Romantic ballet—personalities, anecdotes, performers, impresarios, critical reaction, theaters, etc. Gautier, Jules Janin, and of course the inevitable Scribe figure rather prominently in the world that Guest ably recreates.

Isambert, François-André. *De la Charbonnerie au Saint-Simonisme*. Paris: Editions de Minuit, 1966. Pp. 200. 24 Fr.

Katz, R. A. "Extincta revivisco: 1780-1828." Pp. 146-68 in his *Ronsard's French Critics: 1585-1828*. (Travaux d'Humanisme et Renaissance, LXXXV.) Geneva: Librairie Droz, 1966. Pp. 190. 50 Fr.

For the period covered by this chapter, the *beaux rôles* are played by the elder Viollet-le-Duc, Guizot, and, of course, Sainte-Beuve. The treatment, even of the last named, is brief and so rather superficial. (J.S.P.)

Keil, Erika. *"Cantique" und "Hymne" in der französischen Lyrik seit der Romantik*. (Romanistische Versuche und Vorarbeiten, 18.) Bonn: Romanisches Seminar der Universität Bonn, 1966. Pp. 259.

Kitchin, Joanna. *Un Journal "philosophique": La Décade (1794-1807)*. Paris: M. J. Minard, 1966. Pp. viii + 317.

Rev. by Raymond Birn in *CL*, XIX (1967), 190-91; by Pierre Moreau in *RLC*, XL (1966), 646-51; and by G. Ross Roy in *BA*, XLI (1967), 303-04.

Koplenig, Hilde. *Geburt der Freiheit: Gestalten und Ereignisse Frankreich, 1789-1794*. Berlin: Veb Deutscher Verlag der Wissenschaften, 1964. Pp. 408.

Rev. by Crane Brinton in *JMH*, XXXIX (1967), 184-85.

Maurois, André. "Le Biographe et ses personnages: vérité et poesie." Les *Annales*, n.s. No. 196 (Feb. 1967), pp. 5-19.

A defense of the literary biography by the famous biographer of Chateaubriand, George Sand, Hugo, Dumas, Balzac, *et al*.

Minder, Robert. *Paris in der neueren französischen Literatur (1770-1890)*. (Akademie der Wissenschaften und der Literatur [Mainz]. Abhandlungen der Klasse der Literatur. 1965, No. 2.) Wiesbaden: Franz Steiner, 1965. Pp. 31.

Moreau, Pierre. "Vues sur Montaigne et les Romantiques français." *Bulletin de la Société des Amis de Montaigne*, 4e série, No. 9 (1967), 3-12.

Nearly all the major Romantics are mentioned, but Moreau emphasizes Chateaubriand, whom he sees as most faithful to Montaigne's autobiographical method.

Orlando, Francesco. *Infanzia, memoria e storia da Rousseau ai romantici.* (Biblioteca di Cultura.) Padua: Liviana Editrice, 1966. Pp. 253. L. 2900.

Romantic authors discussed are: Chateaubriand, Nodier, Stendhal, Lamartine, G. Sand, Senancour, Constant, Sainte-Beuve, Nerval.

Pohl, Almut. "Aus der Geschichte des Kainstoffes biz zum Beginn des 19. Jahrhunderts." Pp. 9-45 in his *Das Gedicht "Qain" von Leconte de Lisle: eine literarhistorische Interpretation.* (Hamburger Romanistische Studien. Reihe A. Band 47.) Hamburg: Romanisches Seminar, 1964. Pp. 191.

Reizov, B. G. "U istokov romanticheckoj Estetiki" ("At the sources of Romantic esthetics"). *Izvestija Akademii Nauk S. S. S. R. Serija Literatury i Jazyka,* xxvi (1967), 308-20.

Robichez, Jacques. *Panorama du XIXe siècle français.* Paris: Seghers, 1967. Pp. 252. 12 Fr.

An agreeable but necessarily superficial survey of the period.

Vax, Louis. *La Séduction de l'étrange. Etude sur la littérature fantastique.* Paris: Presses Universitaires de France, 1965. Pp. 316.

Reviews of books previously listed:

BEAUCHAMP, Louis de, *Le Côté de Vinteuil* (see *ELN*, v, Supp., 45), rev. anon. in *SC*, IX, 195-96; CHRISTOUT, Marie-Françoise, *Le Merveilleux et le théâtre du silence en France à partir du XVIIe siècle* (see *ELN*, v, Supp., 45), rev. by André Veinstein in *RHT*, xviii, 258-59; EASTON, Malcolm, *Artists and Writers in Paris: The Bohemian Idea, 1803-1867* (see *ELN*, iv, Supp., 48), rev. by Edward D. Sullivan in *MLJ*, li, 127; ENGLER, Winfrid, *Der französischen Roman von 1800 bis zur Gegenwart* (see *ELN*, v, Supp., 46), rev. by Jesús Cantera in *FMod*, v, 151-52; GIRARD, Alain, *Le Journal intime* (see *ELN*, iv, Supp., 49), rev. by Jean Lacroix in *Le Monde*, Nov. 15-16, 1964, p. 17; KELLER, Luzius, *Piranèse et les Romantiques français* (see *ELN*, v, Supp., 47), rev. in *TLS*, June 8, 1967, pp. 497-98; by Pierre Georgel in *RHL*, lxvii (1967), 847-48; and by Jean Seznec in *FS*, xxi (1967), 166-67; MOREAU, Pierre, *Ames et thèmes romantiques* (see *ELN*, iv, Supp., 50), rev. by R. Fargher in *FS*, xxi (1967), 256-57; by Marius-François Guyard in *RHL*, lxvii (1967), 161-62; and by M[ax]. M[ilner]. in *IL*, xix (1967), 122-23; POULET, Georges, *Trois Essais de mythologie romantique* (see *ELN*, v, Supp., 71), rev. in *TLS*, June 8, 1967, pp. 497-98; RAITT, A.W., *Life and Letters in France: The Nineteenth Century* (see *ELN*, v, Supp., 48), rev. in *TLS*, Feb. 24, 1966, p. 138; by Colin Duckworth in *FS*, xxi (1967), 355-58; by G. Mirandola in *SFr*, xi (1967), 367-68; and by Margaret A. Rees in *MLR*, lxii (1967), 343-44; TOUCHARD, Pierre-Aimé, *Grandes Heures de théâtre à Paris* (see *ELN*, iv, Supp., 51), rev. by Rose-Marie Moudouès in *RHT*, xviii (1967), 256-57; WOOD, John, *Sondages,*

1830-1838. Romanciers français secondaires (see *ELN,* IV, Supp., 51), rev. by R.C. Dale in *ECr,* VII (1967), 60-62; by Henri Godin in *FS,* XXI (1967), 257-58; and by Murray Sachs in *RR,* LVIII (1967), 59-60.

2. STUDIES OF AUTHORS

ALLART

Reviews of works previously listed:

UFFENBECK, Lorin A., ed., *Nouvelles lettres d'Hortense Allart à Sainte-Beuve (1832-1864)* (see *ELN,* IV, Supp., 52), rev. by Albert Delorme in *RdS,* LXXXVII (1966), 378-79; by Raphaël Molho in *RHL,* LXVII (1967), 169-70; and by E.M. Phillips in *FS,* XXI (1967), 258-59.

BALLANCHE

See Fletcher ("General 3. Criticism").

BALZAC

Alvarez Turienzo, S. "Sobre Honorato Balzac y la novela." *RO,* V (Aug. 1967), 221-35.

L'Année Balzacienne 1967. Paris: Garnier, 1967. Pp. 440. 28 F.

Eighth in series. Contains: P. Citron, "Sur deux zones obscures de la psychologie de Balzac," pp. 3-27; R.J.B. Clark, "Un condisciple de Balzac: Paul Duport," pp. 29-35; Bruce Tolley, "Balzac anecdotier. De l' 'Album historique et anecdotique' (1927) à 'La Comédie humaine,'" pp. 37-50; Pierre Barbéris, "L'accueil de la critique aux premières grandes oeuvres de Balzac (1829-1830)," pp. 51-72; Rose Fortassier, "Interview d'un dandy (1830)," pp. 73-87; Léon-François Hoffmann, "Eros en filigrane: 'Le Curé de Tours,'" pp. 89-105; Raymond L. Sullivant, "'La Femme de trente ans': quelques emprunts de Balzac à la littérature et à la vie anglaises," pp. 107-14; Henri Gautier, "Le projet du recueil 'Etudes de femme,'" pp. 115-46; Jean Gaudon, "Sur la chronologie du 'Père Goriot,'" pp. 147-56; Jean-Pierre Barricelli, "Autour de 'Gambara.' I. Balzac et Meyerbeer," pp. 157-63; Pierre Citron, "Autour de 'Gambara.' I. 'Gambara' Strunz et Beethoven," pp. 165-70; Bruce Tolley, "'Une Histoire amoureuse' et 'Dom Gigadas,'" pp. 171-76; René Guise, "Un grand homme du roman à la scène, ou les illusions reparaissantes de Balzac (suite)," pp. 177-214; Anthony R. Pugh, "Un chapitre retrouvé des 'Comédiens sans le savoir': 'La Comédie gratis,'" pp. 215-21; C. Smethurst, "Introduction à l'étude du 'Député d'Arcis,'" pp. 223-40; Francis Ley, "Balzac et Mme Hanska chez les Krüdener, Berne 1846," pp. 241-44; Jean Pommier, "Balzac, 'écrivain révolutionnaire,'" pp. 247-58; P.-J. Tremewan, "Balzac et Shakespeare," pp. 259-303; Albert Prioult, "Balzac et le Père-Lachaise," pp. 306-23; Lucienne Frappier-Mazur, "Espace et regard dans 'La Comédie humaine,'" pp. 325-38; "Notes" by P. Citron, D. Delecolle, H. Godin, R. Guise, A. Lorant, A.-R. Pugh, G. Sagnes, and R.-A. Whelpton; reviews, Balzac bibliography for 1966, and reports on Balzac work abroad.

Barbéris, Pierre. "La Pensée de Balzac: histoire et structures." *RHL,* LXVII (1967), 18-54.

A response to Per Nykrog's *La Pensée de Balzac dans "La Comédie humaine"* (see *ELN,* v, Supp., 53). Although Barbéris reproaches "la nouvelle critique" for not taking advantage of the resources offered by literary scholarship, he concludes that "ce livre important marque peut-être . . . un nouveau départ des études balzaciennes." In the course of his analysis, Barbéris gives a concise assessment of the directions taken by Balzac criticism in recent years. (C.C.)

Caput, Jean-Pol, ed. *Eugénie Grandet.* (Nouveaux Classiques Larousse.) Paris: Larousse, 1965. Illus. 2 vols.
The complete text with notes, introduction, and interesting photographic documentation. (C.C.)

Castex, Pierre-Georges and Pierre Citron, eds. *La Comédie humaine.* (Coll. "L'Intégrale.") Paris: Editions du Seuil, 1965-1966. 7 vols. 16 Fr. ea.
Vols. I and II reviewed by Max Milner in *AnB,* 1966, pp. 420-24.

Castex, Pierre-Georges, ed. *Histoire des Treize: Ferragus; La Duchesse de Langeais; La Fille aux yeux d'or.* Edition augmentée d'un sommaire biographique et enrichie d'illustrations. Paris: Garnier, 1966. Pp. viii + 538.

Citron, Pierre, ed. *Le Contrat de mariage.* Paris: Garnier-Flammarion, 1966.

Citron, Pierre, ed. *Illusions perdues.* Paris: Garnier-Flammarion, 1966.

Citron, Pierre, ed. *Pierrette.* Paris: Garnier-Flammarion, 1967. Pp. 256. 2.45 Fr.

Citron, Pierre, ed. *La Rabouilleuse.* Edition illustrèe de 25 reproductions. Paris: Garnier, 1966. Pp. cix + 601.

Conner, Wayne. "Frame and Story in Balzac." *ECr,* VII (1967), 45-54.
A survey of point of view and reader distance in the short stories. (C.C.)

Cortés, Luis. *Cinco estudios sobre el habla popular en la literatura francesa: Molière, Balzac, Maupassant, Giono, Sartre.* (Acta Salmenticensia. Filosofía y letras, vol. 17, no. 4.) Universidad de Salamanca, 1964. Pp. 134.

Dale, R. C. *"Le Colonel Chabert* between Gothicism and Naturalism." *ECr,* VII (1967), 11-16.

Eaubonne, Françoise d'. *Honoré de Balzac.* Paris: Albin Michel, 1966.

Giles, Anthony E. "On a supposed inadvertence of Balzac in *Eugénie Grandet." RomN,* IX (1967), 66-67.

Gurkin, Janet. "Romance Elements in *Eugénie Grandet." ECr,* VII (1967), 17-24.

Sleeping Beauty and the legend of the Fisher King figured in the "realistic" novel.

Hemmings, F. W. J. *Balzac: An Interpretation of 'La Comédie humaine.'* (Studies in Language and Literature.) New York: Random House, 1967. Pp. 192. $1.95.
A sound reading of *La Comédie humaine.* Not the least of Mr. Hemmings' accomplishments is to have outlined Balzac's treatment of feminine psychology. He skirts the knotty problem of where the main emphasis lies in *Le Père Goriot,* "a novel in which three or four archetypal themes jostle for supremacy. . . ." Judicious and sparing use of good and recent scholarship in support of his own interpretation. (C.C.)

Hönnighausen, Lother. "Dowsons *Seraphita*-Geidtche." *Archiv,* CCIV (1967), 192-201.
A study of two poems by Ernest Dowson inspired by Balzac's *Séraphita.*

Hort, Jean. *Vie de Balzac. Chronique en forme de pièce en trois parties.* Paris: Promotion et Edition, 1967. Pp. 253. 13 Fr.
A biographical dialogue, written for radio performance.

Iwase, Hiroaki. "Une Remarque sur la signification de l'existence de Dieu chez Balzac." *Regards: Revue de Littérature et de Langue Françaises* (Université du Tôhoku. Section de Littérature et Langue Françaises), No. 10 (1967), pp. 20-28.
In Japanese with *résumé analytique* in French (p.79).

Junker, Albert. "Das Thema der Hand in der modernen französischen Literatur." *NS,* n. s. LXVI (1967), 311-23.

Kotchetkova, T. "Un apport à l'histoire de l'oeuvre de Balzac en Russie." *Travaux de la Bibliothèque d'Etat de la R. S. S. de Lettonie* (Riga), I (1964), 113-82.
Rev. by G. Diérenkovskaja and G. Vipper in *AnB,* LXXIII (1966), 465-67.

Lecour, Charles. *Les Personnages de 'la Comédie humaine,'* avec 33 tableaux généalogiques dépliants. (Essais d'Art et de Philosophie.) Paris: J. Vrin, 1966. Pp. 163. 54 Fr.
The genealogical charts come unbound, separate from the text, almost guaranteeing that they will be lost in normal library usage.
The study, like the tables, is primarily focused on the reappearing characters, 515 in all according to Lecour's count (from a total of 2209 characters in the *Comédie humaine*). Many of the non-reappearing characters are linked within the *Comédie* by relations with reappearing ones. A brief but suggestive study; highly condensed. (C.C.)

Lowrie, Joyce Oliver. "Balzac and 'le doigt de Dieu.' " *ECr,* VII (1967), 36-44.

The motif of divine justice as means for counter-balancing the evil deeds of certain characters in the *Comédie humaine*. Author concludes that the motif is useful, whether Balzac sincerely believed in God's finger or not. (C.C.)

Macchia, Giovanni. "Balzac e la strada del romanzo." *Strumenti Critici,* No. 2 (Feb. 1967), pp. 131-57.

Martínez-Estrada, Ezequiel. *Realidad y fantasía en Balzac.* Bahía Blanca (Argentina): Universidad Nacional del Sur, 1964. Pp. 900.
Rev. by Oscar Tacca in *AnB,* LXXIII (1966), 444-46.

Meininger, Anne-Marie. " 'Les Employés': réflexions sur la création balzacienne." *RHL,* LXVII (1967), 754-58.

Mikhajlov, A. D. "Tri pis'ma Bal'zaka (Three Letters from Balzac)." *Izvestija Akademii Nauk S. S. S. R. Serija Literatury i Jazyka,* XXVI (1967), 379-82.
Publishes three letters which are not in the first four volumes of Pierrot's current edition of the *Correspondance*. Mikhajlov supposes the first, to M. Lequien, to have been written in April 1835. The second, to M. de Saint-Julien, is postmarked Oct. 5, 1839; the third, to M. Marie Aycard, is dated Feb. 4, 1840. All three letters have to do with literary business. The originals are in the Government Historical Museum and in the Lenin Library (both in Moscow). (C.C.)

Milly, J. "Les Pastiches de Proust: Structure et correspondances." *FM,* XXXV (1967), 31-52, 125-41.
On Balzac: pp. 44-46 and *passim.*

Petruzzi, Simonetta. "La Sardegna di Balzac." *NA,* CII (1967), 527-37.

Plessen, Jacques. "Quelques remarques sur l'emploi du présent dans le début du *Père Goriot*." *Neophil,* LI (1967), 1-10.

Pugh, Anthony R. "The Complexity of *Le Père Goriot*." *ECr,* VII (1967), 25-35.

Quénelle, Gilbert, ed. *Eugénie Grandet.* (Macmillan's Modern Language Texts.) London: Macmillan; New York: St. Martin's Press, 1967. Pp. xlvii + 201; 8 plates.
A handy, readable text in a sturdy binding, with introductory materials and notes in English. Suitable for high school or undergraduate use. The editor gives an accurate overall view of Balzac's work as well as a summary introduction to various aspects of this novel. (C.C.)

Rays, H. *The Dangerous Sex (The Myth of Feminine Evil).* New York: G. P. Putnam's, 1964.
Pp. 212-19 on *La Peau de chagrin.*

Reboussin, Marcel. *Balzac et le mythe de Foedora.* Paris: A.-G. Nizet, 1966. Pp. 285.
A penetrating essay on the political and social realities of the Restoration and the July Monarchy as depicted in the *Comédie humaine.* Reboussin says that Balzac's myth of society conveys "une catégorie de la sensibilité balzacienne, . . . une réaction instinctive du moi qui, blessé dans ses contacts avec le monde extérieur, se cherche une justification dans le domaine des idées." The confrontation of myth and reality is based on Balzac's theoretical writings as well as on important texts from the *Comédie.* (C.C.)

Sacy, Samuel de, ed. *La Femme de trente ans.* (Le Livre de Poche.) Paris: Librairie Générale Française, 1967. Pp. 382.

Sacy, Samuel de, ed. *La Recherche de l'absolu,* suivi de *La Messe de l'athée.* Introduction de Raymond Abellio. (Le Livre de Poche.) Paris: Librairie Générale Française, 1967. Pp. 384.

Schroder, Maurice Z. "Balzac's Theory of the Novel." *ECr,* VII (1967), 3-10.
Theory distilled from prefaces and articles by Balzac. Perceptive. (C.C.)

Takayama, Tetsuo. *Les Oeuvres romanesques avortées de Balzac 1829-1842.* (Studies in the Humanities and Social Relations, Vol. VIII) Tokyo: The Keio Institute of Cultural and Linguistic Studies, 1966.

Taylor, A. Carey. "Balzac and Manoel António de Almeida. The Beginnings of Realism in Brazil." *RLC,* XLI (1967), 195-203.

Välikangas, Olli. "La personne grammaticale dans les appellations chez Balzac." *NM,* LXVIII (1967), 337-90.

Willett, Maurita. "Henry James's Indebtedness to Balzac." *RLC,* XLI (1967), 204-27.
Comparison of *The American* with *Le Père Goriot.*

See also Fletcher ("General 3. Criticism"); Thérive ("Lamartine").

Reviews of books previously listed:
ADAMSON, Donald, *The Genesis of 'Le Cousin Pons'* (see *ELN,* V, Supp., 49), rev. by André Lacaux in *RHL,* LXVII (1967), 846-47; AFFRON, Charles, *Patterns of Failure in 'La Comédie humaine'* (see *ELN,* V, Supp., 49), rev. by Carrol F. Coates in *FR,* XL (1967), 844-45; ALLEMAND, André, *Unité et structure de l'univers balzacien* (see *ELN,* IV, Supp., 53), rev. by Pierre Citron in *RHL,* LXVII (1967), 645-47; *L'Année Balzacienne 1965* (see *ELN,* IV, Supp., 53), rev. by Pierre Laubriet in *RHL,* LXVII (1967), 165-68; *L'Année Balzacienne 1966,* rev. by Carrol F. Coates in *BA,* XLI (1967), 50; and by André Lacaux in *RHL,* LXVII (1967), 846; BARDÉCHE, Maurice, *Une Lecture de Balzac* (see *ELN,* III, Supp., 52), rev. by Léon-François Hoffmann in *Esprit,* fév. 1967; CASTEX, Pierre-Georges, ed., *Eugénie Grandet* (see *ELN,* IV, Supp., 55), rev. by

Maurice Regard in *RHL*, LXVII (1967), 168-69; GERMAIN, François, ed., *L'Enfant maudit* (see *ELN*, V, Supp., 52), rev. by Raffaele de Cesare in *RLMC*, XX (1967), 69-71; by Stirling Haig in *ECr*, VII (1967), 59-60; and by André Lacaux in *RHL*, LXVII (1967), 847; HOFFMANN, Léon-François, Répertoire *géographique de la Comédie humaine*. I. *L'Etranger* (see *ELN*, IV, Supp., 58), rev. by Neal Oxenhandler in *FR*, XLI (1967), 150-51; LE YOUANC, Moïse, ed., *Le Lys dans la vallée* (see *ELN*, V, Supp., 52), rev. by Bruce Tolley in *FS*, XXI (1967), 171-72; PIERROT, Roger, ed., *Correspondance*, Tome I (see *PQ*, XLIII, 468), rev. by Antonin Zatloukal in *Philologica Pragensia*. *Casopis pro Moderní Filologii*, VII (1964), 96; PIERROT, Roger, ed., *Correspondance*, Tome IV (1840-avril 1845) (see *ELN*, V, Supp., 53), rev. by G. Franceschetti in *SFr*, XI (1967), 168-69; and by James Walt in *BA*, XLI (1967), 306; VALIKANGAS, Olli, *Les Termes d'appellation et d'interpellation dans 'la Comédie Humaine' de Balzac* (see *ELN*, V, Supp., 54), rev. by Carrol Coates in *FR*, XLI (1968), 577; by H.J. Hunt in *FS*, XXI (1967), 68-69; by P. Larthoumas in *FM*, XXXV (1967), 233-34; and by Veikko Väänänen in *NM*, LXVIII (1967), 213-16; WURMSER, André, *La Comédie inhumaine* (see *ELN*, III, Supp., 58), rev. by Pierre Aubery in *FR*, XL (1967), 843-44.

BERANGER

See Grojnowski ("French 1. General").

BONALD

Derré, Jean-René. *En marge de la Sainte Alliance*: *lettres de Bonald au Comte de Senfft*. (Bibliothèque de la Faculté des Lettres de Lyon, Vol. XIV, Série GF.) Paris: Les Belles Lettres, 1967. Pp. 132. 12 Fr.

CHASLES

Reviews of books previously listed:

PICHOIS, Claude, *Philarète Chasles et la vie littéraire au temps du romantisme* (see *ELN*, IV, Supp., 63), rev. by Raffaele de Cesare in *SFr*, XI, 103-05; by M.M. [Max Milner?] in *IL*, XIX, 81-82; and by E.M. Phillips in *FS*, XXI, 70-72.

CHATEAUBRIAND

Amer, Henry. "Littérature et portrait: Retz, Saint-Simon, Chateaubriand, Proust." *Études Françaises*, III (1967), 131-68.

Book, Truett. "The Unacknowledged Source of a Chapter in Chateaubriand's *Essai sur les révolutions*." *RomN*, VIII (1967), 190-196.

Shows the principal source of information for Chapter XVI of the *Essai* ("Jugement et condamnation de Charles 1er, roi d'Angleterre") to be David Hume's *History of England*.

Boutet, Gilbert. "Un 'Art Poétique' de Chateaubriand: *Cynthie*." *LR*, XXI (1967), 311-38.

De Cesare, Raffaele. "A proposito di una lettera di Chateaubriand à Delphine de Girardin." Pp. 309-15 in *Studi in onore di Italo Siciliano*, *I*. Florence: L.S. Olschki, 1966. 2 vols.

Dupuis, G., J. Georgel et J. Moreau, eds. *Politique de Chateaubriand.* Textes choisis et présentés. (Coll. "U," Série: Idées politiques.) Paris: Armand Colin, 1967. Pp. 293. 11.50 Fr.

Rev. in *Bulletin Critique du Livre Français,* XXII (1967), 505; and by Petre Ciureanu in *SFr,* XI (1967), 369-70.

An anthology of political texts of Chateaubriand, with an introduction entitled "Chateaubriand ou la fidélité politique."

Garnier, Jean-Paul. "Chateaubriand et les Bourbons." *RDM,* June 1, 1967, pp. 381-92.

Shows in some detail why the Bourbons lacked confidence in Chateaubriand's "royalisme tapageur."

Grimsley, Ronald. *Soren Kierkegaard and French Literature.* Eight Comparative studies. Cardiff: University of Wales Press, 1966. Pp. ix + 171. 21 s.

Rev. by Colin Smith in *FS,* XXI (1967), 89-90: Cites among the essays one that compares the mentality of Chateaubriand's René with the Diapsalmatist of *Either/Or,* and another on "Kierkegaard and Vigny" that discusses the poet and his mission.

Lebègue, Raymond. "Les archaïsmes dans les trois premiers livres des *Mémoires d'Outre-Tombe.*" *CAIEF,* No. 19 (1967), pp. 59-68.

Lebègue briefly considers Chateaubriand's use of archaisms in the works prior to the *Mémoires* before turning to the latter work. His general conclusion emphasizes Chateaubriand's classical sense of restraint. See the discussion of this paper, pp. 259-63.

Lyautey, Pierre. "L'actualité de Chateaubriand." *RDM,* Oct. 1, 1967, pp. 356-64.

Martin, Paul. "Quelques sources de Chateaubriand." *IL,* XIX (1967), 114-16.

The most plausible suggestions here seem to be those as to the source of two passages in the *Mémoires d'outre-tombe* (3e partie, 2e époque, livre deuxième, 10 [éd. Levaillant, III, 83] and 4e partie, livre IV, 10 [*ibid.,* IV, 247]) respectively in *Aeneid,* XI, 547ff. and in Ovid's *Fasti,* IV, 270-348.

Pozzo di Borgo, Olivier, ed. *De Buonaparte et des Bourbons.* (Collection "Libertés," 44.) [Paris:] Jean-Jacques Pauvert, 1966. Pp. 165.

Rev. by M. M[ilner] in *IL,* XIX (1967), 122.

Reproduces text of the first edition (Paris: Mame [4 avril] 1814) with Chateaubriand's prefaces to the first and second editions and with variants of the second edition in notes at the bottom of the pages. Editor's *présentation* sees Chateaubriand as on occasion here anticipating *Les Châtiments,* but finds *De Buonaparte et des Bourbons* ultimately, in strange paradox, serving the Napoleonic legend.

Reboul, Pierre, ed. *Génie du Christianisme, I.* Paris: Garnier-Flammarion, 1966, Pp. 511.

Rev. by R. Fargher in *FS,* xxi (1967), 358-59.

Fargher notes that the text of this 2 vol. edition is that of Ladvocat (*Oeuvres complètes,* Vols. xi-xv, 1826-28), with the "Notes et Eclaircissements" and Préface of that edition.

Redman, Harry, Jr. "La 'Louisianaise' de Chateaubriand dévoilée." *RdP,* lxxiv (1967), 77-81.

On Mme Soniat Du Fossat (1804-1882, d. in Paris), *née* Célestine Soniat, whom Chateaubriand met in Paris and refers to in the *Mémoires d'outre-tombe* as "Célestine" and "la Louisianaise."

Richard, Jean-Pierre. *Paysage de Chateaubriand.* (Coll. "Pierres vives.") Paris: Ed. du Seuil, 1967. Pp. 189. 15 Fr.

Société Chateaubriand. Bulletin, No. 9 (1965-1966).

Contents listed in *RHL,* lxvii, No. 4 (1967), 904: Mme d'Andlau, "Delphine: une lettre inédite de Mme de Custine, 1802 [à Mme de Staël], and "Quelque re-marques sur les portraits de Dioclétien et de Napoléon (rapprochements entre des fragments inédits des *MOT* et le texte primitif des *Martyrs*]: Jean-Albert Bédé, "Chateaubriand et Washington: a propos d'une lettre récemment décou-verte"; Pierre Clarac, "Une version inédite de l'avant-propos des Mémoires"; J.-R. Derré, "En marge de *L'Avenir*: Chateaubriand, Lamennais et Metter-nich"; Mme Marie-Jeanne Durry, "Deux lettres et un billet inédit de Chateau-briand à Louise Colet, 1835, 1845"; Robert Laulan, "Chateaubriand antiquaire (aperçus)"; Raymond Lebègue, "Chateaubriand et le passage du Nord-Ouest"; Mlle Maija Lehtonen, "L'Evolution du langage imagé de Chateaubriand"; Pierre Riberette, "Chateaubriand et le libraire Piatti" [trois lettres de Chateau-briand, 30 nov. 1803; s.d.; 7 mai 1804]; Rouch (Cap[ne] de vaisseau Jules), "L'Exactitude de Chateaubriand dans l'*Itinéraire de Paris à Jérusalem*"; André Sauvage, "Chateaubriand et Stace" (à propos d'une comparaison des *Martyrs,* vi, éd. Garnier, 1963, p. 109); Jacques Suffel, "La fête de la Villa Médicis pour la grande-duchesse Hélène, 28 avril 1829 [inédit: lettre du peintre Carle Vernet à sa fille Camille]; Revue des autographes; ms. d'oeuvres de Chateau-briand, correspondance de Chateaubriand, Correspondance diverse; publication de lettres inédites de Chateaubriand.

Switzer, Richard. "Chateaubriand and the Foreign Office: Unpublished Correspondence." *FR,* xli (1967), 319-25.

Excerpts from Chateaubriand's correspondence with the British Foreign Office, as Ambassador and then as Foreign Minister. Switzer is preparing an edition of the material (comprising nearly 150 documents), which will complement the general correspondence now being prepared by Clarac and Christophorov.

Vial, André. *Chateaubriand et une autre dame de Pierreclau. Documents inédits et pages oubliées.* Paris: Nizet, 1967. Pp. 188.

See also Moreau ("French 1. General"); Nuñez de Arenas ("Spanish 2. General"); and Monguió ("Spanish. Mora").

Reviews of books previously listed:
GAUTIER, Jean-Maurice, *Le Style des Mémoires d'outre-tombe de Chateaubriand* (see *ELN*, V, Supp., 57), rev. by Maija Lehtonen in *ZRP*, LXXXIII (1967), 178-80: Notes some modifications, abridgements and additions in the new edition; LEHTONEN, Maija, *L'Expression imagée dans l'oeuvre de Chateaubriand* (see *ELN*, III, Supp., 59), rev. by Fritz Nies in *ZRP*, LXXXIII (1967), 181-89.

COLET

Viguié, Pierre. "Louise Colet, 'la Vénus en marbre chaud.'" *RdP*, Sept. 1967, pp. 95-100.

CONSTANT

Cordié, Carlo. "Un maestro di 'libertà.' Constant due secoli dopo." *NA*, No. 1996 (April 1967), pp. 464-73.

Courtney, C. P. "Autour de Benjamin Constant. Lettres inédites de Juste de Constant à Sir Robert Murray Keith." *RHL*, LXVII (1967), 97-100.

Courtney, C. P. "New Light on Benjamin Constant. Three Unpublished Letters from Juste de Constant to J.-B. Suard." *Neophil*, LI (1967), 10-14.

Deguise, Pierre. "Benjamin Constant, Mme Talma, et la 'Lettre sur Julie,'" *RHL*, LXVII (1967), 100-11.

Delbouille, Paul. "A propos d'une correction *d'Adolphe.*" *RHL*, LXVI (1966), 160-62.

Matucci, Mario. "Sul pensiero religioso di Benjamin Constant." *Saggi e Ricerche di Letteratura Francese*, VII (1966), 139-200.

Mönch, Walter. "Benjamin Constant's 'Wallenstein.'" *ZFSL*, LXXVII (1967), 289-95.
A review article on Jean-René Derré, ed., *Wallstein* (see *ELN*, V, Supp., 58).

Oliver, Andrew. "*Cécile* et la genèse *d'Adolphe.*" *RSH*, XXXII (1967), 5-28.

Pardo de Leygonier, G. F. "Bolivar, l'abbé de Pradt et Benjamin Constant." *Revue de l'Institut Napoléon*, No. 87 (April 1963), pp. 62-68.

Pozzo di Borgo, Olivier, ed. *Benjamin Constant polémiste.* Choix de textes politiques. (Coll. "Libertés.") Paris: J.-J. Pauvert, 1966. Pp. 162.
Rev. by M[ax]. M[ilner]. in *IL*, XIX (1967), 122-23.

Reviews of works previously listed:
BASTID, Paul, *Benjamin Constant et sa doctrine* (see *ELN*, V, Supp., 58), rev.

by Pierre Deguise in *FR,* XL (1967), 712-13; and by Carlo Cordié in *SFr,* XI (1967), 289-96; DEGUISE, Pierre, *Benjamin Constant méconnu: le livre "De la religion"* (see *ELN,* V, Supp., 58), rev. by Frank Paul Bowman in *FR,* XL (1967), 569-70; by Alison Fairlie in *FS,* XXI (1967), 251-53; and by Patrice Thompson in *RHL,* LXVII (1967), 159-60; DERRÉ, Jean-René, ed., *Wallstein* (see *ELN,* V, Supp., 58), rev. by Patrice Thompson in *RHL,* LXVII (1967), 158-59; and by Alison Fairlie in *FS,* XXI (1967), 253-55; HOGUE, H[elen]. H.S., *Of Changes in Benjamin Constant's Books on Religions* (see *ELN,* III, Supp., 61), rev. by Paul Delbouille in *RBPH,* XLIV (1966), 1033-37.

DELACROIX

Mras, George P. *Eugène Delacroix's Theory of Art.* (Princeton Monograph in Art and Archaeology, XXXVII.) Princeton University Press, 1966. Pp. xiv + 160; 37 plates. $7.50

DELECLUZE

Baschet, Robert. "Delécluze à Parme." *SC,* X (1967), 55-69.

Extracts from Delécluze's *carnet de route* covering his visit to Piacenza, Parma, Modena, and Bologna (June 1823).

DUMAS

Josserand, Pierre, ed. *Mes Mémoires.* Tomes III, IV. (Coll. "Mémoires du passé pour servir au temps présent.") Paris: Gallimard, 1966-1967.

DURAS

Stavan, Henry A. "Un exemple de wertherisme en France: *Ourika* et *Edouard* de la duchesse de Duras." *RLC,* XLI (1967), 342-50.

No direct influence of Goethe on Madame de Duras is indicated (however, she sent him a copy of *Ourika*).

FAURIEL

Cento, Alberto. "La corrispondenza Fauriel-Mary Clarke." Pp. 195-99 in *Studi di letteratura, storia e filosofia in onore di Bruno Revel* (Biblioteca dell'*Archivum Romanicum,* Series 2, Vol. 74.) Florence: Leo S. Olschki, 1965. Pp. xx + 662.

Galpin, Alfred. *Fauriel in Italy. Unpublished Correspondence (1822-1825).* (Quaderni di Cultura Francese, a cura della Fondazione Primoli, 5.) Rome: Edizioni di Storia e Letteratura, 1962. Pp. 128. L. 2500.

Rev. by Giulio Vallese in *Pel,* VIII, 227-28.

Reviews of book previously listed:

IBROVAC, Miodrag, *Claude Fauriel et la fortune européenne des poésies populaires grecque et serbe* (see *ELN,* V, Supp., 60-61), rev. by Dem. Eliadou-Hemmerdinger in *Balkan Studies,* VII, 244-49; and by R. Warnier in *LR,* XXI, 69-74.

FOURIER

Debout, Simone. "La Terre permise ou l'analyse selon Charles Fourier et la théorie des groupes." *TM,* No. 242 (1966), pp. 1-55.
Fourier as sexologist and precursor of the sexual revolution.

Review of book previously listed:
LEHOUCK, Emile, *Fourier aujourd'hui* (see *ELN,* v, Supp., 61), rev. by Claude Jannoud in *FL,* Jan. 12, 1967, p. 6.

GAUTIER

Babuts, Nicolae. "Une réexamination de la dette de Baudelaire envers Théophile Gautier." *RSH,* n.s. No. 127 (1967), pp. 351-80.
A long study of Gautier's influence on Baudelaire. Reaffirms in conclusion the sincerity of Baudelaire's dedication of *Les Fleurs du Mal* to Gautier, showing that, as different as Baudelaire was from Gautier and as conscious as he was of Gautier's limitations, Baudelaire admired him still, was influenced and inspired by him, and called him his master.

Boschot, Adolphe, ed. *Mademoiselle de Maupin.* Texte complet (1835). (Coll. "Selecta.") Paris: Garnier, 1966.

Cottin, Madeleine. "Autour d'un album romantique." *Nouvelles Littéraires,* Sept. 1, 1966.

Giraud, Raymond. "Winckelmann's Part in Gautier's Perception of Classical Beauty." *YFS,* No. 38 (1967), pp. 172-82.

Guichard, Léon, ed. *Lettres à Judith Gautier par Richard et Cosima Wagner.* Paris: Gallimard, 1964. Pp. 382. 23.50 Fr.
Rev. by E[dward]. L[ockspeiser]. in *Music and Letters,* XLVI (1965), 59-61. Includes published letters to Théophile Gautier from his daughter and from Wagner.

Van den Bogaert, Geneviève, ed. *Le Capitaine Fracasse.* (Collection "G.-F.") Paris: Garnier-Flammarion, 1967. Pp. 506. 3.95 Fr.

Van den Bogaert, Geneviève, ed. *Mademoiselle de Maupin.* Paris: Garnier-Flammarion, 1966. Pp. 380.
Rev. by M.C. Spencer in *FS,* XXI (1967), 359-60. Praised as an excellent edition, with the comment that "there now seems little point in Garnier frères continuing the 'Classiques Garnier' edition of this work unless its present Introduction and notes are both modified and lengthened." One fault cited: a disappointing bibliography.

See also Guest ("French 1. General").

GERANDO

Wilson, John B. "A Fallen Idol of the Transcendentalists: Baron de Gérando." *CL,* XIX (1967), 334-40.

An attempt to rescue Gérando from neglect as a transmitter of German philosophical ideas and to explain this neglect by the Transcendentalists and their historians.

GIRARDIN

Corriere, Alex. "Madame de Girardin as a Dramatist." *RomN,* IX (1967), 68-74.

It appears her best efforts were in comedy, especially one-acters.

GOZLAN

Chaffiol-Debillement, F. "Léon Gozlan." *RDM,* June 15, 1967, pp. 537-43.

A light-weight rehabilitation.

GUÉRIN

Elenberg, Fernando. "Cartas de Maurice de Guérin à Jules Barbey d'Aurevilly." *Boletín de la Academia Argentina de Lettras,* XXXI, No. 120 (1966), 193-251.

Reviews of works previously listed:

MOREAU, Pierre, *Maurice de Guérin ou les métamorphoses d'un centaure* (see *ELN,* IV, Supp., 68), rev. by Edouard Guitton in *RHL,* LXVII (1967), 857-58.

GUIZOT

Weintraub, Karl J. "Guizot, 1787-1874." Pp. 75-114 in his *Visions of Culture: Voltaire, Guizot, Burckhardt, Lamprecht, Huizinga, Ortega y Gasset.* University of Chicago Press, 1966. Pp. 308. $7.50.

Rev. by R. L. Colie in *American Historical Review,* LXXII, 524.

A fine (and sympathetic) essay on Guizot's "philosophical" approach to cultural history.

See also Katz ("French 1. General").

HETZEL

Cordroc'h Marie, et al. *De Balzac à Jules Verne: un grand éditeur du XIXe siècle, P.-J. Hetzel.* Paris: Bibliothèque Nationale, 1966. Pp. xiii + 92.

Rev. by Giles Barber in *FS,* XXI, 69-70.

Catalogue of the exposition organized by the Bibliothèque Nationale.

HUGO

Abraham, Pierre. "Victor Hugo au jour le jour." *Europe,* No. 458 (June 1967), pp. 237-40.

Albouy, Pierre, ed. *Oeuvres poétiques. II: Les Châtiments. Les Contemplations 1852-1870.* (Bibliothèque de la Pléiade.) Paris: Gallimard, 1967.

Albouy, Pierre. "Quelques observations sur la lumière dans l'oeuvre de victor Hugo." *CAIEF,* No. 19 (1967), pp. 205-23.
Clusters of quotations (all from the later Hugo) containing the imagery of light are arranged so as to yield an ultimate identification of God with light, souls with eyes (*le regard*), being with love. See the discussion of this paper, pp. 297-300.

Barrère, Jean-Bertrand. "Etat présent des études sur Victor Hugo." *CAIEF,* No. 19 (1967), pp. 169-76.
A helpful summary of trends and achievements in Hugo scholarship during the last quarter of a century. See discussion of this paper, pp. 285-86.

Cellier, Léon, ed. *La Légende des siècles,* I [II]. (Coll. "G.-F.") Paris: Garnier-Flammarion, 1967. 3.95 Fr.

Cornaille, Roger, and Georges Herscher, eds. *Victor Hugo dessinateur.* Préface de Gaëtan Picon. (Le Cabinet Fantastique, 3.) Paris: Editions du Minotaure, 1963. Pp. 234.
Rev. by Alfred Neumeyer in *JAAC,* xxvi (1967), 262.
Three hundred sixty-five of Hugo's drawings, arranged in a roughly chronological order, are reproduced in this handsome volume.

Descotes, Maurice. *L'Obsession de Napoléon dans le "Cromwell" de Victor Hugo.* (Archives des Lettres Modernes, No. 78.) Paris: Minard, 1967. Pp. 56.
Sees *Cromwell* not as a *pièce à clés,* but as "le fruit d'une contamination," for the drama (alone in this in Hugo's theater) is full of the memory of Napoleon and of those who were his allies and his enemies.

Franceschetti, G. "*Pyrénées,* Victor Hugo nell'estate 1843: cronaca e poesia." In *Contributi dell' Istituto di filologia moderna,* Serie francese, Vol. iv. Milan: Società ed. "Vita e pensiero," 1966.

Gaudon, Jean. "Ambiguïtés hugoliennes." *CAIEF,* No. 19 (1967), pp. 195-203.
Gaudon claims that, by means of his extraordinary poetic ambiguities (e.g., his paradoxical antitheses), Hugo transcended the limitations of rational discourse and fused the bi-polar world of good vs. evil into unity. See discussion of this paper, pp. 292-97.

Grant, Elliott M. *Victor Hugo: A Select and Critical Bibliography.* (University of North Carolina Studies in Romance Languages and Literatures, No. 67.) University of North Carolina Press, 1966. Pp. 94. Paper. $2.75.
A welcome contribution to Hugo scholarship. Contains 511 entries (all annotated, except for a few titles repeated in different categories). Many entries include supplementary references to critical reviews of the works cited. The bibliography is organized under thirteen separate headings: Bibliographies (4

entries), Catalogues (6), Editions (35), Anthologies (3), Biography (89), General Criticism (92), Hugo's Political Career and Social Philosophy (21), Language, Style, Imagery, etc. (18), Poetry (88), The Novel (70), Theater (40), Foreign Influences (19), Miscellaneous (19), and Addenda (7). The volume contains two useful indexes: one of the authors of books and articles cited, the other of writers and persons other than Hugo treated in the various studies.

Hof, Andrée. "Le Sens du mot *ombre* dans *Les Rayons et les ombres*." *RHL,* LXVII (1967), 537-56.

Notes that *les ombres* is in the plural and thus seems to show intended ambiguity on Hugo's part. Author suggests that "les *ombres* recouvrent dans l'ensemble les évocations du passé et de son passé—cher et regretté—, ainsi que les tristesses et les mystérieux desseins de la destinée . . . ."

Hyslop, Lois Boe. "Baudelaire on *Les Misérables*." *FR,* XLI (1967), 23-29.

Plausibly defends Baudelaire against the charge of duplicity in his praise of *Les Misérables* by showing that the praise is above all for the *usefulness* of the book and that Baudelaire did not once "call the novel a great work of art or praise it for anything more than its characterization or its effective propaganda."

Journet, René, ed. *Les Misérables.* Paris: Garnier-Flammarion, 1967. 3 vols.

Journet, René, and Guy Robert. "Pourquoi Victor Hugo n'a-t-il pas publié son poème 'Dieu'?" *CAIEF,* No. 19 (1967), pp. 225-31.

Admittedly failing to answer their question conclusively, the authors emphasize the caution of publishers before the heterodox ideas of the poem. See the discussion of this paper, pp. 300-302.

Koehler, E. "Zu Victor Hugos Gedichte: 'Elle était déchaussée, elle était décoiffée' (*Les Contemplations,* I, XXI)." Pp. 593-97 in *Studi in onore di Italo Siciliano, I,* Florence: Leo S. Olschki, 1966. 2 vols.

Lacretelle, Jacques de. "Hugo." *RDM,* Sept. 1, 1967, pp. 6-21.

Mazaleyrat, J. "Aux limites de deux formes métriques: rejet interne et rhythme ternaire dans l'alexandrin de Victor Hugo." In: *Mélanges de linguistique et de philologie romanes, offerts à Mgr Pierre Gardette.* Strasbourg: Centre de Philologie et de Littérature Romanes de l'Université de Strasbourg, 1966. Pp. 527. (En dépôt à la Librairie C. Klincksieck, 11, rue de Lille, Paris, VIIᵉ.)

Pommier, Jean. "Baudelaire et Hugo: Nouvelles glanes." *RSH,* n.s. No. 127 (1967), pp. 337-49.

A fascinating collection of passages, phrases, or impressively related words from Hugo's writings (*Odes et poésies diverses, Han d'Islande, Le dernier jour d'un condamné, Hernani, Notre-Dame de Paris, Marie Tudor, Le Rhin, Les*

Contemplations, Les Misérables) that seem to have inspired or in some way influenced Baudelaire in *Les Fleurs du Mal.* Most of the suggestions are so persuasive that the pertinent verses of Baudelaire will sound in the thought of those familiar with his poems even before they come upon the citations in the text. Professor Pommier's suggestions are urged less as matters of source-study than as elements in artistic inspiration, and his article affords an impressive demonstration of a very subtle aspect of literary sensibility.

Reizov, B[oris]. "Viktor Gjugo, P'er Leru i 'simvolicheskij stil' " ("Victor Hugo, Pierre Leroux and 'symbolic style.' "). *Izvestija Akademii Nauk S. S. S. R. Serija Literatury i Jazyka,* xxvi (1967), 113-20.

Riffaterre, Michael. "La poétisation du mot chez Victor Hugo." *CAIEF,* No. 19 (1967), pp. 177-94.
An attempt to demonstrate the author's conception of stylistics as the study of linguistic structures internal to each literary work. See the discussion of this paper, pp. 286-92.

Roy, Claude. "Hugo en somme . . . " *RdP,* LXXIV, No. 9 (1967), 20-33.
A part of the author's *Victor Hugo* (Coll. "Génie et Réalités": Hachette).

Sacy, S. de, ed. *Quatre-vingt-treize.* Préface de Michel Mohrt. (Coll. "Le Livre de Poche.") Paris: Librairie Générale Française (exclusivité Hachette), 1967. 2 vols. 3.40 Fr.

Seebacher, Jacques. "Esthétique et politique chez Victor Hugo: 'l'utilité du beau.' " *CAIEF,* No. 19 (1967), 233-46.
Analyzing a passage intended for Hugo's *William Shakespeare* but not utilized, Seebacher sees Hugo as having foreseen several important developments of modern esthetics and criticism. See the discussion of this paper, pp. 302-08.

Reviews of books previously listed:
ALBOUY, Pierre, ed., *L'Ane* (see *ELN,* v, Supp., 62), rev. by Richard M. Chadbourne in *FR,* XL (1967), 847-48; BARRERE, Jean-Bertrand, ed., *Un Carnet des 'Misérables,'* octobre-décembre 1860. *Notes et brouillons* (see *ELN,* IV, Supp., 69), rev. by Jean Gaudon in *MLR,* LXII (1967), 729-30; and by René Journet in *RHL,* LXVII (1967), 854-55; BARRERE, Jean-Bertrand, *Victor Hugo à l'oeuvre* (see ELN, v, Supp., 62), rev. by Jean Gaudon in *RHL,* LXVII (1967), 851-53; and by A.R.W. James in *FS,* XXI (1967), 259-61; JOURNET, R. et G. Robert, eds., *Boîte aux lettres* (see *ELN,* v, Supp., 64), rev. by J.-B. Barrère in *FS,* XXI (1967), 172-74; and by Jacques Seebacher in *RHL,* LXVIII (1967), 853-54; JOURNET, R. et G. Robert, eds., *Journal de ce que j'apprends chaque jour* (see *ELN,* v, Supp., 64), rev. by J.-B. Barrère in *FS,* XXI (1967), 172-74; and by Jacques Seebacher in *RHL,* LXVII (1967), 850-51; LAMBERT, F., ed., *Épîtres* (see *ELN,* v, Supp., 64), rev. by G. Franceschetti in *SFr,* XI (1967), 373-74; MAUROIS, André, *Victor Hugo and His World* (see *ELN,* v, Supp., 64), rev. by H.J. Hunt in *FS,* XXI (1967), 72.

JACQUEMONT

Théodoridès, Jean. "La mission de Victor Jacquemont dans l'Inde anglaise 1828-1832 (documents inédits)." *Revue d'Histoire Diplomatique*, LXXXI (1967), 125-42.
Various documents: Jacquemont's passport, will, etc.

LACORDAIRE

Peyrade, Jean. *La Conversion de Lacordaire ou le baptême du romantisme*. (Conversions Célèbres, 9.) Paris: Wesmael-Charlier, 1966. Pp. 177. 12.90 Fr.
A light-weight, uncritical account of Lacordaire's religious evolution. (J.S.P.)

LAMARTINE

Barbiano di Belgiojoso, Guido. "Un'amicizia italiana di Alphonse de Lamartine." *SFr*, XI (1967), 272-77.
Lamartine and the Marchese Giorgio Pallaviano and his wife. The author gives the text of three letters to the poet from the Marchesa (1850, 1856).

Chervet, Maurice. "Lamartine et le terroir." *RDM*, Jan. 1, 1966, pp. 102-06.
Lamartine's deep, abiding attachment to the "home place" (Milly); his descriptions are really *états d'âme*.

Croisille, Christian. "Sur la date d'un poème des 'Recueillements' de Lamartine: l'Ode á M. Wap.'" *RHL*, LXVII (1967), 784-88.
The poem dates from August, 1838.

des Cognets, Jean, ed. *Recueillements poétiques*. (Classiques Garnier.) Paris: Garnier Frères, 1966. Pp. xx + 393.
Useful as an inexpensive compendium of all the poems which Lamartine published in the various editions of this volume, plus the dozens of miscellaneous lyrics and pieces of occasional verse never integrated into any of his collections, but disappointing in the complete lack of annotation, even bibliographical. (J.S.P.)

Domange, Michel. "La chute de l'Empire vue par la mère de Lamartine." *RdP*, Nov. 1967, pp. 68-76.
Extracts from her journal, with linking commentary.

Guillemin, Henri. "Lamartine en 1824. Lettres inédites." *MedF*, No. 177 (Dec. 1966).
Five letters to the Austrian diplomat, the Count de Senfft.

Mormile, Mario. *L'Idylle épique de Lamartine et de Longfellow. Etude de Jocelyn et d'Evangeline*. Rome: Ricerche (Centenari), 1967. Pp. 49.

Perrochon, Henri. "Lamartine et le pays de Vaud." In his *De Rousseau à Ramuz*. Bienne: Editions du Panorama, 1966. Pp. 308. 12.50 Sw. Fr.

Redman, Harry, Jr. "A Little Known Letter of Lamartine." *RomN*, VIII (1967), 188-89.
A brief letter ca. 1855 to Mademoiselle Alzire.

Thérive, André. "De la facilité." *TR*, No. 204 (1965), pp. 81-84.

Waldinger, Renée. "Lamartine et Voltaire." *FR*, XXXIX (1966), 496-500.
Lamartine's praise of Voltaire (in the *Histoire des Girondins*) can be seen as the logical outgrowth of his break with the Restoration régime ca. 1827.

Reviews of books previously listed:
CHERVET, Maurice, ed., *Secondes Journées européennes d'études lamartiniennes* (see *ELN*, V, Supp., 65), rev. by Petre Ciureanu in *SFr*, XI, 566-67; VERDIER, Abel, *Les Amours italiennes de Lamartine: Graziella et Lena* (see *ELN*, III, Supp., 69), rev. by Maurice Hougardy in *RBPH*, XLIV, 254-55.

LAMENNAIS

Guillemin, Henri, ed. "Lamennais, l'irréductible. Lettres inédites présentées par Henri Guillemin." *Journal de Genève*, Jan. 8-9, 1966.

Hayward, J. E. S. "Lamennais and the Religion of Social Consensus." *Archives de Sociologie des Religions*, XI (1966), 37-46.

Le Guillou, Louis. *Les Discussions critiques. Journal de la crise mennaisienne. Genèse et édition du manuscrit 356 de la Bibliothèque Universitaire de Rennes.* Paris: Armand Colin, 1967. Pp. 111. 12 Fr.
Rev. by Roger Aubert in *Revue d'Histoire Ecclésiastique*, LXII, 538-47.
A critical edition of this manuscript (which is not in Lamennais' hand, however). In his introduction, Le Guillou stresses the influence of Polish affairs in Lamennais' rupture with the Papacy.

Le Guillou, Louis. "L'évolution de la pensée religieuse de Lamennais." *IL*, XVIII (1966), 139-43.
A résumé of the author's thesis bearing the same title (see *ELN*, V, Supp., 67).

Le Guillou, Louis. "Un fidèle ami de Lamennais: le comte Benoît d'Azy. Lettres inédites de Benoît d'Azy à Lamennais (1825-1833)." *AnBret*, LXXIII (1966), 363-427.
Twenty-eight letters, with a brief introduction and a few notes.

Roe, W. G. *Lamennais and England: The Reception of Lamennais's Religious Ideas in England in the 19th Century.* (Oxford Modern Language and Literature Monographs.) Oxford University Press, 1966. Pp. viii + 241. 38s; $6.10.
Rev. anon. in *TLS*, Dec. 1, 1966, p. 1131; by C. Cordié in *SFr*, XI, 165; by Martin E. Marty in *JR*, XLVII, 277-78; by John Ratte in *Commonweal*, Oct. 6, 1967; and by Lancelot Sheppard in *TR*, No. 229 (Feb. 1967), pp. 140-42.

Reviews of books previously listed:

DERRÉ, Jean-René, *Metternich et Lamennais* (see *ELN*, III, Supp., 70), rev. by Roger Aubert in *Revue d'Histoire Ecclésiastique*, LXII, 649-51; LE GUILLOU, Louis, *L'Evolution de la pensée religieuse de Lamennais* (see *ELN*, V, Supp., 67), rev. by Roger Aubert in *Revue d'Histoire Ecclésiastique*, LXII, 538-47; and by Pierre Moreau in *RLC*, XLI, 308-12.

LA MORVONNAIS

Chaffiol-Debillemont, F. "Hippolyte de La Morvonnais, poète breton." *RDM*, Sept. 15, 1967, pp. 211-22.

LAMOTHE-LANGON

De Diesbach, G., ed. *Mémoires et souvenirs d'une femme de qualité sur le Consulat et l'Empire.* (Le Temps Retrouvé.) Paris: Mercure de France, 1966. Pp. 394.

LATOUCHE

See Derche ("Nerval").

Reviews of book previously listed:

HOFFMANN, Léon-François, ed. *Dernières Lettres de deux amans de Barcelone* (see *ELN*, V, Supp., 68), rev. by Albert Delorme in *RdS*, LXXXVII, 374; by G. Jacques in *LR*, XXI, 291-92; and by J. Théodoridès in *RdS*, LXXXVII, 145-46.

LEFEVRE

Chaffiol-Debillemont, F. "Un poète romantique: Jules Lefèvre-Deumier." *RDM*, April 15, 1967, pp. 524-36.

A brief biography and an attempted rehabilitation.

MAISTRE

Branan, A. G. "Six lettres inédites de Joseph de Maistre au comte de Noailles." *RHL*, LXVII (1967), 123-34.

These letters, written from St. Petersburg, Paris, and Turin, date from the period 1816-1818. Matters both personal and literary are treated.

Reviews of books previously listed:

LEBRUN, R.A., *Throne and Altar: The Political and Religious Thought of Joseph de Maistre* (see *ELN*, V, Supp., 68), rev. by J.W. Gough in *EHR*, LXXXII, 182; and by R. Triomphe in *RHL*, LXVII, 160-61; LOVIE, Jacques, and Joannès Chetail, eds., *Du Pape* (see *ELN*, V, Supp., 68), rev. by C. Cordié in *SFr*, XI, 162-63.

MARMIER

Ménard, Jean. *Xavier Marmier et le Canada.* (Relations Franco-Canadiennes au XIXe Siècle.) Quebec: Les Presses de l'Université Laval, 1967. Pp. 210. $4.20.

Rev. by Roger Duhamel in *Revue d'Histoire de l'Amérique Française*, XXI, 312-13.

MÉRIMÉE

Almela Vivès, Francisco. *La Carmen de Mérimée era valenciana.* Valencia: Tip. Moderna, 1966. Pp. 36.

Dale, R. C. *The Poetics of Prosper Mérimée.* (Studies in French Literature, XIV.) The Hague and Paris: Mouton and Co., 1966. Pp. 181. 20 Guilders (28 Fr.).

Mérimée's literary theories are here worked into a system by piecing together the many scattered observations to be found in his works, including his correspondence. Frankly, the author insists on utilizing more quotations than are really needed in order to construct Mérimée's not very startling "poetics." Moreover, in his surrounding commentary, he reworks Mérimée's ideas into monotonous restatements, occasionally tricking these variations out in terminology whose pretentiousness is at odds with Mérimée's dry simplicity and ironic restraint. On the other hand, he often falls into sub-literary flatness (" 'Clara' . . . realized his own theatre had been pretty much of that nature"—p. 115) and at least once into solecism ("he was well aware of the dangers laying in wait"—p. 97). Is the author's spelling or proof-reading to be blamed for "dilletantish" (p. 110) and "Dilletantism" (p. 162)? Getting away from mere nitpicking, we must observe that Dale has very thoroughly studied the corpus of Mérimée's writings and so spared future students of this subject a great deal of searching. For there is a valuable subject here, but this is probably not the definitive treatment of it. (J.S.P.)

Dean, Winton. *Georges Bizet: His Life and Work.* London: J. M. Dent, 1965. Pp. xiv + 304.

Rev. by J.W.K. [John Klein] in *Music and Letters,* XLVI (1965), 336-39. The author deals, somewhat cursorily, with the changes made by Bizet's librettists (Meilhac and Halévy) in the material taken from Mérimée. An appendix ("Catalogue of Works") reveals that Bizet wrote a large number of songs based on poems by Romantic authors, notably Hugo, Lamartine, Arvers, Musset, Gautier, and Desbordes-Valmore.

Hainsworth, G. "West-African Local Colour in *Tamango." FS,* XXI (1967), 16-23.

The influences of Prévost's *Histoire générale des voyages,* Raynal's *Histoire philosophique des Indes,* and several lesser authors are sorted out.

Livermore, Ann. "The Birth of Carmen." *Music Review,* XXVII (1966), 194-201.

Possible influences of Spanish plays and songs for theater on Mérimée's conception of his heroine and her story.

Livermore, Ann. "Carmen and Ulysses." *Music Review,* XXVIII (1967), 300-10.

Parallels with, and allusions to, Bizet's opera and incidentally to Mérimée's story. The connections between the two bodies of material are mostly rather tenuous.

Parturier, Maurice, ed. *Romans et nouvelles*. (Classiques Garnier.) Paris: Garnier Frères, 1967. 2 vols.

Poydenot, Henry. *"Colomba* ou les métamorphoses d'un sujet de roman." *RDM,* July 1, 1966, pp. 90-96.

The real incidents and characters Mérimée utilized in writing his novel; his trip to Corsica (1839); his personal contacts with "Colomba" and her family in later life. Nothing new here.

Raitt, A. W., ed. *The Venus of Ille and Other Stories*. Translated by Jean Kimber. Oxford University Press, 1966. Pp. 238. $4.00.

Rev. anon. in *TLS,* July 21, 1966; by Alfred Cismaru in *Studies in Short Fiction,* v, 86-87.

Redman, Harry. "Quand Mérimée commentait la Guerre de sécession." *RDM,* Aug. 1, 1966, pp. 348-55.

Mérimée's pro-Southern attitude; his Southern friends; his comments on events and protagonists.

See also Nuñez de Arenas ("Spanish 2. General").

Review of book previously listed:

CERMAKIAN, Marianne, and France Achener, eds., *Lettres à Edward Ellice (1857-1863)* (see *PQ,* XLIII, 477), rev. by Jacques Dubois in *RBPH,* XLV, 659-60.

MICHELET

Poulet, Georges. "Michelet et le moment d'Eros." *NRF,* xv (1967), 610-35.

In a typical exercise, Poulet exploits the sexual connotations of Michelet's style. His point: "Bref, à mesure que Michelet identifie plus complètement son activité sexuelle avec son activité d'écrivain, de penseur et d'historien, le point de vue philosophique et historique qui était le sien tend à se transformer, à tenir de plus en plus compte de l'avenir."

Review of book previously listed:

ALFF, Wilhelm, *Michelets Ideen* (see *ELN,* v, Supp., 69), rev. by Manfred Hutter in *RF,* LXXVIII, 593-95.

MOREAU

Vignon, Octave. *Hégésippe Moreau, sa vie, son oeuvre*. Préface de M. Jean Fabre. (Société d'Histoire et d'Archéologie de l'arrondissement de Provins, Seine-et-Marne. Documents et travaux, II-III.) Provins: La Société, 1966. 2 vols. 43 Fr.

MUSSET

Greet, Anne Hyde. "Humor in the Poetry of Alfred de Musset." *SIR,* VI (1967), 175-92.

Hartley, K. H. "Three 'Lorenzacci.'" *AUMLA,* No. 28 (Nov. 1967), pp. 227-34.
Compares three treatments of the theme—Musset's, Benelli's (*La Maschera di Bruto*), and Shirley's (*The Traitor*)—in order to show how each author has twisted the enigmatic central character to his own ends.

Jansen, Steen. "Alfred de Musset, Dramaturge: *A quoi rêvent les jeunes filles* et la technique dramatique d'*Un spectacle dans un fauteuil.*" *Orbis Litterarum,* XXI, (1966), 222-54.
Discovers four elements especially characteristic of Musset's technique here: "grande indépendance de la scène isolée, imprécision du décor, très nette stylisation et renoncement à l'action principale."

Mandach, André von. "Eine wiedergefundene Novelle von Alfred de Musset: Les Amours du Petit Job et de la Belle Blandine (Okt. 1856)." *ZFSL,* LXXXVII (1967), 347-59.
Reprints the story.

Nordon, Pierre. "Alfred de Musset et l'Angleterre (Suite)." *LR,* XXI (1967), 354-68.

See also Reizov ("Staël").

Review of work previously listed:
LEBOIS, André, *Vues sur le théâtre de Musset* (see *ELN,* V, Supp., 70), rev. by André Bourgeois in *BA,* XLI (1967), 423-24.

NERVAL

Bays, Gwendolyn M. "The Orphic Vision of Nerval, Baudelaire, and Rimbaud." *CLS,* IV (1967), 17-26.
The author of *The Orphic Vision* (Lincoln, Nebraska, 1964) cites a distinction from ancient times "between two kinds of seers—the nocturnal or the orphic, the artist who descends into the underworld (the Unconscious) and charms the wild beasts there; and the Platonic-Plotinian experience later cultivated by medieval Christian mystics." She sees this as a "distinction between a waking consciousness and a sleeping or 'unconsciousness' state" and identifies Gérard de Nerval as "the pioneer of this group of seer poets . . . the most purely visionary of them all" and thinks that perhaps Gérard dreams of his ancestral past (rather than of his own) because "he attained a deeper level of the unconscious than Baudelaire or Rimbaud."

Belleli, Maria Luisa. "I viaggi di Nerval in Italia." *RLMC,* XX (1967), 45-52.
Offers interesting details on Gérard's two journeys to Italy, in 1834 and 1843.

Bénichou, Paul. *L'Ecrivain et ses travaux.* Paris: J. Corti, 1967. Pp. xviii + 362. 32 Fr.
Review notice in *Bulletin Critique du Livre Français,* No. 260-261 (Aug.-Sept. 1967), p. 715, notes eleven essays here—among them one on two sonnets of Nerval.

Carofiglio, Vito. *Nerval e il mito della "pureté."* (Pubblicazioni della Facoltà di lettere e filosofia dell'Università di Milano. XL. Sezione a cura dell'Istituto di lingue e letterature moderne, 2.) Florence: La Nuova Italia, 1966.

Chambers, Ross. "Les Nuits mal employées de Gérard de Nerval." *RSH,* n.s. No. 126 (1967), pp. 167-84.
The first of ten articles devoted to Nerval and others in a special issue of the *Revue des Sciences Humaines* ("Autour de Nerval et de l'ésoterisme"). Shows in Nerval's imagination "l'existence d'un *complexe de la nuit mal employée"* which relates his guilty flight toward the dream with images of nocturnal festival, fire in the night, the descent to Hell, a feeling of revolt and guilt, and finally the idea of prison and an expiation.

Constans, François. "Les Sonnets majeurs des *Chimères." RSH,* n.s. No. 126 (1967), pp. 197-213.
On "Artémis" and "El Desdichado."

Derche, Roland. "Deux sources littéraires possibles de 'Myrtho.' " *RHL,* LXVII (1967), 612-17.
Le Prisonnier chanceux ou les Aventures de Jean de la Tour Miracle by le Comte de Gobineau and H. Latouche's poem "A Mme Desbordes-Valmore" in *La Minerve Littéraire* of 1820 (reprinted in *L'Almanach dédié aux Dames pour 1822*).

Glatigny, Michel. "La Place des adjectifs épithètes dans deux oeuvres de Nerval." *FM,* XXXV (1967), 201-20.
A study of the *antéposition* and *postposition* of adjectives in *La Main enchantée* and *Aurélia* ("le premier conte et la dernière oeuvre en prose de Nerval") with conclusions and observations of interest to students of the relationship between syntax and style.

Kaplan, Edward Kiwie. "L'Imagination occulte chez Gérard de Nerval: Une épistémologie de connaissance spirituelle dans *Aurélia." RSH,* n.s. No. 126 (1967), pp. 185-95.
Sees Nerval's experience in dream as well as his experience awake as furnishing him "une perspective métaphysique complète qui nourrissait l'imagination occulte." Thus Gérard constructed "une religion de rêve ratifiée par le christianisme officiel" and, by bringing together all the symbolic forms, "[il] a réalisé son intuition primordiale que toute religion est valide selon l'expérience intérieure."

Krüger, Manfred. *Gérard de Nerval. Darstellung und Deutung des Todes.* Stuttgart, Berlin, Cologne, Mainz: W. Kohlhammer Verlag, 1966. Pp. 230.
Rev. in *ZFSL,* LXXVII (1967), 375-76.
Includes an excellent bibliography of over 200 entries.

Lassaigne, Jean. "Gérard de Nerval et le Périgord." *Bulletin de la Sociéte Historique et Archéologique de Périgord,* 3e livraison, 1966.

Montal, Robert. "Nerval et Gide. De l'*Aurélia* aux *Cahiers d'André Walter." Le Thyrse,* Nov.-Dec., 1966.

Richer, Jean. *Le Carnet de "Dolbreuse":* Essai de lecture. Athens, 1967. Pp. 117.
An edition, with commentary, of the text of Gérard's notebook for the pro-jected novel or play, *Dolbreuse.* The "Répertoire des thèmes et noms propres du carnet" (pp. 113-15) is a precious indication of Nerval's literary references. Richer notes that "la religion de Nerval telle qu'elle apparaît dans ces notations est un christianisme qui s'essaye à concilier certains éléments du rousseauisme avec la croyance au péché originel, le mysticisme théosophique et la religion naturelle." One is not likely to forget such entries as the following: "106.36— Oh! nature qu' on doit reposer doucement dans ton sein. Rendre aux élémens ce que chacun a fourni pour mon corps. Mourir dans quelque fossé imprégné des vapeurs et des parfums du soir. Les oiseaux raseront mon front de l'aile et mon âme se dissoudra dans les vapeurs du soir."

Richer, Jean, ed. *L'Imagier de Harlem.* Paris: Minard (Lettres Mod-ernes), 1967. 30 Fr. (*Oeuvres complémentaires de Gérard de Nerval,* T. V. Théâtre 3.)

Richer, Jean, ed. *Oeuvres complémentaires de Gérard de Nerval, III. Théâtre. I. Piquillo. Les Monténégrins. Ébauches.* Paris: Minard, 1965. Pp. 437.
Rev. by Ross Chambers in *AUMLA,* No. 27 (May 1967), pp. 125-26; by François Constans in *RSH,* n.s. No. 126 (1967), pp. 322-24; and by Henri Lemaitre in *RHL,* LXVII (1967), 861.

Richer, Jean. " 'Sylvie' de Nerval ou la ronde des heures: un récit en forme de voûte étoilée." *Saggi e Ricerche di Letteratura Francese,* VII (1966), 201-37.
Complements Richer's study on the astrological basis of *Aurélia.*

Richer, Jean. "Une lettre inédite de Gérard de Nerval: 'A Madame Mar-tin (du Nord) à Ostende,' présentée par Jean Richer." *Les Nouvelles Littéraires,* Aug. 10, 1967, p. 7.

Schneider, Marcel. "Nerval à la recherche de la nuit noire et blanche." *NRF,* xv (1967), 491-98.
Speculations on Nerval's spiritual quest and death in the light of recent studies by Peyrouzet, Richer, Christian Dédéyan, and Poulet.

Senelier, Jean. *Un amour inconnu de Gérard de Nerval,* avec des docu-ments et des estampes inédits. Préface de Jean Richer. (Nouvelle Bib-liothéque Nervalienne.) Paris: Minard, 1966. Pp. viii + 264.

Rev. by François Constans in *RSH*, n.s. No. 126 (1967), pp. 324-25; by Marcel Françon in *FR*, XL (1967), 713-14; and by M. Milner in *IL*, XIX (1967), 122.

Senelier would identify Gérard's Pandora, not as Marie Pleyel, but as the actress and dancer Esther de Bongars, with whom Gérard may have had a liaison between April 1838 and October 1839.

Serra-Lima, F. "Rubén Darío y Gérard de Nerval." *Revista Hispanica Moderna*, XXXII (1966), 25-32.

Identifies the drama of the mad poet Garcín in Darío's tale "El pájaro azul" (important in the literary revolution called *modernismo*) as not merely an idealized biography of Darío himself, but also as "una verdadera biografía de Gérard de Nerval."

Stierle, Karlheinz. *Dunkelheit und Form in Gérard de Nervals "Chimères."* (Theorie und Geschichte der Literatur und der schönen Künste. Bd 5.) Munich: Wilhelm Fink, 1967. Pp. 123.

Strange, William C. "The Proper Marriage of Allegory and Myth in Nerval's 'Horus.' " *MLQ*, XXVIII (1967), 317-28.

An attempt to find meaning in one of Nerval's less studied poems. Denying the possibility of fixing exact equivalents, the author tries to come to grips with the symbolic identity of Kneph and his rôle in the poem, which he finds telling two stories: "one of a god who dies and is reborn in a myth, and the other of gods whose demise is a matter of historical fact."

Villas, James. "Present State of Nerval Studies: 1957 to 1967." *FR*, XLI (1967), 221-31.

Intended "to offer as complete a critical outline as possible of the most interesting and significant items to appear on Nerval since the publication of Cellier's work in 1957." The author will soon publish a critical bibliography of Nerval studies from 1900 to 1967.

See also Cottin ("Gautier"); Grojnowski ("French I. General"); Junker ("Balzac").

Reviews of books previously listed:

GUILLAUME, Jean, S.J., ed., *"Les Chimères" de Nerval* (see *ELN*, V, Supp., 71), rev. by Edward Ahearn in *FR*, XL (1967), 570-71; MOREAU, Pierre, *Sylvie et ses soeurs nervaliennes* (see *ELN*, V, Supp., 71), rev. by Petre Ciureanu in *SFr*, XI (1967), 375; and by Alison Fairlie in *FS*, XXI (1967), 174-75; PEYROUZET, Édouard, *Gérard de Nerval inconnu* (see *ELN*, IV, Supp., 78), rev. by Raymond Jean in *RSH*, n.s. No. 126 (1967), pp. 325-26; by M[ax]. M[ilner]. in *IL*, XIX (1967), 82; and by Jean Richer in RHL, LXVII (1967), 858-60; RICHER, Jean, et al., eds., *Aurélia, ou Le Réve et la vie* (see *ELN*, IV, Supp., 79), rev. by Ross Chambers in *AUMLA*, No. 27 (1967), pp. 125-26; by François Constans in *RSH*, n.s. No. 126 (1967), p. 321, who finds *Aurélia* "de toute manière . . . en rapport étroit avec le sonnet *Artémis*"; and by Henri Lemaitre in *RHL*, LXVII (1967), 861-63.

NODIER

Nodier, Charles. *Bonaventure Despériers. Cirano de Bergerac.* Geneva: Slatkine Reprints, 1967.
A photographic reproduction of the original (?) edition.

Nodier, Charles. *Infernalia.* Paris: Poche-Club, 1966.

Orlando, Francesco. "Charles Nodier memorialista: una infanzia sotto la Rivoluzione." *Critica Storica,* IV (1965), 279-98.

Review of work previously listed:
OLIVER, A. Richard, *Charles Nodier: Pilot of Romanticism* (see *ELN*, IV, Supp., 80), rev. by R.C. Dale in *ECr*, V (1967), 249-50.

REYNAUD

Review of book previously listed:
GRIFFITHS, David Albert, *Jean Reynaud encyclopédiste de l'époque romantique* (see *ELN*, V, Supp., 72-73), rev. by Pierre Moreau in *RLC*, XL, 145-51.

SAINTE-BEUVE

Bonnerot, Jean, ed. *Correspondance générale,* recueillie, classée et annotée par Jean Bonnerot. Avertissement de Jean Pommier. Tome XV, 1866 (Nouvelle Série, t. IX). Toulouse: Privat; Paris: Didier, 1966. Pp. 473. 78 Fr.
Rev. in *SFr*, XI (1967), 170.

Fayolle, Roger. "Sainte-Beuve et l'Ecole Normale: l'Affaire de 1867." *RHL*, LXVII (1967), 557-76.

Gale, John E. "Sainte-Beuve and Baudelaire on *Madame Bovary.*" *FR*, XLI (1967), 30-37.

Hummel, John and Peter Soehlke. "Sainte-Beuve on Classics and Classicists." *Arion*, VI (1967), 252-65.
Brief introduction and translation of passages from Sainte-Beuve's works and correspondence.

Richard, Jean-Pierre. "Sainte-Beuve, l'objet et la littérature." *Preuves*, April-May, 1967, pp. 18-29, 28-43.

Rowland, Michael. *"Contre Sainte-Beuve* and Character-Presentation in *A la Recherche du temps perdu."* *RomN*, VIII (1967), 183-87.

See also Katz ("French 1. General").

Reviews of works previously listed:
BONNEROT, Jean, ed., *Correspondance générale,* tome XIV (see *ELN*, IV, Supp., 81), rev. by André Vandegans in *RBPH*, XLV (1967), 660-61; MOREAU, Pierre, *La Critique selon Sainte-Beuve* (see *ELN*, IV, Supp., 81), rev. by André Vandegans in *RBPH*, XLV (1967), 295.

SAINT-MARTIN

Raymond, Marcel. "Saint-Martin et l'Illuminisme contre l' 'Illuminismo.' "
LI, XIX (1967), 55-70.
Saint-Martin, says Raymond, "a rappelé à l'homme le sens de sa destinée;
j'ose ajouter: celui de sa destinée éternelle."

SAND

Anon., d. "Lettres de George Sand à François Buloz." *RDM,* April 1,
1967, pp. 354-63.

Carrère, Casimir. *George Sand amoureuse. Ses amants, ses amitiés tendres.*
Préface d'André Maurois. Paris and Geneva: La Palatine, 1967. Pp.
xvi + 452. 30.60 Fr. S.

Lubin, Georges, ed. *Correspondance.* Tome III (juillet 1835-avril 1837).
Paris: Garnier, 1967. Pp. xvii + 979; illus. 38 Fr.
Includes letters numbered 956 to 1460 inclusive, over 500 items. Useful indexes:
there are a biographical index of correspondents and an index to Sand's opinions on various topics as well as an index of names and another of places
cited. Among the well-known correspondents of this period are Musset, Dumas
père, Liszt, Sainte-Beuve, and others. (C.C.)

Lubin, Georges. *George Sand en Berry.* (Albums Littéraires.) Paris:
Hachette, 1967. Pp. 173. 53.50 Fr.
Rev. by René Merker in *FR,* XLI (1967), 420-21.

Marix-Spire, Thérèse. "La femme Sand: George Sand et Baudelaire (documents inédits)." *Europe,* No. 456-457 (1967), pp. 205-16.

Poli, Annarosa. *George Sand vue par les Italiens. Essai de bibliographie
critique.* Florence: Sansoni; Paris: Marcel Didier, 1965. Pp. 262.
L. 3500.
Rev. by Guido Barbiano di Belgioioso in *Aevum,* XLI (1967), 412-14, by Jean
Nicolas in *REI,* n.s. XIII (1967), 200-01.

Poli, Annarosa, ed. *Les Maîtres mosaïstes.* (Collana di Classici Francesi.)
Florence: Sansoni, 1966.

Vernois, Paul. "L'archaïsme dans le roman rustique aux XIXᵉ et
XXᵉ siècles." *CAIEF,* No. 19 (1967), pp. 69-85.
On the interplay of regional and archaic speech in the rustic novels of George
Sand and her leading successors. See discussion of this paper, pp. 263-69.

Reviews of works previously listed:
COLIN, Georges, *Bibliographie des premières publications des romans de George
Sand* (see *ELN, V,* Supp., 73), rev. by René Joly in *RHL,* LXVII (1967), 855-
56; POMMIER, Jean, *George Sand et le rêve monastique. Spiridion* (see *ELN,*
V, Supp., 74), rev. in *SFr,* XI (1967), 374-75; and by Yves Le Hir in *RSH,*
XXXII (1967), 328-29.

SENANCOUR

Grenier, Jean. "La Nuit de Thiel." *NRF*, xiv, No. 166 (1966), 663-67.
On the experience described in the fourth letter of *Oberman* reflecting the July night that Senancour himself spent in 1793 on the lake shore at Thiel which provided "la révélation la plus complète de sa propre nature et de son propre destin." Author would compare this with the famous nights of intuitive revelation of Pascal and Tolstoy, but sees Senancour as at best thereafter merely transforming his torture into somnolence.

Padgett, G. "The Idea of Nature in Senancour's *Sur les générations actuelles.*" *Nottingham French Studies*, v, No. 2 (1966), 52-66.
An attempt "to discuss those aspects of this first known work of Senancour that are relevant to an appreciation of his development as a thinker, and particularly to the understanding of the intricacies of his thought." Shows his ideas of nature here as "in some ways, a form of escapism."

Padgett, G. "Senancour's Ennui and Its Relation to His Ideas." *Nottingham French Studies*, vi, No. 1 (1967), 2-18.
An examination of the melancholy and sense of alienation in Senancour's *Aldomen* and *Oberman*.

Pizzorusso, Arnaldo. "L'allusion biographique dans une lettre d' 'Oberman.' " *CAIEF*, No. 19 (1967), pp. 129-42.
This study of letter lxxxix finds a confusion of *journal intime* with novel which accounts for "le ton vague et indécis de bien des pages d'*Oberman*."

Reviews of books previously listed:
LE GALL, Béatrice, *L'Imaginaire chez Senancour* (see *ELN*, v, Supp., 75), rev. by Pierre Moreau in *RHL*, lxvii (1967), 842-45; RAYMOND, Marcel, *Senancour. Sensations et révélations* (see *ELN*, v, Supp., 75), rev. anon. in *TLS*, June 8, 1967, pp. 497-98; and by Christiane Berkone in *RR*, lviii (1967), 227-29.

SISMONDI

Rappard, William E. *Economistes genevois du XIXᵉ siècle*. Préface de Giovanni Busino. (Travaux de droit, d'économie, de sociologie et de sciences politiques, 43.) Geneva: Droz; Paris: Minard, 1966. Pp. xx + 585. 59 Fr.
A chapter is devoted to Sismondi.

STAEL

Collet, G. P. "Cosmopolitisme et nationalisme chez Madame de Staël." Pp. 552-57 in *Actes du IVᵉ Congrès de l'Association Internationale de Litterature Comparée (Fribourg 1964)*. Vol. II. The Hague: Mouton, 1966.

Cordey, Pierre. *Madame de Staël: le deuil éclatant du bonheur*. (Egéries et femmes de lettres.) Lausanne: Editions Rencontre, 1967. Pp. 295 12 Sw. Fr.

Götze, Alfred. "Goethes Faust und Madame de Staël." *Archiv für das Studium der Neueren Sprachen und Literaturen,* ccIV (1967) 184-191.

Lehtonen, Maija. "Le fleuve du temps et le fleuve de l'enfer: thèmes et images dans *Corinne* de Madame de Staël." *NM,* LXVIII (1967), 225-42.

Machado, José António. *Madame de Staël.* Lisbon: Portugália Ed., 1967. Pp. 379. 11 Fr.

Marshall, J. F. "Madame de Staël et Madame de Tessé." *RHL,* LXVII (1967), 114-22.

Pange, Comtesse Jean de. "Nationalisme et cosmopolitisme dans l'oeuvre de Mme de Staël." Pp. 541-46 in *Actes du IVᵉ Congrès de l'Association Internationale de Littérature Comparée.* The Hague: Mouton, 1966.
Rev. by S. Grotto in *SFr,* XI (1967), 163.

Pange, Comtesse Jean de. "La rencontre de Madame de Staël et de Talma à Lyon en 1809." Pp. 187-195 in *Actes du 5ᵉ Congrès National de la Société Française de Littérature Comparée, Lyon, mai, 1962. Imprimerie, Commerce et Littérature.* Paris: Les Belles Lettres, 1965. Pp. 230.

Pellegrini, Carlo. "L'Italia di Madame de Staël." *La Vita d'Italia,* LXXII (1966), 670-79.

Reizov, B[oris]. "Poeticeskaja Zagadka Zermeny de Stal' (A Poetic Riddle of Germaine de Staël)." *Izvestija Akademii Nauk S. S. S. R. Serija Literatury i Jazyka,* XXV (1966), 406-09.
A four line poem by Mme de Staël ("Tu m'appelles la vie: appelle-moi ton âme") closely resembles one version of a poem by Byron and a couplet of Musset (from *Fantasio*). Reizov suggests the possibility that all three were translated from a Portuguese original. (C.C.)

Starobinski, Jean. "Mme de Staël et la définition de la littérature." *NRF,* XIV (Dec. 1966), 1054-59.

See also Descotes ("1. General"); Doyon ("Stendhal"); and Marcazzan ("Italian 2. General").

Reviews of works previously listed:
BIBLIOTHEQUE NATIONALE, *Madame de Staël et l'Europe* (see *ELN,* V, Supp., 75), rev. by Patrice Thompson in *RHL,* LXVII (1967), 158; CORDEY, Pierre, *Madame de Staël et Benjamin Constant sur les bords du Léman* (see *ELN,* V, Supp., 76), rev. by Ernest Abravanel in *SC,* IX (1967), 200; FORSBERG, Roberta

J. and N.C. Nixon, *Madame de Staël and Freedom Today* (see *ELN*, III, Supp., 78), rev. by Andrée Bergens in *RR*, LVII (1966), 69-70.

STENDHAL

Anon. [V. Del Litto?] "Chronique. Vᵉ Congrès international stendhalien." *SC*, IX (1967), 203-04.
An account of the meeting held in Paris, Sept. 15-17, 1966.

Alciatore, Jules C. "Un petit thème de 'Rouge et Noir': La politesse des grands." *SC*, IX (1967), 323-26.
The author traces Julien's progress in discerning the artificiality of aristocratic courtesy.

Baschet, Robert. "Stendhal et la musique." *RDM*, Sept. 1, 1966, pp. 75-82.

Baschet, Robert. "Stendhal et les arts plastiques." *RDM*, Aug. 1, 1967, pp. 378-92.
A sketch of Stendhal's esthetic.

Bassette, Louis. "Sur une épigraphe de 'Rouge et Noir': Stendhal et Saint-Réal." *SC*, IX (1967), 241-53.
Apropos of the famous definition of the novel as a mirror, Bassette explores the relationship between Stendhal and Saint-Réal. Some phrases in Saint-Réal's *Sur l'usage de l'histoire* may have inspired Stendhal's epigraph.

Baudoin, Henri. "Le Virgile de Henri Beyle (Stendhal et Cⁱᵉ — VI)." *SC*, X (1967), 1-8.
Various considerations, biographical and bibliographical, apropos of a copy of the *Georgics* which Stendhal acquired in 1794.

Bernini, Ferdinando. *Nostalgie stendhaliane*. Parma: Sezione d'Arti Grafiche dell'Istituto Statale d'Arte "Paolo Toschi," 1967. Pp. 30.
Rev. by C. Cordié in *SFr*, XI (1967), 371-72.
Articles originally published in the *Gazzetta di Parma* (Sept.-Nov., 1950).

Bethoux, Félix. "Carnet stendhalien." *Le Valentinois*, Sept. 17, 1966.
See résumé and criticism (by V. Del Litto?) in *SC*, IX (1967), 197.

Bethoux, Félix. "Sur le style de Stendhal." *SC*, IX (1967), 169-74.
A superficial attempt to show a substratum of "style dauphinois" in Stendhal.

Bezzola, Guido. "Intorno alla 'Correspondance' di Stendhal." *Studi Urbinati*, n.s. No. 1-2 (1964), 312-17.

Blin, Georges. "Stendhal et l'idée de 'Morale.' " *SC*, IX (1967), 155-62.

Bosselaers, Remi. "Passion et bonheur selon Stendhal." *SC*, X (1967), 9-21.

Boyer, Ferdinand. "Figures du monde stendhalien vues par Tullio Dandolo (Paris 1821-1823)." *SC*, IX (1967), 299-308.
Dandolo's *Ricordi* (1861) contain references to Cuvier, Destutt de Tracy, Lafayette, La Pasta, etc.

Casamassima, Franco. "En marge d' 'Armance': contribution à la recherche du Mont Kalos." *SC*, IX (1967), 231-39.
The author identifies the mountain referred to in Stendhal's novel with Kaloskopi, near Elis. In the process, he reveals Stendhal's knowledge of the actual military situation in Greece in 1827.

Castex, Pierre-Georges. *"Le Rouge et le noir" de Stendhal.* Paris: Société d'Edition d'Enseignement Supérieur, 1967. Pp. 187. 10 Fr.
Rev. anon. in *Bulletin Critique du Livre Français*, XXII (1967), 507-08; and by V. D[el]. L[itto]. in *SC*, IX (1967), 284-85 (see also p. 194).
A superior example of the manual for students, Castex's book is clear in its presentation of the main features of the novel and the most interesting problems which have beset its critics. In general, he takes a moderate, common-sense position. His principal topics are the materials—current events, literary reminiscences, autobiographical elements—which went into the making of the book, and the character of Julien. His discussion of the latter subject contains Castex's most original contribution: he improves on the widely held Martineau interpretation of Julien's criminal outburst at the climax of the novel. For Castex, Julien did not shoot Madame de Rênal in a trance-like state; rather, in complete lucidity, he pursued his revenge and remained faithful to himself. The principal defect of this study is the brevity with which certain topics are treated; this is especially true for the question of Stendhal's style. (J.S.P.)

Ciureanu, Petre. "Stendhal et Fabio Pallavicini (d'après des documents inédits)." *SC,* X (1967), 23-43.
A brief biography of this friend of Stendhal, interspersed with an account of their relationship.

Coe, Richard N. "Stendhal and the Art of Memory." Pp. 145-63 in J. C. Ireson, ed., *Currents of Thought in French Literature: Essays in Memory of G. T. Clapton.* Oxford: Basil Blackwell, 1965. Pp. xi + 370.
Coe traces Stendhal's gradually emerging realization of the connection between memory and imagination. His discussion is most helpful when it deals with Stendhal's distinction between different sorts of memory and when it demarcates the stages of the novelist's evolution.

Colesanti, Massimo, ed. *Les Cenci e altre Historiettes romaines.* (Biblioteca di Classici Stranieri. Sezione francese.) Milan: U. Mursia, 1966. Pp. 213. L. 1500.
Rev. by C. Cordié in *SFr*, XI (1967), 370-71; and by V. D[el]. L[itto]. in *SC,* IX (1967), 283.

Colesanti, Massimo. *Stendhal a teatro.* (Studi e testi, 1.) Milan: All' insegna del Pesce d'Oro, 1966. Pp. xxxi + 255.
Rev. by C. Cordié in *SFr*, XI (1967), 564; by Paolo Raponi in *Avanti*, Dec. 27, 1966; and by Enzo Siciliano in *Corriere della Sera*, Dec. 4, 1966.
A miscellany of articles on various facets of Stendhal's relationship with the theatre.

Crouzet, Michel, ed. *De l'amour.* (Garnier-Flammarion Texte Intégral, 49.) Paris: Garnier-Flammarion, 1965. Pp. 382.
Rev. by G. Mouillaud in *RHL*, LXVII (1967), 162-65.

Crouzet, Michel, ed. *La Chartreuse de Parme.* (Garnier-Flammarion Texte Intégral, 26.) Paris: Garnier-Flammarion, 1964. Pp. 509.
Rev. by G. Mouillaud in *RHL*, LXVII (1967), 162-65.

Crouzet, Michel. "Misanthropie et vertu: Stendhal et le problème républicain." *RSH*, n.s. No. 125 (1967), pp. 29-52.
Stendhal's dilemma — horror for the common people vs. an earnest desire to improve their welfare — made of him a sort of Romantic Alceste, virtuous, puritanical, hence a republican. But, as in so many things, he is unhappy and uneasy in this rôle, torn between virtue and pleasure, *égoïsme* and humanitarianism, *la logique* and passion.

Crouzet, Michel, ed. *Le Rouge et le noir.* (Garnier-Flammarion Texte Intégral, 11.) Paris: Garnier-Flammarion, 1964. Pp. 505.
Rev. by G. Mouillaud in *RHL*, LXVII (1967), 162-65.

Crouzet, Michel, ed. *La Vie de Henry Brulard.* (Le Monde en 10/18, nos. 175-176-177.) Paris: U. G. E., 1964. Pp. 500.
Rev. by G. Mouillaud in *RHL*, LXVII (1967), 162-65.

Del Litto, V. *Album Stendhal.* Iconographie réunie et commentée par V. Del Litto. (Albums Illustrés de la Pléiade, 5.) Paris: Gallimard, 1966.

Del Litto, V. "Bibliographie stendhalienne: année 1966." *SC,* X (1967), 111-31.
Includes supplement for 1965.

D[el]. L[itto]., V. "Chronique. VIᵉ Congrès international stendhalien." *SC,* IX (1967), 359-64.
Account of the meeting held in Parma, May 22-26, 1967.

Del Litto, Victor, ed. *Communications présentées au Congrès stendhalien de Civitavecchia (IIIᵉˢ Journées du Stendhal Club).* (Publications de l'Institut Français de Florence, 1ʳᵉ série, 16.) Florence: Sansoni; Paris: Marcel Didier, 1966. Pp. 342.
Rev. by Robert Baschet in *SC,* IX (1967), 351-55.
For a complete list of articles contained in this symposium, see *SC,* X (1967), 116-18.

Del Litto, V. "Un épisode inconnu de la vie de Stendhal: Stendhal, Lysimaque et le Gouvernement pontifical (Documents inédits)." *SC,* IX (1967), 119-39.
The documents add substantially to our knowledge of Stendhal's library.

Dethan, Georges. "De la valeur pour l'historien de la correspondance consulaire de Stendhal." Pp. 107-16 in *Mélanges Pierre Renouvin. Etudes d'histoire des relations internationales.* (Publications de la Faculté des lettres et sciences humaines de Paris. Série "Etudes et méthodes." T. 13.) Paris: Presses Universitaires de France, 1966.

d'Huart, Suzanne. "Stendhal et les Daru (d'après des documents privés inédits)." *SC,* IX (1967), 293-97.

Doyon, André. "Le dossier de la mort de Stendhal." *SC,* IX (1967), 317-21.
Details on the streets and buildings at the site of Stendhal's fatal attack.

Doyon, André, and Yves du Parc. "Amitiés parisiennes de Stendhal: les demoiselles de la Bergerie; étude suivie d'une correspondance inédite." *SC,* IX (1967), 141-54, 209-29.
Twenty-six letters of Madame Jules Gaulthier (née Rougier de la Bergerie), Madame Duflos, and Romain Colomb. Completes and corrects article by Louis Hastier in *RDM,* Feb. 1, 1965 (see *ELN,* IV, Supp., 87). There is little here bearing directly on Stendhal.

Doyon, André, and Yves du Parc. "Une cousine marseillaise de Stendhal: Madame Rebuffel." *SC,* X (1967), 45-54.
Account of Stendhal's amours with this lady (he simultaneously flirted with her daughter) in 1802-1804.

du Parc, Yves. "Stendhal chez les Ligures: correspondance inédite avec le Consulat Général de France à Gênes." *Revue d'Histoire Diplomatique,* LXXXI (1967), 143-67, 193-232.
Thirty-one diplomatic letters (1834-1841). Part I of this article introduces the general subject and provides portraits of Stendhal's addressees (le Baron Decazes, Tellier de Blanriez, César Famin, Louis Gros, le Comte de Cancloux).

François-Poncet, André. *Stendhal en Allemagne.* (Les Soirées du Luxembourg, No. 1.) Paris: Hachette, 1967. Pp. 109. 15.50 Fr.
Rev. by Ernest Abravanel in *SC,* X (1967), 74-75; and by Henri Clouard in *RDM,* Aug. 1, 1967, pp. 427-30.
A clear, well-informed, and gracefully written account of Stendhal's German experience, especially his two years in Brunswick (Nov. 1806—Nov. 1808), by the academician who was France's ambassador to Germany in the 1930's. (J.S.P.)

Friedman, Melvin J. "The Cracked Vase." *RomN*, VII (1966), 127-29.
On the significance of an episode in *Le Rouge et le noir* (II, xx); parallels with *The Idiot, The Egoist,* and *Set This House on Fire.*

Gerlach-Nielsen, Merete. *Stendhal théoricien et romancier de l'amour.* (Det Kong. Danske Videns. Selskab, Hist.-filos. Meddelelser, Bd. 40, Nr. 6.) Munksgaard: 1965. Pp. 124. 15 Kr.

Gilman, Stephen. *The Tower as Emblem: Chapters VIII, IX, XIX and XX of the Chartreuse de Parme.* (Analecta Romanica, XXII.) Frankfort: Vittorio Klostermann, 1967. Pp. 63.

González-Ruano, César, ed. *Rojo y negro. La Cartuja de Parma. Del amor.* Trad. Carlos Rivas y Gregorio Lafuerza. Prólogo de César González-Ruano. (Obras Inmortales.) Madrid: E. D. A. F., 1966. Pp. xxiv + 1479.

Grün, Ruth. *'Hommes-copies', 'Dandies' und 'Fausses passions': Ein Beitrag zu Stendhals Kritik an der Gesellschaft.* (Kölner Romanistische Arbeiten, n.s. Vol. 34.) Geneva: Librairie Droz; Paris: Librairie Minard, 1967. Pp. 158. 26 Fr.

Imbert, Henri-François, ed. *Armance.* (Garnier-Flammarion Texte Intégral, 137.) Paris: Garnier-Flammarion, 1967. Pp. 192. 2.45 Fr.
Rev. by V. D[el]. L[itto]. in *SC*, x (1967), 72; and by G. Mouillaud in *RHL*, LXVII (1967), 162-65.

Imbert, Henri-François. *Les Métamorphoses de la liberté ou Stendhal devant la Restauration et le Risorgimento.* Paris: José Corti, 1967. Pp. 670. 45 Fr.
Another study of the political content of Stendhal's work, and perhaps the most searching yet to appear (granting the chronological limits Imbert has set for himself). Ingeniously marshalling countless details, the author follows the thread of Stendhal's reactions to the unfolding history of French and Italian liberty from the fall of Napoleon to *Le Rouge et le noir,* in other words during the Milanese period and the years of Parisian *égotisme.* His study lays bare the surprisingly political implications of Stendhal's early works, recreates the events and tendencies which explain the glancing blows at tyranny and obscurantism. But all this erudition is not displayed for its own sake or even merely to construct Stendhal's evolving political ideas, for Imbert leads us on to those early monuments of Stendhal's career as a novelist, *Armance* and, especially, *Le Rouge et le noir.* Not content simply to explore their political content, he relates it to Stendhal's literary and personal quest for freedom. In all, about a third of this dense, rich book is devoted to these works of fiction; among the many perceptive passages, noteworthy are those which discuss the Tartuffian element in *Le Rouge et le noir,* Julien as a plebeian, the jury system as practiced in France, the parallels with Jesus and Julian the

Apostate. Essentially a work of literary history and intellectual biography, Imbert's book also makes an important contribution to the literary criticism of Stendhal's earlier novels. (J.S.P.)

Jansse, Lucien. "Stendhal et la constitution anglaise." *SC,* IX (1967), 327-48.

An able treatment of Stendhal's knowledge of the English constitution and, generally, of English domestic politics in his own time. Jansse indicates the sources of his knowledge and his changing attitude. Despite certain misjudgments, Stendhal's observations "révèlent chez lui une pensée politique lucide, exigeante et avertie." (J.S.P.)

Jones, Grahame C. *L'Ironie dans les romans de Stendhal.* (Collection stendhalienne, 8.) Lausanne: Editions du Grand Chêne, 1966. Pp. 205. 24 Fr.

Rev. by Carlo Cordié in *SFr,* XI (1967), 372-73.

Jones examines the multiple ironies in Stendhal's fiction, novel by novel, from *Armance* to *Lamiel.* As he says, his purpose is to "étudier l'ironie en action . . . afin de déterminer plus exactement le rôle qu'il a joué dans la conception de tous les romans de Stendhal et de mettre en lumière l'influence qu'elle exerce sur le développement de tous les aspects de ces ouvrages." He discovers ironies that most readers must miss, and he comes to some interesting conclusions about Stendhal's evolving talent for irony in fiction. The main defect of this study is an earnest, plodding manner ill suited to the subject. See Jones's own résumé of his book in *SC,* IX (1967), 163-68. (J.S.P.)

Judrin, Roger. *Moralités littéraires.* Paris: Gallimard, 1966. Pp. 231.

According to Del Litto's review (*SC,* IX [1967], 285-86), Judrin's book contains three chapters on Stendhal: "Le parvenu qui ne parvient à rien" (*Le Rouge et le noir*), "L'amateur de romans" (*La Chartreuse de Parme*), and "Dévotions envers les femmes" (*Lucien Leuwen*).

Kamata, Hiroo. "Impressions de la nature chez Stendhal." *Regards: Revue de Littérature et de Langue Françaises* (Université du Tôhoku. Section de Littérature et Langue Françaises), No. 10 (1967), 12-19.

In Japanese with *résumé analytique* in French (pp. 78-79).

Kotchetkova, Tatiana. "Stendhal en U.R.S.S.: bibliographie (1963-1966)." *SC,* X (1967), 101-02.

Leroy, Pierre. "La politique dans l'oeuvre de Stendhal." *Revue Politique,* Jan. 1967, pp. 53-62.

See résumé by Del Litto in *SC,* IX (1967), 284.

Maquet, Albert. "Stendhal et T. Grossi." *LI,* XVI (1964), 298-321.

Summarized in *RLI,* LXX (1966), 187.

Maranini, Lorenza. "Origine e senso di un personaggio stendhaliano: Lamiel." Pp. 119-92 in his *Il '48 nella struttura della 'Education sentimentale' e altri saggi francesi.* Pisa: Nistri-Lischi, 1963. Pp. 263.
Rev. by V. Del Litto in *SC,* VIII (1966), 192.

Martineau, Henri, and V. Del Litto, eds. *Correspondance.* Tome II: 1821-1834. (Bibliothèque de la Pléiade.) Paris: Gallimard, 1967. Pp. 1180. 45 Fr.

Mason, Haydn T. "Condorcet et Stendhal." *SC,* IX (1967), 255-58.

Meyers, Jeffrey. "The Influence of *La Chartreuse de Parme* on *Il Gattopardo.*" *Italica,* XLIV (1967), 314-25.

Nigay, Gilbert. "Stendhal et les bibliothèques." *SC,* IX (1967), 309-16.
Stendhal frequented the Bibliothèque Nationale, the Vatican Library, etc.

Orlando, Francesco. "Il recente e l'antico nel cap. I, 18 di 'le Rouge et le Noir.'" *Belfagor,* XXII (Nov. 30, 1967), 661-80.

Ortiz Armengol, Pedro. "Cinco cartas stendhalianas." *La Estafeta Literaria* (Madrid), Nos. 363-368 (Feb.-April, 1967).
See *SC,* IX (1967), 358.

Pincherle, Bruno. *In compagnia di Stendhal.* (Biblioteca Stendhaliana, 1.) Milan: All'insegna del Pesce d'Oro, 1967. Pp. 479.
Rev. by Ferdinand Boyer in *SC,* X (1967), 75-76, by C. Cordié in *SFr.* XI (1967), 564-65.
A miscellany of Pincherle's articles on Stendhal published in various places since 1945. Cordié's review in *SFr* gives a complete list and briefly indicates the subject of each.

Prucher, Auda. "Un stendhalien italien: Carlo Placci (avec des lettres inédites de Paul Arbalet, Adolphe Paupe et Léon Bélugou)." *SC,* IX (1967), 259-79.
Placci (1862-1941) was a musician, novelist, essayist, and art critic.

Reizov, Boris. "Pourquoi Stendhal a-t-il intitulé son roman 'Le Rouge et le Noir'?" *SFr,* XI (1967), 296-301.
Reizov passes in review and rejects the principal theories hitherto advanced. His own answer to the question lies in two "prophetic" scenes of the novel, both of which are shown in Monnier's illustrations for the first edition.

Riehn, Christa. "Stendhal en Allemagne: bibliographie (1824-1944)." *SC,* X (1967), 85-100.

Rude, Fernand. *Stendhal et la pensée sociale de son temps.* (Histoire des Mentalités.) Paris: Plon, 1967. Pp. 318. 25 Fr.

Rev. by C. Cordié in *SFr,* xi (1967), 565-66; by V. D[el]. L[itto]. in *SC,* ix (1967), 282-84; by Jacques Franck in *Revue Générale Belge,* June 1967, pp. 109-13; and by Samuel S. de Sacy in *Quinzaine Littéraire,* No. 26 (April 15-30, 1967), p. 14.

After a brief introduction which reviews the emergence among Stendhal scholars and socialist thinkers (e.g., Léon Blum) of a serious view of the novelist's political and social ideas, Rude devotes a long section to a study of Stendhal's readings in political science and economics, and demonstrates the influence of the Ideologues and the classical economists (and their revisionist followers). The central section of the book, "La querelle des industriels (1825)," tells the complex story of Stendhal's generally hostile reaction to Saint-Simonisme and of his treatment at the hands of its adherents. Then Rude examines the writings of Stendhal's literary maturity for their social and economic content: this means, of course, his great novels as well as such lesser productions as the *Mémoires d'un touriste* and even his marginalia to Mrs. Trollope's *Domestic Manners of the Americans.* In his conclusion, after a discussion of Stendhal's fortune in the Soviet Union, he finds a neat formula to describe the novelist's position vis-à-vis society and its problems: "plus qu'un libéral et pas encore un socialiste." There is much of value and interest here, especially in the sections on "La querelle des industriels." The book suffers somewhat from a faulty structure, the result of a compromise between a chronological approach and a thematic one, and from the author's tendency to quote at excessive length from Stendhal's sources and somewhat without regard to their relative importance in his formation. Still, this is an important addition to the fast growing literature on Stendhal as a social scientist. (J.S.P.)

Schweck, Jerome M. "Legal Insanity, Moral Insanity, and Stendhal's 'Le Rouge et le Noir.' " *Medical History,* x (1966), 281-89.

Shattuck, Roger. "The Novelist as Innovator. IV. Stendhal and the Method." *Listener,* lxxv (1966), 467-69.
Shattuck finds the beginning of Stendhal's career as an artist in discoveries which he made about himself in 1804-1805: "acting, *le joué,* need not obliterate feeling, *le naturel.*"

Simone, F. "L'Italia nella letteratura francese. Pugnali e veleni." *La Stampa* (Turin), Nov. 8, 1966.
See summary in *SC,* ix (1967), 198.

Starzynski, Julius, ed. *Du romantisme dans les arts.* (Miroirs de l'Art.) Paris: Hermann, 1966. Pp. 183. 6 Fr.
Rev. anon. in *SC,* ix (1967), 196-97.
Attractive, inexpensive presentation of extracts from Stendhal's writings on art and esthetics.

Vieuille, Marie-Françoise "Stendhal en Tchécoslovaquie: bibliographie (1898-1966)." *SC,* x (1967), 103-09.

See also Garber ("French 1. General").

Reviews of books previously listed:

ATHERTON, John, *Stendhal* (see *ELN*, v, Supp., 78), rev. by William Buchanan in *JR*, XLV (1965), 353; by F.W.J. Hemmings in *MLR*, LXI (1966), 711; by Norman Suckling in *N&Q*, XIII (1966), 275-76; and by George Woodcock in *The New Leader*, June 7, 1965, pp. 23-24; CARACCIO, Armand, *Mélanges franco-italiens de littérature* (see *ELN*, v, Supp., 79), rev. anon. in *SC*, IX (1967), 196; DEL LITTO, V., ed., *La Chartreuse de Parme* (see *ELN*, v, Supp., 79), rev. by C. Cordié in *SFr*, XI (1967), 165-66; DEL LITTO, V., *La Vie de Stendhal* (see *ELN*, v, Supp., 85), rev. by J. Théodoridès in *RdS*, LXXXVII (1966), 374-75; DURAND, Gilbert, *Le Décor mythique de la Chartreuse de Parme* (see *PQ*, XLII, 484), rev. by M. Romano in *SFr*, XI (1967), 168; HEMMINGS, F.W.J., *Stendhal: A Study of His Novels* (see *ELN*, v, Supp., 81), rev. by J. Théodoridès in *RdS*, LXXXVII (1966), 375-77; LAURENT, Jacques, *La Fin de Lamiel* (see *ELN*, v, Supp., 81), see *SC*, x (1967), for list of reviews; MAQUET, Albert, *Deux Amis italiens de Stendhal: Giovanni Plana et Carlo Guasco* (see *PQ*, XLIII, 484), rev. by Aldo Daverio in *Cahiers de l'Alpe*, No. 24 (Feb.-March, 1966), pp. 272-73; STRAUSS, André, *La Fortune de Stendhal en Angleterre* (see *ELN*, v, Supp., 83), rev. anon. in *SC*, IX (1967), 194-95.

VIGNY

Barbera, Giuseppi, ed. *Théâtre*. (Cultura.) Milan: Gastaldi, 1967. Pp. 109. L. 1000.

Bartfeld, Fernande. *Moïse*. ("Archives des Lettres Modernes," No. 83.) Paris: Les Lettres Modernes (Minard), 1967. Pp. 24. 4 Fr.

Castex, Pierre-Georges. *Alfred de Vigny, l'homme et l'oeuvre*. (Connaissance des Lettres.) Nouvelle édition revue et mise au jour. Paris: Hatier, 1967.

See also Grimsley ("Chateaubriand").

Reviews of works previously listed:

GERMAIN, François, ed., *Servitude et grandeur militaires* (see *ELN*, v, Supp., 84), rev. by Raffaele de Cesare in *SFr*, XI (1967), 313-15; PETRONI, Liano, ed., *Chatterton* (see *ELN*, III, Supp., 87), rev. by Gustave Vanwelkenhuyzen in *RBPH*, XLV (1967), 658-59.

GERMAN

(Compilers and reviewers: Ingeborg Carlson, Arizona State Univ.; Ulrich Gaier, University of Konstanz, Germany; Philip Glander, Univ. of Calif., Berkeley; E. Bernell McIntire, Arizona State Univ.; Kenneth Negus, Rutgers Univ., New Brunswick, N. J.; Günther Nerjes, Univ. of Calif., Davis; Laurence R. Radner, Purdue Univ.; Josef S. Thanner, Rutgers Univ., New Brunswick, N. J.)

1. BIBLIOGRAPHY

Arnold, Robert F. *Allgemeine Bücherkunde zur neueren deutschen Literaturgeschichte.* 4. neubearbeitete Auflage von Herbert Jacob. Berlin: de Gruyter, 1966. Pp. 395. DM 32.00.

Rev. by P. M. Mitchell in *JEGP*, LXVI (1967), 627-29.

Revision of the 1931 edition. Academic publications, critical and literary periodicals, literary *Almanache* and *Taschenbücher* are added. Probably too much space is devoted to non-literary topics (e. g. literature on musical instruments). "Darstellung fremder Literaturen" is not up to date. (I.C.)

Germanistik: Internationales Referatenorgan mit bibliographischen Hinweisen. VIII. Jg. Tübingen: Niemeyer, 1967. [=*Germanistik*]

See especially in each of the four issues: "XVIII. Vergleichende Literaturgeschichte," "XXI. Deutsche Literaturgeschichte, Allgemeines," "XXIX. Goethezeit (1770-1830)," and "XXX. Von der Nachromantik bis zum Realismus (1830-1890)." Most books are reviewed. All items are listed by their authors. Coverage includes publications in Europe, South Africa, North and South America, Australia, and Japan.

Hansel, Johannes. *Bücherkunde für Germanisten.* Studienausgabe, vermehrte Ausgabe. Berlin: Erich Schmidt, 1967. Pp. 163. DM 9.80.

Contains a supplement, "Wegweiser für die bibliographische Schulung." Revised and updated, particularly with respect to the bibliographies for more than 300 authors. Included also are references to individual and collective bibliographies, and to recent works containing bibliographies of individual writers. Finally, literary societies, yearbooks, and locations of literary remains are listed. (I.C.)

Henning, Hans and S. Seifert. "Internationale Bibliographie zur deutschen Klassik (1750-1850)." *WB*, x (1965).

Raabe, Paul. *Einführung in die Bücherkunde zur deutschen Literaturwissenschaft.* 5. durchgesehene Auflage. (Sammlung Metzler, M 1.) Stuttgart: J. B. Metzler, 1966. Pp. xii + 308. DM 39.00.

2. GENERAL

Bennholdt-Thomsen, Anke. *Stern und Blume.* (Abhandlungen zur Kunst-, Musik-und Literaturwissenschaft, 39.) Bonn: Bouvier, 1966. Pp. 230. DM 28.00.

Böckmann, Paul. *Formensprache. Studien zur Literarästhetik und Dichtungsinterpretation.* Hamburg: Hoffmann und Campe, 1966. Pp. 559. DM 48.00.

Rev. by H. Praschek in *Germanistik*, VIII (1967), 754-55; and by W. Bender in *GQ*, XL (1967), 409-12.

Böckmann arranges his material methodologically according to the leitmotif "Sprachkunst ist alles." The biographical approach is rejected in favor of an interpretative search for "Kunstgestalt" and "Sprachleistung" of various poets. Ranging from the Reformation, with a primarily historical approach, to more categorical topics such as "Stil- und Formprobleme in der Literatur," the former Heidelberg professor and true humanist still proposes the utopian ideal that "alle Kunst zur Humanisierung des Menschen beiträgt," and concentrates on his favorite and geographically appropriate subject: Hölderlin. The aloof scholar portrays a refreshing personal involvement, concealed somewhat by the *pluralis modestae* in "Das Bild der Nacht in Hölderlins *Brod und Wein*," where he declares the poem to be the starting point of an immense language movement. The image of the night no longer describes "Erlebnis," but becomes Hölderlin's symbol for the unity of nature and spirit, transfigured into "holy night." It further exemplifies the oscillating relationship of man and deity. Nature and Ancient and Christian theology are blended. Most of the Romanticists are discussed. A.W. Schlegel is emphasized—but also Kleist, the "enigmatic one"; Jean Paul, the "humorist"; and Heine, the "disillusionist" are included. There are notes, but no index. (I.C.)

Böschenstein, Bernhard. "Die Transfiguration Rousseaus in der deutschen Dichtung um 1800: Hölderlin—Jean Paul—Kleist." *JJPG,* I (1966), 101-16.

Rousseau's idea of natural man, according to Böschenstein, is embedded in a historical concept for Hölderlin, transplanted into eternity by Jean Paul, and destroyed, in its only apparent reality, by Kleist. While the Hölderlin and Kleist interpretations are convincing, Böschenstein's views on Jean Paul should be modified by consideration of Jean Paul's idylls which, to a certain extent, are experiments in a possible realization of Rousseau's idea. (U.G.)

Brink, Michael and Lambert, eds. *Gedichte der Romantik.* Köln: Hegner, 1967. Pp. 344. DM 12.80.

David, Claude. *Geschichte der deutschen Literatur. Zwischen Romantik und Symbolismus* 1820-1885. Gütersloh: Sigbert Mohn, 1966. Pp. 222. DM 12.80.

The discreetly chosen subtitle includes the complex time span from late Romanticism, through Realism (not evaluated as a historical phenomenon but as omnipresent) and into the abrupt appearance of Modernism, personified in Nietzsche. The Sorbonne scholar gathers the cultural background before he concentrates on literature, which he ambiguously classifies under the aspects of genre, epoch, or even geography. The larmoyant complaint that the great are replaced by the mediocre is counter-balanced by the rebellion of the young. In spite of the importance of the Napoleonic year, 1815, for *Geistesgeschichte* 1832 is the important date. Heine's "les dieux sont morts" refers to the period of fermentation beginning then, resulting in Hegel and leading to our present predicament. The author attempts to prove that symbolism is not simply transposed Neoromanticism, for it struggles to free itself from such epigonal foundations. The profiles of individual poets are cogent. Mörike, the highlights, is given a sharply critical evaluation, but David still places him in the vicinity of Lamartine. The quotations are well chosen, and the apparatus is an extensive, dependable guide for scholars and students. (I.C.)

de Deugh, C. *Het metafysisch grondpatroon van het romantische litraire denken. De fenomenologie van een geestes-gesteldheid.* With a summary in English. (Studia Litteraria Rheno-Traiectina, Vol. X.) Groningen: J.B. Wolters, 1966. Pp. 516. 30.00. Fr.

Emrich, Wilhelm. "Romantik und modernes Bewusstsein." Pp. 236-57 in: *Geist und Widergeist. Wahrheit und Lüge der Literatur. Studien.* Frankfurt: Athenäum, 1965. Pp. 332. DM 29.80.
Rev. by W. Hinck, *Germanistik*, VIII (1967), 301-02.

Haller, R. *Geschichte der deutschen Lyrik vom Ausgang des Mittelalters bis zu Goethes Tod.* Bern: Francke, 1967. Pp. 487. 19.80 S.

Hass, Hans-Egon, ed. *Sturm und Drang, Klassik, Romantik. Texte und Zeugnisse.* (Die deutsche Literatur, Bd. V, erster und zweiter Teilband.) München: Beck, 1966. Pp. 1933. DM 39.00 (each).
Compiled according to the taste of the editor, like most anthologies, the aspects stressed in this one are the characteristic, the useful, and the little-known. This part of a series that covers the period from the Middle Ages to the 20th century presents a surprisingly comprehensive cross-section of its times. It underlines the typical rather than the dilettantishly "beautiful." The introduction pursues the same goal as the selection of texts: to reveal the epoch as a spiritual cosmos in its unity, as well as its diversity. Hass presents his material with the realistic approach that our pace of living does not allow the average reader to submerge at length into the past. But he does it so well that even the most modern Modernist will be forced to recognize his own sources: the late Goethe and the Romanticists. Relatively unknown yet significant selections are made available (e.g., C.G. Jochmann's *Ueber das Klassische und das Romantische*). In spite of the fragmentary character of texts (e.g., only the end of Goethe's *Novelle*), careful editing and source reference qualify the work for scholarly purposes. (I.C.)

Höllerer, Walter. "Die Bedeutung des Augenblicks im modernen Romananfang." Pp. 344-77 in: *Romananfänge. Versuch zu einer Poetik des Romans.* Norbert Miller, ed. Berlin: Literarisches Colloquium, 1965. Pp. 377. DM 24.00.
Rev. by H.H. Reuter in *Germanistik*, VIII (1967), 294-95.
A discussion on Brentano's *Godwi* is included.

Immerwahr, Raymond. "The Ascending Romantic View in the Eighteenth Century." *PEGS*, XXXVI (1966), 1-33.

Kahn, Robert L. "Tieck's *Franz Sternbalds Wanderungen* and Novalis' *Heinrich von Ofterdingen*." *SIR*, VII (1967), 40-64.

Klin, Eugen. *August Ferdinand Bernhardi als Kritiker und Literaturtheoretiker.* (Bonner Arbeiten zur deutschen Literatur Bd. 14.) Bonn: Bouvier, 1966. Pp. 162. DM 19.00.

Rev. by H. Anton in *Germanistik*, VIII (1967), 369.

Klin continues his efforts (see *ELN*, V [1967], 88) to prove the importance of the marginal figure of Bernhardi as catalyst of Romantic ideas, especially for the Berlin group. (I.C.)

Krauss, Werner. "Französische Aufklärung und deutsche Romantik." Pp. 266-84 in: *Perspektiven und Probleme. Zur französischen und deutschen Aufklärung und andere Aufsätze.* Neuwied: Luchterhand, 1965. Pp. 397. DM 28.00.
Rev. by S. Sudhof in *Germanistik*, VIII (1967), 537-38.

Krummacher, Hans-Henrik. *Das 'als ob' in der Lyrik. Erscheinungsformen und Wandlungen einer Sprachfigur der Metaphorik von der Romantik zu Rilke.* (Kölner germanistische Studien, Bd. 1.) Köln: Böhlau, 1965. Pp. 227. DM 28.00.
Rev. by H.H. Reuter in *Germanistik*, VIII (1967), 396-97; and by E.E. George *JEGP*, LXVI (1967), 312-13.
With Rilke considered as the lyrical fulfillment of German literature, Tieck, Brentano, Eichendorff, Uhland, Mörike, Heine, and Lenau of the Romantic era are discussed. Contains notes, but no bibliography. (I.C.)

Kunisch, Hermann, ed. *Literaturwissenschaftliches Jahrbuch.* Im Auftrage der Görres-Gesellschaft, N.S. VI. Berlin: Duncker & Humblot, 1965. Pp. 343. DM 59.00. [=*LJGG, 1965*]
Rev. by W. Segebrecht in *Germanistik*, VIII (1967), 757-58.
The resurrected yearbook maintains its unique tradition. It includes everything from book reviews to essays ranging from Wolfram to Toller with the only poet unmentioned being Görres, though it does deal at length with Romanticism. Egbert Krispyn's "Kleist und Goethe" (109-19) bases Goethe's negative attitude toward Kleist on his own unpleasant experience with Herder. Brentano is represented by three archive studies executed by students under the guidance of Siegfried Sudhof; and by Christa Holst's und S. Sudhof's "Die Lithographien zur ersten Ausgabe von Brentanos Märchen *Gockel, Hinkel, und Gakeleia*" (140-54), Hansjörg Holzamer's "Clemens Brentano: *Der Epheu*" (133-39), and Klaus-Dieter Krabiel's "Die beiden Fassungen von Brentanos *Lureley*" (122-32); Friedrich Carl Scheibe's "Symbolik der Geschichte in Eichendorffs Dichtung" (155-77) is based on the idea of spiritual evolution. Reinhold Wesemeier's "Zur Gestaltung von Eichendorffs satirischer Novelle *Auch ich war in Arkadien*" (179-91) interprets this work as the poet's greatest departure from Romanticism. Gerald Gillespie's "Zum Aufbau von Eichendorffs *Eine Meerfahrt*" (193-206) stresses Eichendorff's Christian inclinations. (I.C.)

Kunz, Josef. *Die deutsche Novelle zwischen Klassik und Romantik.* Berlin: Erich Schmidt, 1966. Pp. 164. DM 9.80.
Rev. by Konrad Kratzsch in *Germanistik*, VIII (1967), 372; and by Gustav Konrad in *Welt und Wort*, XXII (1967), 150.
Romantics discussed are Wackenroder, Tieck, Brentano, Arnim, Eichendorff, Hoffmann, and Kleist.

Mayer, Hans. *Zur deutschen Klassik und Romantik*. Pfullingen: Neske, 1963. Pp. 365.
This is the counterpart and continuation of *Von Lessing bis Thomas Mann* (1959). Mayer highlights certain works of a poet not only for their literary value, but also for their significance with respect to the author's life and their after-effects. Thus *Faust* is classified under Enlightenment, Storm and Stress, Goethe's Italian journey, his epic poems, and *Dichtung und Wahrheit*. Frank is his approach in "Fragen der Romantikforschung," based on a 1962 lecture: "Es herrscht grösster Wirrwarr." This is a typical modernistic attack on traditional attempts to answer fundamental questions by counter-questioning. The critical evaluation of old standard works such as Haym, Hettner, R. Huch or Korff are ranked low because they are totally unpolitical. Sources such as Gorki, Bakunin, and Engels, and the terminology "rationalistischer Aufklärer" (de Quincey), "Aufgabe sozialer Entschlackung" (Brecht's), and the subtitle "Die deutsche Romantik in marxistischer Sicht," betray the origin of this writer's ideas. A surprising hypothesis is that Heine's *Romantische Schule* reveals its author as a classical aesthete! "Heinrich von Kleist, der geschichtliche Augenblick," a reprint of the separate volume of 1962, again proves the author's forte: the essay. There are practically no notes. (I.C.)

Minder, Robert. *Dichter in der Gesellschaft. Erfahrungen mit französischer und deutscher Literatur*. Frankfurt: Insel, 1967. Pp. 424. DM 24.00.
Contains a wide range of interesting topics, treated in the sophisticated style of the author. Parts on Romanticism include: "Jean Paul oder die Verlassenheit des Genius," "Jean Paul in Frankreich," and "Hölderlin unter den Deutschen." (I.C.)

Reiss, Hans Siegbert. *Politisches Denken in der deutschen Romantik*. Bern-München: Francke, 1966. Pp. 96. Fr. 2.80.
Rev. by Waltrand Loos in *Germanistik*, VIII (1967), 819-20.
Treats political views of Fichte, Schelling, Novalis, Fr. Schlegel, A. Müller, Görres, Baader, Schleiermacher, Savigny, and J. Grimm.

Ritter, Johann Wilhelm. *Briefe an Gotthilf Heinrich Schubert und an Karl von Hardenberg: Briefe eins romantischen Physikers*. Ed. Friedrich Klemm et al. München: Heinz Moos Verlag, 1966. Pp. 67. DM 20.00.

Schanze, Helmut. *Die andere Romantik*. Frankfurt: Inselverlag, 1967. Pp. 216. DM 7.00.

Schanze, Helmut. " 'Dualismus unsrer Symphilosophie.' Zum Verhältnis Novalis-Friedrich Schlegel." *JFDH*, 1966, pp. 309-35.
Schanze shows some differences between the ideas of Fr. Schlegel and Novalis as they are made evident by Novalis' criticism of changes which Schlegel made in material which Novalis supplied for the first issue of Athenäum. (B.M.)

Schanze, Helmut. *Romantik und Aufklärung. Untersuchungen zu Friedrich Schlegel und Novalis.* (Erlanger Beiträge zur Sprach-und Kunstwissenschaft. Bd. 27.) Nürnberg: Carl, 1966. Pp. 172. DM 28.00.
Rev. by J.J. Anstett in *EG,* XXII (1967), 630.
Stresses the relationship between Romanticism and Enlightenment, especially the influence of the "Romanlehre" at the end of the 18th century on the development of this genre. (I.C.

Schillemeit, Jost, ed. *Interpretationen.* 4 vols. (Bücher des Wissens.) Vol. I: *Deutsche Lyrik.* (No. 695.) Vol. II: *Deutsche Dramen.* (No. 699.) Vol. III: *Deutsche Romane.* (No. 716.) Vol. IV: *Deutsche Erzählungen.* (No. 721.) Frankfurt am Main and Hamburg: Fischer Bücherei, 1965-66. Pp. 339, 341, 320, and 341, resp. DM 4.80 each.
Rev. by K. Kratzsch in *Germanistik,* VIII (1967), 304-06.
These volumes are very fine, chronologically arranged anthologies of discussions of texts and their authors. It is, however, symptomatic that essays employing a formalistic approach, with clear aesthetic evaluations, are relatively absent in these collections, with a few exceptions such as those by R. Alewyn. To a great extent, the reader is subjected to myths, written in the mythological language of interpreters who actually do not interpret literary texts as art, but rather as vehicles for more or less systematized ideologies, or stimuli for new poeticizing. The style is frequently unnecessarily difficult, sometimes strained and precious. Still, these "Interpretationen" are stimulating reading. Romantic authors dealt with are Hölderlin, Brentano, Eichendorff (Vol. I); Kleist (Vol .II); Jean Paul, Novalis, Eichendorff, Arnim (Vol. III); and Jean Paul, Kleist, Brentano, Arnim, Hoffmann, Eichendorff (Vol. IV). (J.Th. & K.N.)

Schmidt, Arno. *Die Ritter vom Geist. Von vergessenen Kollegen.* Karlsruhe: Stahlberg, 1965. Pp. 316. DM 22.00.
Rev. by Jürgen Brummack in *Germanistik,* VIII (1967), 308-09.
Deals with Hoffmann, Brentano, Fouqué, and, above all, Tieck.

Schmidt, Peter. *Gesundheit und Krankheit in romantischer Medizin und Erzählkunst. JFDH,* 1966, Pp. 197-228.
Medicine, the most Romantic branch of science, puts its mark on aesthetics. The article refers to Arnim, Brentano, Hoffmann, and Novalis. (I.C.)

Sengle, Friedrich. *Arbeiten zur deutschen Literatur 1750-1850.* Stuttgart: Metzler, 1965. Pp. 243. DM 24.50.
Rev. by Jost Hermand in *Monatshefte,* LVIII (1967), 268-72; by J. Wohlleben in *GR,* XLII (1967); by W. Paulsen in *Germanistik,* VIII (1967), 380; and by G. Pons in *EG,* XXII (1967), 373-75.
In his emphasis on the years before 1790 and after 1815, Sengle not only contradicts the "established" view that poets like Wieland are forerunners or those like Lenau are epigones, but also tends to overestimate their importance. In *"Die Braut von Messina"* (94-117), he launches a belligerent campaign against German *Hochklassik.* "Konvention und Ursprünglichkeit in Goethes dichterischem Werk" (9-24) recognizes Goethe's absolute originality, though

the urbane cosmopolitan poet reveals himself even during his Storm and Stress days by a persiflage on the cult of the genius in *Satyros*. "Formen des idyllischen Menschenbildes" (212-31) discusses the idyll from Gessner to Mörike, with Jean Paul as mainstay in between, whose Christian idyll *Das Leben Fibels* is surprisingly claimed as the nucleus of Grillparzer's *Der arme Spielmann*. "Voraussetzungen und Erscheinungsformen der deutschen Restaurationsliteratur" (118-54) assails the dogma of the Hegelian "Dreierschema." Sengle wants to add at least the idyll as a separate addition to the three classical literary genres. In spite of its realistic trends, apparent in its trivial forms, such as Mörike's *Turmhahn*, the idyll reflects the idealistic world of the golden epoch of antiquity as well as contemporary pietistic aspirations. In this idyllic climax, Sengle sees a successful symbiosis of Realism and Individualism. This is the concept of true "Erlebnisdichtung," studded with serene and humorous highlights and set into poetic form after a long, mellowing time span. This is why it turned out to be an idyll, "Wunschbild zufriedener Mittelmässigkeit." In an interesting cultural-political approach Sengle parallels Metternich's restoration of the feudal system with the predominance of aristocratic writers at that time. Can Lenau, whom Hankamer so aptly calls "Lebensnihilist," be recruited by the restoration? But then, his coat of arms was quite new. The preference for the classical epic form reveals traditional tendencies. Structures are less precisely focused, borders of the genres fluctuate. Lenau's poetry, Sengle states, has a cyclical character, betraying epic inclinations, his epic poems lyrical tenor, while Heine is neither praised as a Romanticist nor condemned as a Pseudoromanticist, but is unexpectedly linked to Nestroy and the world of Rococo. Name index is followed by one with the original title "Begriffsregister." Excellent food for thought. (I.C.)

Seybold, Eberhard. *Das Genrebild in der deutschen Literatur.* (Studien zur Poetik und Geschichte der Literatur. Bd. 3.) Stuttgart: Kohlhammer, 1967. Pp. 220. DM 39.00.
The pictorial element, transposed into the world of literature, especially the lyrical realm, is investigated from Opitz to Nestroy, with Romanticism represented by Arnim and Mörike. (I.C.)

Singer, Herbert and Benno von Wiese, eds. *Festschrift für Richard Alewyn.* Köln: Böhlau, 1967. Pp. 423. DM 58.00.
Contributions dealing with Romanticism are A. Henckel, "Was ist eigentlich romantisch?"; P. Küpper, "Unfromme Vigilien: Bonaventuras *Nachtwache*"; C. David, "Achim von Arnims *Isabella von Ägypten*: Essai sur le sens de la littérature fantastique"; E. Lämmert, "Zur Wirkungsgeschichte Eichendorffs in Deutschland" (see also under "German 3. Eichendorff"); H. Henel, "Mörikes *Denk es o Seele,* ein Volkslied?"; and O. Seidlin, "Der junge Joseph und der alte Fontane." (I.C.)

Storz, Gerhard. *Die Schwäbische Romantik*: *Dichter und Dichterkreise im Alten Württemberg.* Stuttgart: Kohlhammer, 1967. Pp. 160. DM. 19.80.

In his historical and interpretative presentation Storz distinguishes between the *Schwäbische Schule* of Uhland and the younger generation of Mörike, Waiblinger, Bauer, Pfizer, and Zimmermann, whom he amazingly ranks as peers. (I.C.)

Weigand, Hermann J. *Surveys and Soundings in European Literature.* Leslie A. Willson, ed. Princeton: Princeton University Press, 1966. Pp. 360.

The fashionable custom of gathering one's brainchildren in book form under a fetching title is different here in that the anthology has an editor, Leslie A. Willson, who furnishes the necessary translations (all quotes are bilingual). In his one-page foreword he states that all essays have been previously published (1942-65). In historical chronology from medieval lore to Broch they favor Schiller in volume. "Shakespeare in German Criticism" (pp. 55-73) stresses the importance of the Schlegel-Tieck translations, whose simplification and reduction of Shakespeare vocabulary result in the fact that Shakespeare is more popular in Germany than in English-speaking countries. Hence, German drama from Goethe to Hauptmann bears the imprint of Shakespeare. *Peter Schlemihl* (pp. 208-22) is understood as a Christian parable and a satire on salesmanship and business ethics that "should have been written by an American." Freud-inspired Weigand sees the work as a psychological case study with Chamisso declared the neurotic protagonist's double, particularly with respect to the Seven League Boots and the wishful thinking of the poet-explorer. Weigand concentrates on structure, and sees in *Schlemihl* a two-act drama where the devil loses his contest with a weak but honest soul because of divine grace. The fantastic basic situation, realistically presented, is rightly classified as a forerunner to Kafka's *The Metamorphosis*. But the Münchhausen braggadogio, narrated with impish lights and generally overlooked by *Schlemihl* interpreters, reveal the work as truly Romantic. (I.C.)

See also Mittner ("Italian 2. General").

Reviews of books previously listed:

BULLING, K., *Die Rezensenten der Jenaischen Allgemeinen Literaturzeitung . . .* (see *ELN*, V, Supp., 87), rev. by L. Uhlig in *Germanistik*, VIII (1967), 353; HARDY, S.L., *Goethe, Calderon und die romantische Theorie des Dramas* (see *ELN*, IV, Supp., 95), rev. by R. Ayrault in *EG*, XXII (1967), 287-88; and by M. Gräfe in *Germanistik*, VIII (1967), 610-11; JENNINGS, L.B., *The Ludicrous Demon* (see *ELN*, IV, Supp., 95), rev. by F. Wood in *Symposium*, XXI (1967), 90-92; KINDERMANN, H., *Theatergeschichte Europas . . .* (see *ELN*, IV, Supp., 95), rev. by R. Girardi in *EG*, XXII (1967), 291; LUDERS, D., ed., *Jahrbuch des Freien Deutschen Hochstifts 1965* (see *ELN*, IV, Supp., 96), rev. by W. Herwig in *Germanistik*, VIII (1967), 366-70; and by R. Ayrault in *EG*, XXII (1967), 394-95; VOERSTER, E., *Märchen und Novellen im klassisch-romantischen Roman* (see *ELN*, IV, Supp., 97), rev. by U.S. Colby in *GR*, XLII (1967), 148-50; and by R. Immerwahr in *JEGP*, LXVI (1967), 313-16.

3. STUDIES OF AUTHORS

ARNIM, ACHIM VON

Brummack, Jürgen. "Zu Arnims 'Melusinen Fragment.'" *GRM,* XLVIII (1967), 208-10.

Proves that a fragment first published by Migge in vol. III of Arnim's works (1965) is actually a continuation of Brentano's fragment *Der arme Raimondin* (*Werke,* ed. Kemp, vol. II, 1963). (P.G.)

Liedke, Herbert R. "Vorstudien Achim von Arnims zur 'Gräfin Dolores.' Zweiter Teil: Entwurf und Quellen zur 'Geschichte der verlorenen Erbprinzessin Wenda' (zweite Abteilung, siebentes Kapitel)," *JFDH,* 1965, pp. 237-313.

Liedke, Herbert R. "Vorstudien Achim von Arnims zur 'Gräfin Dolores.' Dritter Teil: Die Handschrift 'Dichtung in Bildern.' Fragment aus einem Druckmanuscript der 'Gräfin Dolores.'" *JFDH,* 1966, pp. 229-308.

See also Hass, Kunz, Schillemeit, P. Schmidt, Seybold, and Singer ("German 2. General").

Review of book previously listed:

MIGGE, Walther, ed., *Achim von Arnim, Sämtliche Romane und Erzählungen* . . . (see *ELN,* III, Supp., 96), rev. by Wolfgang Hecht in *Euphorion,* LX (1966), 418-20.

ARNIM, BETTINA VON

Küpper, Peter. "Bettina Brentano - 1936." *Euphorion,* LXI (1967), 175-86.

The account of efforts—intentional or otherwise—to trace the Brentano family to Jewish origins. The ironic end of the matter is that Bettina is declared Aryan by the Nazis in 1936. (P.G.)

BERNHARDI, AUGUST FERDINAND

See Klin ("German 2. General").

BONAVENTURA

Brinkmann, Richard. *Nachtwachen von Bonaventura: Kehrseite der Frühromantik?* Pfullingen: Neske, 1966. Pp. 31. DM 2.80.

Rev. by Wolfgang Frühwald in *Germanistik,* VIII (1967), 798.

Sammons, Jeffrey L. *The Nachtwachen von Bonaventura: A Structural Interpretation.* London, The Hague, Paris: Mouton, 1965. Pp. 128. Hfl. 18.00.

Rev. by R. Ayrault in *EG,* XXII (1967), 636; and by William Lillyman in *GQ,* XL (1967), 714-16.

This is a welcome addition to recent first-rate Bonaventura studies by Paulsen and Kohlschmidt. Although primarily a structural analysis, it radiates many a bright light on other parts of this obscure by-way of German Romanticism.

Proceeding from a detailed evaluation of previous scholarship (and taking particular issue with Franz Schultz), Sammons finds the structure of this ostensibly meandering narration to consist mainly of a sequence of five sets of episodes, each of which begins in satire, then gradually sobers, ending with catastrophe and nihilistic despair. He traces in this "external form a cyclical movement boring ever deeper into the empty core of the universe; [there is also a] . . . convergence of two lines of presentation: the intellectual content or *Gehalt* and the personality of the watchman. Both the cyclical process and the process of convergence reach their unmerciful conclusion in the final night-watch, thus providing the structural dynamics of the work with a clearly definable terminal point" (p. 102 f.). Implications of this twofold structure are then examined in separate chapters on the figure of the watchman, the manner of presentation, and the bearing of the *Nachtwachen* on its own time.

Probably the most important conclusion that we can derive from this book for our purposes here is that we are dealing with the most clear-cut form of anti-Romanticism of the period. (Cp. Paulsen's conclusion that the watchman is an "anti-Faust": see *ELN*, v, Supp., 92.) This emerges most impressively on p. 61, where a remarkable parallel between Novalis and the watchman as a child is revealed. But here the child is not father of the man, at least not in a positive sense, for the "hero" of this novel becomes a totally *disillusioned German Romantic*— and already in 1804, when the Romantic movement in Germany was scarcely past its infancy.

Questionable is just one of Sammons' conclusions—the assertion that Bonaventura is *not* a link in the chain of literary history. What about 18th-century skeptics on the one side, Büchner on the other? This point, however, is admittedly peripheral to the main thesis of the book.

Deserving of emphasis are the useful bibliography, and, above all, the exemplary critical method and style, which could serve as models for many English-writing Germanists. (K.N.)

See also Singer ("German 2. General").

BRENTANO

Fetzer, John. "Clemens Brentano's *Godwi*: Variations on the Melos-Eros Theme." *GR*, XLII (1967), 108-23.

Brentano employs musical concepts appropriate to each erotic relationship in the novel. Wherever an erotic theme occurs there is musical imagery descriptive of it.

Holst, Christa, and Siegfried Sudhof. "Die Lithographien zur ersten Ausgabe von Brentanos Märchen 'Gockel, Hinkel, Gakeleja' (1838)." *LJGG*, VI (1965), 140-54.

Holzamer, Hansjörg. "Clemens Brentano: 'Der Epheu.'" *LJGG*, VI (1965), 133-39.

Katann, Oskar. "Die Glaubwürdigkeit von Clemens Brentanos Emmerich Berichten. Zum gegenwärtigen Stand der Quellen und der Forschung." *LJGG*, VII (1966), 145-94.

A comprehensive review of Brentano's years with Anna Katharina Emmerick, followed by an exhaustive survey of the publications about her. Contains a descriptive report of previously unknown notes by Brentano, made in preparation for his *Visionen,* and compares his published accounts of her visions with his own diary entries on them. (P.G.)

Kemp, Friedhelm, ed. *Werke.* Vol. IV. Munich: Hanser, 1966. Pp. 959. DM 31.00.

Krabiel, Klaus-Dieter. "Die beiden Fassungen von Brentanos 'Luerley.' " *LJGG,* VI (1965), 122-32.

Politzer, Heinz. "Das Schweigen der Sirenen." *DVLG,* XLI (1967), 444-67.
Interpretation of Brentano's "Lorelay" (pp. 453-58) and comparison with Heine's "Lorelei."

See also Höllerer, Krummacher, Kunisch, Kunz, Schillemeit, A. Schmidt, and P. Schmidt ("German 2. General"); Brummack ("Arnim, A. v."); and Küpper ("Arnim, B. v.").

Reviews of books previously listed:
FRAENGER, Wilhelm, *Clemens Brentanos Alhambra* . . . (see *ELN,* IV, Supp., 99), rev. by R. Ayrault in *EG,* XXI (1966), 459; KEMP, Friedrich, ed., *Werke,* Vol. III, *Sämtliche Märchen* (see *ELN,* IV, Supp., 99), rev. by Henri Plard in *EG,* XXI (1966), 299-300.

CHAMISSO

Fortunati Glückseckle und Wünschhüttlein. Ein Spiel, 1806. Aus der Handschrift zum ersten Male. Ed. by E. F. Kossmann, 1895 (Deutsche Literaturdenkmale des 18.u.19.Jhdts.Bd. 54-55) Kraus-Reprint, Nendeln 1967. DM 14.00.

Hittier, E. *L'ombre perdue.* Tulle: Orfeuil, 1966. Pp. 80.

See also Hass, Weigand ("German 2. General").

EICHENDORFF

Köhler, Dietmar. "Wiederholung und Variation, zu einem Grundphänomen der Eichendorffschen Erzählkunst." *Aurora,* XXVII (1967), 26-42.
It is not difficult to fill a score of pages with examples of variations and repetitions as they occur in Eichendorff's works. One can agree that the structure of our poet's prose is like a musical composition and even compare it to an opera. It is also agreed that these variations may be viewed as "Chiffern, die alle aufeinander hindeuten, die sich gegenseitig verdeutlichen und die Beschreibung ersetzten" (32). But this simple exercise does not allow the author to reject Kunisch's suggestion that we view his entire production as an organic whole. This perspective might impart to each entity "einem neuen, bisher kaum gesehenen Sinn, eine neue, das Einzelstück übertreffende Bedeutung"

(27). It so happens that Kunisch is correct. *Das Marmorbild* and *Taugenichts* must be viewed as a whole; indeed, one is a continuation of the other. (L.R.)

Lämmert, Eberhard. "Zur Wirkungsgeschichte Eichendorffs in Deutschland." Pp. 346-378 in: *Festschrift für Richard Alewyn*. See Singer ("German 2. General").
"Ich habe zu zeigen versucht, wie besonders leicht es dieser Dichter seinen deutschen Lesern gemacht hat, die Sehnsüchte ihres eigenen Horizontes in seinen Liedern gespiegelt zu finden." With this succinct statement the author explains not only the intent of his article but the condition of Eichendorff scholarship. Via excerpts from a generous bibliography, we are taken from the 19th century when our poet was sung but not read to the early 20th century when he was described as "ein Stück deutscher Volksseele." Beginning with the fourth decade of our century, Eichendorff scholarship slowly acquires the stature of *research*. (L.R.)

Lüthi, Hans Jürg. "Joseph von Eichendorff und Goethe." *Aurora*, XXVII (1967), 15-25.
A selection of Eichendorff's statements evaluating Goethe's works, especially *Wilhelm Meister, Faust*, and *Werther*, is analyzed. Conclusion: Eichendorff the poet praises the beauty of his works while Eichendorff the Christian takes issue with the content. In this relationship to Goethe the author sees "die Dialektik seiner dichterischen Existenz, der Existenz des christlichen Dichters. Der Dichter ist in Gefahr, den tausend verlockenden Stimmen der Natur zu erliegen," but his Christianity saves him. And thus Eichendorff remains a poet "trotz seinem christlichen Geist." I wonder why Lüthi assumes that being a Christian and a poet involves a contradiction. *Must* creativity be tainted with Luciferian denial? And as to these "verlockende Stimmen der Natur," Eichendorff categorically says, "nature's *silence* only points to the mystery of existence." What should we do with this embarrassing statement? (L.R.)

See also Hass, Krummacher, Kunisch, Kunz, Schillemeit, and Singer ("German 2. General"); Helmut Müller ("Hoffmann"); Hellmann ("Kleist"); Schumann ("Fr. Schlegel").

Reviews of books previously listed:
Aurora, XXVI (1966), rev. by G. Pauline in *EG*, XXII (1967), 126-27; LUTHI, Hans Jürg, *Dichtung und Dichter bei Joseph von Eichendorff* (see *ELN*, V, Supp., 93), rev. by Oskar Seidlin in *GQ*, XLI (1968), 108-10.

FICHTE
See Reiss ("German 2. General"); Harich ("Jean Paul").

FOUQUÉ
See A. Schmidt ("German 2. General").

GÖRRES
See Kunisch, Reiss ("German 2. General").

GRIMM, JACOB

Schoof, Wilhelm, ed. *Reden und Aufsätze. Eine Auswahl.* Munich: Winkler, 1966. (Die Fundgrube, 21.) Pp. 196. DM 9.80.
Rev. by Manfred Lemmer in *Germanistik*, VIII (1967), 806-07.

See also Reiss ("German 2. General"); Bravo-Villasante ("Spanish 2. General").

GRIMM, JACOB AND WILHELM

Fründt, Renate. "Die Brüder Grimm als Sammler und Herausgeber altdeutscher Dichtungen." *Wissenschaftliche Zeitchrift der Universität Halle,* XV (1966), 541-47.

Hübner, Rolf. "Unbekannte Briefe der Brüder Grimm an die Weimarer Buchhändler Friedrich Justin und Karl Bertuch." *Forschen und Bilden,* II (1966), 33-39.

Ottendorf-Simrock, Walther, ed. *Die Grimms und die Simrocks in Briefen.* Bonn: Dümmler, 1965. Pp. 175. DM 19.80.
Rev. by Manfred Lemmer in *Germanistik*, VIII (1967), 830-31.

Schroers, Paul. "Die erste Ausgabe der Grimmschen Märchen." *Philobiblon,* IX (1965), 263-69.

HEINE

Atkins, Stuart. "The First Draft of Heine's Newsletter from Paris, May 30, 1840." *HLB,* XV (1967), 353-67.

Beissner, Friedrich. "Lesbare Varianten. Die Entstehung einiger Verse in Heines 'Atta Troll.' " Pp. 15-23 in: Moser, Hugo, Rudolf Schützeichel, and Karl Stackmann, eds. *Festschrift: Josef Quint anlässlich seines 65. Geburtstages überreicht.* Bonn: Semmel, 1964 [1965], DM 50.00.
Rev. by Irmgard Schweikle in *Germanistik,* VIII (1967), 472-73.

Brummack, Jürgen. "Heines Entwicklung zum satirischen Dichter." *DVLG,* XLI (1967), 98-116.

Galley, Eberhard. "Francois Willes Erinnerungen an Heinrich Heine." *HeineJ,* 1967, pp. 3-20.

Guichard, Leon. "Berlioz et Heine." *RLC,* XLI (1967), 5-21.

Hegele, Dr. Wolfgang. "Der romantische Aufklärer Heinrich Heine." *DU,* XIX (1967), 39-63.

Heine-Archiv Düsseldorf, ed. *Heine Jahrbuch* 1967. Hamburg: Hoffmann und Campe, 1967. Pp. 123. DM 12.00. [=*HeineJ, 1967*].
Rev. by Jost Hermand in *Germanistik,* VII (1967), 831.

Hultberg, Helge. "Heines Bewertung der Kunst." *HeineJ,* 1967, pp. 81-89.

Hölderlin-Jahrbuch 1965/66. Eds. Wolfgang Binder and Alfred Kelletat. Tübingen: Mohr, 1967. Pp. 267. [=*HöJb,* xiv (1965/66).]
Apart from the articles discussed individually in this section, the volume contains two reviews, three reports on the Hölderlin archives and the annual meeting of 1965, and the Hölderlin bibliography for 1962-65.

Kirchner, Werner. *Hölderlin: Aufsätze zu seiner Homburger Zeit.* (Kleine Vandenhoeck-Reihe.) Göttingen: Vandenhoeck & Ruprecht, 1967. Pp. 141.
Collection of four previously written essays: "Hölderlins Entwurf 'Die Völker schwiegen, schlummerten' und die Ode 'Der Frieden' " (*HöJb,* xii); "Hölderlin und das Meer" (*HöJb,* xii); "Hölderlins Patmos-Hymne. Dem Landgrafen von Homburg überreichte Handschrift" (1949); and "Das Testament der Prinzessin Auguste von Hessen-Homburg" (*HöJb,* v). Like Kirchner's book on Sinclair, these essays manifest the biographical-historical method which has been rarely used in Hölderlin exegesis and which, sometimes also in Kirchner's other writings, is too uncritically administered on the poems. (U.G.)

Kudszus, Windfried. "Hölderlins 'Friedensfeier.' " *DVLG,* xli (1967), 547-67.
A very enlightening study which relates the father-son relationship between Christ and the "Alllebendiger" with Hölderlin's language problem. Peace, according to Kudszus, can be reached only where the poet refrains from defining and thereby secularizing the son. The problem of the unspoken, however, should be treated in context with many more examples from Hölderlin's poetry (e.g. "Germanien"), and with Hölderlin's philosophical reflections, since what Kudszus treats here is essentially a question of "freie Erfassung der Sphäre." (U.G.)

Minder, Robert. "Hölderlin und die Deutschen." *HöJb,* xiv (1965/66), 1-19.
This lecture not only relates Hölderlin to his own time and traditions, but also describes and criticizes the various epochs of Hölderlin reception and criticism. It offers a very powerful argument for precision and soberness in Hölderlin research. (U.G.)

Mommsen, Momme. "Traditionsbezüge als Geheimschicht in Hölderlins Lyrik. Zu den Gedichten 'Die Weisheit des Traurers,' 'Der Wanderer,' 'Friedensfeier,' 'Brod und Wein.' " *Neophil,* li (1967), 32-42, 156-68.
Some of the motifs discovered by Mommsen were commonly used in Hölderlin's time; others are taken from remote sources (164). Only for the latter ones, therefore, can one speak of a "Geheimschicht." Some of Mommsen's indications really aid understanding, while others tend to obscure it. Mommsen himself has difficulties avoiding a naive identification of text and source. It is doubtful whether the principle of "Motivüberlagerung" and the double sense as here proposed are valid for the interpretation of "Brod und Wein" (1. 156 "Der Syrier"). (U.G.)

Rosteutscher, Joachim. "Hölderlins mythische Spiegelbilder." Pp. 255-98 in: *Sprachkunst als Weltgestaltung. Festschrift für Herbert Seidler.* Ed. Adolf Haslinger. Salzburg: Pustet, 1966. Pp. 415. DM 46.00.
Rev. by D.N. Schmidt in *Germanistik*, viii (1967), 477-79.

Schmidt, Jochen. "Die innere Einheit von Hölderlins 'Friedensfeier.'" *HöJb*, xiv (1965/66), 125-75.
A running exegesis of the poem, commendable for its exactness and ample references to biblical and classical sources. Unconvincing is the identification of "Fürst des Festes" with the Father on which later is superimposed an identification of Christ with the "Fürst." (U.G.)

Schondorff, Joachim, ed. *Antigone: Sophokles, Euripides, Racine, Hölderlin, Hasenclever, Cocteau, Anouilh.* Introduction by Karl Kerenyi. (Theater der Jahrhunderte.) München: Langen-Müller, 1966. Pp. 371. DM 19.80.
Rev. by Ingeborg Carlson, *Germanistik*, viii (1967), 288.
Kerenyi interprets the play as revealing the "heiligtödliche Wahnsinns-Komponente" Hölderlins. (I.C.)

Szondi, Peter. *Hölderlin-Studien. Mit einem Traktat über philologische Erkenntnis.* Frankfurt: Insel, 1967. Pp. 151.
Four of the five essays in this book were previously published: "Über philologische Erkenntnis," "Der andere Pfeil" (rev. in *ELN*, Supp., iii, 109), "Er selbst, der Fürst des Fests," and "Überwindung des Klassizismus" (first publ. as "Hölderlins Brief an Böhlendorff," see my rev., *ibid.*). The last essay, "Gattungspoetik und Geschichtsphilosophie, mit einem Exkurs über Schiller, Schlegel und Hölderlin," discusses the changing parallelism between poetics and history in Hölderlin's work from the Homburg essays onward. One cannot say that Szondi was as strict with himself here as he was with Beissner in his introductory essay on "philologische Erkenntnis." He is eager to see confusion (112) and contradiction (136) in Hölderlin's thought. A thorough investigation, however, would recognize these faults to be Szondi's. Confusion reigns in his understanding of the "tones" and their appearance in the poem. Otherwise the beginning of Pindar's 7th Olympic could not be interpreted as epic (118f.). This is all the more irritating because the "epic" treatment of this poem marks for Szondi the beginning of an epic tendency of the late Hölderlin in general who, according to him, prefers "Nüchternheit" in *all* aspects of his poems. The criterion for "Nüchternheit" is the growing individuality (134-36), which in reality should be understood as a growing objectivation of all three tones, and not as a tendency towards one of them. This tendency, moreover, is viewed by Szondi as a refutation and correction of the thoughts laid down in the letter to Böhlendorff and in the Homburg essays. All these conclusions are unconvincing, because their foundation is dubious. (U.G.)

See also Garber ("General 3. Criticism"); Beck, Böckmann, Böschenstein, Emrich, Enders, Minder, Schillemeit, and Sengle ("German 2. General"); Mittner ("Italian 2. General").

HOFFMANN

Deml, Friedrich. "E. T. A. Hoffmann als lebendige Gegenwart." *MHG,*
XIII (1967), 1-2.
This excerpt from a lecture whets the appetite for more. Yet even in these few
pages Deml should succeed in convincing most readers that Hoffmann writes
of things that are *both* Romantic *and* modern. Those modernists who would
totally "deromanticize" our image of Hoffmann take heed! (K.N.)

Felzmann, Fritz, and Josef Grafenauer. "E. T. A. Hoffmanns Krankheit-
en." *MHG,* XIII (1967), 20-29.
This is a medical history by two physicians, who conclude that Hoffmann, in
all likelihood, did *not* die of syphilis—a disease frequently attributed to him
by critics and biographers far less competent to judge such matters than these
two authors. (K.N.)

Hoefert, Sigfrid. "E. T. A. Hoffmann und Max Halbe. Ein Beitrag zur
Wirkungsgeschichte des ostpreussischen Romantikers." *MHG,* XIII
(1967), 12-19.

Mitteilungen der E. T. A. Hoffmann-Gesellschaft. Sitz in Bamberg. 13.
Heft 1967. Bamberg: Fränkischer Tag GmbH & Co., 1967. Pp. 52.
[=*MHG,* XIII.]
In addition to the articles listed by author in this section, this issue contains
brief miscellanea, including: the usual formidable list of radio and TV programs devoted to Hoffmann; and the encouraging announcement that this
Romanticist has achieved sufficient recognition—at least in Bamberg—to have
a school named after him. There the former "Deutsches Gymnasium" will
henceforth be called "Das E. T. A.-Hoffmann-Gymnasium." (K.N.)

Müller, Helmut. *Untersuchungen zum Problem der Formelhaftigkeit bei
E. T. A. Hoffmann.* (Sprache und Dichtung. N. F. Band 11.) Bern:
Verlag Paul Haupt, 1964. Pp. 128. 9.80. Fr.
Rev. by Eva J. Engel in *GL&L,* xx (1967), 255-56; by J. Giraud in *EG,* xxi
(1966), 616-17; by H. Himmel in *Neophil,* L (1966), 189-92; by Horst Meixner
in *Archiv,* CCIII (1967), 288-89; and by Wulf Segebrecht in *Germanistik,* VI
(1965), 636.
Scholarly discussions of Hoffmann's prose style have often been hesitant,
overqualified, or downright embarrassed. There has been either a reluctance to
probe too deeply for fear of what might be discovered; or, among those whose
hammer could not quite find the nail, we find such clever but forced notions as
Gloor's "style of stylelessness." Müller attacks the problem in a direct manner,
armed with Herman Meyer's and Werner Kohlschmidt's modern weaponry
for "Stilformeln." Hoffmann's "Formeln," like Eichendorff's (though greatly
differing in meaning), are found to constitute an essential and purposeful element of his narrative art. His "Formelhaftigkeit," according to Müller, manifests itself predominantly in the "Konflikt-Formel," which pairs, antithetically
and repeatedly, certain stock words expressive of the agony and ecstasy of this
German Romantic's "Zerrissenheit." Also, as with Eichendorff, a limited
repertoire is shown to be capable of great variation (see esp. p. 114).

One could easily find fault with Müller's choice of works (some major ones indeed are omitted); with his overemphasis of the one type of "Formel," or even with "Formelhaftigkeit" itself to the exclusion of other stylistic concepts; and with several individual interpretations. The book remains nonetheless a considerable achievement, for it establishes at least *one* solid basis for the extremely difficult task of evaluating Hoffmann's stylistic peculiarities. An appendix of typical "Formel" words and a useful bibliography are included. (K.N.)

Paschke, Hans. "E. T. A. Hoffmanns Wohnungen und Hausgenossen zu Bamberg." *MHG,* xiii (1967), 2-11.
Except for a brief passage (p. 11) that could be related to *Kater Murr,* this article contains mainly biographical data. (K.N.)

Pörnbacher, Hans, ed. *E. T. A. Hoffmann: Die Bergwerke zu Falun. Der Artushof.* (Universal-Bibliothek Nr. 8991.) Stuttgart: Reclam, 1966. Pp. 87. DM 0.90.
Rev. by "W.S." in *Germanistik,* viii (1967), 115.
The editor's "Nachwort" provides a concise and informative discussion of the two stories. Some well-considered views on the "Rahmenerzählung" are included. Selective bibliography. (K.N.)

Raraty, Michael Maurice. "Hoffmann und die mimisch-plastische Künstlerin." *MHG,* xiii (1967), 29-45.
The author provides strong evidence for the idea that Berganza's "Dame" in *Nachrichten von den neuesten Schicksalen des Hundes Berganza* is not drawn from life, as was previously assumed, but is a creation that is only partially modeled after *two* women whom Hoffmann knew in Bamberg. Raraty concludes that Hoffmann's artistic aim here was a satire on pantomime and mimicry, which were then in vogue, and which he considered greatly inferior to other performing arts. (K.N.)

Schnapp, Friedrich. "Aus E. T. A. Hoffmanns Bamberger Zeit. Fünf Theater-Kritiken von Adalbert Friedrich Marcus (September-Dezember 1809). Entdeckt und Mitgeteilt von Friedrich Schnapp." *LJGG,* vii (1966), 119-43.
This discovery helps to reduce the almost total lack of information on public and critical reaction to the performances at the Bamberg theater, in which Hoffmann was active in every major capacity other than actor. Schnapp cogently shows that in all probability these reviews and their author are referred to in a passage of *Seltsame Leiden eines Theaterdirektors.* Somewhat more speculative, though certainly well-documented, is Schnapp's surmise that Hoffmann actually collaborated in writing at least two of the five. (The main evidence is stylistic.) The twenty pages of the re-printed texts of the reviews contain a wealth of detailed information on performances, authors, titles, and highly eloquent and cogent pronouncements on the theater by Marcus (and Hoffmann?). Schnapp's annotations thereto are thorough and valuable. (K.N.)

Schnapp, Friedrich, ed. *E. T. A. Hoffmanns Briefwechsel.* Gesammelt und erläutert von Hans von Müller (†) und Friedrich Schnapp. Erster

Band: *Königsberg bis Leipzig 1794-1814.* München: Winkler-Verlag, 1967. Pp. 495. DM 38.00.

This is the first of three volumes and includes the correspondence from its need for a new scholarly collection of his correspondence has been apparent since almost the very publication date of Hans von Müller's hitherto standard edition of 1912, the now scarcely recognizable original of this one. Müller's work—a considerable feat for its time—was rapidly outdated by the discovery of dozens of Hoffmann letters (some during its printing!), most of which were published in lesser-known periodicals. These scattered findings have since been largely overlooked or ignored (as in Harich's edition of the works, letters, and diaries in 1924).

This is the first of three volumes and includes the correspondence from its beginning in 1794 to the end of Hoffmann's stay in Leipzig in 1814. The second will complete the correspondence proper, with letters from Hoffmann's final years in Berlin (1814-1822). The third will contain a variety of legal, journalistic, and other documents of his authorship; biographical miscellanea; geneology; and the index to all three volumes.

In this first volume, Schnapp has abandoned Müller's separation of the letters to Hippel from the remaining correspondence. The principle of chronological order is thus here (and otherwise) maintained from beginning to end. This includes insertion of letters *to* Hoffmann, as well as information on other letters known to have existed, but no longer extant. Space limitation here precludes a truly adequate description of the wealth of new materials that this collection offers. The following may suggest it.

Müller's edition contained 182 actual letters *from* Hoffmann, 28 *to* him; Schnapp has increased the numbers to 423 and 50, resp. Of the additional letters, 91 *from* Hoffmann and 22 *to* him have never been published. Added to this first volume are such important segments of the correspondence as the bulk of the letters between him and "Härtel und Rochlitz," his publishers who opened the door to his career as a music critic, leading to such early literary works as *Ritter Gluck* and the first Kreisler fragments. Also especially enlightening among the new letters are those few close to the creation of his first two master works—*Der goldne Topf* and *Die Elixiere des Teufels.* These letters were written on May 10, 1813, to Kunz (accompanied by a copy of *Ritter Gluck,* but of interest also for the description of military actions in the Battle of Leipzig, and Hoffmann's state of mind during it); and on May 13, 1813, to Härtel, with similar contents. These two letters—along with that of March 7, 1814, to Rochlitz—also relate much about the disastrous Seconda affair, which essentially signaled the end of Hoffmann's career as a professional musician. Furthermore, the summer of 1814—up to now an almost total hiatus in Hoffmann's correspondence—has been partially filled. This has some biographical significance in that these months were a transition period in preparation for Hoffmann's new mode of life as a civil servant and popular author. Müller's annotations were retained when still applicable, and revised appropriately when necessary. The volume is further enhanced by a small selection of illustrations.

We should be grateful to Friedrich Schnapp for his many years of labor (over 40!) culminating in this publication. We can look forward to a truly major work of scholarship when it is completed. (K.N.)

Segebrecht, Wulf. *Autobiographie und Dichtung*: *Eine Studie zum Werk E. T. A. Hoffmanns.* Mit einem Geleitwort von Professor Dr. Walter Müller-Seidel. Stuttgart: Metzler, 1967. Pp. x + 240. DM 31.00.
We are warned from the start against understanding this book as an old-fashioned quest into the "life-sources" of literature. Segebrecht wishes rather to determine and analyze "Art und Verwendung autobiographischer Formen und Bezüge" (p. 42).
The book is divided into two main parts: "E. T. A. Hoffmann und die Auto-biographie" and "Das autobiographische Verfahren E. T. A. Hoffmanns." In Part I, it is clearly established that Hoffmann did indeed cultivate highly so-phisticated forms of autobiography: the diary, the letter, and "die Lebens-beschreibung." It is also clear that they entered into his writing of fiction. Thus Hoffmann's diaries become more than diaries: they contain "Urformen Hoffmannscher Poesie," especially when dealing with such characteristically self-analytical concepts as "Exaltation, Ironie, Fantasma, Erinnerung, Überle-gung und Poesie" (p. 46). Likewise the letters frequently exceed the limits tacitly imposed by the personality of the addressee, and by the relationship between him and the writer, and they seem frequently to be aimed at a wider audience than the recipient himself. A long list of the letters that are most "autobio-graphical" (in this special sense) is given on pp. 50-52. (How unfortunate that Schnapp's collection [see above] was not available to Segebrecht!) Conversely, epistolary fiction is well represented in Hoffmann's literary writings. The third category, "Lebensbeschreibung," drifts from life over into literature, and is illustrated mainly by Hoffmann's many works presented to the reader as biography. It is shown that such "autobiographical" tendencies were strong in writers with whose works Hoffmann was quite familiar (Rousseau, Hamann, Lichtenberg, Karl Philipp Moritz, Goethe, and others). The main theme in all of Hoffmann's autobiographical preoccupations is the conflict of life and art.
Part II is less successful than Part I. (The logic of its organization simply escaped this reviewer.) *Die Elixiere des Teufels* and *Lebensansichten des Katers Murr* figure most predominantly here, both being fictitious biographies. It is difficult, however, to gain a coherent and detailed image of these novels from Segebrecht's point of view, because the section is divided not according to work, but by categories of the autobiographical. At least the overall aim is apparent: in Hoffmann's "autobiographical" fiction, the goal is self-knowledge, both for the author and for the characters; and this self-knowledge again con-sists primarily of insights into the conflict of life and art.
This reviewer must also state a few reservations. They are, admittedly, some-what peripheral to the main thesis of the book. Opposition to Hans von Müller's biographical approach—now simply outdated—is belabored and needlessly ir-ritable. Did not Müller, after all, accomplish enough for one lifetime—includ-ing the discovery and publication of most of Segebrecht's biographical source materials?! The same applies also, though in lesser measure, to the attacks on Hans Georg Werner (p. 136ff.), whose shortcomings could also be qualified at least slightly for having written one of the better Hoffmann books of recent years. Finally, this reviewer again finds himself compelled to object to an attempt to "deromanticize" Hoffmann. This time it is on the basis of a tacit

definition of German Romanticism that is simply incorrect. He quotes from an early letter to Hippel: " 'Ich habe zuviel Wirklichkeit,' schrieb dieser Dichter des Phantastischen, *den man als 'Romantiker' so gern von aller Wirklichkeit entfernt sieht. . . .* " (Italics added.) It could be rather easily proven that in German Romanticism (Novalis, Arnim, Eichendorff, and others) a certain positive relationship with reality is an indispensable element. In its *highest* forms, one might even contend, the writer of this movement "romanticizes" reality, and this is by no means tantamount to writing pure fantasy.

Such objections do not, however, override the book's new insights, interconnections, and assemblage of materials (including an exceptionally valuable bibliography at the end). All of this easily places it among the most valuable contributions to Hoffmann studies of recent years. (K.N.)

Voerster, Jürgen. *160 Jahre E. T. A. Hoffmann-Forschung: 1805-1965. Eine Bibliographie mit Inhaltserfassung und Erläuterungen.* Stuttgart: Verlag Fritz Eggert, 1967. Pp. 227. DM 58.00.
Rev. by Thomas Cramer in *Euphorion,* LXI (1967), 370-74 (containing a 2-page list of major omissions); and by Klaus Kanzog in *Germanistik,* VIII (1967), 629-30.
In spite of conspicuous omissions and other glaring deficiencies (see reviews listed above), this courageous attempt at a concise, descriptive, and usefully organized Hoffmann bibliography is a definite step forward. Most entries are listed at least twice—once or more in the "systematic" section, where the grouping is by subject matter; and once in the alphabetical section, by author. For the first stage in gathering bibliography in a given area, this book definitely recommends itself; and for a great many topics it would provide the *only* coherent and relatively complete listings available. For subsequent, deeper investigation, the more conventional, nearly complete, and less arbitrary Hoffmann bibliographies (Salomon, Goedeke, Kanzog) should be consulted. (K.N.)

Wiese, Benno von, ed. *E. T. A. Hoffmann: Doge und Dogaresse.* Stuttgart: Reclam, 1965. Pp. 79. DM 0.90.
Rev. by "W.S." in *Germanistik,* VIII (1967), 116-17.
Includes helpful notes, and a welcome analysis and evaluation of this seldom-discussed tale. Particularly interesting is the section on sea-symbolism, in which the merit of the story primarily consists. (K.N.)

Wittkopp-Ménardeau, Gabrielle. *E. T. A. Hoffmann in Selbstzeugnissen und Bilddokumenten.* Reinbeck bei Hamburg: Rowohlt, 1966. Pp. 113. DM 2.80.
Rev. by W. Segebrecht in *Germanistik,* VII (1966), 614-15.
This is definitely *not* a scholarly book, but has its place in the scholar's library largely because of the illustrations, most of which are contemporary to Hoffmann and form a numerous and unique collection in this readily accessible little volume. Also a section of "Zeugnisse" is useful, though it hardly begins to match Schollenheber's much fuller selection. The authoress' attempt at a Hoffmann biography, however, leaves much to be desired. It is highly speculative, amateurish in its one-sided psychologizing tendency, and often

downright inaccurate. Some ingenious phrasings ("Plock. Ein Name, der klingt, als ob ein plumper Stein in einen Sumpf fällt") and some less so ("seine Geschichten sind mit einem gefrorenen Teich vergleichbar, auf dem alltägliche Menschen Schlittschuh laufen . . . ") may indicate the unevenness of the book. Interpretations of important controversial matters range from a sensitive and astute revaluation of *Das öde Haus,* to crude and naive assumptions relating to Hoffmann's supposed case of syphilis (see "Felzmann" above). The bibliography is extensive, and organized in a useful fashion, though apparently little of it was used for the writing of the biography. Would that it had been! (K.N.)

See also Kunz, Schillemeit, A. Schmidt, and P. Schmidt ("German 2. General").

Reviews of books previously listed:

CRAMER, Thomas, *Das Groteske bei E. T. A. Hoffmann* (see *ELN,* V, Supp., 97-98), rev. by G. Bianquis in *EG,* XXII (1967), 393-94; by Kenneth Negus in *GR,* XLIII (1968), 64-67; and by "I.P." in *Studi Germanici,* n.s. V (1967), 138; MULLER-SEIDEL, Walter, Wolfgang KRON and Friedrich SCHNAPP, eds., *E. T. A. Hoffmann: Sämtliche Werke in Fünf Einzelbänden* (see *ELN,* III, Supp., 110 [Schnapp], and IV, Supp., 106), Vol. III, rev. by Jean Giraud in *EG,* XXII (1967), 122-24; and Vols. III, IV, and V by Alfred Kelletat in *Germanistik,* VIII (1967), 613-14; NEGUS, Kenneth, *E. T. A. Hoffmann's Other World* (see *ELN,* IV, Supp., 107), rev. by Charles Passage in *JEGP,* LXVI (1967), 92-94; by S. S. Prawer in *GL&L,* XX (1967), 257-58; and by "V.P." in *Studi Germanici,* V (1967), 346-47; REBER, Natalie, *Studien zum Motiv des Doppelgängers bei Dostojevskij und E. T. A. Hoffmann* (see *ELN,* V, Supp., 99), rev. by Raymond Furness in *GL&L,* XX (1966), 77-78.

JEAN PAUL

Harich, Wolfgang, ed. *Jean Paul: Kritik des philosophischen Egoismus: Satirische und philosophische Beiträge zur Erkenntnistheorie.* Leipzig: Reclam 1967. Pp. 290.

A collection of excerpts elucidating Jean Paul's position towards subjective idealism, especially Fichte's. The only complete works printed are *Clavis Fichtiana* and *Brief über die Philosophie;* everything else is taken out of context. In his introductory essay, Harich tries first to vindicate Jean Paul as a philosopher who can fight against subjectivism on Lenin's and Engels' side (p. 8)— only to reduce him to a mere "poet" (pp. 64-70) where he does not fit the progressive picture. The poet, he asserts, should not have rejected Fichte's ethics along with his epistemology because, as he reasons, the ethics of action foreshadows Marxism. While Jean Paul recognizes the immediate link between these two parts of Fichte's teachings and rejects both of them (esp. *Clavis,* §13), Harich hides his own eclecticism by accusing Jean Paul of confusion and poetic quietism. (U.G.)

Harich, Wolfgang. "Satire und Politik beim jungen Jean Paul." *SuF,* XIX (1967), 1482-1527.

It is a pity that this study on Jean Paul's early satires—the only one that can be taken seriously—should be so one-sided. Harich takes into consideration only the political and social aspect of the satires though being conscious of thus not doing them justice (1493). This method, he asserts, leads us to a correct judgment on the whole of Jean Paul's work! The discussion of philosophical influences disregards completely the intense influence of the English theory of imagination which could have led Harich to recognize the real butt of Jean Paul's early satires, stupidity and dullness (in Hobbes' and Locke's sense), as the origins of everything antispiritual, oppressive, and corporeal (fettering the spirit). But surely recognition of this would have led Harich too far away from his Marxist and materialistic intent. (U.G.)

Jeune, Simon. "Sur une traduction romantique inconnue du 'Songe' de Jean-Paul." *RLC,* XLI (1967), 401-11.
Jeune deals with a translation by a group of Alsacian professors of the volume by F. Noël and E. Stoeber, *Leçons allemandes de littérature et de morale* (1828), carefully examining the relationship between this text and the translations by Madame de Staël (*De l'Allemagne*) and Loève-Veimars (*Revue de Paris,* July 4, 1830).

Rasch, Wolfdietrich. "Die Poetik Jean Pauls." Pp. 98-111 in: *Die deutsche Romantik*: *Poetik, Formen und Motive.* Ed. Hans Steffen. (Kleine Vandenhoeck-Reihe.) Göttingen: Vandenhoeck & Ruprecht, 1967. Pp. 250.
Beginning with some interesting points of comparison between Jean Paul and the early Romantics, Rasch centers on a commendably clear definition of Jean Paul's humor. One misunderstanding, however, should be noted. Jean Paul's sentence "Wenn Schlegel mit Recht behauptet, dass das Romantische nicht eine Gattung der Poesie, sondern diese selber immer jenes sein müsse; so gilt dasselbe noch mehr vom Komischen; nämlich alles muss romantisch, d. h. humoristisch werden" (p. 105) indicates only that everything *comical* should become humorous, not *all poetry*, as Rasch interprets it. This misreading somewhat obscures some of his arguments. (U.G.)

Smeed, J. W. "Jean Paul und die Tradition des Theophrastschen 'Charakters.'" *JJPG,* I (1966), 53-77.
The tradition of this "character" is interesting enough in itself, as well as Jean Paul's adherence to it; but very little results from it for *Schmelzle* and for other similar character drawings in Jean Paul's works. What, for instance, is the difference between this "character" itself and that in a "Charakternovelle," ominously hinted at by Smeed at the end of his study? (U.G.)

Wölfel, Kurt. "'Ein Echo, das sich selber in das Unendliche nachhallt.' Eine Betrachtung zu Jean Pauls Poetik und Poesie." *JJPG,* I (1966), 7-52.
Mainly a discussion of the function of reality as a stimulus for the soul's tendency toward the infinite and eternal. Some slight misrepresentations arise from the fact that Wölfel appears to select fitting quotations at random and to interpret them sometimes out of context. (U.G.)

Wölfel, Kurt, ed. *Jahrbuch der Jean-Paul-Gesellschaft.* 1. Jahrgang. Bayreuth, 1966. Pp. 180. [=*JJPG,* I].

A very good start for the long-desired yearbook which supersedes *Hesperus*. Apart from the papers discussed individually in this section, the yearbook contains "Ungedruckte Aphorismen aus Jean Pauls 'Gedanken'-Sammlung"; Rudolf Kassel, "Die Lampe des Aristophanes"; Heinz Schlaffer, "Das Schäfertrauerspiel. Klopstocks Drama *Der Tod Adams* und die Probleme einer Mischform im 18. Jahrhundert" (both of the latter two papers only touch on Jean Paul); two documents of contemporary literary criticism concerning Jean Paul, and a continuation of the Berend-Krogoll bibliography for the years 1963-65. (U.G.)

Wuthenow, Ralph-Rainer. "Gefährdete Idylle." *JJPG,* I (1966), 79-94.
Shows that the realistic trend in Jean Paul's idylls is a strong element of criticism against the genre. The interpretations, however, are rather superficial and, in *Wutz* for instance, neglect the all-important difference between the narrator and his character. (U.G.)

See also Böschenstein, Hass, Mayer, Minder, Schillemeit, and Sengle ("German 2. General").

KERNER

See David ("German 2. General").

KLEIST

Böckmann, Paul. "Kleists Aufsatz 'Über das Marionettentheater.'" In: Sembdner, *Kleist's Aufsatz über das Marionettentheater* (see below), pp. 32-53.
Revised from a previously published essay, this study attempts to refute Hellmann's (see below) romanticization of Kleist. Rather than proceeding from a Romantic basis, Böckmann singles out Kleist with the aim of showing that the description of the marionette fits Kleist's artistic production, and that the artistic product, "ohne die unsicheren Halbheiten des Alltags," confronts life in a fashion that seems to indicate that the human being, throughout, may travel around the world and get back into paradise "from the other end." This reviewer feels that this point seems to be very hard to prove and that the basic premise for such argumentation is a romantic and romantically utopian one, differing from Miss Hellmann's arguments only in style. In his artistic endeavors every Romanticist is trying desperately to show, if not to regain, paradisical innocence—a quality in which the pre-logical and the logical become a sound, harmonious whole again. (J.Th.)

Dabcovich, Elena. "Die Marionette. Die Lösung eines künstlerischen und moralischen Problems durch einen technischen Gedanken." In: Sembdner, *Kleists Aufsatz über das Marionettentheater* (see below), pp. 88-98.
An impenetrable essay; the point of departure is the contemplation of a navel, the comprehension of which is automatically restricted. Also some of the footnotes are dictated by feminine exuberance rather than penetration of the problem. (J.Th.)

Ellis, J. M. "Der Herr lässt regnen über Gerechte und Ungerechte: Kleist's 'Michael Kohlhaas.' " *Monatshefte, LIX* (1967), 35-40.

Ellis, J. M. "The Heidelberger Ms. of Kleist's 'Prinz Friedrich von Homburg.' " *Euphorion,* LX (1966), 383-87.

Emrich, Wilhelm. "Heinrich von Kleist: Selbstbewusstsein als Pflicht." Pp. 120-46 in: *Geist und Widergeist. Wahrheit und Lüge der Literatur.* Frankfurt (Main): Athenäum, 1965.

Hardy, Swana L. "Heinrich von Kleist: Portrait of a Mannerist." *SIR,* VI (1967), 203-13.

Hellmann, Hanna. "Über das Marionettentheater." In: Sembdner, *Kleists Aufsatz über das Marionettentheater* (see below), pp. 17-31.
This essay is part of Hanna Hellmann's *Heinrich von Kleist. Darstellung des Problems* (Heidelberg, 1911), pp. 13-30. The central theme is the romantic quality of Kleist's essay; in proving this—unfortunately in a somewhat disjointed style—Miss Hellmann cites the theses of classicistic and romantic contemporaries. It makes for unwonted and unusually fruitful reading, fascinating also despite Böckmann's objections inasmuch as she simply shows how the artistic endeavor of the whole Romantic Movement can be reduced to, in our case, Kleist's concept of the development of human existence: "Marionette, Mensch und Gott." Esthetically, this provides for the romantic thesis that art is the divine synthesis, the representation of the pre-logical harmony or the return to it. And Miss Hellmann produces thus the common ideological and esthetic bond between the beginnings (Wackenroder's *Berglinger*) and the end (Eichendorff's *Lockung*) of the movement. However, the problem remains that Kleist may not have been as philosophically serious in his essay as Miss Hellmann indicates. (J.Th.)

Hertling, Gunter H. "Kleists 'Michael Kohlhaas' und Fontanes 'Grete Minde': Freiheit und Fügung." *GQ,* XL (1967), 24-40.

Heselhaus, Clemens. "Das Kleistsche Paradox." In: Sembdner, *Kleists Aufsatz über das Marionettentheater* (see below), pp. 112-31.
The author examines the paradox in Kleist's essay. He concludes that the paradox and Kleist are anti-classicistic, that the paradox destroys the old (and classicistic) anthropological conception, i.e. the notion that the universe is comprehensible, and that this paradox—the structural formula of the "Marionettentheater"—is also the core of Kleist's production. Heselhaus sees the paradox as a structural as well as an ideological premise in Kleist's production and infers three stringent qualities: (1) Kleist's sublimation of the theatrical "in die Einbildungskraft der Sprache ist zugleich die höchste Vergeistigung, die es in deutscher Dramatik gibt"; (2) Kleist elevates improbability to the extent of making it the criterion of his paradoxical actions; incalculability becomes the criterion of the character; chance is then the criterion of fate; this all diminishes tragic necessity; and (3) Kleist's dramatic production is, therefore, seen as an attempt at a "Bühne der Phantasie," quite similar to that of Tieck.

Kleist's concept of the paradox is further compared with Adam Müller's "Lehre vom Gegensatz." (J.Th.)

Kleist, Heinrich von, and Hermann von Pückler-Muskau. *Ansichten von Würzburg.* (Bauwerke, Städte und Landschaften mit bekannten Künstlern erlebt, Bd. 5.) Heidelberg: Edition Europäische Kulturstätten, 1965/66. Pp. 32; 11 illus.

Kunz, Josef. "Kleists Gespräch 'Über das Marionettentheater.' " In: Sembdner, *Kleists Aufsatz über das Marionettentheater* (see below), pp. 76-87.
Kunz interprets Kleist's essay in its historical context. He sees, like Hellmann, the basic premise and the relationship to Romanticism; however, he sets Kleist apart from Romanticism since he misses the romantically utopian element (or the flight into art). Therefore, the ending of Kleist's essay is understood not as a possibility of human endeavor but as a happening for which man can only wait patiently. (J.Th.)

Marson, Eric. "Justice and the Obsessed Character in 'Michael Kohlhaas,' 'Der Prozess,' and 'L'Etranger.' " *Seminar,* II (1967), 21-33.

Peters, F. G. "Kafka and Kleist: a Literary Relationship." *OGS,* I (1966), 114-62.

Plügge, Herbert. "Grazie und Anmut. Ein biologischer Exkurs über das Marionettentheater von Heinrich v. Kleist." In: Sembdner, *Kleists Aufsatz über das Marionettentheater* (see below), pp. 54-75.
First appeared as individual edition under the same title (Hamburg: Claassen & Goverts, 1947). A biological or neuro-physiological excursis on Kleist's "Marionettentheater" and on the particular qualities of "Grazie" and the interchangeable "Anmut." Plügge uncovers structures which clarify the two biological layers of the "vis motrix" and their qualities, and in doing so arrives at a highly fascinating correspondence of the biological process with Kleist's intuitive assertions which Kleist himself half-supported empirically. The author obviously does not detect any utopian yearning in Kleist's essay. Nor does he negate—from his neuro-physiological vantage point—the clear possibility of regaining part of an "unendliches Bewusstsein." (J.Th.)

Ryan, Lawrence. "Die Marionette und das 'unendliche Bewusstsein' bei Heinrich von Kleist." In: Sembdner, *Kleists Aufsatz über das Marionettentheater* (see below), pp. 171-95.
The point of departure is the "antigrav" quality of the marionette, enlarged through a further dimension; Ryan is convinced that Kleist had some philosophical conception in mind. The author, therefore, explains the essay as a tool for the comprehension of Kleist's fictional production. He arrives at the conclusion that Kleist attempted (particularly in "Homburg" and "Amphitryon") to regain for the dissonant world "einige wenige Durchblicke auf ein ersehntes neues Kapitel in ihrer Geschichte." This means a correction of the more common ideas on the Kleistian "Gefühl," in as much as Ryan sees the "Gefühl" not

as determined by the "antigrav" lightness of the human being (or of Kleist's fictitious characters), but as "[legitimiert] von der Zugehörigkeit zu einer übergeordneten Ganzheit, die einen zukünftigen Weltzustand ahnend vorwegnimmt." The utopian streak—or the wishful romantic streak—in Kleist's imagination is thus re-established. (J.Th.)

Schaub, Martin. *Heinrich von Kleist und die Bühne.* Zürich: Juris, 1966. Pp. 113.
Of interest is the vantage point, i.e. in particular the reconstructive illumination of Kleist's attempt at producing a drama of "Innerlichkeit." The difficulties—the unification of language, plot, setting, character in theatrical fashion that is to make "Innerlichkeit" comprehensible and visible to the general audience—seem to have overwhelmed Kleist. Schaub finds the perfected union only in *Prinz von Homburg,* not before. Although stimulating, the study as a whole is too compact, at the same time too superficial and too badly annotated. (J.Th.)

Schlawe, Fritz, Helmut Sembdner, and Beda Allemann. " 'Schmerz' order 'Schmutz'? Diskussion einer Briefstelle Kleists." *Euphorion,* LX (1967), 388-401.

Schondorff, Joachim, ed. *Amphitryon. Plautus. - Molière, Dryden. - Kleist. - Giraudoux. - Kaiser.* Introduction by Peter Szondi. (Theater der Jahrhunderte). München: Langen-Müller, 1964 [recte 1965]. Pp. 428. DM 19.80.
Rev. by Ingeborg Carlson in *Germanistik,* VIII (1967), 186-88.
Though Alkmene has the last word in Kleist's version, the play receives the title from the "Joseph" character, Amphitryon. Originally planned as a translation of the Molière comedy, Kleist turns back to tragical mythological origin. Parallels referring to the immaculate conception in reference to the savior figure of Herakles are not mentioned by Szondi. (I.C.)

Sembdner, H., ed. *Kleists Aufsatz über das Marionettentheater. Studien und Interpretationen.* Berlin: E. Schmidt, 1967. Pp. 226.
A most excellently realized idea to combine the significant interpretations of Kleist's "Über das Marionettentheater" and some contributions to the subject from technical, biological, and literary-historical vantage points; with concluding remarks by the editor. See reviews of individual interpretations (listed by author) in this section. (J.Th.)

Sembdner, Helmut. *Kleist-Bibliographie 1803-62. Heinrich von Kleists Schriften in frühen Drucken und Erstveröffentlichungen.* Stuttgart: Eggert, 1966. Pp. 61. DM 45.00.
Rev. by K. Kratsch in *Germanistik,* VIII (1967), 822.

Silz, Walter. "Die Mythe von den Marionetten." In: Sembdner, *Kleists Aufsatz über das Marionettentheater* (see above), pp. 99-111.
Silz doubts that any stringent logic can be found in Kleist's essay and his images and, therefore, categorically denies any esthetic and ideological import-

ance. Silz' firm assertions are not always cogent; however, his anger is quite understandable. (J.Th.)

Steiner, Jacob. "Das Motiv der Puppe bei Rilke." In: Sembdner, *Kleists Aufsatz über das Marionettentheater* (see above), pp. 132-70.
An original contribution. The essay deals with the clarification of Rilke's early art-nouveau treatment of the doll/marionette-motif. This doll/marionette-motif develops, through Rilke's predisposition, through Rilke's intensive reading of Kleist, and through his fascination with the essay on the marionette theater, into an adaptation of Kleist's notions. (J.Th.)

Streller, Siegfried. *Das dramatische Werk Heinrich von Kleists.* (Neue Beiträge zur Literaturwissenschaft. Bd. 27.) Berlin: Rütten & Loening, 1967.

Wiese, Benno von. "Das verlorene und wieder zu findende Paradies. Eine Studie über den Begriff der Anmut bei Goethe, Kleist und Schiller." In: Sembdner, *Kleists Aufsatz über das Marionettentheater* (see above), pp. 196-220.
After a cursory interpretation of Goethe's use of the word "Anmut"—which von Wiese describes as "Form und Bewegung, Geistiges und Sinnliches" and therefore "Voraussetzung für menschliche Kultur"—Kleist's and Schiller's concepts are discussed at length. Kleist's marionette, with its "Anmut," is interpreted as essentially a "Freiheit des Daseins" versus Schiller's ethical principle of "Freiheit der Entscheidung." However, von Wiese discerns quite cogently in both the desire for the lost paradise; he thus draws, almost inadvertently, the line of transition from classicism and classicistic idealism to romanticism. (J.Th.)

See also Böckmann, Böschenstein, Emrich, Kunisch, Kunz, Mayer, Schillemeit, Sengle, and Weigand ("German 2. General").

LENAU

Dietze, Walter, ed. *Lenau, Nikolaus. Die Albigenser: Freie Dichtungen.* Mit einem Nachwort von Walter Dietze. (Insel-Bücherei Nr. 471.) Leipzig: Insel Verlag, 1965. Pp. 134. MDN 1.25.
Rev. by F. Apetsberger in *Germanistik,* VIII (1967), 148.
The text is *not* according to the critical edition (Castle, Leipzig, 1911). Dietze discusses only the *Albigenser* of history, and is not concerned with Lenau's epic poem at all. (I.C.)

Hohl, Egbert, ed. *Nikolaus Lenau: Werke in einem Band.* Mit dem Essay *Der Katarakt* von Reinhold Schneider. (Campe Klassiker.) Hamburg: Hoffmann und Campe, 1966. Pp. 514. DM 13.80.
Rev. by W. Dietze in *Germanistik,* VIII (1967), 833-34.
Hohl selects 200 Lenau-poems, *Faust, Savonarola, Don Juan* and *Schlussgesang* of *Albigenser.* It is an arbitrary selection with no notes. Hohl's concluding essay attempts a middle-of-the-road interpretation of the *Weltschmerz-Dichter,* locating him somewhat vaguely between Reinhold Schneider and Turoczy-Trostler. (I.C.)

Oehlmann, Werner, ed. *Don Juan.* Mit dem Text der Komödie 'Don Juan' von Molière in der Übersetzung von Eugen Nieresheimer. (Dichtung und Wirklichkeit 14.) Berlin: Ullstein, 1965. Pp. 206. DM 3.20.
Rev. by Ch. Jauslin in *Germanistik,* VIII (1967), 56.

See also David, Krummacher, and Sengle ("German 2. General").

MÜLLER, ADAM
See Reiss ("German 2. General"); Heselhaus ("Kleist").

NOVALIS
Albertsen, Leif Ludwig. "Novalismus." *GRM,* XVII (1967), 272-85.
Discussion of trivial literature written after Novalis' death which bears the imprint of his style.

Dauer, Dorothea W. "Early romanticism and India as seen by Herder and Novalis." *KFLQ,* XII (1967), 218-24.

Ehrensperger, Oskar Serge. *Die epische Struktur von Novalis' 'Heinrich von Ofterdingen.' Eine Interpretation des Romans.* Winterthur: Schellenberg, 1965. Pp. 109. Sw. Fr. 14.40.
Rev. by Konrad Kratzsch in *Germanistik,* VIII (1967), 605-06.

Frye, Lawrence O. "Spatial Imagery in Novalis' 'Hymnen an die Nacht.' " *DVLG,* XLI (1967), 568-91.
Frye carefully analyzes variations with regard to movement and space found in each of the hymns, thereby providing valuable assistance in their interpretation. (B.M.)

Hamburger, Käthe. *Philosophie der Dichter. Novalis/Schiller/Rilke.* Stuttgart: Kohlhammer, 1966. Pp. 280. DM 24.80.
Revised from the 1929 edition; recent scholarship is taken into consideration.

Kimura, Uichi. "Novâlis - Bungaku no Shi to Ai ni tsiute. 'Yoru no Sanka' o chûskin ni" ["Liebe und Tod in den 'Hymnen an die Nacht' "]. *Kakyo,* XII (1965-66), 37-47.

Kluckhohn, Paul and Richard Samuel, eds. *Die Werke Friedrich von Hardenbergs.* 3 Vols. Stuttgart: Kohlhammer, 1965.
Rev. by Ernst Behler in *GRM,* XVII (1967), 214-19.

Kohlschmidt, Werner, ed. *Novalis. Gesammelte Werke.* Güterloh: S. Mohn, 1967. Pp. 671. DM 19.80.
This collection is based on the four-volume edition of J. Minor. It includes not only Novalis' important works but also the paralipomena to the *Lehrling* and *Ofterdingen.* Only a few of Novalis' early lyrics and a selected group of his fragments have been included. There is also some biographical material by Tieck and Just. In his introduction, Kohlschmidt gives a brief, sensitive analysis of each work without attempting to present final answers. (B.M.)

Mähl, Hans-Joachim. *Die Idee des goldenen Zeitalters im Werke Novalis.* Heidelberg: Winter, 1965. DM 54.00.
Rev. by Richard Samuel in *Germanistik,* VIII (1967), 609-21; by Furuccio Masini in *Studi Germanici,* V (1967), 342-43; and by R. Ayrault in *EG,* XXII (1967), 361.

Malsch, Wilfried. *'Europa,' Poetische Rede des Novalis.* Stuttgart: Metzler, 1965. Pp. 206. DM 28.00.
Rev. by Richard Samuel in *Germanistik,* VIII (1967), 609-21; by Furuccio

Mason, Eudo Colecestra. "New Light on the thought of Novalis—Volume 2 of the Stuttgart Edition." *MLR,* LXII (1967), 86-91.
Mason's evaluation places the second volume of the Stuttgart Novalis edition in proper perspective as not only a valuable aid to Romantic scholarship but also as a means of perceiving in Novalis a more systematic writer than was previously supposed. (B.M.)

Ritter, Heinz. *Der unbekannte Novalis: Friedrich von Hardenberg im Spiegel seiner Dichtung.* Göttingen: Sachse & Pohl, 1967. Pp. 365. DM 28.00.
Rev. by Gonthier-Louis Fink in *Germanistik,* VIII (1967), 625-26.
Ritter has based his new ordering of many of Hardenberg's lyrics on a study of discrete changes in handwriting found in Hardenberg's diaries and *Studienhefte,* as well as official documents discovered in Tennstedt. Using these external aids, by re-evaluating biographical information, and by analyzing internal relationships, Ritter has proposed sequential changes in the "Vermischten Gedichte" and "Geistliche Lieder." He has also suggested new interpretations of other lyric poems. Working with care and sensitivity, the author has successfully placed Hardenberg's Sophie experience in more realistic perspective. Occasional generalizations with regard to interpretation only tend to point up the soundness of his analyses. This volume constitutes a significant contribution in understanding Novalis as a poet and a man. (B.M.)

Shimbo, Sukeyoshi. "Die Unendlichkeit bei Goethe und Novalis." *Kairosu,* V (1965-66), 1-12.

Zelinsky, Hartmut. "Thomas Bernhards 'Amras' und Novalis, mit besonderer Berücksichtigung von dessen Krankheitsphilosophie." *Literatur und Kritik,* I (1966-67), 38-42.

See also Fletcher ("General 3. Criticism"); Hass Kahn, Reiss, Schanze, Schillemeit, and P. Schmidt ("German 2. General"); Sammons ("Bonaventura").

Reviews of books previously listed:
GRUTZMACHER, C., *Novalis und Philipp Otto Runge* . . . (see *ELN,* IV, Supp., 111), rev. by M. Dyck in *JEGP,* LXVI (1967), 423-27; and by Marianne Zerner in *Monatshefte,* LIX (1967), 56.

SAVIGNY

See Reiss ("German 2. General").

SCHELLING

See Reiss ("German 2. General").

SCHLEGEL, A. W.

Jolles, Frank, ed. *A. W. Schlegels 'Sommernachtstraum' in der ersten Fassung vom Jahre 1789.* Nach den Handschriften herausgegeben. (Palaestra Vol. 244.) Göttingen: Vandenhoeck & Ruprecht, 1967. Pp. 248. DM 28.00.

Lohner, Edgar, ed. *August Wilhelm Schlegel. Kritische Schriften und Briefe.* Vol. VI: *Vorlesungen über dramatische Kunst und Literatur.* Zweiter Teil: *17. - 37. Vorlesung.* Stuttgart: Kohlhammer, 1967. Pp. 303. DM 18.00.

This volume contains a discussion of the French theater and includes the works of Corneille, Racine, Voltaire, Molière, the Elizabethan theater, and the plays of Calderon, Cervantes, and Lope de Vega. The German theater from Hans Sachs to Schiller's late dramas is discussed in two lectures.

Nagavajara, Chetana. *August Wilhelm Schlegel in Frankreich.* Tübingen: Niemeyer, 1966. Pp. 362. DM 40.00.

With careful documentation, sensitive evaluations, and laudable objectivity, Chetana Nagavajara went beyond his stated goal of presenting A.W. Schlegel as a literary mediator between France and Germany. On the basis of comparisons between statements and opinions of critics and authors found in French publications covering nearly 30 years, the author reveals therein a familiarity with Schlegel's ideas which was at first very limited and highly critical, but eventually led to general acceptance and understanding in breadth if not in depth. Nagavajara examined attitudes as well as opinions which could have only developed as a result of acquaintanceship with Schlegel's works. A short foreword by Kurt Wais re-emphasizes Schlegel's position as a pioneer in comparative literature as well as criticism. (B.M.)

See also Böckmann, Hass, and Weigand ("German 2. General").

SCHLEGEL, F.

Behler, Ernst. *Friedrich Schlegel in Selbstzeugnissen und Bilddokumenten.* Reinbek: Rowohlt Taschenbuch Verlag, 1966. Pp. 185.

Making free use of citations from Schlegel's own works written throughout his life as well as excerpts from Schlegel's contemporaries, the author has presented a well-written, carefully organized biography which is a worthwhile addition to recent Schlegel research following the leads of Josef Körner. Behler does much to show the productivity of Friedrich Schlegel as a writer, critic, philosopher, and as a leader of Romantic thought throughout his life. He includes a brief chapter which summarizes the direction and quality of Schlegel research through the years, as well as a useful, selective bibliography of all aspects of Schlegel research through 1966. (B.M.)

Behler, Ernst, and Hans Eichner, eds. *Kritische Friedrich-Schlegel-Ausgabe*. Bd. 2: *Charakteristiken und Kritiken I: 1796-1801*. Paderborn: Ferdinand Schöningh; Zürich: Thomas Verlag, 1967. Pp. cx + 450. DM 54.00.

Friedrich Schlegel's most significant critical works, which are contained in this volume, are made more accessible for use in conjunction with the scholarship of the past 80 years by the inclusion of the pagination from Minor's edition in the margins. The foreword by Hans Eichner is a valuable supplement which places each section of the book in proper perspective with regard to literary problems of the time. His discussion of the *Athenäum-Fragmente* are particularly valuable. (B.M.)

Belgardt, Raimund. " 'Romantische Poesie' in Friedrich Schlegels Aufsatz über das Studium der griechischen Poesie." *GQ*, XL (1967), 165-85.

On the basis of Schlegel's "Aufsatz" (1794-96), Belgardt shows the tenuous nature of the traditional view of Schlegel's life divided into three well-defined periods: Classical, Romantic, and Religious. Belgardt also points up Schlegel's concept of literature in which the classical and the romantic are not polarities but rather a synthesis by which the poetry of the time might be elevated to the Greek level. (B.M.)

Mennemeier, Franz Norbert. "Unendliche Fortschreitung und absolutes Gesetz. Das Schöne und das Hässliche in der Kunstauffassung des jungen F. Schlegel." *WW*, VI (1967), 393-409.

Patsch, Hermann. "Friedrich Schlegels 'Philosophie der Philologie' und Schleiermachers frühe Entwürfe zur Hermeneutik. Zur Frühgeschichte der romantischen Hermeneutik." *Zeitschrift für Theologie und Kirche*, LXIII (1966), 434-72.

Pohlheim, Karl Konrad. *Die Arabeske: Ansichten und Ideen aus Friedrich Schlegels Poetik*. München/Paderborn/Wien: Schöningh, 1966. Pp. 406. DM 34.00.

Rev. by R. Ayrault in *EG*, XXII (1967), 628-30; and by Ernst Behler in *ZDA*, XCVI (1967), 139-41.

Schumann, Detlev W. "Friedrich Schlegels Bedeutung für Eichendorff." *JFDH*, 1966, pp. 336-83.

The author describes the considerable influence which Fr. Schlegel had, as a poet and as a man, upon Joseph von Eichendorff. He shows the similarity of themes and images which exist in the poetry of the two men. Schumann concludes that the mediocre poetry of Fr. Schlegel likely exerted influences upon Eichendorff for more than a decade after he had initially read it. Parallels *do* exist in the language and imagery; but do they represent influence by Schlegel or are they the result of the idealized, stereotyped imagery of the time? (B.M.)

See also Hass, Reiss, and Schanze ("German 2. General"); Brüggemann ("Spanish 2. General").

SCHLEIERMACHER
See Reiss ("German 2. General").

TIECK
Matenko, Percy, Edwin H. Zeydel and Bertha M. Masche, eds. *Letters to and from Ludwig Tieck and his Circle.* Unpublished letters from the period of German Romanticism including the unpublished correspondence of Sophie and Ludwig Tieck. Chapel Hill: University of North Carolina Press, 1967. Pp. 395. $10.00.

Segebrecht, Wulf. "Ludwig Tieck an Eduard von Bülow: Dreiundzwanzig Briefe." *JFDH,* 1966, pp. 384-456.
These letters to Bülow represent an important supplement to Tieck's life and literary activity between the years 1832 and 1850. (B.M.)

See also Kahn, Krummacher, Kunz, A. Schmidt, and Weigand ("German 2. General"); Kohlschmidt ("Novalis"); Lippuner ("Wackenroder").

Reviews of books previously listed:
TIECK, Ludwig, *Franz Sternbalds Wanderungen* (see *ELN,* V, Supp., 110), rev. by Gerhard Schulz in *Germanistik,* VIII (1967), 384-85; TRAINER, James, *Ludwig Tieck: From Gothic to Romantic* (see *ELN,* III, Supp., 121), rev. by Raymond Immerwahr in *GQ,* XL (1967), 716-18.

UHLAND
See David, Krummacher, and Storz ("German 2. General").

VARNHAGEN VON ENSE, K.
Schultze, Christa. "Theodor Fontane und K. A. Varnhagen von Ense im Jahre 1848 (mit einem Brief Varnhagens an Fontane vom 11. Februar 1852)." *Fontane-Blätter,* I, 4 (1967), 139-53.
Recalls Fontane's enthusiasm for the 1848 revolution (later denied by him) and supports this observation with excerpts from letters and early political essays. Compares his attitude to Varnhagen's and discovers similar political views. Letter refers to writer Alexander Jung and publication of his essay on Goethe's *Wanderjahre.*

VARNHAGEN VON ENSE, RAHEL
Reviews of books previously listed:
KEMP, Friedhelm, ed., *Rahel Varnhagen, Briefwechsel mit Alexander von der Marwitz* . . . (see *ELN,* V, Supp., 110-11), rev. by Hans Grössel in *Neue Deutsche Hefte,* XIV (1966), 147-52 (Heft 113 der Gesamtreihe); SCURLA, Herbert, *Begegnungen mit Rahel* . . . (see *ELN,* III, Supp., 121-22), rev. by G. Bianquis *EG,* XXI (1966), 305.

WACKENRODER

Lippuner, Heinz. *Wackenroder/Tieck und die bildende Kunst. Grundlegung der romantischen Ästhetik.* Zürich: Juris, 1965. Pp. 225. Fr. 22.50.
Rev. by Gerhard Schulz in *Germanistik,* VIII (1967), 373-74.

See also Kunz ("German 2. General"); Hellmann ("Kleist"); Mittner ("Italian 2. General").

ITALIAN

(By Olga Ragusa, Columbia University, and William T. Starr, Northwestern University.)

1. BIBLIOGRAPHY

Goffis, Cesare Federico. "Primo Ottocento." *RLI,* LXX (1966), 469-77.

2. GENERAL

Baldi, Guido. *Giuseppe Rovani e il problema del romanzo dell'Ottocento.* Saggi di "Lettere Italiane," XI. Firenze: Olschki, 1967. Pp. 236.
Especially the first chapter is relevant to Romantic studies. Baldi shows how Rovani in his rejection of the historical novel consciously parodies its narrative structure and its *topoi.* The discussion thus focusses on the dissolution of the plot and of the novelistic devices through the author's ironic commentary on them, and on the transformation into bourgeois "heroes" of such familiar figures as the noble outlaw, the demon lover, *la belle dame sans merci,* and the angelic woman. Later chapters deal with Rovani's formulation in the preface to *I cento anni* of the poetics of a new kind of novel, which Baldi, in the wake of recent discussions of the novel, describes—perhaps unnecessarily—as "romanzo saggio." The passages which discuss levels of style and tonal changes, and author-novel/author-reader relationships are proof of Baldi's freshness of approach. His study supersedes almost everything that has been written on Rovani. To the bibliographical note listing works on the theory of the Italian novel in the 19th century (p. 76), I would add Bertacchini's *Il romanzo italiano dell'Ottocento* (see *ELN,* V, Supp., 112). (O.R.).

Blasucci, Luigi. "Studi manzoniani e leopardiani." *GSLI.* CXLIV (1967), 420-39.
Reviews in depth Getto's *Letture manzoniane* (*ELN,* III, Supp., 131) and Getto's *Saggi leopardiani* (below).

Derla, Luigi. "Le idee economiche e sociali del *Conciliatore.*" *NA,* DI (1967), 182-207.
Italian Romanticism in the *Conciliatore* was not conservative but progressive. The bourgeois *élite* viewed its task essentially as the transformation of the economic, social, and political structures of Italy.

Falzone, Gaetano. *Battaglie romantiche e antiromantiche in Sicilia.* La polemica de 'La Ruota' di Palermo. Bologna: Pàtron, 1965. Pp. 86.

Frattarolo, Renzo. "Per una storia della critica dantesca. Dante nell'età romantica." *Accademie e biblioteche d'Italia,* 5-6 (1966), pp. 302-23.

Marcazzan, Mario. *Le origini lombarde nel romanticismo italiano.* Milano: La Goliardica, 1967. Pp. 386.
A sensitive reading of the Romantic manifestoes which results in an excellent reconstruction of the seminal milieu of Italian Romanticism and in a careful differentiation of the positions of writers who were momentarily united by the program of *Il Conciliatore.* Marcazzan is especially successful at interrelating writers and ideas that are usually considered antithetical (Foscolo, Monti, and Leopardi; Foscolo and Manzoni; Lombard and Piedmontese Romanticism; Protestantism and Catholicism as equal ingredients in Milanese Romanticism), and at correcting value judgments born of hasty generalizations (see, for instance, his whole discussion of Austrian cultural politics in Italy). Marcazzan's single most important contribution is probably the revaluation of the role of Di Breme as spokesman in Milan for the ideas of Mme de Staël and the group of Coppet and as the great strategist who gave its direction to *Il Conciliatore.* But the work as a whole is rich in insights and proves the viability and the value of cultural history. (O.R.)

Mariani, Gaetano. *Storia della scapigliatura.* Caltanissetta-Roma: Sciascia, 1967. Pp. 908.
Rev. by Piero Nardi in *LI,* xix (1967), 391-94.

Mittner, Ladislao. "L'Italia nella letteratura tedesca dell'età classico-romantica." *LI,* xix (1967), 71-82.
Excellent synthesis of the importance of the myth of Italy for German esthetic thought in early Romanticism: relation of the southern landscape to the pantheistic poetry of nature in Goethe and Hölderlin; Italy as the medium of German recapture of the ideal of Greek beauty; Wackenroder's simultaneous discovery of Raphael and Dürer. (O.R.)

Mostra della Scapigliatura. Pittura. Scultura. Letteratura. Musica. Architettura (Palazzo della Permanente. Milano, 1966, Maggio-Giugno). Milano: Società per le Belle Arti ed Esposizione Permanente, 1966. Pp. 116.
In a dense introduction, "La scapigliatura artistica," Anna Maria Brizio points out the necessity of reformulating the problem of the artistic nature of the scapigliatura within the broad framework of the crises in Lombard society of the latter part of the 19th century, and, from this, there comes an interesting contribution to the understanding of the culture of the period. Dante Isella's "La Scapigliatura letteraria lombarda, un nome, una definizione" is also worthy of note. (W.T.S.)

Negri, Renzo. *Gusto e poesia delle rovine in Italia fra il sette e l'ottocento.* Milano: Ceschina, 1965. Pp. 254.

Rev. by Giovanna Gronda, *GSLI,* cxliv (1967), 137-40; and by Walter Binni, *RLI,* lxx (1966), 467-68.
A study of the theme of ruins in Italian pre-Romantic and Romantic poetry. The origin of interest in the theme is seen in 16th and 17th century landscape painting. Parallel developments in garden landscaping, stage design, and esthetic theory. The high points of the book are the discussions of the themes in Foscolo and in Leopardi. An excellent corrective to the persistent notion that Romanticism in Italy differed substantially from the concomitant movement in other European nations. (O.R.)

Pagliai, Marena. "Un manifesto della Scapigliatura. *Il libro dei versi di Arrigo Boito." Letteratura,* xxxi (1967), 125-34.
Typically Romantic themes in Boito's poetry, and Pagliai notes a certain Sturm und Drang atmosphere; he makes further suggestions about the influence of Baudelaire.

Pellegrini, Carlo. "Il Risorgimento italiano visto dall'altra parte." *NA,* di (1967), 20-37.

Petrocchi, Giorgio. *Il romanzo storico nell'ottocento italiano.* Torino: Edizioni Radio Italiana, 1967.

Petronio, Giuseppe. "Proposte e ipotesi di lavoro per uno studio sul romanticismo." *Beiträge zur Romanischen Philologie,* ii (1963), 116-26.

Timpanaro, Sebastiano. *Classicismo e illuminismo nell'Ottocento italiano.* Pisa, Nistri-Lischi, 1965. Pp. 387.
Rev. by Lanfranco Caretti in *L'Approdo letterario,* 34 (1966), pp. 121-22.

3. Studies of Authors

BELLI

Belli, G. G. "Dico una cosa che nun è bbuscìa." *Studi romani,* xii (1964), 415-24.

Colombo, Achille. "Il Porta e il Belli: Note per la lettura delle poesie di Carlo Porta e dei sonetti di G. Giovacchino Belli." *Letture,* xx (1965), 587-602.

Gallardo, Piero, ed. *G. G. Belli. Sonetti scelti.* Tornio: UTET, 1964. Pp. 575.

Lodolini Tupputi, Carla. "Il testamento segreto del Belli." *Palatino,* ix, No. 8-12 (1965), 174-185.
Lodolini Tupputi here publishes the copy of Belli's will of Aug. 22, 1837, deposited by Belli with the notary Fratocchi, and recently found by Lodolini Tupputi in the Archivio di Stato, Rome. The autograph copy is in the B.N. Vittorio Emmanuele.

Orioli, Giovanni. "G.G. Belli oggi." *C&S,* v, No. 18 (1966), 50-59.
A thoughtful review of recent studies of Belli's poetry.

Studi belliani nel centenario di Gioacchino Belli. Atti del primo convegno di studi belliani e contributi vari pubblicati con la collaborazione dell'Istituto di Studi romani a cura del Comune di Roma. Roma: Editore Carlo Colombo, 1965. Pp. xxxvii + 1013, con 36 tavole nel testo e 84 fuori testo.
A very important collection of contributions to Belli studies and criticism. The following are among the important ones in Part I, which concerns the life and and time of Belli: A.M. Ghisalberti, "La Roma di Gregorio XVI," pp. 21-38; G. Orioli, "Belli e i moti del '31," pp. 49-60 (Ghisalberti affirms that Belli was not interested in political and social facts. Orioli disputes some of Ghisalberti's conclusions); A. Lazzarini, "G.G. Belli 'clericale,'" pp. 161-74 (concerns the same problem); E. Amadei, "Scritti dedicati al figlio," pp. 61-66; N. Vian, "L'estate del '59 nella vita del Belli," pp. 75-100 (Vian attempts a reconstruction of Belli's sentiments at that time).
In Part II,, "L'opera del Belli. Problemi di storia, di critica e di filologia," almost all the contributions contain new material: R. Vighi, "Il peso dell'ironia nell'interpretazione dei sonetti," pp. 279-310; E. Francia, "La religiosità romana del Belli," pp. 405-26; F. Felcini, "Note sulla poetica del Belli," pp. 311-28; L. Felici, "La storia e gli storici nella formazione culturale del Belli," pp. 387-404; J. Moestrup, "Stile e struttura nel sonetto belliano," pp. 269-78; E. Mazzali, "La comunicabilità del linguaggio poetico-dialettale e la poesia del Belli," pp. 459-64; B. Migliorini, "Lessicografia romanesca," pp. 465-72.

BORSIERI

Alessandrini, Giorgio, ed. Pietro Borsieri. *Avventure letterarie di un giorno e altri scritti editi ed inediti.* Prefazione di Carlo Muscetta. Roma: Edizioni dell'Ateneo, 1967. Pp. xv + 432.
Rev. by Mariso Scotti in *GSLI*, cxlv (1968), 137-42.
Borsieri's pamphlet, one of the principal documents of the Romantic debate, is here reprinted from Bellorini's edition without the addition of notes. In his *Testi di poetica romantica* (Milano: Marzorati, 1960), Febo Allevi reprinted only Chap. I and the long letter inserted in Chap. II, but supplied explanatory notes essential to the comprehension of the text. The present edition contains a choice piece, previously unpublished, Borsieri's Introduction to the *Biblioteca italiana,* set in print and then abandoned in favor of an editorial statement signed, among others, by Monti and Acerbi. There is a good selection of letters, many previously unpublished; others that have appeared in scattered publications and are here brought together for the first time. The Preface is unfortunately hasty and perfunctory. A much finer study of the intellectual profile of Borsieri is contained in Marcazzan's *Le origini lombarde nel romanticismo italiano* (see above). A correction: the Verri mentioned on p. 99 is Alessandro, not Pietro (cf. Index, p. 428). (O.R.)

CATTANEO

Review of book previously listed:
Boneschi, ed., *C. Cattaneo. Scritti politici* (see *ELN*, v, Supp., 113), rev. by Sergio Camerani in *Archivio storico italiano,* cxxiii (1965), 114-16.

D'AZEGLIO

Fantasia, Matteo. *Massimo d'Azeglio pittore, scrittore e statista del Risorgimento italiano.* Conferenza . . . l'8 novembre 1966 al Leggio di Bari. Malfetta: Scuola tipografica Istituto provinciale Apicella, 1967. Pp. 34.

Ferrari, Bernardino. *Eugène Rendu e Massimo d'Azeglio.* Il Risorgimento italiano visto da un cattolico liberale francese (1849-1865). Santena: Fondazione Camillo Cavour, 1967. Pp. 199.

Marshall, Ronald. *Massimo d'Azeglio, an Artist in Politics.* Oxford University Press, 1966. Pp. 328.
Rev. by Nina Ruffini in *NA*, DI (1967), 521-25.

Petrocchi, Giorgio. "D'Azeglio. Il romanzo storico." *FLe,* XLII (March 9, 1967), 18.
A review of *Massimo D'Azeglio. Opera completa,* ed. by Alberto Mario Ghisalberti. Milano: Mursia, 1966.

Vincent, E. R., trans. and ed. *Things I Remember (I miei ricordi).* Oxford Library of Italian Classics. Oxford University Press, 1966. Pp. 349.

DE SANCTIS

Izzi, Giuseppe. "La critica di F. De Sanctis." *C&S,* v, No. 19 (1966), 21-29.

Scuderi, Ermanno. "Note intorno all'estetica del De Sanctis ed alla sua critica dantesca." *Ausonia,* XXII, No. 1-2 (1967), 58-61.

DI BREME

Camporesi, Piero, ed. Ludovico Di Breme. *Lettere.* Torino: Einaudi, 1966. Pp. xxviii + 708.
Rev. by Mario Fubini in *GSLI,* CXLIV (1967), 447-456; by S. Timpanaro in *Belfagor,* XXII (1967), 240-44; and by R. Bertacchini in *NA,* CDXCVIII (1966), 540-43.

Laurent, M.-H. "Cinq Lettres inédites de Ludovico de Breme et cinq opuscules relatifs à son débat avec le comte G. Fr. Galeani Napione de Cocconato." *GSLI,* CXLIV (1967), 99-115.
Letters written between 1812 and 1818 to Luigi Andrioli, Gaetano Cattaneo, and Carlo Boucheron. Bibliographical information on pamphlets now in Vatican Library.

See Marcazzan ("Italian 2. General").

FOSCOLO

Bezzola, Guido. "Appendice Foscoliana." *GSLI,* CXLIV (1967), 149-53.
Completes bibliographical information for a number of items in his edition of Foscolo's *Tragedie e poesie minori* (see *PQ,* XLIII, 506).

Derla, Luigi. "Interpretazione dell'*Ortis.*" *Conv,* XXXV (1967), 556-76.
Proposes an interpretation of the "sociological structure" of the novel as seen through the categories of Marx-Lukács and of Freud. The cause for Foscolo's fascination with "Erostratism" in *Ortis,* that is, with destructive and self-destructive violence, is seen as resulting from Foscolo's inability to accept the dynamics of revolutionary change.

Frattini, Alberto. *Il neoclassicismo e Ugo Foscolo.* Bologna: Cappelli, 1965. Pp. 234.
Written for a collection ("Universale Cappelli") the purpose of which is to interest a broad public, this work is of high quality. In the first part, Frattini explains the genesis and meaning of neo-classicism, and examines the innovating tendencies of Italian esthetics of the 18th century. In the second, he deals with the renewal of Italian culture, with pre-Romanticism, and with the neo-classicism of V. Monti. The third part treats Foscolo. The concept of neo-classicism perhaps is not clarified quite adequately, and there are some lacunae; the arrangement causes some repetition (W.T.S.)

See also Marcazzan ("Italian 2. General"); Negri ("Italian 2. General").

LEOPARDI

Abbadessa, Silvio. *Le 'due voci' delle "Operette morali."* Arezzo: Pellegrini, 1965.
An attempt at constructing a type of philosophical dualism in the *Operette morali* by contrasting the attitudes of various characters (e.g. Porfirio—Plotino) and the internal contradictions of others (esp. Parini). The eclectic nature of Abbadessa's approach dilutes the value of these random observations.

Agosti, Stefano. "Per un repertorio delle 'fonti' leopardiane: Iacopo Sannazaro." *Paragone,* XVIII, 30 (1967), 89-103.
Agosti shows the importance of Maria Corti's "Passero solitario in Arcadia" (see *ELN,* V, Supp., 116), and indicates other evidence of the influence of Sannazaro, Petrarch, and Vergil.

Bertacchini, Renato. "Rassegna leopardiana." *Studium,* LXIII (1967), 659-66.

Consoli, Domenico. *Cultura, coscienza letteraria e poesia in Giacomo Leopardi.* Firenze: Le Monnier, 1967. Pp. 212.
Seventeen essays spanning chronologically nearly the entire *corpus* of Leopardi's poetic and prose production; intended as both a "risultato e premessa" of a reading of the *Canti;* contains both specific analyses of particular works and more general essays on the poet's philosophy.

Figurelli, Fernando. "La canzone di G. Leopardi 'Alla sua donna.'" Pp. 105-24 in: *Studi in memoria di Carmelo Sgroi.* Torino: Bottega d'Erasmo, 1965.
The author interprets the "donna" and the "cara beltà" of Leopardi's poem as an "immaginazione della beatitudine," a chimerical form of "felicità."

Stylistically, "Alla sua donna" is seen as evidence of Leopardi's having achieved poetic maturity.

Frattini, Alberto. "Leopardi e Dante." *Scuola e Cultura nel mondo,* October 1965, pp. 5-21.
Dante reminiscences in Leopardi.

Getto, Giovanni. *Saggi leopardiani.* Firenze: Vallecchi, 1966. Pp. 279.
This collection includes four essays previously published: "Poesia e letteratura nelle *Operette morali"* (see *ELN,* IV, Supp., 120); "Per un'interpretazione di 'A Silvia' " (see *ELN,* III, Supp., 128); " 'D'in su la vetta della torre antica' " (see *ELN,* III, Supp., 128); and "Gli 'Inni cristiani,' " which appeared in *Studi in onore di Vittorio Lugli e Diego Valeri* (1961). In addition, there is a fifth essay, occupying more than half of the volume, entitled "La storia della poesia leopardiana," intended as part of the volume *Leopardi* in the Mursia series *Classici italiani.* The latter traces the development of Leopardi's literary interests in their evolution and the relationship of his writings to those changing preferences. Extensive citations of texts are well chosen.

Marzot, Giulio. *Storia del riso leopardiano.* Firenze: D'Anna, 1966. Pp. 222.
A detailed study of Leopardian irony in its internal development and in relation to outside influences. Six essays with an appendix devoted to the critical fortune of Leopardi's prose writings.

Molinaro, Julius A. "A Note on Leopardi's *Il passero solitario."* *SP,* LXIV (1967), 640-53.
A review of the appearance of the binomials *sollazzo e riso* and *diletto e giogo* in early Romance literatures, as an example of Leopardi's creative reuse of a cliché.

Russo, Vittorio, ed. Antonio Ranieri. *Sette anni di sodalizio con Giacomo Leopardi.* Napoli: Berisio, 1965. Pp. 140.
A reprint of the 1920 Ricciardi edition, including Ranieri's "Notizia intorno alla vita ed agli scritti di Giacomo Leopardi" and its supplements, an appendix with letters of Leopardi to Ranieri (previously published by Antonio Carafa), letters of Ranieri to Conte Monaldo Leopardi (published by Gennaro Buonanno) and to Alessandro D'Ancona, and a short preface by Russo describing Ranieri's career and his relationship with Leopardi.

Solmi, Raffaella and Sergio, eds. Giacomo Leopardi. *Opere,* Vol. II. Milano: Ricciardi, 1966. Pp. 1270.
This is the second volume in the Ricciardi edition and includes extensive selections from the *Zibaldone* (with emphasis on the moral and philosophical passages in contrast with strictly philological material) and from the *Lettere* (1816-1837), the latter annotated with frequent references to correspondence received by Leopardi. There is an index to the principal themes of the *Zibaldone* and a list of the letters selected.

Travi, Ernesto. "Leopardi lettore delle opere di Alessandro Verri." Pp. 497-520 in: *Leopardi e il settecento.* Firenze: Olschki, 1964.

In line with recent interest in the important transitional figure of A. Verri, Travi traces his influence not only on the conception of Leopardi's Brutus and Sappho but especially on Leopardi's preference for an "indefinite" poetic language.

Vallese, Giulio. *Le canzoni patriottiche del Leopardi.* Napoli, A. Morra editore, 1967. Pp. 21.
Shows the relationship of the so-called "patriotic" *Canti* to those that followed and claims that the fundamental theme of Leopardi's poetry is the unhappiness of the individual as it derives from the injustice of "a shameful political deficiency."

See also Blasucci ("Italian 2. General"); Marcazzan ("Italian 2. General"); Negri ("Italian 2. General").

MANZONI

Bàccolo, Luigi. "Riletture curiose in margine a *I Promessi sposi,* La Monaca di Monza di Giovanni Rosini." *FLe,* XLII (Feb. 2, 1967), 8.

Baldacci, Luigi. "Il romanzo giallo degli scapigliati." *FLe,* XLII (1967), 21.

Belotti, Giuseppe. *Il messaggio politico-sociale di Alessandro Manzoni.* Bologna: Ed. Zanichelli, 1966. Pp. viii + 535.
Rev. by G.B. Bonelli in *Studium,* LXIII (1967), 177-80.

Bertacchini, Renato. "Nuove edizioni e saggi manzoniani." *Studium,* LXII (1966), 835-44.

Bezzola, Guido. "I Sermoni manzoniani. Testo e critica." *LI,* XVIII (1966), 361-77.
Establishes the textual history of the four poems on the basis of the only positive documents extant. Places the poems in their historical context by referring to other polemical works and invectives in verse for the period 1796-1800. Singles out *A.G.B. Pagani* as the artistically most successful of the four.

Biagini, Mario. "Echi e richiami della *Bibbia,* dai Padri della Chiesa, dal*Breviario* nell'opera del Manzoni." Pp. 273-90 in: *Studi manzoniani. Atti del VI Congresso Nazionale.* Lecco: Comune di Lecco, 1965.

La biblioteca di Don Ferrante. Mostra bibliografica. Milano, marzo 1967. Biblioteca Comunale di Milano, 1967. Pp. 78.
Exhibition catalogue with introductory essay by GianFranco Grechi. A reconstruction of Don Ferrante's library on the basis of works and authors cited by Manzoni, with additional works of the period that could have been part of the library.

Bonora, Ettore. "Su una fonte dell'Introduzione dei *Promessi Sposi.*" *GSLI,* CXLIV (1967), 55-70.

On the stylistic elaboration of the pastiche paragraph in 17th century Milanese prose and the probable use made by Manzoni of Tadino's *Raguaglio*. An important contribution on a frequently overlooked passage in the novel. (O.R.)

Bosco, Leonardo, ed. *Colloqui su* I promessi sposi. Palermo: Mori, 1964. Pp. 43.

Caretti, Lanfranco, ed. *Alessandro Manzoni. I promessi sposi.* Edizione integrale commentata. Milano: U. Mursia, 1966. Pp. 592.

Casnati, Franceso. "Un'amica del Manzoni," *Ausonia*, XXII, No. 1-2 (1967), 53-57.

Colesanti, M. "Manzoni, Voltaire e l'invito a pranzo." Pp. 153-58 in: *Lettura e critica. Studi e postille.* Napoli, 1966.
Suggests an episode in *Zadig* as possible source for the dinner invitation extended to Renzo, Lucia et al. in Chap. XXXVIII.

Colombo, Umberto. *Itinerario manzoniano.* Milano: Edizioni Paoline, 1965. Pp. 375.

De Michelis, Eurialo. "Raccordi narrativi nei *Promessi Sposi.*" *NA*, CDXCIX (1967), 186-204.
Focusses on the chapters that are links rather than pauses in the narrative (Chap. IV would be an example of the latter). Discusses especially Chaps. XVIII and XIX, emphasizing the dialogue between the "conte zio" and the "padre provinciale." Points out parallels with other dialogues in the novel: Agnese and Perpetua's and Renzo and Azzecca-garbugli's. Remarks on the similarity of the "political" behavior of Don Abbondio and the "padre provinciale," and on the significance of the 1840 revision.

Derla, Luigi. *Realismo storico di Alessandro Manzoni.* Milano: Ist. Ed. Cisalpino, 1965. Pp. 225.
Derla proposes an interpretation of Manzoni based on a new formulation of the problem. Manzoni's poetry and religion, and his thinking, beyond the attempt to reconcile practical reason with theoretical Christian reason, is supposed to have been based on historical methodology; he is supposed to have conceived of history neither in the Christian tradition nor in the Pascalian sense. The fact is that the historical world is revealed as an autonomous sphere, omnipresent, only when one is freed from teleological thinking. The usefulness of the volume is principally in the detailed examination of Manzoni's tendency towards the historical world, a tendency which served to turn him aside from fruitless wanderings in sterile theories.
Many interesting themes for the student of Manzoni are suggested but the subject announced in the title is not demonstrated, indeed perhaps cannot be because the historical world of Manzoni cannot be freed from a teleological perspective. Derla's solution is that historical realism, or Manzonian historicism, never theoretically formulated, was realized in his masterpieces. This means that in the interpretation and representation of historic facts, Manzoni was not a consistent Christian. The thesis tends to transfer completeness from the

plane of the work to that of historical methodology and affirms that there is a Manzonian system with a theoretical base, after elimination of teleological elements. (W.T.S.)

Esposito, Enzo. "Recenti edizioni del Manzoni." *L'Italia che scrive*, XLIX, Nos. 2-3 (1966), 28-29.

Ferrucci, Franco. "Il giardino di Renzo." *Paragone*, XVIII, 26 (1967), 59-86.
A reading of *I promessi sposi* which reflects the malaise felt by many contemporary students of Manzoni who find it impossible to accept his Christian orthodoxy. Interesting observations on Renzo as the "comet-like" protagonist of the novel. (O.R.)

Gambini, Ruggiero. *Alessandro Manzoni, economista*. Spezia: Tip. moderna, 1967. Pp. 7.

Getto, Giovanni. "Manzoni e Shakespeare." *LI*, XIX (1967), 187-236.
An important contribution to an important subject. Getto examines Manzoni's direct references to Shakespeare in the *Lettre à M. Chauvet* and points out innumerable echoes and reminiscences in the tragedies and especially in *I promessi sposi*. His conclusion is that Manzoni did not use Shakespeare as a source but as an authority to justify the treatment of certain subject matter. Getto does not consider a related problem I would like to see treated: Shakespeare's influence on the rhythm and formal structure of *I promessi sposi*. I feel that when this relationship is once established the extent of Scott's influence on Manzoni will be seen in a more proper and reduced perspective. (O.R.)

Girardi, Enzo Noé. *Manzoni "reazionario."* Bologna: Cappelli, 1966.
Rev. by E. Dolce, *Aevum*, XLI (1967), 575-77; and by Renzo Negri, *Conv*, XXXV (1967), 374-75.
Contains "Il tumulto di S. Martino," Renzo agl'Inferi" (on Chap. XIV), "Il Manzoni capovolto dal Moravia," "Nota sul Manzoni e l'economia," and "Manzoni e Cervantes."

Goffsi, Cesare Federico, ed. Manzoni. *Opere*. Bologna: Zanichelli, 1967. Pp. 1033.
Includes *I promessi* sposi in its entirety, Chaps. V-VI of Book II of *Fermo e Lucia*, a selection from the youthful poems and the *Inni sacri*, Chap. VII of *Osservazioni sulla morale cattolica*, the tragedies, the political poems, the Introduction to *Storia della Colonna infame*, and the letters on Romanticism, the historical novel, and the Italian language. Excellent introduction, bibliographies, and notes. The work of one of the best and least eccentric of Manzoni scholars. (O.R.)

Goudet, Jacques. "Il ritmo della conversione del Manzoni e il ritmo della conversione dei suoi personaggi." Pp. 23-30 in: *Studi manzoniani. Atti del VI Congresso Nazionale*. Lecco: Comune di Lecco, 1965.

Grimm, Jürgen. "Manzoni." Pp. 192-207 in: *Die literarische Darstellung der Pest in der Antike und in der Romania*. München: Wilhelm Fink Verlag, 1965. Pp. 243.
Rev. by Frédéric O'Brady, in *RR*, LVIII (1967), 315-16.
The plague episode in *I promessi sposi*, studied by Nicolini for its historical veracity and by Mazzitelli for its medical precision, is considered by Grimm from the strictly literary point of view. He finds Manzoni's treatment of the theme—one of the aspects of the struggle between good and evil in the novel—the most magnificent (*grossartig*) since Vergil's use of the same theme in the *Georgics*. This tight and lucid chapter must henceforth be included in all Manzoni bibliographies. (O.R.)

Jenni, Adolfo. "Il motivo della conversione nel Manzoni e nella letteratura italiana." Pp. 47-70 in: *Studi manzoniani. Atti del VI Congresso Nazionale*. Lecco: Comune di Lecco, 1965.

Lugli, Vittorio. "Anticipazione manzoniane." *L'Approdo Letterario*, XIII, No. 38 (1967), 59-63.

Melli, Grazia. "Note manzoniane sul *Fermo e Lucia*." *Conv*, XXXV (1967), 196-223.
Excellent analysis of Claudio Varese's *Fermo e Lucia. Un'esperienza manzoniana interrotta* (see *ELN*, IV, Supp., 126-27). Contrary to Varese, Melli argues in favor of a continuity between *Fermo e Lucia* and *I promessi sposi*. She brings evidence from *Adelchi* and *La pentecoste* as well as from *Fermo e Lucia* itself to show that *I promessi sposi* is a restatement of the themes of the first draft without the polemical insistence which accompanied their initial formulation. To be commended for its exceptional stylistic clarity. (O.R.)

Negri, Renzo. "Dante e Manzoni di fronte al lettore." *VII Congresso Manzoniano*. Lecco, 9/11 Ottobre 1965. Pp. 14.
Author-reader relationships in Dante and Manzoni compared and evaluated. Valuable insights into the narrative techniques of Manzoni. (O.R.)

Paratore, Ettore. "Lettura del capitolo XXXVIII dei *Promessi Sposi*." *LI*, XVIII (1966), 378-402.
Points out the fundamental symmetries that give important structural value to the last chapter of the novel, making it a *summa* of the more significant episodes. Important also for the incidental comparisons with Balzac, Dostoevski, Tolstoy, and Flaubert. Corrects a tendentious interpretation given by Allegretti in his commentary of *I promessi sposi* (see *ELN*, V, Supp., 120), which, being contained in a widely used edition of Manzoni's works, can be presumed to contribute to the already overwhelming mass of misreadings of the novel. (O.R.)

Pasquazi, Silvio. "Il voto in Dante e in Manzoni." *Rassegna di cultura e vita scolastica*, XX, No. 1 (1966), 1-2.
On Dante's Piccarda episode and Lucia's night at the castle of the Innominato.

Peirone, Luigi. "La linguistica del Manzoni vista oggi." *Studium,* LXIII (1967), 455-59.
Review and evaluation of recent work in this field.

Randazzo, Basilio. *La sociologia del romanzo.* I promessi sposi *di Alessandro Manzoni.* Firenze: Città di Vita, 1965. Pp. 271.

Rolfini, Mario. *Divagazioni manzoniane.* Ferrara: Tip. Sociale Saletti, 1963. Pp. 199.
Although presented modestly as a guide for secondary school students, this is an intelligent commentary on the many themes connected with *I promessi sposi* that criticism has repeatedly considered. Very abundant bibliographical indications, arranged thematically. (O.R.)

Rondi, Gian Luigi. "La lingua di Manzoni è sacra per Riccardo Bacchelli e Bolchi." *FLe,* XLII (Feb. 9, 1967), 26.
I Promessi sposi on T.V.

Rosselini, Aldo. "Note sul francese di Alessandro Manzoni, con un' appendice sugli scritti in francese." *Contributi dell'Istituto di Filologia Moderna.* Serie francese. Università Cattolica del Sacro Cuore. Vol. III. Milano: Soc. Ed. "Vita e Pensiero," 1964, pp. 21-52.
A thorough and detailed study of Manzoni's knowledge of French and of French writers he knew and discussed, or quoted from.

Sansone, Mario. "La crisi dell'uomo del Rinascimento e la conversione manzoniana." Pp. 259-72 in: *Studi manzoniani. Atti del VI Congresso Nazionale.* Lecco: Comune di Lecco, 1965.

Tortoreto, Alessandro. "Tasso e Manzoni." Pp. 303-10 in: *Studi manzoniani. Atti del VI Congresso Nazionale.* Lecco: Comune di Lecco 1965.

Travi, Ernesto. "La presenza della lirica barocca nel rinnovamento religioso e poetico manzoniano." Pp. 97-106 in: *Studi manzoniani. Atti del VI Congresso Nazionale.* Lecco: Comune di Lecco, 1965.

Ulivi, Ferruccio. *Figure e protagonisti dei Promessi Sposi.* Torino: ERI, 1967. Pp. 180.
An intelligent first chapter discusses the relationship between "characters" and the novel in general, and between Manzoni's characters and his novel in particular. Ulivi proposes a structural rather than a psychological analysis. Ulivi recognizes the primary importance of Manzoni's religious ethic, but the thrust of his discussion often concerns the historical truthfulness of the characters: there is in this sense an element of discontinuity, if not of actual opposition, between Ulivi's statement of his subject and his development of it. I found his analysis of padre Cristoforo original and particularly illuminating. A good companion volume to the novel itself. (O.R.)

Ulivi, Ferruccio. "Natura caduta e figurazione naturale in Manzoni" (see *ELN,* IV, Supp., 126). In: *Il manierismo del Tasso e altri studi.* Firenze: Olschki, 1966.

Zaniboni, Maria R. "La Rivincita delle vedove nel capolavoro manzoniano." *FLe,* XLII (Feb. 2, 1967), 9.
A brief study of the effects of Manzoni's childhood circumstances on his writings: the mother has the rôle of honor; fathers are few and insignificant; the principal male characters are confirmed bachelors; widows are prominent; the portrayal of father-son relationship is poor. Zaniboni suggests the possibility of an oedipal complex.

See also Blasucci and Marcazzan ("Italian 2. General").

Reviews of books previously listed:
BARBERI-SQUAROTTI, Giorgio, *Teoria e prove dello stile del Manzoni* (see *ELN,* v, Supp., 118), rev. by Adrani Colombo in *Il Verri,* 23 (1967), 147-51; DE CASTRIS, A., *L'impegno del Manzoni* (see *ELN,* v, Supp., 119), rev. by Piero De Tommaso in *Letteratura,* XXXI (1967), 118-24.

MAZZINI

Battaglia, Salvatore. "L'idea di Dante nel pensiero di G. Mazzini." *Filologia e letteratura,* No. 46 (1966), pp. 113-23.

MONTI

See Marcazzan ("Italian 2. General").

PORTA

Isella, Dante, ed. *Le lettere di Carlo Porta e degli amici della cameretta.* Milano: Ricciardi, 1967. Pp. xxii + 485.

Sioli, Legnani, Emilio. "L'edizione originale milanese di 'La porta di Meneghino' di Carlo Porta rappresentata alla Scala la sera del 26 luglio 1818." *Archivio storico lombardo,* Serie IX, IV (1963), 399-424.
Reproduces the dialect version which appears in vol. VII of the *Nuova raccolta teatrale* . . . (Milano, 1821-1822), and credits Barbieri with the attribution to Porta of that version. Sioli Legnani also publishes in photocopy and in a diplomatic edition a draught of Porta's letter, from which it appears that his contribution was a revision of orthography and of a few sentences in the text prepared by Petracchi.

See also Colombo ("Belli").

TOMMASEO

Di Biase, Carmine. *Tommaseo e Dante. Ritratto di Dante ovvero autoritratto di Tommaseo.* Marcianise: Ed. "La Diana," 1966. Pp. 154.

PORTUGUESE
(By Heitor Martins, Indiana University.)

1. BIBLIOGRAPHY

Carvalho, Pérola de. "Biblioteca Municipal Mário de Andrade, São Paulo-S.P.: Catálogo de periódicos da secção de livros raros." *Revista do Instituto de Estudos Brasileiros,* II (1967), 131-53.

List of Brazilian serials (1809-1880) in the Mário de Andrade Municipal Library, in São Paulo. One hundred and twenty-eight items are briefly described. In an addendum, twelve periodicals published outside of Brazil but in the Portuguese language are listed.

2. GENERAL

Barboza, Onédia C. de C. "Revista da Sociedade Filomática." *ESPSL,* March 18, 1967, p. 4.

Short study of one of the first Brazilian reviews showing romantic tendencies.

Coelho, Nelly Novaes. *O ensino da literatura.* São Paulo: Editôra F.T.D., 1966.

"Methodological suggestions" for the teaching of literature in secondary schools. Very good, although entirely traditional as the audience for this book would require, are the interpretation and criticism of *O Guarani,* by José de Alencar (pp. 35-65); *A morte do lidador,* by Alexandre Herculano (pp. 77-87); *Amor de perdição,* by Camilo Castelo Branco (pp. 135-169); and the early novels by Machado de Assis (pp. 210-216).

Ferreira, Alberto. *Bom senso e bom gosto (Questão Coimbrã). Textos integrais da polêmica.* Recolha, notas e biobibliografia por Maria José Marinho. Vol. I (1865). Lisboa: Portugália, 1966.

This first volume of a set comprises an introduction (Perspectives of Romanticism: 1834-1865), the reproduction of 12 pamphlets of the "questão coimbrã," and some notes and addenda. Six illustrations are also presented. In his introduction (pp. xiii-cxxxviii), Ferreira leans heavily on the ideas first set forth by Augusto da Costa Dias, analysing Portuguese romanticism as an expression of the period between the victory of the bourgeoisie over the monarchic-feudal institutions (1834) and the final victory of the liberal over the radical faction of that same bourgeoisie (1865). This ideological interpretation of romanticism modifies the accepted standards in some ways: Garrett becomes a champion of radicalism, and Herculano is considered as the most typical of the ultra-romantics. Castilho, on the other side, although remaining the conservative depicted by the literary historians, is viewed also under a different light as a kind of self-elected poet laureate. The basic line of romantic development passes through Herculano and not Garrett. Following the example of the former, the authors of 1840 and 1850 avoid consideration of the contemporary state of Portuguese society, hiding themselves in a "barbaric" medievalism. When the shock waves of 1848 reach Portugal the struggle is inevitable. Hence, the protest of the "escola coimbrã," which, in spirit if not in matter, repeats the attitude of Garrett. This is probably the best interpretation of romanticism in Portugal now available, and, although it leans dramatically towards the history of ideas and avoids purely literary considerations, we are sure future historians and critics will have to review many accepted positions on the new basis proposed by Alberto Ferreira. Maria José Marinho did a very careful scholarly job of collecting and annotating the elements of the 1865 polemics. An index and bibliography are promised as part of the last volume scheduled for publication.

Goes, Fernando. "Notícia (incompleta) sobre a literatura do café." *O espelho infiel*. São Paulo: Conselho Estadual de Cultura, 1966, pp. 195-241.

The first part of the article is a good study of a mediocre novella (*O capitão Silvestre e frei Veloso ou A plantação do café no Rio de Janeiro*) by a minor writer (Luís da Silva Alves de Azambuja Susano), who was the first to deal with the coffee theme in Brazilian literature. Susano, according to Goes, "se não era brilhante mostra vivacidade de espírito e certa liberdade de linguagem." References are made to the theme of coffee as it appears sporadically in works by Alencar, Taunay, Castro Alves, and Fagundes Varela.

Ramos, Péricles Eugênio da Silva, ed. *Poesia romântica*. Com introd. e notas. São Paulo: Melhoramentos, 1965.

Following *Antologia dos poetas brasileiros da fase romântica,* by Manuel Bandeira, and *Panorama de poesia brasileira. O romantismo,* by Edgard Cavalheiro, this new anthology of Brazilian romantic poetry has all the good qualities of its predecessors plus more scholarly editing. The "introduction" (pp. 9-28) presents a brief survey of the romantic period in Brazilian poetry, more or less in accord with the standards universally accepted, calling attention also to features of poetic diction and versification. Most notable is the restraint in dealing with Joaquim de Sousandrade, a fresh breeze for the enthusiasts so common among recent Brazilian critics. The anthology offers 9 poets in the "first generation" (and two considered as marginal), 27 in the "second generation," and 6 in the "third generation." The selections from each poet are preceded by a biography and critical appraisal, a list of his publications, a bibliography, and editorial information on the texts presented. The texts are profusely annotated. The best represented poet is Conçalves Dias (with 8 selections), followed by Álvares de Azevedo, Casimiro de Abreu, Fagundes Varela, Castro Alves (7 each), and Junqueira Feire (6). The minor names, making up about half of the authors, are represented by a single selection.

Silva, Vítor Manuel de Aguiar e. "Pré-romantismo e romantismo." *Teoria da literatura*. Coimbra: Livraria Almedina, 1967, pp. 370-408.

A very broad examination of the concept of romanticism and its elements. The author accepts the position of Wellek (unified romanticism) against Lovejoy's (romanticisms), and develops a rather traditionalistic outlook of the movement. Although quoted in the bibliography at the end of the volume, no use was made in this chapter of M.H. Abrams' basic work, *The Mirror and the Lamp*. Considering the fact that this book is intended for Portuguese students or students of Portuguese literature, it is odd indeed that no examples are drawn from artists or critics who wrote in that language.

Tengarrinha, José. "La presse illégale portugaise pendant la guerre civile de 1846-47." *Bulletin des Etudes Portugaises et de l'Institut Français au Portugal,* XXVII (1966), 137-56.

3. STUDIES OF AUTHORS

a. *Portuquese*

ALORNA

Roberts, K. S. "The Marquesa de Alorna and the English Poets." *KFLQ,* XIII (1966), 145-55.

BRAGA

Cidade, Hernani. "Teófilo Braga e João de Deus." *Ocidente,* LXXII (1967), 121-27.

Teófilo Braga, although representing a very different philosophical attitude, was able to see João de Deus as the best representative of Portuguese lyricism in his time.

See also Ferreira ("2. General").

CASTELO BRANCO

Cabral, Alexandre, ed. *As polêmicas de Camilo.* Vol. III. Com introd. Lisboa: Portugália, 1967.

This third volume of the complete polemical works of Camilo Castelo Branco comprises the text of twelve pieces (1849-54), scholarly editing and annotating.

Ferro, Túlio Ramires. *Tradição e modernidade em Camilo.* Lisboa: Parceria António Maria Pereira, 1966.

A new printing of the introduction to the author's edition of *A queda de um anjo.*

Mendes, João, ed. "Sete cartas de Camilo." *Brotéria,* LXXXIII (1966), 679-82.

Letters addressed to D. António Pereira da Cunha, lamenting poor health and other sufferings, physical and spiritual.

Ramos, Vítor. "As 'Novelas do Minho' de Camilo e a integração rural no romance português do século XIX." *Estudos em três planos.* São Paulo: Conselho Estadual de Cultura, 1966, pp. 85-122.

A very broad review of the rural novel in Portuguese romanticism. Ramos links its development with the integration of rural communities in the Portuguese political life after 1832 and Mousinho da Silveira's reforms. Following this reasoning the author draws an ascending line starting in *Pároco da aldeia* (by Herculano), through the novels of Julio Dinis, *A felicidade pela agricultura* (by Castilho), and culminating in the novels of Camilo. Before Camilo, country life is idealized (although the authors consider themselves engaged in the reformist spirit), and it is an irony that the "verdade, mesmo a verdade sociológica, a representação fiel da época fornecida aos vindouros," comes from the least engaged of these authors (Camilo). Ramos provides a very detailed analysis of the *Novelas do Minho* and their rural elements, concluding that the integration of the rural sector of Portuguese life in the novel takes place only with Camilo's book. In the representation of this rustic world, Camilo is richer than his predecessors not only in aesthetic values but also in moral and social ones. Vítor Ramos' work is the best tentative interpretation of the *roman rustique* in Portugal, and draws attention to the links of that genre to the political realities of the time. Unfortunately, the author does not consider purely literary elements (the change in taste, and possible foreign influences, such as George Sand's) in his interpretation.

Silva, Domingos Carvalho da. "Laet e Camilo." *ESPSL,* Dec. 3, 1966, p. 2.

Souza, José de Campos. *Camilo e a princesa do Corgo.* Porto: Comissão de Turismo da Serra do Marão, 1967.

Xavier, Alberto. *Camilo e outras figuras e fatos da literatura nacional e internacional.* Lisboa: Férin, 1967.

See also Coelho ("2. General"); Neves ("3b. Laet").

CASTILHO
See Ferreira ("2. General").

DEUS
Mourão-Ferreira, David. "Evocação de João de Deus." *Ocidente,* LXXII (1967), 131-44.

See also Cidade ("3a. Braga").

GAMA
Simões, João Gaspar. "Arnaldo Gama e o romance histórico." *ESPSL,* Dec. 24, 1966, p. 4.

GARRETT
Garcia, Mario. "Dialéctica do fogo em Almeida Garrett." *Brotéria,* LXXXV (1967), 3-17.
The works of Garrett (*Viagens, Folhas Caídas, Frei Luís de Sousa*) are seen as a document of deep religious preoccupation. The author analyses the dichotomy present in the fire metaphor (bright light, burning flame) as a bivalent analogy for heaven and hell.

Dias, Augusto da Costa. "As 'luzes' e a batuta ou um grande vulto ignorado do iluminismo português." *Seara Nova,* XLVI (1967), 73-79.
This article is a brief but excellent summary of an introduction to *Roubo das Sabinas,* an unpublished long poem of Garrett's early years. Costa Dias considers Garrett as the direct heir to Bocage's "linha libertina" and promises a critical edition of the poem.

Martins, Heitor. "Garrett censor dramatico." *ESPSL,* April 1, 1967, p. 5.
Includes the only known example of Garrett's theatrical report, in which a more liberal linquistic policy is defended.

See also Ferreira ("2. General").

HERCULANO

Martins, Heitor. "Gonçalves Dias e Herculano." *ESPSL,* Jan. 21, 1967, p. 4.
A description of personal relationship between the young Gonçalves Dias and Herculano. Includes an unpublished letter of Herculano to the editors of *O Trovador.*

See also Coelho ("2. General"); Ferreira ("2. General").

MENDONCA

Santos, Julio Eduardo dos. "Algumas notas sôbre três escritores olisiponenses: Manuel de Galhegos—Francisco Leitão Ferrira—António Pedro Lopes de Mendonça." *Olisipo,* XXX (1967), 108-29.
Lopes de Mendonça considered as a writer native to Lisbon. For the author, Mendonça is the best Portuguese critic of the romantic period.

QUENTAL

See Ferreira ("2. General").

REBELO DA SILVA

Simões, João Gaspar. "Herói de um romance histórico." *ESPSL,* Jan. 28, 1967, p. 1.
Rebelo da Silva used Beckford as a model for a character in *Rausso por homizio.*

b. *Brazilian*

ABREU

Massa, Jean-Michel. "Casimiro de Abreu, un poète 'engagé'?" *Bulletin de la Faculté des Lettres de Strasbourg,* XLV (1967), 658-60.

ALENCAR

Martins, Heitor. "As leituras juvenis de Alencar." *ESPSL,* Feb. 18, 1967, p. 4.
Identification of the three anonymous novels cited by Alencar in *Como e porque sou romancista* as *Celestina* (1791), by Charlotte Smith; *The Children of the Abbey* (1796), by Regina Maria Roche; and *Saint-Clair of the Isles* (1803), by Elizabeth Helme.

Myer, Marlyse. "Para brindar Iracema." *Pireneus, caiçaras* . . . São Paulo: Conselho Estadual de Cultura, 1967, pp. 75-85.
Brief study, stressing the influence of Chateaubriand's *Les Natchez* on *Iracema* and *O Guarani.* Another possible source, according to the author, is *Oderahi,*

histoire américaine (Paris: Boiste, 1802). Well constructed, although major part of material used is already known.

Proença, M. Cavalcânti. *José de Alencar na literatura brasileira*. Rio de Janeiro: Civilização, 1966.
A separate edition of the introduction to the *Obras completas of Alencar* (Rio: Aguilar, 1959).

See also Coelho ("2. General").

ALMEIDA

Taylor, A. Carey. "Balzac and Manoel António de Almeida; The beginnings of Realism in Brazil." *RLC,* XLI (1967), 195-203.

CASTRO ALVES

Meyer, Augusto. "Navios negreiros." *ESPL,* Aug. 5, 1967, p. 4.
Slightly ironic considerations on the possible sources of *O navio negreiro,* by Castro Alves, the best known of all Brazilian abolitionist poems.

ASSIS

Moraes, Carlos Dante de. "Machado." *ESPSL,* July 15, 1967, p. 6.

Neves, João Alves das. "Machado de Assis e os portuguêses." *ESPSL,* Feb. 11, 1967, p. 2; Feb. 18, 1967, p. 2.

Woll, Dieter. "Machado de Assis oder Moreira de Azevedo? Zur Frage ihrer Autorschaft in der *Marmota Fluminense, A Marmota,* und *O Espelho.*" *RF,* LXXIX (1967), 28-61.

See also Coelho ("2. General").

BARRETO

Nunes, Benedito. "A Escola do Recife." *ESPSL,* July 15, 1967, p. 4.

Paim, Antônio. *A filosofia da Escola do Recife.* Rio de Janeiro: Saga, 1966.

Paim, Antônio. "Importância e limitação da obra filosófica de Tobias Barreto." *Revista do Livro,* XXVII-XXVIII (1965), 81-105.

Torres, João Camilo de Oliveira. "Tobias Barreto e o poder moderador." *Revista do Livro,* XXIX-XXX (1966), 9-17.

DIAS

Nunes, Cassiano. "Gonçalves Dias e a estética do Indianismo." *Luso-Brazilian Review,* IV, 1 (1967), 35-50.
Text of a lecture delivered in the Brazilian Institute of New York University (1964). The author repeats the standard interpretation of Indianism as the first truly national literary manifestation in Brazil.

See also Martins ("3a. Herculano").

LAET

Neves, João Alves das. "A polêmica de Carlos Laet com Camilo Castelo Branco." *Colóquio,* XLII (1967), 60-61.
Brief description of the major arguments of that famous grammatical polemic.

See also Silva ("3a. Castelo Branco").

MARTINS PENA

Beiguelman, Paula. "Análise literária e investigação sociológica." *Viagem sentimental a Dona Guidinha do Poço.* São Paulo: Editôra Centro Universitário, 1966, pp. 67-77.
Following Lucàks' methods, the author tries to give a brief example of how literary material can be used for sociological investigation. "The period that followed Independence was characterized by the growth of commercial and financial activities which, in view of the type of economy then prevalent in Brazil, favoured the capital connected with slavery traffic and speculation; and the intensification or urbanization, with disintegrating effects on the traditional crafts of the Court" (p. 71). Martins Pena, according to Beiguelman, understands this process and develops it, in his plays, around a basic axis: the break in traditional austerity and decorum. A very short though illuminating study.

Damasceno, Darci, and Maria Figueiras, eds. *Comédias.* Rio de Janeiro: Ouro, 1966.
A separate printing, comprising only the comedies, of Damasceno's standard critical edition of the works of Martins Pena.

MONTE ALVERNE

Lopes, Hélio. "Monte Alverne e o Instituto Histórico da França." *ESPSL,* Feb. 11, 1967, p. 4.
Study of the relationship between Monte Alverne and Monglave and the French Historical Institute.

Lopes, Hélio. "Monte Alverne e Massillon." *ESPSL,* April 29, 1967, p. 4.
Brief analysis of the possible influence of Massillon on the oratory style of Monte Alverne.

PARANPIACABA

Ramos, Péricles Eugênio da Silva, ed. *Poesias escolhidas.* Com. introd. e notas. São Paulo: Conselho Estadual de Cultura, 1965.
Paranapiacaba was the most revered translator of Byron into Portuguese and a very popular romantic poet in his own right. His longevity, however—born in 1827, he died in 1915—made him a strange case: being one of the earliest romantics he was able to see the forerunners of contemporary art. This anthology, prepared with scholarly care, consists of an introduction, 16 original poems, 6 pieces of translation (bilingual edition), and an appendix with variants and a curious prose work about "poesia pantagruélica" (a type of macaronic, nonsense poetry written by students during the ultra-romantic period). The introduction is too self-defensive. The position of Paranapiacaba

as a Byron popularizer and one of the first Indianist poets in Brazil is reason enough for this long needed anthology. It is a pity that such gothic tales as "Octavio e Branca ou A maldição materna" could not be included, for they have much to say about the taste and sensibility of the Brazilian romantics at the middle of the century.

TAUNAY, A. E.

Diamante, Hélio. "Uma retirada esquecida: a da Laguna." *ESPSL,* Aug. 12, 1967, p. 3.

Brief considerations on *La retraite de Laguna,* first major book by Taunay, calling attention to the centennial of the historical event narrated in that work. There are clear links between the experiences narrated in *Retraite* and Taunay's *Inocência.*

TAUNAY, C. A.

Meyer, Marlyse. "Uma novela brasileira de 1830." *Revista do Instituto de Estudos Brasileiros,* II (1967), 125-30.

Very well documented article, in which the author attributes the authorship of *Olaya e Julio,* first published in *O Beija-Flor* (1830-31), to Charles Auguste Taunay.

VARELA

Azevedo, Vicente de P. V. de. " 'Poeta!' " *ESPSL,* Jan. 28, 1967, p. 4; Feb. 4, 1967, p. 4.

The non-conformist life of Fagundes Varela is seen as having been responsible for the popular attitude in Brazil that poets are always bohemian.

SPANISH

(By Brian J. Dendle, University of Michigan.)

1. Bibliography

Iniesta Oneca, Antonio. "Sobre algunas traducciones españolas de novelas." *RL,* XXVII (1965), 79-84.

Lists certain translators and translations of novels in the first half of the 19th century; mainly gleaned from references in the contemporary press.

See also Rodrîguez-Moñino, Antonio ("Gallardo").

2. General

Aronson, Theo. *The Royal Vendetta. The Crown of Spain 1829-1965.* New York: The Bobbs-Merrill Company, 1966. Pp. 246.

Readable, popular account of Bourbon personalities, quarrels, and scandals.

Azcárate, Pablo de. "Pronunciamiento del Teniente don Cayetano Cardero." *BRAH,* CLIX (July 1966), 117-33.

Cardero's own account of the liberals' seizure of the *Casa de Correos.*

Badillo, Pedro E. "Problemática espiritual del s. XIX." *Revista de Estudios Generales* (Universidad de Puerto Rico), VIII (May 1966), 25-36.
Internal contradictions in the 19th century *bourgeoisie*: their Romantic sentimental interest in the Middle Ages contrasts with their utilitarianism. A century of revolution (political and industrial), secularization, social problems, and novel philosophies of history.

Bravo-Villasante, Carmen. "Los hermanos Grimm en España." *CHA,* Nos. 175-76 (1965), pp. 184-95.
A brief examination of German Romantic interest in Spain, Jacob Grimm's *Silva de romances viejos,* the tales of the Brothers Grimm, and the fortunes of this type of *cuento* in the Spain of the 19th and 20th centuries, notably in the work of Fernán Caballero and in the folk-lore movement led by Antonio Machado y Alvarez.

Brüggemann, Werner. "Friedrich Schlegel y su concepción de la literatura española como quintaesencia del arte romántico." *FMod,* Nos. 15-16 (1964), pp. 241-64.
Friedrich Schlegel considered the *Quijote* to be the archetypal Romantic novel and the *romancero* to be the paradigm of Romantic poetry. He found in Calderón the perfect blend of "lo romántico, lo cristiano y lo español." With the revaluation of Spanish literature by German Romantic critics and their doctrine that literature expresses national character, the myth of Romantic Spain is born.

Christiansen, Eric. *The Origins of Military Power in Spain 1800-1854.* London: Oxford University Press, 1967. Pp. 193.
A scholarly analysis of the situation of the Spanish soldier during this troubled period. Grievances were many: the private soldiers were unwilling conscripts; officers were ill-paid and dependent on patronage. In times of crisis, troops were neither paid nor adequately supplied. The Army's involvement in the political life of Spain became a question of economic survival in the prevailing spoils system; hence the conflict between generals and civilian politicians with their differing ambitions and interests. Nevertheless, the situation of the military did improve and their rôle in politics was not necessarily harmful. Despite occasional lapses (for example, contrary to Mr. Christiansen's assertion, Serrano was never President of the First Republic), Mr. Christiansen's fresh vantage-point and detailed scholarship make this work of unusual interest for all students of the period. Appendices cover the Ministry of War and the promotion system, the mutiny of La Granja, the Seville *pronunciamiento,* and the military press. Prime Ministers and War Ministers are listed. Useful critical bibliography.

Cuenca Toribio, José Manuel. "Algunos aspectos de la segunda restauración fernandina en Sevilla (1823-25)." *ArH,* No. 131 (1965), pp. 203-27.
Cultural and social conditions in Sevilla, 1823-25. The theatre was restored, although considered by some members of the *Ayuntamiento* to be "el seminario de todos los pecados."

Effross, Susi Hillburn. "The Influence of Alexander Pope in Eighteenth-Century Spain." *SP,* LXIII (1966), 78-92.
Spanish familiarity with Pope in the last third of the 18th century, with study of Lista's translation of *The Dunciad.*

Elorza, Antonio. "La Sociedad Bascongada de los Amigos del País en la ilustración española." *CHA,* No. 185 (1965), pp. 325-57.
The ideological tendencies of the members of the *Sociedad Bascongada,* their social background, the foundation of the Seminario de Vergara, the polemics on *el lujo* and commerce, and the anticlericalism of Samaniego.

Esquer Torres, Ramón. "Dos álbumes inéditos del Romanticismo." *RL,* XXVIII (1965), 163-227.
Text of poems, some inedited, by Campoamor, Espronceda, la Avellaneda, Hartzenbusch, Rodríguez Rubí, E. F. Sanz, García Gutiérrez, and others, and fragment of comedy by Bretón.

García, Salvador. "Una revista romántica: *El Observatorio Pintoresco,* de 1837." *BBMP,* XL (1964), 337-59.
Contents of and contributors to this imitation of *El Semanario Pintoresco.* Text of Estébanez Calderón's sonnet "El despecho del español."

Holt, Edgar. *The Carlist Wars in Spain.* Chester Springs, Pennsylvania: Dufour Editions, 1967. Pp. 303.
Chapters I-XVI present a general, well-organized account of the First Carlist War. Details, based on Foreign Office papers and contemporary accounts, are given of the conduct of the British Legion.

Kiernan, Victor Gordon. *The Revolution of 1854 in Spanish History.* Oxford: Clarendon Press, 1966. Pp. 266.
Rev. by Josep Fontana Làzaro, *BHS,* XLIV (1967), 295-97.
Chronological account of the confused events of the *bienio.* Liberal ineptitude and fears of anarchism opened the way for O'Donnell's counter-revolution.

Maravall, José Antonio. "Las tendencias de reforma política en el siglo XVIII español." *RO,* V, No. 52 (1967), pp. 53-82.
Professor Maravall disagrees with Herr's thesis that there were no attacks on the absolute monarchy in Spain before 1789. Rationalist critics in the reign of Charles III considered the monarchy to be only one element in the social order. Despite the great power of the monarchy, gropings toward political affiliation are apparent before 1789. The *Sociedades Económicas* reveal a *bourgeois* mentality in their criticism of the nobility and ecclesiastical organization. As early as 1741, Amor de Soria attacks absolute monarchic power and advocates the summoning of *Cortes.* About 1780, Ibáñez de la Rentería, favoring the English system, calls for a general reform of the *constitución* of Spain. Foronda, inspired by the Constitution of the United States, opposes despotism and defends a system of individual liberty.

Marco, Joaquín. "Notas a una estética de la novela española (1795-1842)." *BRAE,* XLVI (1966), 113-24.

The translators of *Pamela Andrews* (1795), *El castillo negro* (1803), and *Foblas* (1836) reveal in prologues their concept of the novel: the novel is utilitarian, moral, and intended for the young. The translators emended the novels to fit the demands of Spanish morality.

Mateos, María Dolores. *Salamanca.* (Fasc. O of *La España del Antiguo Régimen.*) Prologue by Miguel Artola. Salamanca: Universidad de Salamanca, 1966. Pp. 65.
The present volume, the first in the series of studies of the *antiguo régimen* edited by Miguel Artola, analyzes the demography, seigniorial privileges, and economic structure of the Province of Salamanca in the 18th and first third of the 19th centuries.

Molas, Joaquim, ed. *Poesia catalana romàntica.* (Antologia Catalana, Vol. VII.) Barcelona: Edicions 62, 1965. Pp. 127.
The poems of this useful anthology have been selected for their literary value and representative nature. The arrangement is chronological (1833-1859, 1859-1874) and thematic (*La Pàtria, Els sentiments de l'home, Imitacions de poesia tradicional, Poesia narrativa*). In the brief but lucid prologue, Molas relates Catalan Romanticism to its historical background. Molas notes the failure of Catalan Romanticism to become an instrument of progress and finds that after 1844 " . . . un Romanticisme pusillànime i eclèctic monopolitzà pràcticament les lletres catalanes." Molas also discusses the themes, forms, and sources of the Catalan Romantic poets. Essential bibliography, bio-bibliographical notes, and chronological tables are included.

Montoliu, Manuel de. *Aribau i el seu temps.* Barcelona: Editorial Alpha, 1962. Pp. 170.
Essays on the life and works of Aribau, and (a briefer treatment) the intellectual and literary environment in Catalonia at the end of the 18th and beginning of the 19th centuries, the Catalan Romantics who wrote in Castillian, Cabanyes, Piferrer, Quadrado, and lesser figures. Catalan Romanticism is characterised by "l'equilibri i la ponderació." Aribau was always faithful to his humanistic schooling and can be considered a Romantic only in his *Oda a la pàtria.* The *Oda* is analyzed in detail; it can no longer be considered ingenuous, for Aribau composed it with full artistic consciousness in an attempt to give dignity to the Catalan tongue. Montoliu examines the circumstances of composition of the *Oda* (Aribau's "exile" to Madrid, 1827-1828), its themes, its form (the French *alexandrin,* with predominance of *rima aguda*), and its sources (March, Manzoni). Montoliu explains the strange reference to Aribau's employer in line 46: the *Oda* originally read "ma pàtria" and not "mon patró"; Aribau's political opposition to Catalan nationalism led him to conserve the temporary emendation. The subsequent fortunes of the *Oda* are traced. Aribau must be considered only as one of several precursors to the *Renaixença;* his *Oda* was not intended as a manifesto. Bibliography.

Montoliu, Manuel de. *La Renaixença i els Jocs Florals. Verdaguer.* Epíleg d'Octavi Saltor. Barcelona: Editorial Alpha, 1962. Pp. 226.

Essays on Rubió i Ors, the *Renaixença* in Mallorca and Valencia, Marian Aguiló, and Milà i Fontanals. Lengthier treatments of the *Jocs Florals* in their "època heroica" between 1859 and 1877 (polemics, themes, genres), and of Verdaguer (life, works, his return to the early Romantic themes of *Fe* and *Patria*). Appendix lists translations of Verdaguer's works. Bibliography. Saltor's epilogue pays tribute to the labors of Montoliu.

Morales Oliver, Luis. "Resonancias africanas en el romanticismo literario español." Lecture V, pp. 67-77, in Morales Oliver, Luis. *Africa en la literatura española* (Vol. III, "Del siglo de oro a la época contemporánea"). Madrid: Consejo Superior de Investigaciones Científicas, 1964.
Eighteenth-century writers show an interest in primitive man (for example, *Sélico*, a *novela africana* of 1797) and in Oriental themes (the *romances moriscos* of García de la Huerta and the Conde de Noroña). Zorrilla, Martínez de la Rosa, Arolas, Rivas, and Mauri, as well as various Latin American Romantics, write on Oriental and African themes. Trueba creates the *novela morisca* in his *Gómez Arias*.

Núñez de Arenas, Manuel. *L'Espagne des Lumières au Romantisme.* Etudes réunies par Robert Marrast. Paris: Centre de Recherches de l'Institut d'Etudes Hispaniques, 1963. Pp. 434.
Collection of 37 historical and literary studies by the late D. Manuel Núñez de Arenas. Detailed studies of Teresa Cabarrús, Vicente María Santiváñez, Goya's stay in France, French police records of the Expedition of Vera, and briefer mention of Peñaflorida, Amorós, Gimbernat, Llorente, Bernabeu, El Empecinado, Blanqui's visit to Spain in 1826, Chateaubriand and Scott in Spain, Rivas, Mérimée, Gallego, García Villalta, Salas y Quiroga, Fernán Caballero, and Mesonero Romanos. All articles have been previously published, but some are difficult of access.

Olivera, Miguel Alfredo. "El siglo XVIII español." *Sur,* No. 300 (1966), pp. 54-67.
Eighteenth-century Spain, with its profound spiritual revolution and material progress, compares favorably with the Spain of the following century.

Palacio Atard, Vicente. *Los españoles de la Ilustración.* Madrid: Ediciones Guadarrama, 1964. Pp. 333; 48 plates.
The presence of Protestant workers in Catalonia in 1773, Charles III's unsuccessful attempt to reform the universities, Olavide, German settlers, attempts to abolish the bullfight, the rôle of the *tertulia,* Floridablanca, diet, and Charles III's maritime policies are among the topics treated in these essays on the 18th century. Of particular interest to students of Romanticism are the following chapters: I. "Los españoles de la Ilustración" (the clash of Catholic upbringing, Enlightenment, and a commercial, rather than aristocratic, ideal helps to explain the contradictory nature of the Spaniard of the 18th century); II. "Estilo de vida aristocrático y mentalidad burguesa" (the zeal for economic change, attacks on the Golden Age theatre for its immoral, i.e. reactionary, nature when viewed in the light of a reformist ideology, the survival in all classes of the

aristocratic ideal, the clash of this ideal with Christian and *bourgeois* attitudes);
VIII. "La educación de la mujer en Moratín" (the rôle of women in the 18th
century, Moratín's advocacy of free choice of husband, Moratín's sincerity and
passion tempered with reflection).

Rincón, Carlos. "Reseña de los estudios sobre el siglo XVIII español."
Beitræge zur Romanischen Philologie, V (1966 Heft 1), 37-65.
Summary of opinions on the 18th century, ranging from the Romantic period
(Böhl von Faber, Larra, Donoso Cortés, Alcalá Galiano, Gómez Hermosilla)
to the present day. Marxist viewpoint.

Romero Mendoza, Pedro. *Siete ensayos sobre el romanticismo español.*
Vol. II. Cáceres: Servicios Culturales de la Excma. Diputación Provin-
cial de Cáceres, 1966. Pp. 466; 14 plates.
In his sixth essay, the first of this volume, Romero Mendoza summarizes, and
offers judicious criticism of, the literary theories of the pre-Romantic critics
(Luzán, Quintana, Lista, Martínez de la Rosa, Silvela, Durán, Hermosilla), of
those whom he terms the *clásico-románticos* (Gil y Zárate, Aribau, Mesonero
Romanos, Donoso Cortés, Hartzenbusch, Madrazo, Pedro José Pidal, Tabino
Tejado, Quadrado), and of the Romantics (Larra, Molíns, Escosura, Alcalá
Galiano, Ochoa, Gil y Carrasco, Pastor Díaz, Ros de Olano, Piferrer, Ferrer
del Río). In his final essay, Romero Mendoza studies the Spanish novel of
the Romantic period. After an examination of the influence of foreign works
(including a list of foreign novels translated into Spanish in the first third of
the 19th century) and a discussion of Scott's contribution to the novel, Romero
Mendoza analyzes the novelistic works of the following: Trueba y Cossío,
López Soler, Larra, Escosura, García Villalta, Espronceda, Estébanez Calderón,
Martínez de la Rosa, Ochoa, Miguel de los Santos Alvarez, la Avellaneda,
Aguiló, Gil y Carrasco, Antonio Hurtado, Navarro Villoslada, Carolina Coronado, Antonio Flores, Fernández y González, Vicente Boix, Castelar, Pastor
Díaz, Ros de Olano, Cánovas del Castillo. While the essays are as much a
work of love as of erudition, Romero Mendoza does not hesitate to indicate
what he considers to be the defects of the works studied. Taken as a whole,
the essays form, in their scholarship and understanding of the Romantic attitude, a useful introduction to Spanish Romanticism. The studies of individual
authors offer fresh insights into the works of the more well-known Romantics,
and a valuable presentation of the theories and works of such neglected figures
as Ros de Olano and the Marqués de Molíns. Bibliography. Index to both
volumes.

Schwartz, Kessel. "A Fascist View of Nineteenth-Century Spanish Literature (1936-1939)." *RomN,* VII (1966), 117-22.
Zorrilla and Bécquer acclaimed, Larra and Espronceda attacked in the Seville
edition of *ABC,* 1936-1939.

Sebold, Russell P. "Contra los mitos anticlásicos españoles." *PSA,* XXXV
(1964), 83-114.
Professor Sebold is alarmed at the present tendency to study the literature of
the 18th century merely for survivals of forms of the *siglo de oro* or for signs
of pre-Romanticism, while neoclassical literary theory is neglected. The propaganda of such Romantic critics as Durán is in part to blame for this hostility

to neoclassicism: the Romantics confused the issue by using the emotionally charged term *afrancesado* as a synonym of *clásico* or *seudoclásico;* imitating the prejudices of the French Romantics, they sought "classics" to attack. Professor Sebold indicates the popularity of national and sentimental themes in the drama of the 18th century. He cogently argues that the term *neoclásico* should not be used pejoratively, but rather in its strict sense of "nuevo clasicismo español."

Torrent, Joan, and Rafael Tasis. *Història de la premsa catalana.* Pròleg de Dr. Agustí Pedro Pons. Barcelona: Editorial Bruguera, 1966. 2 vols. Illus.

Comprehensive listing and treatment of all newspapers, journals, calendars, almanacs, and even comic magazines published in *catalán,* both inside and outside Spain, 1640-1965. Of particular interest to students of Romanticism are the following sections: "L'esperit de la Renaixença a les publicacions castellanes de la primera meitat del segle XIX," I, 37-48 (the pre-Romanticism of the *Periódico Universal de Ciencias, Literatura y Artes,* historical background and contributors to *El Europeo,* the "Oda a la pàtria" and *El Vapor,* journalistic contributions of Milà, Balaguer, Rubió, et al.); "Els primers periòdics catalans," I, 51-59 (*renaixentista* tendencies in *Lo Pare Arcàngel* and *Lo Verdader Català*); "La premsa catalana a les illes balears," II, 481-83, 490-92; and "La premsa catalana a les terres valencianes," II, 542-45, 563-64. Numerous illustrations, some in color. Bibliography. Separate indices of publications, editors, journalists and contributors, illustrators, and printers (although regrettably, in such a beautifully-produced work, occasional inaccuracies in page numbers are given in the indices). An invaluable tool of research and reference.

Tudisco, Antonio. "América en la poesía española del siglo XVIII." *RHM,* XXXI (1965), 431-38.

Lack of originality in Spanish poets' treatment of such American themes as Columbus, the *Conquista,* the *indio,* and the *criollo.* The few allusions to the Wars of Independence reveal hostility and incomprehension.

Ubieto, Antonio, Juan Reglá and José María Jover. *Introducción a la historia de España.* Barcelona: Editorial Teide, 1963. Pp. 798.

A useful general history of Spain. Professor Jover Zamora, in the section dealing with the contemporary period, 1808-1931 (pages 417-765), analyzes in detail social and ideological changes. Romanticism is briefly discussed in Chapter III of this section (pages 470-85). Romanticism is "una determinada concepción del mundo y una determinada forma de comportamiento humano" which appears in the last third of the 18th century; it is therefore a collective phenomenon, expressed not only in literature but also in the military tactics of the War of Independence, in the works of Goya, and in the political attitudes of the liberals. Numerous illustrations. Brief bibliography. Index.

Vidart, Daniel D. "El renacimiento romántico." Pp. 123-32 in Vidart, Daniel D., *Regionalismo y universalismo de la cultura gallega.* Ediciones del Banco de Galicia (Uruguay), 1961.

The late flowering of the *Volksgeist* in Galicia; the contributions of **Pondal**, Rosalía de Castro, and Curros Enríquez.

Zavala, Iris. "Francia en la poesía del XVIII español." *BH,* LXVIII (1966), 49-68.
Spanish poets' opinion of France. Jovellanos and Forner fear the French Revolution. Spanish attitudes change with the *Cortes* of Cádiz and the acceptance of liberal ideas.

3. STUDIES OF AUTHORS

ALCALA GALIANO

See Rincon, Carlos ("2. General").

ARENAL

Martín, Elvira. "Concepción Arenal." Pp. 17-86 in Martín, Elvira, *Tres mujeres gallegas del siglo XIX.* Barcelona: Editorial Aedos, 1962.
Sympathetic biography, although somewhat novelized.

ARIBAU

See Montoliu, Manuel de ("2. General").

AVELLANEDA

Carlos, Albert J. "El *Mal du Siècle* en un soneto de la Avellaneda." *RomN,* VII (1966), 134-38.
Tedio in sonnet "Mi Mal."

See also Esquer Torres, Ramón ("2. General"); Gulsoy, J. ("Bécquer").

BÉCQUER

Balbín, Rafael de. "Sobre un influjo germanista en G. A. Bécquer." Pp. 851-66 in: *Homenaje a Johannes Vincke.* Madrid: Consejo Superior de Investigaciones Científicas, 1962-1963.
Rima XV ("Cendal flotante . . .") compared with E.F. Sanz's "Tú, El y Yo." Thematic, stylistic, and lexical analysis of both poems.

González-Gerth, Miguel. "The Poetics of Gustavo Adolfo Bécquer." *MLN,* LXXX (1965), 185-201.
Bécquer's essentially Platonic poetic theories as revealed in *rimas* and prose works.

Gulsoy, J. "La fuente comú de *Los ojos verdes y El rayo de luna* de G. A. Bécquer." *BHS,* XLIV (1967), 96-106.
Both *leyendas* have their source in la Avellaneda's *La ondina del lago azul.*

Hartsook, John H. "Bécquer and the Creative Imagination." *HR,* XXXV (1967), 252-69.
Light thrown by Bécquer on the psychology of the creative process.

Navarro, Alberto. "Dos andaluces universales: Bécquer y Juan Ramón Jiménez." *Arbor,* IV (May 1966), 262-77.
The influence of Andalucía on the two poets. Their attitudes toward nature, eternity, and death.

Soria, Andrés. "Bécquer y Dante." *CHA,* No. 189 (1965), pp. 377-82.
Bécquer's treatment of the episode of Paolo and Francesca in *Rima XXIX.*

Soria, Andrés. "La vida de la letra (Bécquer y Dante)." *RL,* XXVIII (1965), 67-73.
Almost identical article to above.

See also Cubero Sanz, Manuela ("Ferrán"); Nogales de Muñiz, María ("Castro").

BLANCO WHITE

Sánchez-Castañer, Francisco. "José María Blanco White y Alberto Lista en las Escuelas de Cristo hispalenses." *ArH,* No. 131 (1965), pp. 229-47.
The piety of Blanco White and Alberto Lista established by their membership of the *Escuela de Cristo* in Seville: "una indudable sinceridad religiosa, volcada hacia el ascetismo y perfección cristiana más profundos, en momentos vitales de los citados presbíteros."

BÖHL VON FABER

See Rincón, Carlos ("2. General"); Rodríguez-Moñino, Antonio ("Gallardo").

BRETON DE LOS HERREROS

See Esquer Torres, Ramón ("2. General").

CADALSO

Glendinning, Nigel. "Cartas inéditas de Cadalso a un P. Jesuíta en inglés, francés, español y latín." *BBMP,* XLII (1966), 97-116.
Text of letters written in affectionate vein by Cadalso to his former teacher, Lozano, in 1760. Also Cadalso's bills in the Real Semanario de Madrid.

Gómez del Prado, Carlos. "José Cadalso, las *Noches Lúgubres,* y el Determinismo literario." *KFLQ,* XIII (1966), 209-19.
Cadalso's work is very different from Young's. For Cadalso, Man is determined by Nature.

CAPMANY

Alvarez Junco, José. "Capmany y su informe sobre la necesidad de una constitución (1809)." *CHA,* No. 210 (1967), pp. 520-51
The revolutionary situation which existed in 1809. The somewhat reactionary ideas of Capmany in the *Informe.* The text of the *Informe.*

Glendinning, Nigel. "A Note on the Authorship of the *Comentario sobre el Doctor festivo y maestro de los Eruditos a la Violeta, para desengaño de los españoles que leen poco y malo.*" *BHS,* XLIII (1966), 276-83.
Capmany identified as author of the *Comentario.* The Europeanizing spirt of Capmany in the 1770's. Appendix: Capmany's inedited *Carta al padre Gil* of 1773.

CASTRO

Díez-Canedo, Enrique. "Una precursora: Rosalía de Castro." Pp. 21-26 in Díez-Canedo, Enrique, *Estudios de poesía española contemporánea.* Mexico: Joaquín Mortiz, 1965.
Metrical innovations and mastery in *En las orillas del Sar.*

Martín, Elvira. "Rosalía de Castro." Pp. 87-154 in Martín, Elvira, *Tres mujeres gallegas del siglo XIX.* Barcelona: Editorial Aedos, 1962.
Her life, marriage, works, and the themes in her works.

Nogales de Muñiz, María Antonia. *Irradiación de Rosalía de Castro.* Barcelona: (Distribuido por IBER-AMER, Publicaciones Hispano-americanas), 1966. Pp. 304.
Rosalí has been belittled by critics who see her purely as a representative of Celtic regionalism. Her *dolor* is to be explained by her personal experience of injustice, not by mysticism of race or soil. In the first part of this somewhat confused doctoral dissertation, Sra. Nogales declares that the underlying themes of Rosalía's work are *amor desgraciado* and social protest. Rosalía's humor and concept of religion are also examined. In Part Two, Sra. Nogales examines Rosalía's similarities to Bécquer (Heine influenced both poets; Rosalía is more intellectual than Bécquer), and Rosalía as a precursor of Antonio Machado and of the socially committed poets of the 1940's and 1950's. Bibliography.

See also Vidart, Daniel D. ("2. General").

CIENFUEGOS

Cano, José Luis. "Un prerromántico: Cienfuegos." *CHA,* No. 195 (1966), pp. 462-74.
Cienfuegos' life, the influence of Rousseau, his friendships (with Quintana and others), his courageous attitude towards Murat, and his sufferings at the hands of the French.

DONOSO CORTÉS

Comellas, José Luis. "Donoso Cortés, doctrinario" and "La teoría de las aristocracias legítimas." Chapts. I and II, pp. 13-66, in Comellas, José Luis. *La teoría del régimen liberal español.* Madrid: Instituto de Estudios Políticos, 1962.
Donoso's doctrinaire liberalism, as expounded 1834-36. Donoso sees history from the Redemption to the French Revolution as a gigantic liberating process, culminating in a contemporary society freed from the prejudices of earlier centuries. Rejecting both the divine right of kings and the sovereignty of the people, Donoso believes in the *soberanía de la inteligencia* or government by

the intelligent. His political ideal is the France of Louis-Philippe. Donoso's theories were known to Bravo Murillo, Cánovas, and Costa.

See also Rincón, Carlos ("2. General").

DURAN

See Sebold, Russell ("2. General").

ESCOSURA

Redonet, Luis. "Bárbara de Blomberg." *BRAH,* CLVIII (1966), 121-45.
This account of the historical Bárbara Blomberg might be of interest to students of Escosura.

ESPRONCEDA

Caravaca, Francisco. "Dramatis personae en *El Diablo Mundo* de Espronceda." *CHA*, No. 177 (1964), pp. 356-72.
Seeking philosophical coherence in Espronceda's portrayal of Adán, Caravaca discusses such problems as Adán's knowledge of good and evil, Adán's immortality, and the involvement of an immortal being in vulgar enterprises. Name-dropping of philosophers from Plato to Sartre fails to solve the problem of Adán's immortality; hence, Caravaca's conclusion that: "Adán es, más aún que una abstracción, un verdadero rompecabezas." Espronceda's portrayal of Salada, however, is worthy of Dostoevski.

Caravaca, Francisco. "Notas sobre el humorismo de Espronceda en 'El Diablo Mundo.' " *RHM*, XXX (1964), 119-25.
Espronceda, while not a humorist in the British sense, reveals a certain irony. He obtains a burlesque effect with his choice of rhymes and by exaggeration.

Martinengo, Alessandro. "Para una nueva edición de Espronceda." *Thesaurus,* XIX (1964), 147-52, 565-70.
Variants of texts of Espronceda's poems.

See also Esquer Torres, Ramón ("2. General").

ESTÉBANEZ CALDERON

Estébanez Calderón. *La Andalucía de Estébanez Calderón (Antología)*. Recopilación de Jorge Campos. Madrid: Taurus, 1963. Pp. 144.
Brief prologue discusses the life, literary style, *costumbrismo,* and personality of Estébanez Calderón, and the Romantic vision of picturesque Andalucía. Texts of the *Escenas andaluzas,* with certain omissions; Estébanez' sonnet to Seville; and article "El sombrero."

Pabón, J. "De 'El Solitario.' (En el centenario de Estébanez Calderón: 1867-1967)." *BRAH,* CLX (1967), 123-55.
Estébanez' admiration for and political involvement with General Córdova; the background to the *escena* "Asamblea general de los caballeros y damas de Triana . . . " and his treatment of Romantic Andalusia; the authenticity of his Andalusia; his labors for the *Academia de la Historia;* his manuscripts in the *Academia.*

See also García, Salvador ("2. General"); Rodríguez-Moñino, Antonio ("Gallardo").

FERNAN CABALLERO

See Bravo-Villasante, Carmen ("2. General"); Nuñez de Arenas, Manuel ("2. General").

FERRAN

Cubero Sanz, Manuela. *Vida y obra de Augusto Ferrán.* Madrid: Consejo Superior de Investigaciones Científicas, 1965. Pp. 303.

Rev. by R. Pageard in *BH,* LXVIII (1966), 389-94; and by Rica Brown in *HR,* XXXV (1967), 378-81.

Life of Ferrán. Exhaustive treatment of his works, including his translations of the Brothers Grimm, Mickiewicz, Hoffmann, Heine, and Nordic ballads. His collection of *cantares populares* compared with other collections. The style and themes of Ferrán's own *cantares populares.* The influence of Heine on Ferrán. The reciprocal influence of Bécquer and Ferrán. Bibliography. Text of *La Soledad* and variants; texts of minor works by Ferrán and of his translation of Heine.

FORNER

Peñuelas, Marcelino C. "Personalidad y obra de Forner." *Hispano,* No. 26 (1966), pp. 23-31.

Forner's family background, unbalanced temperament, violent and futile polemics, attitude of shortsighted reaction.

See also Zavala, Iris ("2. General").

GALLARDO

Rodríguez-Moñino, Antonio. *Historia de una infamia bibliográfica. La de San Antonio de 1823.* Madrid: Editorial Castalia, 1965. Pp. 250.

Rev. by Ramón Esquer Torres in *Arbor,* LXV (1966), 152-53; and by Edward M. Wilson in *BHS,* XLIV (1967), 68-69.

Detailed and scholarly rebuttal of charges of mendacity, theft, and sloth levelled against Gallardo. Gallardo is vindicated; Böhl von Faber comes out well; Xavier de Burgos and Estévanez Calderón appear in less favorable light. Catalogue of works looted from Gallardo and their present location. Appendices: works in Gallardo's library, two letters from Fernán Nuñez relating his efforts to suppress a work by Gallardo, and a letter written by Gallardo in 1824. An index would have been helpful.

GALLEGO

See Núñez Arenas, Manuel ("2. General").

GARCIA GUTIÉRREZ

See Esquer Torres, Ramón ("2. General").

GOMEZ HERMOSILLA

See Rincón, Carlos ("2. General").

GOROSTIZA

Martínez Berrones, María Guadalupe. "En torno al teatro de Don Manuel Eduardo de Gorostiza." *Hum* (Universidad de Nuevo León), VIII (1967), 203-18.
Confused biographical notes. List of Gorostiza's works and synopses of plots of three of his plays.

HARTZENBUSCH

See Esquer Torres, Ramón ("2. General").

HUMARA SALAMANCA

Lloréns, Vicente. "Sobre una novela histórica: *Ramiro, Conde de Lucena* (1823)." *RHM*, XXXI (1965), 286-93.
Professor Lloréns confirms that *Ramiro, Conde de Lucena* was first published in 1823 and is thus Spain's first historical novel. Lloréns summarises the novel (conventional orientalism) and gives the text of the *Discurso preliminar*. The *Discurso* illuminates the state of the novel in Spain at this time: the moral significance of the novel, Húmara's views on Scott, Chateaubriand, Byron, et al., Spanish ignorance of many foreign novels, the feminine reading public.

JOVELLANOS

Caso González, José. *"El delincuente honrado,* drama sentimental." *Arch,* XIV (1964), 103-33.
El delincuente honrado enjoyed great success in the late 18th and early 19th centuries. The themes of the play are analyzed, and Jovellanos' concept of honor and justice is discussed. In form, the play owes much to Diderot's theories: it is both *comédie larmoyante* and *comedia sentimental,* it is written in prose and character is subordinated to *condiciones.*

Caso González, José. "Escolásticos e innovadores a finales del siglo XVIII (Sobre el catolicismo de Jovellanos)." *PSA,* XXXVII (1965), 25-48.
Caso González sees Jovellanos as a representative of "el catolicismo de centro." The theological works which Jovellanos recommended in the *Reglamento para el Colegio de Calatrava* were not heretical; the polemics around these works were part of the struggle between scholastics and innovators within the Church. Jovellanos wished to give seminarians an intellectual foundation in dogma which, with the Spanish stress on moral theology, they had not hitherto received.

Knowlton, John F. "Two Epistles: Nuñez de Arce and Jovellanos." *RomN,* VII (1966), 130-33.
Nuñez' "La duda" may have been influenced by Jovellanos' "Fabio a Anfriso." Nuñez' poem is less concrete.

See also Zavala, Iris ("2. General").

LAFUENTE

Caro Baroja, Julio. "Don Modesto Lafuente y sus escritos de carácter social (1966)." *BRAH,* CLX (1967), 89-99.

In the *Viajes de Fray Gerundio, por Francia, Bélgica, Holanda y orillas del Rhin* (1842), and the *Teatro social del siglo XIX* (1846), Lafuente escapes the limitations of *costumbrismo* to become a pioneer of sociology.

LARRA

Alvarez Guerrero, Osvaldo. "Larra e Hispanoamérica. Generación de 1837." *RO*, v, No. 50 (1967), 230-38.
Similarity of thought between Larra and the Argentinian Generation of 1837. Larra's influence on Juan Bautista Alberdi and on Sarmiento.

Brent, Albert. "Larra's Dramatic Works." *RomN*, VIII (1967), 207-12.
Chronological list of plays, with dates of composition and staging.

Carpintero, Helio. "Larra, entre dos fuegos." *RO*, v, No. 50 (1967), 217-29.
Larra sees the backwardness, frivolity, despotism, and lack of true patriotism in Spain.

Dieterich Arenas, Genoveva. "Lo romántico y lo moderno en Larra." *RO*, v, No. 50 (1967), 205-16.
Larra was a liberal and, after 1832, a Romantic. As an outsider, he approaches modern man. His was not a sterile rebellion for his political attitude was constructive.

Fabra Barreiro, Gustavo. "El pensamiento vivo de Larra." *RO*, v, No. 50 (1967), 129-52.
Fabra Barreiro, recognizing that critics have been more concerned with Larra's life and attitude than with his ideology, attempts to portray Larra as an advanced thinker. The keys to Larra's method are (a) an analytical mentality which studies facts in their internal relations, (b) a secularised historical consciousness, i.e., belief in the relativity and strictly human origins of all change and progress, (c) literature and art as the expression of the spirit of the times, and (d) all cultural phenomena seen *sub specie societatis*. With these criteria, Fabra examines certain aspects of Larra's ideas: Larra believes that literature can transform as well as express society; Larra, like Ortega, cannot consider Spain as forming a true society; Larra is a revolutionary, not a reformer; the revolution must be social, not only political; Larra's concept of history is sociological.

Johnson, Robert. "Larra, Martínez de la Rosa and the *Colección de artículos* of 1835-37." *Neophil*, L (1966), 316-24.
Professor Johnson finds stylistic and ideological justification for Larra's revisions of his review of Martínez de la Rosa's *Los celos infundados*. There is no evidence for Seco Serrano's charge that Larra's revisions were motivated by malice.

Lorenzo-Rivero, Luis. "Paralelismo entre la crítica literaria de Larra y Sarmiento." *CHA*, No. 208 (April 1967), pp. 59-74.
Resumes the critical ideas of Larra. Sarmiento, living in similar circumstances, agrees with Larra's judgments. Students of Larra may be surprised to learn

that: "La crítica literaria de Larra se caracterizaba por su moderación, su falta de hostilidad y por su disposición de espíritu sano."

Lorenzo-Rivero, Luis. "La sinfronía de Azorín y Larra." *Hispano,* No. 28 (1966), pp. 27-38.
Trite argument that Azorín and Larra reveal similar attitudes because they live in similar circumstances.

Mateo del Peral, Diego. "Larra: compromiso y libertad en el escritor." *CHA,* No. 193 (1966), pp. 40-58.
Sartrian analysis of Larra as "hombre comprometido y libre." Larra symbolizes the Romantic awareness of European change; conscious of the historical moment, he accuses the social system as the conscience of his group. Mateo del Peral rejects Umbral's theory of Larra's demonism; rather, Larra represents "un profundo entendimiento del sentido racional de la religión cristiana."

Mateo del Peral, Diego Ignacio. "Larra y el presente." *RO,* v, No. 50 (1967), 181-204.
The relevance of Larra to the Generation of 1898 and to Cernuda. The actuality of his criticism. Larra as rebel, non-conformist; his bitterness, his anguish.

Miró Llull, José María. "Aproximación a Larra." *RO,* v, No. 50 (1967), 239-49.
Larra's actuality, inconstancy, refusal to accept limitations, and stylistic mastery. Constants in Larra: his critical spirit, hatred of hypocrisy, acceptance of a class system, tenderness towards the underprivileged, love of Spain. His suicide caused by the conflict between his lucidity and his passionate nature.

Oguiza, Tomás. "Larra-Ganivet." *CHA,* No. 192 (1965), pp. 440-55.
Larra's ideology (satiric rather than ironic), fundamental pessimism, debt to the 18th century. (Followed by examination of Ganivet's analysis of Spain.)

Ortiz Sánchez, Lourdes. "Larra, el hombre." *RO,* v, No. 50 (1967), 153-71.
Larra as outsider. His suicide.

Sánchez Reboredo, José. "Larra y los seres irracionales." *RO,* v, No. 50 (1967), 172-80.
Larra, with his belief in reason and in the importance of education, owes much to the ideology of the Enlightenment. He can only retreat into an attitude of humor before the irrationality of Spanish life.

Seator, Lynette. "Larra and Daumier." *RomN,* vii, No. 2 (1966), 139-43.
Larra and Daumier are satirical, scathingly critical, and share Romantic anguish. Daumier has greater compassion for the downtrodden; Larra feels no kinship with the lower classes.

LISTA

See Effross, Susi Hillburn ("2. General"); Sánchez-Castañer, Francisco ("Blanco White").

MARCHENA

Montiel, Isidoro. "El abate Marchena, traductor de Ossián." *Hispano,*
No. 30 (1967), pp. 15-19.

MARTINEZ DE LA ROSA

See Morales Oliver, Luis ("2. General").

MELÉNDEZ VALDÉS

Demerson, Georges. *D. Juan Meléndez Valdés. Correspondance Relative*
à la Réunion des Hôpitaux d'Avila. (Bibliothèque de l'Ecole des Hautes
Etudes Hispaniques, Université de Bordeaux, Fasc. XXXV.) Bordeaux: Féret et Fils, 1964. Pp. 199.
Rev. by P.-J. Guinard in *BH*, LXIX (1967), 238-45.
Text of Meléndez' correspondence and related documents concerning Meléndez'
attempts to reform the charitable foundations of Avila, 1792-93. Demerson,
in a useful introduction, discusses Meléndez' pragmatism, belief in law, and difficult relations with the clergy. Also text of Meléndez' proposals in 1796 for
a reform of *mayorazgos.*

Forcione, Alban. "Meléndez Valdés and the *Essay on Man." HR,* XXXIV
(1966), 291-306.
Meléndez' debt to Pope in *Oda XII* "Vanidad de las quejas del hombre contra
su Hacedor."

MESONERO ROMANOS

See Nuñez de Arenas, Manuel ("2. General").

MOLINS

See Romero Mendoza, Pedro ("2. General").

MORA

Monguió, Luis. "Aquel fecundo escritor de arlequinadas . . . " *RHM,* XXX
(1964), 1-11.
Mora's poem "El Melancólico" exists in three versions (1825, 1836, 1853). In
the first version, Mora attacks Chateaubriand, not d'Arlincourt. The later
Mora, while less hostile to Chateaubriand, dislikes the Romantic novels of
Chateaubriand and d'Arlincourt. Text of "El Melancólico" (1825), with variants.

Monguió, Luis. "Don José Joaquín de Mora en Buenos Aires en 1827."
RHM, XXXI (1965), 303-28.
Professor Monguió discusses, with ample quotations, the articles on literary
subjects which Mora published in Buenos Aires. Mora's approach is rationa-
listic, if not neoclassical in the strictest sense. Mora finds inacceptable the
metaphysical intent of Calderonian drama, and thus rejects Schlegel's ex-
travagant praise of Calderón. Nevertheless, in his article on Shakespeare,
Mora's criticism approaches that of the Romantics, for Mora expresses his admiration for genius, local color, and national spirit in literature. A valuable
supplement to Lloréns' *Liberales y románticos.*

MORATIN

Aubrun, Charles V.*"El sí de las niñas* o más allá de la mecánica de una comedia." *RHM,* XXXI (1965), 29-35.

An amusing, but penetrating, comparison between *El sí de las niñas* and two plays of the Golden Age, Lope's *El acero de Madrid* and Calderón's *La vida es sueño,* serves to indicate the change in social assumptions between the 17th century and the Enlightenment. Thus, in *El sí de las niñas,* it is the aged, paternalistic, *ilustrado* Don Diego who leads the action, rather than the pair of young lovers. A revealing study.

See also Palacio Atard, Vicente ("2. General").

RIVAS

Pattison, Walter T. "The Secret of Don Alvaro." *Symposium,* XXI (1967), 67-81.

Professor Pattison claims to have solved a long-standing critical problem, the meaning of "fate" in *Don Alvaro.* "Fate" in *Don Alvaro* is not a mysterious, vague, external force but is merely Don Alvaro's lot in life. The key to the play and to Don Alvaro's psychology is the fact that he is a *mestizo;* the workings of "fate" in the drama hinge on Don Alvaro's unwillingness to reveal his racial origins. The theme may have been suggested to Rivas by the presence in Córdoba of the tomb of Garcilaso de la Vega el Inca.

Ribbans, Geoffrey. "El regreso de Angel Saavedra de su destierro en 1834." *RFE,* XLVII (1964), 421-27.

Alexander Slidell MacKenzie describes, in *Spain Revisited* (London, 1836), Rivas' return to Madrid. Rivas found Spanish conditions greatly improved since his departure ten years before.

See also Morales Oliver, Luis ("2. General"); Nuñez de Arenas, Manuel ("2. General").

RODRIGUEZ RUBI

See Esquer Torres, Ramón ("2. General").

ROS DE OLANO

See Romero Mendoza, Pedro ("2. General").

RUBIO I ORS

See Montoliu, Manuel de ("2. General").

SANZ

See Balbín, Rafael de ("Bécquer"); Esquer Torres, Ramón ("2. General").

TRUEBA

See Morales Oliver, Luis ("2. General").

ZORRILLA

Adams, Nicholson B. "Don Juan Tenorio: 1877." *RHM,* xxxi (1965), 5-10.
Zorrilla's *zarzuela.*

Bequero, Arturo. Pp. 171-96 and 391-95 in Vol. II of Bequero, Arturo, *Don Juan y su evolución dramática.* Editora Nacional, 1966.
Introductions to the texts of *Don Juan Tenorio* and the *zarzuela* of the same title. Sources, critical views, characters, contemporary reception, Zorrilla's own opinion of *Don Juan Tenorio.* Text of Zorrilla's open letter to the press giving his reasons for writing the *zarzuela.*

Mancini, Giudo. "Sulla semplicità di Zorrilla." Pp. 81-97 in: *Studi di Lingua e Letteratura Spagnola.* (Quaderni Ibero-Americani, XXXI.) Torino: Giappichelli, 1965.
A sympathetic study of Zorrilla's character. Isabeline society could safely idolize Zorrilla. His exaltation of religion, patriotism, and sentiment, when combined with his fundamental moderation, simplicity, and lack of political spirit threatened no one.

See also Morales Oliver, Luis ("2. General").